AUTOMOTIVE FUEL AND EMISSIONS CONTROL SYSTEMS

AUTOMOTIVE FUEL AND EMISSIONS CONTROL SYSTEMS

James D. Halderman

Sinclair Community College

Jim Linder

Linder Technical Services

Upper Saddle River, New Jersey
Columbus, Ohio

Library of Congress Cataloging-in-Publication Data

Halderman, James D.
  Automotive fuel and emissions control systems / James D. Halderman, Jim Linder.—1st ed.
    p. cm.
  Includes index.
  ISBN 0-13-110442-X (pbk.)
    1. Automobiles—Fuel systems. 2. Automobiles—Pollution control devices. I. Linder, Jim.
  II. Title
  TL214.F8H35 2006

                                                                        2004065973

Production Editor: Christine Buckendahl
Production Coordination: Carlisle Publishers Services
Design Coordinator: Diane Ernsberger
Cover Designer: Ali Mohrman
Production Manager: Deidra Schwartz
Marketing Manager: Mark Marsden

This book was set in ITC Century Book by Carlisle Communications, Ltd. It was printed and bound by Banta Book Group. The cover was printed by The Lehigh Press, Inc.

Pearson Education Ltd.
Pearson Education Singapore Pte. Ltd.
Pearson Education Canada, Ltd.
Pearson Education—Japan

Pearson Education Australia Pty. Limited
Pearson Education North Asia Ltd.
Pearson Educación de Mexico, S.A. de C.V.
Pearson Education Malaysia Pte. Ltd.

10 9 8 7 6 5 4 3 2
0-13-110442-X

PREFACE

Automotive Fuel and Emissions Control Systems is organized around the A8 ASE automobile test content area for Engine Performance (A8) with a major emphasis on fuels and emissions. Terminology throughout the text reflects the SAE J1930 standard.

ASE and NATEF Correlated

This comprehensive textbook is correlated to the task list as specified by the National Institute for Automotive Service Excellence (ASE) and the National Automotive Technicians Education Foundation (NATEF). The ASE certification test topics are listed in the objectives at the beginning of each chapter, and all laboratory worksheets are correlated to the NATEF task list. The ASE Engine Performance (A8) test content includes:

A. **Engine Diagnosis** (Chapters 3, 4, 5, 6, 7, and 8)
B. **Ignition System Diagnosis and Repair** (Chapters 17, 22, and 23)
C. **Fuel, Air Induction, and Exhaust Systems Diagnosis and Repair** (Chapters 5, 6, 7, 18, 20, and 21)
D. **Emission Control Systems** (Chapters 19, 25, 26, 27, and 28)
E. **Computerized Engine Controls** (Chapters 11, 12, 13, 14, 15, 16, and 17)
F. **Engine Electrical Systems Diagnosis and Repair** (Chapters 9 and 10)

Diagnostic Approach

The primary focus of this textbook is to satisfy the need for problem diagnosis. Time and time again, the author has heard that technicians need more training in diagnostic procedures and skill development. To meet this need and to help illustrate how real problems are solved, diagnostic stories are included throughout. Each new topic covers the parts involved plus their purpose, function, and operation, as well as how to test and diagnose each system.

Multimedia System Approach

The multimedia CD-ROM that accompanies and supplements the textbook is informative and also makes learning more fun for the student. The CD includes:

1. PowerPoint presentations covering all aspects of the textbook material.
2. Live action videos and animation to help students understand complex systems.
3. A glossary of automotive terms.

4. Sample ASE test questions with immediate correct answer feedback.
5. Sample worksheets.
6. Crossword and word search puzzles.
7. ASE content list for Engine Performance (A8).
8. NATEF task lists for Engine Performance (A8).

Internet (World Wide Web) Approach

The book includes a coupon that entitles the owner to *free* access to an ASE test preparation website for an extended time period. Now you can practice and take the ASE certification tests with confidence. Included at this website are ASE-type questions for Engine Performance (A8). The questions are presented 10 at a time, then graded (marked). The correct answer is then given as you scroll back through the questions. This feature allows students to study at their own pace.

Worktext Approach

A worktext is also available with the book, and each activity sheet is correlated to the NATEF task list. The activity sheets are illustrated and help instructors and students apply the material presented to everyday-type activities and typical service and testing procedures. The worksheets show typical results and a listing of what could be defective if the test results are not within the acceptable range. These sheets help build diagnostic and testing skills. A NATEF checksheet is included so the students and the instructor can track student progress.

Chapter Components

- Each chapter opens with a list of learning *objectives*, including the ASE content topics covered by the chapter. These objectives identify the topics covered and goals to be achieved in the chapter.
- Most chapters contain *tech tips, diagnostic stories, frequently asked questions, high-performance tips,* and *guru tips.*
- All chapters contain a *summary* at the end that highlights the material covered in the chapter.
- *Review questions* (discussion-type questions) are offered at the end of each chapter.
- Each chapter contains *ASE certification-type questions.*

Type Styles Used in This Text

Various type styles are used throughout this text to emphasize words, identify important terms, and highlight figure references. *Italic type* is used to emphasize words and terms. For example, the word *not* is often printed in italic type when it is important that an operation be avoided. New terms appear in **bold type** at first usage. These terms are defined when introduced, and most are listed in the glossary at the back of the text.

Troubleshooting Charts

Troubleshooting charts have been added to the end of each service chapter. These charts will help the reader diagnose and repair common problems.

Color Use

Color is used extensively throughout this text to enhance understanding and highlight important information. This makes the textbook easier to read and helps illustrate important aspects of technical content.

Instructor Package

A comprehensive *instructor package* is available free when the text is adopted for classroom use from Prentice Hall (call 1-800-526-0485 or visit Prentice Hall online at **http://autotech.prenhall.com**).

This instructor package includes the following:

- PowerPoint presentations on all topics covered in the text.
- Instructor CD with suggested student activities, a test bank, an image library with hundreds of digital color photos, as well as line drawings and many other useful elements for the classroom.
- Answers to the crossword and word search puzzles.
- Answers to all questions in the textbook.

ACKNOWLEDGMENTS

A large number of people and organizations have cooperated in providing the reference material and technical information used in this text. The authors wish to express sincere thanks to the following persons and organizations for their special contributions:

Automotive Video Inc.
Fluke
Linder Technical Services, Inc.
John Thornton
Gary Smith

Technical and Content Reviewers

The following people reviewed the manuscript before production and checked it for technical accuracy and clarity of presentation. Their suggestions and recommendations were included in the final draft of the manuscript, and their input helped make this textbook clear and technically accurate while maintaining the easy-to-read style that has made other books from the same authors so popular.

Jim Anderson
Greenville High School

Victor Bridges
Umpqua Community College

Dr. Roger Donovan
Illinois Central College

A. C. Durdin
Moraine Park Technical College

Herbert Ellinger
Western Michigan University

Al Engledahl
College of Dupage

Larry Hagelberger
Upper Valley Joint Vocational School

Oldrick Hajzler
Red River College

Betsy Hoffman
Vermont Technical College

Steven T. Lee
Lincoln Technical Institute

Carlton H. Mabe, Sr.
Virginia Western Community College

Roy Marks
Owens Community College

Tony Martin
University of Alaska Southeast

Kerry Meier
San Juan College

Fritz Peacock
Indiana Vocational Technical College

Dennis Peter
NAIT (Canada)

Kenneth Redick
Hudson Valley Community College

Mitchell Walker
St. Louis Community College at Forest Park

Jennifer Wise
Sinclair Community College

Photo Sequences

The authors wish to thank Blaine Heeter, Frank Clay, Tony Martin, and Rick Henry, who photographed many of the photo sequences. Special thanks to all who helped, including:

B P ProCare
Dayton, Ohio

Rodney Cobb Chevrolet
Eaton, Ohio

Foreign Car Service
Huber Heights, Ohio

Genuine Auto Parts
Machine Shop
Dayton, Ohio

Import Engine and
Transmission
Dayton, Ohio

Dare Automotive
Specialists
Centerville, Ohio

Electric Garage
Beavercreek, Ohio

J and B Transmission
Service
Dayton, Ohio

Saturn of Orem
Orem, Utah

University of Alaska
Southeast
Juneau, Alaska

We want to thank Michele Winn, Doug Garriot, and Randy Dillman from Linder Technical Services, Inc., as well as John Thornton from Protec Auto Repair for their contributions to this book. We also wish to thank the faculty and students at Sinclair Community College in Dayton, Ohio, for their ideas and suggestions, as well as Richard Reaves for all of his help. Most of all, we wish to thank Michelle Halderman for her assistance in all phases of manuscript preparation.

James D. Halderman
Jim Linder

CONTENTS

Chapter 21 FUEL-INJECTION SYSTEM DIAGNOSIS AND SERVICE   362

Chapter 22 IGNITION SYSTEM COMPONENTS AND OPERATION   394

Chapter 23 IGNITION SYSTEM DIAGNOSIS AND SERVICE   416

TECH TIPS, FREQUENTLY ASKED QUESTIONS, DIAGNOSTIC STORIES, GURU TIPS AND SAFETY TIPS

PHOTO SEQUENCES

◀ Chapter 1 ▶

SERVICE INFORMATION, TOOLS, AND SAFETY

OBJECTIVES

After studying Chapter 1, the reader should be able to:

1. Prepare for ASE knowledge content for vehicle identification and the proper use of tools and shop equipment.
2. Retrieve vehicle service information.
3. Explain the strength ratings of threaded fasteners.
4. Describe how to safely hoist a vehicle.
5. Discuss how to safely use hand tools.
6. List the personal protective equipment (PPE) that all service technicians should wear.

VEHICLE IDENTIFICATION

All service work requires that the vehicle, including the engine and accessories, be properly identified. The most common identification is knowing the make, model, and year of the vehicle.

Make e.g., Chevrolet
Model e.g., Trailblazer
Year e.g., 2003

The year of the vehicle is often difficult to determine exactly. A model may be introduced as the next year's model as soon as January of the previous year. Typically, a new model year starts in September or October of the year prior to the actual new year, but not always. This is why the **vehicle identification number,** usually abbreviated **VIN,** is so important. See Figure 1-1. Since 1981 all vehicle manufacturers have used a VIN that is 17 characters long. Although every vehicle manufacturer assigns various letters or numbers within these 17 characters, there are some constants, including:

- The first number or letter designates the **country of origin.**

1 = United States	5 = United States
2 = Canada	6 = Australia
3 = Mexico	8 = Argentina
4 = United States	9 = Brazil

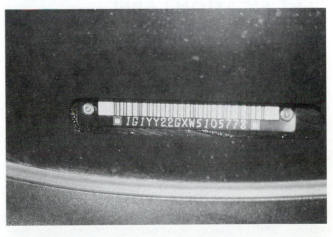

FIGURE 1-1 Typical vehicle identification number (VIN) as viewed through the windshield.

J = Japan
U = Romania
K = Korea
V = France
L = China
W = Germany
R = Taiwan
X = Russia
S = England
Y = Sweden
T = Czechoslovakia
Z = Italy

- The model of the vehicle is commonly the fourth and/or fifth character.
- The eighth character is often the engine code. (Some engines cannot be determined by the VIN number.)
- The tenth character represents the year on all vehicles. See the following chart.

VIN Year Chart
(The pattern repeats every 30 years.)

A = 1980/2010	S = 1995/2025
B = 1981/2011	T = 1996/2026
C = 1982/2012	V = 1997/2027
D = 1983/2013	W = 1998/2028
E = 1984/2014	X = 1999/2029
F = 1985/2015	Y = 2000/2030
G = 1986/2016	1 = 2001/2031
H = 1987/2017	2 = 2002/2032
J = 1988/2018	3 = 2003/2033
K = 1989/2019	4 = 2004/2034
L = 1990/2020	5 = 2005/2035
M = 1991/2021	6 = 2006/2036
N = 1992/2022	7 = 2007/2037
P = 1993/2023	8 = 2008/2038
R = 1994/2024	9 = 2009/2039

VEHICLE SAFETY CERTIFICATION LABEL

A vehicle safety certification label is attached to the left side pillar post on the rearward-facing section of the left front door. This label indicates the month and year of manufacture as well as the gross vehicle weight rating (GVWR), the gross axle weight rating (GAWR), and the vehicle identification number (VIN).

VECI LABEL

The **vehicle emissions control information (VECI)** label under the hood of the vehicle shows informative settings and emission hose routing information. See Figure 1-2. The VECI label (sticker) can be located on the bottom side of the hood, the radiator fan shroud, the

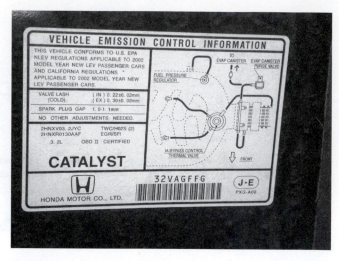

FIGURE 1-2 The vehicle emissions control information (VECI) sticker is placed under the hood.

radiator core support, or the strut towers. The VECI label usually includes the following information:

- Engine identification
- Emissions standard that the vehicle meets
- Vacuum hose routing diagram
- Base ignition timing (if adjustable)
- Spark plug type and gap
- Valve lash
- Emission calibration code

CALIBRATION CODES

Calibration codes are usually located on power train control modules (PCMs) or other controllers. Some calibration codes are only accessible with a scan tool. Whenever diagnosing an engine operating fault, it is often necessary to know the calibration code to be sure that the vehicle is the subject of a technical service bulletin or other service procedure. See Figure 1-3.

CASTING NUMBERS

Whenever an engine part such as a block is cast, a number is put into the mold to identify the casting. See Figure 1-4. These casting numbers can be used to check dimensions such as the cubic inch displacement and other information. Sometimes changes are made to the mold, yet the casting number is not changed. Most often the casting number is the best piece of identifying in-

FIGURE 1-3   A typical calibration code sticker on the case of a controller. The information on this sticker is often needed when ordering parts or a replacement controller.

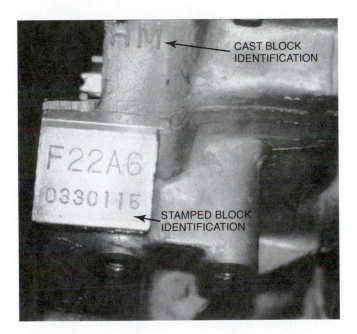

CAST BLOCK IDENTIFICATION

STAMPED BLOCK IDENTIFICATION

FIGURE 1-4   Engine block identification can be either cast or stamped or both.

formation that the service technician can use for identifying an engine.

SERVICE INFORMATION

Service information is needed by the service technician to determine specifications and service procedures, as well as learn about any necessary special tools.

FIGURE 1-5   A factory service manual contains all specifications and procedures for a particular vehicle or model in one or more volumes.

Service Manuals

Factory and aftermarket service manuals contain specifications and service procedures. While factory service manuals cover just one year and one or more models of the same vehicle, most aftermarket service manufacturers cover multiple years and/or models in one manual. See Figure 1-5. Included in most service manuals are the following:

- Capacities and recommended specifications for all fluids
- Specifications including engine and routine maintenance items
- Testing procedures
- Service procedures including the use of special tools when needed

Electronic Service Information

Electronic service information is available mostly by subscription and provides access to an Internet site where service manual-type information is available. See Figure 1-6. Most vehicle manufacturers also offer electronic service information to their dealers and to most schools and colleges that offer corporate training programs.

Technical Service Bulletins

Technical service bulletins, often abbreviated TSBs, are issued by the vehicle manufacturer to notify service technicians of a problem and include the necessary corrective action. Technical service bulletins are designed

FIGURE 1-6 Electronic service information is available from aftermarket sources such as All-Data and Mitchell-on-Demand as well as on websites hosted by the vehicle manufacturer.

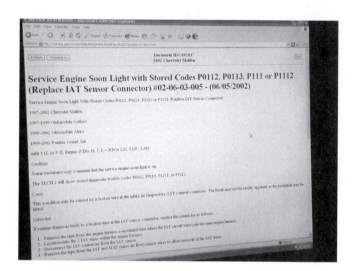

FIGURE 1-7 Technical service bulletins are issued by vehicle manufacturers when a fault occurs that affects many vehicles with the same problem.

for dealership technicians but are republished by aftermarket companies and made available along with other service information to shops and vehicle repair facilities. See Figure 1-7.

Internet

The Internet has opened the field for information exchange and access to technical advice. One of the most useful websites is the International Automotive Technician's Network at www.iatn.net. This is a free site but service technicians need to register to join.

For a small monthly sponsor fee, the shop or service technician can gain access to the archives, which include thousands of successful repairs in the searchable database.

Recalls and Campaigns

A recall or campaign is issued by a vehicle manufacturer and a notice is sent to all owners in the event of a safety or emission-related fault or concern. While these faults may be repaired by independent shops, it is generally handled by a local dealer. Items that have created recalls in the past have included potential fuel system leakage problems, exhaust leakage, or electrical malfunctions that could cause a possible fire or the engine to stall. Unlike technical service bulletins whose cost is only covered when the vehicle is within the warranty period, a recall or campaign is always done at no cost to the vehicle owner.

THREADED FASTENERS

Most of the threaded fasteners used on vehicles are cap screws. They are called **cap screws** when they are threaded into a casting. Automotive service technicians usually refer to these fasteners as **bolts,** regardless of how they are used. In this chapter, they are called bolts. Sometimes, studs are used for threaded fasteners. A **stud** is a short rod with threads on both ends. Often, a stud will have coarse threads on one end and fine threads on the other end. The end of the stud with coarse threads is screwed into the casting. A nut is used on the opposite end to hold the parts together.

The fastener threads *must* match the threads in the casting or nut. The threads may be measured either in fractions of an inch (called fractional) or in metric units. The size is measured across the outside of the threads, called the **crest** of the thread. See Figure 1-8.

Fractional threads are either coarse or fine. The coarse threads are called Unified National Coarse (UNC), and the fine threads are called Unified National Fine (UNF). Standard combinations of sizes and number of threads per inch (called **pitch**) are used. Pitch can be measured with a thread pitch gauge as shown in Figure 1-9. Bolts are identified by their diameter and length as measured from below the head, and not by the size of the head or the size of the wrench used to remove or install the bolt. Bolts and screws have many different-shaped heads. See Figure 1-10.

Fractional thread sizes are specified by the diameter in fractions of an inch and the number of threads per inch. Typical UNC thread sizes would be 5/16-18

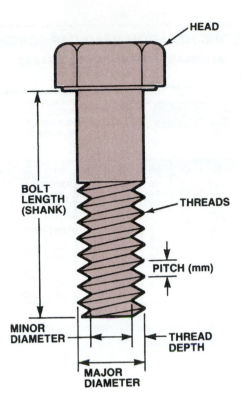

FIGURE 1-8   The dimensions of a typical bolt showing where sizes are measured.

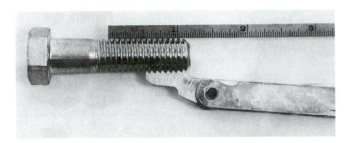

FIGURE 1-9   Thread pitch gauge used to measure the pitch of the thread. This bolt is 1/2-in. diameter with 13 threads to the inch (1/2-13).

and 1/2-13. Similar UNF thread sizes would be 5/16-24 and 1/2-20. See Figure 1-11.

METRIC BOLTS

The size of a metric bolt is specified by the letter *M* followed by the diameter in millimeters (mm) across the outside (crest) of the threads. Typical metric sizes would be M8 and M12. Fine metric threads are specified by the thread diameter followed by X and the distance between the threads measured in millimeters (M8 X 1.5). See Figure 1-12.

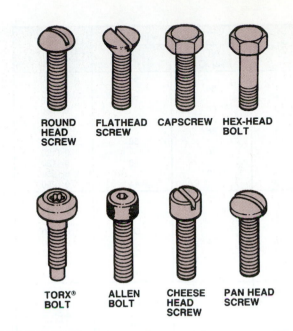

FIGURE 1-10   Bolts and screws have many different heads which determine what tool must be used.

GRADES OF BOLTS

Bolts are made from many different types of steel, and for this reason some are stronger than others. The strength or classification of a bolt is called the **grade.** The bolt heads are marked to indicate their grade strength.

The actual grade of bolts is two more than the number of lines on the bolt head. Metric bolts have a decimal number to indicate the grade. More lines or a higher grade number indicate a stronger bolt. Higher grade bolts usually have threads that are rolled rather than cut, which also makes them stronger. See Figure 1-14. In some cases, nuts and machine screws have similar grade markings.

CAUTION: *Never use hardware store (nongraded) bolts, studs, or nuts on any vehicle steering, suspension, or brake component. Always use the exact size and grade of hardware that is specified and used by the vehicle manufacturer.*

TENSILE STRENGTH

Graded fasteners have a higher tensile strength than nongraded fasteners. **Tensile strength** is the maximum stress used under tension (lengthwise force) without causing failure of the fastener. Tensile strength is specified in pounds per square inch (psi). See the chart that shows the grade and specified tensile strength.

Size	Threads per inch		Outside Diameter Inches
	NC UNC	NF UNF	
0	..	80	0.0600
1	64	..	0.0730
1	..	72	0.0730
2	56	..	0.0860
2	..	64	0.0860
3	48	..	0.0990
3	..	56	0.0990
4	40	..	0.1120
4	..	48	0.1120
5	40	..	0.1250
5	..	44	0.1250
6	32	..	0.1380
6	..	40	0.1380
8	32	..	0.1640
8	..	36	0.1640
10	24	..	0.1900
10	..	32	0.1900
12	24	..	0.2160
12	..	28	0.2160
1/4	20	..	0.2500
1/4	..	28	0.2500
5/16	18	..	0.3125
5/16	..	24	0.3125
3/8	16	..	0.3750
3/8	..	24	0.3750
7/16	14	..	0.4375
7/16	..	20	0.4375
1/2	13	..	0.5000
1/2	..	20	0.5000
9/16	12	..	0.5625
9/16	..	18	0.5625
5/8	11	..	0.6250
5/8	..	18	0.6250
3/4	10	..	0.7500
3/4	..	16	0.7500
7/8	9	..	0.8750
7/8	..	14	0.8750
1	8	..	1.0000
1	..	12	1.0000
1 1/8	7	..	1.1250
1 1/8	..	12	1.1250
1 1/4	7	..	1.2500
1 1/4	..	12	1.2500
1 3/8	6	..	1.3750
1 3/8	..	12	1.3750
1 1/2	6	..	1.5000
1 1/2	..	12	1.5000
1 3/4	5	..	1.7500
2	4 1/2	..	2.0000
2 1/4	4 1/2	..	2.2500
2 1/2	4	..	2.5000
2 3/4	4	..	2.7500
3	4	..	3.0000
3 1/4	4	..	3.2500
3 1/2	4	..	3.5000
3 3/4	4	..	3.7500
4	4	..	4.0000

FIGURE 1-11 The American National System is one method of sizing fasteners.

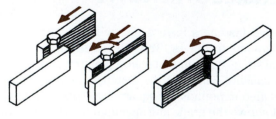

ROLLING THREADS

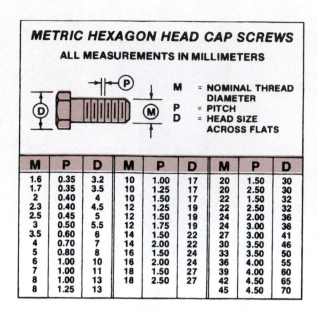

METRIC HEXAGON HEAD CAP SCREWS

ALL MEASUREMENTS IN MILLIMETERS

M = NOMINAL THREAD DIAMETER
P = PITCH
D = HEAD SIZE ACROSS FLATS

M	P	D	M	P	D	M	P	D
1.6	0.35	3.2	10	1.00	17	20	1.50	30
1.7	0.35	3.5	10	1.25	17	20	2.50	30
2	0.40	4	10	1.50	17	22	1.50	32
2.3	0.40	4.5	12	1.25	19	22	2.50	32
2.5	0.45	5	12	1.50	19	24	2.00	36
3	0.50	5.5	12	1.75	19	24	3.00	36
3.5	0.60	6	14	1.50	22	27	3.00	41
4	0.70	7	14	2.00	22	30	3.50	46
5	0.80	8	16	1.50	24	33	3.50	50
6	1.00	10	16	2.00	24	36	4.00	55
7	1.00	11	18	1.50	27	39	4.00	60
8	1.00	13	18	2.50	27	42	4.50	65
8	1.25	13				45	4.50	70

FIGURE 1-12 The metric system specifies fasteners by diameter, length, and pitch.

◀ TECH TIP ▶

THE WINTERGREEN OIL TRICK

Synthetic wintergreen oil, available at drugstores everywhere, makes an excellent penetrating oil. So the next time you can't get that rusted bolt loose, head for the drugstore. See Figure 1-13.

FIGURE 1-13 Synthetic wintergreen oil can be used as a penetrating oil to loosen rusted bolts or nuts.

FIGURE 1-14 Stronger threads are created by cold-rolling a heat-treated bolt blank instead of cutting the threads using a die.

The strength and type of steel used in a bolt is supposed to be indicated by a raised mark on the head of the bolt. The type of mark depends on the standard to which the bolt was manufactured. Most often, bolts used in machinery are made to SAE standard J429.

Metric bolt tensile strength property class is shown on the head of the bolt as a number, such as 4.6, 8.8, 9.8, and 10.9; the higher the number, the stronger the bolt. See Figure 1-15.

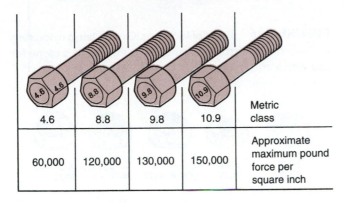

				Metric class
4.6	8.8	9.8	10.9	
60,000	120,000	130,000	150,000	Approximate maximum pound force per square inch

FIGURE 1-15 Metric bolt (cap screw) grade markings and approximate tensile strength.

SAE Bolt Designations

SAE Grade No.	Size Range	Tensile Strength, psi	Material	Head Marking
1	1/4 through 1-1/2	60,000	Low or medium carbon steel	
2	1/4 through 3/4	74,000		
	7/8 through 1-1/2	60,000		
5	1/4 through 1	120,000	Medium carbon steel, quenched & tempered	
	1-1/8 through 1-1/2	105,000		
5.2	1/4 through 1	120,000	Low carbon martensite steel[*], quenched & tempered	
7	1/4 through 1-1/2	133,000	Medium carbon alloy steel, quenched & tempered	
8	1/4 through 1-1/2	150,000	Medium carbon alloy steel, quenched & tempered	
8.2	1/4 through 1	150,000	Low carbon martensite steel[*], quenched & tempered	

[*]Martensite steel is steel that has been cooled rapidly, thereby increasing its hardness. It is named after a German metallurgist, Adolf Martens.

A 1/2-INCH WRENCH DOES NOT FIT A 1/2-INCH BOLT

A common mistake made by persons new to the automotive field is to think that the size of a bolt or nut is the size of the head. The size of the bolt or nut (outside diameter of the threads) is usually smaller than the size of the wrench or socket that fits the head of the bolt or nut. Examples are given in the following table:

Wrench Size	Thread Size
7/16 in.	1/4 in.
1/2 in.	5/16 in.
9/16 in.	3/8 in.
5/8 in.	7/16 in.
3/4 in.	1/2 in.
10 mm	6 mm
12 mm or 13 mm*	8 mm
14 mm or 17 mm*	10 mm

* European (Systeme International d'Unites-SI) metric.

HINT: An open-end wrench can be used to gauge bolt sizes. A 3/8-in. wrench will closely fit the threads of a 3/8-in. bolt.

NUTS

Most nuts used on cap screws have the same hex size as the cap screw head. Some inexpensive nuts use a hex size larger than the cap screw head. Metric nuts are often marked with dimples to show their strength. More dimples indicate stronger nuts. Some nuts and cap screws use interference fit threads to keep them from accidentally loosening. This means that the shape of the nut is slightly distorted or that a section of the threads is deformed. Nuts can also be kept from loosening with a nylon washer fastened in the nut or with a nylon patch or strip on the threads. See Figure 1-16.

NOTE: Most of these "locking nuts" are grouped together and are commonly referred to as **prevailing torque nuts**. This means that the nut will hold its tightness or torque and not loosen with movement or vibra-

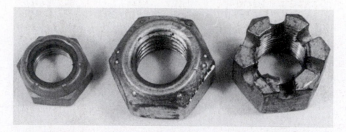

FIGURE 1-16 Types of lock nuts. On the left, a nylon ring; in the center, a distorted shape; and on the right, a castle for use with a cotter key.

HEX NUT — JAM NUT — NYLON LOCK NUT — CASTLE NUT — ACORN NUT

FLAT WASHER — LOCK WASHER — STAR WASHER — STAR WASHER

FIGURE 1-17 Various types of nuts (top) and washers (bottom) serve different purposes and all are used to secure bolts or cap screws.

tion. Most prevailing torque nuts should be replaced whenever removed to ensure that the nut will not loosen during service. Always follow the manufacturer's recommendations. Anaerobic sealers, such as Loctite, are used on the threads where the nut or cap screw must be both locked and sealed.

WASHERS

Washers are often used under cap screw heads and under nuts. See Figure 1-17. Plain flat washers are used to provide an even clamping load around the fastener. Lock washers are added to prevent accidental loosening. In some accessories, the washers are locked onto the nut to provide easy assembly.

ELECTRICAL TOOLS

Electrical-related tools include various types of soldering guns.

- **Electric soldering gun** This type of soldering gun is usually powered by 110-volt AC and often has two power settings expressed in watts. A typical electric soldering gun will produce from 85 to 300 watts of heat at the tip, which is more than adequate for soldering. See Figure 1-18.

- **Electric soldering pencil** This type of soldering iron is less expensive and creates less heat than an electric soldering gun. A typical electric soldering pencil (iron) creates 30 to 60 watts of heat and is suitable for soldering most smaller wires and connections. See Figure 1-19.

- **Butane-powered soldering iron** A butane-powered soldering iron is portable and very useful for automotive service work because an electrical cord is not needed. Most butane-powered soldering irons produce about 60 watts of heat, which is enough for most automotive soldering.

In addition to a soldering iron, most service technicians who do electrical-related work should have the following:

- Wire cutters
- Wire strippers
- Wire crimpers
- Heat gun

A digital meter is a necessary tool for any electrical diagnosis and troubleshooting. A digital multimeter, abbreviated DMM, is usually capable of measuring the following units of electricity:

- DC volts
- AC volts
- Ohms
- Amperes

See Chapter 10 for details on digital meters and meter usage.

BASIC HAND TOOL LIST

Hand tools are used to turn fasteners (bolts, nuts, and screws). The following is a list of hand tools every automotive technician should possess. Specialty tools are not included. See Figures 1-20 through 1-38.

FIGURE 1-18   A typical 110-volt electric soldering gun.

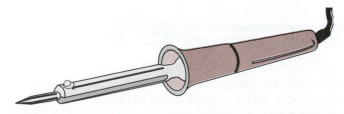

FIGURE 1-19   A typical 110-volt electric soldering pencil.

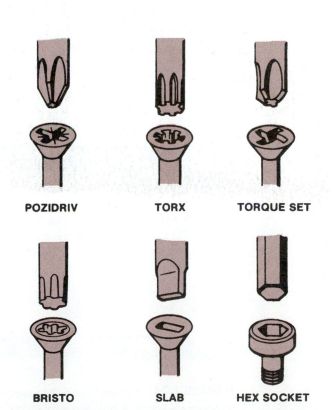

POZIDRIV   TORX   TORQUE SET

BRISTO   SLAB   HEX SOCKET

FIGURE 1-20   Many different types of screw heads have been used over the years in a variety of applications.

FIGURE 1-21 Combination wrench. The openings are the same size at both ends. Notice the angle of the open end to permit use in close spaces.

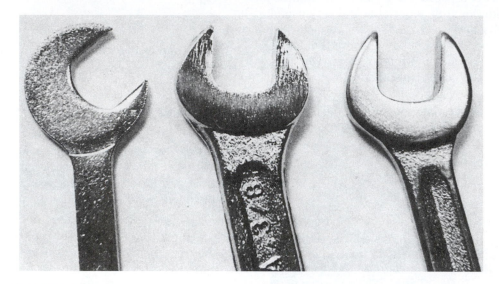

FIGURE 1-22 Three different qualities of open-end wrenches. The cheap wrench on the left is made from weaker steel and is thicker and less accurately machined than the standard in the center. The wrench on the right is of professional quality (and price).

FIGURE 1-23 Flare-nut wrench; also known as a *line wrench, fitting wrench,* or *tube-nut wrench*. This style of wrench is designed to grasp most of the flats of a six-sided (hex) tubing fitting to provide the most grip without damage to the fitting.

FIGURE 1-24 Box-end wrench; recommended to loosen or tighten a bolt or nut where a socket will not fit. A box-end wrench has a different size at each end and is better to use than an open-end wrench because it touches the bolt or nut around the entire head instead of at just two places.

FIGURE 1-25   Open-end wrench. Each end has a different-sized opening and is recommended for general usage. Do not attempt to loosen or tighten bolts or nuts from or to full torque with an open-end wrench because it could round the flats of the fastener.

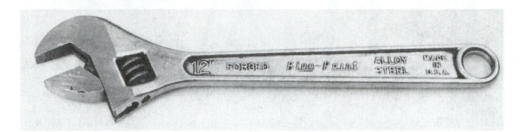

FIGURE 1-26   Adjustable wrench. The size (12 inches) is the *length* of the wrench, not how far the jaws open!

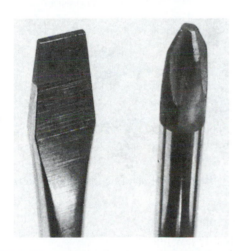

FIGURE 1-27   A flat-blade (or straight-blade) screwdriver (on the left) is specified by the length of the screwdriver and width of the blade. The width of the blade should match the width of the screw slot of the fastener. A Phillips-head screwdriver (on the left) is specified by the length of the handle and the size of the point at the tip. A #1 is a sharp point, a #2 is most common (as shown), and a #3 Phillips is blunt and is only used for larger sizes of Phillips-head fasteners.

Safety glasses
Tool chest
1/4-inch drive socket set (1/4 in. to 9/16 in. standard and deep sockets; 6 mm to 15 mm standard and deep sockets)
1/4-inch drive ratchet
1/4-inch drive 2-inch extension

1/4-inch drive 6-inch extension
1/4-inch drive handle
3/8-inch drive socket set (3/8 in. to 7/8 in. standard and deep sockets; 10 mm to 19 mm standard and deep sockets)
3/8-inch drive Torx set (T40, T45, T50, and T55)
3/8-inch drive 13/16-inch plug socket
3/8-inch drive 5/8-inch plug socket
3/8-inch drive ratchet
3/8-inch drive 1 1/2-inch extension
3/8-inch drive 3-inch extension
3/8-inch drive 6-inch extension
3/8-inch drive 18-inch extension
3/8-inch drive universal
1/2-inch drive socket set (1/2 in. to 1 in. standard and deep sockets)
1/2-inch drive ratchet
1/2-inch drive breaker bar
1/2-inch drive 5-inch extension
1/2-inch drive 10-inch extension
3/8-inch to 1/4-inch adapter
1/2-inch to 3/8-inch adapter
3/8-inch to 1/2-inch adapter
Crowfoot set (fractional inch)
Crowfoot set (metric)
3/8- through 1-inch combination wrench set
10 millimeters through 19 millimeters combination wrench set

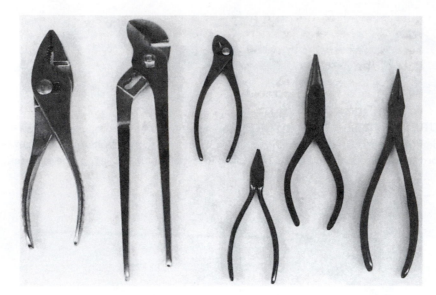

FIGURE 1-28 Assortment of pliers. Slip-joint pliers (far left) are often confused with water pump pliers (second from left).

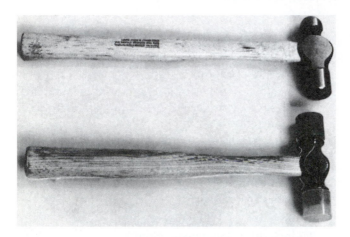

FIGURE 1-29 A ball-peen hammer (top) is purchased according to the weight (usually in ounces) of the head of the hammer. At bottom is a soft-faced (plastic) hammer. Always use a hammer that is softer than the material being driven. Use a block of wood or similar material between a steel hammer and steel or iron engine parts to prevent damage to the engine parts.

1/16-inch through 1/4-inch hex wrench set
2 millimeters through 12 millimeters hex wrench set
3/8-inch hex socket
13 millimeters to 14 millimeters flare nut wrench
15 millimeters to 17 millimeters flare nut wrench
5/16-inch to 3/8-inch flare nut wrench
7/16-inch to 1/2-inch flare nut wrench
1/2-inch to 9/16-inch flare nut wrench
Diagonal pliers

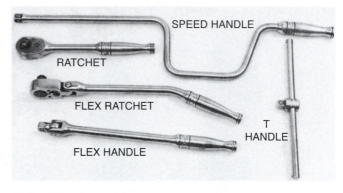

FIGURE 1-30 Typical drive handles for sockets.

Needle pliers
Adjustable-jaw pliers
Locking pliers
Snap-ring pliers
Stripping or crimping pliers
Ball-peen hammer
Rubber hammer
Dead-blow hammer
Five-piece standard screwdriver set
Four-piece Phillips screwdriver set
#15 Torx screwdriver
#20 Torx screwdriver
Awl
Mill file
Center punch
Pin punches (assorted sizes)

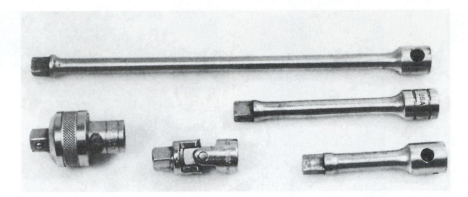

FIGURE 1-31 Various socket extensions. The universal joint (U-joint) in the center (bottom) is useful for gaining access in tight areas.

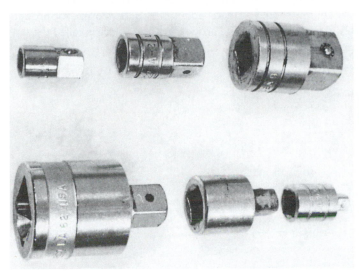

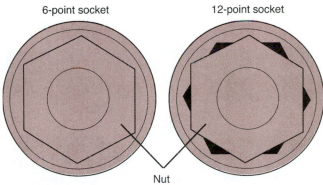

FIGURE 1-33 A 6-point socket fits the head of the bolt or nut on all sides. A 12-point socket can round off the head of a bolt or nut if a lot of force is applied.

FIGURE 1-32 Socket drive adapters. These adapters permit the use of a 3/8-inch drive ratchet with 1/2-inch drive sockets, or other combinations as the various adapters permit. Adapters should *not* be used where a larger tool used with excessive force could break or damage a smaller-sized socket.

Chisel

Utility knife

Valve core tool

Filter wrench (large filters)

Filter wrench (smaller filters)

Test light

Feeler gauge

Scraper

Pinch bar

Magnet

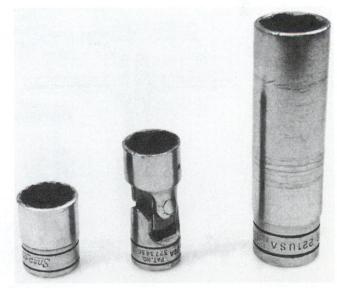

FIGURE 1-34 Standard 12-point short socket (left), universal joint socket (center), and deep-well socket (right). Both the universal and deep well are 6-point sockets.

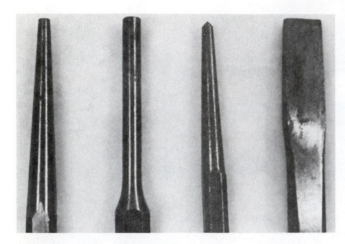

FIGURE 1-35 Various punches on the left and a chisel on the right.

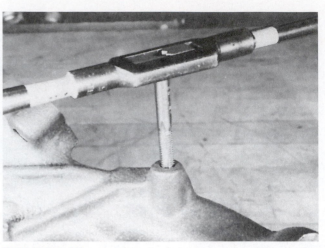

FIGURE 1-38 Starting a tap in a drilled hole. The hole diameter should be matched exactly to the tap size for proper thread clearance. The proper drill size to use is called the tap drill size.

FIGURE 1-36 Using a die to cut threads on a rod.

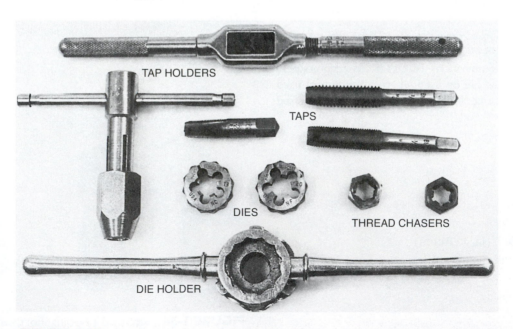

TAP HOLDERS

TAPS

DIES

THREAD CHASERS

DIE HOLDER

FIGURE 1-37 Dies are used to make threads on the outside of round stock. Taps are used to make threads inside holes. A thread chaser is used to clean threads without removing metal.

TOOL SETS AND ACCESSORIES

A beginning service technician may wish to start with a small set of tools before spending a lot of money on an expensive, extensive toolbox. See Figures 1-39 through 1-41.

(a)

(b)

FIGURE 1-39 (a) A beginning technician can start with some simple basic hand tools. (b) An experienced, serious technician often spends several thousand dollars a year for tools such as those found in this large (and expensive) toolbox.

◀ TECH TIP ▶

HIDE THOSE FROM THE BOSS

An apprentice technician started working for a dealership and put his top toolbox on a workbench. Another technician observed that, along with a complete set of good-quality tools, the box contained several adjustable wrenches. The more experienced technician said, "Hide those from the boss." If any adjustable wrench is used on a bolt or nut, the movable jaw often moves or loosens and starts to round the head of the fastener. If the head of the bolt or nut becomes rounded, it becomes that much more difficult to remove.

FIGURE 1-40 An inexpensive muffin tin can be used to keep small parts separated.

FIGURE 1-41 A good fluorescent trouble light is essential. A fluorescent light operates cooler than an incandescent light and does not pose a fire hazard as when gasoline is accidentally dropped on an unprotected incandescent bulb used in some trouble lights.

◀ **TECH TIP** ▶

NEED TO BORROW A TOOL MORE THAN TWICE? BUY IT!

Most service technicians agree that it is okay for a beginning technician to borrow a tool occasionally. However, if a tool has to be borrowed more than twice, then be sure to purchase it as soon as possible. Also, whenever a tool is borrowed, be sure that you clean the tool and let the technician you borrowed the tool from know that you are returning the tool. These actions will help in any future dealings with other technicians.

◀ **TECH TIP** ▶

THE VALVE GRINDING COMPOUND TRICK

Apply a small amount of valve grinding compound to a Phillips or Torx screw or bolt head. The gritty valve grinding compound "grips" the screwdriver or tool bit and prevents the tool from slipping up and out of the screw head. Valve grinding compound is available in a tube from most automotive parts stores.

BRAND NAME VERSUS PROPER TERM

Technicians often use slang or brand names of tools rather than the proper term. This results in some confusion for new technicians. Some examples are given in the following table.

Brand Name	Proper Term	Slang Name
Crescent wrench	Adjustable wrench	Monkey wrench
Vise Grips	Locking pliers	
Channel Locks	Water pump pliers or multigroove adjustable pliers	Pump pliers
	Diagonal cutting pliers	Dikes or side cuts

◀ **TECH TIP** ▶

IT JUST TAKES A SECOND

Whenever removing any automotive component, it is wise to screw the bolts back into the holes a couple of threads by hand. This ensures that the right bolt will be used in its original location when the component or part is put back on the vehicle. Often, the same diameter of fastener is used on a component, but the length of the bolt may vary. Spending just a couple of seconds to put the bolts and nuts back where they belong when the part is removed can save a lot of time when the part is being reinstalled. Besides making certain that the right fastener is being installed in the right place, this method helps prevent bolts and nuts from getting lost or kicked away. How much time have you wasted looking for that lost bolt or nut?

SAFETY TIPS FOR USING HAND TOOLS

The following safety tips should be kept in mind whenever you are working with hand tools:

- Always *pull* a wrench toward you for best control and safety. Never push a wrench.
- Keep wrenches and all hand tools clean to help prevent rust and to allow for a better, firmer grip.
- Always use a 6-point socket or a box-end wrench to break loose a tight bolt or nut.
- Use a box-end wrench for torque and an open-end wrench for speed.
- Never use a pipe extension or other type of "cheater bar" on a wrench or ratchet handle. If more force is required, use a larger tool or use penetrating oil and/or heat on the frozen fastener. (If heat is used on a bolt or nut to remove it, always replace it with a new part.)
- Always use the proper tool for the job. If a specialized tool is required, use the proper tool and do not try to use another tool improperly.
- Never expose any tool to excessive heat. High temperatures can reduce the strength ("draw the temper") of metal tools.
- Never use a hammer on any wrench or socket handle unless you are using a special "staking face" wrench designed to be used with a hammer.
- Replace any tools that are damaged or worn.

AIR AND ELECTRICALLY OPERATED TOOLS

Impact Wrench

An impact wrench, either air (pneumatic) or electrically powered, is a tool that is used to remove and install fasteners. The air-operated 1/2-inch drive impact wrench is the most commonly used unit. See Figure 1-42. The direction of rotation is controlled by a switch. See Figure 1-43. Electrically powered impact wrenches commonly include:

- Battery-powered units. See Figure 1-44.

- 110-volt AC-powered units. This type of impact is very useful, especially if compressed air is not readily available.

CAUTION: Always use impact sockets with impact wrenches, and be sure to wear eye protection in case the socket or fastener shatters. Impact sockets are thicker walled and constructed with premium alloy steel. They are hardened with a black oxide finish to help prevent corrosion and distinguish them from regular sockets. See Figure 1-45.

FIGURE 1-42 A typical 1/2-inch drive air impact wrench.

FIGURE 1-44 A typical battery-powered 3/8-inch drive impact wrench.

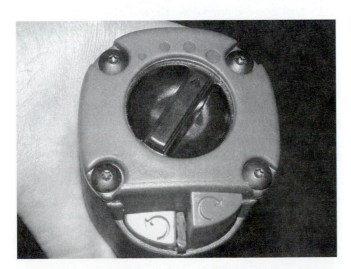

FIGURE 1-43 This air impact wrench features a variable torque setting using a rotary knob; the direction of rotation can be changed by pressing the buttons at the bottom.

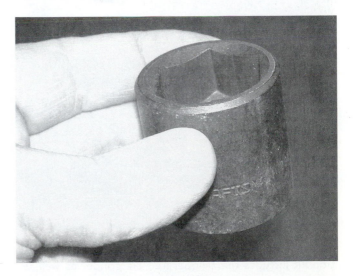

FIGURE 1-45 A black impact socket. Always use impact-type sockets whenever using an impact wrench to avoid the possibility of shattering the socket, which can cause personal injury.

Air Ratchet

An air ratchet is used to remove and install fasteners that would normally be removed or installed using a ratchet and a socket. An air ratchet is much faster, yet has an air hose attached, which reduces accessibility to certain places. See Figure 1-46.

Die Grinder

A die grinder is a commonly used air-powered tool which can also be used to sand or remove gaskets and rust. See Figure 1-47.

FIGURE 1-46 An air ratchet is a very useful tool that allows fast removal and installation of fasteners, especially in areas that are difficult to reach or do not have room enough to move a hand ratchet wrench.

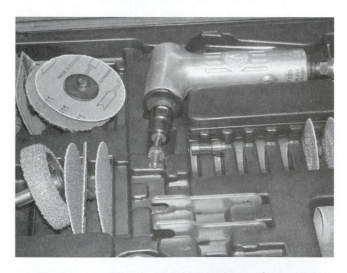

FIGURE 1-47 This typical die grinder surface preparation kit includes the air-operated die grinder as well as a variety of sanding disks for smoothing surfaces or removing rust.

Bench- or Pedestal-Mounted Grinder

These high-powered grinders can be equipped with a wire brush wheel and/or a stone wheel.

- A **wire brush wheel** is used to clean threads of bolts as well as to remove gaskets from sheet metal engine parts.
- A **stone wheel** is used to grind metal or to remove the mushroom from the top of punches or chisels. See Figure 1-48.

CAUTION: Always wear a face shield when using a wire wheel or a grinder. Also keep the port support ledge (table) close to the stone.

◀ TECH TIP ▶

WEARING GLOVES SAVES YOUR HANDS

Many technicians wear gloves not only to help keep their hands clean but also to help protect their skin from the effects of dirty engine oil and other possibly hazardous materials. Several types of gloves and their characteristics include:

- **Latex surgical gloves**—These gloves are relatively inexpensive, but tend to stretch, swell, and weaken when exposed to gas, oil, or solvents.
- **Vinyl gloves**—These gloves are also inexpensive and are not affected by gas, oil, or solvents.
- **Polyurethane gloves**—These gloves are more expensive, yet very strong. Even though these gloves are also not affected by gas, oil, or solvents, they do tend to be slippery.
- **Nitrile gloves**—These gloves are exactly like latex gloves, but are not affected by gas, oil, or solvents, yet they tend to be expensive.
- **Mechanic's gloves**—These gloves are usually made of synthetic leather and spandex and provide thermal protection, as well as protection from dirt and grime.

See Figure 1-49.

FIGURE 1-48 A typical pedestal grinder with a wire wheel on the left side and a stone wheel on the right side. Even though this machine is equipped with guards, safety glasses or a face shield should always be worn whenever working using a grinder or wire wheel.

SAFETY TIPS FOR TECHNICIANS

Safety is not just a buzzword on a poster in the work area. Safe work habits can reduce accidents and injuries, ease the workload, and keep employees pain free. Suggested personal protection equipment (PPE) and safety tips include the following:

- *Safety glasses that meet standard ANSI Z87.1 should be worn at all times while servicing any vehicle.* See Figure 1-50.

NOTE: Prescription glasses are not considered safety glasses even if they state "shatter proof" unless they meet the ANSI specifications.

FIGURE 1-49 Protective gloves such as these vinyl gloves are available in several sizes. Select the size that allows the gloves to fit snugly. Vinyl gloves last a long time and often can be worn all day to help protect your hands from dirt and possible hazardous materials.

- Watch your toes—always keep your toes protected with steel-toed safety shoes. See Figure 1-51. If safety shoes are not available, then leather-topped shoes offer more protection than canvas or cloth.
- Wear gloves to protect your hands from rough or sharp surfaces. Thin rubber gloves are recommended when working around automotive liquids

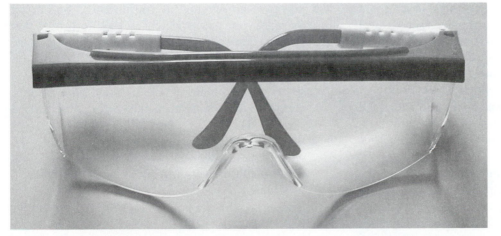

FIGURE 1-50 Safety glasses should be worn at all times when working on or around any vehicle or servicing any component.

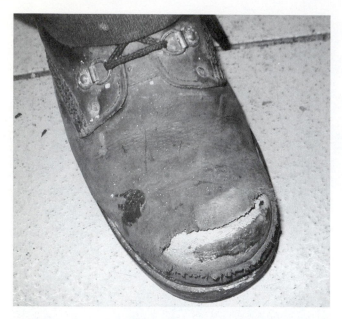

FIGURE 1-51 Steel-toed shoes are a worthwhile investment to help prevent foot injury due to falling objects. Even these well-worn shoes can protect the feet of this service technician.

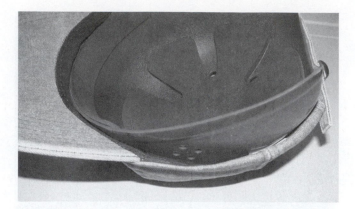

FIGURE 1-52 One version of a bump cap is this padded plastic insert that is worn inside a regular cloth cap.

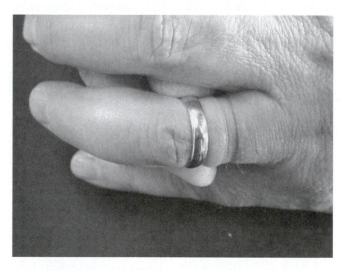

FIGURE 1-53 Remove all jewelry before performing service work on any vehicle.

such as engine oil, antifreeze, transmission fluid, or any other liquids that may be hazardous.

- Service technicians working under a vehicle should wear a **bump cap** to protect the head against under-vehicle objects and the pads of the lift. See Figure 1-52.
- Remove jewelry that may get caught on something or act as a conductor to an exposed electrical circuit. See Figure 1-53.
- Take care of your hands. Keep your hands clean by washing with soap and hot water that is at least 110°F (43°C).
- Avoid loose or dangling clothing.
- Ear protection should be worn if the sound around you requires that you raise your voice (sound level higher than 90 dB). (A typical lawnmower produces noise at a level of about 110 dB. This means that everyone who uses a lawnmower or other lawn or garden equipment should wear ear protection.)
- When lifting any object, get a secure grip with solid footing. Keep the load close to your body to minimize the strain. Lift with your legs and arms, not your back.
- Do not twist your body when carrying a load. Instead, pivot your feet to help prevent strain on the spine.
- Ask for help when moving or lifting heavy objects.

- Push a heavy object rather than pull it. (This is opposite to the way you should work with tools— never push a wrench! If you do and a bolt or nut loosens, your entire weight is used to propel your hand(s) forward. This usually results in cuts, bruises, or other painful injury.)
- Always connect an exhaust hose to the tailpipe of any running vehicle to help prevent the buildup of carbon monoxide inside a closed garage space. See Figure 1-54.
- When standing, keep objects, parts, and tools with which you are working between chest height and waist height. If seated, work at tasks that are at elbow height.
- Always be sure the hood is securely held open. See Figure 1-55.

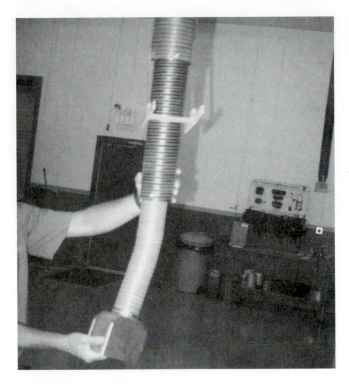

FIGURE 1-54 Always connect an exhaust hose to the tailpipe of the engine of a vehicle to be run inside a building.

◀ **TECH TIP** ▶

SHOP CLOTH DISPOSAL

Always dispose of oily shop cloths in an enclosed container to prevent a fire. See Figure 1-56. Whenever oily cloths are thrown together on the floor or workbench, a chemical reaction can occur which can ignite the cloth even without an open flame. This process of ignition without an open flame is called **spontaneous combustion.**

◀ **TECH TIP** ▶

SHOCK CONTROL

To avoid impact damage from your impact wrench on your hand, take the rubber covering from an old electric fuel pump and fit it on the handle of the gun. This tremendously softens the blow.

(a)

HOOD STRUT
CLAMP

(b)

FIGURE 1-55 (a) A crude but effective method is to use locking pliers on the chrome-plated shaft of a hood strut. Locking pliers should only be used on defective struts because the jaws of the pliers can damage the strut shaft. (b) A commercially available hood clamp. This tool uses a bright orange tag to help remind the technician to remove the clamp before attempting to close the hood. The hood could be bent if force is used to close the hood with the clamp in place.

FIGURE I-56 All oily shop cloths should be stored in a metal container equipped with a lid to help prevent spontaneous combustion.

SAFETY IN LIFTING (HOISTING) A VEHICLE

Many chassis and underbody service procedures require that the vehicle be hoisted or lifted off the ground. The simplest methods involve the use of drive-on ramps or a floor jack and safety (jack) stands, whereas in-ground or surface-mounted lifts provide greater access.

Setting the pads is a critical part of this procedure. All automobile and light-truck service manuals include recommended locations to be used when hoisting (lifting) a vehicle. Newer vehicles have a triangle decal on the driver's door indicating the recommended lift points. The recommended standards for the lift points and lifting procedures are found in SAE Standard JRP-2184. See Figure 1-57. These recommendations typically include the following points:

1. The vehicle should be centered on the lift or hoist so as not to overload one side or put too much force either forward or rearward. See Figure 1-58.
2. The pads of the lift should be spread as far apart as possible to provide a stable platform.
3. Each pad should be placed under a portion of the vehicle that is strong and capable of supporting the weight of the vehicle.
    a. Pinch welds at the bottom edge of the body are generally considered to be strong.

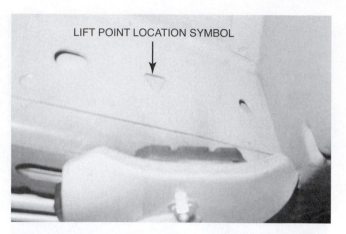

FIGURE I-57 Most newer vehicles have a triangle symbol indicating the recommended hoisting lift points.

b. On trucks, SUVs, and other vehicles that use a frame, place the pads on the frame rails.

CAUTION: Even though pinch weld seams are the recommended location for hoisting many vehicles with unitized bodies (unit-body), care should be taken not to place the pad(s) too far forward or rearward. Incorrect placement of the vehicle on the lift could cause the vehicle to be imbalanced, and the vehicle could fall. This is exactly what happened to the vehicle in Figure 1-59.

---

c. Boxed areas of the body are the best places to position the pads on a vehicle without a frame. Be careful to note whether the arms of the lift might come into contact with other parts of the vehicle before the pad touches the intended location. Commonly damaged areas include the following:
    1. Rocker panel moldings
    2. Exhaust system (including catalytic converter)
    3. Tires or body panels (See Figures 1-60 and 1-61.)
4. The vehicle should be raised about a foot (30 centimeters [cm]) off the floor, then stopped and shaken to check for stability. If the vehicle seems to be stable when checked at a short distance from the floor, continue raising the vehicle and continue to view the vehicle until it has reached the desired height. The hoist should be lowered onto the mechanical locks, and then raised off of the locks before lowering.

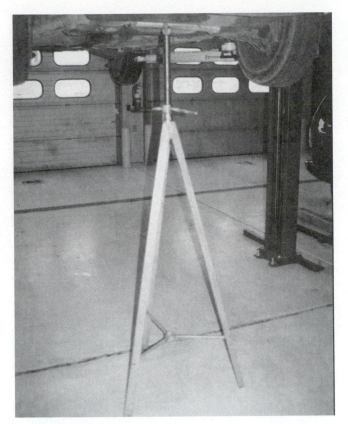

(a)

(b)

FIGURE 1-58   (a) Tall safety stands can be used to provide additional support for a vehicle while on a hoist. (b) A block of wood should be used to avoid the possibility of doing damage to components supported by the stand.

CAUTION: Do not look away from the vehicle while it is being raised (or lowered) on a hoist. Often one side or one end of the hoist can stop or fail, resulting in the vehicle being slanted enough to slip or fall, creating physical damage not only to the vehicle and/or hoist but also to the technician or others who may be nearby.

FIGURE 1-59   This vehicle fell from the hoist because the pads were not set correctly. No one was hurt, but the vehicle was a total loss.

(a)

(b)

FIGURE 1-60   (a) An assortment of hoist pad adapters that are often necessary to safely hoist many pickup trucks, vans, and sport utility vehicles. (b) A view from underneath a Chevrolet pickup truck showing how the pad extensions are used to attach the hoist lifting pad to contact the frame.

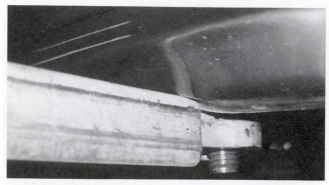
(a)

(b)

FIGURE 1-61 (a) In this photo the pad arm is just contacting the rocker panel of the vehicle. (b) This photo shows what can occur if the technician places the pad too far inward underneath the vehicle. The arm of the hoist has dented in the rocker panel.

HINT: Most hoists can be safely placed at any desired height. For ease while working, the area in which you are working should be at chest level. When working on brakes or suspension components, it is not necessary to work on them down near the floor or over your head. Raise the hoist so that the components are at chest level.

---

5. Before lowering the hoist, the safety latch(es) must be released and the direction of the controls reversed. The speed downward is often adjusted to be as slow as possible for additional safety.

JACKS AND SAFETY STANDS

Floor jacks properly rated for the weight of the vehicle being raised are a common vehicle lifting tool. Floor jacks are portable and relatively inexpensive and must be used with safety (jack) stands. The floor

(a)

(b)

FIGURE 1-62 (a) A typical 3-ton (6000-pound) capacity hydraulic floor jack. (b) Whenever a vehicle is raised off of the ground, a safety stand should be placed under the frame, axle, or body to support the weight of the vehicle.

jack is used to raise the vehicle off the ground and safety stands should be placed under the frame on the body of the vehicle. The weight of the vehicle should never be kept on the hydraulic floor jack because a failure of the jack could cause the vehicle to fall. See Figure 1-62. The jack is then slowly released to allow the vehicle weight to be supported on the safety stands. If the front or rear of the vehicle is being raised, the opposite end of the vehicle must be blocked.

CAUTION: Safety stands should be rated higher than the weight they support.

DRIVE-ON RAMPS

Ramps are an inexpensive way to raise the front or rear of a vehicle. See Figure 1-63. Ramps are easy to store, but they can be dangerous because they can "kick out" when driving the vehicle onto the ramps.

CAUTION: Professional repair shops do not use ramps because they are dangerous to use. Use only with extreme care.

◀ TECH TIP ▶

POUND WITH SOMETHING SOFTER

If you must pound on something, be sure to use a tool that is softer than what you are about to pound on to avoid damage. Examples are given in the following table.

The Material Being Pounded	*What to Pound With*
Steel or cast iron	Brass or aluminum hammer or punch
Aluminum	Plastic or rawhide mallet or plastic-covered dead-blow hammer
Plastic	Rawhide mallet or plastic dead-blow hammer

ELECTRICAL CORD SAFETY

Use correctly grounded three-prong sockets and extension cords to operate power tools. Some tools use only two-prong plugs. Make sure these are double insulated and repair or replace any electrical cords that are cut or damaged to prevent the possibility of an electrical shock. When not in use, keep electrical cords off the floor to prevent tripping over them. Tape the cords down if they are placed in high foot traffic areas.

JUMP STARTING AND BATTERY SAFETY

To jump start another vehicle with a dead battery, connect good quality copper jumper cables as indicated in Figure 1-64 or a jump box. The last connection made should always be on the engine block or an engine bracket as far from the battery as possible. It is normal for a spark to be created when the jumper cables finally complete the jumping circuit, and this spark could cause an explosion of the gases around the battery. Many newer vehicles have special negative and positive terminals built away from the battery just for the purpose of jump starting. Check the owner's manual or service information for the exact location.

Batteries contain acid and should be handled with care to avoid tipping them greater than a 45-degree angle. Always remove jewelry when working around a battery to avoid the possibility of electrical shock or burns, which can occur when the metal comes in contact with a 12-volt circuit and ground, such as the body of the vehicle.

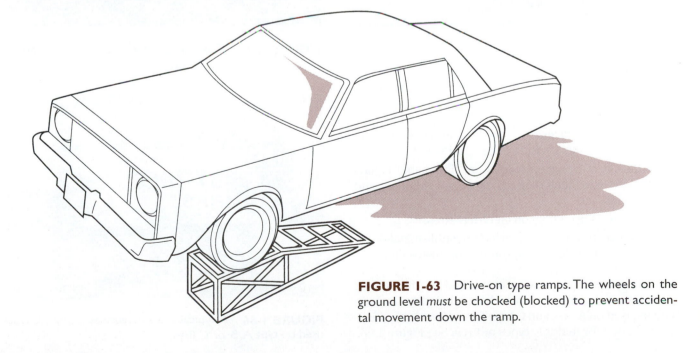

FIGURE 1-63 Drive-on type ramps. The wheels on the ground level *must* be chocked (blocked) to prevent accidental movement down the ramp.

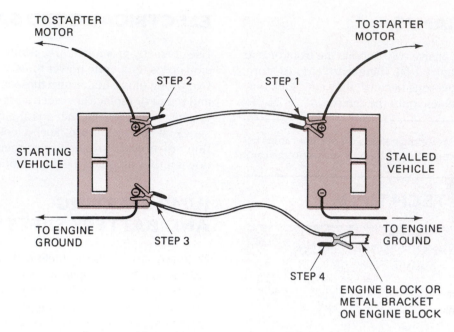

FIGURE 1-64   Jumper cable usage guide.

◀ **SAFETY TIP** ▶

AIR HOSE SAFETY

Improper use of an air nozzle can cause blindness or deafness. Compressed air must be reduced to less than 30 psi (206 kPa). See Figure 1-65. If an air nozzle is used to dry and clean parts, make sure the airstream is directed away from anyone else in the immediate area. Coil and store air hoses when they are not in use. Only use OSHA approved air nozzles.

FIRE EXTINGUISHERS

There are four classes of fire extinguishers. Each class should be used on specific fires only:

- **Class A** is designed for use on general combustibles, such as cloth, paper, and wood.
- **Class B** is designed for use on flammable liquids and greases, including gasoline, oil, thinners, and solvents.
- **Class C** is used only on electrical fires.
- **Class D** is effective only on combustible metals such as powdered aluminum, sodium, or magnesium.

The class rating is clearly marked on the side of every fire extinguisher such as those labeled ABC which can be used on A-, B-, and C-type fires. Many extinguishers are good for multiple types of fires. See Figure 1-66.

FIGURE 1-65   The air pressure going to the nozzle should be reduced to 30 psi or less.

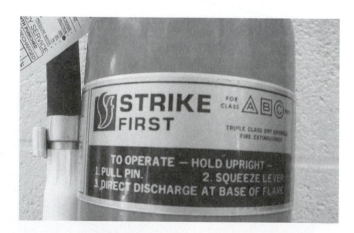

FIGURE 1-66   A typical fire extinguisher designed to be used on type A, B, or C fires.

FIGURE 1-67 A CO_2 fire extinguisher being used on a fire set in an open steel drum during a demonstration at a fire department training center.

FIGURE 1-68 A treated wool blanket is kept in this easy-to-open wall-mounted holder and should be placed in a centralized location in the shop.

When using a fire extinguisher, remember the word "PASS."

P = Pull the safety pin.
A = Aim the nozzle of the extinguisher at the base of the fire.
S = Squeeze the lever to actuate the extinguisher.
S = Sweep the nozzle from side-to-side.

See Figure 1-67.

Types of Fire Extinguishers

Types of fire extinguishers include the following:

- **Water** A water fire extinguisher, usually in a pressurized container, is good to use on Class A fires by reducing the temperature to the point where a fire cannot be sustained.
- **Carbon dioxide (CO_2)** A carbon dioxide fire extinguisher is good for almost any type of fire, especially Class B or Class C materials. A CO_2 fire extinguisher works by removing the oxygen from the fire and the cold CO_2 also helps reduce the temperature of the fire.
- **Dry chemical (yellow)** A dry chemical fire extinguisher is good for Class A, B, or C fires by coating the flammable materials, which eliminates the oxygen from the fire. A dry chemical fire extinguisher tends to be very corrosive and will cause damage to electronic devices.

FIRE BLANKETS

Fire blankets are required in the shop areas. If a person is on fire, a fire blanket should be removed from its storage bag and thrown over and around the victim to smother the fire. See Figure 1-68 showing a typical fire blanket.

FIRST AID AND EYE WASH STATIONS

All shop areas must be equipped with a first aid kit and an eye wash station centrally located and kept stocked with emergency supplies.

First Aid Kit

A first aid kit should include:

- Bandages (variety)
- Gauze pads
- Roll gauze
- Iodine swab sticks
- Antibiotic ointment
- Hydrocortisone cream
- Burn gel packets
- Eye wash solution
- Scissors
- Tweezers
- Gloves
- First aid guide

See Figure 1-69. Every shop should have a person trained in first aid. If there is an accident, call for help immediately.

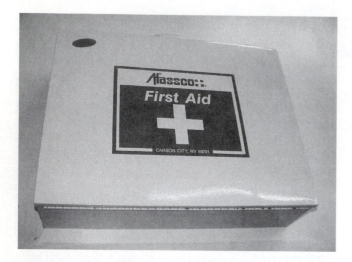

FIGURE 1-69 A first aid box should be centrally located in the shop and kept stocked with the recommended supplies.

Eye Wash Station

An eye wash station should be centrally located and used whenever any liquid or chemical gets into the eyes. If such an emergency does occur, keep eyes in a constant stream of water and call for professional assistance. See Figure 1-70.

◀ TECH TIP ▶

MARK OFF THE SERVICE AREA

Some shops rope off the service bay area to help keep traffic and distractions to a minimum, which could prevent personal injury. See Figure 1-71. Tape should be placed on the floor indicating vehicle traffic areas in all shops.

◀ SAFETY TIP ▶

INFECTION CONTROL PRECAUTIONS

Working on a vehicle can result in personal injury including the possibility of being cut or hurt enough to cause bleeding. Some infections such as hepatitis B, HIV (which can cause acquired immunodeficiency syndrome, or AIDS), hepatitis C virus, and others are transmitted in the blood. These infections are commonly called blood-borne pathogens. Report any injury that involves blood to your supervisor and take the necessary precautions to avoid coming in contact with blood from another person.

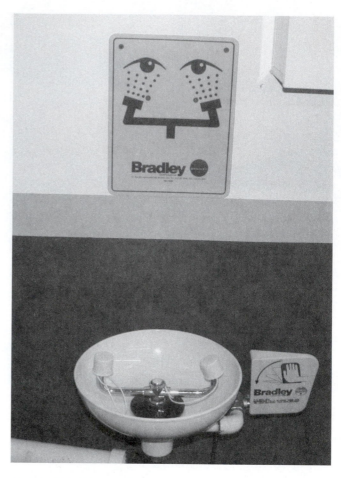

FIGURE 1-70 A typical eye wash station. Often a thorough flushing of the eyes with water is the best treatment in the event of eye contamination.

FIGURE 1-71 This area has been blocked off to help keep visitors from the dangerous work area.

PHOTO SEQUENCE Hoisting the Vehicle

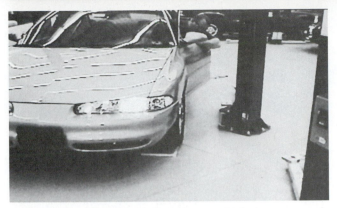

PS 1-1 The first step in hoisting a vehicle is to properly align the vehicle in the center of the stall.

TIRE PAD

PS 1-2 Most vehicles will be correctly positioned when the left front tire is centered on the tire pad.

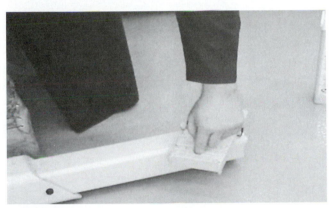

PS 1-3 Most pads at the end of the hoist arms can be rotated to allow for many different types of vehicle construction.

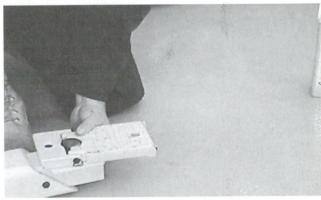

PS 1-4 The arms of the lifts can be retracted or extended to accommodate vehicles of many different lengths.

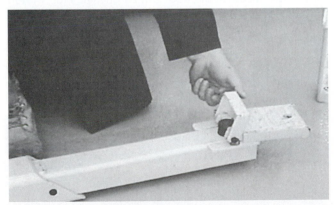

PS 1-5 Most lifts are equipped with short pad extensions that are often necessary to use to allow the pad to contact the frame of a vehicle without causing the arm of the lift to hit and damage parts of the body.

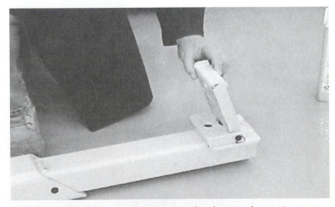

PS 1-6 Tall pad extensions can also be used to gain access to the frame of a vehicle. This position is needed to safely hoist many pickup trucks, vans, and sport utility vehicles.

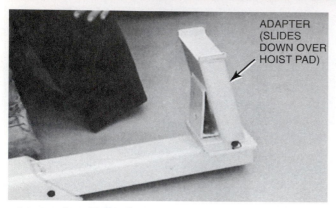

PS 1-7 An additional extension may be necessary to hoist a truck or van equipped with running boards to give the necessary clearance.

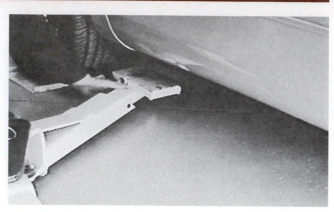

PS 1-8 Position the front hoist pads under the recommended locations as specified in the owner's manual and/or service information for the vehicle being serviced.

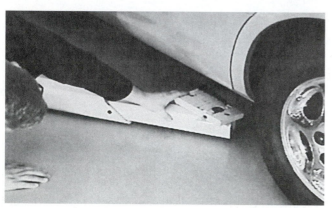

PS 1-9 Position the rear pads under the vehicle under the recommended locations.

PS 1-10 This photo shows an asymmetrical lift where the front arms are shorter than the rear arms. This design is best used for passenger cars and allows the driver to exit the vehicle easier because the door can be opened wide without it hitting the vertical support column.

PS 1-11 After being sure all pads are correctly positioned, use the electromechanical controls to raise the vehicle.

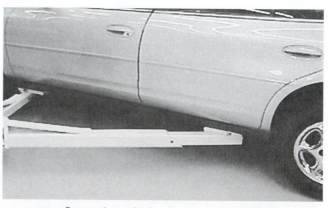

PS 1-12 Raise the vehicle about one foot (30 cm) and stop to double-check that all pads contact the body or frame in the correct positions.

PHOTO SEQUENCE   Hoisting the Vehicle—*Continued*

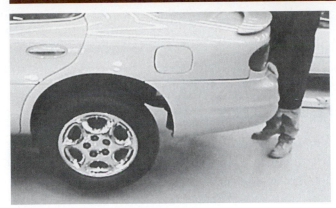

PS 1-13 With the vehicle raised about one foot off the ground, push down on the vehicle to check to see if it is stable on the pads. If the vehicle rocks, lower the vehicle and reset the pads. If the vehicle is stable, the vehicle can be raised to any desired working level. Be sure the safety is engaged before working on or under the vehicle.

PS 1-14 This photo shows the pads set flat and contacting the pinch welds of the body. This method spreads the load over the entire length of the pad and is less likely to dent or damage the pinch weld area.

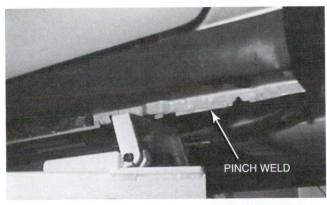

PS 1-15 Where additional clearance is necessary for the arms to clear the rest of the body, the pads can be raised and placed under the pinch weld area as shown.

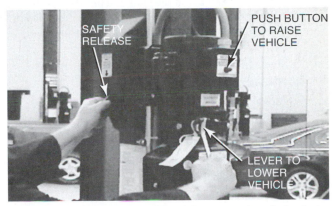

PS 1-16 When the service work is completed, the hoist should be raised slightly and the safety released before using the hydraulic lever to lower the vehicle.

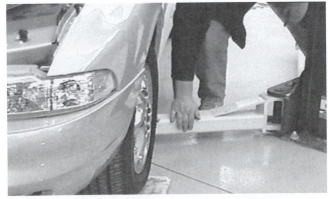

PS 1-17 After lowering the vehicle, be sure all arms of the lift are moved out of the way before driving the vehicle out of the work stall.

PS 1-18 Carefully back the vehicle out of the stall. Notice that all of the lift arms have been neatly moved out of the way to provide clearance so that the tires will not contact the arms when the vehicle is driven out of the stall.

SUMMARY

1. Bolts, studs, and nuts are commonly used as fasteners in the chassis. The sizes for fractional and metric threads are different and are not interchangeable. The grade is the rating of the strength of a fastener.

2. Whenever a vehicle is raised above the ground, it must be supported at a substantial section of the body or frame.

REVIEW QUESTIONS

1. List three precautions that must be taken whenever hoisting (lifting) a vehicle.

2. Describe how to determine the grade of a fastener, including how the markings differ between fractional and metric bolts.

3. List four items that are personal protective equipment (PPE).

4. List the types of fire extinguishers and their usage.

ASE CERTIFICATION-TYPE QUESTIONS

1. Two technicians are discussing the hoisting of a vehicle. Technician A says to put the pads of a lift under a notch at the pinch weld seams of a unit-body vehicle. Technician B says to place the pads on the frame rails of a full-frame vehicle. Which technician is correct?
   a. Technician A only
   b. Technician B only
   c. Both Technicians A and B
   d. Neither Technician A nor B

2. The correct location for the pads when hoisting or jacking the vehicle can often be found in the _____.
   a. Service manual
   b. Shop manual
   c. Owner's manual
   d. All of the above

3. For the best working position, the work should be _____.
   a. At neck or head level
   b. At knee or ankle level
   c. Overhead by about 1 foot
   d. At chest or elbow level

4. When working with hand tools, always _____.
   a. Push the wrench—don't pull toward you
   b. Pull a wrench—don't push a wrench

5. A high-strength bolt is identified by _____.
   a. A UNC symbol
   b. Lines on the head
   c. Strength letter codes
   d. The coarse threads

6. A fastener that uses threads on both ends is called a _____.
   a. Cap screw
   b. Stud
   c. Machine screw
   d. Crest fastener

7. The proper term for Channel Locks is _____.
   a. Vise Grips
   b. Crescent wrench
   c. Locking pliers
   d. Multigroove adjustable pliers

8. The proper term for Vise Grips is _____.
   a. Locking pliers
   b. Slip-joint pliers
   c. Side cuts
   d. Multigroove adjustable pliers

9. What is *not* considered to be personal protective equipment (PPE)?
   a. Air impact wrench
   b. Safety glasses
   c. Rubber gloves
   d. Hearing protection

10. Which tool listed is a brand name?
    a. Locking pliers
    b. Monkey wrench
    c. Side cutters
    d. Vise Grips

◀ Chapter 2 ▶

ENVIRONMENTAL AND HAZARDOUS MATERIALS

OBJECTIVES

After studying Chapter 2, the reader should be able to:

1. Prepare for the ASE assumed knowledge content required by all service technicians to adhere to environmentally appropriate actions and behavior.
2. Define the Occupational Safety and Health Act (OSHA).
3. Explain the term Material Safety Data Sheet (MSDS).
4. Identify hazardous waste materials in accordance with state and federal regulations and follow proper safety precautions while handling hazardous waste materials.
5. Define the steps required to safely handle and store automotive chemicals and waste.

Safety and the handling of hazardous waste material are extremely important in the automotive shop. The improper handling of hazardous material affects us all, not just those in the shop. Shop personnel must be familiar with their rights and responsibilities regarding hazardous waste disposal. Right-to-know laws explain these rights. Shop personnel must also be familiar with hazardous materials in the automotive shop, and the proper way to dispose of these materials according to state and federal regulations.

OCCUPATIONAL SAFETY AND HEALTH ACT

The United States Congress passed the **Occupational Safety and Health Act (OSHA)** in 1970. This legislation was designed to assist and encourage the citizens of the United States in their efforts to assure safe and healthful working conditions by providing research, information, education, and training in the field of occupational safety and health, as well as to assure safe and healthful working conditions for working men and women by authorizing enforcement of the standards developed under the Act. Since approximately 25% of workers are exposed to health and safety hazards on the job, the OSHA standards are necessary to monitor, control, and educate workers regarding health and safety in the workplace.

HAZARDOUS WASTE

CAUTION: When handling hazardous waste material, one must always wear the proper protective clothing and equipment detailed in the right-to-know laws. This includes respirator equipment. All recommended procedures must be followed accurately. Personal injury may result from improper clothing, equipment, and procedures when handling hazardous materials.

Hazardous waste materials are chemicals, or components, that the shop no longer needs that pose a danger to the environment and people if they are disposed of in ordinary garbage cans or sewers. However, one should note that no material is considered hazardous waste until the shop has finished using it and is ready to dispose of it. The **Environmental Protection Agency (EPA)** publishes a list of hazardous materials that is included in the Code of Federal Regulations (CFR). The EPA considers waste hazardous if it is included on the EPA list of hazardous materials, or it has one or more of the following characteristics.

Reactive

Any material which reacts violently with water or other chemicals is considered hazardous.

Corrosive

If a material burns the skin, or dissolves metals and other materials, a technician should consider it hazardous. A pH scale is used, with the number 7 indicating neutral. Pure water has a pH of 7. Lower numbers indicate an acidic solution and higher numbers indicate a caustic (basic) solution. If a material releases cyanide gas, hydrogen sulfide gas, or similar gases when exposed to low pH acid solutions, it is considered hazardous.

Toxic

Materials are hazardous if they leak one or more of eight different heavy metals in concentrations greater than 100 times the primary drinking water standard.

Ignitable

A liquid is hazardous if it has a flash point below 140°F (60°C), and a solid is hazardous if it ignites spontaneously.

Radioactive

Any substance that emits measurable levels of radiation is radioactive. When individuals bring containers of a highly radioactive substance into the shop environment, qualified personnel with the appropriate equipment must test them.

WARNING: Hazardous waste disposal laws include serious penalties for anyone responsible for breaking these laws.

RESOURCE CONSERVATION AND RECOVERY ACT (RCRA)

Federal and state laws control the disposal of hazardous waste materials. Every shop employee must be familiar with these laws. Hazardous waste disposal laws include the *Resource Conservation and Recovery Act (RCRA)*. This law states that hazardous material users are responsible for hazardous materials from the time they become a waste until the proper waste disposal is completed. Many shops hire an independent hazardous waste hauler to dispose of hazardous waste material. The shop owner, or manager, should have a written contract with the hazardous waste hauler. Rather than have hazardous waste material hauled to an approved hazardous waste disposal site, a shop may choose to recycle the material in the shop. Therefore, the user must store hazardous waste material properly and safely, and be responsible for the transportation of this material until it arrives at an approved hazardous waste disposal site, where it can be processed according to the law. The RCRA controls these types of automotive waste:

- Paint and body repair products waste
- Solvents for parts and equipment cleaning
- Batteries and battery acid
- Mild acids used for metal cleaning and preparation
- Waste oil, engine coolants, or antifreeze
- Air-conditioning refrigerants and oils
- Engine oil filters

The **right-to-know laws** state that employees have a right to know when the materials they use at work are hazardous. The right-to-know laws started with the **Hazard Communication Standard** published by the Occupational Safety and Health Administration (OSHA) in 1983. Originally, this document was intended for chemical companies and manufacturers that required employees to handle hazardous materials in their work situation. Meanwhile, the federal courts have decided to apply these laws to all companies, including automotive service shops. Under the right-to-know laws, the employer has responsibilities regarding the handling of hazardous materials by their employees. All employees must be trained about the types of hazardous materials they will encounter in the workplace. The employees must be informed about their rights under legislation regarding the handling of hazardous materials.

CLEAN AIR ACT

Air-conditioning (A/C) systems and refrigerant are regulated by the Clean Air Act, Title VI, Section 609. Technician certification and service equipment are also regulated. Any technician working on automotive A/C systems must be certified. A/C refrigerants must not be released or vented into the atmosphere, and used refrigerants must be recovered.

MATERIAL SAFETY DATA SHEETS (MSDS)

All hazardous materials must be properly labeled, and information about each hazardous material must be posted on **Material Safety Data Sheets (MSDS)** available from the manufacturer. See Figure 2-1. In Canada, MSDS sheets are called **Workplace Hazardous Materials Information Systems (WHMIS).**

FIGURE 2-1 Material Safety Data Sheets (MSDS) should be readily available for use by anyone in the area who may come into contact with hazardous materials.

The employer has a responsibility to place MSDS sheets where they are easily accessible by all employees. The MSDS sheets provide the following information about the hazardous material: chemical name, physical characteristics, protective handling equipment, explosion/fire hazards, incompatible materials, health hazards, medical conditions aggravated by exposure, emergency and first-aid procedures, safe handling, and spill/leak procedures.

The employer also has a responsibility to make sure that all hazardous materials are properly labeled. The label information must include health, fire, and reactivity hazards posed by the material, as well as the protective equipment necessary to handle the material. The manufacturer must supply all warning and precautionary information about hazardous materials. This information must be read and understood by the employee before handling the material.

THE DANGERS OF EXPOSURE TO ASBESTOS

Friction materials such as brake and clutch linings often contain asbestos. While asbestos has been eliminated from most original equipment friction materials, the automotive service technician cannot know whether or not the vehicle being serviced is or is not equipped with friction materials containing asbestos. It is important that all friction materials be handled as if they do contain asbestos.

Asbestos exposure can cause scar tissue to form in the lungs. This condition is called **asbestosis.** It gradually causes increasing shortness of breath, and the scarring to the lungs is permanent.

Even low exposures to asbestos can cause **mesothelioma,** a type of fatal cancer of the lining of the chest or abdominal cavity. Asbestos exposure can also increase the risk of **lung cancer** as well as cancer of the voice box, stomach, and large intestine. It usually takes 15 to 30 years or more for cancer or asbestos lung scarring to show up after exposure. (Scientists call this the **latency period.**)

Government agencies recommend that asbestos exposure should be eliminated or controlled to the lowest level possible. These agencies have developed recommendations and standards that the automotive service technician and equipment manufacturer should follow. These U.S. federal agencies include the National Institute for Occupational Safety and Health (NIOSH), Occupational Safety and Health Administration (OSHA), and Environmental Protection Agency (EPA).

ASBESTOS OSHA STANDARDS

The Occupational Safety and Health Administration (OSHA) has established three levels of asbestos exposure. Any vehicle service establishment that does either brake or clutch work must limit employee exposure to asbestos to less than 0.2 fibers per cubic centimeter (cc) as determined by an air sample.

If the level of exposure to employees is greater than specified, corrective measures must be performed and a large fine may be imposed.

NOTE: Research has found that worn asbestos fibers such as those from automotive brakes or clutches may not be as hazardous as first believed. Worn asbestos fibers do not have sharp flared ends that can latch onto tissue, but rather are worn down to a dust form that resembles talc. Grinding or sawing operations on unworn brake shoes or clutch discs *will* contain *harmful* asbestos fibers. To limit health damage, always use proper handling procedures while working around any component that may contain asbestos.

ASBESTOS EPA REGULATIONS

The federal Environmental Protection Agency (EPA) has established procedures for the removal and disposal of asbestos. The EPA procedures require that products containing asbestos be "wetted" to prevent the asbestos fibers from becoming airborne. According to the EPA, asbestos-containing materials can be disposed of as regular waste. Only when asbestos becomes airborne is it considered to be hazardous.

ASBESTOS HANDLING GUIDELINES

The air in the shop area can be tested by a testing laboratory, but this can be expensive. Tests have determined that asbestos levels can easily be kept below the recommended levels by using a solvent or a special vacuum.

NOTE: Even though asbestos is being removed from brake and clutch lining materials, the service technician cannot tell whether or not the old brake pads, shoes, or clutch disc contain asbestos. Therefore, to be safe, the technician should assume that all brake pads, shoes, or clutch discs contain asbestos.

HEPA Vacuum

A special high-efficiency particulate air (HEPA) vacuum system has been proven to be effective in keeping asbestos exposure levels below 0.1 fibers per cubic centimeter.

Solvent Spray

Many technicians use an aerosol can of brake cleaning solvent to wet the brake dust and prevent it from becoming airborne. Commercial brake cleaners are available that use a concentrated cleaner that is mixed with water. See Figure 2-2.

The waste liquid is filtered, and when dry, the filter can be disposed of as solid waste.

CAUTION: Never use compressed air to blow brake dust. The fine talc-like brake dust can create a health hazard even if asbestos is not present or is present in dust rather than fiber form.

FIGURE 2-2 All brakes should be moistened with water or solvent to help prevent brake dust from becoming airborne.

Disposal of Brake Dust and Brake Shoes

The hazard of asbestos occurs when asbestos fibers are airborne. Once the asbestos has been wetted down, it is then considered to be solid waste, rather than hazardous waste. Old brake shoes and pads should be enclosed, preferably in a plastic bag, to help prevent any of the brake material from becoming airborne. *Always follow current federal and local laws concerning disposal of all waste.*

USED BRAKE FLUID

Most brake fluid is made from polyglycol, is water soluble, and can be considered hazardous if it has absorbed metals from the brake system.

- Collect brake fluid in containers clearly marked to indicate that they are dedicated for that purpose.
- If the waste brake fluid is hazardous, manage it appropriately and use only an authorized waste receiver for its disposal.
- If the waste brake fluid is nonhazardous (such as old, but unused), determine from your local solid waste collection provider what should be done for its proper disposal.
- Do not mix brake fluid with used engine oil.
- Do not pour brake fluid down drains or onto the ground.
- Recycle brake fluid through a registered recycler.

USED OIL

Used oil is any petroleum-based or synthetic oil that has been used. During normal use, impurities such as dirt, metal scrapings, water, or chemicals can get mixed in with the oil. Eventually, this used oil must be replaced with virgin or re-refined oil. The EPA's used oil management standards include a three-pronged approach to determine if a substance meets the definition of used oil. To meet the EPA's definition of used oil, a substance must meet each of the following three criteria.

- **Origin** The first criterion for identifying used oil is based on the oil's origin. Used oil must have been refined from crude oil or made from synthetic materials. Animal and vegetable oils are excluded from the EPA's definition of used oil.

- **Use** The second criterion is based on whether and how the oil is used. Oils used as lubricants, hydraulic fluids, heat transfer fluids, and for other similar purposes are considered used oil. Unused oil, such as bottom clean-out waste from virgin fuel oil storage tanks or virgin fuel oil recovered from a spill, does not meet the EPA's definition of used oil because these oils have never been "used." The EPA's definition also excludes products used as cleaning agents, as well as certain petroleum-derived products like antifreeze and kerosene.
- **Contaminants** The third criterion is based on whether or not the oil is contaminated with either physical or chemical impurities. In other words, to meet the EPA's definition, used oil must become contaminated as a result of being used. This aspect of the EPA's definition includes residues and contaminants generated from handling, storing, and processing used oil.

NOTE: The release of only one gallon of used oil (a typical oil change) can make a million gallons of fresh water undrinkable.

If used oil is dumped down the drain and enters a sewage treatment plant, concentrations as small as 50 to 100 PPM (parts per million) in the waste water can foul sewage treatment processes. Never mix a listed hazardous waste, gasoline, waste water, halogenated solvent, antifreeze, or an unknown waste material with used oil. Adding any of these substances will cause the used oil to become contaminated, which classifies it as hazardous waste.

DISPOSAL OF USED OIL

Once oil has been used, it can be collected, recycled, and used over and over again. An estimated 380 million gallons of used oil are recycled each year. Recycled used oil can sometimes be used again for the same job or can take on a completely different task. For example, used engine oil can be re-refined and sold at the store as engine oil or processed for furnace fuel oil. After collecting used oil in an appropriate container (e.g., a 55-gallon steel drum), the material must be disposed of in one of two ways:

- Shipped offsite for recycling
- Burned in an onsite or offsite EPA-approved heater for energy recovery

USED OIL STORAGE

Used oil must be stored in compliance with an existing **underground storage tank (UST)** or an **aboveground storage tank (AGST)** standard, or kept in separate containers. See Figure 2-3. Containers are portable receptacles, such as a 55-gallon steel drum.

Keep Used Oil Storage Drums in Good Condition

This means that they should be covered, secured from vandals, properly labeled, and maintained in compliance with local fire codes. Frequent inspections for leaks, corrosion, and spillage are an essential part of container maintenance.

Never Store Used Oil in Anything Other Than Tanks and Storage Containers

Used oil may also be stored in units that are permitted to store regulated hazardous waste.

Used Oil Filter Disposal Regulations

Used oil filters contain used engine oil that may be hazardous. Before an oil filter is placed into the trash or sent to be recycled, it must be drained using one of the following hot draining methods approved by the EPA.

- Puncture the filter antidrain back valve or filter dome end and hot drain for at least 12 hours
- Hot drain and crushing

FIGURE 2-3 A typical aboveground oil storage tank.

- Dismantling and hot draining
- Any other hot draining method, which will remove all the used oil from the filter

After the oil has been drained from the oil filter, the filter housing can be disposed of in any of the following ways:

- Sent for recycling
- Pickup by a service contract company
- Disposed of in regular trash

SOLVENTS

The major sources of chemical danger are liquid and aerosol brake cleaning fluids that contain chlorinated hydrocarbon solvents. Several other chemicals that do not deplete the ozone, such as heptane, hexane, and xylene, are now being used in nonchlorinated brake cleaning solvents. Some manufacturers are also producing solvents they describe as environmentally responsible, which are biodegradable and noncarcinogenic.

Sources of Chemical Poisoning

The health hazards presented by brake cleaning solvents occur from three different forms of exposure: ingestion, inhalation, or physical contact. It should be obvious that swallowing brake cleaning solvent is harmful, and such occurrences are not common. Still, brake cleaning solvents should always be handled and stored properly, and kept out of the reach of children. The dangers of inhalation are perhaps the most serious problem, as even very low levels of solvent vapors are hazardous.

Allowing brake cleaning solvents to come in contact with the skin presents a danger because these solvents strip natural oils from the skin and cause irritation of the tissues, plus they can be absorbed through the skin directly into the bloodstream. The transfer begins immediately upon contact, and continues until the liquid is wiped or washed away.

There is no specific standard for physical contact with chlorinated hydrocarbon solvents or the chemicals replacing them. All contact should be avoided whenever possible. The law requires an employer to provide appropriate protective equipment and ensure proper work practices by an employee handling these chemicals.

Effects of Chemical Poisoning

The effects of exposure to chlorinated hydrocarbon and other types of solvents can take many forms. Short-term exposure at low levels can cause headache, nausea, drowsiness, dizziness, lack of coordination, or unconsciousness. It may also cause irritation of the eyes, nose, and throat, and flushing of the face and neck. Short-term exposure to higher concentrations can cause liver damage with symptoms such as yellow jaundice or dark urine. Liver damage may not become evident until several weeks after the exposure.

Health Care Rights

The OSHA regulations concerning on-the-job safety place certain responsibilities on the employer, and give employees specific rights. Any person who feels there might be unsafe conditions where he or she works, whether asbestos exposure, chemical poisoning, or any other problem, should discuss the issue with fellow workers, their union representative (where applicable), and their supervisor or employer. If no action is taken and there is reason to believe the employer is not complying with OSHA standards, a complaint can be filed with OSHA and it will investigate.

◀ SAFETY TIP ▶

HAND SAFETY

Service technicians should wash their hands with soap and water after handling engine oil or differential or transmission fluids, or wear protective rubber gloves. Another safety hint is that the service technician should not wear watches, rings, or other jewelry that could come in contact with electrical or moving parts of a vehicle. See Figure 2-4.

FIGURE 2-4 Washing hands and removing jewelry are two important safety habits all service technicians should practice.

The law forbids employers from taking action against employees who file a complaint concerning a health or safety hazard. However, if workers fear reprisal as the result of a complaint, they may request that OSHA withhold their names from the employer.

SOLVENT HAZARDOUS AND REGULATORY STATUS

Most solvents are classified as hazardous wastes. Other characteristics of solvents include the following.

- Solvents with flash points below 140°F are considered flammable and, like gasoline, are federally regulated by the Department of Transportation (DOT).
- Solvents and oils with flash points above 140°F are considered combustible and, like engine oil, are also regulated by the DOT. See Figure 2-5.

It is the responsibility of the repair shop to determine if its spent solvent is hazardous waste. Waste solvents that are considered hazardous waste have a flash point below 140°F (60°C). Hot water or aqueous parts cleaners may be used to avoid disposing of spent solvent as hazardous waste. Solvent-type parts cleaners with filters are available to greatly extend solvent life and reduce spent solvent disposal costs. Solvent reclaimers are available that clean and restore the solvent so it lasts indefinitely.

FIGURE 2-5 Typical fireproof flammable storage cabinet.

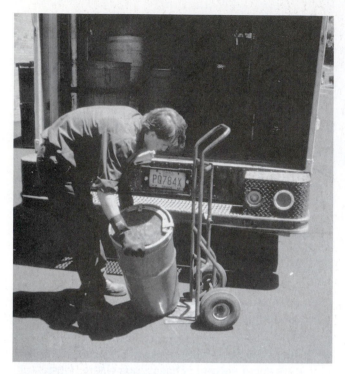

FIGURE 2-6 All solvents and other hazardous waste should be disposed of properly.

FIGURE 2-7 Used antifreeze coolant should be kept separate and stored in a leakproof container until it can be recycled or disposed of according to federal, state, and local laws. Note that the storage barrel is placed inside another container to catch any coolant that may spill out of the inside barrel.

USED SOLVENTS

Used or spent solvents are liquid materials that have been generated as waste and may contain xylene, methanol, ethyl ether, and methyl isobutyl ketone (MIBK). These materials must be stored in OSHA-approved safety containers with the lids or caps closed tightly. These storage receptacles must show no signs of leaks or significant damage due to dents or rust. In addition, the containers must be stored in a protected area equipped with secondary containment or a spill protector, such as a spill pallet. Additional requirements include the following:

- Containers should be clearly labeled "Hazardous Waste" and the date the material was first placed into the storage receptacle should be noted.
- Labeling is not required for solvents being used in a parts washer.
- Used solvents will not be counted toward a facility's monthly output of hazardous waste if the vendor under contract removes the material.
- Used solvents may be disposed of by recycling with a local vendor, such as *SafetyKleen*, to have the used solvent removed according to specific terms in the vendor agreement. See Figure 2-6.
- Use aqueous-based (nonsolvent) cleaning systems to help avoid the problems associated with chemical solvents.

COOLANT DISPOSAL

Coolant is a mixture of antifreeze and water. New antifreeze is not considered to be hazardous even though it can cause death if ingested. Used antifreeze may be hazardous due to dissolved metals from the engine and other components of the cooling system. These metals can include iron, steel, aluminum, copper, brass, and lead (from older radiators and heater cores).

1. Coolant should be recycled either onsite or offsite.
2. Used coolant should be stored in a sealed and labeled container. See Figure 2-7.
3. Used coolant can often be disposed of into municipal sewers with a permit. Check with local authorities and obtain a permit before discharging used coolant into sanitary sewers.

LEAD-ACID BATTERY WASTE

About 70 million spent lead-acid batteries are generated each year in the United States alone. Lead is classified as a toxic metal and the acid used in lead-acid batteries is highly corrosive. The vast majority (95 to 98%) of these batteries are recycled through lead reclamation operations and secondary lead smelters for use in the manufacture of new batteries.

BATTERY HAZARDOUS AND REGULATORY STATUS

Used lead-acid batteries must be reclaimed or recycled in order to be exempt from hazardous waste regulations. Leaking batteries must be stored and transported as hazardous waste. Some states have more strict regulations, which require special handling procedures and transportation. According to the Battery Council International (BCI), battery laws usually include the following rules.

- Lead-acid battery disposal is prohibited in landfills or incinerators.
- Batteries must be delivered to a battery retailer, wholesaler, recycling center, or lead smelter.
- All retailers of automotive batteries are required to post a sign that displays the universal recycling symbol and indicates the retailer's specific requirements for accepting used batteries.

CAUTION: Battery electrolyte contains sulfuric acid, which is a very corrosive substance capable of causing serious personal injury, such as skin burns and eye damage. In addition, the battery plates contain lead, which is highly poisonous. For this reason, disposing of batteries improperly can cause environmental contamination and lead to severe health problems.

BATTERY HANDLING AND STORAGE

Batteries, whether new or used, should be kept indoors if possible. The storage location should be an area specifically designated for battery storage and must be well ventilated (to the outside). If outdoor storage is the only alternative, a sheltered and secured area with acid-resistant secondary containment is strongly recommended. It is also advisable that acid-resistant secondary containment be used for indoor storage. In addition, batteries should be placed on acid-resistant pallets and never stacked!

FUEL SAFETY AND STORAGE

Gasoline is a very explosive liquid. The expanding vapors that come from gasoline are extremely dangerous. These vapors are present even in cold temperatures. Vapors formed in gasoline tanks on many vehicles are controlled, but vapors from gasoline storage may escape from the can, resulting in a hazardous situation.

FIGURE 2-8 This red gasoline container holds about 30 gallons of gasoline and is used to fill vehicles used for training.

Therefore, place gasoline storage containers in a well-ventilated space. Although diesel fuel is not as volatile as gasoline, the same basic rules apply to diesel fuel and gasoline storage. These rules include the following:

- Approved gasoline storage cans have a flash-arresting screen at the outlet. These screens prevent external ignition sources from igniting the gasoline within the can when someone pours the gasoline or diesel fuel.
- Technicians must always use *red* approved gasoline containers to allow for proper hazardous substance identification. See Figure 2-8.
- Do not fill gasoline containers completely full. Always leave the level of gasoline at least one inch from the top of the container. This action allows expansion of the gasoline at higher temperatures. If gasoline containers are completely full, the gasoline will expand when the temperature increases. This expansion forces gasoline from the can and creates a dangerous spill.
- If gasoline or diesel fuel containers must be stored, place them in a designated storage locker or facility.
- Never leave gasoline containers open, except while filling or pouring gasoline from the container.

- Never use gasoline as a cleaning agent.
- Always connect a ground strap to containers when filling or transferring fuel or other flammable products from one container to another to prevent static electricity that could result in explosion and fire. These ground wires prevent the buildup of a static electric charge, which could result in a spark and disastrous explosion.

AIRBAG HANDLING

Airbag modules are pyrotechnic explosive devices that can be ignited if exposed to an electrical charge or the body of the vehicle is subjected to a shock. Airbag safety should include the following precautions:

1. Disarm the airbag(s) if you will be working in the area where a discharged bag could make contact with any part of your body. Consult service information for the exact procedure to follow for the vehicle being serviced. The usual procedure is to deploy the airbag using a 12-volt power supply, such as a jump start box, using long wires to connect to the module to ensure a safe deployment.
2. Do not expose an airbag to extreme heat or fire.
3. Always carry an airbag with the bag pointing away from your body.
4. Place an airbag module facing upward.
5. Always follow the manufacturer's recommended procedure for airbag disposal or recycling, including the proper packaging to use during shipment.
6. Always wash your hands or body well if exposed to a deployed airbag. The chemicals involved can cause skin irritation and possible rash development.
7. Wear protective gloves if handling a deployed airbag.

USED TIRE DISPOSAL

Used tires are an environmental concern because of several reasons, including the following:

1. In a landfill, they tend to "float" up through the other trash and rise to the surface.
2. The insides of tires trap and hold rainwater, which is a breeding ground for mosquitoes. Mosquito-borne diseases include **encephalitis** and **dengue fever.**

3. Used tires present a fire hazard and, when burned, create a large amount of black smoke that contaminates the air.

Used tires should be disposed of in one of the following ways:

1. Used tires can be reused until the end of their useful life.
2. Tires can be retreaded.
3. Tires can be recycled or shredded for use in asphalt.
4. Derimmed tires can be sent to a landfill (most landfill operators will shred the tires because it is illegal in many states to landfill whole tires).
5. Tires can be burned in cement kilns or other power plants where the smoke can be controlled.
6. A registered scrap tire handler should be used to transport tires for disposal or recycling.

AIR-CONDITIONING REFRIGERANT OIL DISPOSAL

Air-conditioning refrigerant oil contains dissolved refrigerant and is therefore considered to be hazardous waste. This oil must be kept separated from other waste oil or the entire amount of oil must be treated as hazardous. Used refrigerant oil must be sent to a licensed hazardous waste disposal company for recycling or disposal. See Figure 2-9.

FIGURE 2-9 Air-conditioning refrigerant oil must be kept separated from other oils because it contains traces of refrigerant and must be treated as hazardous waste.

SUMMARY

1. Hazardous materials include common automotive chemicals, liquids, and lubricants, especially those whose ingredients contain *chlor* or *fluor* in their name.
2. Right-to-know laws require that all workers have access to Material Safety Data Sheets (MSDS).
3. Asbestos fibers should be avoided and removed according to current laws and regulations.
4. Used engine oil contains metals worn from parts and should be handled and disposed of properly.
5. Solvents represent a serious health risk and should be avoided as much as possible.
6. Coolant should be recycled.
7. Batteries are considered to be hazardous waste and should be discarded to a recycling facility.

REVIEW QUESTIONS

1. List five common automotive chemicals or products that may be considered hazardous materials.
2. List five precautions to which every technician should adhere when working with automotive products and chemicals.

ASE CERTIFICATION-TYPE QUESTIONS

1. Hazardous materials include all of the following except _____.
   a. Engine oil
   b. Asbestos
   c. Water
   d. Brake cleaner

2. To determine if a product or substance being used is hazardous, consult _____.
   a. A dictionary
   b. An MSDS
   c. SAE standards
   d. EPA guidelines

3. Exposure to asbestos dust can cause what condition?
   a. Asbestosis
   b. Mesothelioma
   c. Lung cancer
   d. All of the above are possible

4. Wetted asbestos dust is considered to be _____.
   a. Solid waste
   b. Hazardous waste
   c. Toxic
   d. Poisonous

5. An oil filter should be hot drained for how long before disposing of the filter?
   a. 30 to 60 minutes
   b. 4 hours
   c. 8 hours
   d. 12 hours

6. Used engine oil should be disposed of by all *except* the following methods.
   a. Disposed of in regular trash
   b. Shipped offsite for recycling
   c. Burned onsite in a waste oil-approved heater
   d. Burned offsite in a waste oil-approved heater

7. All of the following are the proper ways to dispose of a drained oil filter *except* _____.
   a. Sent for recycling
   b. Picked up by a service contract company
   c. Disposed of in regular trash
   d. Considered to be hazardous waste and disposed of accordingly

8. Which act or organization regulates air conditioning refrigerant?
   a. Clean Air Act (CAA)
   b. MSDS
   c. WHMIS
   d. Code of Federal Regulations (CFR)

9. Gasoline should be stored in approved containers that include what color(s)?

    a. A red container with yellow lettering

    b. A red container

    c. A yellow container

    d. A yellow container with red lettering

10. Infections that can be transmitted in the blood are called _____.

    a. HIV

    b. Blood-borne pathogens

    c. Blood virus

    d. SARS

Chapter 3

GASOLINE ENGINE OPERATION

OBJECTIVES

After studying Chapter 3, the reader should be able to:

1. Prepare for ASE Engine Performance (A8) certification test content area "A" (General Engine Diagnosis).
2. Explain how a 4-stroke cycle gasoline engine operates.
3. List the various characteristics by which vehicle engines are classified.
4. Describe how engine power is measured and calculated.
5. Discuss how a compression ratio is calculated.
6. Explain how engine size is determined.

The engine converts part of the fuel energy to useful power. This power is used to move the vehicle.

ENERGY AND POWER

Energy is used to produce power. The chemical energy in fuel is converted to heat by the burning of the fuel at a controlled rate. This process is called **combustion.** If engine combustion occurs within the power chamber, the engine is called an **internal combustion engine.**

NOTE: An **external combustion engine** is an engine that burns fuel outside of the engine itself, such as a steam engine.

Engines used in automobiles are internal combustion heat engines. They convert the chemical energy of the gasoline into heat within a power chamber that is called a **combustion chamber.** Heat energy released in the combustion chamber raises the temperature of the combustion gases within the chamber. The increase in gas temperature causes the pressure of the gases to increase. The pressure developed within the combustion chamber is applied to the head of a piston or to a turbine wheel to produce a usable **mechanical force,** which is then converted into useful **mechanical power.**

4-STROKE CYCLE OPERATION

Most automotive engines use the 4-stroke cycle of events, begun by the starter motor which rotates the engine. The 4-stroke cycle is repeated for each cylinder of the engine. See Figure 3-1.

- **Intake stroke** The intake valve is open and the piston inside the cylinder travels downward, drawing a mixture of air and fuel into the cylinder.
- **Compression stroke** As the engine continues to rotate, the intake valve closes and the piston moves upward in the cylinder, compressing the air-fuel mixture.
- **Power stroke** When the piston gets near the top of the cylinder (called **top dead center** [**TDC**]), the spark at the spark plug ignites the air-fuel mixture, which forces the piston downward.

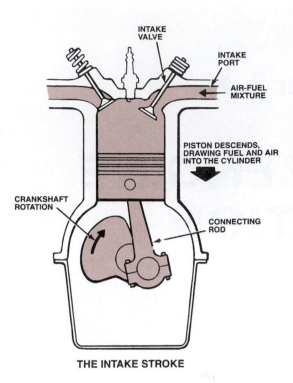

INTAKE VALVE

INTAKE PORT

AIR-FUEL MIXTURE

PISTON DESCENDS, DRAWING FUEL AND AIR INTO THE CYLINDER

CRANKSHAFT ROTATION

CONNECTING ROD

THE INTAKE STROKE

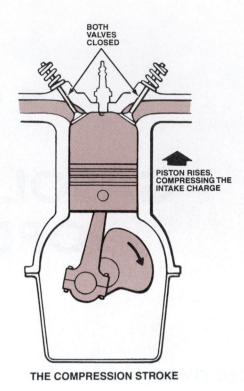

BOTH VALVES CLOSED

PISTON RISES, COMPRESSING THE INTAKE CHARGE

THE COMPRESSION STROKE

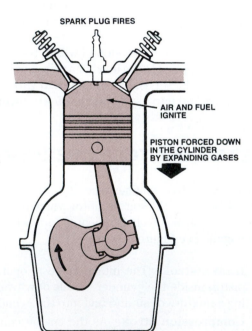

SPARK PLUG FIRES

AIR AND FUEL IGNITE

PISTON FORCED DOWN IN THE CYLINDER BY EXPANDING GASES

THE POWER STROKE

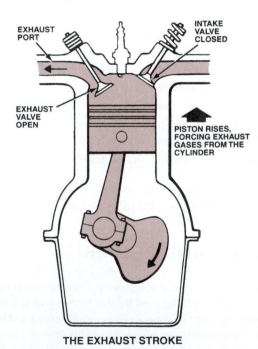

EXHAUST PORT

INTAKE VALVE CLOSED

EXHAUST VALVE OPEN

PISTON RISES, FORCING EXHAUST GASES FROM THE CYLINDER

THE EXHAUST STROKE

FIGURE 3-1 The downward movement of the piston draws the air-fuel mixture into the cylinder through the intake valve on the intake stroke. On the compression stroke, the mixture is compressed by the upward movement of the piston with both valves closed. Ignition occurs at the beginning of the power stroke, and combustion drives the piston downward to produce power. On the exhaust stroke, the upward-moving piston forces the burned gases out the open exhaust valve.

FIGURE 3-2 Cutaway of an engine showing the cylinder, piston, connecting rod, and crankshaft.

- **Exhaust stroke** The engine continues to rotate, and the piston again moves upward in the cylinder. The exhaust valve opens, and the piston forces the residual burned gases out of the **exhaust valve** and into the exhaust manifold and exhaust system.

This sequence repeats as the engine rotates. To stop the engine, the electricity to the ignition system is shut off by the ignition switch.

A piston that moves up and down, or reciprocates, in a **cylinder** can be seen in Figure 3-2. The piston is attached to a **crankshaft** with a **connecting rod.** This arrangement allows the piston to reciprocate (move up and down) in the cylinder as the crankshaft rotates. The combustion pressure developed in the combustion chamber at the correct time will push the piston downward to rotate the crankshaft.

THE 720° CYCLE

Each cycle of events requires that the engine crankshaft make two complete revolutions or 720° (360° × 2 = 720°). The greater the number of cylinders, the closer together the power strokes occur. To find the angle between cylinders of an engine, divide the number of cylinders into 720°.

Angle with 3 cylinders = 720°/3 = 240°
Angle with 4 cylinders = 720°/4 = 180°
Angle with 5 cylinders = 720°/5 = 144°
Angle with 6 cylinders = 720°/6 = 120°
Angle with 8 cylinders = 720°/8 = 90°
Angle with 10 cylinders = 720°/10 = 72°

This means that in a 4-cylinder engine, a power stroke occurs at every 180° of the crankshaft rotation (every 1/2 rotation). A V-8 is a much smoother operating engine because a power stroke occurs twice as often (every 90° of crankshaft rotation).

Engine cycles are identified by the number of piston strokes required to complete the cycle. A **piston stroke** is a one-way piston movement between the top (top dead center or TDC) and bottom (bottom dead center or BDC) of the cylinder. During one stroke, the crankshaft revolves 180° (1/2 revolution). A **cycle** is a complete series of events that continually repeat. Most automobile engines use a **4-stroke cycle.**

ENGINE CLASSIFICATION

Engines are classified by several characteristics including:

- **Number of strokes** Most automotive engines use the 4-stroke cycle.
- **Cylinder arrangement** An engine with more cylinders is smoother operating because the power pulses produced by the power strokes are more closely spaced. An inline engine places all cylinders in a straight line. Commonly manufactured inline engines include 4-, 5-, and 6-cylinder engines. A V-type engine, such as a V-6 or V-8, has the number of cylinders split and built into a V-shape. See Figure 3-3. Horizontally opposed 4- and 6-cylinder engines have two banks of cylinders that are horizontal, resulting in a low engine and a lower center of gravity in the vehicle. This style of engine is used in Porsche and Subaru engines and are often called a **boxer** or **pancake** engine design. See Figure 3-4.
- **Longitudinal or transverse mounting** Engines may be mounted either parallel with the length of the vehicle (longitudinally) or crosswise (transversely). See Figures 3-5 and 3-6. The same engine may be mounted in various vehicles in either direction.

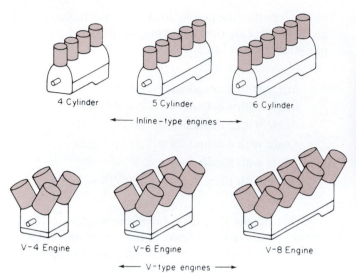

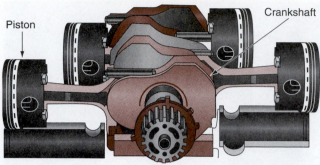

FIGURE 3-4   A horizontally opposed engine design helps to lower the vehicle's center of gravity.

FIGURE 3-3   Automotive engine cylinder arrangements.

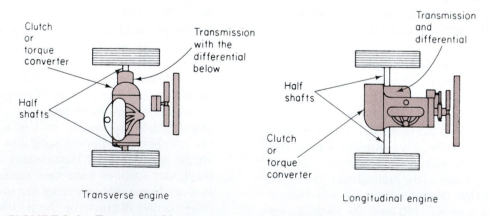

FIGURE 3-5   Automotive engine cylinder arrangements.

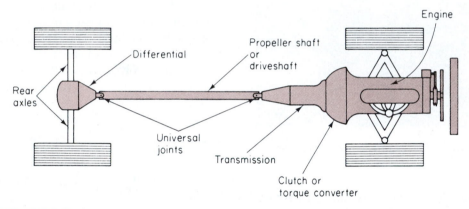

FIGURE 3-6   Two types of front-engine, front-wheel drive.

NOTE: Although it might be possible to mount an engine in different vehicles both longitudinally and transversely, the engine component parts may *not* be interchangeable. Differences can include different engine blocks and crankshafts, as well as different water pumps.

- **Valve and camshaft number and location** The number of valves and the number and location of camshafts are a major factor in engine operation. A typical older-model engine uses one intake valve and one exhaust valve per cylinder. Many newer engines use two intake and two exhaust valves per cylinder. The valves are opened by a **camshaft.** For high-speed engine operation, the camshaft should be overhead (over the valves). Some engines use one camshaft for the intake valves and a separate camshaft for the exhaust valves. When the camshaft is located in the block, the valves are operated by lifters, pushrods, and rocker arms. See Figure 3-7. This type of engine is called a **pushrod engine.** An overhead camshaft engine has the camshaft above the valves in the cylinder head. When one overhead camshaft is used, the design is called a **single overhead camshaft (SOHC)** design. When two overhead camshafts are used, the design is called a **double overhead camshaft (DOHC)** design. See Figures 3-8 and 3-9.

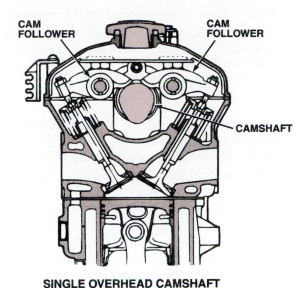

SINGLE OVERHEAD CAMSHAFT

FIGURE 3-7 Cutaway of a V-8 engine showing the lifters, pushrods, roller rocker arms, and valves.

DOUBLE OVERHEAD CAMSHAFT

FIGURE 3-8 SOHC engines usually require additional components such as a rocker arm to operate all of the valves. DOHC engines often operate the valves directly.

FIGURE 3-9 A dual overhead camshaft (DOHC) V-8 engine with part of the cam cover cut away.

NOTE: A V-type engine uses two banks or rows of cylinders. An SOHC design therefore uses two camshafts, but only one camshaft per bank (row) of cylinders. A DOHC V-6 therefore has four camshafts, two for each bank.

- **Type of fuel** Most engines operate on gasoline, whereas some engines are designed to operate on methanol, natural gas, propane, or diesel fuel.
- **Cooling method** Most engines are liquid cooled, but some older models were air cooled.
- **Type of induction pressure** If atmospheric air pressure is used to force the air-fuel mixture into the cylinders, the engine is called **naturally** or **normally aspirated.** Some engines use a **turbocharger** or **supercharger** to force the air-fuel mixture into the cylinder for even greater power.

◀ FREQUENTLY ASKED ▶ QUESTION

WHAT IS A ROTARY ENGINE?

A successful alternative engine design is the **rotary engine,** also called the **Wankel engine** after its inventor. The Mazda RX-7 and RX-8 represents the only long-term use of the rotary engine. The rotating combustion chamber engine runs very smoothly, and it produces high power for its size and weight.

The basic rotating combustion chamber engine has a triangular-shaped rotor turning in a housing. The housing is in the shape of a geometric figure called a **two-lobed epitrochoid.** A seal on each corner, or apex, of the rotor is in constant contact with the housing, so the rotor must turn with an eccentric motion. This means that the center of the rotor moves around the center of the engine. The eccentric motion can be seen in Figure 3-10.

ENGINE ROTATION DIRECTION

The SAE standard for automotive engine rotation is counterclockwise (CCW) as viewed from the flywheel end (clockwise as viewed from the front of the engine). The flywheel end of the engine is the end to which the power is applied to drive the vehicle. This is called the **principal end** of the engine. The **nonprincipal** end of the engine is opposite the principal end and is generally referred to as the *front* of the engine, where the accessory belts are used. See Figure 3-11 on page 52. In most rear-wheel-drive vehicles, therefore, the engine is mounted longitudinally with the principal end at the rear of the engine. Most transversely mounted engines also adhere to the same standard for direction of rotation. Many Honda engines and some marine applications may differ from this standard.

◀ FREQUENTLY ASKED ▶ QUESTION

WHERE DOES AN ENGINE STOP?

When the ignition system is turned off, the firing of the spark plugs stops and the engine will rotate until it stops due to the inertia of the rotating parts. The greatest resistance that occurs in the engine happens during the compression stroke. It has been determined that an engine usually stops when one of the cylinders is about 70 degrees before top dead center (BTDC) on the compression stroke with a variation of plus or minus 10 degrees.

This explains why technicians discover that the starter ring gear is worn at two locations on a 4-cylinder engine. The engine stops at one of the two possible places on a 4-cylinder engine, one of three areas for a 6-cylinder engine, and one of four areas on a V-8 engine depending on which cylinder is on the compression stroke.

BORE

The diameter of a cylinder is called the **bore.** The larger the bore, the greater the area on which the gases have to work. Pressure is measured in units, such as pounds per square inch (psi). The greater the area (in square inches), the higher the force exerted by the pistons to rotate the crankshaft. See Figure 3-12 on page 52.

STROKE

The distance the piston travels down in the cylinder is called the **stroke.** The longer this distance is, the greater the amount of air-fuel mixture that can be drawn into the cylinder. The more air-fuel mixture inside the cylinder, the more force will result when the mixture is ignited.

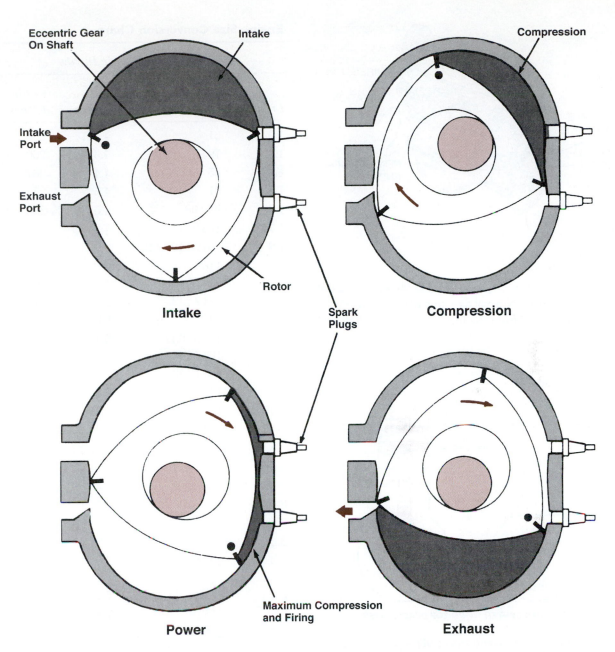

FIGURE 3-10 A rotary engine operates on the 4-stroke cycle but uses a rotor instead of a piston and crankshaft to achieve intake, compression, power, and exhaust strokes.

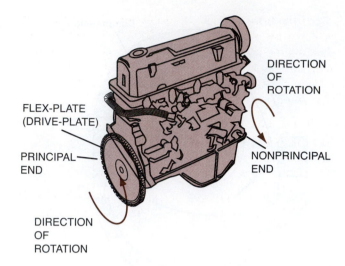

FIGURE 3-11 Inline 4-cylinder engine showing principal and nonprincipal ends. Normal direction of rotation is clockwise (CW) as viewed from the front or accessory belt end (nonprincipal end).

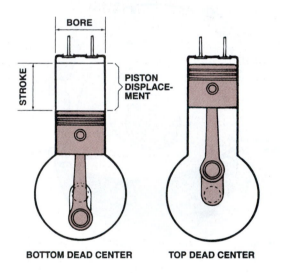

FIGURE 3-12 The bore and stroke of pistons are used to calculate an engine's displacement.

ENGINE DISPLACEMENT

Engine size is described in terms of displacement. **Displacement** is the cubic inch (cu. in.) or cubic centimeter (cc) volume displaced or swept by all of the pistons. A liter (L) is equal to 1000 cubic centimeters; therefore, most engines today are identified by their displacement in liters.

$$1\ L = 1000\ cc$$
$$1\ L = 61\ cu.\ in.$$
$$1\ cu.\ in. = 16.4\ cc$$

Engine Size Conversion Chart

Liters to Cubic Inches			
Liters	Cubic Inches	Liters	Cubic Inches
1.0	61	4.2	255 / 258
1.3	79	4.3	260 / 262 / 265
1.4	85	4.4	267
1.5	91	4.5	273
1.6	97 / 98	4.6	280 / 281
1.7	105	4.8	292
1.8	107 / 110 / 112	4.9	300 / 301
1.9	116	5.0	302 / 304 / 305 / 307
2.0	121 / 122	5.2	318
2.1	128	5.3	327
2.2	132 / 133 / 134 / 135	5.4	330
2.3	138 / 140	5.7	350
2.4	149	5.8	351
2.46	150	5.9	359 / 360 / 361
2.5	150 / 153	6.0	366 / 368
2.6	156 / 159	6.1	370
2.8	171 / 173	6.2	381
2.9	177	6.4	389 / 390 / 391
3.0	181 / 182 / 183	6.5	396
3.1	191	6.6	400
3.2	196	6.9	420
3.3	200 / 201	7.0	425 / 427 / 428 / 429
3.4	204	7.2	440
3.5	215	7.3	445
3.7	225	7.4	454
3.8	229 / 231 / 232	7.5	460
3.9	239 / 240	7.8	475 / 477
4.0	241 / 244	8.0	488
4.1	250 / 252	8.8	534

How to convert cubic inches to liters: 61.02 cubic inches = 1 liter

The formula to calculate the displacement of an engine is basically the formula for determining the volume of a cylinder multiplied by the number of cylinders. However, because the formula has been publicized in many different forms, it seems somewhat confusing.

Regardless of the method used, the results will be the same. The easiest and most commonly used formula is

Bore × Bore × Stroke × 0.7854 × number of cylinders

For example, take a 6-cylinder engine where:

Bore = 4.000 in., Stroke = 3.000 in.

Applying the formula:

4.000 in. × 4.000 in. × 3.000 in. × 0.7854 × 6 = 226 cu. in.

Because 1 cubic inch equals 16.4 cubic centimeters, this engine displacement equals 3706 cubic centimeters or, rounded to 3700 cubic centimeters, 3.7 liters.

Example: From liter to cubic inch—5.0 L × 61.02 = 305 CID
From cubic inch to liter—305 ÷ 61.02 = 5.0 L

Engine Size versus Horsepower

The larger the engine, the more power the engine is capable of producing. Several sayings are often quoted about engine size:

"There is no substitute for cubic inches."
"There is no replacement for displacement."

Although a large engine generally uses more fuel, making an engine larger is often the easiest way to increase power.

Engine Size if Bored or Stroked

If an engine is bored oversize compared to stock, material is removed from the cylinder walls and a larger piston is installed. The displacement and compression ratio are both increased when the engine is bored. A stock 6-cylinder engine (like the one used in the previous displacement example) with a bore of 4.000 inches and a stroke of 3.000 inches has a displacement of 226 cubic inches. If the engine is bored to 0.060 inches oversize, the size of the bore now becomes 4.060 inches. The formula for displacement in cubic inches remains the same except that 4.060 is substituted for 4.000.

Cubic inch displacement = Bore × Bore × Stroke × 0.7854 × Number of cylinders
4.060 in. × 4.060 in. × 3.000 in. × 0.7854 × 6 = 233 cu. in. = 3818 cc

If the bore remains the same and the stroke is increased by changing the crankshaft, the cubic inch displacement will increase and the compression ratio will also increase. If the stroke is increased 1/8 inch (0.125 in.), keeping the same stock bore, the new displacement will be calculated as follows:

Cubic inch displacement = Bore × Bore × Stroke × 0.7854 × Number of cylinders
4.000 in. × 4.000 in. × 3.125 in. × 0.7854 × 6 = 236 cu. in. = 3867 cc

If the engine is both bored and stroked (bored 0.060 inches, stroked 0.125 inches), the resultant displacement will be:

4.060 in. × 4.060 in. × 3.125 in. × 0.7854 × 6 = 243 cu. in. = 3982 cc

◀ TECH TIP ▶

ALL 3.8-LITER ENGINES ARE NOT THE SAME!

Most engine sizes are currently identified by displacement in liters. However, not all 3.8-liter engines are the same. See, for example, the following table:

Engine	Displacement
Chevrolet-built 3.8-L, V-6	229 cu. in.
Buick-built 3.8-L, V-6 (also called 3800 cc)	231 cu. in.
Ford-built 3.8-L, V-6	232 cu. in.

The exact conversion from liters (or cubic centimeters) to cubic inches is 231.9 cubic inches. However, due to rounding of exact cubic-inch displacement and rounding of the exact cubic-centimeter volume, several entirely different engines can be marketed with the exact same liter designation. To reduce confusion and reduce the possibility of ordering incorrect parts, the vehicle identification number (VIN) should be noted for the vehicle being serviced. The VIN should be visible through the windshield on all vehicles. Since 1980, the *engine* identification number or letter is usually the eighth digit or letter from the left.

Smaller, 4-cylinder engines can also cause confusion because many vehicle manufacturers use engines from both overseas and domestic manufacturers. Always refer to service manual information to be assured of correct engine identification.

COMPRESSION RATIO

The compression ratio of an engine is an important consideration when rebuilding or repairing an engine. **Compression ratio (CR)** is the ratio of the volume in the cylinder above the piston when the piston is at the bottom of the stroke (BDC) to the volume in the cylinder above the piston when the piston is at the top of the stroke. (TDC) See Figure 3-13.

If Compression Is Lower	If Compression Is Higher
Lower power	Higher power possible
Poorer fuel economy	Better fuel economy
Easier engine cranking	Harder to crank engine, especially when hot
More advanced ignition timing possible without spark knock (detonation)	Less ignition timing required to prevent spark knock (detonation)

$$CR = \frac{\text{Volume in cylinder with piston at bottom of cylinder}}{\text{Volume in cylinder with piston at top center}}$$

See Figure 3-14. For example: What is the compression ratio of an engine with 50.3-cu. in. displacement in one cylinder and a combustion chamber volume of 6.7 cu. in.?

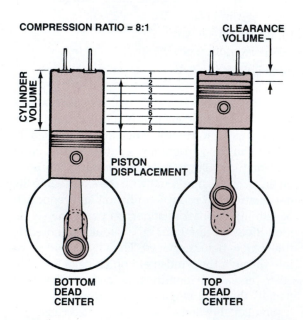

FIGURE 3-13 Compression ratio is the ratio of the total cylinder volume (when the piston is at the bottom of its stroke) to the clearance volume (when the piston is at the top of its stroke).

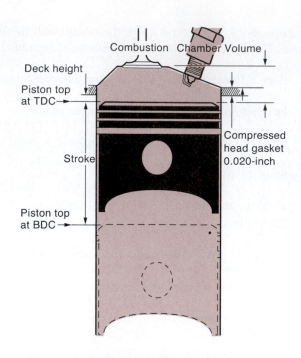

FIGURE 3-14 Combustion chamber volume is the volume above the piston with the piston at top dead center.

$$CR = \frac{50.3 + 6.7 \text{ cu. in.}}{6.7 \text{ cu. in.}} = \frac{57.0}{6.7} = 8.5$$

See Chapter 14 for additional information on calculating compression ratio.

THE CRANKSHAFT DETERMINES THE STROKE

The stroke of an engine is the distance the piston travels from top dead center (TDC) to bottom dead center (BDC). This distance is determined by the throw of the crankshaft. The throw is the distance from the centerline of the crankshaft to the centerline of the crankshaft rod journal. The throw is one-half of the stroke. See Figure 3-15 for an example of a crankshaft as installed in a GM V-6 engine.

If the crankshaft is replaced with one with a greater stroke, the pistons will be pushed up over the height of the top of the block (deck). The solution to this problem is to install replacement pistons with the piston pin relocated higher on the piston. Another alternative is to replace the connecting rod with a shorter one to prevent the piston from traveling too far up in the cylinder. Changing the connecting rod length does *not* change the stroke of an engine. Changing the connecting rod only changes the position of the piston in the cylinder.

FIGURE 3-15 The distance between the centerline of the main bearing journal and the centerline of the connecting rod journal determines the stroke of the engine. This photo is a little unusual because this is from a V-6 with a splayed crankshaft used to even out the impulses on a 90°, V-6 engine design.

TORQUE

Torque is the term used to describe a rotating force that may or may not result in motion. Torque is measured as the amount of force multiplied by the length of the lever through which it acts. If a one-foot-long wrench is used to apply 10 pounds of force to the end of the wrench to turn a bolt, then you are exerting 10 pound-feet of torque. See Figure 3-16. The metric unit for torque is Newton-meters because Newton is the metric unit for force and the distance is expressed in meters.

one pound-foot = 1.3558 Newton-meters
one Newton-meter = 0.7376 pound-foot

Newton-Meters to Pound-Feet Conversion Chart

(1 N-m = 0.074 lb-ft)

N-m	Lb-ft	N-m	Lb-ft	N-m	Lb-ft	N-m	Lb-ft
1	0.74	26	19.2	51	37.7	76	56.2
2	1.5	27	20.0	52	38.5	77	57.0
3	2.2	28	20.7	53	39.2	78	57.7
4	3.0	29	21.5	54	40.0	79	58.5
5	3.7	30	22.2	55	40.7	80	59.2
6	4.4	31	22.9	56	41.4	81	59.9
7	5.2	32	23.7	57	42.2	82	60.7
8	5.9	33	24.4	58	42.9	83	61.4
9	6.7	34	25.2	59	43.7	84	62.2
10	7.4	35	25.9	60	44.4	85	62.9
11	8.1	36	26.6	61	45.1	86	63.6
12	8.9	37	27.4	62	45.9	87	64.4
13	9.6	38	28.1	63	46.6	88	65.1
14	10.4	39	28.9	64	47.4	89	65.9
15	11.1	40	29.6	65	48.1	90	66.6
16	11.8	41	30.3	66	48.8	91	67.3
17	12.6	42	31.1	67	49.6	92	68.1
18	13.3	43	31.8	68	50.3	93	68.8
19	14.1	44	32.6	69	51.0	94	69.6
20	14.8	45	33.3	70	51.8	95	70.3
21	15.5	46	34.0	71	52.5	96	71.0
22	16.3	47	34.8	72	53.3	97	71.8
23	17.0	48	35.5	73	54.0	98	72.5
24	17.8	49	36.3	74	54.8	99	73.3
25	18.5	50	37.0	75	55.5	100	74.0

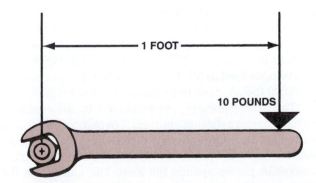

FIGURE 3-16 Torque is a twisting force equal to the distance from the pivot point times the force applied expressed in units called pound-feet (lb-ft) or Newton-meters (N-m).

Pound-Feet to Newton-Meters Conversion Chart

(1 lb-ft = 1.4 N-m)

Lb-ft	N-m	Lb-ft	N-m	Lb-ft	N-m	Lb-ft	N-m
1	1.4	26	36.4	51	71.4	76	106.4
2	2.8	27	37.8	52	72.8	77	107.8
3	4.2	28	39.2	53	74.2	78	109.2
4	5.6	29	40.6	54	75.6	79	110.6
5	7.0	30	42.0	55	77.0	80	112.0
6	8.4	31	43.4	56	78.4	81	113.4
7	9.8	32	44.8	57	79.8	82	114.8
8	11.2	33	46.2	58	81.2	83	116.2
9	12.6	34	47.6	59	82.6	84	117.6
10	14.0	35	49.0	60	84.0	85	119.0
11	15.4	36	50.4	61	85.4	86	120.4
12	16.8	37	51.8	62	86.8	87	121.8
13	18.2	38	53.2	63	88.2	88	123.2
14	19.6	39	54.6	64	89.6	89	124.6
15	21.0	40	56.0	65	91.0	90	126.0
16	22.4	41	57.4	66	92.4	91	127.4
17	23.8	42	58.8	67	93.8	92	128.8
18	25.2	43	60.2	68	95.2	93	130.2
19	26.6	44	61.6	69	96.6	94	131.6
20	28.0	45	63.0	70	98.0	95	133.0
21	29.4	46	64.4	71	99.4	96	134.4
22	30.8	47	65.8	72	100.8	97	135.8
23	32.2	48	67.2	73	102.2	98	137.2
24	33.6	49	68.6	74	103.6	99	138.6
25	35.0	50	70.0	75	105.0	100	140.0

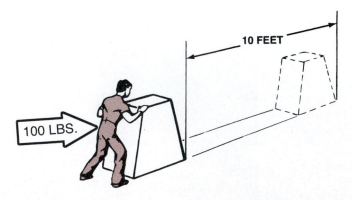

FIGURE 3-17 Work is calculated by multiplying force times distance. If you exert 100 pounds of force for 10 feet, you have done 1000 foot-pounds of work.

WORK

Work is defined as actually accomplishing movement when torque or force is applied to an object. A service technician can apply torque to a bolt in an attempt to loosen it, yet no work is done until the bolt actually moves. Work is calculated by multiplying the applied force (in pounds) by the distance the object moves (in feet). If you applied 100 pounds of force to move an object 10 feet, then you accomplished 1000 foot-pounds of work (100 pounds × 10 feet = 1000 foot pounds). See Figure 3-17.

NOTE: The designations for torque and work are often confusing. Torque is expressed in pound-feet because it represents a force exerted a certain distance from the object and acts as a lever. Work, however, is expressed in foot-pounds because work is the movement over a certain distance (feet) multiplied by the force applied (pounds). Engines produce torque and service technicians exert torque represented by the unit pound-feet.

POWER

The term **power** means the rate of doing work. Power equals work divided by time. Work is achieved when a certain amount of mass (weight) is moved a certain distance by a force. Whether the object is moved in 10 seconds or 10 minutes does not make a difference in the amount of work accomplished, but it does affect the amount of power needed. Power is expressed in units of foot-pounds per minute.

HORSEPOWER

The power an engine produces is called horsepower (hp). One **horsepower** is the power required to move 550 pounds one foot in one second, or 33,000 pounds one foot in one minute (550 lb. × 60 sec = 33,000 ft.-lb.). This is expressed as 550 foot-pounds (ft.-lb.) per second or 33,000 foot-pounds per minute. See Figure 3-18.

The actual horsepower produced by an engine is measured with a **dynamometer**. A dynamometer (often abbreviated as **dyno** or **dyn**) places a load on the engine and measures the amount of twisting force the engine crankshaft places against the load. The load holds the engine speed, so it is called a **brake**. The horsepower derived from a dynamometer is called **brake horsepower (bhp)**. The dynamometer actually measures the torque output of the engine. Torque is a rotating force

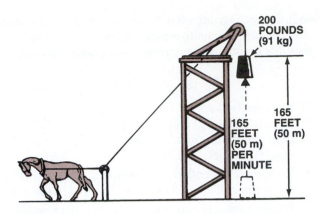

FIGURE 3-18 One horsepower is equal to 33,000 foot-pounds (200 lbs. × 165 ft.) of work per minute (60 seconds).

that may or may not cause movement. The horsepower is calculated from the torque readings at various engine speeds (in revolutions per minute or RPM).

Horsepower is torque times RPM divided by 5252.

$$\text{Horsepower} = \frac{\text{Torque} \times \text{RPM}}{5252}$$

Torque is what the driver "feels" as the vehicle is being accelerated. A small engine operating at a high RPM may have the same horsepower as a large engine operating at a low RPM.

NOTE: As can be seen by the formula for horsepower, the higher the engine speed for a given amount of torque, the greater the horsepower. Many engines are high revving. To help prevent catastrophic damage due to excessive engine speed, most manufacturers limit the maximum RPM by programming fuel injectors to shut off if the engine speed increases past a certain level. Sometimes this cutoff speed can be as low as 3000 RPM if the transmission is in neutral or park. Complaints of high-speed "miss" or "cutting out" may be normal if the engine is approaching the "rev limiter."

SAE Gross versus Net Horsepower

SAE standards for measuring horsepower include gross and net horsepower ratings. **SAE gross horsepower** is the maximum power an engine develops without some accessories in operation. **SAE net horsepower** is the power an engine develops as installed in the vehicle. A summary of the differences is given in the following table.

SAE Gross Horsepower	SAE Net Horsepower
No air cleaner or filter	Stock air cleaner or filter
No cooling fan	Stock cooling fan
No alternator	Stock alternator
No mufflers	Stock exhaust system
No emission controls	Full emission and noise control

Ratings are about 20% lower for the net rating method. Before 1971, most manufacturers used gross horsepower rating (the higher method) for advertising purposes. After 1971, the manufacturers started advertising only SAE net-rated horsepower.

HORSEPOWER AND ALTITUDE

Because the density of the air is lower at high altitude, the power that a normal engine can develop is greatly reduced at high altitude. According to SAE conversion factors, a nonsupercharged or nonturbocharged engine loses about 3% of its power for every 1000 feet (300 meters [m]) of altitude.

◄ TECH TIP ►

QUICK-AND-EASY EFFICIENCY CHECK

A good, efficient engine is able to produce a lot of power from little displacement. A common rule of thumb is that an engine is efficient if it can produce *1 horsepower per cubic inch* of displacement. Many engines today are capable of this feat, such as the following:

Ford	4.6-L V-8 (281 cu. in.)	—300 hp
Chevrolet	3.4-L V-6 (207 cu. in.)	—210 hp
Daimler Chrysler	3.5-L V-6 (214 cu. in.)	—214 hp
Acura	3.2-L V-6 (195 cu. in.)	—270 hp

An engine is very powerful for its size if it can produce *100 hp per liter*. This efficiency goal is harder to accomplish. Most factory stock engines that can achieve this feat are supercharged or turbocharged.

Therefore, an engine that develops 150 brake horsepower at sea level will only produce about 85 brake horsepower at the top of Pike's Peak in Colorado at 14,110 feet (4300 meters). Supercharged and turbocharged engines are not as greatly affected by altitude as normally aspirated engines. Normally aspirated, remember, means engines that breathe air at normal atmospheric pressure.

SUMMARY

1. The four strokes of the 4-stroke cycle are intake, compression, power, and exhaust.
2. Engines are classified by number and arrangement of cylinders and by number and location of valves and camshafts, as well as by type of mounting, fuel used, cooling method, and induction pressure.
3. Most engines rotate clockwise as viewed from the front (accessory) end of the engine. The SAE standard is counterclockwise as viewed from the principal (flywheel) end of the engine.
4. Engine size is called displacement and represents the volume displaced or swept by all of the pistons.
5. Engine power is expressed in horsepower, which is a calculated value based on the amount of torque or twisting force the engine produces.

REVIEW QUESTIONS

1. Name the strokes of a 4-stroke cycle.
2. What does a dynamometer actually measure?
3. What is the difference between SAE net and SAE gross horsepower?
4. If an engine at sea level produces 100 horsepower, how many horsepower would it develop at 6,000 feet of altitude?

ASE CERTIFICATION-TYPE QUESTIONS

1. All overhead valve engines _____.
   a. Use an overhead camshaft
   b. Have the overhead valves in the head
   c. Operate by the 2-stroke cycle
   d. Use the camshaft to close the valves

2. An SOHC V-8 engine has how many camshafts?
   a. One
   b. Two
   c. Three
   d. Four

3. Brake horsepower is calculated by which of the following?
   a. Torque times RPM
   b. 2π times stroke
   c. Torque times RPM divided by 5252
   d. Stroke times bore times 3300

4. Torque is expressed in units of _____.
   a. Pound-feet
   b. Foot-pounds
   c. Foot-pounds per minute
   d. Pound-feet per second

5. Horsepower is expressed in units of _____.
   a. Pound-feet
   b. Foot-pounds
   c. Foot-pounds per minute
   d. Pound-feet per second

6. A normally aspirated automobile engine loses about _____ power per 1000 feet of altitude.
   a. 1%
   b. 3%
   c. 5%
   d. 6%

7. One cylinder of an automotive 4-stroke cycle engine completes a cycle every _____.
   a. 90°
   b. 180°
   c. 360°
   d. 720°

8. How many rotations of the crankshaft are required to complete each stroke of a 4-stroke cycle engine?
   a. One-fourth
   b. One-half
   c. One
   d. Two

9. A rotating force is called _____.
   a. Horsepower
   b. Torque
   c. Combustion pressure
   d. Eccentric movement

10. Technician A says that power is expressed in units of ft.-lbs. per second (or minute). Technician B says that torque is expressed in units of lb.-ft. per second (or minute). Which technician is correct?
    a. Technician A only
    b. Technician B only
    c. Both Technicians A and B
    d. Neither Technician A nor B

◄ **Chapter 4** ►

DIESEL ENGINE OPERATION

OBJECTIVES

After studying Chapter 4, the reader should be able to:

1. Prepare for ASE Engine Performance (A8) certification test content area "C" (Fuel, Air Induction, and Exhaust Systems Diagnosis and Repair).
2. Explain how a diesel engine works.
3. Describe the difference between direct injection (DI) and indirect injection (IDI) diesel engines.
4. List the parts of the typical diesel engine fuel system.
5. Explain how glow plugs work.
6. List the advantages and disadvantages of a diesel engine.
7. Describe how diesel fuel is rated and tested.

DIESEL ENGINES

In 1892, a German engineer named Rudolf Diesel perfected the compression-ignition engine that bears his name. The diesel engine uses heat created by compression to ignite the fuel, so it requires no spark ignition system.

The diesel engine requires compression ratios of 16:1 and higher. Incoming air is compressed until its temperature reaches about 1,000°F (540°C). This is called **heat of compression.** As the piston reaches the top of its compression stroke, fuel is injected into the cylinder, where it is ignited by the hot air. See Figure 4-1. As the fuel burns, it expands and produces power. Because of the very high compression and torque output of a diesel engine, it is made heavier and stronger than the same size gasoline powered engine.

A common diesel engine uses a fuel system precision **injection pump** and individual fuel injectors. The pump delivers fuel to the injectors at a high pressure and at timed intervals. Each injector sprays fuel into the combustion chamber at the precise moment required for efficient combustion. See Figure 4-2.

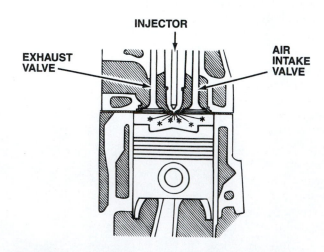

FIGURE 4-1 Diesel combustion occurs when fuel is injected into the hot, highly compressed air in the cylinder.

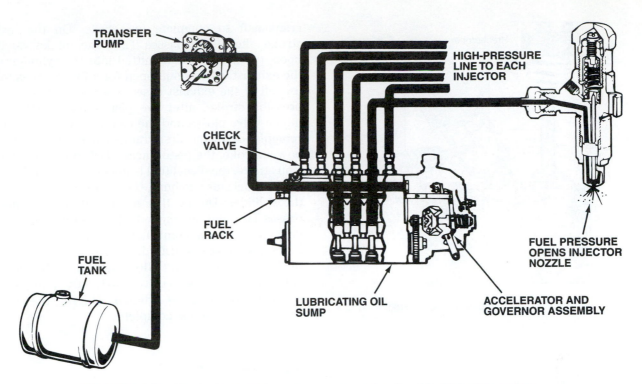

FIGURE 4-2   A typical injector-pump-type automotive diesel fuel injection system.

In a diesel engine, air is not controlled by a throttle as in a gasoline engine. Instead, the amount of fuel injected is varied to control power and speed. The air-fuel mixture of a diesel can vary from as lean as 85:1 at idle to as rich as 20:1 at full load. This higher air-fuel ratio and the increased compression pressures make the diesel more fuel-efficient than a gasoline engine in part because diesel engines do not suffer from throttling losses. Throttling losses involve the power needed in a gasoline engine to draw air past a closed or partially closed throttle.

In a gasoline engine, the speed and power are controlled by the throttle valve, which controls the amount of air entering the engine. Adding more fuel to the cylinders of a gasoline engine without adding more air (oxygen) will not increase the speed or power of the engine. In a diesel engine, speed and power are not controlled by the amount of air entering the cylinders because the engine air intake is always wide open. Therefore, the engine always has enough oxygen to burn the fuel in the cylinder and will increase speed (and power) when additional fuel is supplied.

Diesel engines are built in both 2-stroke and 4-stroke versions. The most common 2-stroke diesels were the truck and industrial engines made by Detroit Diesel. In these engines, air intake is through ports in the cylinder wall. Exhaust is through poppet valves in the head. A blower pushes air into the air box surrounding liner ports to supply air for combustion and to blow the exhaust gases out of the exhaust valves.

Indirect and Direct Injection

In an indirect injection (abbreviated **IDI**) diesel, fuel is injected into a small prechamber, which is connected to the cylinder by a narrow opening. The initial combustion takes place in this prechamber. This has the effect of slowing the rate of combustion, which tends to reduce noise. See Figure 4-3. All indirect diesel injection engines require the use of a glow plug.

In a direct injection (abbreviated DI) diesel engine, fuel is injected directly into the cylinder. The piston incorporates a depression where initial combustion takes place. Direct injection diesel engines are generally more efficient than indirect injection engines, but have a tendency to produce greater amounts of noise. See Figure 4-4. While some direct injection diesel engines use glow plugs to help cold starting and to reduce emissions, many direct injection diesel engines do not use glow plugs.

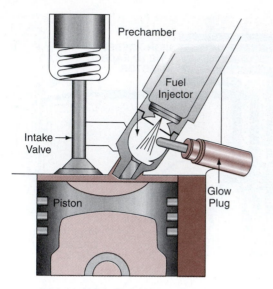

FIGURE 4-3 An indirect injection diesel engine uses a prechamber and a glow plug.

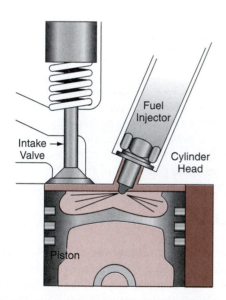

FIGURE 4-4 A direct injection diesel engine injects the fuel directly into the combustion chamber. Many designs do not use a glow plug.

Diesel Fuel Ignition

Ignition occurs in a diesel engine by injecting fuel into the air charge which has been heated by compression to a temperature greater than the ignition point of the fuel or about 1000°F (538°C). The chemical reaction of burning the fuel liberates heat, which causes the gases to expand, forcing the piston to rotate the crankshaft. A 4-stroke diesel engine requires two rotations of the crankshaft to complete one cycle. On the intake stroke, the piston passes TDC, the intake valve(s) open, the fresh air is admitted into the cylinder, and the exhaust valve is still open for a few degrees to allow all of the exhaust gases to escape. On the compression stroke, after the piston passes BDC, the intake valve closes and the piston travels up to TDC (completion of the first crankshaft rotation). On the power stroke, the piston nears TDC on the compression stroke, the diesel fuel is injected by the injectors, and the fuel starts to burn, further heating the gases in the cylinder. During this power stroke, the piston passes TDC and the expanding gases force the piston down, rotating the crankshaft. On the exhaust stroke, as the piston passes BDC, the exhaust valves open and the exhaust gases start to flow out of the cylinder. This continues as the piston travels up to TDC, pumping the spent gases out of the cylinder. At TDC, the second crankshaft rotation is complete.

THREE PHASES OF COMBUSTION

There are three distinct phases or parts to the combustion in a diesel engine.

1. **Ignition delay.** Near the end of the compression stroke, fuel injection begins, but ignition does not begin immediately. This period is called delay.
2. **Rapid combustion.** This phase of combustion occurs when the fuel first starts to burn, creating a sudden rise in cylinder pressure. It is this rise in combustion chamber pressure that causes the characteristic diesel engine knock.
3. **Controlled combustion.** After the rapid combustion occurs, the rest of the fuel in the combustion chamber begins to burn and injection continues. This is an area near the injector that contains fuel surrounded by air. This fuel burns as it mixes with the air.

DIESEL ENGINE CONSTRUCTION

Diesel engines must be constructed heavier than gasoline engines because of the tremendous pressures that are created in the cylinders during operation. The torque output of a diesel engine is often double or more than the same size gasoline powered engines. See the comparison chart.

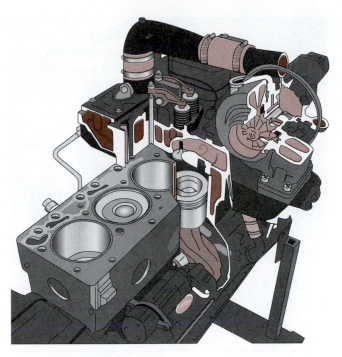

FIGURE 4-5 The common rail on a Cummins diesel engine. A high-pressure pump (up to 30,000 psi) is used to supply diesel fuel to this common rail, which has tubes running to each injector. Note the thick cylinder walls and heavy-duty construction.

System or Component	Diesel Engine	Gasoline Engine
Block	Cast iron and heavy in weight See Figure 4-5.	Cast iron or aluminum and as light as possible
Cylinder head	Cast iron or aluminum	Cast iron or aluminum
Compression ratio	17:1 to 25:1	8:1 to 12:1
Peak engine speed	2000 to 2500	5000 to 8000
Pistons and connecting rods	Aluminum with combustion pockets and heavy duty rods. See Figure 4-6.	Aluminum, usually flat top or with valve relief but no combustion pockets

FUEL TANK AND LIFT PUMP

A fuel tank used on a vehicle equipped with a diesel engine differs from the one used with a gasoline engine in several ways, including:

FIGURE 4-6 A rod/piston assembly from a 5.9-liter Cummins diesel engine used in a Dodge pickup truck.

- A larger filler neck for diesel fuel. Gasoline filler necks are smaller for the unleaded gasoline nozzle.
- No evaporative emission control devices or charcoal (carbon) canister. Diesel fuel is not as volatile as gasoline and, therefore, diesel vehicles do not have evaporative emission control devices.

The diesel fuel is drawn from the fuel tank by a **lift pump** and delivers the fuel to the injection pump. Between the fuel tank and the lift pump is a **water-fuel separator.** Water is heavier than diesel fuel and sinks to the bottom of the separator. Part of normal routine maintenance on a vehicle equipped with a diesel engine is to drain the water from the water-fuel

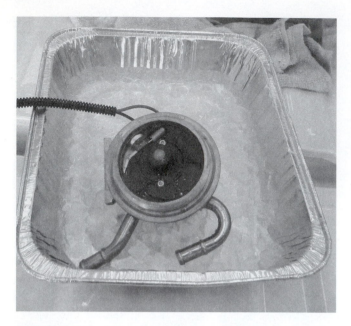

FIGURE 4-7 Using an ice bath to test the fuel temperature sensor.

FIGURE 4-8 A typical distributor-type diesel injection pump showing the pump, lines, and fuel filter.

separator. A float is usually used inside the separator, which is connected to a warning light on the dash that lights if the water reaches a level where it needs to be drained.

NOTE: Water can cause corrosive damage as well as wear to diesel engine parts because water is not a good lubricant. Water cannot be atomized by a diesel fuel injector nozzle and will often "blow out" the nozzle tip.

Many diesel engines also use a fuel temperature sensor. The computer uses this information to adjust fuel delivery based on the density of the fuel. See Figure 4-7.

INJECTION PUMP

A diesel engine injection pump is used to increase the pressure of the diesel fuel from very low values from the lift pump to the extremely high pressures needed for injection.

Injection pumps are usually driven by the camshaft at the front of the engine. As the injection pump shaft rotates, the diesel fuel is fed from a fill port to a high-pressure chamber. If a distributor-type injection pump is used, the fuel is forced out of the injection port to the correct injector nozzle through the high-pressure line. See Figure 4-8.

NOTE: Because of the very tight tolerances in a diesel engine, the smallest amount of dirt can cause excessive damage to the engine and to the fuel injection system.

Distributor Injection Pump

A distributor diesel injection pump is a high-pressure pump assembly with lines leading to each individual injector. The high-pressure lines between the distributor and the injectors must be the exact same length to ensure proper injection timing. The injection pump itself creates the injection advance needed for engine speeds above idle and the fuel is discharged into the lines. The high-pressure fuel causes the injectors to open. Due to the internal friction of the lines, there is a slight delay before fuel pressure opens the injector nozzle. See Figure 4-9.

NOTE: The lines expand some during an injection event. This is how timing checks are performed. The pulsing of the injector line is picked up by a probe used to detect the injection event similar to a timing light used to detect a spark on a gasoline engine.

Common Rail

Newer diesel engines use a fuel delivery system referred to as a **common rail** design. Diesel fuel under

Fuel Flow

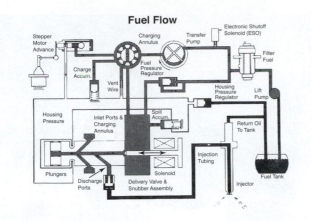

FIGURE 4-9 A schematic of a Stanadyne diesel fuel injection pump assembly showing all of the related components. *(Courtesy of Stanadyne Corporation)*

high pressure, over 20,000 psi (138,000 kPa), is applied to the injectors, which are opened by a solenoid controlled by the computer. Because the injectors are computer controlled, the combustion process can be precisely controlled to provide maximum engine efficiency with the lowest possible noise and exhaust emissions. See Figure 4-10.

DIESEL INJECTOR NOZZLES

Diesel injector nozzles are spring-loaded closed valves that spray fuel directly into the combustion chamber or pre-combustion chamber. Injector nozzles are threaded into the cylinder head, one for each cylinder, and are replaceable as an assembly.

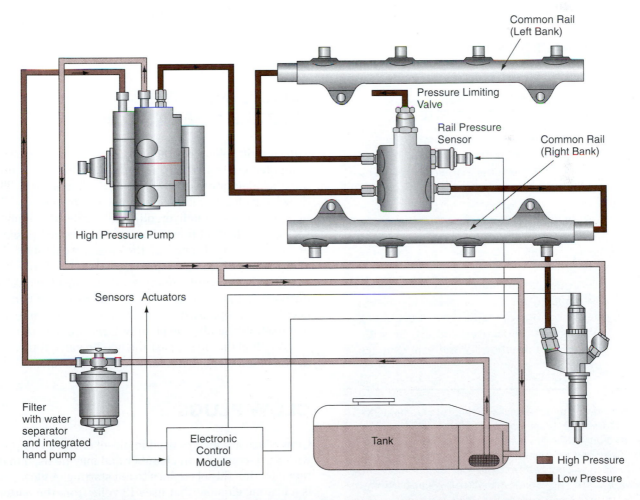

FIGURE 4-10 Overview of a computer-controlled common rail V-8 diesel engine.

The top of the injector nozzle has many holes to deliver an atomized spray of diesel fuel into the cylinder. Parts of a diesel injector nozzle include:

- **Heat shield** This is the outer shell of the injector nozzle and has external threads where it seals in the cylinder head.
- **Injector body** This is the inner part of the nozzle and contains the injector needle valve and spring, and threads into the outer heat shield.
- **Diesel injector needle valve** This precision machined valve and the tip of the needle seal against the injector body when it is closed. When the valve is open, diesel fuel is sprayed into the combustion chamber. This passage is controlled by a solenoid on diesel engines equipped with computer-controlled injection.
- **Injector pressure chamber** The pressure chamber is a machined cavity in the injector body around the tip of the injector needle. Injection pump pressure forces fuel into this chamber, forcing the needle valve open.

FIGURE 4-11 Typical computer-controlled diesel engine fuel injectors.

◀ TECH TIP ▶

NEVER ALLOW A DIESEL ENGINE TO RUN OUT OF FUEL

If a gasoline-powered vehicle runs out of gasoline, it is an inconvenience and a possible additional expense to get some gasoline. However, if a vehicle equipped with a diesel engine runs out of fuel, it can be a major concern.

Besides adding diesel fuel to the tank, the other problem is getting all of the air out of the pump, lines, and injectors so the engine will operate correctly.

The procedure usually involves cranking the engine long enough to get liquid diesel fuel back into the system, but at the same time keeping cranking time short enough to avoid overheating the starter. Consult service information for the exact service procedure if the diesel engine is run out of fuel.

NOTE: Some diesel engines such as the General Motors Duramax V-8 are equipped with a priming pump located under the hood on top of the fuel filter. Pushing down and releasing the priming pump with a vent valve open will purge any trapped air from the system. Always follow the vehicle manufacturer's instructions.

DIESEL INJECTOR NOZZLE OPERATION

The electric solenoid attached to the injector nozzle is computer controlled and opens to allow fuel to flow into the injector pressure chamber. See Figure 4-11. The diesel injector nozzle is mechanically opened by the high-pressure fuel delivered to the nozzle by the injector pump. The fuel flows down through a fuel passage in the injector body and into the pressure chamber. The high fuel pressure in the pressure chamber forces the needle valve upward, compressing the needle valve return spring and forcing the needle valve open. When the needle valve opens, diesel fuel is discharged into the combustion chamber in a hollow cone spray pattern.

Any fuel that leaks past the needle valve returns to the fuel tank through a return passage and line.

GLOW PLUGS

Glow plugs are always used in diesel engines equipped with a pre-combustion chamber and may be used in direct injection diesel engines to aid starting. A glow plug is a heating element that uses 12 volts from the battery and aids in the starting of a cold engine. As the temperature of the glow plug increases, the resistance of the

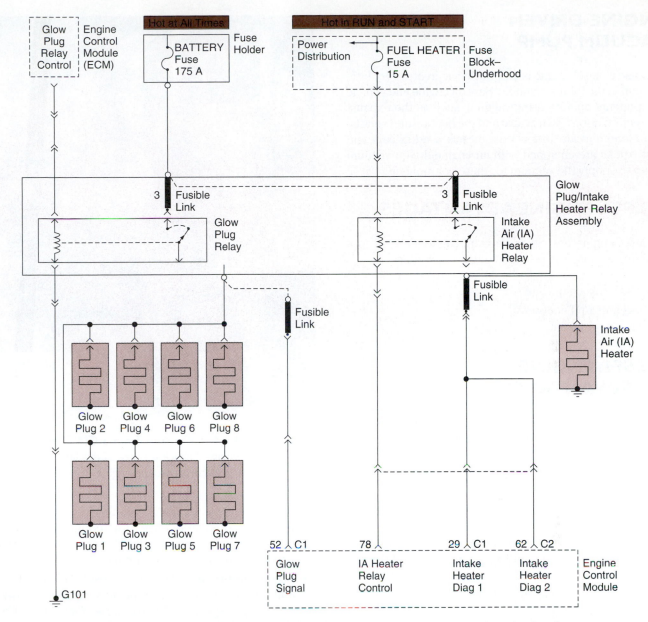

FIGURE 4-12 A schematic of a typical glow plug circuit. Notice that the relay for the glow plug and intake air heater are both computer controlled.

heating element inside increases, thereby reducing the current in amperes needed by the glow plugs.

Most glow plugs used in newer vehicles are controlled by the power train control module (PCM), which monitors coolant temperature and intake air temperature. The glow plugs are turned on or pulsed on or off depending on the temperature of the engine. The PCM will also keep the glow plug turned on after the engine starts to reduce white exhaust smoke (unburned fuel) and to improve idle quality after starting. See Figure 4-12.

The "wait to start" lamp will light when the engine and the outside temperature is low to allow time for the glow plugs to get hot. The wait to start lamp will not come on when the glow plugs are operating after the engine starts.

NOTE: The glow plugs are removed to test cylinder compression using a special high-pressure reading gauge.

ENGINE-DRIVEN VACUUM PUMP

Because a diesel engine is unthrottled, it creates very little vacuum in the intake manifold. Several engine and vehicle components operate using vacuum, such as the exhaust gas recirculation (EGR) valve and the heating and ventilation blend and air doors. Most diesels used in cars and light trucks are equipped with an engine-driven vacuum pump to supply the vacuum for these components.

DIESEL ENGINE ADVANTAGES

A diesel engine has several advantages compared to a similar size gasoline powered engine including:

1. More torque output
2. Greater fuel economy
3. Long service life

DIESEL ENGINE DISADVANTAGES

A diesel engine has several disadvantages compared to a similar size gasoline powered engine including:

1. Engine noise, especially when cold and/or at idle speed
2. Exhaust smell
3. Cold weather startability
4. A vacuum pump is needed to supply the vacuum needs of the heat, ventilation, and air-conditioning system
5. Heavier than a gasoline engine (See Figure 4-13.)
6. Fuel availability

DIESEL FUEL

Diesel fuel must meet an entirely different set of standards than gasoline. The fuel in a diesel engine is not ignited with a spark, but is ignited by the heat generated by high compression. The pressure of compression (400 to 700 psi or 2800 to 4800 kilopascals) generates temperatures of 1200° to 1600°F (700° to 900°C) which speeds the preflame reaction to start the ignition of fuel injected into the cylinder.

All diesel fuel must be clean, be able to flow at low temperatures, and be of the proper cetane rating.

- **Cleanliness** It is imperative that the fuel used in a diesel engine be clean and free from water. Unlike the case with gasoline engines, the fuel is the lubricant and coolant for the diesel injector pump and in-

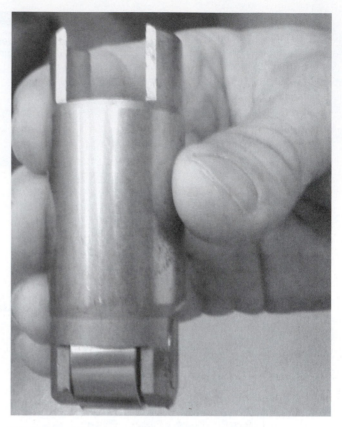

FIGURE 4-13 A roller lifter from a GM Duramax 6.6-liter V-8 diesel engine. Notice the size of this lifter compared to a roller lifter used in a gasoline engine.

jectors. Good-quality diesel fuel contains additives such as oxidation inhibitors, detergents, dispersants, rust preventatives, and metal deactivators.

- **Low-temperature fluidity** Diesel fuel must be able to flow freely at all expected ambient temperatures. One specification for diesel fuel is its "pour point," which is the temperature below which the fuel would stop flowing. **Cloud point** is another concern with diesel fuel at lower temperatures. Cloud point is the low-temperature point at which the waxes present in most diesel fuel tend to form wax crystals that clog the fuel filter. Most diesel fuel suppliers distribute fuel with the proper pour point and cloud point for the climate conditions of the area.

- **Cetane number** The cetane number for diesel fuel is the opposite of the octane number for gasoline. The **cetane number** is a measure of the ease with which the fuel can be ignited. The cetane rating of the fuel determines, to a great extent, its ability to start the engine at low temperatures and to provide smooth warm-up and even combustion. The cetane rating of diesel fuel should be between 45 and 50. The higher the cetane rating, the more easily the fuel is ignited, whereas the higher the octane rating, the more slowly the fuel burns.

Other diesel fuel specifications include its flash point, sulfur content, and classification. The **flash point** is the temperature at which the vapors on the surface of the fuel will ignite if exposed to an open flame. The flash point does *not* affect diesel engine operation. However, a lower than normal flash point could indicate contamination of the diesel fuel with gasoline or a similar substance.

The sulfur content of diesel fuel is very important to the life of the engine. Most engine manufacturers specify that only fuel containing less than about 0.3% sulfur be used. The current limit as set by the American Society for Testing and Materials (ASTM) is 0.5% maximum. Sulfur in the fuel creates sulfuric acid during the combustion process, which can damage engine components and cause piston ring wear. Federal regulations are getting extremely tight on sulfur content. High sulfur fuel contributes to acid rain.

ASTM also classifies diesel fuel by volatility (boiling range) into the following grades:

Grade #1. This grade of diesel fuel has the lowest boiling point and the lowest cloud and pour points; it also has a lower BTU content—less heat per pound of fuel. As a result, grade #1 is suitable for use during low-temperature (winter) operation. Grade #1 produces less heat per pound of fuel compared to grade #2 and may be specified for use in diesel engines involved in frequent changes in load and speed, such as those found in city buses and delivery trucks.

Grade #2. This grade has a higher boiling range, cloud point, and pour point as compared with grade #1. It is usually specified where constant speed and high loads are encountered, such as in long-haul trucking and automotive diesel applications.

DIESEL FUEL SPECIFIC GRAVITY TESTING

The density of diesel fuel should be tested whenever there is a driveability concern. The density or specific gravity of diesel fuel is measured in units of **API gravity.** API gravity is an arbitrary scale expressing the gravity or density of liquid petroleum products devised jointly by the American Petroleum Institute and the National Bureau of Standards. The measuring scale is calibrated in terms of degrees API. Oil with the least specific gravity has the highest API gravity. The formula for determining API gravity is as follows:

Degrees API gravity = (141.5/specific gravity at 60°F) − 131.5

The normal API gravity for #1 diesel fuel is 39 to 44 (typically 40).

The normal API gravity for #2 diesel fuel is 30 to 39 (typically 35). A hydrometer calibrated in API gravity units should be used to test diesel fuel. See Figure 4-14.

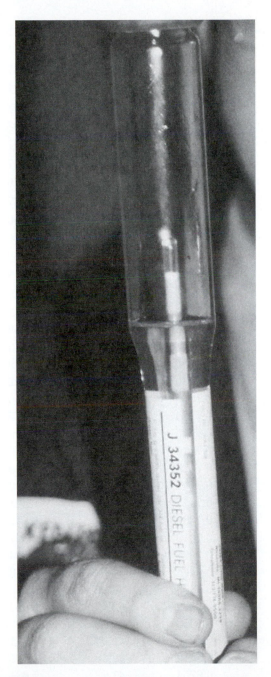

FIGURE 4-14 A hydrometer is used to measure the API specific gravity of diesel fuel. The unit of measure is usually the American Petroleum Institute (API) scale.

API Gravity Comparison Chart

Values for API Scale Oil

API Gravity Scale	Specific Gravity S	Weight Density, lb/ft P	Pounds per Gallon
0			
2			
4			
6			
8			
10	1.0000	62.36	8.337
12	0.9861	61.50	8.221
14	0.9725	60.65	8.108
16	0.9593	59.83	7.998
18	0.9465	59.03	7.891
20	0.9340	58.25	7.787
22	0.9218	57.87	7.736
24	0.9100	56.75	7.587
26	0.8984	56.03	7.490
28	0.8871	55.32	7.396
30	0.8762	54.64	7.305
32	0.8654	53.97	7.215
34	0.8550	53.32	7.128
36	0.8448	52.69	7.043
38	0.8348	51.06	6.960
40	0.8251	51.46	6.879
42	0.8155	50.86	6.799
44	0.8030	50.28	6.722
46	0.7972	49.72	6.646
48	0.7883	49.16	6.572
50	0.7796	48.62	6.499
52	0.7711	48.09	6.429
54	0.7628	47.57	6.359
56	0.7547	47.07	6.292
58	0.7467	46.57	6.225
60	0.7389	46.08	6.160
62	0.7313	45.61	6.097
64	0.7238	45.14	6.034
66	0.7165	44.68	5.973
68	0.7093	44.23	5.913
70	0.7022	43.79	5.854
72	0.6953	43.36	5.797
74	0.6886	42.94	5.741
76	0.6819	42.53	5.685
78	0.6754	41.72	5.631
80	0.6690	41.33	5.577
82	0.6628	41.12	5.526
84	0.6566	40.95	5.474
86	0.6506	40.57	5.424
88	0.6446	40.20	5.374
90	0.6388	39.84	5.326
92	0.6331	39.48	5.278
94	0.6275	39.13	5.231
96	0.6220	38.79	5.186
98	0.6116	38.45	5.141
100	0.6112	38.12	5.096

◄ FREQUENTLY ASKED ► QUESTION

HOW CAN YOU TELL IF GASOLINE HAS BEEN ADDED TO THE DIESEL FUEL BY MISTAKE?

If gasoline has been accidentally added to diesel fuel and is burned in a diesel engine, the result can be very damaging to the engine. The gasoline can ignite faster than diesel fuel, which would tend to increase the temperature of combustion. This high temperature can harm injectors and glow plugs, as well as pistons, head gaskets, and other major diesel engine components. If contaminated fuel is suspected, first smell the fuel at the filler neck. If the fuel smells like gasoline, then the tank should be drained and refilled with diesel fuel. If the smell test does not indicate a gasoline (or any rancid smell), then test a sample for proper API gravity.

NOTE: Diesel fuel designed for on-road use should be green in color. Red diesel fuel (high sulfur) should only be found in off-road or farm equipment.

DIESEL FUEL HEATERS

Diesel fuel heaters help prevent power loss and stalling in cold weather. The heater is placed in the fuel line between the tank and the primary filter. Some coolant

FIGURE 4-15 A wire wound electrical heater is used to warm the intake air on some diesel engines.

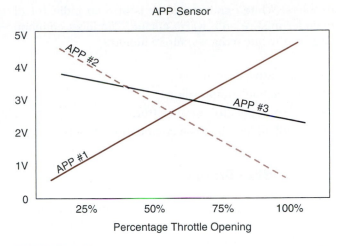

FIGURE 4-16 A typical accelerator pedal position (APP) sensor uses three different sensors in one package with each creating a different voltage as the accelerator is moved.

heaters are thermostatically controlled, which allows fuel to bypass the heater once it has reached operating temperature.

HEATED INTAKE AIR

Some diesels, such as the General Motors 6.6-liter Duramax V-8, use an electrical heater wire to warm the intake air to help in cold weather starting and running. See Figure 4-15.

ACCELERATOR PEDAL POSITION SENSOR

Some light truck diesel engines are equipped with an electronic throttle to control the amount of fuel injected into the engine. Because a diesel engine does not use a throttle in the air intake, the only way to control engine speed is by controlling the amount of fuel being injected into the cylinders. Instead of a mechanical link from the accelerator pedal to the diesel injection pump, a throttle-by-wire system uses an accelerator pedal position sensor. To ensure safety, it consists of three separate sensors that change in voltage as the accelerator pedal is depressed. See Figure 4-16.

The computer checks for errors by comparing the voltage output of each of the three sensors inside the APP and compares them to what they should be if there are no faults. If an error is detected, the engine and vehicle speed are often reduced.

DIESEL EXHAUST SMOKE DIAGNOSIS

While some exhaust smoke is considered normal operation for many diesel engines, especially older units, the cause of excessive exhaust smoke should be diagnosed and repaired.

Black Smoke

Black exhaust smoke is caused by incomplete combustion because of a lack of air or a fault in the injection system that could cause an excessive amount of fuel in the cylinders. Items that should be checked include the following:

- Check the fuel specific gravity (API gravity).
- Perform an injector balance test to locate faulty injectors using a scan tool.
- Check for proper operation of the engine coolant temperature (ECT) sensor.
- Check for proper operation of the fuel rail pressure (FRP) sensor.
- Check for restrictions in the intake or turbocharger.
- Check to see if the engine is using oil.

White Smoke

White exhaust smoke occurs most often during cold engine starts because the smoke is usually condensed fuel droplets. White exhaust smoke is also an indicator of cylinder misfire on a warm engine. The most common causes of white exhaust smoke include:

- Inoperative glow plugs
- Low engine compression
- Incorrect injector spray pattern
- A coolant leak into the combustion chamber

Gray or Blue Smoke

Blue exhaust smoke is usually due to oil consumption caused by worn piston rings, scored cylinder walls, or defective valve stem seals. Gray or blue smoke can also be caused by a defective injector(s).

SCAN TOOL DIAGNOSIS

Diesel engines since the late 1980s have been computer controlled and are equipped with sensors and activators to control functions that were previously mechanically controlled. All light truck diesels since 1996 have also adhered to on-board diagnostic (second generation [OBD-II]). The use of a scan tool to check for diagnostic trouble codes (DTCs) and to monitor engine operation is one of the first diagnostic steps. See Figure 4-17.

COMPRESSION TESTING

A compression test, as described in detail in Chapter 8, is fundamental for determining the mechanical condition of a diesel engine. Worn piston rings can cause low power and excessive exhaust smoke. A diesel engine should produce at least 300 psi of compression pressure and all cylinders should be within 50 psi of each other. See Figure 4-18.

GLOW PLUG RESISTANCE BALANCE TEST

Glow plugs increase in resistance as their temperature increases. All glow plugs should have about the same resistance when checked with an ohmmeter. A similar test of the resistance of the glow plugs can be used to detect a weak cylinder. This test is particularly helpful on a diesel engine that is not computer controlled. To test for even cylinder balance using glow plug resistance, perform the following on a warm engine.

1. Unplug, measure, and record the resistance of all of the glow plugs.
2. With the wires still removed from the glow plugs, start the engine.
3. Allow the engine to run for several minutes to allow the combustion inside the cylinder to warm the glow plugs.

FIGURE 4-17 A scan tool is used to retrieve diagnostic trouble codes and to perform injector balance tests.

FIGURE 4-18 A compression gauge designed for the higher compression rate of a diesel engine should be used when checking the compression.

4. Measure the plugs and record the resistance of all of the glow plugs.

5. The resistance of all of the glow plugs should be higher than at the beginning of the test. A glow plug that is in a cylinder that is not firing correctly will not increase in resistance as much as the others.

6. Another test is to measure exhaust manifold temperature at each exhaust port. Misfiring cylinders will run cold. This can be done with a contact or non-contact thermometer.

◄ **TECH TIP** ►

SWAP INJECTORS

If a cylinder is misfiring, swap the injector from a good cylinder. If the problem moves to the other cylinder, the injector is the cause of the misfire. If the problem continues, the bad cylinder likely has a loss of compression due to a mechanical fault.

INJECTOR POP TESTING

A **pop tester** is a device used for checking a diesel injector nozzle for proper spray pattern. The handle is depressed and pop off pressure is displayed on the gauge. See Figure 4-19. The spray pattern should be a hollow cone. This will vary depending on design. The nozzle should also be tested for leakage—dripping of the nozzle while under pressure. If the spray pattern is not correct, cleaning, repairing, or replacing the injector nozzle may be necessary.

DIESEL EMISSION TESTING

The most commonly used diesel exhaust emission test used in state or local testing programs is called the **opacity** test. Opacity means the percentage of light that is blocked by the exhaust smoke.

- A 0% opacity means that the exhaust has no visible smoke and does not block light from a beam projected through the exhaust smoke.
- A 100% opacity means that the exhaust is so dark that it completely blocks light from a beam projected through the exhaust smoke.
- A 50% opacity means that the exhaust blocks half of the light from a beam projected through the exhaust smoke.

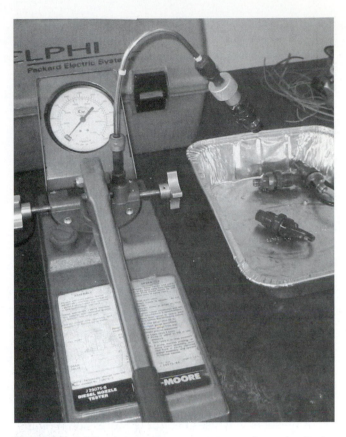

FIGURE 4-19   A typical pop tester used to check the spray pattern of a diesel engine injector.

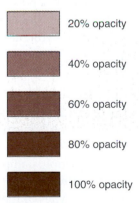

20% opacity

40% opacity

60% opacity

80% opacity

100% opacity

Snap Acceleration Test

In a snap acceleration test, the vehicle is held stationary with wheel chocks and brakes released as the engine is rapidly accelerated to high idle with the transmission in neutral while smoke emissions are measured. This test is conducted a minimum of six times and the three most consistent measurements are averaged together for a final score.

Rolling Acceleration Test

Vehicles with a manual transmission are rapidly accelerated in low gear from an idle speed to a maximum governed RPM while the smoke emissions are measured.

Stall Acceleration Test

Vehicles with automatic transmissions are held in a stationary position with the parking brake and service brakes applied while the transmission is placed in "drive." The accelerator is depressed and held momentarily while smoke emissions are measured.

The standards for diesels vary according to the type of vehicle and other factors, but usually include a 40% opacity or less.

◄ **FREQUENTLY ASKED QUESTION** ►

DO DIESEL PERFORMANCE REPROGRAMMED COMPUTERS REALLY WORK?

Yes. The manufacturers of these reprogrammed computers claim very impressive torque and horsepower gains over the stock factory rating. When factory engineers were asked about this type, they acknowledge that the gains are true, but that the changes "take the engine exhaust emission out of compliance." Therefore, before installing any high-performance upgrades, be sure to check the local or state emissions regulations in your area or the manufacturer of the replacement component to be sure that they comply with all emissions regulations.

SUMMARY

1. A diesel engine uses heat of compression to ignite the diesel fuel when it is injected into the compressed air in the combustion chamber.

2. There are two basic designs of combustion chambers used in diesel engines. Indirect injection (IDI) uses a pre-combustion chamber whereas a direct injection (DI) occurs directly into the combustion chamber.

3. The three phases of diesel combustion include:
   a. Ignition delay
   b. Rapid combustion
   c. Controlled combustion

4. The typical diesel engine fuel system consists of the fuel tank, lift pump, water-fuel separator, and fuel filter.

5. The engine-driven injection pump supplies high-pressure diesel fuel to the injectors.

6. The two most common types of fuel injection used in automotive diesel engines are:
   a. Distributor-type injection pump
   b. Common rail design where all of the injectors are fed from the same fuel supply from a rail under high pressure

7. Injector nozzles are either opened by the high-pressure pulse from the distributor pump or electrically by the computer on a common rail design.

8. Glow plugs are used to help start a cold diesel engine and help prevent excessive white smoke during warm-up.

9. The higher the cetane rating of diesel fuel, the more easily the fuel is ignited.

10. Most automotive diesel engines are designed to operate on grade #2 diesel fuel in moderate weather conditions.

11. The API specific gravity of diesel fuel should be 30 to 39 with a typical reading of 35 for #2 diesel fuel.

12. Diesel engines can be tested using a scan tool, as well as measuring the glow plug resistance or compression reading to determine a weak or nonfunctioning cylinder.

REVIEW QUESTIONS

1. What is the difference between direct injection and indirect injection?

2. What are the three phases of diesel ignition?

3. What are the two most commonly used types of automotive diesel injection systems?

4. Why are glow plugs kept working after the engine starts?

5. What is the advantage of using diesel fuel with a high cetane rating?

6. How is the specific gravity of diesel fuel tested?

ASE CERTIFICATION-TYPE QUESTIONS

1. How is diesel fuel ignited in a warm diesel engine?
   a. Glow plugs
   b. Heat of compression
   c. Spark plugs
   d. Distributorless ignition system

2. Which type of diesel injection produces less noise?
   a. Indirect injection (IDI)
   b. Common rail
   c. Direct injection
   d. Distributor injection

3. Which diesel injection system requires the use of a glow plug?
   a. Indirect injection (IDI)
   b. Common rail
   c. Direct injection
   d. Distributor injection

4. The three phases of diesel ignition include _____.
   a. Glow plug ignition, fast burn, slow burn
   b. Slow burn, fast burn, slow burn
   c. Ignition delay, rapid combustion, controlled combustion
   d. Glow plug ignition, ignition delay, controlled combustion

5. What fuel system component is used in a vehicle equipped with a diesel engine that is not usually used on the same vehicle when it is equipped with a gasoline engine?
   a. Fuel filter
   b. Fuel supply line
   c. Fuel return line
   d. Water-fuel separator

6. The diesel injection pump is driven by a _____.
   a. Gear off the camshaft
   b. Belt off the crankshaft
   c. Shaft drive off of the crankshaft
   d. Chain drive off of the camshaft

7. Which diesel system supplies high-pressure diesel fuel to all of the injectors all of the time?
   a. Distributor
   b. Inline
   c. Common rail
   d. Rotary

8. Glow plugs should have high resistance when _____ and lower resistance when _____.
   a. Cold/warm
   b. Warm/cold
   c. Wet/dry
   d. Dry/wet

9. Technician A says that glow plugs are used to help start a diesel engine and are shut off as soon as the engine starts. Technician B says that the glow plugs are turned off as soon as a flame is detected in the combustion chamber. Which technician is correct?
   a. Technician A only
   b. Technician B only
   c. Both Technicians A and B
   d. Neither Technician A nor B

10. What part should be removed to test cylinder compression on a diesel engine?
   a. An injector
   b. An intake valve rocker arm and stud
   c. An exhaust valve
   d. A glow plug

◀ Chapter 5 ▶

GASOLINE AND ALTERNATIVE FUELS

OBJECTIVES

After studying Chapter 5, the reader should be able to:

1. Prepare for ASE Engine Performance (A8) certification test content area "C" (Fuel, Air Induction, and Exhaust Systems Diagnosis and Repair).
2. Describe how the proper grade of gasoline affects engine performance.
3. List gasoline purchasing hints.
4. Discuss how volatility affects driveability.
5. Explain how oxygenated fuels can reduce CO exhaust emissions.
6. Discuss the advantages and disadvantages of alternative fuels and hybrid vehicles.

The quality of the fuel any engine uses is important to its proper operation and long life. If the fuel is not right for the air temperature or if the tendency of the fuel to evaporate is incorrect, severe driveability problems can result. An engine burns about 10,000 cubic feet of air (a box 10 ft × 10 ft × 100 ft) for every cubic foot of gasoline (about 7.5 gallons or 9,000 cu ft per gallon of gasoline).

GASOLINE

Gasoline is a term used to describe a complex mixture of various hydrocarbons refined from crude petroleum oil for use as a fuel in engines. The word **petroleum** means "rock oil." The refinery where gasoline is produced removes undesirable ingredients such as paraffins and puts in additives such as octane improvers. Most gasoline is "blended" to meet the needs of the local climates and altitudes.

◀ FREQUENTLY ASKED ▶ QUESTION

WHAT IS A CALIFORNIA GAS CAN?

When researching for ways to reduce hydrocarbon emissions in California, it was discovered that leakage from small gasoline containers used to refill small lawnmowers and other power equipment was a major source of unburned gasoline entering the atmosphere. As a result of this discovery, a new design for a gas can (container) was developed that is kept closed by a spring and uses O-rings to seal the opening. To use this container, the nozzle release lever is held against the side of the fuel opening and, when depressed, allows air to enter the container and fuel to flow. The flow of fuel stops automatically when the tank is full, eliminating any spillage. See Figure 5-1.

FIGURE 5-1 A gas can that meets the California Resources Board (CARB) approval uses a spring-loaded sealed nozzle that eliminates gasoline spillage and leaks into the atmosphere.

VOLATILITY

Volatility describes how easily the gasoline evaporates (forms a vapor). The definition of volatility assumes that the vapors will remain in the fuel tank or fuel line and will cause a certain pressure based on the temperature of the fuel.

Winter Blend

Reid vapor pressure (RVP) is the pressure of the vapor above the fuel when the fuel is at 100°F (38°C). Increased vapor pressure permits the engine to start in cold weather. Gasoline without air will not burn. Gasoline must be vaporized (mixed with air) to burn in an engine. Cold temperatures reduce the normal vaporization of gasoline; therefore, winter-blended gasoline is specially formulated to vaporize at lower temperatures for proper starting and driveability at low ambient temperatures. The **American Society for Testing and Materials (ASTM)** standards for winter-blend gasoline allow volatility of up to 15 pounds per square inch (psi) RVP.

Summer Blend

At warm ambient temperatures, gasoline vaporizes easily. However, the fuel system (fuel pump, carburetor, fuel-injector nozzles, etc.) is designed to operate with liquid gasoline. The volatility of summer-grade gasoline should be about 7.0 psi RVP. According to ASTM standards, the maximum RVP should be 10.5 psi for summer-blend gasoline.

Volatility Problems

At higher temperatures, liquid gasoline can easily vaporize, which can cause **vapor lock.** Vapor lock is a *lean* condition caused by vaporized fuel in the fuel system. This vaporized fuel takes up space normally occupied by liquid fuel. Vapor lock is caused by bubbles that form in the fuel, preventing proper operation of the fuel-injection system.

Bubbles in the fuel can be caused by heat or by sharp bends in the fuel system. Heat causes some fuel to evaporate, thereby causing bubbles. Sharp bends cause the fuel to be restricted at the bend. When the fuel flows past the bend, the fuel can expand to fill the space after the bend. This expansion drops the pressure, and bubbles form in the fuel lines. When the fuel is full of bubbles, the engine is not being supplied with enough fuel and the engine runs lean. A lean engine will stumble during acceleration, will run rough, and may stall. Warm weather and alcohol-blended fuels both tend to increase vapor lock and engine performance problems.

If winter-blend gasoline (or high-RVP fuel) is used in an engine during warm weather, the following problems may occur:

1. Rough idle
2. Stalling
3. Hesitation on acceleration
4. Surging

The RVP can be tested using the test kit shown in Figure 5-2.

DISTILLATION CURVE

Besides Reid vapor pressure, another method of classifying gasoline volatility is the **distillation curve.** A curve on a graph is created by plotting the temperature where the various percentage of the fuel evaporates. A typical distillation curve is shown in Figure 5-3.

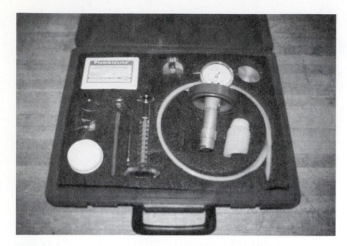

FIGURE 5-2 A gasoline testing kit. Included is an insulated container where water at 100°F is used to heat a container holding a small sample of gasoline. The reading on the pressure gauge is the Reid vapor pressure (RVP).

◀ **FREQUENTLY ASKED** ▶
QUESTION

WHY DO I GET LOWER GAS MILEAGE IN THE WINTER?

Several factors cause the engine to use more fuel in the winter than in the summer, including:

- Gasolines blended for use in cold climates are designed for ease of starting and contain fewer heavy molecules, which contribute to fuel economy. The heat content of winter gasoline is lower than summer-blended gasoline.

- In cold temperatures, all lubricants are stiff, causing more resistance. These lubricants include the engine oil, as well as the transmission and differential gear lubricants.

- Heat from the engine is radiated into the outside air more rapidly when the temperature is cold, resulting in longer run time until the engine has reached normal operating temperature.

- Road conditions, such as ice and snow, can cause tire slippage or additional drag on the vehicle.

◀ **TECH TIP** ▶

THE SNIFF TEST

Problems can occur with stale gasoline from which the lighter parts of the gasoline have evaporated. Stale gasoline usually results in a no-start situation. If stale gasoline is suspected, sniff it. If it smells rancid, replace it with fresh gasoline.

NOTE: If storing a vehicle, boat, or lawnmower over the winter, put some gasoline stabilizer into the gasoline to reduce the evaporation and separation that can occur during storage. Gasoline stabilizer is frequently found at lawnmower repair shops or marinas.

Some experts recommend that a diesel fuel additive be used to kill bacteria and fungi growth that occurs in fuels when moisture is present. To kill algae and stop bacterial growth, use from 0.25 to 0.50 fl. oz. in each 20 gallons. While algae growth is usually associated with diesel fuel when water collects at the bottom of the tank, gasoline tanks can still be a source of algae, especially when vehicles are stored.

NORMAL AND ABNORMAL COMBUSTION

The **octane rating** of gasoline is the measure of its antiknock properties. **Engine knock** (also called **detonation, spark knock,** or **ping**) is a metallic noise an engine makes, usually during acceleration, resulting from abnormal or uncontrolled combustion inside the cylinder.

Normal combustion occurs smoothly and progresses across the combustion chamber from the point of ignition. See Figure 5-4. Normal combustion propagation is between 45 and 90 MPH (72 and 145 km/h). The speed of the flame front depends on air-fuel ratio, combustion chamber design (determining amount of turbulence), and temperature.

During periods of spark knock (detonation), the combustion speed increases by up to 10 times to near the speed of sound. The increased combustion speed also causes increased temperatures and pressures, which can damage pistons, gaskets, and cylinder heads. See Figure 5-5.

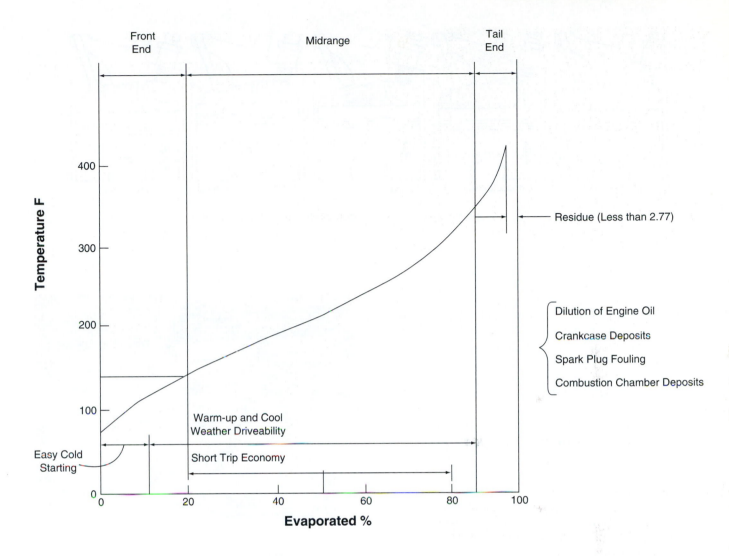

FIGURE 5-3 A typical distillation curve. Heavier molecules evaporate at higher temperatures and contain more heat energy for power, whereas the lighter molecules evaporate easier for starting.

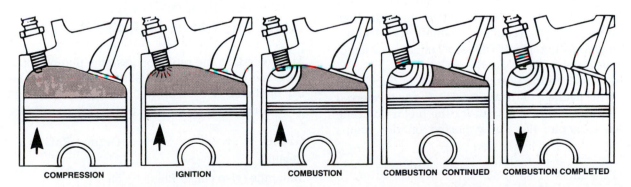

FIGURE 5-4 Normal combustion is a smooth, controlled burning of the air-fuel mixture.

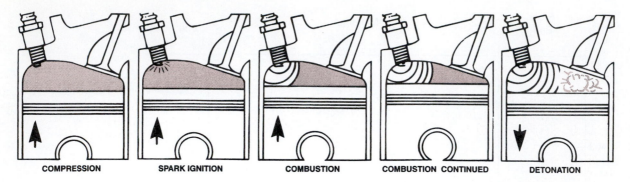

| COMPRESSION | SPARK IGNITION | COMBUSTION | COMBUSTION CONTINUED | DETONATION |

FIGURE 5-5 Detonation is a secondary ignition of the air-fuel mixture. It is also called spark knock or pinging.

One of the first additives used in gasoline was **tetraethyl lead (TEL).** TEL was added to gasoline in the early 1920s to reduce the tendency to knock. It was often called *ethyl* or *high-test* gasoline.

OCTANE RATING

The antiknock standard or basis of comparison was the knock-resistant hydrocarbon isooctane, chemically called trimethylpentane (C_8H_{18}), also known as 2-2-4 trimethylpentane. If a gasoline tested had the exact same antiknock characteristics as isooctane, it was rated as 100-octane gasoline. If the gasoline tested had only 85% of the antiknock properties of isooctane, it was rated as 85 octane. Remember, octane rating is only a comparison test.

The two basic methods used to rate gasoline for antiknock properties (octane rating) are the *research method* and the *motor method*. Each uses a model of the special cooperative fuel research (CFR) single-cylinder engine. The research method and the motor method vary as to temperature of air, spark advance, and other parameters. The research method typically results in readings that are six to ten points higher than those of the motor method. For example, a fuel with a research octane number (RON) of 93 might have a motor octane number (MON) of 85.

The octane rating posted on pumps in the United States is the average of the two methods and is referred to as (R + M)/2, meaning that, for the fuel used in the previous example, the rating posted on the pumps would be

$$\frac{RON + MON}{2} = \frac{93 + 85}{2} = 89$$

FIGURE 5-6 A typical fuel pump showing regular (87 octane), midgrade (89 octane), and premium (92 octane). These ratings can vary with brand as well as in different parts of the country, especially in high altitude areas where the ratings are lower.

GASOLINE GRADES AND OCTANE NUMBER

The posted octane rating on gasoline pumps is the rating achieved by the average of the research and the motor methods. See Figure 5-6. Except in high-altitude areas, the grades and octane ratings are as follows:

Grades	Octane Rating
Regular	87
Midgrade (also called Plus)	89
Premium	91 or higher

◄ TECH TIP ►

HORSEPOWER AND FUEL FLOW

To produce 1 hp, the engine must be supplied with 0.50 lb of fuel per hour (lb/hr). Fuel injectors are rated in pounds per hour. For example, a V-8 engine equipped with 25 lb/hr fuel injectors could produce 50 hp per cylinder (per injector) or 400 hp. Even if the cylinder head or block is modified to produce more horsepower, the limiting factor may be the injector flow rate.

The following are flow rates and resulting horsepower for a V-8 engine:

30 lb/hr: 60 hp per cylinder or 480 hp
35 lb/hr: 70 hp per cylinder or 560 hp
40 lb/hr: 80 hp per cylinder or 640 hp

Of course, injector flow rate is only one of many variables that affect power output. Installing larger injectors without other major engine modification could decrease engine output and drastically increase exhaust emissions.

SEASONALLY BLENDED GASOLINE

All gasoline is seasonally blended to match the volatility of the gasoline to the seasonal temperature range of the area. See the following chart showing which class of volatility is specified for each part of the country.

1 = 140°F start of vaporization
2 = 133°F start of vaporization
3 = 124°F start of vaporization

OCTANE IMPROVERS

When gasoline companies, under federal EPA regulations, removed tetraethyl lead from gasoline, other methods were developed to help maintain the antiknock properties of gasoline. Octane improvers (enhancers) can be grouped into three broad categories:

1. Aromatic hydrocarbons (hydrocarbons containing the benzene ring) such as xylene and toluene

◄ DIAGNOSTIC STORY ►

THE STALLING ACURA

On a warm day in March, a customer walked into an automotive repair shop and asked for help. The car was parked on the street just outside the shop. A service technician accompanied the owner to check out the situation. The owner complained that the engine would start, then immediately stall. The engine would again start, then stall during another attempt.

The service technician slid into the driver's seat and turned the ignition key. When the engine started, the technician depressed the accelerator slightly and the engine continued to run without any apparent problem. The car owner had never depressed the accelerator pedal and had never had any previous engine trouble.

The technician suspected winter-grade (high-RVP) gasoline was the problem. The owner replied that the present tank of fuel had been purchased during the last week in February. The technician explained that the uncommonly warm weather caused the fuel to vaporize in the fuel rail. Enough condensed fuel was available to start the engine, but the fuel injectors were designed to handle liquid fuel—not vapor—so the engine stalled.

The technician was probably lucky because by the third start enough of the remaining vapor had been drawn into the engine that all that remained was liquid gasoline.

Geographical Fuel-marketing Regions

Volatility Class by Month

State and Fuel Marketing Region	Jan	Feb	March	April	May	June	July	Aug	Sept	Oct	Nov	Dec
Alabama	2	2	2	2	2/1	1	1	1	1	1/2	2	2
Alaska												
Southern Region	3	3	3	3	3/2	2/1	1	1/2	2/3	3	3	3
South Mainland	3	3	3	3	3/2	2/1	1/2	2	2/3	3	3	3
Arizona												
North of 34° lat & E. of 111° long	3	3	3	3/2	2	2/1	1	1	1/2	2/3	3	3
Remainder south of 34°	2	2	2	2/1	1	1	1	1	1	1/2	2	2
Arkansas	3	3	3/2	2/1	1	1	1	1	1/2	2	2/3	3
California												
North Coast	2	2	2	2	2	2/1	1	1	1	1/2	2	2
South Coast	2	2	2	2	2/1	1	1	1	1	1/2	2	2
Southeast	3	3/2	2	2	2/1	1	1	1	1/2	2	2/3	3
Interior	2	2	2	2	2	2/1	1	1	1	1/2	2	2
Colorado												
East of 105° longitude	3	3	3	3/2	2	2/1	1	1	1/2	2/3	3	3
West of 105° longitude	3	3	3	3	3/2	2	2/1	1/2	2/3	3	3	3
Connecticut	3	3	3	3/2	2	2/1	1	1	1/2	2	2/3	3
Delaware	3	3	3/2	2	2/1	1	1	1	1/2	2	2/3	3
District of Columbia	3	3	3/2	2	2/1	1	1	1	1/2	2	2/3	3
Florida												
North of 29° latitude	2	2	2	2/1	1	1	1	1	1	1/2	2	2
South of 29° latitude	2	2/1	1	1	1	1	1	1	1	1	1/2	2
Georgia	3	3/2	2	2/1	1	1	1	1	1	1/2	2	2/3
Hawaii	1	1	1	1	1	1	1	1	1	1	1	1
Idaho	3	3	3	3/2	2	2	2/1	1/2	2	2/3	3	3
Illinois												
North of 40° latitude	3	3	3	3/2	2	2/1	1	1	1/2	2/3	3	3
South of 40° latitude	3	3	3	3/2	2/1	1	1	1	1/2	2/3	3	3
Indiana	3	3	3	3/2	2/1	1	1	1	1/2	2/3	3	3
Iowa	3	3	3	3/2	2	2/1	1	1	1/2	2/3	3	3
Kansas	3	3	3	3/2	2	2/1	1	1	1/2	2/3	3	3
Kentucky	3	3	3/2	2	2/1	1	1	1	1.2	2	2/3	3
Louisiana	2	2	2	2/1	1	1	1	1	1	1/2	2	2
Maine	3	3	3	3/2	2	2/1	1	1/2	2	2/3	3	3
Maryland	3	3	3/2	2	2/1	1	1	1	1/2	2	2/3	3
Massachusetts	3	3	3	3/2	2	2/1	1	1	1/2	2	2/3	3
Michigan												
Lower Peninsula	3	3	3	3/2	2	2/1	1	1/2	2	2/3	3	3
Upper Peninsula	3	3	3	3	3/2	2/1	1	1/2	2	2/3	3	3
Minnesota	3	3	3	3	3/2	2/1	1	1/2	2	2/3	3	3
Mississippi	2	2	2	2/1	1	1	1	1	1	1/2	2	2

State and Fuel Marketing Region	Jan	Feb	March	April	May	June	July	Aug	Sept	Oct	Nov	Dec
Missouri	3	3	3	3/2	2/1	1	1	1	1/2	2/3	3	3
Montana	3	3	3	3	3/2	2	2/1	1/2	2/3	3	3	3
Nebraska	3	3	3	3/2	2	2/1	1	1/2	2	2/3	3	3
Nevada												
North of 38° latitude	3	3	3	3/2	2	2	2/1	1/2	2	2/3	3	3
South of 38° latitude	3	3	3/2	2	2/1	1	1	1	1/2	2	2/3	3
New Hampshire	3	3	3	3/2	2	2/1	1	1/2	2	2/3	3	3
New Jersey	3	3	3/2	2	2/1	1	1	1	1/2	2	2/3	3
New Mexico												
North of 34° latitude	3	3	3	3/2	2	2/1	1	1	1/2	2/3	3	3
South of 34° latitude	3	3	3/2	2/1	1	1	1	1	1	1/2	2/3	3
New York												
North of 42° latitude	3	3	3	3/2	2	2/1	1	1/2	2	2/3	3	3
South of 42° latitude	3	3	3	3/2	2/1	1	1	1	1/2	2	2/3	3
North Carolina	3	3	3/2	2	2/1	1	1	1	1/2	2/3	3	3
North Dakota	3	3	3	3	3/2	2/1	1	1/2	2	2/3	3	3
Ohio	3	3	3	3/2	2/1	1	1	1	1/2	2/3	3	3
Oklahoma	3	3	3	3/2	2/1	1	1	1	1/2	2	2/3	3
Oregon												
East of 122° longitude	3	3	3	3/2	2	2	2/1	1/2	2	2/3	3	3
West of 122° longitude	3	3/2	2	2	2	2/1	1	1	1/2	2	2	2/3
Pennsylvania												
North of 41° latitude	3	3	3	3/2	2	2/1	1	1/2	2	2/3	3	3
South of 41° latitude	3	3	3	3/2	2	2/1	1	1	1/2	2	2/3	3
Rhode Island	3	3	3	3/2	2/1	1	1	1	1/2	2	2/3	3
South Carolina	2	2	2	2/1	1	1	1	1	1	1/2	2	2
South Dakota	3	3	3	3/2	2	2/1	1	1/2	2	2/3	3	3
Tennessee	3	3	3/2	2	2/1	1	1	1	1/2	2	2/3	3
Texas												
North of 31° latitude	3	3	3/2	2	2/1	1	1	1	1/2	2	2/3	3
South of 31° latitude	2	2	2	2/1	1	1	1	1	1	1/2	2	2
Utah	3	3	3	3/2	2	2/1	1	1	1/2	2/3	3	3
Vermont	3	3	3	3/2	2	2/1	1	1/2	2	2/3	3	3
Virginia	3	3	3/2	2	2/1	1	1	1	1/2	2	2/3	3
Washington												
East of 122° longitude	3	3	3/2	2	2	2/1	1	1	1/2	2/3	3	3
West of 122° longitude	3	3/2	2	2	2	2/1	1	1	1/2	2	2	2/3
West Virginia	3	3	3	3/2	2	2/1	1	1/2	2	2/3	3	3
Wisconsin	3	3	3	3/2	2	2/1	1	1/2	2	2/3	3	3
Wyoming	3	3	3	3	3/2	2	2/1	1.2	2	2/3	3	3

2. Alcohols such as ethanol (ethyl alcohol), methanol (methyl alcohol), and tertiary butyl alcohol (TBA)
3. Metallic compounds such as methylcyclopentadienyl manganese tricarbonyl (MMT)

NOTE: MMT has been proven to be harmful to catalytic converters and can cause spark plug fouling. However, MMT is currently one of the active ingredients commonly found in octane improvers available to the public and in some gasoline sold in Canada. If an octane boost additive has been used that contains MMT, the spark plugs will be rust colored.

Propane and butane, which are volatile by-products of the refinery process, are also often added to gasoline as octane improvers. The increase in volatility caused by the added propane and butane often leads to hot-weather driveability problems.

◀ FREQUENTLY ASKED ▶ QUESTION

CAN REGULAR GRADE GASOLINE BE USED IF PREMIUM IS THE RECOMMENDED GRADE?

Yes. It is usually possible to use regular or midgrade (plus) grade gasoline in most newer vehicles without danger of damage to the engine. Most vehicles built since the 1990s are equipped with at least one knock sensor. If a lower octane gasoline than specified is used, the engine ignition timing setting will usually cause the engine to spark knock, also called detonation or ping. This spark knock is detected by the knock sensor(s), which sends a signal to the computer. The computer then retards the ignition timing until the spark knock stops.

NOTE: Some scan tools will show the "estimated octane rating" of the fuel being used, which is based on knock sensor activity.

As a result of this spark timing retardation, the engine torque is reduced. While this reduction in power is seldom noticed, it will reduce fuel economy, often by 4 to 5 miles per gallon. If premium gasoline is then used, the PCM will gradually permit the engine to operate at the more advanced ignition timing setting. Therefore, it may take several tanks of premium gasoline to restore normal fuel economy. For best overall performance, use the grade of gasoline recommended by the vehicle manufacturer.

OXYGENATED FUELS

Oxygenated fuels contain oxygen in the molecule of the fuel itself. Examples of oxygenated fuels include methanol, ethanol, methyl tertiary butyl ether (MTBE), tertiary-amyl methyl ether (TAME), and ethyl tertiary butyl ether (ETBE).

Oxygenated fuels are commonly used in high-altitude areas to reduce carbon monoxide (CO) emissions. The extra oxygen in the fuel itself is used to convert harmful CO into carbon dioxide (CO_2). The extra oxygen in the fuel helps ensure that there is enough oxygen to convert all the CO into CO_2 during the combustion process in the engine or catalytic converter.

Methyl Tertiary Butyl Ether (MTBE)

MTBE is manufactured by means of the chemical reaction of methanol and isobutylene. Unlike methanol, MTBE does not increase the volatility of the fuel, and is not as sensitive to water as are other alcohols. The maximum allowable volume level, according to the EPA, is 15% but is currently being phased out due to concern with MTBE contamination of drinking water if spilled from storage tanks.

Tertiary-Amyl Methyl Ether

Tertiary-amyl methyl ether (TAME) is often added to gasoline as an oxygenater.

Ethyl Tertiary Butyl Ether

ETBE is derived from ethanol. The maximum allowable volume level is 17.2%. The use of ETBE is the cause of much of the odor from the exhaust of vehicles using reformulated gasoline.

FIGURE 5-7 This fuel tank indicates that the gasoline is blended with 10% ethanol (ethyl alcohol).

FIGURE 5-8 This container holds pure gasoline and water. Notice how the water separates and sinks to the bottom.

Ethanol

Ethyl alcohol is drinkable alcohol made from grain. Adding 10% ethanol (ethyl alcohol or grain alcohol) increases the (R + M)/2 octane rating by three points. The alcohol added to the base gasoline, however, also raises the volatility of the fuel about 0.5 psi. Most automobile manufacturers permit up to 10% ethanol if driveability problems are not experienced. The oxygen content of a 10% blend of ethanol in gasoline is 3.5% oxygen by weight. See Figure 5-7.

Methanol

Methyl alcohol is made from wood (wood alcohol), natural gas, or coal. Methanol is poisonous if ingested and tends to be more harmful to the materials in the fuel system and tends to separate when combined with gasoline unless used with a cosolvent. A cosolvent is another substance (usually another alcohol) that is soluble in both methanol and gasoline and is used to reduce the tendency of the liquids to separate.

Methanol can damage fuel system parts. Methanol is corrosive to lead (used as a coating of fuel tanks), aluminum, magnesium, and some plastics and rubber. Methanol can also cause rubber products (elastomers) to swell and soften. Methanol itself is 50% oxygen. Gasoline containing 5% methanol would have an oxygen content of 2.5% by weight.

CAUTION: All alcohols can absorb water, and the alcohol-water mixture can separate from the gasoline and sink to the bottom of the fuel tank. This process is called **phase separation**. To help avoid engine performance problems, try to keep at least a quarter tank of fuel at all times, especially during sea-

sons when there is a wide temperature span between daytime highs and nighttime lows. These conditions can cause moisture to accumulate in the fuel tank as a result of condensation of the moisture in the air. See Figure 5-8. Keeping the fuel tank full reduces the amount of air and moisture in the tank.

ALCOHOL ADDITIVES— ADVANTAGES AND DISADVANTAGES

The advantages and disadvantages of using alcohol as an additive to gasoline can be summarized in the following manner.

Advantages

1. Alcohol absorbs moisture in the fuel tank.
2. Ten percent alcohol added to gasoline raises the octane rating—(R + M)/2—by three points.
3. Alcohol cleans the fuel system.
4. Alcohol reduces CO emissions because it contains oxygen.

Disadvantages

1. The use of alcohol can result in the clogging of fuel filters with dirt and other debris cleaned from the fuel tank, pump, and lines.
2. Alcohol raises the volatility of fuel about 0.5 psi; this can cause hot-weather driveability problems.
3. Alcohol reduces the heat content of the resulting fuel mixture (it has about one-half of the energy content of gasoline): 60,000 to 75,000 **British thermal units (BTUs)** per gallon for alcohol versus about 130,000 BTUs per gallon for gasoline.
4. Alcohol absorbs water and then separates from the gasoline, especially as the temperature drops. Separated alcohol and water on the bottom of the tank can cause hard starting during cold weather. Alcohol does not vaporize easily at low temperatures.

TESTING GASOLINE FOR ALCOHOL CONTENT

Take the following steps when testing gasoline for alcohol content.

1. Pour suspect gasoline into a small clean beaker or glass container.
   DO NOT SMOKE OR RUN THE TEST AROUND SOURCES OF IGNITION!
2. Carefully fill the graduated cylinder to the 10-mL mark.
3. Add 2 mL of water to the graduated cylinder by counting the number of drops from an eyedropper. (Before performing the test, the eyedropper must be calibrated to determine how many drops equal 2.0 mL.)
4. Put the stopper in the cylinder and shake vigorously for 1 minute. Relieve built-up pressure by occasionally removing the stopper. Alcohol dissolves in water and will drop to the bottom of the cylinder.
5. Place the cylinder on a flat surface and let it stand for 2 minutes.
6. Take a reading near the bottom of the cylinder at the boundary between the two liquids.
7. For percent of alcohol in gasoline, subtract 2 from the reading and multiply by 10.
   For example,

   The reading is 3.1 mL: $3.1 - 2 = 1.1 \times 10 = 11\%$ alcohol

The reading is 2.0 mL: $2 - 2 = 0 \times 10 = 0\%$ alcohol (no alcohol)

If the increase in volume is 0.2% or less, it may be assumed that the test gasoline contains no alcohol. Alcohol content can also be checked using an electronic tester. See the photo sequence at the end of the chapter.

◀ FREQUENTLY ASKED ▶ QUESTION

HOW DOES ALCOHOL CONTENT IN THE GASOLINE AFFECT ENGINE OPERATION?

In most cases, the use of gasoline containing 10% or less of ethanol (ethyl alcohol) has little or no effect on engine operation. However, because the addition of 10% ethanol raises the volatility of the fuel slightly, occasional rough idle or stalling may be noticed, especially during warm weather. The rough idle and stalling may also be noticeable after the engine is started, driven, then stopped for a short time. Engine heat can vaporize the alcohol-enhanced fuel causing bubbles to form in the fuel system. These bubbles in the fuel prevent the proper operation of the fuel injection or carburetor and result in a hesitation during acceleration, rough idle, or in severe cases repeated stalling until all the bubbles have been forced through the fuel system replaced by cooler fuel from the fuel tank.

COMBUSTION CHEMISTRY

Internal combustion engines burn an organic fuel to produce power. The term **organic** refers to a product (gasoline) from a source that originally was alive. Because crude oil originally came from living plants and animals, all products of petroleum are considered organic fuels and are composed primarily of hydrogen (H) and carbon (C).

The combustion process involves the chemical combination of oxygen (O_2) from the air (about 21% of the atmosphere) with the hydrogen and carbon from the fuel. In a gasoline engine, a spark starts the combustion process, which takes about 3 ms (0.003 sec) to be completed inside the cylinder of an engine. The chemical reaction that takes place can be summarized as follows: hydrogen (H) plus carbon (C) plus oxygen (O_2) plus nitrogen (N) plus spark equals heat plus water (H_2O) plus carbon monoxide (CO) plus carbon dioxide (CO_2) plus hydrocarbons (HC) plus oxides of nitrogen (NO_X) plus many other chemicals.

AIR-FUEL RATIOS

Fuel burns best when the intake system turns it into a fine spray and mixes it with air before sending it into the cylinders. In fuel-injected engines, the fuel becomes a spray and mixes with the air in the intake ports. There is a direct relationship between engine airflow and fuel requirements; this is called the **air-fuel ratio.**

The air-fuel ratio is the proportion by weight of air and gasoline that the injection system mixes as needed for engine combustion. The mixtures with which an engine can operate without stalling range from 8 to 1 to 18.5 to 1. See Figure 5-9. These ratios are usually stated by weight, such as:

- 8 parts of air by weight combined with 1 part of gasoline by weight (8:1), which is the richest mixture that an engine can tolerate and still fire regularly.
- 18.5 parts of air mixed with 1 part of gasoline (18.5:1), which is the leanest. Richer or leaner air-fuel ratios cause the engine to misfire badly or not run at all.

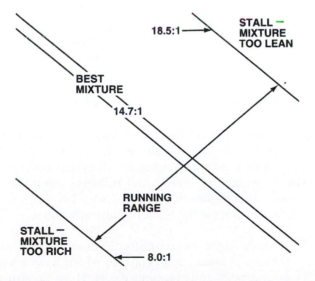

FIGURE 5-9 An engine will not run if the air-fuel mixture is either too rich or too lean.

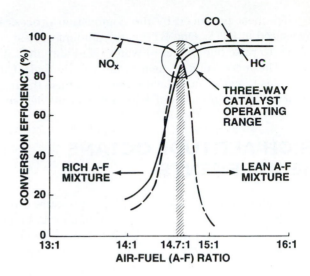

FIGURE 5-10 With a three-way catalytic converter, emission control is most efficient with an air-fuel ratio between 14.65:1 and 14.75:1.

Stoichiometric Air-Fuel Ratio

The ideal mixture or ratio at which all of the fuel combines with all of the oxygen in the air and *burns completely* is called the **stoichiometric ratio**—a chemically perfect combination. In theory, this ratio is an air-fuel mixture of 14.7 to 1. See Figure 5-10. In reality, the exact ratio at which perfect mixture and combustion occurs depends on the molecular structure of gasoline, which can vary. The stoichiometric ratio is a compromise between maximum power and maximum economy.

Stoichiometric Air-Fuel Ratio for Various Fuels

If the combustion process is complete, all gasoline or HCs will be completely combined with all the available oxygen. This total combination of all components of the fuel is called **stoichiometric air-fuel ratio.** The stoichiometric quantities for gasoline are 14.7 parts air for 1 part gasoline by weight. Different fuels have different stoichiometric proportions. See the table comparing the heat and stoichiometric ratio for alcohol versus gasoline.

Fuel	Heat energy (BTU/gal)	Stoichiometric ratio
Gasoline	About 130,000	14.7:1
Ethyl alcohol (Ethanol)	About 76,000	9.0:1
Methyl alcohol (Methanol)	About 60,000	6.4:1

The heat produced by the combustion process is measured in BTUs. One BTU is the amount of heat required to raise one pound of water one Fahrenheit degree. The metric unit of heat is the calorie (cal). One calorie is the amount of heat required to raise the temperature of one gram (g) of water one Celsius degree.

HIGH-ALTITUDE OCTANE REQUIREMENTS

As the altitude increases, atmospheric pressure drops. The air is less dense because a pound of air takes more volume. The octane rating of fuel does not need to be as high because the engine cannot intake as much air. This process will reduce the combustion (compression) pressures inside the engine. In mountainous areas, gasoline (R + M)/2 octane ratings are two or more numbers lower than normal (according to SAE, about one octane number lower per 1000 ft or 300 m in altitude). See Figure 5-11. A secondary reason for the lowered octane requirement of engines running at higher altitudes is the normal enrichment of the air-fuel ratio and lower engine vacuum with the decreased air density. Some problems, therefore, may occur when driving out of high-altitude areas into lower-altitude areas where the octane rating must be higher. Most computerized engine control systems can compensate for changes in altitude and modify air-fuel ratio and ignition timing for best operation.

Because the combustion burn rate slows at high altitude, the ignition (spark) timing can be advanced to improve power. The amount of timing advance can be about 1 degree per 1000 ft over 5000 ft. Therefore, if

FIGURE 5-11 Photo of gasoline pump taken in a high-altitude area. Note the lower than normal octane ratings. The "ethanol" sticker reads that all grades contain 10% ethanol from November 1 through February 28 each year to help reduce CO exhaust emissions.

driving at 8000 ft of altitude, the ignition timing can be advanced 3 degrees.

High altitude also allows fuel to evaporate more easily. The volatility of fuel should be reduced at higher altitudes to prevent vapor from forming in sections of the fuel system, which can cause driveability and stalling problems. The extra heat generated in climbing to higher altitudes plus the lower atmospheric pressure at higher altitudes combine to cause vapor lock problems as the vehicle goes to higher altitudes.

VALVE RECESSION AND UNLEADED FUEL

Unleaded fuel has been available since the early 1970s and since that time has caused concern about valve problems related to its use. However, back in the 1920s when "leaded" gasoline was first introduced, the main problem concerned the valves. In the 1920s, the lead deposits in the engine prevented the valves from fully seating, which resulted in overheated valves since the major place where valves got rid of their heat was through the valve face or seat area. The solution to valve burning in the 1920s with leaded fuel was to increase the valve spring tension. This increased pressure smashed the lead deposits into a thin lubricating film, allowing the valve to fully close and thereby transfer heat to the seat area.

Without lead, the valve movement against the seat tears away tiny iron oxide particles during engine operation. The valve movement causes these particles of iron oxide to act like valve grinding compound, cutting into the valve seat surface. As the valve seat erodes, the valve recedes further into the cylinder head.

Vehicle engines produced after 1971 for sale in the United States were required to operate on unleaded fuel. Most engine manufacturers started induction hardening of valve seats to help prevent valve recession.

REFORMULATED GASOLINE

Reformulated gasoline (RFG) is manufactured by refiners to help reduce emissions. The gasoline refiners reformulate gasoline by using additives that contain at least 2% oxygen by weight and reducing the additive benzenes to a maximum of 1% by value. Two other major changes done at the refineries are as follows:

1. **Reduce light compounds.** Refineries eliminate butane, pentane, and propane, which have a low boiling point and evaporate easily. These unburned hydrocarbons are released into the atmosphere during refueling and through the fuel tank vent system, contributing to smog formation.

2. **Reduce heavy compounds.** Refineries eliminate heavy compounds with high boiling points such as aromatics and olefins. The purpose of this reduction is to reduce the amount of unburned hydrocarbons that enter the catalytic converter.

Because many of the heavy compounds are eliminated, a drop in fuel economy of about 1 mpg has been reported in areas where reformulated gasoline is being used. Formaldehyde is formed when RFG is burned, and the vehicle exhaust has a unique smell when reformulated gasoline is used.

GENERAL GASOLINE RECOMMENDATIONS

The fuel used by an engine is a major expense in the operation cost of the vehicle. The proper operation of the engine depends on clean fuel of the proper octane rating and vapor pressure for the atmospheric conditions.

To help ensure proper engine operation and keep fuel costs to a minimum, follow these guidelines:

1. Purchase fuel from a busy station to help ensure that it is fresh and less likely to be contaminated with water or moisture.
2. Keep the fuel tank above one-quarter full, especially during seasons in which the temperature rises and falls by more than 20°F between daytime highs and nighttime lows. This helps to reduce condensed moisture in the fuel tank and could prevent gas line freeze-up in cold weather.

NOTE: Gas line freeze-up occurs when the water in the gasoline freezes and forms an ice blockage in the fuel line.

---

3. Do not purchase fuel with a higher octane rating than is necessary. Try using premium high-octane fuel to check for operating differences. Most newer engines are equipped with a detonation (knock) sensor that signals the vehicle computer to retard the ignition timing when spark knock occurs. Therefore, an operating difference may not be noticeable to the driver when using a low-octane fuel, except for a decrease in power and fuel economy. In other words, the engine with a knock sensor will tend to operate knock free on regular fuel, even if premium, higher octane fuel is specified. Using premium fuel may result in more power and greater fuel economy. The increase in fuel economy, however, would have to be substantial to justify the increased cost of high-octane premium fuel. Some drivers find a good compromise by using midgrade (plus) fuel to benefit from the engine power and fuel economy gains without the cost of using premium fuel all the time.

4. Avoid using gasoline with alcohol in warm weather, even though many alcohol blends do not affect engine driveability. If warm-engine stumble, stalling, or rough idle occurs, change brands of gasoline.

5. Do not purchase fuel from a retail outlet when a tanker truck is filling the underground tanks. During the refilling procedure, dirt, rust, and water may be stirred up in the underground tanks. This undesirable material may be pumped into your vehicle's fuel tank.

6. Do not overfill the gas tank. After the nozzle clicks off, add just enough fuel to round up to the next dime. Adding additional gasoline will cause the excess to be drawn into the charcoal canister. This can lead to engine flooding and excessive exhaust emissions.

7. Be careful when filling gasoline containers. Always fill a gas can on the ground to help prevent the possibility of static electricity buildup during the refueling process. See Figure 5-12.

◄ FREQUENTLY ASKED ► QUESTION

WHY SHOULD I KEEP THE FUEL GAUGE ABOVE ONE-QUARTER TANK?

The fuel pickup inside the fuel tank can help keep water from being drawn into the fuel system unless water is all that is left at the bottom of the tank. Over time, moisture in the air inside the fuel tank can condense, causing liquid water to drop to the bottom of the fuel tank (water is heavier than gasoline—about 8 lb per gallon for water and about 6 lb per gallon for gasoline). If alcohol-blended gasoline is used, the alcohol can absorb the water and the alcohol-water combination can be burned inside the engine. However, when water combines with alcohol, a separation layer occurs between the gasoline at the top of the tank and the alcohol-water combination at the bottom. When the fuel level is low, the fuel pump will draw from this concentrated level of alcohol and water. Because alcohol and water do not burn as well as pure gasoline, severe driveability problems can occur such as stalling, rough idle, hard starting, and missing.

FIGURE 5-12 Many gasoline service stations have signs posted warning customers to place plastic fuel containers on the ground while filling. If placed in a trunk or pickup truck bed equipped with a plastic liner, static electricity could build up during fueling and discharge from the container to the metal nozzle, creating a spark and possible explosion. Some service stations have warning signs not to use cell phones while fueling to help avoid the possibility of an accidental spark creating a fire hazard.

◄ TECH TIP ►

DO NOT OVERFILL THE FUEL TANK

Gasoline fuel tanks have an expansion volume area at the top. The volume of this expansion area is equal to 10 to 15% of the volume of the tank. This area is normally not filled with gasoline, but rather is designed to provide a place for the gasoline to expand into, if the vehicle is parked in the hot sun and the gasoline expands. This prevents raw gasoline from escaping from the fuel system. A small restriction is usually present to control the amount of air and vapors that can escape the tank and flow to the charcoal canister.

This volume area could be filled with gasoline if the fuel is slowly pumped into the tank. Since it can hold an extra 10% (2 gallons in a 20-gallon tank), some people deliberately try to fill the tank completely. When this expansion volume is filled, liquid fuel (rather than vapors) can be drawn into the charcoal canister. When the purge valve opens, liquid fuel can be drawn into the engine, causing an excessively rich air-fuel mixture. Not only can this liquid fuel harm vapor recovery parts, but overfilling the gas tank could also cause the vehicle to fail an exhaust emission test, particularly during an enhanced test when the tank could be purged while on the rollers.

ALTERNATIVE FUELS

Alternative fuels include a number of fuels besides gasoline for use in passenger vehicles.

E-85

Vehicle manufacturers have available vehicles that are capable of operating on gasoline plus ethanol or a combination of gasoline and ethanol called **E-85.** E-85 is composed of 85% ethanol and 15% gasoline. The gasoline in this blend helps the engine start, especially in cold weather. Vehicles equipped with this capability are commonly referred to as **flexible fuel vehicles** or **FFV.** See Figure 5-13. These vehicles are equipped with an electronic sensor that detects the presence and percentage of ethanol and then programs the fuel injector on-time and ignition timing to match the needs of the fuel being used.

E-85 contains less heat energy and, therefore, will use more fuel, but the benefits include a lower cost of the fuel and the environmental benefit associated with using an oxygenated fuel.

General Motors, Ford, DaimlerChrysler, Mazda, and Honda are a few of the manufacturers offering E-85 compatible vehicles. E-85 vehicles use fuel system parts designed to withstand the additional alcohol content, modified driveability programs that adjust fuel delivery and timing to compensate for the various percentages of ethanol fuel, and a **fuel compensation sensor** that measures both the percentage of ethanol blend and the temperature of the fuel. This sensor is also called a **variable fuel sensor.** See Figures 5-14 and 5-15.

FIGURE 5-13 A vehicle emission control information (VECI) sticker on a flexible fuel vehicle indicating the percentage of ethanol with which it is able to operate.

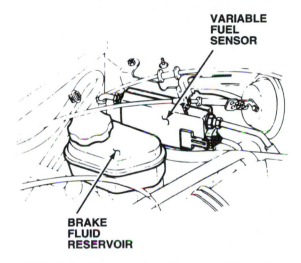

FIGURE 5-14 The location of the variable fuel sensor can vary, depending on the make and model of vehicle, but it is always in the fuel line between the fuel tank and the fuel injectors.

Most E-85 vehicles are very similar to non-E-85 vehicles. Fuel system components may be redesigned to withstand the effects of higher concentrations of ethanol. In addition, since the stoichiometric point for ethanol is 9:1 instead of 14.7:1 as for gasoline, the air-fuel mixture has to be adjusted for the percentage of ethanol present in the fuel tank. In order to determine this percentage of ethanol in the fuel tank, a composition sensor is used. The fuel composition sensor is the only additional piece of hardware required on an E-85 vehicle. The fuel composition sensor provides both the ethanol percentage and the fuel temperature to the PCM. The

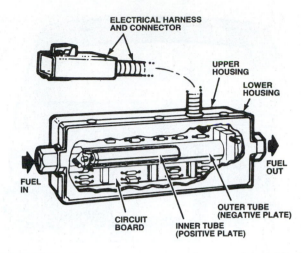

FIGURE 5-15 A cutaway view of a typical variable fuel sensor.

PCM uses this information to adjust both the ignition timing and the quantity of fuel delivered to the engine. The fuel compensation sensor uses a microprocessor to measure both the ethanol percentage and the fuel temperature. This information is sent to the PCM on the signal circuit. The compensation sensor produces a square wave frequency and pulse width signal. The normal frequency range of the fuel composition sensor is 50 hertz, which represents 0% ethanol, and 150 hertz, which represents 100% ethanol. The pulse width of the signal varies from 1 millisecond to 5 milliseconds. One millisecond would represent a fuel temperature of $-40°F$ ($-40°C$) and 5 milliseconds would represent a fuel temperature of 257°F (125°C). Since the PCM knows both the fuel temperature and the ethanol percentage of the fuel, it can adjust fuel quantity and ignition timing for optimum performance and emissions. The benefits of E-85 vehicles are less pollution, less CO_2 production, and less dependence on oil. Ethanol-fueled vehicles generally produce the same pollutants as gasoline vehicles; however, they produce less CO and CO_2 emissions. In addition, evaporative emissions are lower from ethanol than gasoline. While CO_2 is not considered a pollutant, it does lead to global warming and is called a greenhouse gas.

M-85

Some flexible fuel vehicles are designed to operate on 85% methanol and 15% gasoline. Methanol, also called **methyl alcohol,** is very corrosive and requires that the fuel system components be constructed of stainless steel and other alcohol-resistant rubber and plastic components. The heat content of M-85 is about 60% of that of gasoline.

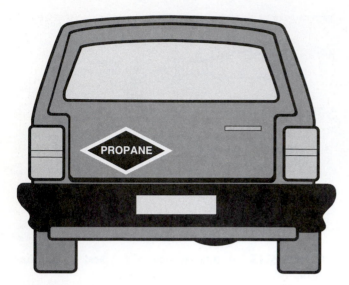

FIGURE 5-16 Some taxi companies operate their fleets on propane.

Propane

Propane, also referred to as **liquefied petroleum gas (LPG),** is commonly used in forklifts and other equipment used inside warehouses and factories because the exhaust from the engine using propane is not harmful. Propane comes from a by-product of petroleum refining of natural gas. In order to liquefy the fuel, it is stored in strong tanks at about 300 psi (2000 kPa). The heating value of propane is less than that of gasoline; therefore, more is required, which reduces the miles per gallon economy. See Figure 5-16. However, the cost of propane is less than the cost of gasoline and does not create carbon particles or sulfuric acid, which tends to shorten the life of engine oil.

CNG

Another alternative fuel that is often used in fleet vehicles is **compressed natural gas.** Natural gas has to be compressed to about 3000 psi (20,000 kPa) or more so that the weight and the cost of the storage container is a major factor when it comes to preparing a vehicle to run on CNG. The tanks needed for CNG are typically constructed of 0.5 inch (3 mm)-thick aluminum reinforced with fiberglass. The octane rating of CNG is about 130 and the cost per gallon is about half of the cost of gasoline, but the heat value of CNG is also less; therefore, more is required to produce the same power and the miles per gallon is less.

Compressed natural gas is made up of a blend of methane, propane, ethane, N-butane, carbon dioxide, and nitrogen. Once it is processed, it is at least 93% methane. Natural gas is nontoxic, odorless, and colorless

in its natural state. It is odorized during processing using morcaptan ("skunk") to allow for easy leak detection. Natural gas is lighter than air and will rise when released into the air. Since CNG is already a vapor, it does not need heat to vaporize before it will burn, which improves cold start-up and results in lower emissions during cold operation. However, because it is already in a gaseous state, it does replace some of the air charge in the intake manifold. This leads to about a 10% reduction in engine power as compared to an engine operating on gasoline. Natural gas also burns slower than gasoline; therefore, the ignition timing must be advanced more when the vehicle operates on natural gas. Natural gas has an octane rating of about 115 octane. The stoichiometric ratio, the point at which all the air and fuel is used or burned, is 16.5:1 compared to 14.7:1 for gasoline. This means that more air is required to burn one pound of natural gas than is required to burn one pound of gasoline.

When completely filled, the CNG tank has 3600 psi of pressure in the tank. When the ignition is turned on, the alternate fuel electronic control unit activates the high-pressure lock-off, which allows high-pressure gas to pass to the high-pressure regulator. The high-pressure regulator reduces the high-pressure CNG to approximately 170 psi and sends it to the low-pressure lock-off. The low-pressure lock-off is also controlled by the alternate fuel electronic control unit and is activated at the same time that the high-pressure lock-off is activated. From the low-pressure lock-off, the CNG is directed to the low-pressure regulator. This is a two-stage regulator that first reduces the pressure to approximately 4 to 6 psi in the first stage and then to 4.5 to 7 inches of water in the second stage. From here, the low-pressure gas is delivered to the gas mass sensor/mixture control valve. This valve controls the air-fuel mixture. The CNG gas distributor adapter then delivers the gas to the intake stream.

CNG vehicles are designed for fleet use that usually have their own refueling capabilities. One of the drawbacks to using CNG is the time that it takes to refuel a vehicle. The ideal method of refueling is the slow fill method. The slow filling method compresses the natural gas as the tank is being fueled. This method ensures that the tank will receive a full charge of CNG; however, this method can take three to five hours to accomplish. If more than one vehicle needs filling, the facility will need multiple CNG compressors to refuel the vehicles.

The fast fill method uses CNG that is already compressed. However, as the CNG tank is filled rapidly, the internal temperature of the tank will rise, which causes a rise in tank pressure. Once the temperature drops in the CNG tank, the pressure drops, resulting in an incomplete charge in the CNG tank. This refueling method may take only about five minutes; however, it will result in an incomplete charge to the CNG tank, reducing the driving range.

FIGURE 5-17   Mild parallel-hybrid vehicles use an integrated starter/alternator located at the rear of the engine.

FIGURE 5-18   The dash display on a Toyota Prius, which shows the driver the distribution of power.

HYBRID ELECTRIC VEHICLES

Hybrid electric vehicles (HEV) use an electric motor and a gasoline or diesel internal combustion engine to power the vehicle. The term *hybrid* means made from different kinds of materials or sources. In this case, a hybrid electric vehicle uses both the power from batteries and an electric motor with an engine.

Series-Hybrid Vehicles

A series-hybrid vehicle uses an engine such as a small gasoline or diesel engine to power a generator, which charges batteries. The vehicle itself is powered by an electric motor(s) taking power from the storage batteries. Series-hybrid vehicles are not in production and are somewhat limited by the capacity of the generator alone to create enough electrical energy to power the vehicle.

Parallel-Hybrid Vehicles

All of the hybrids available to the public today are parallel-hybrid vehicles. With a parallel-hybrid vehicle, the electric motor can assist the gasoline engine in the propulsion of the vehicle. If the electric motor cannot propel the vehicle by itself, it is often referred to as a **mild parallel-hybrid vehicle.** See Figure 5-17. In hybrid vehicles built by Toyota (Prius) and Lexus (RX 400H), the electric motor is capable of propelling the vehicle without the use of the gasoline engine. See Figure 5-18.

FIGURE 5-19   The electronic controller on the Toyota Prius is located under the hood and has its own cooling system to help keep the electronics cool.

CAUTION: Many hybrid vehicles are capable of starting the engine if the battery voltage drops below a certain level. Use caution when working under the hood of a hybrid vehicle to prevent personal injury if the gasoline engine starts. In a Toyota or Lexus hybrid, the gasoline engine may or may not start when the "start" button is pushed. Also, use caution around all electrical components on a hybrid vehicle. See Figure 5-19.

In most mild parallel-hybrid vehicles, the motor/generator combination is attached to the engine crankshaft at the rear of the block and is mounted between

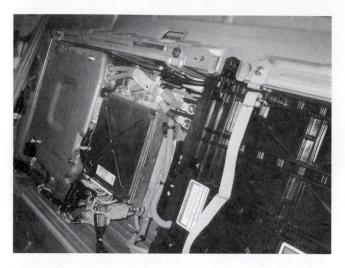

FIGURE 5-20   The electronics and the battery pack are located behind the rear seat on the Honda Civic hybrid vehicle.

FIGURE 5-21   A warning label on the cover of the battery pack on a Honda Insight hybrid vehicle.

the engine and the transmission. One of the features of the General Motors hybrid pickup trucks is the availability of 110-volt electrical outlets in the bed of the pickup that allow the use of power equipment at construction sites and other uses.

Hybrid Batteries

Most hybrid electrical vehicles use sealed nickel-metal hydride (Ni-MH) batteries. The batteries are arranged in groups and located under the floor or backseat area of the vehicle. The life of the batteries is estimated to be 8 to 10 years. The voltage of the battery pack varies from 144 volts to 274 volts or higher. All high-voltage electrical wiring is covered with orange-colored plastic conduit to help service technicians identify potential high-voltage wiring. See Figures 5-20 and 5-21.

FUEL CELLS

A fuel cell is a unit that generates electricity without any moving parts and produces zero emissions. The only thing that a fuel cell produces, besides electricity, is pure water and heat. The fuel needed for a fuel cell is hydrogen. The three main parts of a fuel cell include:

- **Anode.**   This is the negative portion of the fuel cell and it conducts the electrons that are released from the hydrogen molecules so they can be converted to outside electrical load.
- **Cathode.**   This is the positive portion of the fuel cell.
- **Catalyst.**   A catalyst starts a chemical reaction but does not enter into nor is consumed by the chemical reaction.
- **Electrolyte.** The electrolyte in a fuel cell is also called a **proton exchange membrane** and it conducts only positively charged ions (atoms missing electron[s]).

Fuel Cell Operation

The electrolyte is also called the membrane electrode assembly (MEA).

A fuel cell combines hydrogen fuel and oxygen from the air to create electricity and heat. Hydrogen flows into the fuel cell anode where a platinum coating (catalyst) helps separate the gas into protons (hydrogen ions) and electrons. The electrolyte in the center allows only the proton to pass through to the cathode side of the fuel cell. The electrons must flow through an external circuit, creating electron flow (electric current flow). This electrical current can power an electrical load, such as a light bulb or any other electrical devices. Oxygen from the outside air flows into the fuel cell into the cathode where another platinum coating helps the oxygen and protons from the anode side combine to form pure water and heat. See Figure 5-22.

These chemical reactions produce only about 0.7 volts. In order to achieve reasonable fuel cell voltage levels, many separate fuel cells are combined to form a **fuel cell stack.**

One of the major disadvantages of a fuel cell is that it produces water; therefore, if it is used to power a vehicle, some method must be used to heat the fuel cell above 32°F (0°C) in cold weather.

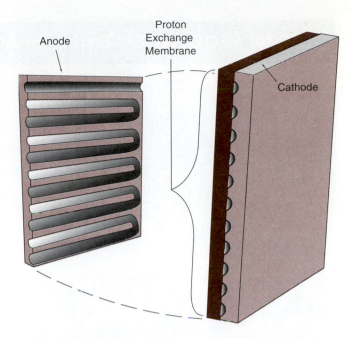

FIGURE 5-22 A fuel cell has no moving parts and converts hydrogen fuel and the oxygen from the air to create electricity, heat, and pure water.

PHOTO SEQUENCE   Testing for Alcohol Content in Gasoline

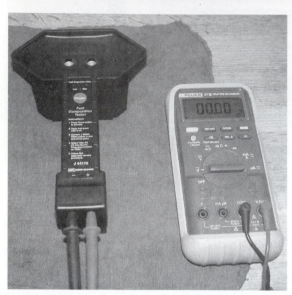

PS 2-1   A fuel composition tester is the tool recommended by General Motors to use to test the alcohol content of gasoline.

PS 2-2   This battery-powered tester uses light-emitting diodes (LEDs), meter lead terminals and two small openings for the fuel sample.

PS 2-3   The first step is to verify the proper operation of the tester by measuring the air frequency by selecting AC hertz on the meter. The air frequency should be between 35 Hz and 48 Hz.

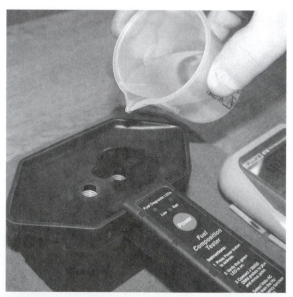

PS 2-4   After verifying that the tester is capable of correctly reading the air frequency, gasoline is poured into the testing cell of the tool.

PHOTO SEQUENCE   Testing for Alcohol Content in Gasoline—*Continued*

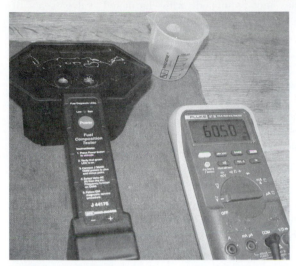

PS 2-5   Record the AC frequency as shown on the meter and subtract 50 from the reading. (60.50-50.00 = 10.5). This number (10.5) is the percentage of alcohol in the gasoline sample.

PS 2-6   Adding additional amounts of ethyl alcohol (ethanol) increases the frequency reading.

SUMMARY

1. Gasoline is a complex blend of hydrocarbons. Gasoline is blended for seasonal usage to gain the correct volatility for easy starting and maximum fuel economy under all driving conditions.
2. Winter-blend fuel used in a vehicle during warm weather can cause a rough idle and stalling because of its higher Reid vapor pressure (RVP).
3. Abnormal combustion (also called detonation or spark knock) increases both the temperature and the pressure inside the combustion chamber.
4. Most regular-grade gasoline today, using the (R + M)/2 rating method, is 87 octane, midgrade (plus) is 89, and premium grade is 91 or higher.

5. Oxygenated fuels contain oxygen in its content to lower CO exhaust emissions.
6. Gasoline should always be purchased from a busy station, and the tank should not be overfilled.
7. Flexible fuel vehicles are designed to operate on gasoline or E-85.
8. Hybrid vehicles use both a small gasoline or diesel engine and an electric motor to propel the vehicle.
9. Fuel cells produce electrical power from hydrogen fuel and oxygen from the air.

REVIEW QUESTIONS

1. What is the difference between summer-blend and winter-blend gasoline?
2. What is Reid vapor pressure?
3. What is vapor lock?
4. What does the (R + M)/2 gasoline pump octane rating indicate?
5. What are five octane improvers that may be used during the refinery process?

6. What is stoichiometric?
7. How can valves recede into the head on engines using unleaded gasoline without hardened valve seats?
8. What is the difference between a mild- and a full-parallel hybrid vehicle?
9. What are the advantages of fuel cells?

ASE CERTIFICATION-TYPE QUESTIONS

1. Winter-blend gasoline _____.
   a. Vaporizes more easily than summer-blend gasoline
   b. Has a higher RVP
   c. Can cause engine driveability problems if used during warm weather
   d. All of the above

2. Vapor lock can occur _____.
   a. As a result of excessive heat near fuel lines
   b. If a fuel line is restricted
   c. During both a and b
   d. During neither a nor b

3. Technician A says that spark knock, ping, and detonation are different names for abnormal combustion. Technician B says that any abnormal combustion raises the temperature and pressure inside the combustion chamber and can cause severe engine damage. Which technician is correct?
   a. Technician A only
   b. Technician B only
   c. Both Technicians A and B
   d. Neither Technician A nor B

4. Technician A says that the research octane number is higher than the motor octane number. Technician B says that the octane rating posted on fuel pumps is an average of the two ratings. Which technician is correct?
   a. Technician A only
   b. Technician B only
   c. Both Technicians A and B
   d. Neither Technician A nor B

5. Technician A says that in going to high altitudes, a non-computer-controlled engine becomes richer and lower on power. Technician B says that most computerized engine control systems can compensate for changes in altitude. Which technician is correct?
   a. Technician A only
   b. Technician B only
   c. Both Technicians A and B
   d. Neither Technician A nor B

6. Valve seat recession is most likely to occur with older engines not equipped with hardened valve seats if _____.
   a. Driven at high speeds and with heavy loads
   b. Driven at slow speeds and with light loads
   c. Used at idle most or all of the time
   d. Both a and c

7. The use of premium high-octane gasoline in an engine designed to use regular grade gasoline will increase engine power.
   a. True
   b. False

8. To avoid problems with the variation of gasoline, all government testing uses _____ as a fuel during testing procedures.
   a. MTBE (methyl tertiary butyl ether)
   b. Indolene
   c. Xylene
   d. TBA (tertiary butyl alcohol)

9. Avoid topping off the fuel tank because _____.
   a. It can saturate the charcoal canister
   b. The extra fuel simply spills onto the ground
   c. The extra fuel increases vehicle weight and reduces performance
   d. The extra fuel goes into the expansion area of the tank and is not used by the engine

10. Using ethanol-enhanced or reformulated gasoline can result in reduced fuel economy.
    a. True
    b. False

◀ Chapter 6 ▶

INTAKE AND EXHAUST SYSTEMS

OBJECTIVES

After studying Chapter 6, the reader should be able to:

1. Prepare for ASE Engine Performance (A8) certification test content area "C" (Air Induction and Exhaust Systems Diagnosis and Repair).

2. Discuss the purpose and function of intake manifolds.

3. Explain the differences between throttle fuel-injection manifolds and port fuel-injection manifolds.

4. Describe the operation of the exhaust gas recirculation system in the intake manifold.

5. List the materials used in exhaust manifolds and exhaust systems.

6. Discuss the need for intake manifold heating.

Gasoline must be mixed with air to form a combustible mixture. Air movement into an engine occurs due to low pressure (vacuum) being created in the engine. See Figure 6-1. Like gasoline, air contains dirt and other materials which cannot be allowed to reach the engine. Just as fuel filters are used to clean impurities from gasoline, an air cleaner and filter are used to remove contaminants from the air. The three main jobs of the air cleaner and filter are to:

- Clean the air before it is mixed with fuel
- Silence intake noise
- Act as a flame arrester in case of a backfire

AIR INTAKE FILTRATION

The automotive engine uses about 9000 gallons (34,069 liters) of air for every gallon of gasoline burned at an air-fuel ratio of 14.7 to 1. Without proper filtering of the air before intake, dust and dirt in the air seriously damage engine parts and shorten engine life.

While abrasive particles can cause wear any place inside the engine where two surfaces move against each

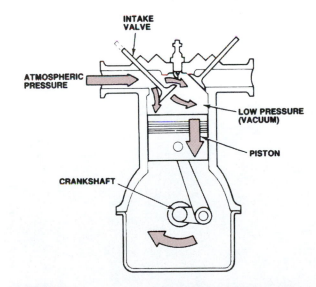

FIGURE 6-1 Downward movement of the piston lowers the air pressure inside the combustion chamber. The pressure differential between the atmosphere and the inside of the engine forces air into the engine.

other, they first attack piston rings and cylinder walls. Contained in the blowby gases, they pass by the piston rings and into the crankcase. From the crankcase, the particles circulate throughout the engine in the oil. Large amounts of abrasive particles in the oil can damage other moving engine parts.

THE AIR CLEANER

The filter that cleans the intake air is in a two-piece air cleaner housing made either of stamped steel or composite materials. The air cleaner housing is located on top of the throttle-body injection (TBI) unit or is positioned to one side of the engine. See Figure 6-2.

Filter Replacement

Manufacturers recommend cleaning or replacing the air filter element at periodic intervals, usually listed in terms of distance driven or months of service. The distance and time intervals are based on so-called normal driving. More frequent air filter replacement is necessary when the vehicle is driven under dusty, dirty, or other severe conditions.

It is best to replace a filter element before it becomes too dirty to be effective. A dirty air filter passes contaminants that cause engine wear.

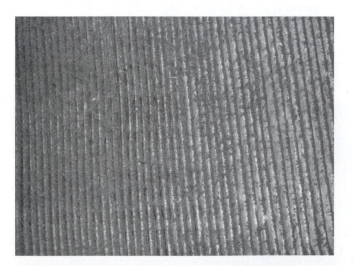

FIGURE 6-2   Dust and dirt in the air are trapped in the air filter so they do not enter the engine.

Air Filter Elements

The paper air filter element is the most common type of filter. It is made of a chemically treated paper stock that contains tiny passages in the fibers. These passages form an indirect path for the airflow to follow. The airflow passes through several fiber surfaces, each of which traps microscopic particles of dust, dirt, and carbon. Most air filters are capable of trapping dirt and other particles larger than 10 to 25 microns in size. One micron is equal to 0.000039 in.

NOTE: A person can only see objects that are 40 microns or larger in size. A human hair is about 50 microns in diameter.

NOTE: Do not attempt to clean a paper element filter by rapping it on a sharp object to dislodge the dirt, or blowing compressed air through the filter. This tends to clog the paper pores and further reduce the airflow capability of the filter.

Remotely Mounted Air Filters and Ducts

Air cleaner and duct design depend on a number of factors such as the size, shape, and location of other engine compartment components, as well as the vehicle body structure.

Port fuel-injection systems generally use a horizontally mounted throttle body. Some systems also have a mass airflow (MAF) sensor between the throttle body and the air cleaner. See Figure 6-3. Because placing the air cleaner housing next to the throttle body would cause engine and vehicle design problems, it is more efficient to use this remote air cleaner placement.

Turbocharged engines present a similar problem. The air cleaner connects to the air inlet elbow at the turbocharger. However, the tremendous heat generated by the turbocharger makes it impractical to place the air cleaner housing too close to the turbocharger. For better protection, the MAF sensor is installed between the turbocharger and the air cleaner in some vehicles. Remote air cleaners are connected to the turbocharger air inlet elbow or fuel-injection throttle body by composite ducting which is usually retained by clamps. The ducting used may be rigid or flexible, but all connections must be airtight.

FIGURE 6-3 Most air filter housings are located on the side of the engine compartment and use flexible rubber hose to direct the airflow into the throttle body of the engine.

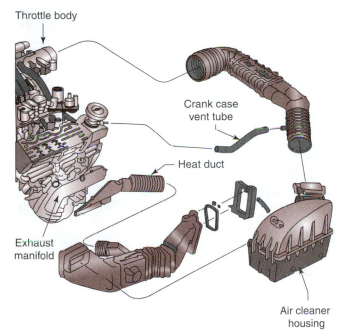

Throttle body

Crank case vent tube

Heat duct

Exhaust manifold

Air cleaner housing

FIGURE 6-4 Some port fuel-injected engines use heated air taken from around the exhaust manifold.

ENGINE AIR TEMPERATURE REQUIREMENTS

Some form of **thermostatic** control has been used on vehicles equipped with a throttle-body fuel injection to control intake air temperature for improved driveability. In a throttle-body fuel injection system, the fuel and air are combined above the throttle plate and must travel through the intake manifold before reaching the cylin-

ders. Air temperature control is needed under these conditions to help keep the gas and air mixture combined.

Heat radiating from the exhaust manifold is retained by the heat stove and sent to the air cleaner inlet to provide heated air to the throttle body.

An air control valve or damper permits the air intake of:

- Heated air from the heat stove
- Cooler air from the snorkel or cold-air duct
- A combination of both

While the air control valve generally is located in the air cleaner snorkel, it may be in the air intake housing or ducting of remote air cleaners. See Figure 6-4 for an example of heated air intake systems on a port fuel-injected engine. Most fuel-injection systems do not use air intake temperature control.

◄ TECH TIP ►

"NUTS"

Always inspect the air filter and the air intake system carefully during routine service. Debris or objects deposited by animals can cause a restriction to the airflow and can reduce engine performance. See Figure 6-5.

◄ FREQUENTLY ASKED ► QUESTION

WHAT DOES THIS TUBE DO?

What is the purpose of the odd-shaped tube attached to the inlet duct between the air filter and the throttle body, as seen in Figure 6-6? The tube shape is designed to dampen out certain resonant frequencies that can occur at certain engine speeds. The length and shape of this tube are designed to absorb shock waves that are created in the air intake system and to provide a reservoir for the air that will then be released into the airstream during cycles of lower pressure. This resonance tube is often called a **Helmholtz resonator,** named for the discoverer of the relationship between shape and value of frequency Herman L. F. von Helmholtz (1821–1894) of the University of Hönizsberg in East Prussia. The overall effect of these resonance tubes is to reduce the noise of the air entering the engine.

(a)

(b)

FIGURE 6-5 (a) Note the discovery as the air filter housing was opened during service on a Pontiac Bonneville. The nuts were obviously deposited by squirrels (or some other animal). (b) Not only was the housing filled with nuts, but also this air filter was extremely dirty, indicating that this vehicle had not been serviced for a long time.

THROTTLE-BODY INJECTION INTAKE MANIFOLDS

The *intake manifold* is also called *inlet manifold.*

Smooth operation can only occur when each combustion chamber produces the same pressure as every other chamber in the engine. For this to be achieved, each cylinder must receive a charge exactly like the charge going into the other cylinders in quality and quantity. The charges must have the same physical properties and the same air-fuel mixture.

A throttle-body fuel injector forces finely divided droplets of liquid fuel into the incoming air to form a

FIGURE 6-6 A resonance tube, called a Helmholtz resonator, is used on the intake duct between the air filter and the throttle body to reduce air intake noise during engine acceleration.

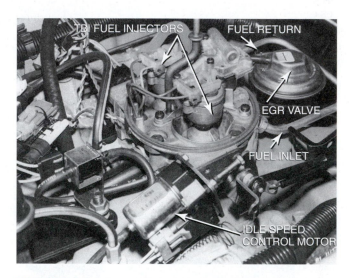

FIGURE 6-7 A typical throttle-body injection (TBI) unit. This TBI uses two injectors. Most V-6 and V-8 engines require two throttle-body injectors, whereas 4-cylinder engines use one injector.

combustible air-fuel mixture. See Figure 6-7 for an example of a typical throttle-body injection (TBI) unit. These droplets start to evaporate as soon as they leave the throttle-body injector nozzles. *The droplets stay in the charge as long as the charge flows at high velocities.* At maximum horsepower, these velocities may reach 300 feet per second. Separation of the droplets from the charge as it passes through the manifold occurs when the velocity drops below 50 feet per second. Intake charge velocities at idle speeds are often below this value. When separation occurs—at low engine speeds—

extra fuel must be supplied to the charge in order to have a combustible mixture reach the combustion chamber.

Manifold sizes represent a compromise. They must have a cross-section large enough to allow charge flow for maximum power. The cross-section must be small enough that the flow velocities of the charge will be high enough to keep the fuel droplets in suspension. This is required so that equal mixtures reach each cylinder. Manifold cross-sectional size is one reason why engines designed especially for racing will not run at low engine speeds. Racing manifolds must be large enough to reach maximum horsepower. This size, however, allows the charge to move slowly, and the fuel will separate from the charge at low engine speeds. Fuel separation leads to poor accelerator response. See Figure 6-8. Standard passenger vehicle engines are primarily designed for economy during light-load, partial-throttle operation. Their manifolds, therefore, have a much smaller cross-sectional area than do those of racing engines. This small size will help keep flow velocities of the charge high throughout the normal operating speed range of the engine.

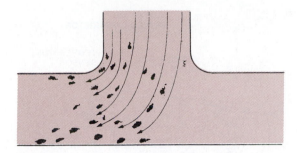

FIGURE 6-8 Heavy fuel droplets separate as they flow around an abrupt bend in an intake manifold.

◀ TECH TIP ▶

THE GLUE AND ANTISEIZE COMPOUND TRICK

A common problem with using aluminum intake manifolds on a V-type cast-iron engine is that the gasket often fails. Aluminum expands at twice the rate of cast iron (0.0012 inch per 100°F for aluminum versus 0.0006 inch per 100°F for cast iron). As a result, when the engine gets warm, the intake manifold expands and tends to move upward, sliding over the surface of the cast-iron cylinder heads.

To help prevent premature intake manifold gasket failure, use a contact adhesive to glue the gasket to the cast-iron head. This helps hold the gasket in place for easier installation and prevents movement of the gasket against the cast iron. Then, before installing the aluminum intake manifold, coat the gasket and/or the sealing surface of the intake manifold with antiseize compound. This will allow movement without damage to the gasket.

◀ TECH TIP ▶

EVERY OTHER CYLINDER

All engines of four or more cylinders are furnished fuel according to firing order. The intake manifold on a V-type engine is designed so that each side of the TBI unit supplies the air-fuel mixture to every other cylinder in the *firing order* for each barrel (venturi) of the throttle-body fuel-injection unit. It is easy to determine which cylinders are fed an air-fuel mixture from the same side of a throttle-body injector unit.

Step 1. Write out the cylinder numbers in their firing order: 1 6 5 4 3 2

Step 2. Mark every other cylinder in the firing order: 1̲ 6 5̲ 4 3̲ 2

The marked cylinders share the same bore of the throttle body, and the unmarked cylinders share the other bore of the throttle body.

NOTE: Most V-6 engines are split so that the left bank of cylinders is on one runner and the right bank is on the other runner. Most V-8s have two cylinders on each side of the engine sharing a barrel with two cylinders of the opposite bank.

MANIFOLD HEAT

Heat is required in the manifold so that liquid fuel in the charge will evaporate as the charge travels from the intake to the combustion chamber. When heat is taken from the air in the intake charge by fuel evaporation, the charge temperature is lowered. Additional fuel will not evaporate from the cooled charge as rapidly as it would from a warm charge. Additional heat is supplied to the charge when it is needed. The added heat gives good fuel evaporation for smooth engine operation when the engine is cold. An intake charge temperature range of about 100° to 130°F (38° to 55°C) is necessary to give good fuel evaporation. In some engines, heat is supplied to the intake manifold during low-temperature operation by a system known as a **thermostatic air cleaner**

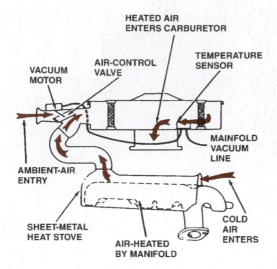

FIGURE 6-9 Heat radiating from the exhaust manifold heats the intake air on engines equipped with a carburetor or throttle-body-type fuel injection.

(TAC). Heat is picked up from around the exhaust manifold and routed to the air cleaner inlet. A thermostatically controlled bimetallic switch adjusts a **vacuum motor.** It controls the amount of heated air used. Parts of this system are shown in Figure 6-9. Another thermostatic valve, called a **heat riser,** directs exhaust gases against the underside of the intake manifold. On V-type engines, exhaust gas is routed through a passage called an exhaust **heat crossover.** Part of the exhaust gas is directed against the intake manifold directly under the throttle body. This can be seen in Figure 6-10.

NOTE: Port fuel-injected engines do not require an exhaust heat crossover because there is no fuel in the air flowing through the intake runner.

◀ TECH TIP ▶

CHECK THE INTAKE IF AN EXHAUST NOISE

Because many V-type engines equipped with a throttle-body injection and/or EGR valve use a crossover exhaust passage, a leak around this passage will create an exhaust leak and noise. Always check for evidence of an exhaust leak around the intake manifold whenever diagnosing an exhaust sound.

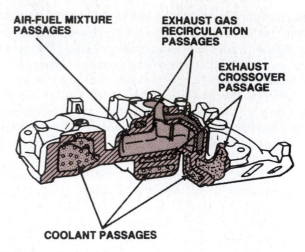

FIGURE 6-10 The heat crossover passage allows exhaust gases to flow under and heat the manifold to improve cold engine operation.

PORT FUEL-INJECTION INTAKE MANIFOLDS

The size and shape of port fuel-injected engine intake manifolds can be optimized because the only thing in the manifold is air. The fuel injection is located in the intake manifold about 3 to 4 inches (70 to 100 mm) from the intake valve. Therefore, the runner length and shape are designed for tuning only. There is no need to keep an air-fuel mixture homogenized throughout its trip from the TBI unit to the intake valve.

- Long runners build low-RPM torque.
- Shorter runners provide maximum high-RPM power.

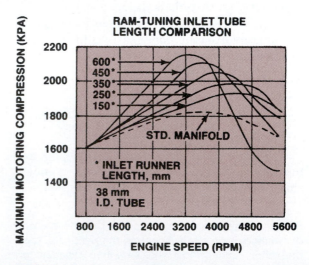

FIGURE 6-11 The graph shows the effect of sonic tuning of the intake manifold runners. The longer runners increase the torque peak and move it to a lower RPM. The .600-mm-long intake runner is about 24 inches long.

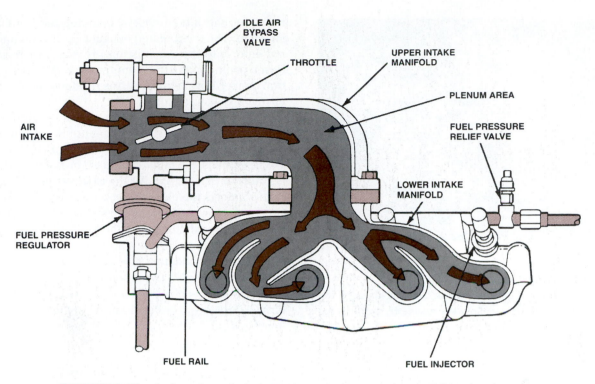

FIGURE 6-12 Airflow through the large diameter upper intake manifold is distributed to smaller diameter individual runners in the lower manifold in this two-piece manifold design.

See Figures 6-11 and 6-12. Some engines with four valve heads utilize a dual or variable intake runner design. At lower engine speeds, long intake runners provide low-speed torque. At higher engine speeds, shorter intake runners arc opened by means of a computer-controlled valve to increase high-speed power.

◀ TECH TIP ▶

THE ALUMINUM EPOXY TRICK

Often, aluminum intake manifolds are corroded around the coolant passages. Rather than replacing the manifold, simply apply an 80% aluminum epoxy to fill the pitted area. Be sure that the area to be repaired is thoroughly cleaned, and mix the epoxy according to the manufacturer's instructions. The epoxy can be applied with a putty knife or other similar tool. After the epoxy has hardened, the area can be surfaced as usual. Epoxy can also be used to repair pitted water pumps.

PLASTIC INTAKE MANIFOLDS

Most thermoplastic intake manifolds are molded from fiberglass-reinforced nylon. The plastic manifolds can be cast or injection molded. Some manifolds are molded in two parts and bonded together. Plastic intake manifolds are lighter than aluminum manifolds and can better insulate engine heat from the fuel injectors.

Plastic intake manifolds have smoother interior surfaces than do other types of manifolds, resulting in greater airflow. See Figure 6-13.

EXHAUST GAS RECIRCULATION PASSAGES

To reduce the emission of oxides of nitrogen (NO_x), engines have been equipped with **exhaust gas recirculation (EGR)** valves. From 1973 until recently, they were used on almost all vehicles. Because of the efficiency of computer-controlled fuel injection, some newer engines do not require an EGR system to meet emission standards. Some engines use intake

FIGURE 6-13 This DaimlerChrysler V-6 engine uses an intake manifold tuning valve that is controlled by the engine computer to switch where the air is directed through the passages of the manifold to allow the engine to produce the most torque possible at every engine speed.

and exhaust valve overlap as a means of trapping some exhaust in the cylinder as an alternative to using an EGR valve.

The EGR valve opens at speeds above idle on a warm engine. When open, the valve allows a small portion of the exhaust gas (5 to 10%) to enter the intake manifold. Here, the exhaust gas mixes with and takes the place of some of the intake charge. This leaves less room for the intake charge to enter the combustion chamber. The recirculated exhaust gas is inert and does *not* enter into the combustion process. The result is a lower peak combustion temperature. As the combustion temperature is lowered, the production of oxides of nitrogen is also reduced.

The EGR system has some means of interconnecting the exhaust and intake manifolds. The interconnecting passage is controlled by the EGR valve. On V-type engines, the intake manifold crossover is used as a source of exhaust gas for the EGR system. A cast passage connects the exhaust crossover to the EGR valve. On inline-type engines, an external tube is generally used to carry exhaust gas to the EGR valve. This tube is often designed to be long so that the exhaust gas is cooled before it enters the EGR valve. The exhaust gases are more effective in reducing oxide of nitrogen (NO_x) emissions if the exhaust is cooled before being drawn into the cylinder. Figure 6-14 shows a typical long EGR tube.

UPPER AND LOWER INTAKE MANIFOLDS

Many intake manifolds are constructed in two parts.

- A lower section, usually called the **plenum,** attaches to the cylinder heads and includes passages from the intake ports.

FIGURE 6-14 The exhaust gas recirculation system is more efficient at controlling NO_x emissions if the exhaust gases are cooled. A long metal tube between the exhaust manifold and the intake manifold allows the exhaust gases to cool before entering the engine.

- An upper manifold connects to the lower unit and includes the long passages needed to help provide the ram effect that helps the engine deliver maximum torque at low engine speeds. The throttle body attaches to the upper intake.

The use of a two-part intake manifold allows for easier manufacturing as well as assembly, but can create additional locations for leaks.

If the lower intake manifold gasket leaks, not only could a vacuum leak occur affecting the operation of the engine, but a coolant leak or an oil leak can also occur. A leak at the gasket(s) of the upper intake manifold usually results in a vacuum (air) leak only.

EXHAUST MANIFOLD DESIGN

The exhaust manifold is designed to collect high-temperature spent gases from the head exhaust ports. See Figure 6-15. The hot gases are sent to an exhaust pipe, then to a catalytic converter, to the muffler, to a resonator, and on to the tailpipe, where they are vented to the atmosphere. This must be done with the least possible amount of restriction or back pressure while keeping the exhaust noise at a minimum.

Exhaust gas temperature will vary according to the power produced by the engine. The manifold must be designed to operate at both engine idle and continuous full power. Under full-power conditions, the exhaust manifold will become red-hot, causing a great deal of expansion.

NOTE: The temperature of an exhaust manifold can exceed 1500°F (815°C).

At idle, the exhaust manifold is just warm, causing little expansion. After casting, the manifold may be annealed. **Annealing** is a heat-treating process that takes out the brittle hardening of the casting to reduce the chance of cracking from the temperature changes. During vehicle operation, manifold temperatures usually reach the high-temperature extremes. Most exhaust manifolds are made from cast iron to withstand extreme and rapid temperature changes. The manifold is bolted to the head in a way that will allow expansion and contraction. In some cases, hollow-headed bolts are used to maintain a gas-tight seal while still allowing normal expansion and contraction.

The exhaust manifold is designed to allow the free flow of exhaust gas. Some manifolds use internal cast-rib deflectors or dividers to guide the exhaust gases toward the outlet as smoothly as possible.

Some exhaust manifolds are designed to go above the spark plug, whereas others are designed to go below. The spark plug and carefully routed ignition wires are usually shielded from the exhaust heat with sheet-metal deflectors. Typical deflectors can be seen in Figure 6-16.

Exhaust systems are especially designed for the engine-chassis combination. The exhaust system length, pipe size, and silencer are designed, where possible, to

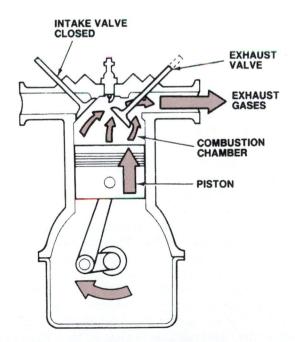

FIGURE 6-15 The exhaust gases are pushed out of the cylinder by the piston on the exhaust stroke.

FIGURE 6-16 Example of heat deflector shields placed between the exhaust manifold and the spark plugs and plug wires. Even high-temperature-resistant silicone jacket spark plug wires cannot withstand the high exhaust manifold temperatures.

FIGURE 6-17 Original-equipment (OE) type of tubular steel exhaust manifold.

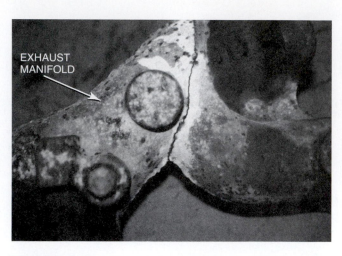

FIGURE 6-18 A crack in an exhaust manifold is often not this visible. A crack in the exhaust manifold upstream of the oxygen sensor can fool the sensor and affect engine operation.

make use of the tuning effect of the gas column resonating within the exhaust system. Tuning occurs when the exhaust pulses from the cylinders are emptied into the manifold between the pulses of other cylinders. See Figure 6-17.

◄ FREQUENTLY ASKED ► QUESTION

HOW CAN A CRACKED EXHAUST MANIFOLD AFFECT ENGINE PERFORMANCE?

A crack in an exhaust manifold will not only allow exhaust gases to escape and cause noise but the crack can also allow air to enter the exhaust manifold. See Figure 6-18. Exhaust flows from the cylinders as individual puffs or pressure pulses. Behind each of these pressure pulses, a low pressure (below atmospheric pressure) is created. Outside air at atmospheric pressure is then drawn into the exhaust manifold through the crack. This outside air contains 21% oxygen and is measured by the oxygen sensor (O2S). The air passing the O2S signals the engine computer that the engine is operating too lean (excess oxygen) and the computer, not knowing that the lean indicator is false, adds additional fuel to the engine. The result is that the engine will be operating richer (more fuel than normal) and spark plugs could become fouled causing poor engine operation.

EXHAUST MANIFOLD GASKETS

Exhaust heat will expand the manifold more than it will expand the head. It causes the exhaust manifold to slide on the sealing surface of the head. The heat also causes thermal stress. When the manifold is removed from the engine for service, the stress is relieved and this may cause the manifold to warp slightly. Exhaust manifold gaskets are included in gasket sets to seal slightly warped exhaust manifolds. These gaskets *should* be used, even if the engine did not originally use exhaust manifold gaskets. When a perforated core exhaust manifold gasket has facing on one side only, put the facing side against the head and put the manifold against the perforated metal core. The manifold can slide on the metal of the gasket just as it slid on the sealing surface of the head.

Gaskets are used on new engines with tubing- or header-type exhaust manifolds. The gaskets often include heat shields to keep exhaust heat from the spark plugs and spark plug cables. They may have several layers of steel for high-temperature sealing. The layers are spot-welded together. Some are embossed where special sealing is needed. See Figure 6-19. Many new engines do not use gaskets with cast exhaust manifolds. The flat surface of the new cast-iron exhaust manifold fits tightly against the flat surface of the new head.

FIGURE 6-19 Typical exhaust manifold gaskets. Note how they are laminated to allow the exhaust manifold to expand and contract due to heating and cooling.

FIGURE 6-20 An exhaust manifold spreader tool is a tool that is absolutely necessary to use when reinstalling exhaust manifolds. When they are removed from the engine, they tend to warp slightly even though the engine is allowed to cool before being removed. The spreader tool allows the technician to line up the bolt holes without doing any harm to the manifold.

◀ TECH TIP ▶

THE CORRECT TOOLS SAVE TIME

When cast-iron exhaust manifolds are removed, the stresses built up in the manifolds often cause the manifolds to twist or bend. This distortion even occurs when the exhaust manifolds have been allowed to cool before removal. Attempting to reinstall distorted exhaust manifolds is often a time-consuming and frustrating exercise.

However, special spreading jacks can be used to force the manifold back into position so that the fasteners can be lined up with the cylinder head. See Figure 6-20.

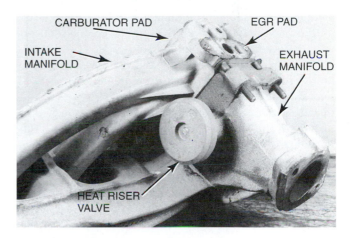

FIGURE 6-21 A heat riser at the junction of the intake and exhaust manifold.

HEAT RISERS

A heat riser is used on carburetor-equipped engines and some throttle-body fuel-injected engines. The purpose of the heat riser is to divert some exhaust to warm the intake manifold. The extra heat that this provides improves cold-engine driveability. If the heat riser was to become stuck in the open position (no heat to the intake manifold), the engine could idle roughly, stall, or hesitate during acceleration. If the heat riser were to become stuck in the closed position (constant heat to the intake manifold), the engine would operate correctly when cold, but there could be spark knock (ping) or stalling when the engine was warm. On some inline engines, the intake manifold is attached to the exhaust manifold. See Figure 6-21. On V-type engines, the heat riser valve partially blocks one exhaust manifold exit, increasing the exhaust pressure in the exhaust manifold on that side of the engine. This forces the exhaust gases to flow through the intake manifold exhaust heat crossover passage to the opposite exhaust manifold.

MUFFLERS

When the exhaust valve opens, it rapidly releases high-pressure gas. This sends a strong air pressure wave through the atmosphere, which produces a sound we call an explosion. It is the same sound produced when the high-pressure gases from burned gunpowder are released from a gun. In an engine, the pulses are released one after another. The explosions come so fast that they blend together in a steady roar.

Sound is air vibration. When the vibrations are large, the sound is loud. The muffler catches the large bursts of high-pressure exhaust gas from the cylinder, smoothing out the pressure pulses and allowing them to be released at an even and constant rate. It does this through the use of perforated tubes within the muffler chamber. The smooth-flowing gases are released to the tailpipe. In this way, the muffler silences engine exhaust noise. Sometimes resonators are used in the exhaust system and the catalytic converter also acts as a muffler. See Chapter 28 for details about catalytic converters. They provide additional expansion space at critical points in the exhaust system to smooth out the exhaust gas flow. See Figure 6-22.

Most mufflers have a larger inlet diameter than outlet diameter. As the exhaust enters the muffler, it expands and cools. The cooler exhaust is more dense and occupies less volume. The diameter of the outlet of the muffler and the diameter of the tailpipe can be reduced with no decrease in efficiency.

The tailpipe carries the exhaust gases from the muffler to the air, away from the vehicle. In most cases, the tailpipe exit is at the rear of the vehicle, below the rear bumper. In some cases, the exhaust is released at the side of the vehicle, just ahead of or just behind the rear wheel.

The muffler and tailpipe are supported with brackets called **hangers.** The hangers are made of rubberized fabric with metal ends that hold the muffler and tailpipe in position so that they do not touch any metal part. This helps to isolate the exhaust noise from the rest of the vehicle.

◀ FREQUENTLY ASKED ▶ QUESTION

WHY IS THERE A HOLE IN MY MUFFLER?

Many mufflers are equipped with a small hole in the lower rear part to drain accumulated water. About 1 gallon of water is produced in the form of steam for each gallon of gasoline burned. The water vapor often condenses on the cooler surfaces of the exhaust system unless the vehicle has been driven long enough to fully warm the muffler above the boiling point of water (212°F [100°C]). See Figure 6-23.

◀ HIGH-PERFORMANCE TIP ▶

MORE AIRFLOW = MORE POWER

One of the most popular high-performance modifications is to replace the factory exhaust system with a low-restriction design and to replace the original air filter and air filter housing with a low-restriction unit as shown in Figure 6-24. The installation of one of these aftermarket filters not only increases power, but also increases air induction noise, which many drivers prefer. The aftermarket filter housing, however, may not be able to effectively prevent water from being drawn into the engine if the vehicle is traveling through deep water.

Just remember that almost every modification that increases performance has a negative effect on some other part of the vehicle, or else the manufacturer would include the change at the factory.

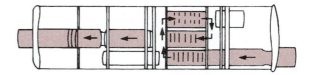

FIGURE 6-22 Exhaust gases expand and cool as they travel through the passages in the muffler.

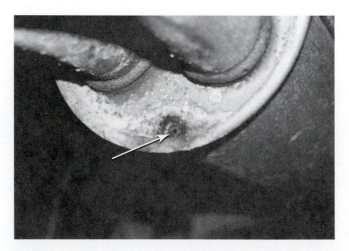

FIGURE 6-23 A hole in the muffler allows condensed water to escape.

FIGURE 6-24 A high-performance aftermarket air filter often can increase the airflow into the engine for more power.

SUMMARY

1. All air entering an engine must be filtered.
2. Engines that use throttle-body injection units are equipped with intake manifolds that keep the airflow speed through the manifold at 50 to 300 feet per second.
3. Most intake manifolds have an EGR valve that regulates the amount of recirculated exhaust that enters the engine to reduce NO_x emissions.
4. Exhaust manifolds can be made from cast iron or stainless steel.
5. The exhaust system also contains a catalytic converter, exhaust pipes, and muffler. The entire exhaust system is supported by rubber hangers that isolate the noise and vibration of the exhaust from the rest of the vehicle.

REVIEW QUESTIONS

1. Why is it necessary to have intake charge velocities of about 50 feet per second?
2. Why can fuel-injected engines use larger (and longer) intake manifolds and still operate at low engine speed?
3. What is a tuned runner in an intake manifold?
4. How does a muffler quiet exhaust noise?

ASE CERTIFICATION-TYPE QUESTIONS

1. Intake charge velocity has to be _____ to prevent fuel droplet separation.
   a. 25 feet per second
   b. 50 feet per second
   c. 100 feet per second
   d. 300 feet per second

2. The intake manifold of a port fuel-injected engine _____.
   a. Uses a dual heat riser
   b. Contains a leaner air-fuel mixture than does the intake manifold of a TBI system
   c. Contains only fuel (gasoline)
   d. Contains only air

3. Why are the EGR gases cooled before entering the engine on some engines?
   a. Cool exhaust gas is more effective at controlling NO_X emissions
   b. To help prevent the exhaust from slowing down
   c. To prevent damage to the intake valve
   d. To prevent heating the air-fuel mixture in the cylinder

4. A heated air intake system is usually necessary for proper cold-engine driveability on _____.
   a. Port fuel-injection systems
   b. Throttle-body fuel-injection systems
   c. Both a port-injected and throttle-body injected engine
   d. Any fuel-injected engine

5. Air filters can remove particles and dirt as small as _____.
   a. 5 to 10 microns
   b. 10 to 25 microns
   c. 30 to 40 microns
   d. 40 to 50 microns

6. Why do many port fuel-injected engines use long intake manifold runners?
   a. To reduce exhaust emissions
   b. To heat the incoming air
   c. To increase high-RPM power
   d. To increase low-RPM torque

7. Exhaust passages are included in some intake manifolds. Technician A says that the exhaust passages are used for exhaust gas recirculation (EGR) systems. Technician B says that the exhaust heat is used to warm the intake charge on some engines equipped with a throttle-body-type fuel-injection system. Which technician is correct?
   a. Technician A only
   b. Technician B only
   c. Both Technicians A and B
   d. Neither Technician A nor B

8. The lower portion of a two-part intake manifold is often called the _____.
   a. Housing
   b. Lower part
   c. Plenum
   d. Vacuum chamber

9. Technician A says that a cracked exhaust manifold can affect engine operation. Technician B says that a leaking lower intake manifold gasket could cause a vacuum leak. Which technician is correct?
   a. Technician A only
   b. Technician B only
   c. Both Technicians A and B
   d. Neither Technician A nor B

10. Technician A says that some intake manifolds are plastic. Technician B says that some intake manifolds are constructed in two parts or sections: upper and lower. Which technician is correct?
    a. Technician A only
    b. Technician B only
    c. Both Technicians A and B
    d. Neither Technician A nor B

◀ Chapter 7 ▶

TURBOCHARGING AND SUPERCHARGING

OBJECTIVES

After studying Chapter 7, the reader should be able to:

1. Prepare for ASE Engine Performance (A8) certification test content area "C" (Fuel, Air Induction, and Exhaust Systems Diagnosis and Repair).
2. Explain the difference between a turbocharger and a supercharger.
3. Describe how the boost levels are controlled.
4. Discuss maintenance procedures for turbochargers and superchargers.

Naturally aspirated engines with throttle bodies rely on atmospheric pressure to push an air-fuel mixture into the combustion chamber vacuum created by the down stroke of a piston. The mixture is then compressed before ignition to increase the force of the burning, expanding gases. The greater the mixture compression, the greater the power resulting from combustion.

AIRFLOW REQUIREMENTS

All gasoline automobile engines share certain air-fuel requirements. For example, a 4-stroke engine can take in only so much air, and how much fuel it consumes depends on how much air it takes in. Engineers calculate engine airflow requirements using these three factors:

- Engine displacement
- Engine revolutions per minute (rpm)
- Volumetric efficiency

Volumetric Efficiency

Volumetric efficiency is a comparison of the actual volume of air-fuel mixture drawn into an engine to the theoretical maximum volume that could be drawn in. Volumetric efficiency is expressed as a percentage, and changes with engine speed. For example, an engine might have 75% volumetric efficiency at 1000 RPM. The same engine might be rated at 85% at 2000 RPM and 60% at 3000 RPM.

If the engine takes in the airflow volume slowly, a cylinder might fill to capacity. It takes a definite amount of time for the airflow to pass through all the curves of the intake manifold and valve port. Therefore, volumetric efficiency decreases as engine speed increases. At high speed, it may drop to as low as 50%. See Figure 7-1.

The average street engine never reaches 100% volumetric efficiency. With a street engine, the volumetric efficiency is about 75% at maximum speed, or 80% at the torque peak. A high-performance street engine is about 85% efficient, or a bit more efficient at peak torque. A race engine usually has 95% or better volumetric efficiency. These figures apply only to naturally aspirated engines, however, and turbocharged and supercharged engines easily achieve more than 100% volumetric efficiency.

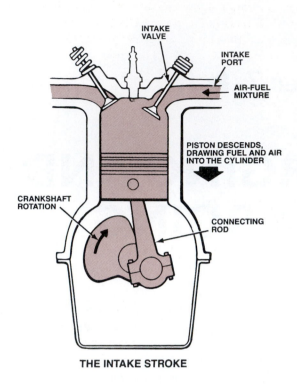

INTAKE
VALVE

INTAKE
PORT

AIR-FUEL
MIXTURE

PISTON DESCENDS,
DRAWING FUEL AND AIR
INTO THE CYLINDER

CRANKSHAFT
ROTATION

CONNECTING
ROD

THE INTAKE STROKE

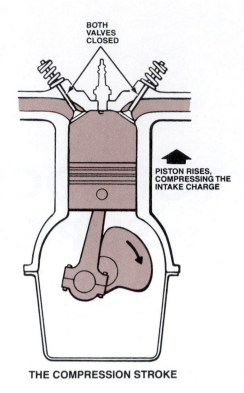

BOTH
VALVES
CLOSED

PISTON RISES,
COMPRESSING THE
INTAKE CHARGE

THE COMPRESSION STROKE

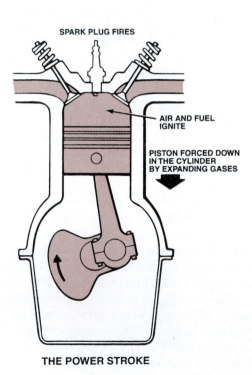

SPARK PLUG FIRES

AIR AND FUEL
IGNITE

PISTON FORCED DOWN
IN THE CYLINDER
BY EXPANDING GASES

THE POWER STROKE

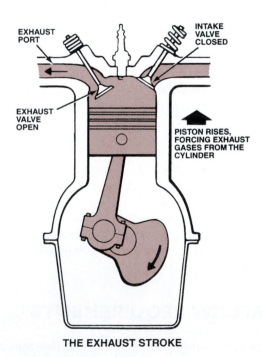

EXHAUST
PORT

INTAKE
VALVE
CLOSED

EXHAUST
VALVE
OPEN

PISTON RISES,
FORCING EXHAUST
GASES FROM THE
CYLINDER

THE EXHAUST STROKE

FIGURE 7-1 The greater the amount of air into the cylinders, the more fuel that can be added, thereby increasing the torque output of the engine.

Engine Compression

Higher compression increases the thermal efficiency of the engine because it raises compression temperatures, resulting in hotter, more complete combustion. However, a higher compression can cause an increase in NO_X emissions and would require the use of high-octane gasoline with effective antiknock additives.

SUPERCHARGING PRINCIPLES

The amount of force an air-fuel charge produces when it is ignited is largely a function of the charge density. Density is the mass of a substance in a given amount of space. See Figure 7-2. The greater the density of an air-fuel charge forced into a cylinder, the greater the force it produces when ignited, and the greater the engine power.

An engine that uses atmospheric pressure for intake is called a naturally **(normally) aspirated** engine. A better way to increase air density in the cylinder is to use a pump.

When air is pumped into the cylinder, the combustion chamber receives an increase of air pressure known as **boost** and is measured in pounds per square inch (psi) atmosphere (ATM) or bar. While boost pressure increases air density, friction heats air in motion and causes an increase in temperature. This increase in temperature works in the opposite direction, decreasing air density. Because of these and other variables, an increase in pressure does not always result in greater air density.

Another way to achieve an increase in mixture compression is called **supercharging.** This method uses a pump to pack a denser air-fuel charge into the cylinders. Since the density of the air-fuel charge is greater, so is its weight—and power is directly related to the weight

of an air-fuel charge consumed within a given time period. The result is similar to that of a high compression ratio, but the effect can be controlled during idle and deceleration to avoid high emissions.

Air is drawn into a naturally aspirated engine by atmospheric pressure forcing it into the low-pressure area of the intake manifold. The low pressure or vacuum in the manifold results from the reciprocating motion of the pistons. When a piston moves downward during its intake stroke, it creates an empty space, or vacuum, in the cylinder. Although atmospheric pressure pushes air to fill up as much of this empty space as possible, it has a difficult path to travel. The air must pass through the air filter, the throttle body, the manifold, and the intake port before entering the cylinder. Bends and restrictions in this pathway limit the amount of air reaching the cylinder before the intake valve closes; therefore, the volumetric efficiency is less than 100%.

Pumping air into the intake system under pressure forces it through the bends and restrictions at a greater speed than it would travel under normal atmospheric pressure, allowing more air to enter the intake port before it closes. By increasing the airflow into the intake, more fuel can be mixed with the air while still maintaining the same air-fuel ratio. The denser the air-fuel charge entering the engine during its intake stroke, the greater the potential energy released during combustion. In addition to the increased power resulting from combustion, there are several other advantages of supercharging an engine including:

- It increases the air-fuel charge density to provide high-compression pressure when power is required, but allows the engine to run on lower pressures when additional power is not required.
- The pumped air pushes the remaining exhaust from the combustion chamber during intake and exhaust valve overlap.
- The forced airflow and removal of hot exhaust gases lowers the temperature of the cylinder head, pistons, and valves, and helps extend the life of the engine.

A supercharger pressurizes air to greater than atmospheric pressure. The pressurization above atmospheric pressure, or boost, can be measured in the same way as atmospheric pressure. Atmospheric pressure drops as altitude increases, but boost pressure remains the same. If a supercharger develops 12 psi (83 kPa) boost at sea level, it will develop the same amount at a 5000-foot altitude because boost pressure is measured inside the intake manifold. See Figure 7-3.

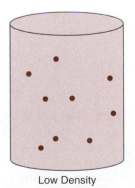
Low Density

High Density

FIGURE 7-2 The more air and fuel that can be packed in a cylinder, the greater the density of the air-fuel charge.

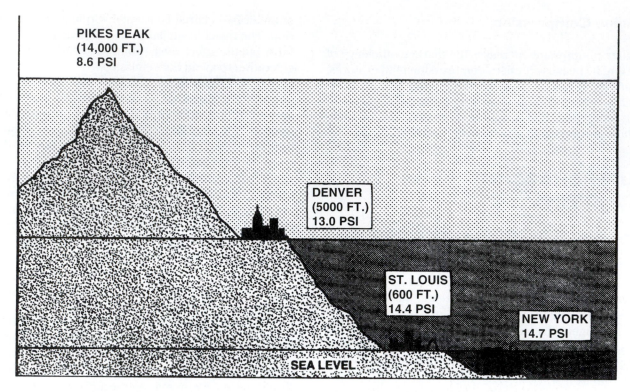

FIGURE 7-3 Atmospheric pressure decreases with increases in altitude.

Final Compression Ratio Chart @ Various Boost Levels

Comp Ratio	Blower Boost (psi)									
	2	*4*	*6*	*8*	*10*	*12*	*14*	*16*	*18*	*20*
6.5	7.4	8.3	9.2	10	10.9	11.8	12.7	13.6	14.5	15.3
7	8	8.9	9.9	10.8	11.8	12.7	13.6	14.5	15.3	16.2
7.5	8.5	9.5	10.6	11.6	12.6	13.6	14.6	15.7	16.7	17.8
8	9.1	10.2	11.3	12.4	13.4	14.5	15.6	16.7	17.8	18.9
8.5	9.7	10.8	12	13.1	14.3	15.4	16.6	17.8	18.9	19.8
9	10.2	11.4	12.7	13.9	15.1	16.3	17.6	18.8	20	21.2
9.5	10.8	12.1	13.4	14.7	16	17.3	18.5	19.8	21.1	22.4
10	11.4	12.7	14.1	15.4	16.8	18.2	19.5	20.9	22.2	23.6

Boost and Compression Ratios

Boost increases the amount of air drawn into the cylinder during the intake stroke. This extra air causes the effective compression ratio to be greater than the mechanical compression ratio designed into the engine. The higher the boost pressure, the greater the compression ratio. See the following table for an example of how much the effective compression ratio is increased compared to the boost pressure.

SUPERCHARGERS

A supercharger is an engine-driven air pump that supplies more than the normal amount of air into the intake manifold and boosts engine torque and power. A supercharger provides an instantaneous increase in power without the delay or lag often associated with turbochargers. However, a supercharger, because it is driven by the engine, does require horsepower to operate and is not as efficient as a turbocharger.

In basic concept, a supercharger is nothing more than an air pump mechanically driven by the engine itself. Gears, shafts, chains, or belts from the crankshaft can be used to turn the pump. This means that the air pump or supercharger pumps air in direct relation to engine speed.

There are two general types of superchargers:

- **Roots-type.** Named for Philander and Francis Roots, two brothers from Connersville, Indiana, who patented the design in 1860 as a type of water pump to be used in mines. Later it was used to move air and is used today on 2-stroke cycle Detroit diesel engines and other supercharged engines. The roots-type supercharger is called a **positive-displacement** design because all of the air that enters is forced through the unit. Examples of a roots-type supercharger include the GMC 6-71 (used originally on GMC diesel engines that had six cylinders each with 71 cu. in.) and Eaton used on supercharged 3800 V-6 General Motors engines. See Figure 7-4.
- **Centrifugal supercharger.** A centrifugal supercharger is similar to a turbocharger but is mechanically driven by the engine instead of being powered by the hot exhaust gases. A centrifugal supercharger is not a positive displacement pump and all of the air that enters is not forced through the unit. Air enters a centrifugal supercharger housing in the center and exits at the outer edges of the compressor wheels at a much higher speed due to centrifugal force. The speed of the blades has to be higher than engine speed so a smaller pulley is used on the supercharger and the crankshaft overdrives the impeller through an internal gear box achieving about seven times the speed of the engine. Examples of centrifugal superchargers include Vortech and Paxton.

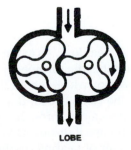

LOBE

FIGURE 7-4 A roots-type supercharger uses two lobes to force the air around the outside of the housing and forces it into the intake manifold.

Supercharger Boost Control

Many factory installed superchargers are equipped with a **bypass valve** that allows intake air to flow directly into the intake manifold bypassing the supercharger. The computer controls the bypass valve actuator. See Figure 7-5. The airflow is directed around the supercharger whenever any of the following conditions occur:

- The boost pressure, as measured by the MAP sensor, indicates that the intake manifold pressure is reaching the predetermined boost level.
- During deceleration.
- Whenever reverse gear is selected.

Supercharger Service

Superchargers are usually lubricated with synthetic engine oil inside the unit. This oil level should be checked and replaced as specified by the vehicle or supercharger manufacturer. The drive belt should also be inspected and replaced as necessary.

TURBOCHARGERS

The major disadvantage of a supercharger is its reliance on engine power to drive the unit. In some installations, as much as 20% of the engine's power is used by a mechanical supercharger. However, by connecting a centrifugal supercharger to a turbine drive wheel and installing it in the exhaust path, the lost engine horsepower is regained to perform other work and the combustion heat energy lost in the engine exhaust (as much as 40 to 50%) can be harnessed to do useful work. This is the concept of a **turbocharger.**

The turbocharger's main advantage over a mechanically driven supercharger is that the turbocharger does not drain power from the engine. In a naturally aspirated engine, about half of the heat energy contained in the fuel goes out the exhaust system. See Figure 7-6. Another 25% is lost through radiator cooling. Only about 25% is actually converted to mechanical power. A mechanically driven pump uses some of this mechanical output, but a turbocharger gets its energy from the exhaust gases, converting more of the fuel's heat energy into mechanical energy.

A turbocharger turbine looks much like a typical centrifugal pump used for supercharging. See Figure 7-7. Hot exhaust gases flow from the combustion chamber to the turbine wheel. The gases are heated and expanded as they leave the engine. It is not the

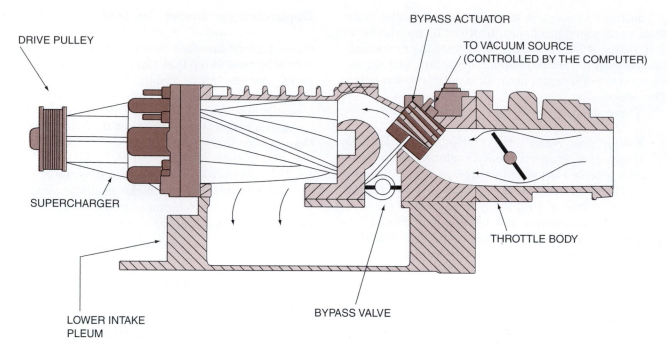

FIGURE 7-5　The bypass actuator opens the bypass valve to control boost pressure.

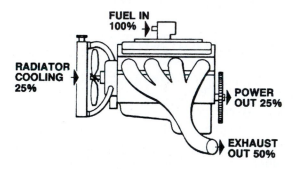

FIGURE 7-6　A turbocharger uses some of the heat energy that would normally be wasted.

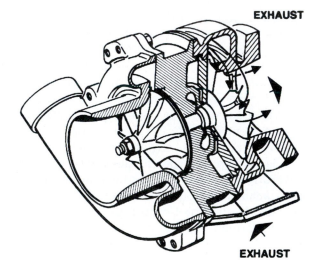

FIGURE 7-7　A turbine wheel is turned by the expanding exhaust gases.

speed of force of the exhaust gases that forces the turbine wheel to turn, as is commonly thought, but the expansion of hot gases against the turbine wheel's blades.

Turbocharger Design and Operation

A turbocharger consists of two chambers connected by a center housing. The two chambers contain a turbine wheel and a compressor wheel connected by a shaft which passes through the center housing.

To take full advantage of the exhaust heat which provides the rotating force, a turbocharger must be positioned as close as possible to the exhaust manifold. This allows the hot exhaust to pass directly into the unit

with a minimum of heat loss. As exhaust gas enters the turbocharger, it rotates the turbine blades. The turbine wheel and compressor wheel are on the same shaft so that they turn at the same speed. Rotation of the compressor wheel draws air in through a central inlet and centrifugal force pumps it through an outlet at the edge of the housing. A pair of bearings in the center housing supports the turbine and compressor wheel shaft, and is lubricated by engine oil. See Figure 7-8.

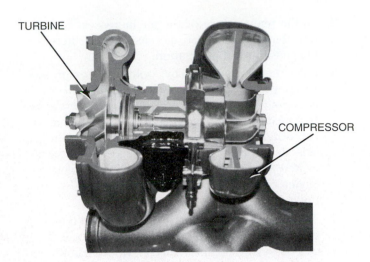

TURBINE

COMPRESSOR

FIGURE 7-8 A cutaway of a typical turbocharger. The exhaust from the engine turns the turbine on the left side over 100,000 revolutions per minute. The turbine is connected by a shaft to a compressor located on the right side of the turbocharger. The compressor blades draw air from the air filter housing and force it into the intake manifold to give the engine extra power.

Both the turbine and compressor wheels must operate with extremely close clearances to minimize possible leakage around their blades. Any leakage around the turbine blades causes a dissipation of the heat energy required for compressor rotation. Leakage around the compressor blades prevents the turbocharger from developing its full boost pressure.

When the engine is started and runs at low speed, both exhaust heat and pressure are low and the turbine runs at a low speed (approximately 1000 RPM). Because the compressor does not turn fast enough to develop boost pressure, air simply passes through it and the engine works like any naturally aspirated engine. As the engine runs faster or load increases, both exhaust heat and flow increases, causing the turbine and compressor wheels to rotate faster. Since there is no brake and very little rotating resistance on the turbocharger shaft, the turbine and compressor wheels accelerate as the exhaust heat energy increases. When an engine is running at full power, the typical turbocharger rotates at speeds between 100,000 and 150,000 RPM.

Engine deceleration from full power to idle requires only a second or two because of its internal friction, pumping resistance, and drive train load. The turbocharger, however, has no such load on its shaft, and is already turning many times faster than the engine at top speed. As a result, it can take as much as a minute or more after the engine has returned to idle speed before the turbocharger also has returned to idle. If the en-

gine is decelerated to idle and then shut off immediately, engine lubrication stops flowing to the center housing bearings while the turbocharger is still spinning at thousands of rpm. The oil in the center housing is then subjected to extreme heat and can gradually "coke" or oxidize. The coked oil can clog passages and will reduce the life of the turbocharger.

The high rotating speeds and extremely close clearances of the turbine and compressor wheels in their housings require equally critical bearing clearances. The bearings must keep radial clearances of 0.003–0.006 inch (0.08–0.15 mm). Axial clearance (endplay) must be maintained at 0.001–0.003 inch (0.025–0.08 mm). If properly maintained, the turbocharger also is a trouble-free device. However, to prevent problems, three conditions must be met:

- The turbocharger bearings must be constantly lubricated with clean engine oil—turbocharged engines should have regular oil changes at half the time or mileage intervals specified for non-turbocharged engines.
- Dirt particles and other contamination must be kept out of the intake and exhaust housings.
- Whenever a basic engine bearing (crankshaft or camshaft) has been damaged, the turbocharger must be flushed with clean engine oil after the bearing has been replaced.
- If the turbocharger is damaged, the engine oil must be drained and flushed and the oil filter replaced as part of the repair procedure.

Late-model turbochargers all have liquid-cooled center bearings to prevent heat damage. In a liquid-cooled turbocharger, engine coolant is circulated through passages cast in the center housing to draw off the excess heat. This allows the bearings to run cooler and minimize the probability of oil coking when the engine is shut down.

Turbocharger Size and Response Time

A time lag occurs between an increase in engine speed and the increase in the speed of the turbocharger. This delay between acceleration and turbo boost is called **turbo lag.** Like any material, moving exhaust gas has inertia. Inertia also is present in the turbine and compressor wheels, as well as the intake airflow. Unlike a supercharger, the turbocharger cannot supply an adequate amount of boost at low speed.

Turbocharger response time is directly related to the size of the turbine and compressor wheels. Small wheels accelerate rapidly; large wheels accelerate slowly. While small wheels would seem to have an advantage over larger ones, they may not have enough airflow capacity for an engine. To minimize turbo lag, the intake and exhaust breathing capacities of an engine must be matched to the exhaust and intake airflow capabilities of the turbocharger.

BOOST CONTROL

Both supercharged and turbocharged systems are designed to provide a pressure greater than atmospheric pressure in the intake manifold. This increased pressure forces additional amounts of air into the combustion chamber over what would normally be forced in by atmospheric pressure. This increased charge increases engine power. The amount of "boost" (or pressure in the intake manifold) is measured in pounds per square inch (psi), in inches of mercury (in. Hg), in BAR's, or in atmospheres.

> 1 atmosphere = 14.7 psi
> 1 atmosphere = 30 in. Hg
> 1 atmosphere = 1.0 BAR
> 1 BAR = 14.7 psi

The higher the level of boost (pressure), the greater the horsepower potential. However, other factors must be considered when increasing boost pressure:

1. As boost pressure increases, the temperature of the air also increases.

FIGURE 7-9 An intercooler on a vehicle equipped with an aftermarket turbocharger shown with the bumper and grill removed.

INTERCOOLER

2. As the temperature of the air increases, combustion temperatures also increase, which increases the possibility of detonation.

3. Power can be increased by cooling the compressed air after it leaves the turbocharger. *The power can be increased about 1% per 10°F by which the air is cooled.* A typical cooling device is called an **intercooler** and is similar to a radiator, wherein outside air can pass through, cooling the pressurized heated air. See Figure 7-9. Some intercoolers use engine coolant to cool the hot compressed air that flows from the turbocharger to the intake.

4. As boost pressure increases, combustion temperature and pressures increase, which, if not limited, can do severe engine damage. The maximum exhaust gas temperature must be 1550°F (840°C). Higher temperatures decrease the durability of the turbocharger *and* the engine.

◄ HIGH-PERFORMANCE TIP ►

BOOST IS THE RESULT OF RESTRICTION

The boost pressure of a turbocharger (or supercharger) is commonly measured in pounds per square inch. If a cylinder head is restricted because of small valves and ports, the turbocharger will quickly provide boost. Boost results when the air being forced into the cylinder heads cannot flow into the cylinders fast enough and "piles up" in the intake manifold, increasing boost pressure. If an engine had large valves and ports, the turbocharger could provide a much greater *amount* of air into the engine at the same boost pressure as an identical engine with smaller valves and ports. Therefore, by increasing the size of the valves, a turbocharged or supercharged engine will be capable of producing much greater power.

Wastegate

A turbocharger uses exhaust gases to increase boost, which causes the engine to make more exhaust gases, which in turn increases the boost from the turbocharger. To prevent overboost and severe engine damage, most turbocharger systems use a wastegate. A wastegate is a valve similar to a door that can open and close. The wastegate is a bypass valve at the exhaust inlet to the turbine. It allows all of the exhaust into the turbine, or it can route part of the exhaust past the turbine to the exhaust

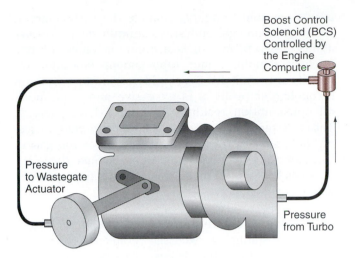

Boost Control Solenoid (BCS) Controlled by the Engine Computer

Pressure to Wastegate Actuator

Pressure from Turbo

FIGURE 7-10 The boost pressure on most turbocharged engines is controlled by the engine computer by pulsing the boost control solenoid on and off based on signals received by the computer from the manifold absolute pressure (MAP) sensor.

system. If the valve is closed, all of the exhaust travels to the turbocharger. When a predetermined amount of boost pressure develops in the intake manifold, the wastegate valve is opened. As the valve opens, most of the exhaust flows directly out the exhaust system, bypassing the turbocharger. With less exhaust flowing across the vanes of the turbocharger, the turbocharger decreases in speed and boost pressure is reduced. When the boost pressure drops, the wastegate valve closes to direct the exhaust over the turbocharger vanes and again allow the boost pressure to rise. Wastegate operation is a continuous process to control boost pressure.

The wastegate is the pressure control valve of a turbocharger system. The wastegate is usually controlled by the onboard computer through a boost control solenoid. See Figure 7-10.

Relief Valves

A wastegate controls the exhaust side of the turbocharger. A relief valve controls the intake side. A relief valve vents pressurized air from the connecting pipe between the outlet of the turbocharger and the throttle whenever the throttle is closed during boost, such as during shifts. If the pressure is not released, the turbocharger turbine wheel will slow down, creating a lag when the throttle is opened again after a shift has been completed. There are two basic types of relief valves including:

- **Compressor bypass valve or CBV.** This type of relief valve routes the pressurized air to the inlet

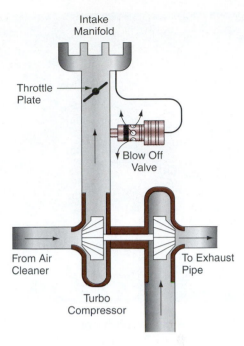

Intake Manifold

Throttle Plate

Blow Off Valve

From Air Cleaner

To Exhaust Pipe

Turbo Compressor

FIGURE 7-11 A blow-off valve vents pressure to the atmosphere when the throttle is closed to help keep the turbine blade from slowing when the pressurized air backs up after striking the closed throttle plate.

side of the turbocharger for reuse and is quiet during operation.

- **Blow-off valve or BOV.** This is also called a **dump valve** or **vent valve** and features an adjustable spring design that keeps the valve closed until a sudden release of the throttle. The resulting pressure increase opens the valve and vents the pressurized air directly into the atmosphere. This type of relief valve is noisy in operation and creates a whooshing sound when the valve opens. See Figure 7-11.

◄ HIGH-PERFORMANCE TIP ►

IF ONE IS GOOD, TWO ARE BETTER

A turbocharger uses the exhaust from the engine to spin a turbine, which is connected to an impeller inside a turbocharger. This impeller then forces air into the engine under pressure higher than is normally achieved without a turbocharger. The more air that can be forced into an engine, the greater the power potential. A V-type engine has two exhaust manifolds and so two, small turbochargers can be used to help force greater quantities of air into an engine, as shown in Figure 7-12.

FIGURE 7-12 A dual turbocharger system installed on a small block Chevrolet V-8 engine.

TURBOCHARGER FAILURES

When turbochargers fail to function correctly, a drop in power is noticed. To restore proper operation, the turbocharger must be rebuilt, repaired, or replaced. It is not possible to simply remove the turbocharger, seal any openings, and still maintain decent driveability. Bearing failure is a common cause of turbocharger failure, and replacement bearings are usually only available to rebuilders. Another common turbocharger problem is excessive and continuous oil consumption resulting in blue exhaust smoke. Turbochargers use small rings similar to piston rings on the shaft to prevent exhaust (combustion gases) from entering the central bearing. Because there are no seals to keep oil in, excessive oil consumption is usually caused by:

1. A plugged positive crankcase ventilation (PCV) system resulting in excessive crankcase pressures forcing oil into the air inlet. This failure is not related to the turbocharger, but the turbocharger is often blamed.

2. A clogged air filter, which causes a low-pressure area in the inlet, which can draw oil past the turbo shaft rings and into the intake manifold.

3. A clogged oil return (drain) line from the turbocharger to the oil pan (sump), which can cause the engine oil pressure to force oil past the turbocharger's shaft rings and into the intake *and* exhaust manifolds. Obviously, oil being forced into both the intake and exhaust would create lots of smoke.

SUMMARY

1. Volumetric efficiency is a comparison of the actual volume of air-fuel mixture drawn into the engine to the theoretical maximum volume that can be drawn into the cylinder.

2. A supercharger operates from the engine by a drive belt and, while it does consume some engine power, it forces a greater amount of air into the cylinders for even more power.

3. A turbocharger uses the normally wasted heat energy of the exhaust to turn an impeller at high speed. The impeller is linked to a turbine wheel on the same shaft and is used to force air into the engine.

4. There are two types of superchargers: roots-type and centrifugal.

5. A bypass valve is used to control the boost pressure on most factory installed superchargers.

6. An intercooler is used on many turbocharged and some supercharged engines to reduce the temperature of air entering the engine for increased power.

7. A wastegate is used on most turbocharger systems to limit and control boost pressures, as well as a relief valve, to keep the speed of the turbine wheel from slowing down during engine deceleration.

REVIEW QUESTIONS

1. What are the reasons why supercharging increases engine power?

2. How does the bypass valve work on a supercharged engine?

3. What are the advantages and disadvantages of supercharging?

4. What are the advantages and disadvantages of turbocharging?

5. What turbocharger control valves are needed for proper engine operation?

ASE CERTIFICATION-TYPE QUESTIONS

1. Boost pressure is generally measured in _____.
   a. in. Hg
   b. psi
   c. in. H$_2$O
   d. in. lb.

2. Two types of superchargers include _____.
   a. Rotary and reciprocating
   b. Roots-type and centrifugal
   c. Double and single acting
   d. Turbine and piston

3. Which valve is used on a factory supercharger to limit boost?
   a. A bypass valve
   b. A wastegate
   c. A blow-off valve
   d. An air valve

4. How are most superchargers lubricated?
   a. By engine oil under pressure through lines from the engine
   b. By an internal oil reservoir
   c. By greased bearings
   d. No lubrication is needed because the incoming air cools the supercharger

5. How are most turbochargers lubricated?
   a. By engine oil under pressure through lines from the engine
   b. By an internal oil reservoir
   c. By greased bearings
   d. No lubrication is needed because the incoming air cools the supercharger

6. Two technicians are discussing the term "turbo lag." Technician A says that it refers to the delay between when the exhaust leaves the cylinder and when it contacts the turbine blades of the turbocharger. Technician B says that it refers to the delay in boost pressure that occurs when the throttle is first opened. Which technician is correct?
   a. Technician A only
   b. Technician B only
   c. Both Technicians A and B
   d. Neither Technician A nor B

7. What is the purpose of an intercooler?
   a. To reduce the temperature of the air entering the engine
   b. To cool the turbocharger
   c. To cool the engine oil on a turbocharged engine
   d. To cool the exhaust before it enters the turbocharger

8. Which type of relief valve used on a turbocharged engine is noisy?
   a. A bypass valve
   b. A BOV
   c. A dump valve
   d. Both b and c

9. Technician A says that a stuck-open wastegate can cause the engine to burn oil. Technician B says that a clogged PCV system can cause the engine to burn oil. Which technician is correct?
   a. Technician A only
   b. Technician B only
   c. Both Technicians A and B
   d. Neither Technician A nor B

10. What service operation is *most* important on engines equipped with a turbocharger?
    a. Replacing the air filter regularly
    b. Replacing the fuel filter regularly
    c. Regular oil changes
    d. Regular exhaust system maintenance

ENGINE CONDITION DIAGNOSIS

OBJECTIVES

After studying Chapter 8, the reader should be able to:

1. Prepare for ASE Engine Performance (A8) certification test content area "A" (General Engine Diagnosis).
2. List the visual checks to determine engine condition.
3. Discuss engine noise and its relation to engine condition.
4. Describe how to perform a dry and a wet compression test.
5. Explain how to perform a cylinder leakage test.
6. Discuss how to measure the amount of timing chain slack.
7. Describe how an oil sample analysis can be used to determine engine condition.

If there is an engine operation problem, then the cause could be any one of many items, including the engine itself. The condition of the engine should be tested anytime the operation of the engine is not satisfactory.

TYPICAL ENGINE-RELATED COMPLAINTS

Many driveability problems are *not* caused by engine mechanical problems. A thorough inspection and testing of the ignition and fuel systems should be performed before testing for mechanical engine problems.

Typical engine problem complaints include the following:

- Excessive oil consumption
- Engine misfiring
- Loss of power
- Smoke from the engine or exhaust
- Engine noise

◄ TECH TIP ►

THE BINDER CLIP TRICK

It is important to use fender covers whenever working on an engine. The problem is few covers remain in place and they often become more of a hindrance than a help. A binder clip, available at most office supply stores, can be used to hold fender covers to the lip of the fender of most vehicles. See Figure 8-1. When clipped over the lip, the cover is securely attached and cannot be pulled loose. This method works with cloth and vinyl covers.

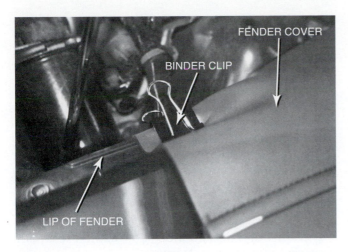

FIGURE 8-1 It is very important to use fender covers to protect the paint of the vehicle from being splashed with brake fluid. Use a binder clip, available at local office supply stores, to clip the fender cover to the lip of the fender, preventing the fender cover from slipping.

ENGINE SMOKE DIAGNOSIS

The color of engine exhaust smoke can indicate what engine problem might exist.

Typical Exhaust Smoke Color	Possible Causes
Blue	Blue exhaust indicates that the engine is burning oil. Oil is getting into the combustion chamber either past the piston rings or past the valve stem seals. Blue smoke only after start-up is usually due to defective valve stem seals. See Figure 8-2.
Black	Black exhaust smoke is due to excessive fuel being burned in the combustion chamber. Typical causes include a defective or misadjusted throttle body, leaking fuel injector, or excessive fuel-pump pressure.
White (steam)	White smoke or steam from the exhaust is normal during cold weather and represents condensed steam. Every engine creates about 1 gallon of water for each gallon of gasoline burned. If the steam from the exhaust is excessive, then water (coolant) is getting into the combustion chamber. Typical

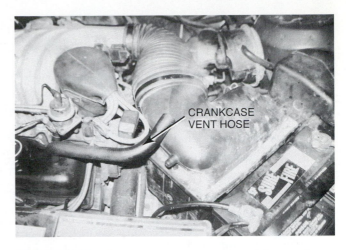

FIGURE 8-2 Blowby gases coming out of the crankcase vent hose. Excessive amounts of combustion gases flow past the piston rings and into the crankcase.

FIGURE 8-3 White steam is usually an indication of a blown (defective) cylinder head gasket that allows engine coolant to flow into the combustion chamber where it is turned to steam.

causes include a defective cylinder head gasket, a cracked cylinder head, or in severe cases a cracked block. See Figure 8-3.

NOTE: White smoke can also be created when automatic transmission fluid (ATF) is burned. A common source of ATF getting into the engine is through a defective vacuum modulator valve on the automatic transmission.

THE DRIVER IS YOUR BEST RESOURCE

The driver of the vehicle knows a lot about the vehicle and how it is driven. *Before* diagnosis is started, always ask the following questions:

- When did the problem first occur?
- Under what conditions does it occur?
  1. Cold or hot?
  2. Acceleration, cruise, or deceleration?
  3. How far was it driven?

After the nature and scope of the problem are determined, the complaint should be verified before further diagnostic tests are performed.

VISUAL CHECKS

The first and most important "test" that can be performed is a careful visual inspection.

Oil Level and Condition

The first area for visual inspection is oil level and condition.

1. Oil level—oil should be to the proper level
2. Oil condition
   a. Using a match or lighter, try to light the oil on the dipstick; if the oil flames up, gasoline is present in the engine oil.
   b. Drip some of the engine oil from the dipstick onto the hot exhaust manifold. If the oil bubbles or boils, there is coolant (water) in the oil.
   c. Check for grittiness by rubbing the oil between your fingers.

Coolant Level and Condition

Most mechanical engine problems are caused by overheating. The proper operation of the cooling system is critical to the life of any engine.

NOTE: Check the coolant level in the radiator only if the radiator is cool. If the radiator is hot and the radiator cap is removed, the drop in pressure above the coolant will cause

the coolant to boil immediately and can cause severe burns when the coolant explosively expands upward and outward from the radiator opening.

1. The coolant level in the coolant recovery container should be within the limits indicated on the overflow bottle. If this level is too low or the coolant recovery container is empty, then check the level of coolant in the radiator (only when cool) and also check the operation of the pressure cap.
2. The coolant should be checked with a hydrometer for boiling and freezing temperature. This test indicates if the concentration of the antifreeze is sufficient for proper protection.
3. Pressure test the cooling system and look for leakage. Coolant leakage can often be seen around hoses or cooling system components because it will often cause
   a. A grayish white stain
   b. A rusty color stain
   c. Dye stains from antifreeze (usually greenish)
4. Check for cool areas of the radiator indicating clogged sections.
5. Check operation and condition of the fan clutch, fan, and coolant pump drive belt.

◄ TECH TIP ►

WHAT'S LEAKING?

The color of the leaks observed under a vehicle can help the technician determine and correct the cause. Some leaks, such as condensate (water) from the air-conditioning system, are normal, whereas a brake fluid leak is very dangerous. The following are colors of common leaks:

Sooty black	Engine oil
Yellow, green, blue, or orange	Antifreeze (coolant)
Red	Automatic transmission fluid
Murky brown	Brake or power steering fluid or very neglected antifreeze (coolant)
Clear	Air-conditioning condensate (water) (normal)

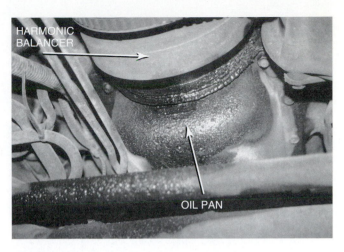

FIGURE 8-5 A leaking front crankshaft seal.

FIGURE 8-4 Typical valve (rocker cover) gasket leak. Always check the *highest* and *most forward* parts of the engine that are wet when attempting to find a fluid leak.

Oil Leaks

Oil leaks can lead to severe engine damage if the resulting low oil level is not corrected. Besides causing an oily mess where the vehicle is parked, the oil leak can cause blue smoke to occur under the hood as leaking oil drips on the exhaust system. *Finding* the location of the oil leak can often be difficult. See Figures 8-4 and 8-5. To help find the source of oil leaks follow these steps:

Step 1 Clean the engine or area around the suspected oil leak. Use a high-powered hot water spray to wash the engine. While the engine is running, spray the entire engine and the engine compartment. Avoid letting the water come into direct contact with the air inlet and ignition distributor or ignition coil(s).

HINT: If the engine starts to run rough or stalls when the engine gets wet, then the secondary ignition wires (spark plug wires) or distributor cap may be defective or have weak insulation. Be certain to wipe all wires and the distributor cap dry with a soft, dry cloth if the engine stalls.

An alternative method is to spray a degreaser on the engine, then start and run the engine until warm. Engine heat helps the degreaser penetrate the grease and dirt. Use a water hose to rinse off the engine and engine compartment.

Step 2 If the oil leak is not visible or oil seems to be coming from "everywhere," use a white talcum powder. The leaking oil will show as a dark area on the white powder. See the Tech Tip, "The Foot Powder Spray Trick."

Step 3 Fluorescent dye can be added to the engine oil. Add about 1/2 oz (15 cc) of dye per 5 quarts of engine oil. Start the engine and allow it to run about 10 minutes to thoroughly mix the dye throughout the engine. A black light can then be shown around every suspected oil leak location. The black light will easily show all oil leak locations because the dye will show as a bright yellow/green area.

HINT: Fluorescent dye works best with clean oil.

◀ TECH TIP ▶

THE FOOT POWDER SPRAY TRICK

The source of an oil or other fluid leak is often difficult to determine. A quick and easy method that works is the following. First, clean the entire area. This can best be done by using a commercially available degreaser to spray the entire area. Let it soak to loosen all accumulated oil and greasy dirt. Clean off the degreaser with a water hose. Let the area dry. Start the engine, and using spray foot powder or other aerosol powder product, spray the entire area. The leak will turn the white powder dark. The exact location of any leak can be quickly located.

ENGINE NOISE DIAGNOSIS

An engine knocking noise is often difficult to diagnose. Several items that can cause a deep engine knock include:

- **Valves clicking** because of lack of oil to the lifters. This noise is most noticeable at idle when the oil pressure is the lowest. See Figure 8-6.
- **Torque converter** attaching bolts or nuts loose on the flex plate. This noise is most noticeable at idle or when there is no load on the engine.
- **Cracked flex plate.** The noise of a cracked flex plate is often mistaken for a rod or main bearing noise. See Figure 8-7.
- **Loose or defective drive belts.** If an accessory drive belt is loose or defective, the flopping noise often sounds similar to a bearing knock. See Figures 8-8 and 8-9.
- **Piston pin knock.** This knocking noise is usually not affected by load on the cylinder. If the clearance is too great, a double knock noise is heard when the engine idles. If all cylinders are grounded out one at a time and the noise does not change, a defective piston pin could be the cause.
- **Piston slap.** A piston slap is usually caused by an undersized or improperly shaped piston or oversized cylinder bore. A piston slap is most noticeable

FIGURE 8-6 Pushrod worn through a rocker arm.

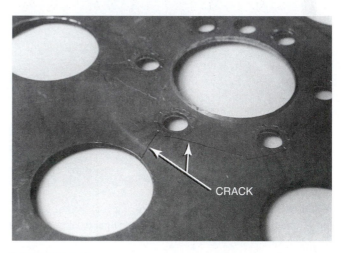

CRACK

FIGURE 8-7 Cracked drive (flex) plate. The noise this plate made was similar to a rod-bearing knocking noise.

when the engine is cold and tends to decrease or stop making noise as the piston expands during engine operation.

- **Timing chain noise.** An excessively loose timing chain can cause a severe knocking noise when the chain hits the timing chain cover. This noise can often sound like a rod-bearing knock.
- **Heat riser noise.** A loose (worn) or defective heat riser valve in the exhaust can make a knocking noise similar to a bearing noise. Even a vacuum-controlled heat riser [also called an **early fuel evaporation (EFE)** valve] can make a knocking noise, especially under load, as the result of slight vacuum variations applied to the actuator diaphragm. To eliminate the heat riser as a possible cause, remove the vacuum

FIGURE 8-8   An accessory drive belt tensioner. Most tensioners have a mark that indicates normal operating location. If the belt has stretched, this indicator mark will be outside of the normal range. Anything wrong with the belt or the tensioner can cause noise.

FIGURE 8-9   A defective serpentine belt can cause a variety of noises including squealing and knocking, similar to a main-bearing knock.

hose to the actuator or retain the thermostatic valve with a wire or other suitable means.

- **Rod-bearing noise.** The noise from a defective rod bearing is usually load sensitive and changes in intensity as the load on the engine increases and decreases. A rod-bearing failure can often be detected by grounding out the spark plugs one cylinder at a time. If the knocking noise decreases or is eliminated when a particular cylinder is grounded (disabled), then the grounded cylinder is the one from which the noise is originating.

Typical Noises	*Possible Causes*
Clicking noise—like the clicking of a ballpoint pen	1. Loose spark plug
	2. Loose accessory mount (for air-conditioning compressor, alternator, power steering pump, etc.)
	3. Loose rocker arm
	4. Worn rocker arm pedestal
	5. Fuel pump (broken mechanical fuel pump return spring)
	6. Worn camshaft
	7. Exhaust leak
	8. Ping (detonation)
Clacking noise—like tapping on metal	1. Worn piston pin
	2. Broken piston
	3. Excessive valve clearance
	4. Timing chain hitting cover

continued

Typical Noises	*Possible Causes*
Knock—like knocking on a door	1. Rod bearing(s)
	2. Main bearing(s)
	3. Thrust bearing(s)
	4. Loose torque converter
	5. Cracked flex plate (drive plate)
Rattle—like a baby rattle	1. Manifold heat control valve
	2. Broken harmonic balancer
	3. Loose accessory mounts
	4. Loose accessory drive belt or tensioner
Clatter—like rolling marbles	1. Rod bearings
	2. Piston pin
	3. Loose timing chain
Whine—like an electric motor running	1. Alternator bearing
	2. Drive belt
	3. Power steering
	4. Belt noise (accessory or timing)
Clunk—like a door closing	1. Engine mount
	2. Drive axle shaft U-joint or constant velocity (CV) joint

■ **Main-bearing knock.** A main-bearing knock often cannot be isolated to a particular cylinder. The sound can vary in intensity and may disappear at times depending on engine load.

Regardless of the type of loud knocking noise, after the external causes of the knocking noise have been eliminated, the engine should be disassembled and carefully inspected to determine the exact cause.

◄ TECH TIP ►

ENGINE NOISE AND COST

A light ticking noise often heard at one-half engine speed and associated with valve train noise is a less serious problem than many deep-sounding knocking noises. Generally, the deeper the sound of the engine noise, the more the owner will have to pay for repairs. A light "tick tick tick," though often not cheap, is usually far less expensive than a deep "knock knock knock" from the engine.

OIL PRESSURE TESTING

Proper oil pressure is very important for the operation of any engine. *Low oil pressure can cause engine wear, and engine wear can cause low oil pressure.*

If main and rod bearings are worn, oil pressure is reduced because of leakage of the oil around the bearings. Oil pressure testing is usually performed with the following steps:

Step 1 Operate the engine until normal operating temperature is achieved.

Step 2 With the engine off, remove the oil pressure sending unit or sender, usually located near the oil filter. Thread an oil pressure gauge into the threaded hole. See Figure 8-10.

HINT: An oil pressure gauge can be made from another gauge, such as an old air-conditioning gauge, and a flexible brake hose. The threads are often the same as those used for the oil pressure sending unit.

Step 3 Start the engine and observe the gauge. Record the oil pressure at idle and at 2500 RPM.

Most vehicle manufacturers recommend a minimum oil pressure of 10 psi per 1000 RPM. Therefore, at 2500 RPM, the oil pressure should be at least 25 psi. Always

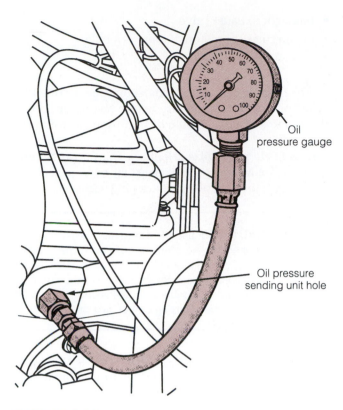

FIGURE 8-10 To measure engine oil pressure, remove the oil pressure sending (sender) unit usually located near the oil filter. Screw the pressure gauge into the oil pressure sending unit hole.

compare your test results with the manufacturer's recommended oil pressure.

Besides engine bearing wear, other possible causes for low oil pressure include:

- Low oil level
- Diluted oil
- Stuck oil pressure relief valve

OIL PRESSURE WARNING LAMP

The red oil pressure warning lamp in the dash usually lights when the oil pressure is less than 4 to 7 psi, depending on vehicle and engine. The oil light should not be on during driving. If the oil warning lamp is on, stop the engine immediately. Always confirm oil pressure with a reliable mechanical gauge before performing engine repairs. The sending unit or circuit may be defective. See Figure 8-11.

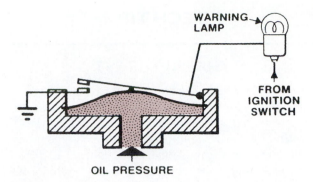

FIGURE 8-11 The oil pressure switch is connected to the warning lamp indicating to the driver that the oil pressure is low.

◄ TECH TIP ►

USE THE KISS TEST METHOD

Engine testing is done to find the cause of an engine problem. All the simple things should be tested first. Just remember KISS—"keep it simple, stupid." A loose alternator belt or loose bolts on a torque converter can sound just like a lifter or rod bearing. A loose spark plug can make the engine perform as if it had a burned valve. Some simple items that can cause serious problems include the following:

Oil burning

- Low oil level
- Clogged PCV valve or system, causing blowby and oil to be blown into the air cleaner
- Dirty oil that has not been changed for a long time (Change the oil and drive for about 1000 miles (1600 kilometers) and change the oil and filter again.)

Noises

- Loose torque-to-flex plate bolts (or nuts), causing a loud knocking noise

---

HINT: Often this problem will cause noise only at idle; the noise tends to disappear during driving or when the engine is under load.

- A loose and/or defective drive belt, which may cause a rod or main bearing knocking noise (A loose or broken mount for the alternator, power steering pump, or air-conditioning compressor can also cause a knocking noise.)

THE PAPER TEST

A soundly running engine should produce even and steady exhaust at the tailpipe. Hold a piece of paper or a 3×5 card (even a dollar bill works), within 1 inch (2.5 centimeters) of the tailpipe with the engine running at idle. See Figure 8-12. The paper should blow out evenly without "puffing." If the paper is drawn *toward* the tailpipe at times, the valves in one or more cylinders could be burned. Other reasons why the paper might be sucked toward the tailpipe include the following:

1. The engine could be misfiring because of a lean condition that could occur normally when the engine is cold.
2. Pulsing of the paper toward the tailpipe could also be caused by a hole in the exhaust system. If exhaust escapes through a hole in the exhaust system, air could be drawn in during the intervals between the exhaust puffs from the tailpipe to the hole in the exhaust, causing the paper to be drawn toward the tailpipe.
3. Ignition fault causing misfire.

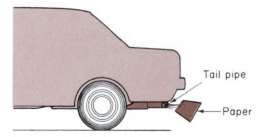

FIGURE 8-12 The paper test involves holding a piece of paper near the tailpipe of an idling engine. A good engine should produce even outward puffs of exhaust. If the paper is sucked in toward the tailpipe, a burned valve is a possibility.

COMPRESSION TEST

Testing an engine for proper compression is one of the fundamental engine diagnostic tests that can be performed. For smooth engine operation, all cylinders must have equal compression. An engine can lose compression by leakage of air through one or more of only three routes:

- Intake or exhaust valve
- Piston rings (or piston, if there is a hole)
- Cylinder head gasket

For best results, the engine should be warmed to normal operating temperature before testing. An accurate compression test should be performed as follows:

Step 1 Remove all spark plugs. This allows the engine to be cranked to an even speed. Be sure to label all spark plug wires.

CAUTION: Disable the ignition system by disconnecting the primary leads from the ignition coil or module or by grounding the coil wire after removing it from the center of the distributor cap. Also disable the fuel-injection system to prevent the squirting of fuel into the cylinder.

Step 2 Block open the throttle. This permits the maximum amount of air to be drawn into the engine. This step also ensures consistent compression test results.

Step 3 Thread a compression gauge into one spark plug hole and crank the engine. See Figure 8-13. Continue cranking the engine through *four* compression strokes. Each compression stroke makes a puffing sound.

HINT: Note the reading on the compression gauge after the first puff. This reading should be at least one-half the final reading. For example,

FIGURE 8-13 A two-piece compression gauge set. The threaded hose is screwed into the spark plug hole after removing the spark plug. The gauge part is then snapped onto the end of the hose.

if the final, highest reading is 150 psi, then the reading after the first puff should be higher than 75 psi. A low first-puff reading indicates possible weak piston rings. Release the pressure on the gauge and repeat for the other cylinders.

Step 4   Record the highest readings and compare the results. Most vehicle manufacturers specify the minimum compression reading and the maximum allowable variation among cylinders. Most manufacturers specify a maximum difference of 20% between the highest reading and the lowest reading. For example:

If the high reading is	150 psi
Subtract 20%	−30 psi
Lowest allowable compression is 120 psi	

HINT: To make the math quick and easy, think of 10% of 150, which is 15 (move the decimal point to the left one place). Now double it: 15 × 2 = 30. This represents 20%.

NOTE: During cranking, the oil pump cannot maintain normal oil pressure. Extended engine cranking, such as that which occurs during a compression test, can cause hydraulic lifters to collapse. When the engine starts, loud valve clicking noises may be heard. This should be considered normal after performing a compression test, and the noise should stop after the vehicle has been driven a short distance.

◄ TECH TIP ►

THE HOSE TRICK

Installing spark plugs can be made easier by using a rubber hose on the end of the spark plug. The hose can be a vacuum hose, fuel line, or even an old spark plug wire end. See Figure 8-14. The hose makes it easy to start the threads of the spark plug into the cylinder head. After starting the threads, continue to thread the spark plug for several turns. Using the hose eliminates the chance of cross-threading the plug. This is especially important when installing spark plugs in aluminum cylinder heads.

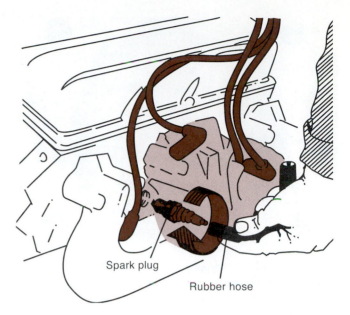

Spark plug

Rubber hose

FIGURE 8-14   Use a vacuum or fuel line hose over the spark plug to install it without danger of cross-threading the cylinder head.

WET COMPRESSION TEST

If the compression test reading indicates low compression on one or more cylinders, add three squirts of oil to the cylinder and retest. This is called a **wet compression test,** when oil is used to help seal around the piston rings.

CAUTION: Do not use more oil than three squirts from a hand-operated oil squirt can. Too much oil can cause a hydrostatic lock, which can damage or break pistons or connecting rods or even crack a cylinder head.

Perform the compression test again and observe the results. If the first-puff readings greatly improve and the readings are much higher than without the oil, the cause of the low compression is worn or defective piston rings. If the compression readings increase only slightly (or not at all), then the cause of the low compression is usually defective valves. See Figure 8-15.

RUNNING COMPRESSION TEST

The compression test is commonly used to help determine engine condition. A compression test is usually performed with the engine cranking.

What is the RPM of a cranking engine? An engine idles at about 600 to 900 RPM, and the starter motor

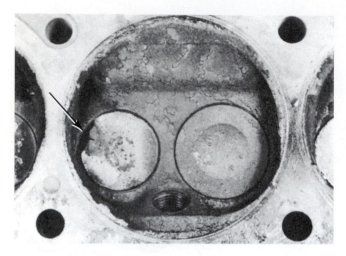

FIGURE 8-15 A compression test could have detected this badly burned exhaust valve, and a cylinder leakage test (leak-down test) could have been used to determine the exact problem.

obviously cannot crank the engine as fast as the engine idles. Most manufacturers' specifications require the engine to crank at 80 to 250 cranking RPM. Therefore, a check of the engine's compression at cranking speed determines the condition of an engine that does not run at such low speeds.

But what should be the compression of a running engine? Some would think that the compression would be substantially higher, because the valve overlap of the cam is more effective at higher engine speeds which would tend to increase the compression.

Actually, the compression pressure of a running engine is much *lower* than cranking compression pressure. This results from the volumetric efficiency. The engine is revolving faster, and therefore, there is less *time* for air to enter the combustion chamber. With less air to compress, the compression pressure is lower. Typically, the higher the engine RPM, the lower the running compression. For most engines, the value ranges are as follows:

- Compression during cranking: 125 to 160 psi
- Compression at idle: 60 to 90 psi
- Compression at 2000 RPM: 30 to 60 psi

As with cranking compression, the running compression of all cylinders should be equal. Therefore, a problem is not likely to be detected by single compression values, but by *variations* in running compression values among the cylinders. Broken valve springs, worn valve guides, bent pushrods, and worn cam lobes are some items that would be indicated by a low running compression test reading on one or more cylinders.

Performing a Running Compression Test

To perform a running compression test, remove just one spark plug at a time. With one spark plug removed from the engine, use a jumper wire to *ground* the spark plug wire to a good engine ground. This prevents possible ignition coil damage. Start the engine, push the pressure release on the gauge, and read the compression. Increase the engine speed to about 2000 RPM and push the pressure release on the gauge again. Read the gauge. Stop the engine, reattach the spark plug wire, and repeat the test for each of the remaining cylinders. Just like the cranking compression test, the running compression test can inform a technician of the *relative* compression of all the cylinders.

CYLINDER LEAKAGE TEST

One of the best tests that can be used to determine engine condition is the cylinder leakage test. This test involves injecting air under pressure into the cylinders one at a time. The amount and location of any escaping air helps the technician determine the condition of the engine. The air is injected into the cylinder through a cylinder leakage gauge into the spark plug hole. See Figure 8-16.

Step 1   For best results, the engine should be at normal operating temperature (upper radiator hose hot and pressurized).

Step 2   The cylinder being tested must be at top dead center (TDC) of the compression stroke.

NOTE: The greatest amount of wear occurs at the top of the cylinder because of the heat generated near the top of the cylinders. The piston ring flex also adds to the wear at the top of the cylinder.

Step 3   Calibrate the cylinder leakage unit as per manufacturer's instructions.

Step 4   Inject air into the cylinders one at a time, rotating the engine as necessitated by firing order to test each cylinder at TDC on the compression stroke.

Step 5   Evaluate the results:

         Less than 10% leakage: good

         Less than 20% leakage: acceptable

FIGURE 8-16   A typical handheld cylinder leakage tester.

Less than 30% leakage: poor
More than 30% leakage: definite
problem

HINT: If leakage seems unacceptably high, repeat the test, being certain that it is being performed correctly and that the cylinder being tested is at TDC on the compression stroke.

Step 6   Check the source of air leakage.
   a. If air is heard escaping from the oil filler cap, the *piston rings* are worn or broken.
   b. If air is observed bubbling out of the radiator, there is a possible blown *head gasket* or cracked *cylinder head*.
   c. If air is heard coming from the throttle body or air inlet on fuel injection-equipped engines, there is a defective intake valve(s).
   d. If air is heard coming from the tailpipe, there is a defective *exhaust valve(s)*.

CYLINDER POWER BALANCE TEST

Most large engine analyzers have a cylinder power balance feature. The purpose of a cylinder balance test is to determine if all cylinders are contributing power equally. It determines this by shorting out one cylinder at a time. If the engine speed (RPM) does not drop as

much for one cylinder as for other cylinders of the same engine, then the shorted cylinder must be weaker than the other cylinders. For example:

Cylinder number	RPM drop when ignition is shorted
1	75
2	70
3	15
4	65
5	75
6	70

Cylinder #3 is the weak cylinder.

NOTE: Most automotive test equipment uses automatic means for testing cylinder balance. Be certain to correctly identify the offending cylinder. Cylinder #3 as identified by the equipment may be the third cylinder in the firing order instead of the actual cylinder #3.

POWER BALANCE TEST PROCEDURE

When point-type ignition was used on all vehicles, the common method for determining which, if any, cylinder was weak was to remove a spark plug wire from one spark plug at a time while watching a tachometer and a vacuum gauge. This method is not recommended on any vehicle with any type of electronic ignition. If any of the spark plug wires are removed from a spark plug with the engine running, the ignition coil tries to supply increasing levels of voltage attempting to jump the increasing gap as the plug wires are removed. This high voltage could easily track the ignition coil, damage the ignition module, or both.

The acceptable method of canceling cylinders, which will work on all types of ignition systems, including distributorless, is to *ground* the secondary current for each cylinder. See Figure 8-17. The cylinder with the least RPM drop is the cylinder not producing its share of power.

VACUUM TESTING

Vacuum is pressure below atmospheric pressure and is measured in **inches** (or millimeters) **of Mercury** (Hg). An engine in good mechanical condition will run with high manifold vacuum. Manifold vacuum is developed

FIGURE 8-17 Using a vacuum hose and a test light to ground one cylinder at a time on a distributorless ignition system works on all types of ignition systems and provides a method for grounding out one cylinder at a time without fear of damaging any component.

FIGURE 8-18 A typical vacuum gauge showing about 19 in. Hg of vacuum at idle—well within the normal reading of 17 to 21 in. Hg.

by the pistons as they move down on the intake stroke to draw the charge from the throttle body and intake manifold. Air to refill the manifold comes past the throttle plate into the manifold. Vacuum will increase anytime the engine turns faster or has better cylinder sealing while the throttle plate remains in a fixed position. Manifold vacuum will decrease when the engine turns more slowly or when the cylinders no longer do an efficient job of pumping.

Cranking Vacuum Test

Measuring the amount of manifold vacuum during cranking is a quick and easy test to determine if the piston rings and valves are properly sealing. (For accurate results, the engine should be warm and the throttle closed.)

Step 1 Disable the ignition.
Step 2 Connect the vacuum gauge to a manifold vacuum source.
Step 3 Crank the engine while observing the vacuum gauge.

Cranking vacuum should be higher than 2.5 inches of Mercury. (Normal cranking vacuum is 3 to 6 inches Hg.) If it is lower than 2.5 inches Hg, then the following could be the cause:

- Too slow a cranking speed
- Worn piston rings
- Leaking valves
- Excessive amounts of air bypassing the throttle plate (This could give a false low vacuum reading. Common sources include a throttle plate partially open or a high-performance camshaft with excessive overlap.)

Idle Vacuum Test

An engine in proper condition should idle with a steady vacuum between 17 and 21 inches Hg. See Figure 8-18.

NOTE: Engine vacuum readings vary with altitude. A reduction of 1 inch Hg per 1000 feet (300 meters) of altitude should be subtracted from the expected values if testing a vehicle above 1000 feet (300 meters).

Low and Steady Vacuum

If the vacuum is lower than normal, yet the gauge reading is steady, the most common causes include:

- Retarded ignition timing
- Retarded cam timing (check timing chain for excessive slack or timing belt for proper installation; see Figure 8-19).

Fluctuating Vacuum

If the needle drops, then returns to a normal reading, then drops again, and again returns, this indicates a sticking valve. A common cause of sticking valves is lack of lubrication of the valve stems. See Figures 8-20 through 8-29.

HINT: A common trick that some technicians use is to squirt some automatic transmission fluid (ATF) down the throttle body or into the air inlet of a warm engine. Often the idle quality improves and normal vacuum gauge readings are restored. The use of ATF does create excessive exhaust smoke for a short time, but it should not harm oxygen sensors or catalytic converters.

If the vacuum gauge fluctuates above and below a center point, burned valves or weak valve springs may be indicated. If the fluctuation is slow and steady, unequal fuel mixture could be the cause.

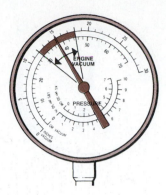

FIGURE 8-21 A gauge reading with the needle fluctuating 3 to 9 in. Hg below normal often indicates a vacuum leak in the intake system.

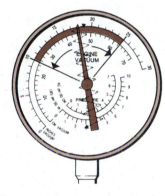

FIGURE 8-22 A leaking head gasket can cause the needle to vibrate as it moves through a range from below to above normal.

FIGURE 8-19 An engine in good mechanical condition should produce 17 to 21 in. Hg of vacuum at idle at sea level.

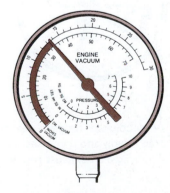

FIGURE 8-20 A steady but low reading could indicate retarded valve or ignition timing.

FIGURE 8-23 An oscillating needle 1 or 2 in. Hg below normal could indicate an incorrect air-fuel mixture (either too rich or too lean).

FIGURE 8-24   A rapidly vibrating needle at idle that becomes steady as engine speed is increased indicates worn valve guides.

FIGURE 8-27   A steady needle reading that drops 2 or 3 in. Hg when the engine speed is increased slightly above idle indicates that the ignition timing is retarded.

FIGURE 8-25   If the needle drops 1 or 2 in. Hg from the normal reading, an engine valve is burned or not seating properly.

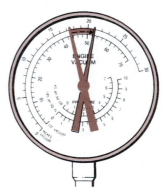

FIGURE 8-28   A steady needle reading that rises 2 or 3 in. Hg when the engine speed is increased slightly above idle indicates that the ignition timing is advanced.

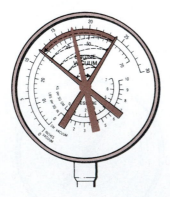

FIGURE 8-26   Weak valve springs will produce a normal reading at idle, but as engine speed increases, the needle will fluctuate rapidly between 12 and 24 in. Hg.

FIGURE 8-29   A needle that drops to near zero when the engine is accelerated rapidly and then rises slightly to a reading below normal indicates an exhaust restriction.

EXHAUST RESTRICTION TEST

If the exhaust system is restricted, the engine will be low on power, yet smooth. Common causes of restricted exhaust include the following:

- **Clogged catalytic converter.** Always check the ignition system for faults that could cause excessive amounts of unburned fuel to be exhausted. Excessive unburned fuel can overheat the catalytic converter and cause the beads or structure of the converter to fuse together, creating the restriction. A defective fuel delivery system could also cause excessive unburned fuel to be dumped into the converter.
- **Clogged or restricted muffler.** This can cause low power. Often a defective catalytic converter will shed particles that can clog a muffler. Broken internal baffles can also restrict exhaust flow.
- **Damaged or defective piping.** This can reduce the power of any engine. Some exhaust pipe is constructed with double walls, and the inside pipe can collapse and form a restriction that is not visible on the outside of the exhaust pipe.

TESTING BACK PRESSURE WITH A VACUUM GAUGE

A vacuum gauge can be used to measure manifold vacuum at a high idle (2000 to 2500 RPM). If the exhaust system is restricted, pressure increases in the exhaust system. This pressure is called **back pressure.** Manifold vacuum will drop gradually if the engine is kept at a constant speed if the exhaust is restricted.

The reason the vacuum will drop is that all exhaust leaving the engine at the higher engine speed cannot get through the restriction. After a short time (within 1 minute), the exhaust tends to "pile up" above the restriction and eventually remains in the cylinder of the engine at the end of the exhaust stroke. Therefore, at the beginning of the intake stroke, when the piston traveling downward should be lowering the pressure (raising the vacuum) in the intake manifold, the extra exhaust in the cylinder *lowers* the normal vacuum. If the exhaust restriction is severe enough, the vehicle can become undriveable because cylinder filling cannot occur except at idle.

TESTING BACK PRESSURE WITH A PRESSURE GAUGE

Exhaust system back pressure can be measured directly by installing a pressure gauge into an exhaust opening. This can be accomplished in one of the following ways:

- **With an oxygen sensor.** Use a back pressure gauge and adapter or remove the inside of an old discarded oxygen sensor and thread in an adapter to convert to a vacuum or pressure gauge.

NOTE: An adapter can be easily made by inserting a metal tube or pipe. A short section of brake line works great. The pipe can be brazed to the oxygen sensor housing or it can be glued in with epoxy. An 18-millimeter compression gauge adapter can also be adapted to fit into the oxygen sensor opening. See Figure 8-30.

- **With the exhaust gas recirculation (EGR) valve.** Remove the EGR valve and fabricate a plate to connect to a pressure gauge.
- **With the air-injection reaction (AIR) check valve.** Remove the check valve from the exhaust tubes leading down to the exhaust manifold. Use a rubber cone with a tube inside to seal against the exhaust tube. Connect the tube to a pressure gauge.

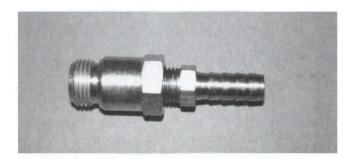

FIGURE 8-30 A back pressure testing tool can be assembled by using an 18-mm air-holding fitting and a ¼-inch male barb fitting. Most oxygen sensors use an 18-mm thread and the barb fitting can be used to attach a rubber hose leading to a pressure gauge. Both of these low-cost parts are available at most automotive parts stores.

At idle, the maximum back pressure should be less than 1.5 psi (10 kPa), and it should be less than 2.5 psi (15 kPa) at 2500 RPM.

TIMING CHAIN SLACK DIAGNOSIS

Engines with high mileage often have timing chains with slack that is excessive for proper operation. As the timing chain stretches, the cam retards in relation to the position of the crankshaft and pistons. Because the camshaft operates the valves, this also causes the valves to open and close later in the stroke than they were designed to do. (This discussion does *not* involve engines equipped with timing *belts*.) This retarded or late closing of the intake valve and late closing of the exhaust valve tends to lower available power at low speeds. However, the retarded cam timing does tend to slightly improve high-engine speed performance. A typical comment from an owner of a vehicle with excessive timing chain stretch is that the engine performs best after "getting it going faster."

To determine the condition of a timing chain, follow this simple procedure:

Step 1   With the ignition off, rotate the engine by hand clockwise as viewed from the front or accessory belt end (nonprincipal end) until the timing mark aligns with top dead center (TDC). See Figure 8-31. If the crankshaft pulley does not have any timing marks, make a mark that can be seen on the pulley and the engine.

NOTE: Do not turn the engine counterclockwise if turned past TDC! This will loosen the tension on the chain, and the results of the test will not be accurate. If the engine is accidentally turned beyond TDC, continue clockwise rotation until the timing mark once again lines up with TDC.

Step 2   Remove the distributor cap.

NOTE: If the engine is not equipped with a distributor, remove the oil filler cap to gain access to the rocker arms to detect movement.

Step 3   Slowly rotate the engine counterclockwise as viewed from the front of the engine (nonprincipal end) while observing for any movement of the distributor rotor.

Step 4   As soon as the rotor starts to move, note the distance of the timing mark from TDC.

A distance of less than 5 degrees is normal and acceptable, especially for a high-mileage engine. A distance of 5 to 8 degrees is acceptable for a high-mileage engine, but not acceptable for a low-mileage engine. Very little change in the operation of the engine would be noticed if the timing chain were replaced. If the distance is over 8 degrees, the timing chain definitely requires replacement for proper engine operation and to prevent severe engine damage that could occur if the timing chain and/or gear should fail during engine operation.

NOTE: Eight degrees usually translates to about 0.5 inch (13 mm) of slack as measured at the crankshaft pulley. See Figure 8-32.

FIGURE 8-32 Excessive timing chain wear was observed on a Ford V-8 (over 10 degrees of slack). After replacing the timing chain, the real cause of the slack was finally discovered— a worn distributor gear.

FIGURE 8-31 Typical timing mark on the crankshaft pulley.

DIAGNOSING HEAD GASKET FAILURE

Several items can be used to help diagnose a head gasket failure:

- **Exhaust gas analyzer.** With the radiator cap removed, place the probe from the exhaust analyzer above the radiator filler neck. If the HC reading increases, the exhaust (unburned hydrocarbons) is getting into the coolant from the combustion chamber.
- **Chemical test.** A chemical tester using blue liquid is also available. The liquid turns yellow if combustion gases are present in the coolant. See Figure 8-33.
- **Bubbles in the coolant.** Remove the coolant pump belt to prevent pump operation. Remove the radiator cap and start the engine. If bubbles appear in the coolant before it begins to boil, a defective head gasket or cracked cylinder head is indicated.
- **Excessive exhaust steam.** If excessive water or steam is observed coming from the tailpipe, this means that coolant is getting into the combustion chamber from a defective head gasket or a cracked head. If there is leakage between cylinders, the engine usually misfires and a power balancer test and/or compression test can be used to confirm the problem.

If any of the preceding indicators of head gasket failure occur, remove the cylinder head(s) and check all of the following:

1. Head gasket
2. Sealing surfaces—for warpage
3. Castings—for cracks

FIGURE 8-33 A typical combustion leak detector which uses color-changing indicating fluid.

HINT: A leaking thermal vacuum valve can cause symptoms similar to those of a defective head gasket. Most thermal vacuum valves thread into a coolant passage, and they often leak only after they get hot.

DASH WARNING LIGHTS

Most vehicles are equipped with several dash warning lights often called "telltale" or "idiot" lights. These lights are often the only warning a driver receives that there may be engine problems. A summary of typical dash warning lights and their meanings follows.

Oil (Engine) Light

The red oil light indicates that the engine oil pressure is too low [usually lights when oil pressure is 4 to 7 psi (20 to 50 kPa)]. Normal oil pressure should be 10 to 60 psi (70 to 400 kPa) or 10 psi per 1000 engine RPM.

When this light comes on, the driver should shut off the engine immediately and check the oil level and condition for possible dilution with gasoline caused by a fuel system fault. If the oil level is okay, then there is a possible serious engine problem or a possible defective oil pressure sending (sender) unit. The automotive technician should always check the oil pressure using a reliable mechanical oil pressure gauge if low oil pressure is suspected.

NOTE: Some automobile manufacturers combine the dash warning lights for oil pressure and coolant temperature into one light, usually labeled "engine." Therefore, when the engine light comes on, the technician should check for possible coolant temperature and/or oil pressure problems.

Coolant Temperature Light

Most vehicles are equipped with a coolant temperature gauge or dash warning light. The warning light may be labeled "coolant," "hot," or "temperature." If the coolant temperature warning light comes on during driving, this usually indicates that the coolant temperature is above a safe level, or above about 250°F (120°C). Normal coolant temperature should be about 200° to 220°F (90° to 105°C).

If the coolant temperature light comes on during driving, the following steps should be followed to prevent possible engine damage:

1. Turn off the air conditioning and turn on the heater. The heater will help get rid of some of the heat in the cooling system.
2. Raise the engine speed in neutral or park to increase the circulation of coolant through the radiator.
3. If possible, turn the engine off and allow it to cool (this may take over an hour).
4. Do not continue driving with the coolant temperature light on (or the gauge reading in the red warning section or above 260°F) or serious engine damage may result.

NOTE: If the engine does not feel or smell hot, it is possible that the problem is a faulty coolant temperature sensor or gauge.

Charge Light

The red charge warning light indicates that the charging system is not operating. The charge light may also be labeled "gen" or "alt" (alternator). Because most batteries are capable of supplying the electrical needs of the vehicle for a short time, it is not necessary to stop the engine if this warning light comes on.

If, however, the charging system is not repaired or serviced, the engine will eventually cease running because the ignition system, which ignites the spark plugs, requires a certain level of voltage to operate (usually a minimum of 9 volts).

Computer Warning Light

Most vehicles with an engine control computer use dash warning lights to warn the driver that some computer sensor, actuator, or engine parameter is not within acceptable range.

The computer dash warning light called a malfunction indicator lamp (MIL) is usually orange in color and indicates a less than serious problem, whereas some computer warning lights may be red, indicating more serious engine problems. For example, some computer systems monitor oil pressure versus engine RPM, battery voltage, and coolant temperature. The computer warning lights might be labeled

Check Engine
Check Engine Soon
Check Engine Now
Power Loss
Power Limited

If an orange engine computer light comes on, continue driving and check for any stored trouble codes as per the vehicle manufacturer's procedures. If a *red* engine computer light comes on, it is best to stop the engine and check all vital engine systems before continuing operation. Follow the manufacturer's recommended procedures for determining the cause and corrective action required.

Maintenance Reminder Light

Many vehicles are equipped with a maintenance reminder light notifying the driver that some service is required.

Routine service that should be done when the service reminder light comes on usually include an oil change plus other items recommended by the vehicle manufacturer. These additional items could include:

- Air filter replacement
- Coolant change
- Tire rotation

NOTE: The maintenance reminder light and the check engine light are often confusing to drivers. Before attempting service work, make certain that the service is appropriate for the warning light.

◄ GURU TIP ►

Carbon on valves will cause stalling after start and poor operation when the engine is cold.

◄ GURU TIP ►

If a misfire goes away with propane added to the air inlet, suspect a lean injector.

PS 3-1 Always use a vacuum "T" at the end of the vacuum gauge to make sure that the gauge is measuring the engine as it is normally operating. The gauge being used is from an old engine analyzer.

PS 3-2 Locate a good manifold vacuum source. A common location that is often easy to access is the vacuum line at the fuel-pressure regulator.

PS 3-3 Be sure all vacuum hoses fit snugly onto the fittings.

PS 3-4 Start the engine and observe the vacuum gauge. The vacuum at idle (engine warm) should be 17 to 21 in. Hg (at sea level) and steady. This reading of slightly over 20 in. Hg indicates that the condition of the engine is sound.

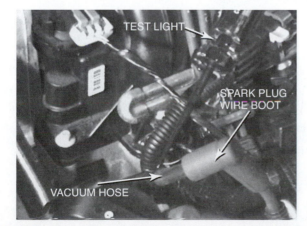

PS 3-5 An ignition misfire will often cause the vacuum gauge needle to occasionally drop less than 1 in. Hg. A test light is being used to ground out a spark plug wire to show how a vacuum gauge reacts to an ignition misfire. (By attaching a 2-inch length of vacuum hose between the coil and a plug wire, a test light is used to ground out the spark.)

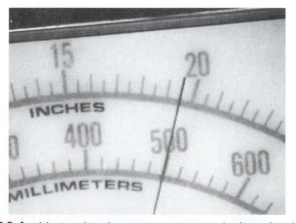

PS 3-6 Notice that the vacuum gauge reads about 1 in. Hg lower than normal every time the plug was grounded.

PS 3-7 An engine mechanical fault such as a sticking valve or broken valve spring will cause the vacuum gauge to drop more than 1 in. Hg and fluctuate. A low vacuum reading can also be caused by a restricted intake or exhaust system. Placing a hand partially over the intake throttle plate causes the vacuum to decrease.

PS 3-8 A lower-than-normal reading is usually a result of retarded ignition or valve timing. A misadjusted distributor or a worn (stretched) timing chain can cause both the valve and the ignition timing to be retarded. An incorrectly installed timing belt could also cause the vacuum to be steady, but lower than normal.

PS 3-9 Rapidly accelerating the engine (or driving the vehicle at wide-open throttle) should cause the vacuum gauge to read zero.

PS 3-10 If greater than 1 in. Hg of vacuum is observed during rapid acceleration, look for a restricted intake system.

PS 3-11 During deceleration, the vacuum should increase above the idle reading. Just remember that a vacuum gauge senses engine load. Light load (such as deceleration) is indicated by a high vacuum reading whereas a heavy load (such as driving at wide-open throttle) results in a very low or zero reading.

PS 3-12 After testing, be sure to reinstall the vacuum connector at the fuel pressure regulator and keep the T fitting attached to the hose of the vacuum gauge for future use.

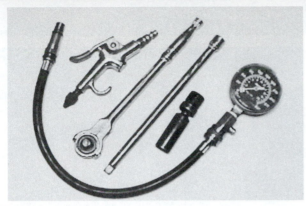

PS 4-1 The tools and equipment needed to perform a compression test include a compression gauge, an air nozzle, and the socket ratchets and extensions that may be necessary to remove the spark plugs from the engine.

PS 4-2 To prevent ignition and fuel-injection operation while the engine is being cranked, remove both the fuel-injection fuse and the ignition fuse. If the fuses cannot be removed, disconnect the wiring connectors for the injectors and the ignition system.

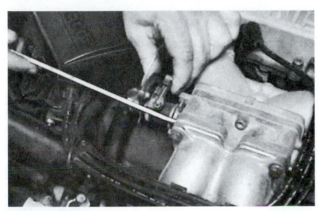

PS 4-3 Block open the throttle (and choke, if the engine is equipped with a carburetor). Here a screwdriver is being used to wedge the throttle linkage open. Keeping the throttle open ensures that enough air will be drawn into the engine so that the compression test results will be accurate.

PS 4-4 Before removing the spark plugs, use an air nozzle to blow away any dirt that may be around the spark plug. This step helps prevent debris from getting into the engine when the spark plugs are removed.

PS 4-5 Remove all of the spark plugs. Be sure to mark the spark plug wires so that they can be reinstalled onto the correct spark plugs after the compression test has been performed.

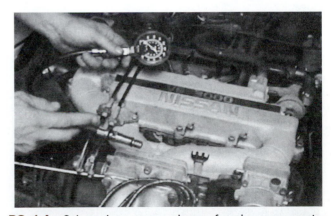

PS 4-6 Select the proper adapter for the compression gauge. The threads on the adapter should match those on the spark plug.

PHOTO SEQUENCE   Compression Test—*Continued*

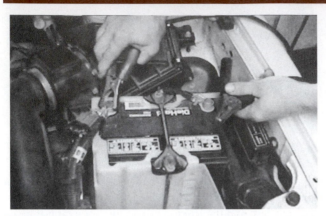

PS 4-7   If necessary, connect a battery charger to the battery before starting the compression test. It is important that consistent cranking speed be available for each cylinder being tested.

PS 4-8   Have an assistant use the ignition key to crank the engine while you are observing the compression gauge. Make a note of the reading on the gauge after the first "puff," which indicates the first compression stroke that occurred on that cylinder as the engine was being rotated. An engine with good piston rings should indicate at least one-half the final reading on the first puff. If the first puff reading is low and the reading gradually increases with each puff, weak or worn piston rings may be indicated.

PS 4-9   After the engine has been cranked for four "puffs," stop cranking the engine and observe the compression gauge.

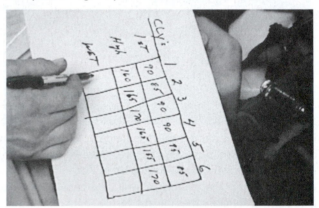

PS 4-10   Record the first puff and this final reading for each cylinder. The final readings should all be within 20% of each other.

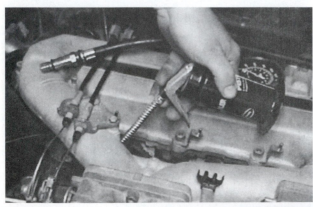

PS 4-11   If a cylinder(s) is lower than most of the others, use an oil can and squirt two squirts of engine oil into the cylinder and repeat the compression test. This is called performing a wet compression test.

PS 4-12   If the gauge reading is now much higher than the first test results, then the cause of the low compression is due to worn or defective piston rings. The oil in the cylinder temporarily seals the rings which causes the higher reading.

PHOTO SEQUENCE Oil Pressure Measurement

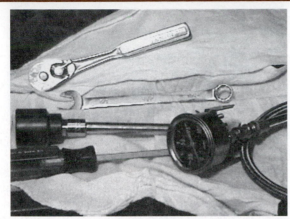

PS 5-1 The tools needed to measure engine oil pressure include an oil pressure gauge, oil pressure sending unit socket, and a ratchet with an extension.

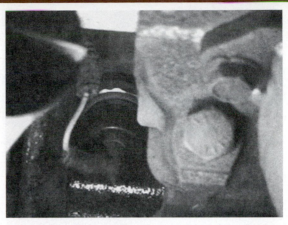

PS 5-2 To measure the oil pressure, the oil pressure warning sending unit has to be located. On this Lincoln, the oil pressure sending unit is located near the oil filter with one wire attached that leads to the dash warning light.

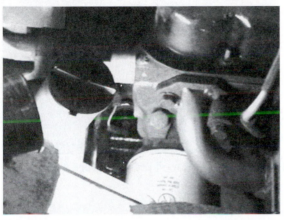

PS 5-3 To gain access to the oil pressure sending unit, the air cleaner housing duct was removed.

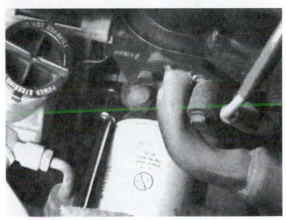

PS 5-4 Be sure the ignition is off before using an oil pressure sending unit socket (or a 1 1/16-in., 6-point socket) to remove the oil pressure sending unit.

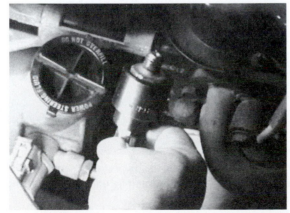

PS 5-5 The original sending unit had sealant around the threads to prevent oil from leaking from around the threads.

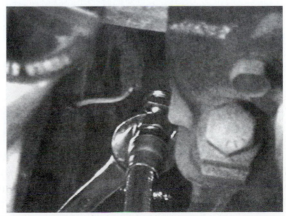

PS 5-6 Attach the threaded end of the oil pressure gauge into the threaded opening where the oil pressure sending unit was removed.

PS 5-7 Be sure that the gauge is out of the way of any moving parts and then start the engine.

PS 5-8 Observe the oil pressure gauge. This is normal oil pressure for a cold engine. Normal oil pressure should be about 10 psi per 1000 RPM.

PS 5-9 After allowing the engine to reach normal operating temperature and observing that the oil pressure is within the normal range at idle and at higher engine speeds, the ignition key can be turned off.

PS 5-10 Remove the oil pressure gauge assembly.

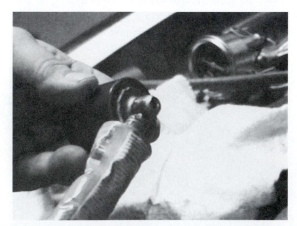

PS 5-11 Apply sealant to the threads of the oil pressure sending unit. Most vehicle manufacturers warn against using Teflon® tape because the threads can cut through the tape and cause strips of the tape to travel through the oil system, possibly causing a partial blockage which can create a major engine mechanical fault.

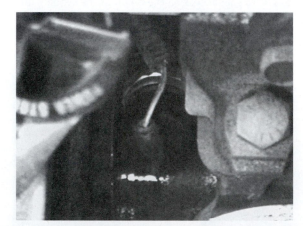

PS 5-12 After threading the oil pressure sending unit back into the block, reattach the sending unit wire. Start the engine and check for leaks.

SUMMARY

1. The first step in diagnosing engine condition is to perform a thorough visual inspection, including a check of oil and coolant levels and condition.
2. Oil leaks can be found by using a white powder or a fluorescent dye and a black light.
3. Many engine-related problems make a characteristic noise.
4. Oil analysis by an engineering laboratory can reveal engine problems by measuring the amount of dissolved metals in the oil.
5. A compression test can be used to test the condition of valves and piston rings.
6. A cylinder leakage test fills the cylinder with compressed air, and the gauge indicates the percentage of leakage.
7. A cylinder balance test indicates whether all cylinders are working.
8. Testing engine vacuum is another procedure that can help the service technician determine engine condition.
9. If the timing chain has worn and stretched, the engine cannot produce normal power.
10. Exhaust analysis testing is another diagnostic tool that can tell the service technician whether the engine is performing correctly and efficiently.

REVIEW QUESTIONS

1. Describe four visual checks that should be performed on an engine if a mechanical malfunction is suspected.
2. List three simple items that could cause excessive oil consumption.
3. List three simple items that could cause engine noises.
4. Describe how to perform a compression test and how to determine what is wrong with an engine based on a compression test result.
5. Describe the cylinder leakage test.
6. Describe how a vacuum gauge would indicate if the valves were sticking in their guides.
7. Describe the test procedure for determining if the exhaust system is restricted (clogged) using a vacuum gauge.

ASE CERTIFICATION-TYPE QUESTIONS

1. Technician A says that the paper test could detect a burned valve. Technician B says that a grayish white stain on the engine could be a coolant leak. Which technician is correct?
   a. Technician A only
   b. Technician B only
   c. Both Technicians A and B
   d. Neither Technician A nor B

2. Two technicians are discussing oil leaks. Technician A says that an oil leak can be found using a fluorescent dye in the oil with a black light to check for leaks. Technician B says that a white spray powder can be used to locate oil leaks. Which technician is correct?
   a. Technician A only
   b. Technician B only
   c. Both Technicians A and B
   d. Neither Technician A nor B

3. An increase in engine oil viscosity can be due to _____.
   a. Wear metals in the oil
   b. Fuel dilution of the oil
   c. A clogged air filter
   d. All of the above

4. Antifreeze in the engine oil can cause _____.
   a. The oil to become thinner (decrease viscosity)
   b. The oil to become thicker (increase viscosity)
   c. The oil to congeal
   d. Both b and c

5. A smoothly operating engine depends on _____.
   a. High compression on most cylinders
   b. Equal compression between cylinders
   c. Cylinder compression levels above 100 psi (700 kPa) and within 70 psi (500 kPa) of each other
   d. Compression levels below 100 psi (700 kPa) on most cylinders

6. A good reading for a cylinder leakage test would be _____.

   a. Within 20% between cylinders

   b. All cylinders below 20% leakage

   c. All cylinders above 20% leakage

   d. All cylinders above 70% leakage and within 7% of each other

7. Technician A says that during a power balance test, the cylinder that causes the biggest RPM drop is the weak cylinder. Technician B says that if one spark plug wire is grounded out and the engine speed does not drop, a weak or dead cylinder is indicated. Which technician is correct?

   a. Technician A only

   b. Technician B only

   c. Both Technicians A and B

   d. Neither Technician A nor B

8. *Cranking* vacuum should be _____.

   a. 2.5 inches Hg or higher

   b. Over 25 inches Hg

   c. 17 to 21 inches Hg

   d. 6 to 16 inches Hg

9. Technician A says that a worn (stretched) timing chain and worn gears will cause the valve and ignition timing to be retarded. Technician B says that if the timing chain slack is over 8 degrees, the timing chain and gears should be replaced. Which technician is correct?

   a. Technician A only

   b. Technician B only

   c. Both Technicians A and B

   d. Neither Technician A nor B

10. The low oil pressure warning light usually comes on _____.

   a. Whenever an oil change is required

   b. Whenever oil pressure drops dangerously low (4 to 7 psi)

   c. Whenever the oil filter bypass valve opens

   d. Whenever the oil filter antidrain back valve opens

◀ Chapter 9 ▶

ELECTRICAL AND ELECTRONIC FUNDAMENTALS

OBJECTIVES

After studying Chapter 9, the reader should be able to:

1. Prepare for ASE Engine Performance (A8) certification test content area "F" (Engine Electrical Systems Diagnosis and Repair).
2. Define electricity.
3. Explain the units of electrical measurement.
4. Discuss the relationship among volts, amperes, and ohms.
5. Explain how magnetism is used in automotive electrical system applications.
6. Explain voltage drops.
7. Discuss where various electronic and semiconductor devices are used in vehicles.

The electrical system is one of the most important systems in a vehicle today. Every year more and more components and systems use electricity.

ELECTRICITY

Electricity is the movement of electrons from one atom to another. An atom is the smallest unit of all matter in the universe. See Figure 9-1.

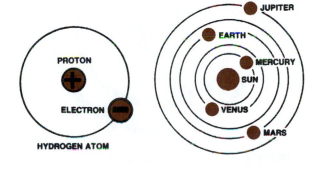

FIGURE 9-1 In an atom (left), electrons orbit protons in the nucleus just as planets orbit the sun in our solar system (right).

Positive and Negative Charges

The parts of the atom have different charges. The orbiting electrons are negatively charged, while the protons are positively charged. Positive charges are indicated by the "plus" sign (+), negative charges by the "minus" sign (−), as shown in Figure 9-2. These same + and − signs are used to identify parts of an electrical circuit. Neutrons have no charge at all. They are neutral. In a normal, or balanced, atom, the number of negative particles equals the number of positive particles. That is, there are as many electrons as there are protons. See

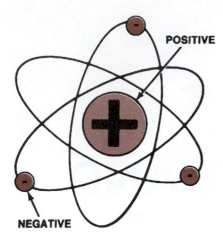

FIGURE 9-2 The nucleus of an atom has a positive ($+$) charge and the surrounding electrons have a negative ($-$) charge.

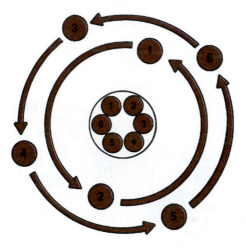

FIGURE 9-3 A balanced atom.

Figure 9-3. The number of neutrons varies according to the type of atom.

The charges within an atom behave like the poles of a magnet. An ordinary magnet has two ends, or poles. One end is called the south pole, and the other is called the north pole. If two magnets are brought close to each other with like poles together (south to south or north to north), the magnets will push each other apart. This is because like poles repel each other. If the opposite poles of the magnets are brought close to each other, south to north, the magnets will snap together. This is because unlike poles attract each other.

The positive and negative charges within an atom are like the north and south poles of a magnet. Charges that are alike will repel each other, similar to the poles of a magnet. See Figure 9-4. That is why the negatively-

FIGURE 9-4 Unlike charges attract and like charges repel.

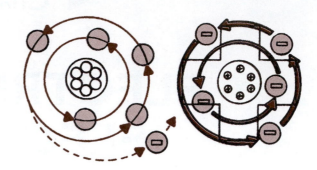

FIGURE 9-5 An unbalanced, positively charged atom (ion) will attract electrons from neighboring atoms.

charged electrons continue to orbit around the positively-charged protons. They are attracted and held by the opposite charge of the protons. The electrons keep moving in orbit because they repel each other.

When an atom loses electrons, it becomes unbalanced. It will have more protons than electrons and, therefore, will have a positive charge. If it gains more electrons than protons, the atom will be negatively charged. When an atom is not balanced, it becomes a charged particle called an **ion.** Ions try to regain their balance of equal protons and electrons. They do this by exchanging electrons with neighboring atoms. See Figure 9-5. This is the flow of electric current or electricity.

Electron Shells

Electrons orbit around the nucleus in definite paths. These paths form **shells,** like concentric rings, around the nucleus. Only a specific number of electrons can orbit within each shell. If there are too many electrons for the first and closest shell to the nucleus, the others will orbit in additional shells until all electrons have an orbit within a shell. There can be as many as seven shells around a single nucleus. See Figure 9-6.

Free and Bound Electrons

The outermost electron shell, or ring, is the most important to our study of electricity. It is called the **valence ring.** The number of electrons in this ring determines the valence of the atom, and indicates its capacity to combine with other atoms.

If the valence ring of an atom has three or fewer electrons in it, the ring has room for more. The electrons

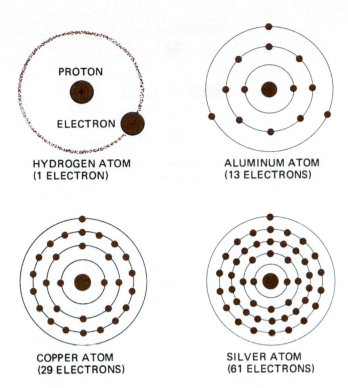

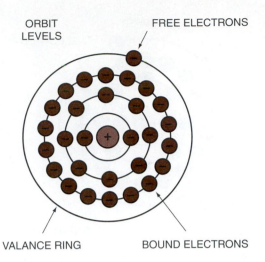

FIGURE 9-6 The hydrogen atom is the simplest atom, with only one proton, one neutron, and one electron. More complex elements contain higher numbers of protons, neutrons, and electrons.

there are held very loosely, and it is easy for a drifting electron to join the valence ring and push another electron away. These loosely held electrons are called **free electrons.** When the valence ring has five or more electrons in it, it is fairly full. The electrons are held tightly, and it is hard for a drifting electron to push its way into the valence ring. These tightly held electrons are called **bound electrons.** See Figures 9-7 and 9-8.

The movement of these drifting electrons is called current. Current can be small, with only a few electrons moving, or it can be large, with a tremendous number of electrons moving. However, current only flows in a conductor. Electric current is the controlled, directed movement of electrons from atom to atom within a conductor.

Conductors

Conductors are materials with fewer than four electrons in their atom's outer orbit. See Figure 9-9. Copper is an excellent conductor because it has only one electron in its outer orbit. This orbit is far enough away from the nucleus of the copper atom that the pull or force holding the outermost electron in orbit is relatively weak. See Figure 9-10. Copper is the conductor most

FIGURE 9-7 As the number of electrons increases, they occupy increasing energy levels that are further from the center of the atom.

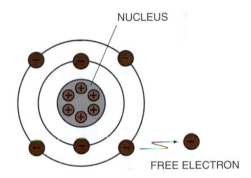

FIGURE 9-8 Electrons in the outer orbit, or shell, can often be drawn away from the atom and become free electrons.

FIGURE 9-9 A conductor is any element that has one to three electrons in its outer orbit.

used in vehicles because the price of copper is reasonable compared to the relative cost of other conductors with similar properties.

Insulators

Insulators are materials with more than four electrons in their atom's outer orbit. Because they have more than

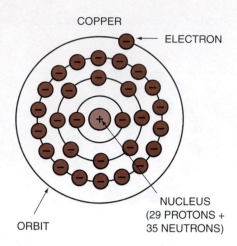

COPPER

ELECTRON

NUCLEUS
(29 PROTONS +
35 NEUTRONS)

ORBIT

FIGURE 9-10   Copper is an excellent conductor of electricity because it has just one electron in its outer orbit, making it easy to be knocked out of its orbit and flow to other nearby atoms causing electron flow, which is the definition of electricity.

INSULATORS

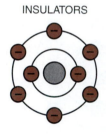

FIGURE 9-11   Insulators are elements with five to eight electrons in the outer orbit.

four electrons in their outer orbit, it becomes easier for these materials to acquire (gain) electrons than to release electrons. See Figure 9-11. Examples of insulators include plastics, wood, glass, rubber, ceramics (spark plugs), and varnish for covering (insulating) copper wires in alternators and starters.

Semiconductors

Materials with exactly four electrons in their outer orbit are neither conductors nor insulators and are called *semiconductor* materials. See Figure 9-12.

How Electrons Move Through a Conductor

If an outside source of power, such as a battery, is connected to the ends of a conductor, a positive charge (lack of electrons) is placed on one end of the conduc-

SEMICONDUCTORS

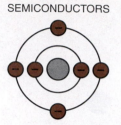

FIGURE 9-12   Semiconductor elements contain exactly four electrons in the outer orbit.

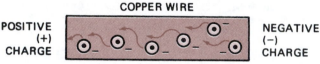

COPPER WIRE

POSITIVE
(+)
CHARGE

NEGATIVE
(−)
CHARGE

FIGURE 9-13   Current electricity is the movement of electrons through a conductor.

tor and a negative charge is placed on the opposite end of the conductor. The negative charge will repel the free electrons from the atoms of the conductor, whereas the positive charge on the opposite end of the conductor will attract electrons. As a result of this attraction of opposite charges and repulsion of like charges, electrons will flow through the conductor. See Figure 9-13.

Conventional Theory versus Electron Theory

It was once thought that electricity had only one charge and moved from positive to negative. This theory of the flow of electricity through a conductor is called the **conventional theory** of current flow. See Figure 9-14. After the discovery of the electron and its negative charge came the **electron theory,** which states that there is electron flow from negative to positive. Most automotive applications use the conventional theory. This book will use the conventional theory unless stated otherwise.

Amperes

The **ampere** is the unit used throughout the world as a measure of the amount of current flow. When 6.28 billion billion electrons (the name for this large number of electrons is a **coulomb**) move past a certain point in one second, this represents one ampere of current. See Figure 9-15. The ampere, named for the French electrician André Marie Ampére (1775–1836), is the electrical unit for the amount of electron flow just as "gallons per

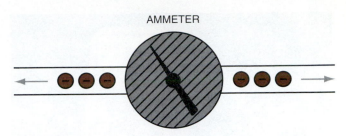

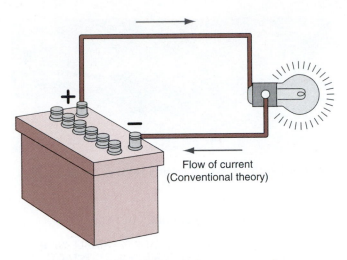

FIGURE 9-14   Conventional theory states that current flows through a circuit from positive (+) to negative (−). Automotive electricity uses the conventional theory in all electrical diagrams and schematics.

FIGURE 9-16   An ammeter is installed in the path of the electrons similar to a water meter used to measure the flow of water in gallons per minute. The ammeter displays current flow in amperes.

FIGURE 9-15   One ampere is the movement of 1 coulomb (6.28 billion billion electrons) past a point in 1 second.

FIGURE 9-17   Voltage is the electrical pressure that causes the electrons to flow through a conductor.

minute" is the unit that can be used to measure the quantity of water flow. The conventional abbreviations and measurement for amperes are summarized as follows:

1. The ampere is the unit of measurement for the amount of current flow.
2. *A* and *amps* are acceptable abbreviations for *amperes.*
3. The capital letter *I,* for *intensity,* is used in mathematical calculations to represent amperes.
4. Amperes are measured by an **ammeter** (not ampmeter). See Figure 9-16.

Volts

The **volt** is the unit of measurement for electrical pressure. It is named for Alessandro Volta (1745–1827), an Italian physicist. The comparable unit using water as an example would be pounds per square inch (psi). It is possible to have very high pressure (volts) and low or no water flow (amperes). It is also possible to have high water flow (amperes) and low pressure (volts). Voltage is also called **electrical potential,** because if there is

voltage present in a conductor, there is a potential (possibility) for current flow. Voltage does *not* flow through conductors, but voltage does cause current (in amperes) to flow through conductors. See Figure 9-17. The conventional abbreviations and measurement for voltage are as follows:

1. The volt is the unit of measurement for the amount of electrical pressure.
2. **Electromotive force,** abbreviated **EMF,** is another way of indicating voltage.
3. *V* is the generally accepted abbreviation for *volts.*
4. The symbol used in calculations is *E,* for *electromotive force.*
5. Volts are measured by a **voltmeter.** See Figure 9-18.

Ohms

Resistance to the flow of current through a conductor is measured in units called **ohms,** named after the German physicist Georg Simon Ohm (1787–1854). The resistance to the flow of free electrons through a conductor results from the countless collisions the electrons cause within the atoms of the conductor. See

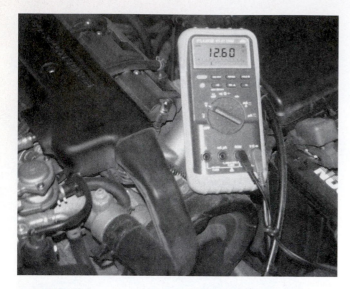

FIGURE 9-18 A digital multimeter set to read DC volts and being used to test the voltage of a vehicle battery. Most multimeters can also measure resistance (ohms) and current flow (amperes).

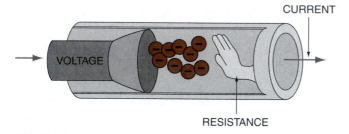

FIGURE 9-19 Resistance to the flow of electrons through a conductor is measured in ohms.

Figure 9-19. The conventional abbreviations and measurement for resistance are as follows:

1. The ohm is the unit of measurement for electrical resistance.
2. The symbol for ohms is Ω (Greek capital letter omega), the last letter of the Greek alphabet.
3. The symbol used in calculations is R, for *resistance*.
4. Ohms are measured with an **ohmmeter.**

Resistors

Resistance is the opposition to current flow. Resistors represent an electrical load, or resistance, to current flow. Most electrical and electronic devices use resistors of specific values to limit and control the flow of current. Resistors can be made from carbon or from

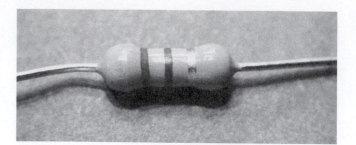

FIGURE 9-20 A typical carbon resistor.

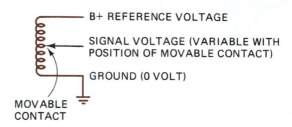

FIGURE 9-21 A three-wire variable resistor is called a potentiometer.

other materials that restrict the flow of electricity and are available in various sizes and resistance values. Most resistors have a series of painted color bands around them. These color bands are coded to indicate the degree of resistance. See Figure 9-20.

Variable Resistors

Two basic types of mechanically operated variable resistors are used in automotive applications. A **potentiometer** is a three-terminal variable resistor where the majority of the current flow travels through the resistance of the unit and a wiper contact provides a variable voltage output. See Figure 9-21.

Potentiometers are most commonly used as throttle-position (TP) sensors on computer-equipped engines.

CIRCUITS

A **circuit** is a path that electrons travel from a power source (such as a battery) through a resistance or load (such as a light bulb) and back to the power source. It is called a *circuit* because the current must start and finish at the same place (power source). See Figure 9-22.

For *any* electrical circuit to work at all, it must be continuous from the battery (power), through all the wires and components, and back to the battery (ground). A circuit that is continuous throughout is said to have **continuity.**

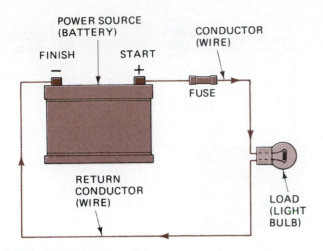

FIGURE 9-22   All complete circuits must have a power source, a power path, protection (fuse), an electrical load (light bulb in this case), and a return path back to the power source.

Parts of a Complete Circuit

Every **complete circuit** contains the following parts:

1. A **power source**, such as a vehicle's battery.
2. **Protection** from harmful overloads (excessive current flow). Fuses, circuit breakers, and fusible links are examples of electrical circuit protection devices.
3. A **path** for the current to flow through from the power source to the resistance. This path from a power source to the resistance (a light bulb in this example) is usually an insulated copper wire.
4. The **electrical load** or resistance—the object the electrical current is operating or lighting.
5. A **return path** for the electrical current from the load back to the power source so that there is a *complete* circuit. This return path is usually the metal body, frame, and engine block of the vehicle. This is called the **ground return path.** See Figure 9-23.
6. Switches and controls to turn the circuit on and off. See Figure 9-24.

CIRCUIT FAILURES

Open Circuits

An **open circuit** is any circuit that is *not* complete, or that lacks continuity. See Figure 9-25. *No current at all* will flow through an incomplete circuit. An open circuit may be created by a break in the circuit or by a switch that opens (turns off) the circuit and prevents the flow of current. In any circuit containing a power load and ground, an opening anywhere in the circuit will cause

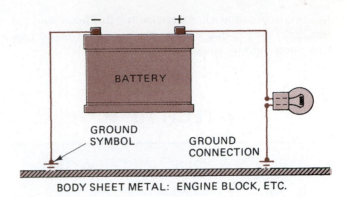

FIGURE 9-23   The return path back to the battery can be any electrical conductor, such as the metal frame or body of the vehicle.

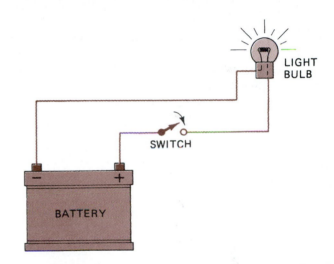

FIGURE 9-24   An electrical switch opens the circuit and no current flows. The switch could also be on the return (ground) path wire.

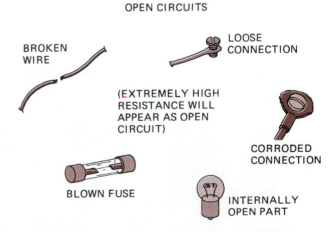

FIGURE 9-25   Examples of common causes of open circuits. Some of these causes are often difficult to find.

the circuit not to work. A light switch in a home and the headlight switch in a vehicle are examples of devices that open a circuit to control its operation.

◀ **TECH TIP** ▶

OPEN IS A FOUR-LETTER WORD

An open in a circuit breaks the path of current flow. The open can be any break in the power side, load, or ground side of a circuit. A switch is often used to close and open a circuit (i.e., to turn it on and off). Just remember these facts.

open = no current flow

closed = current flow

Trying to locate an open circuit in a vehicle is often difficult and may cause the technician to use other four-letter words such as "HELP!"

Short-to-Voltage

If a wire (conductor) or component is shorted to voltage, it is commonly called **shorted.** See Figure 9-26. A short circuit has the following characteristics.

1. It is a complete circuit in which the current bypasses *some* or *all* of the resistance in the circuit.
2. It involves the power side of the circuit.
3. It involves a copper-to-copper connection.
4. It is also called a *short-to-voltage.*

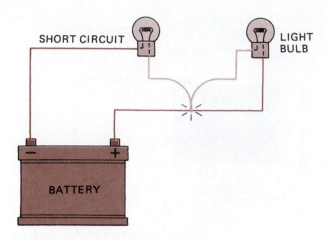

FIGURE 9-26 A short circuit permits electrical current to bypass some or all of the resistance in the circuit.

5. It usually affects more than one circuit.
6. It *may* or *may not* blow a fuse. See Figure 9-27.

Short-to-Ground

A **short-to-ground** is a type of short circuit wherein the current bypasses part of the normal circuit and flows directly to ground. Because the ground return circuit is metal (vehicle frame, engine, or body), this type of circuit is identified as having current flowing from copper to steel. A defective component or circuit that is shorted to ground is commonly called **grounded.** For example, if a penny was accidentally inserted into a cigarette lighter socket, the current would flow through the penny to ground. Because the penny has little resistance, an excessive amount of current flow causes the fuse to blow. See Figure 9-28.

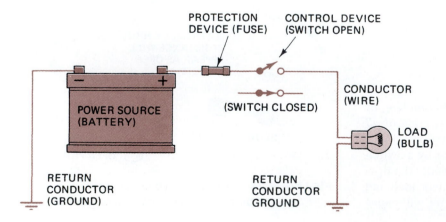

FIGURE 9-27 A fuse or circuit breaker opens the circuit to prevent possible overheating damage in the event of a short circuit.

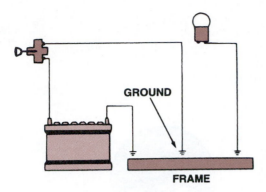

FIGURE 9-28 A short-to-ground affects the power side of the circuit. Current flows directly to the ground return, bypassing some or all of the electrical loads in the circuit. There is no current in the circuit past the short.

◄ **TECH TIP** ►

THINK OF A WATERWHEEL

A beginner technician cleaned the positive terminal of the battery when the starter was cranking the engine slowly. When questioned by the shop foreman as to why only the positive post had been cleaned, the technician responded that the negative terminal was "only a ground." The foreman reminded the technician that the current, in amperes, is constant throughout a series circuit (such as the cranking motor circuit). If 200 amperes leave the positive post of the battery, then 200 amperes must return to the battery through the negative post.

The technician just could not understand how electricity can do work (crank an engine), yet return the same amount of current, in amperes, as left the battery. The shop foreman explained that even though the current is constant throughout the circuit, the voltage (electrical pressure or potential) is dropped to zero in the circuit. To explain further, the shop foreman drew a waterwheel. See Figure 9-29.

As water drops from a higher level to a lower level, high potential energy (or voltage) is used to turn the waterwheel and results in low potential energy (or lower voltage). The same amount of water (or amperes) reaches the pond under the waterwheel as started the fall above the waterwheel. As current (amperes) flows through a conductor, it performs work in the circuit (turns the waterwheel) while its voltage (potential) is dropped.

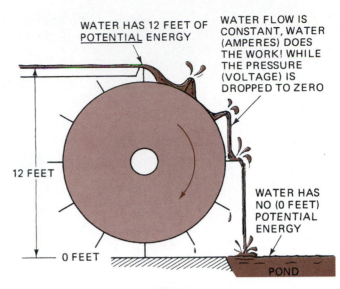

FIGURE 9-29 Electrical flow through a circuit is similar to water flowing over a waterwheel. The more water (amperes in electricity), the greater the amount of work (waterwheel). The amount of water remains constant, yet the pressure (voltage in electricity) drops as the current flows through the circuit.

OHM'S LAW

The German physicist, Georg Simon Ohm, established that electric pressure (EMF) in volts, electrical resistance in ohms, and the amount of current in amperes flowing through any circuit are all related. See Figure 9-30. According to **Ohm's law,** it requires 1 volt to push 1 ampere through 1 ohm of resistance. This means that if the voltage is doubled, then the number of amperes of current flowing through a circuit will also double if the resistance of the circuit remains the same.

Ohm's law can also be stated as a simple formula used to calculate one value of an electrical circuit if the other two are known:

$$I = \frac{E}{R}$$

where

I = Current in amperes (A)
E = Electromotive force (EMF) in volts (V)
R = Resistance in ohms (Ω)

1. Ohm's law can determine the resistance if the voltage and current are known: $R = E/I$.
2. Ohm's law can determine the *voltage* if the resistance (ohms) and current are known: $E = I \times R$.
3. Ohm's law can determine the current if the resistance and voltage are known: $I = E/R$.

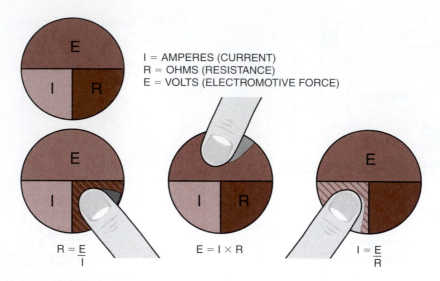

I = AMPERES (CURRENT)
R = OHMS (RESISTANCE)
E = VOLTS (ELECTROMOTIVE FORCE)

$R = \dfrac{E}{I}$ $E = I \times R$ $I = \dfrac{E}{R}$

FIGURE 9-30 To calculate one unit of electricity when the other two are known, simply use your finger and cover the unit you do not know. For example, if both voltage (*E*) and resistance (*R*) are known, cover the letter *I* (amperes). Notice that the letter *E* is above the letter *R*, so divide the resistor's value into the voltage to determine the current in the circuit.

See the following table for a quick summary of relationships under Ohm's law.

Voltage	*Resistance*	*Amperage*
Up	Down	Up
Up	Same	Up
Up	Up	Same
Same	Down	Up
Same	Same	Same
Same	Up	Down
Down	Up	Down
Down	Same	Down

Ohm's Law Applied to Simple Circuits

If a battery with 12 volts is connected to a light bulb with a resistance of 4 ohms, how many amperes will flow through the circuit? Using Ohm's law, we can calculate the number of amperes that will flow through the wires and the bulb. Remember, if two factors are known (volts and ohms in this example), the remaining factor (amperes) can be calculated using Ohm's law.

$$I = E/R = 12 \text{ V}/4 \ \Omega$$

The values for the voltage (12) and the resistance (4) were substituted for the variables *E* and *R*, and *I* is thus 3 amperes (12/4 = 3).

If we want to connect a light bulb to a 12-volt battery, we now know that this simple circuit requires 3 amperes to operate. This may help us for two reasons:

1. We can now determine the wire diameter that we will need based on the number of amperes flowing through the circuit.
2. The correct fuse rating can be selected to protect the circuit.

◄ TECH TIP ►

FARSIGHTED QUALITY OF ELECTRICITY

Electricity almost seems to act as if it knows what resistances are ahead on the long trip through a circuit. If the trip through the circuit has many high-resistance components, very few electrons (amperes) will choose to attempt to make the trip. If a circuit has little or no resistance (for example, a short circuit), then as many electrons (amperes) as possible attempt to flow through the complete circuit. If the flow exceeds the capacity of the fuse or the circuit breaker, then the circuit is opened and all current flow stops.

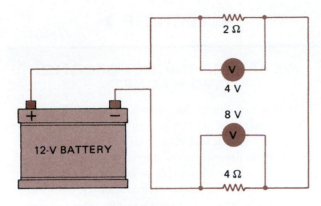

A. I = E/R (TOTAL "R" = 6 Ω)
  = 12/6 = 2 A

B. E = IR (VOLTAGE DROP)
  AT 2 Ω RESISTANCE =
  E = 2 X 2 = 4 V
  AT 4 Ω RESISTANCE =
  E = 2 X 4 = 8 V

C. 4 + 8 = 12 V
  SUM OF VOLTAGE DROP
  EQUALS APPLIED VOLTAGE

FIGURE 9-31 A voltmeter reads the differences of voltage between the test leads. The voltage read across a resistance is the voltage drop that occurs when current flows through a resistance. A voltage drop is also called an "IR" drop because it is calculated by multiplying the current (*I*) through the resistance (electrical load) by the value of the resistance (*R*).

VOLTAGE DROPS AS A TESTING METHOD

Any resistance in a circuit causes the voltage to drop in proportion to the amount of the resistance. Because a high resistance will drop the voltage more than a lower resistance, we can use a voltmeter to measure the effect of the resistance. See Figure 9-31.

CAPACITORS OR CONDENSERS

Capacitors (also called **condensers**) are electrical components that can be used to perform a variety of functions. Electrons can be "stored" on the inside of a capacitor on two or more conductor plates separated by an insulator called a **dielectric.** See Figure 9-32.

If a capacitor is connected to a battery or another electrical power source, it is capable of storing the electrons from the power source. See Figure 9-33. This storage capacity is called **capacitance,** and it is measured in the unit called a **farad,** named for Michael Faraday

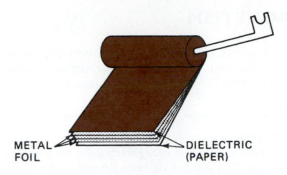

FIGURE 9-32 A foil and paper condenser (capacitor) can store electrons on the surface of the foil.

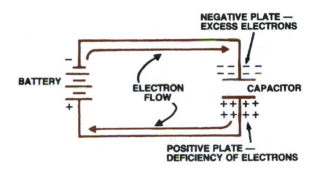

FIGURE 9-33 As the capacitor is charging, the battery forces electricity through the circuit.

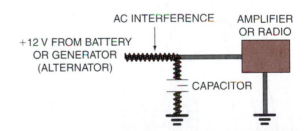

FIGURE 9-34 A capacitor blocks direct current (DC) but passes alternating current (AC). A capacitor makes a very good noise suppressor because most of the interference is AC and the capacitor will conduct this AC to ground before it can reach the radio or amplifier.

(1791–1867), an English physicist. A farad is the capacity to store 1 coulomb of electrons at 1 volt of potential difference between the plates of the capacitor. This is a very large number, so most capacitors for automotive use list values measured in microfarads (one-millionth of a farad). A capacitor can pass current that is constantly changing its direction of flow (alternating current, or AC), but blocks the flow of direct current (DC). See Figure 9-34.

MAGNETISM

Like electricity, magnetism is sometimes difficult to visualize. Although electricity and magnetism cannot be seen, the *effects* of both can be seen and felt.

NOTE: Magnetism is extremely important to automotive applications because everything electrical in the automobile, except the lights and the cigarette lighter, work as a result of magnetism.

Because a magnet shows attraction for metal objects such as tacks, nails, and iron filings, it is clear that a force surrounds the magnetic material. Magnetic lines of force are invisible, but when iron filings are placed on a piece of paper held above a magnet, the filings move and then become stationary along a definite pattern formed between and around both the north and south poles. See Figure 9-35. The poles of a magnetic substance act similarly to electrostatic charges: Like poles repel each other, whereas opposite poles are attracted. See Figure 9-36.

◀ TECH TIP ▶

A CRACKED MAGNET BECOMES TWO MAGNETS

Magnets are commonly used in vehicle crankshaft, camshaft, and wheel speed sensors. If a magnet is struck and cracks or breaks, the result is two smaller-strength magnets. Because the strength of the magnetic field is reduced, the sensor output voltage is also reduced. A typical problem occurs when a magnetic crankshaft sensor becomes cracked, resulting in a no-start condition. Sometimes the cracked sensor works well enough to start an engine that is cranking at normal speeds but will not work when the engine is cold. See Figure 9-37.

Electromagnetism

Around 1820, it was discovered that a wire carrying an electrical current had an effect on a compass. See Figure 9-38. Until that time, the only thing known to af-

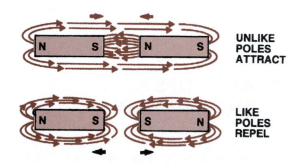

FIGURE 9-36 Magnetic poles behave like electrically charged particles—unlike poles attract and like poles repel.

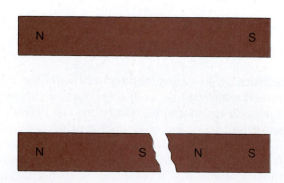

FIGURE 9-37 If a magnet breaks or is cracked, it becomes two weaker magnets.

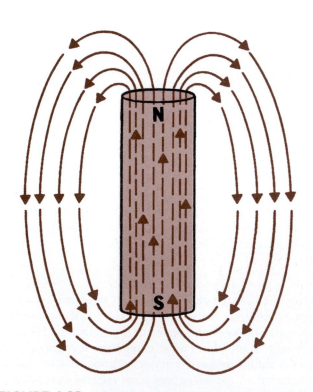

FIGURE 9-35 Magnetic lines of force leave the north pole and return to the south pole of a bar magnet.

fect a compass was a magnetic field. Further study revealed that a magnetic field surrounds any conductor (wire) that carries an electrical current. A magnetic field created by current flow is called **electromagnetism.**

Whenever there is electricity flowing through a conductor, magnetic lines of force are produced (induced) around the conductor. Whenever there is a conductor near a *moving* magnetic field, electricity is produced in the conductor. If a wire (conductor) is coiled and current is sent through the wire, the same magnetic fields that would surround straight wires combine to form one larger magnetic field with true north and south poles.

The iron in the center of the coil provides an excellent conductor for the magnetic field that travels through the center of the wire coil. This is the reason all ignition coils use laminated iron cores in their construction. See Figure 9-39.

Electromagnetic Switches

Electromagnets are widely used in automotive electrical systems in the form of electromagnetic switches. An electromagnetic switch is one that opens or closes electrical contacts using an electromagnet. See Figure 9-40.

A low-current electromagnetic switch is usually used to control (open or close) a high-current circuit. For example, an ignition switch circuit (low current) can control a high-current starter motor circuit by using an electromagnetic switch. When the electromagnetic wires are connected to a power source, the resulting magnetic pull on the upper movable contact point forces the switch into contact with the lower contact point. These contact points complete (close) another circuit. Because the electromagnetic switch controls a higher current than the control current, it is often called a **relay:** it "relays" heavy current in the circuit.

If an electromagnetic switch has a movable arm (armature), it is called a relay. See Figure 9-41. If an electromagnetic switch uses a movable iron core, it is called a **solenoid.** A solenoid, besides operating as a switch,

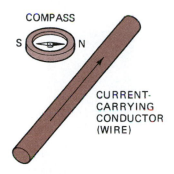

FIGURE 9-38 Surrounding any conductor carrying an electrical current is a magnetic field.

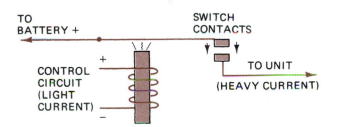

FIGURE 9-40 Electromagnetic switch. A light current (low amperes) produces an electromagnet and causes the contact points to close. The contact points then conduct a heavy current (high amperes) to an electrical unit.

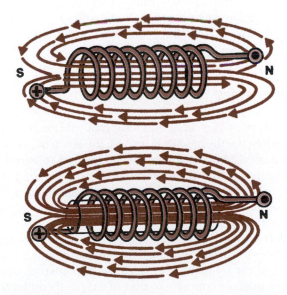

FIGURE 9-39 An iron core concentrates the magnetic lines of force surrounding a coil.

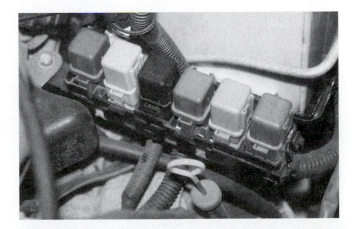

FIGURE 9-41 A row of relays as found in a vehicle. The different colors represent different ratings and therefore different applications for each color of relay.

FIGURE 9-42 Cutaway of a typical automotive solenoid. A solenoid uses a marble core to force a disc into contact with the two terminals of the solenoid.

can also use a movable core to perform mechanical work, such as engaging a starter pinion gear. Solenoids are usually constructed to transfer heavier current than a movable arm relay. See Figure 9-42.

Electromagnetic Induction

In 1831, Michael Faraday (1867) discovered that electrical energy can be induced from one circuit to another by using magnetic lines of force. When a conductor cuts across magnetic lines of force, a difference of potential is set up between the ends of the conductor, and a voltage is induced. This action is called **electromagnetic induction.** See Figure 9-43. This voltage exists only when the magnetic field *or* the conductor is in motion.

The induced voltage can be increased by increasing:

- The *speed* with which the magnetic lines of force cut the conductor
- The *number of conductors* that are cut
- The *strength of the magnetic field*

Electromagnetic induction is the principle behind the operation of all ignition systems, coils, starter motors, generators, alternators, and relays.

Diodes

A **diode** is an electrical one-way check valve. The word *diode* means "having two electrodes." Electrodes are electrical connections. The positive electrode is called the **anode** and the negative electrode is called the **cathode.** See Figure 9-44.

If the positive terminal of a battery were connected to the diode positive (anode), current would

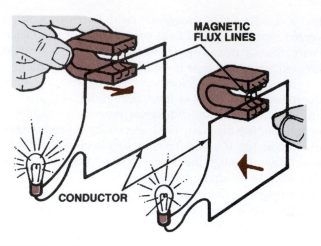

FIGURE 9-43 Voltage can be induced by the relative motion between a conductor and magnetic lines of force.

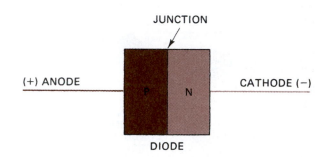

FIGURE 9-44 A diode is a component with P- and N-type material together. The negative electrode is called the cathode and the positive electrode is called the anode.

flow through the diode with low resistance. This condition is called **forward bias.** If the battery connections were reversed, the diode offers very high resistance to current flow, and this condition is called **reverse bias.**

Thermistors

A **thermistor** is a semiconductor material such as silicon. When the thermistor is heated, the electrons within the material gain energy and electrons are released. If voltage is applied to a thermistor, its resistance decreases because the thermistor itself is acting as a current carrier rather than as a resistor at higher temperatures.

A thermistor is commonly used as a temperature-sensing device for coolant temperature and intake manifold air temperature. Because thermistors operate in a manner opposite to that of a typical conductor, they are called **negative temperature coefficient (NTC)** and their resistance decreases as the temperature increases. Thermistor symbols are shown in Figure 9-45.

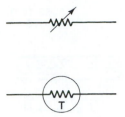

FIGURE 9-45 Symbols used to represent a thermistor.

◀ **TECH TIP** ▶

ELECTRONIC DEVICES DIE IN INFANCY

All solid-state electronic components are constructed of silicon chips, which include thousands of circuits. Due to the high density of these circuits, it is not unusual for a failure to occur when the circuit is first placed into service. Because most electronic failures occur in infancy, manufacturers operate the circuits for 24 to 48 hours to help prevent these components from failing after they are sold to a customer. This process of operating the component or circuit is called **burn in**.

TRANSISTORS

A **transistor** is a semiconductor device that can perform the following electrical functions:

1. An electrical switch in a circuit
2. An amplifier of current in a circuit
3. A regulator of current in a circuit

The word *transistor*, derived from the words *transfer* and *resistor*, is used to describe the transfer of current across a resistor.

A transistor is made of three alternating sections or layers of P- and N-type material. See Figure 9-46. A transistor that has P-type material on each end, with N-type material in the center, is called a **PNP transistor**. Another type, with an arrangement exactly opposite, is an **NPN transistor**.

The center section of a transistor is called the **base**, and it controls current flow through the transistor. The material at one end of a transistor is called the **emitter**, and the material at the other end is called the **collector**. On all symbols for a transistor, there is an arrow indicating the emitter part of the transistor. The arrow points in the direction of current flow (conventional theory).

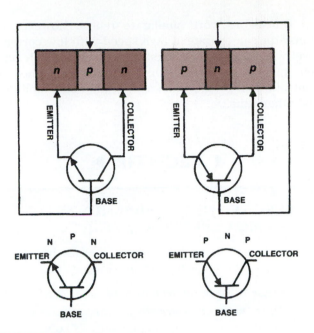

FIGURE 9-46 Transistor symbols and construction.

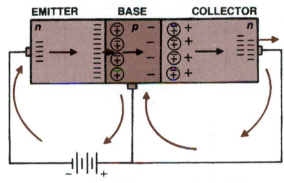

INPUT-OUTPUT CIRCUIT INTERACTION

FIGURE 9-47 When a transistor is forward biased (+ to base of an NPN transistor), electrons from the emitter pass through the base to the collector and greater overall forward current flows. Note that greater reverse current flows in the output circuit because more holes in the collector are filled by free electrons.

A transistor will allow current flow if the electrical conditions allow it to switch on, in a manner similar to the working of an electromagnetic relay. If the base current is turned off or on, the current flow from collector to emitter is turned off or on.

The current flowing through a transistor can also be regulated or controlled just as a valve on a water faucet controls the flow of water—by varying the current to the base, the current flowing through the collector and emitter are also controlled. See Figure 9-47.

Transistors work similar to relays. However, a transistor can operate at high speed with low current level whereas a relay is used for low speed, high current applications. Transistors are used as switches to control other circuits such as fuel injection, ignition, and other units.

◀ TECH TIP ▶

ELECTRONIC COMPONENTS DO NOT LIKE THREE THINGS

Computers are sensitive electronic devices that can be damaged if subjected to the following things:

- **High voltage.** Especially static electricity
- **High current (amperes).** Current through a computer circuit is usually limited to one ampere or less
- **High heat.** Electronic devices work best when isolated from extreme heat

There is another item that may be of interest. While troubleshooting a computer-related problem, this author found the vehicle computer full of water because of a leaky windshield. So add another item to the list—computers can't swim!

FUSES AND CIRCUIT PROTECTION DEVICES

Fuses should be used in every circuit to protect the wiring from overheating and damage caused by excessive current flow as a result of a short circuit or other malfunction. The symbol for a fuse is a wavy line between two points: ⎯∿⎯

A fuse is constructed of a fine tin conductor inside a glass, plastic, or ceramic housing. The tin is designed to melt and open the circuit if excessive current flows through the fuse. Each fuse is rated according to its maximum current-carrying capacity.

Many fuses are used to protect more than one circuit of the automobile. A typical example is the fuse for the cigarette lighter that also protects many other circuits such as those for the courtesy lights, clock, and other circuits. A fault in one of these circuits can cause this fuse to melt, which will prevent the operation of all other circuits that are protected by the fuse.

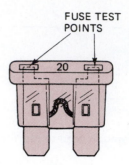

FIGURE 9-48 Blade-type fuses can be tested through openings in the plastic at the top of the fuse.

Testing Fuses

It is important to test the condition of a fuse if the circuit being protected by the fuse does not operate. Most blown fuses can be detected quickly because the center conductor is melted. Fuses can also fail and open the circuit because of a poor connection in the fuse itself or in the fuse holder. Therefore, just because a fuse "looks okay" does not mean that it *is* okay. All fuses should be tested with a test light. The test light should be connected to first one side of the fuse and then the other. A test light should light on both sides. If the test light only lights on one side, the fuse is blown or open. See Figure 9-48. If the test light does not light on either side of the fuse, then that circuit is not being supplied power.

Circuit Breakers

Circuit breakers are used to prevent harmful overload (excessive current flow) in a circuit by opening the circuit and stopping the current flow to prevent overheating and possible fire caused by hot wires or electrical components. Circuit breakers are mechanical units made of two different metals (bimetallic) that deform when heated and open a set of contact points that work in the same manner as an "off" switch. See Figure 9-49.

Circuit breakers, therefore, are reset when the current stops flowing, which causes the bimetallic strip to cool and the circuit to close again. A circuit breaker is used in circuits that could affect the safety of passengers if a conventional nonresetting fuse were used. The headlight circuit is an excellent example of the use of a circuit breaker rather than a fuse. A short or grounded circuit anywhere in the headlight circuit could cause excessive current flow and, therefore, the

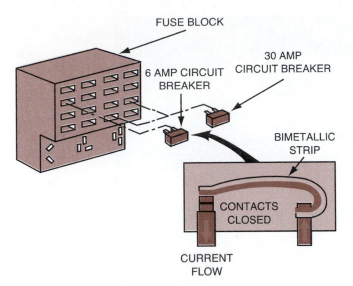

FUSE BLOCK

30 AMP
CIRCUIT BREAKER

6 AMP CIRCUIT
BREAKER

BIMETALLIC
STRIP

CONTACTS
CLOSED

CURRENT
FLOW

FIGURE 9-49   A typical blade circuit breaker fits into the same space as a blade fuse. If excessive current flows through the bimetallic strip, the strip bends and opens the contacts and stops current flow. When the circuit breaker cools, the contacts close again, completing the electrical circuit.

opening of the circuit. A sudden loss of headlights at night could have disastrous results. A circuit breaker opens and closes the circuit rapidly, thereby protecting the circuit from overheating and also providing sufficient current flow to maintain at least partial headlight operation.

Fusible Links

A fusible link is a type of fuse that consists of a short length of standard copper-strand wire covered with a special nonflammable insulation. This wire is usually four wire sizes smaller than the wire of the circuits it protects. The special thick insulation over the wire may make it look larger than other wires of the same gauge number. See Figure 9-50.

If excessive current flow (caused by a short to ground or a defective component) occurs, the fusible link will melt in half and open the circuit to prevent a fire hazard. Some fusible links are identified with "fusible link" tags at the junction between the fusible link and the standard chassis wiring, which represent only the junction. Fusible links are the backup system for circuit protection.

◀ **TECH TIP** ▶

LOOK FOR THE "GREEN CRUD"

Corroded connections are a major cause of intermittent electrical problems and open circuits. The usual sequence of conditions is as follows:

1. Heat causes expansion. This heat can be from external sources such as connectors being too close to the exhaust system. Another possible source of heat is a poor connection at the terminal, causing a voltage drop and heat due to the electrical resistance.
2. Condensation is created when a connector cools. The moisture in the condensation causes rust and corrosion.

The solution is, if corroded connectors are noticed, the terminal should be cleaned and the condition of the electrical connection to the wire terminal end(s) confirmed. Many automobile manufacturers recommend using a dielectric silicone or lithium-based grease inside connectors to prevent moisture from getting into and attacking the connector.

TERMINALS AND CONNECTORS

A **terminal** is a metal fastener attached to the end of a wire. The term **connector** usually refers to the plastic portion that snaps or connects together. Wire terminal ends usually snap into and are held by a connector. Male and female connectors can then be snapped together, thereby completing an electrical connection. Connectors exposed to the environment are also equipped with a weather-tight seal.

A typical repair often involves removing a wire's terminal from a connector and replacing that terminal on the end of the lead (wire). A terminal may be corroded or has lost its tension or grip on the mating terminal. Terminals are usually retained in a connector by a locking tang or tab that must be depressed to release the terminal end from the plastic connector. See Figures 9-51 and 9-52 on page 169.

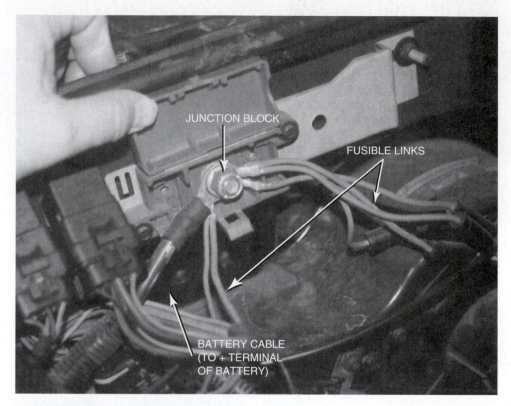

FIGURE 9-50 Fusible links are usually located close to the battery and are usually attached to a junction block. Notice that they are only 6 to 9 inches long and feed more than one fuse from each fusible link.

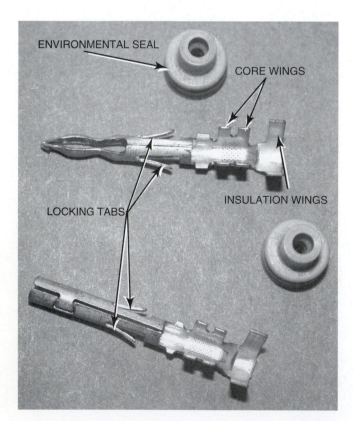

FIGURE 9-51 Male (top) and female (bottom) weatherpack terminals. The insulation is stripped from the end of the wire (core) and crimped under the core wings. The insulation is then crimped over the insulation to help prevent the wire from being pulled out of the terminal.

WIRING DIAGRAMS

Automotive manufacturers' service manuals include wiring diagrams of all the electrical circuits. These wiring diagrams may include all of the circuits combined on several large fold-out sheets, or they may be broken down to show individual circuits. All circuit diagrams include the power-side wiring of the circuit and all splices, connectors, electrical components, and ground return paths. The gauge and color of the wiring are also included on most wiring diagrams.

Circuit Information

Many wiring diagrams include numbers and letters near components and wires that may confuse readers of the diagram. Most letters used near or on a wire identify the

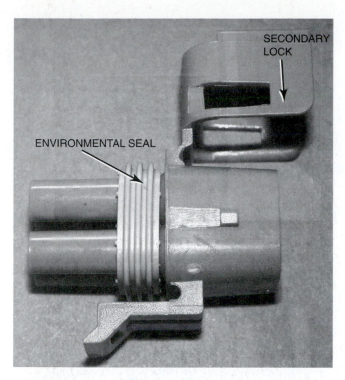

FIGURE 9-52 A male weather-pack connector. The plastic connector holds the metal terminals in position and locks to the female connector to make a good tight connection.

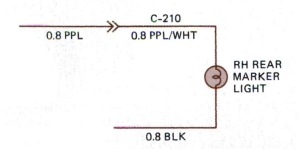

FIGURE 9-53 Typical section of a wiring diagram. Notice that the wire color changes at connection C210. The ".8" represents the metric wire size in square millimeters.

color or colors of the wire. The first color or color abbreviation is the color of the wire insulation, and the second color (if mentioned) is the color of the strip or tracer on the base color.

Wires with different-color tracers are indicated by both colors with a slash (/) between them. For example, BRN/WHT means a brown wire with a white stripe or tracer.

Figure 9-53 illustrates a rear side-marker bulb circuit diagram where ".8" indicates the metric wire gauge size in square millimeters (mm²) and "PPL" indicates a solid purple wire.

The wire diagram also shows that the color of the wire changes at the number C210. This stands for "connector #210" and is used for reference purposes. The symbol for the connection can vary depending on the manufacturer. The color change from purple (PPL) to purple with a white tracer (PPL/WHT) is not important except for knowing where the wire changes color in the circuit. The wire gauge has remained the same on both sides of the connection (0.8 square millimeters or 18-gauge). The ground circuit is the ".8 BLK" wire. Figure 9-54 shows electrical and electronic symbols that are used in wiring and circuit diagrams.

SWITCHES

Electrical switches are drawn on a wiring diagram in their normal position. This can be one of two possible positions:

- **Normally Open.** The switch is not connected to a terminal and no current flows in this position. This type of switch is labeled **N.O.**
- **Normally Closed.** The switch is electrically connected to a contact and current will flow through the switch. This type of switch is labeled **N.C.**

Other switches can use more than two contacts.

The **poles** refer to the number of circuits completed by the switch, and the **throws** refer to the number of output circuits. A single-pole, single-throw (SPST) switch has only two positions—on or off. A single-pole, double-throw (SPDT) switch has three terminals—one wire in and two wires out. A headlight dimmer switch is an example of a typical SPDT switch. In one position, the current flows to the low-filament headlight; in the other, the current flows to the high-filament headlight. There are also double-pole, single-throw (DPST) switches and double-pole, double-throw (DPDT) switches. See Figure 9-55.

RELAY TERMINAL IDENTIFICATION

Most automotive relays adhere to common terminal identification. Knowing this terminal information will help in the correct diagnosis and troubleshooting of any circuit containing a relay. See Figure 9-56.

The schematic is often printed or embossed on the side of the relay. The terminals are labeled to help the technician test and check for proper operation, as shown in Figure 9-57. The identification of relay terminals also helps when trying to diagnose a circuit that contains a relay.

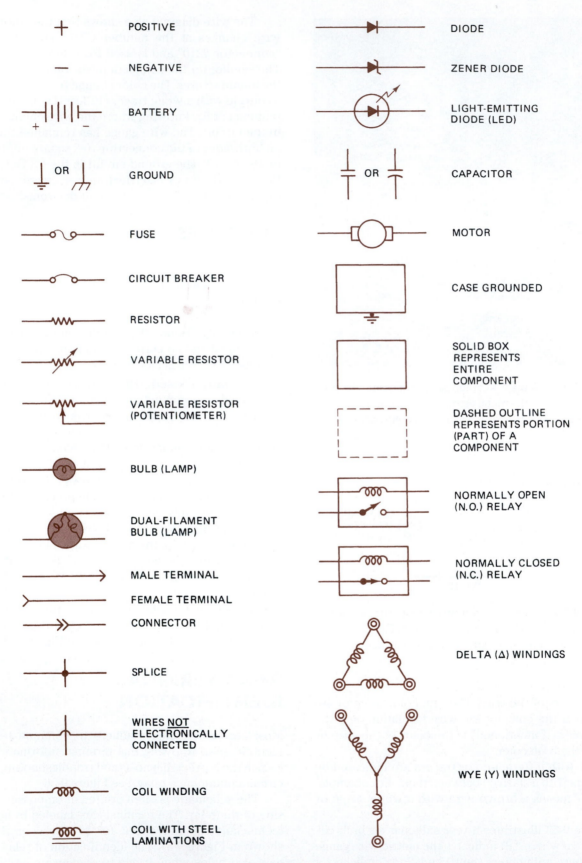

FIGURE 9-54 Typical electrical and electronic symbols used in automotive wiring and circuit diagrams.

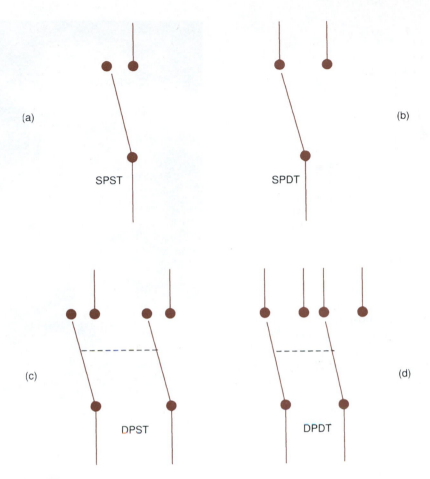

FIGURE 9-55 (a) A symbol for a single-pole, single-throw (SPST) switch. This type of switch is normally open (N.O.) because nothing is connected to the terminal that the switch is contacting in its normal position. (b) A single-pole, double-throw (SPDT) switch has three terminals. (c) A double-pole, single-throw (DPST) switch has two positions (off and on) and can control two separate circuits. (d) A double-pole, double-throw (DPDT) switch has six terminals—three for each pole.

◀ FREQUENTLY ASKED QUESTION ▶

WHERE TO START?

The common question is, where does a technician start the troubleshooting when using a wiring diagram (schematic)?

HINT 1: If the circuit contains a relay, start your diagnosis at the relay. The entire circuit can be tested at the terminals of the relay.

HINT 2: The easiest first step is to locate the unit on the schematic that is not working at all or not working correctly.

1. Trace where the unit gets its ground connection.
2. Trace where the unit gets its power connection.

Often a ground is used by more than one component. Therefore, ensure that everything else is working correctly. If not, then the fault may lie at the common ground (or power) connection.

HINT 3: Divide the circuit in half by locating a connector or a part of the circuit that can be accessed easily. Then check for power and ground at this midpoint. This step could save you much time.

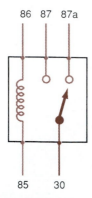

86–POWER SIDE OF THE COIL
85–GROUND SIDE OF THE COIL

(MOST RELAY COILS
HAVE BETWEEN
50–150 OHMS
OF RESISTANCE.)

30–COMMON POWER FOR RELAY CONTACTS
87–NORMALLY OPEN OUTPUT (N.O.)
87a–NORMALLY CLOSED OUTPUT (N.C.)

FIGURE 9-56   A relay uses a movable arm to complete a circuit whenever there is a power at terminal 86 and a ground at terminal 85. A typical relay only requires about 1/10 ampere through the relay coil. The movable arm then closes the contacts (#30 to #87) and can relay 30 amperes or more.

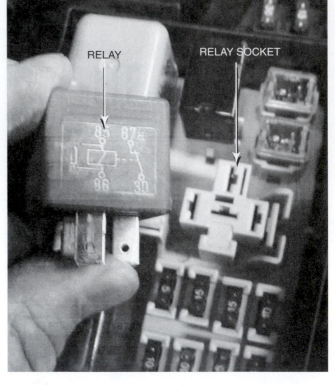

FIGURE 9-57   A typical relay showing the schematic of the wiring in the relay. Terminals #30 and #87 are electrically connected when the relay is energized.

◄ TECH TIP ►

WIGGLE TEST

Intermittent electrical problems are common yet difficult to locate. To help locate these hard-to-find problems, try operating the circuit and then start wiggling the wires and connections that control the circuit. If in doubt where the wiring goes, try moving all the wiring starting at the battery. Pay particular attention to wiring running near the battery or the windshield washer container. Corrosion can cause wiring to fail, and battery acid fumes and alcohol-based windshield washer fluid can start or contribute to the problem. If you notice any change in the operation of the device being tested while wiggling the wiring, look closer in the area you were wiggling until the actual problem is located and corrected.

ELECTRICAL TROUBLESHOOTING GUIDE

When troubleshooting any electrical component, remember the following hints to find the problem faster and more easily:

1. For a device to work, it must have two things: power and ground.
2. If there is no power to a device, an open power side (blown fuse, etc.) is indicated.
3. If there is power on both sides of a device, an open ground is indicated.
4. If a fuse blows immediately, a grounded power-side wire is indicated.
5. Most electrical faults result from heat or movement.
6. Most noncomputer-controlled devices operate by opening and closing the power side of the circuit.
7. Most computer-controlled devices operate by opening and closing the ground side of the circuit.

SUMMARY

1. Electricity is the movement of electrons from one atom to another.
2. Automotive electricity uses the conventional theory that electricity flows from positive to negative.
3. The ampere is the measure of the amount of current flow.
4. Voltage is the unit of electrical pressure.
5. The ohm is the unit of electrical resistance.
6. All complete electrical circuits have a power source (such as a battery), a circuit protection device (such as a fuse), a power-side wire or path, an electrical load, a ground return path, and a switch or a control device.
7. A short-to-voltage involves a copper-to-copper connection and usually affects more than one circuit.
8. A short-to-ground involves a copper-to-steel connection and usually causes the fuse to blow.
9. An open is a break in the circuit resulting in no current flow at all through the circuit.
10. The greater the resistance, the greater the voltage drop.
11. Ohm's law states: "It requires 1 volt to push 1 ampere through 1 ohm of resistance."
12. Capacitors can store electrons and this storage capacity is measured in farads.
13. Magnetism and electricity are related. Electricity creates magnetism and magnetism creates electricity.
14. Diodes can be used to direct and control current flow in circuits and to provide despiking protection.
15. Transistors are electronic relays that can also amplify.

REVIEW QUESTIONS

1. List the parts of a complete electrical circuit.
2. Describe the difference between a short-to-voltage and a short-to-ground.
3. Describe the difference between an open and a short.
4. State Ohm's law.
5. Explain what happens to current flow (amperes) and wattage if the resistance of a circuit is increased because of a corroded connection.
6. Define electricity.
7. Define ampere, volt, and ohm.
8. List three functions that a capacitor (condenser) can perform.
9. Explain the difference between P-type material and N-type material.
10. Explain how a transistor works.
11. Describe how a relay works and how it can be tested.

ASE CERTIFICATION-TYPE QUESTIONS

1. If an insulated wire rubbed through a part of the insulation and the wire conductor touched the steel body of a vehicle, the type of failure would be called _____.
   a. A short-to-voltage
   b. A short-to-ground
   c. An open
   d. A chassis ground

2. If two insulated wires were to melt together where the copper conductors touched each other, the type of failure would be called _____.
   a. A short-to-voltage
   b. A short-to-ground
   c. An open
   d. A floating ground

3. If 12 volts are being applied to a resistance of 3 ohms, _____ amperes will flow.
   a. 12
   b. 3
   c. 4
   d. 36

4. Like charges _____.
   a. Attract
   b. Repel
   c. Neutralize each other
   d. Add

5. Technician A says that a relay is an electromagnetic switch that uses a movable arm. Technician B says that a solenoid is an electromagnetic switch that uses a movable core. Which technician is correct?

   a. Technician A only
   b. Technician B only
   c. Both Technicians A and B
   d. Neither Technician A nor B

6. Current is able to flow through a diode when that diode is _____.

   a. Forward biased
   b. Reversed biased
   c. Turned on
   d. Heated

7. Technician A says that a connector is the plastic part and provides a mechanical connection. Technician B says that a terminal is the metal part of an electrical connection. Which technician is correct?

   a. Technician A only
   b. Technician B only
   c. Both Technicians A and B
   d. Neither Technician A nor B

8. The _____ is a unit of electrical pressure.

   a. Coulomb
   b. Volt
   c. Ampere
   d. Ohm

9. Capacitors are measured in units called _____.

   a. Watts
   b. Farads
   c. Coulombs
   d. Dielectrics

10. Two technicians are discussing a wiring schematic that is labeled 0.8, red, C142. Technician A says that the 0.8 represents the wire gauge size in square millimeters (mm^2). Technician B says that the C142 represents the length of the wire in inches. Which technician is correct?

    a. Technician A only
    b. Technician B only
    c. Both Technicians A and B
    d. Neither Technician A nor B

◄ Chapter 10 ►

DIGITAL METER AND SCOPE USAGE

OBJECTIVES

After studying Chapter 10, the reader should be able to:

1. Prepare for ASE Engine Performance (A8) certification test content area "E" (Computerized Engine Controls Diagnosis and Repair).
2. Explain how to set a digital meter to read volts, amperes, and ohms.
3. List the precautions necessary when working with test equipment.
4. Explain how a digital storage scope differs from an analog scope.
5. Describe how to safely connect test equipment or a meter to a circuit or component without doing any harm.

Test equipment must be used by the service technician because electrical signals cannot be seen or felt and therefore must be measured. This chapter reviews the basics of electrical measurement and provides the background for measuring the components and circuits in the remaining chapters.

TEST LIGHTS

A test light is simply a light bulb with two wires attached. See Figure 10-1. It is used to test for low-voltage (6 to 12 volts) current. Battery voltage cannot be seen or felt and can be detected only with test equipment. See Figure 10-2.

A test light can be purchased or homemade. A purchased test light could be labeled as a 6- to 12-volt test

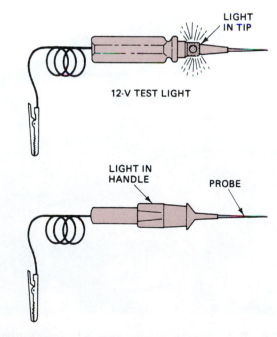

FIGURE 10-1 Examples of probe-type test lights.

light. Do not purchase a test light designed for household current (110 or 220 volts). It will not light with 12 volts.

ALWAYS TEST YOUR TEST EQUIPMENT

More than one technician has misdiagnosed a problem because the test equipment did not work correctly. Examples include the following:

- **Test light bulb burned out**—A test light bulb can be easily checked by regularly testing the test light bulb across a battery. A burned out test light bulb will not be able to detect voltage.

- **Meter fuse blown**—If an ammeter fuse is blown (open), the meter will simply read 0.0 amperes (A) and not conduct current in the circuit. If an inline fuse is used in the meter leads, all functions of the meter will not work. Volts will read 0.0 all the time and often will read OL (over limit) on all ohmmeter scales.

FIGURE 10-2 Always test the test light before using! Connecting the test light across the vehicle battery assures the technician that the leads and bulb are functioning before further testing with the test light.

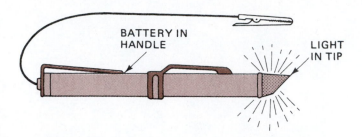

FIGURE 10-3 A self-powered test light should not be used on computer circuits because the applied voltage can damage delicate electronic components or circuits.

SELF-POWERED TEST LIGHTS

A self-powered test light, also called a continuity light, is similar to a test light but includes a battery. A self-powered light will light when connected to both ends of a wire that has continuity or that is not broken. See Figure 10-3.

CAUTION: The use of a continuity test light is not recommended on any electronic circuit. Because a continuity light contains a battery and applies voltage, it may harm delicate electronic components.

LED TEST LIGHT

Another type of test light uses an LED instead of a standard automotive bulb for a visual indication of voltage. An LED test light requires only about 25 mA (0.025 A) to light, so it can be used on electronic circuits and on standard circuits. See Figure 10-4 for construction details.

LOGIC PROBE

A logic probe is an electronic device that lights up a red (usually) LED if the probe is touched to battery voltage. If the probe is touched to ground, a green (usually) LED lights. See Figures 10-5 and 10-6. A logic probe can "sense" the difference between high- and low-voltage levels, thus the term *logic*. A typical logic probe can also light another light (a "pulse" light) when a change in voltage levels occurs. This feature is helpful when checking for a variable voltage output from a computer or ignition sensor.

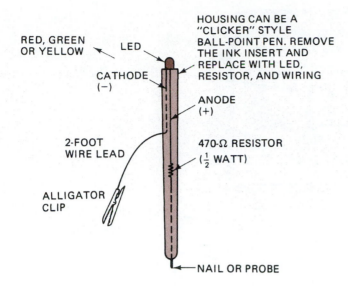

FIGURE 10-4 High-impedance test light. An LED test light can be easily made using low-cost components and an old ink pen. With the 470-ohm resistor in series with the LED, this tester only draws 0.025 A (25 mA) from the circuit being tested. This low current draw helps assure the technician that the circuit or component being tested will not be damaged by excessive current flow.

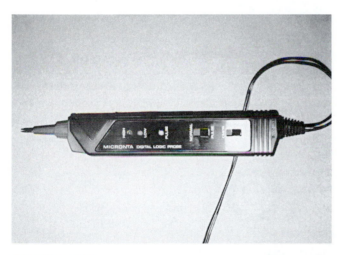

FIGURE 10-5 A typical logic probe can detect voltage and ground, plus show if the signal being measured is being pulsed on or off. A logic probe is a great tool for checking a fuel injector or computer mixture control solenoid being pulsed by the computer.

A logic probe must be first connected to a power source (vehicle battery). This connection powers the probe and gives it a reference low (ground).

Most logic probes also make a distinctive sound for each high- and low-voltage level, which makes troubleshooting easier when probing connectors or compo-

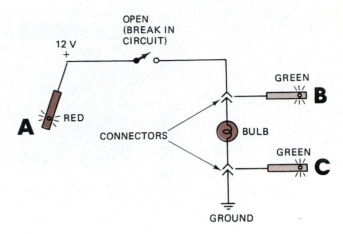

FIGURE 10-6 A logic probe will show green (in this example) if a ground is detected, such as at B and C. A standard (or LED) test light would only indicate to a technician a lack of power at B and could not determine if C was, in fact, connected to a ground.

nent terminals. A sound (usually a beep) is heard when the probe tip is touched to a voltage source that is changing. The changing voltage also usually lights the pulse light on the logic probe. Therefore, the probe can be used to check components such as pickup coils, Hall-effect sensors, magnetic sensors, and many other circuits.

DIGITAL MULTIMETERS

Digital multimeter (DMM) and **digital volt-ohm-milliammeter (DVOM)** are terms commonly used for electronic high-impedance test meters, which have a high internal resistance. Most digital meters have 10 megohms (MΩ) (10 million ohms) or more of internal resistance. *Analog (needle-type) meters are almost always lower than 10 (MΩ) and should not be used to measure any computer circuit.* A high-impedance meter can be used to measure any automotive circuit within the ranges of the meter. See Figures 10-7 through 10-9.

MEASURING AMPERES

An ammeter measures the flow of **current** through a complete circuit in units of amperes. The ammeter has to be installed in series in the circuit so that it can measure all the current flow in that circuit, just as a water flow meter would measure the amount of water flow (cubic feet per minute, for example).

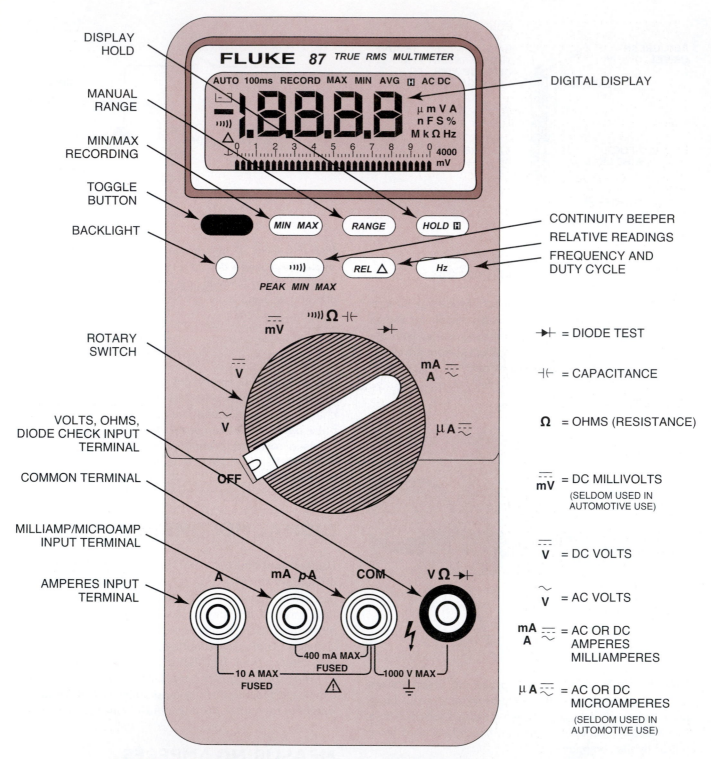

FIGURE 10-7 Typical digital multimeter. The black meter lead always is placed in the COM terminal. Except when measuring the current in amperes, the red meter test lead remains in the V Ω terminal.

SYMBOL	MEANING
AC	Alternating current or voltage
DC	Direct current or voltage
V	Volts
mV	Millivolts (1/1000 volts)
A	Ampere (amps). Current
mA	Milliampere (1/1000 amps)
%	Percent (for duty cycle readings only)
Ω	Ohms. Resistance
kΩ	Kilohm (1000 ohms). Resistance
MΩ	Megohm (1,000,000 ohms). Resistance
Hz	Hertz (1 cycle/sec). Frequency
kHz	Kilohertz (1000 cycles/sec). Frequency
RPM 1	Revolutions/minute. Counting one cycle per spark.
RPM 2	Revolutions/minute. Counting 2 cycles per spark
ms	Milliseconds (1/1000 sec) for Pulse Width measurements.

FIGURE 10-8   Common abbreviations used on the display face of many digital multimeters. *(Courtesy of Fluke Corporation)*

SYSTEM & COMPONENTS	MEASUREMENT TYPES				
	Voltage Presence & Level	Voltage Drop	Current (Amps)	Resistance (Ohms)	Frequency (Hz)
Charging System					
Alternators	●		●		●
Connectors	●	●		●	
Diodes		●		●	
Regulators	●				●
Cooling System					
Connectors	●	●		●	
Fan Motors	●		●	●	
Relays	●	●		●	
Temperature Switches	●	●		●	
Ignition System					
Coils	●			●	
Condensors	●			●	
Connectors	●	●		●	
Contact Set (points)	●			●	
MAF Sensors	●			●	
Magnetic Pick-up	●		●	●	
MAP/BP Sensors	●			●	●
O$_2$ Sensors	●			●	
Starting System					
Batteries	●	●			
Connectors		●	●		
Interlocks			●		
Solenoids	●	●		●	
Starters	●	●	●		

FIGURE 10-9   A summary chart indicating what measurement type may be used to test which vehicle system. *(Courtesy of Fluke Corporation)*

CAUTION: An ammeter must be installed in the circuit to measure the current flow in the circuit. If a meter set to read amperes is connected in parallel, such as across a battery, the meter or the leads may be destroyed by the current available across the battery.

Digital meters require that the meter leads be moved to the ammeter terminals. Most digital meters have an ampere scale that can accommodate a maximum of 10 A. See the Tech Tip, "Fuse Your Meter Leads."

Many ammeters are the **inductive** type. See Figure 10-10. Inductive means that the meter probe surrounds the wire(s) carrying the current and measures the strength of the magnetic field that surrounds any conductor carrying a current.

FIGURE 10-10 A Sun VAT-40 (volt amp tester, model 40) is an example of an analog voltmeter and ammeter. An inductive amp probe is used to measure current (amperes).

◀ TECH TIP ▶

FUSE YOUR METER LEADS

Most digital meters include an ammeter capability. When reading amperes, the leads of the meter must be changed from volts or ohms (V or Ω) to amperes (A), milliamperes (mA), or microamperes (μA).

A common problem may then occur the next time voltage is measured. Although the technician may switch the selector to read volts, often the red test lead is not switched back to the volt or ohm position. Because the ammeter lead position results in 0 ohms of resistance to current flow through the meter, the meter or the fuse inside the meter will be destroyed if the meter is connected to a battery. Many meter fuses are expensive and difficult to find.

To solve this problem, simply solder an inline blade fuse holder into one meter lead. See Figure 10-11. Do not think that this fuse is necessary only for beginners. Experienced technicians often get in a hurry and forget to switch the lead. A blade fuse is faster, easier, and less expensive to replace than a meter fuse or the meter itself. Also, if the soldering is done properly, the addition of an inline fuse holder and fuse does not increase the resistance of the meter leads. All meter leads have some resistance. If the meter is measuring very low resistance, simply touch the two leads together and read the resistance (usually only a couple of tenths of an ohm). Simply subtract the resistance of the leads from the resistance of the component being measured.

FIGURE 10-11 Tie a knot in the test leads near the meter to help prevent the leads from becoming tangled.

AC/DC CLAMP-ON DIGITAL MULTIMETER

An AC/DC clamp-on DMM is a useful meter for automotive diagnostic work. See Figure 10-12.

The major advantage of the clamp-on type meter is that there is no need to break the circuit to measure current (amperes). Simply clamp the jaws of the meter around the power lead(s) or ground lead(s) of the component being measured and read the display. Most clamp-on meters can also measure AC, which is helpful in the diagnosis of a generator (alternator) problem. Volts, ohms, frequency, and temperature can also be measured with the typical clamp-on DMM.

FIGURE 10-12 A mini clamp-on DMM. This small hand-held meter can measure over 200 A DC or AC current as well as measure voltage and resistance similar to other DMMs. This meter is especially helpful for measuring battery electrical drain. In this case, the battery drain is 0.02 A (20 mA) which is normal for most vehicles.

MEASURING VOLTAGE

A voltmeter measures the *pressure* or potential of electricity and measures in units of volts. A voltmeter is connected to a circuit in parallel. All voltmeters have a large, built-in resistance so that the current flow through the meter will not affect either the circuit being tested or the meter. Most digital meters have an internal resistance of

10 MΩ or more on the voltmeter scale only. This is called the *impedance* of the meter and represents the total internal resistance of the meter circuit due to internal coils, capacitors, and resistors. A typical analog voltmeter has only about 12,000 ohms of internal resistance. Although this may sound like a lot of resistance, it is too low for electronic and computer circuit measurement. When a voltmeter is connected to measure voltage, the meter itself becomes a part of the circuit. This is the reason why vehicle manufacturers specify that a high-impedance digital meter be used. The high internal resistance has little effect on the circuit or component being measured. See Figures 10-13 and 10-14.

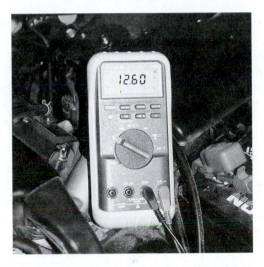

FIGURE 10-13 Typical DMM set to read DC volts.

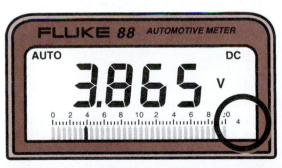

(a)

Since the signal your meter's reading is below 4 volts, the meter autoranges to the 4-volt scale. In this scale, the meter provides you with three decimal places.

(b)

When the voltage exceeded 4 volts, the meter autoranges into the 40-volt scale. The decimal point moves one place to the right, leaving you with only two decimal places.

FIGURE 10-14 A typical auto-ranging digital multimeter automatically selects the proper scale to read the voltage being tested. The scale selected is usually displayed on the meter face. (a) Note that the display indicates "4" meaning that this range can read up to 4 volts. (b) The range is now set to the 40-volt scale meaning that the meter can read up to 40 volts on the scale. Any reading above this level will cause the meter to reset to a higher scale. If not set on autoranging, the meter display would indicate OL if a reading exceeds the limit of the scale selected. (*Courtesy of Fluke Corporation*)

NOTE: The input impedance of any meter can be measured by using another meter and measuring the resistance on the voltmeter scale.

Remember, the resistance of any meter is only effective when the meter is set on the voltmeter scales. This is the major reason why most automobile manufacturers recommend testing *voltage* at selected points instead of resistance or current.

◀ TECH TIP ▶

THE T-PIN ADVANTAGE

T-pins are commonly found in discount stores and craft shops. See Figure 10-15. These low-cost pins are extremely helpful in gaining access to signals without doing any harm. These T-pins are commonly found in 1.5-in. and 1.75-in. lengths.

To use a T-pin, carefully push the sharp end alongside the wire and push toward the connector. The sharp end of the T-pin will slide alongside the insulation and contact the metal terminal inside the plastic connector. See Figure 10-16. The T shape of the pin makes it easy to attach scope probes or meter alligator clips to it. After scope or voltage measurements have been completed, the T-pin can be easily pulled out without damaging the environmental seal of the connector.

CAUTION: Do not use T-pins on high-voltage secondary ignition cables or components. These ignition systems represent a serious shock hazard. Only use T-pins on voltages less than 30 volts AC or 60 volts DC.

MEASURING RESISTANCE

An ohmmeter measures the resistance in ohms of a component or circuit section in parallel when power has been disconnected from the circuit. An ohmmeter contains a battery (or other power source). When the leads are connected to a component, current flows through the test leads and actually measures the difference in voltage (voltage drop) between the leads, which the meter registers as resistance on its scale. Zero ohms mean no resistance between the test leads, indicating that there is continuity or a continuous path for the cur-

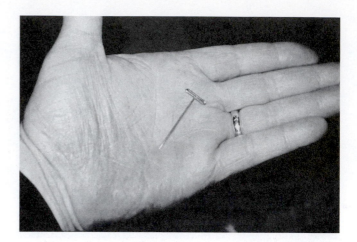

FIGURE 10-15   A typical T-pin.

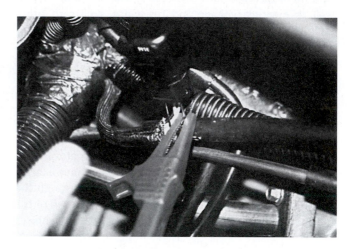

FIGURE 10-16   To measure voltage at an electrical connector, simply use a T-pin and gently slide the tip alongside the signal wire toward the metal terminal inside the plastic connector.

rent to flow in a closed circuit. Infinity means no connection, as in an open circuit.

With a closed circuit (low ohms), maximum current from the built-in battery causes a low reading, whereas an open circuit prevents any current from flowing. Different meters have different ways of indicating infinite resistance, or a reading higher than the scale allows. For example, most meters read OL, meaning "over limit," whereas others may show a number 1 or 3 on the left side of the display. See Figure 10-17. To summarize open and zero readings, remember:

$0.00 \ \Omega$ = zero resistance

OL   = an open circuit (no current flows)

See Figure 10-18 for an example of how to zero your digital meter to read very low resistances accurately. See Figure 10-19 for a summary of meter hookup.

◄ **TECH TIP** ►

"OL" DOES NOT MEAN THE METER IS READING "NOTHING"

Beginner technicians often confuse the meaning of the display on a digital meter. When asked what the meter is reading when OL is displayed on the meter face, the response often heard is "nothing." Many meters indicate OL on the display to indicate *over limit* or *overload*. Over limit means that the reading is over the maximum that can be displayed for the selected range. For example: OL is displayed if 12 volts is being read, but the meter has been set to read a maximum of 4 volts.

Autoranging meters adjust the range to match what is being measured. Here OL means a value higher than the meter can read (unlikely on the voltage scale for automobile usage) or infinity while measuring resistance (ohms). Therefore, OL means infinity while measuring resistance or an open circuit is being indicated. The meter will read 00.0 if the resistance is zero. "Nothing" in this case indicates continuity (zero resistance), whereas OL indicates infinity resistance. Therefore, when talking with another technician about a meter reading, make sure you know exactly what the reading on the face of the meter means.

◄ **FREQUENTLY ASKED** ► **QUESTION**

HOW MUCH VOLTAGE DOES AN OHMMETER APPLY?

Most digital meters that are set to measure ohms (resistance) apply a voltage of from 0.3 to 1.0 volt to the component being measured. The voltage comes from the meter itself to measure the resistance. Two things are important to remember about an ohmmeter:

1. The component or circuit must be disconnected from any electrical circuit while the resistance is being measured.
2. Because the meter itself applies a voltage (even though it is relatively low), a meter set to measure ohms can damage electronic circuits. Computer or electronic chips can be easily damaged if subjected to only a few milliamperes of current similar to the amount an ohmmeter applies when a resistance measurement is being performed.

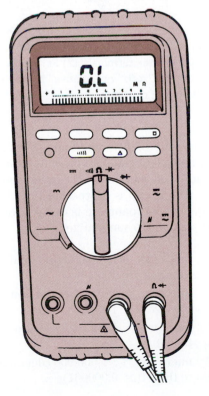

FIGURE 10-17 Typical DMM showing OL (over limit) on the readout with the ohms (Ω) unit selected. This usually means that the unit being measured is open (infinity resistance) and has no continuity.

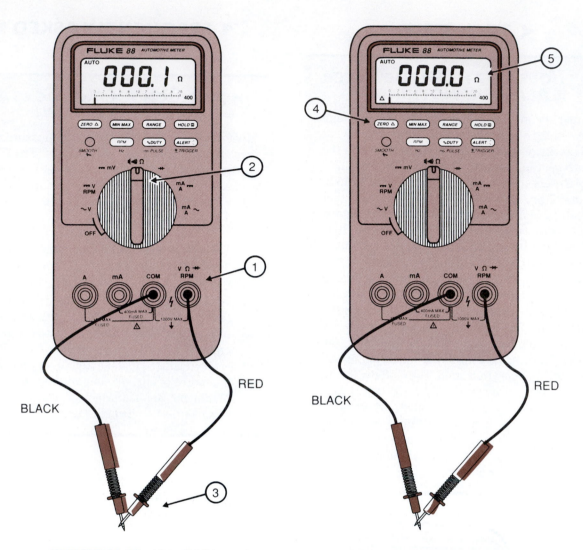

FIGURE 10-18 Many DMMs can have the display indicate zero to compensate for test lead resistance. (1) Connect leads in the VΩ and COM meter terminals. (2) Select the Ω scale. (3) Touch the two meter leads together. (4) Push the "zero" or "relative" button on the meter. (5) The meter display will now indicate 0 ohm of resistance.
(Courtesy of Fluke Corporation)

ELECTRICAL UNIT PREFIXES

Electrical units are measured in numbers such as 12 volts, 150 amperes, and 470 ohms. Large units over 1000 may be expressed in kilo units. The prefix *kilo* means "thousand."

> 1100 volts = 1.1 kilovolts (kV)
> 4700 ohms = 4.7 kilohms (kΩ)

If the value is over 1 million (1,000,000), then the prefix *mega* (M) is often used.

> 1,100,000 volts = 1.1 megavolts (MV)
> 4,700,000 ohms = 4.7 megohms (MΩ)

See Figure 10-20. Sometimes a circuit conducts so little current that a smaller unit of measure is required. Small units of measure of 1/1000 are called *milli* (m).

The *micro* is represented by the Greek letter *mu* (μ). One microampere is one-millionth (1/1,000,000) of an ampere. To summarize:

> mega (M) = 1,000,000 (decimal point six places to the right = 1000000.)
> kilo (k) = 1000 (decimal point three places to the right = 1000.)
> milli (m) = 1/1000 (decimal point three places to the left = 0.001)
> micro (μ) = 1/1,000,000 (decimal point six places to the left = 0.000001)

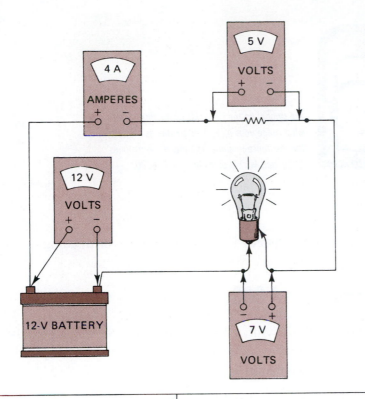 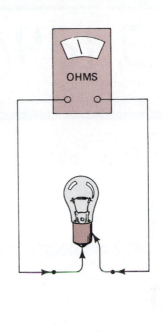

AMMETER	VOLTMETER	OHMMETER
1. Connected in series IN a circuit according to polarity.	1. Connected in parallel to a circuit or part of a circuit according to polarity.	1. Has its own supply of power.
2. Measures current flow.	2. Measures voltage drop: This is the difference between voltage at its two leads.	2. USED ONLY WHEN UNIT IS DISCONNECTED from its original circuit.
3. Used in a closed circuit.	3. Used in a closed circuit.	3. Measures resistance directly on meter.
		4. Low ohms means continuity.
		5. Infinity reading means open circuit.

ALWAYS USE A LARGE ENOUGH AMMETER AND VOLTMETER

FIGURE 10-19 Summary of test meter hookup.

HINT: Lowercase *m* equals a small unit (milli), whereas a capital *M* represents a large unit (mega).

These prefixes can be confusing because most digital meters can express values in more than one prefix, especially if the meter is autoranging. For example, an ammeter reading may show 36.7 mA on autoranging. When the scale is changed to amperes ("A" in the window of the display), the number displayed will be 0.037 A. Note that the resolution of the value is reduced.

HINT: Always check the face of the meter display for the unit being measured. To best understand what is being displayed on the face of a digital meter, select a manual scale and move the selector until *base units* appear, such as A for amperes instead of mA for milliamperes.

HOW TO READ DIGITAL METERS

Getting to know and use a digital meter takes time and practice. The first step is to read, understand, and follow all safety and operational instructions that come with the meter. Use of the meter usually involves the following steps.

1. **Select the proper unit of electricity for what is being measured:** volts, ohms (resistance), or amperes (amount of current flow) as well as to AC or DC. If the meter is not autoranging, select the proper scale for the anticipated reading. For example, if a 12-volt battery is being measured, select a meter reading range that is higher than the voltage but not too high. A 20- or 30-volt range will accurately show the voltage of a 12-volt battery. If a 1000-volt scale is selected, a 12-volt reading may not be accurate.

The symbol on the right side of the display tells you what range your meter's in. Ω means the display is the resistance in ohms; kΩ means ohms times 1,000, and MΩ is ohms times 1,000,000.

Ω = ohms

If the only symbol on the display is the ohms symbol, the reading on the display is exactly the resistance in ohms.

kΩ = kilohms = ohms times 1,000

A "k" in front of the ohms symbol means "kilohms"; the reading on the display is in kilohms. You have to multiply the reading on the display by 1,000 to get the resistance in ohms.

MΩ = megohms = ohms times 1,000,000

An "M" in front of the ohms symbol means "megohms"; the reading on the display is in megohms. You have to multiply by one million (1,000,000) to get the resistance in ohms.

FIGURE 10-20   Always look at the meter display when a measurement is being made, especially if using an autoranging meter. *(Courtesy of Fluke Corporation)*

NOTE: For most automotive applications, select DC volts.

---

2. **Place the meter leads into the proper input terminals.**

   - The black lead usually is inserted into the common (COM) terminal, and stays in this location for all meter functions.
   - The red lead is inserted into the volt, ohm, or diode check terminal usually labeled "V Ω," when voltage, resistance, or diodes are being measured.
   - When current flow in amperes is being measured, most digital meters require that the red test lead be inserted in the ammeter terminal, usually labeled "A" or "mA."

CAUTION: If the meter leads are inserted into ammeter terminals, even though the selector is set to

volts, the meter may be damaged or an internal fuse may blow if the test leads touch both terminals of a battery.

---

3. **Measure the component being tested.** Carefully note the decimal point and the unit on the meter face.

   - **Correct scale.** A 12-volt battery is measured with a low-voltage scale selected. The proper reading of 12.0 is given.
   - **Incorrect scale.** A 12-volt battery is measured with a high-voltage scale selected. Use of the incorrect scale results in a reading of 0.012.

   If a 12-volt battery is measured with an autoranging meter, the correct reading of 12.0 is given. "AUTO" and "V" should show on the face of the meter.

4. **Interpret the reading.** This is especially difficult on autoranging meters, where the meter itself se-

lects the proper scale. The following are two examples of different readings:

- A voltage drop is being measured. The specifications indicate a maximum voltage drop of 0.2 volt. The meter reads "AUTO" and "43.6 mV." This reading means that the voltage drop is 0.0436 volt, or 43.6 mV, which is far lower than the 0.2 volt (200 mV). Because the number showing on the meter face is much larger than the specifications, many beginner technicians are led to believe that the voltage drop is excessive.

HINT: Pay attention to the units displayed on the meter face and convert to base units.

- A spark plug wire is being measured. The reading should be less than 10,000 ohms for each foot in length if the wire is okay. The wire being tested is 3 ft long (maximum allowable resistance is 30,000 ohms). The meter reads "AUTO" and "14.85 KΩ." This reading is equivalent to 14,850 ohms.

HINT: When converting from kilohms to ohms, make the decimal point a comma.

Because this reading is well below the specified maximum allowable, the spark plug wire is okay.

◀ **TECH TIP** ▶

PURCHASE A DIGITAL METER THAT WILL WORK FOR AUTOMOTIVE USE

Purchase a digital meter that is capable of reading the following:

- DC volts
- AC volts
- DC amperes (up to 10 A or more is helpful)
- Ohms up to 40 MΩ (40 million ohms)
- Diode check

Additional features for advanced automotive diagnosis include:

- Frequency [hertz (Hz)]
- Temperature probe (°F and/or °C)
- Pulse width [millisecond (ms)]
- Duty cycle (%)

If working on older model vehicles, select a meter that includes:

- RPM (engine speed)
- Dwell (degrees)

◀ **TECH TIP** ▶

THINK OF MONEY

Digital meter displays can often be confusing. A battery being measured as 12.5 volts would be displayed as 12.50 V, just as $12.50 is 12 dollars and 50 cents. A 0.5-volt reading on a digital meter will be displayed as 0.50 V, just as $0.50 is half of a dollar.

Low-value displays can be even more confusing. For example, if a voltage reading is 0.063 volt, an autoranging meter will display 63 mV or 63/1000 of a volt or $63 of $1000. (It takes 1000 mV to equal 1 volt.) Millivolts are like one-tenth of a cent with 1 volt being $1.00. Therefore, 630 mV is equal to $0.63 of $1.00 (630 1/10's cent or 63 cents).

To avoid confusion, manually range the meter to read base units (whole volts). If the meter is ranged to base unit volts, 63 mV would be displayed as 0.063 or maybe just 0.06 depending on the display capabilities of the meter.

RMS VERSUS AVERAGE

Alternating current voltage waveforms can be true sinusoidal or nonsinusoidal. A true sine wave pattern measurement will be the same for both **root-mean-square (RMS)** and average reading meters. RMS and averaging are two methods used to measure the true effective rating of a signal that is constantly changing. See Figure 10-21.

RESOLUTION, DIGITS, AND COUNTS

Resolution refers to how small or fine a measurement the meter can make. By knowing the resolution of a DMM, you can determine if the meter could measure down to 1 volt or to 1 millivolt (1/1000 of a volt).

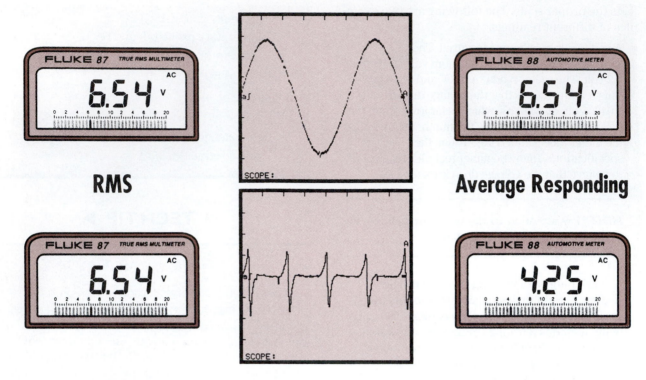

FIGURE 10-21 When reading AC voltage signals, a true RMS meter (such as a Fluke 87) provides a different reading than an average responding meter (such as a Fluke 88). The only time this difference is important is when a reading is to be compared with a specification. *(Courtesy of Fluke Corporation)*

You would not buy a ruler marked in 1-in. segments (or centimeters) if you had to measure down to .25 in. (or 1 mm). A thermometer that measures only in whole degrees is of little use when your normal temperature is 98.6°F. You need a thermometer with 0.1° *resolution.*

The terms *digits* and *counts* are used to describe a meter's resolution. DMMs are grouped by the number of counts or digits they display. A 3.5-digit meter can display three full digits ranging from 0 to 9, and one "half" digit which displays only a 1 or is left blank. A 3.5-digit meter will display up to 1999 counts of resolution. A 4.5-digit meter can display up to 19,000 counts of resolution.

It is more precise to describe a meter by counts of resolution rather than by 3.5 or 4.5 digits. Some 3.5-digit meters have enhanced resolution of up to 3200 or 4000 counts.

Meters with more counts offer better resolution for certain measurements. For example, a 1999-count meter cannot measure down to a tenth of 0.10 volt when measuring 200 volts or more. See Figure 10-22. However, a 3200-count meter will display 0.10 volt up to 320 volts. Digits displayed to the far right of the display may at times flicker or constantly change. This is called *digit rattle* and represents a changing voltage being measured on the ground (COM terminal of the meter lead). High-quality meters are designed to reject this unwanted voltage.

ACCURACY

Accuracy is the largest allowable error that will occur under specific operating conditions. In other words, it is an indication of how close the DMM's displayed measurement is to the actual value of the signal being measured.

Accuracy for a DMM is usually expressed as a percent of reading. An accuracy of ±1% of reading means that for a displayed reading of 100.0 V, the actual value of the voltage could be anywhere between 99.0 to 101.0 volts. Thus, a lower accuracy percentage is better.

- Unacceptable = 1.00%
- Okay = 0.50% (1/2%)
- Good = 0.25% (1/4%)
- Excellent = 0.10% (1/10%)

For example, if a battery had 12.6 volts, a meter could read between the following, based on its accuracy.

FIGURE 10-22 This meter display shows 052.2 volts AC. Notice that the zero beside the 5 indicates that the meter can read over 100 volts AC with a resolution of 0.1 volt.

± 0.1%	high = 12.61
	low = 12.59
± 0.25%	high = 12.63
	low = 12.57
± 0.50%	high = 12.66
	low = 12.54
± 1.00%	high = 12.73
	low = 12.47

Before you purchase a meter, check the accuracy. Accuracy is usually indicated on the specifications sheet for the meter.

ANALOG VERSUS DIGITAL STORAGE OSCILLOSCOPE

An **oscilloscope** (usually called a **scope**) is a visual voltmeter with a timer (clock) that shows when a voltage changes. An *analog scope* uses a **cathode ray tube (CRT)** similar to a television screen to display voltage patterns. The scope screen displays the electrical signal constantly. A *digital scope* commonly uses an LCD (liquid crystal display), but a CRT may also be used on some digital scopes. A digital scope takes samples of the signals that can be stopped or stored; hence the term **digital storage oscilloscope (DSO).** Because an analog scope displays all voltage signals and does not take samples, it cannot miss an occurrence. A digital storage scope can miss glitches that may occur between samples; thus, a DSO with a high "sampling rate" is preferred.

NOTE: Some digital storage scopes such as the Fluke 98 increase the capture rate of 25 million samples per second, which means that the scope can capture a glitch (fault) that lasts just 40 nano seconds (0.00000040 sec).

For example, if a throttle-position sensor was to be tested on an analog and a DSO, the results would be as shown in Figures 10-23 and 10-24.

OSCILLOSCOPE DISPLAY GRID

A typical scope face has 8 grids vertically (up and down) and 10 grids horizontally. The grid lines on the scope screen are used as a reference scale, which is called a **graticule.** This arrangement is commonly called an **8 × 10 display.**

NOTE: These numbers represent the metric dimensions of the graticule in centimeters. Therefore, the display would be 8 cm (80 mm or 3.14 in.) high and 10 cm (100 mm or 3.90 in.) wide.

Voltage is displayed on a scope as a line vertically from the bottom. The scope illustrates time left to right as shown in Figure 10-25.

SETTING THE TIME BASE

Most scopes use 10 divisions from left to right on the display. The **time base** indicates how much time will be displayed in each division. For example, if the scope is set to read 200 mV (0.200 V) per division, then the total displayed would be 2 sec (0.200 × 10 divisions = 2 sec). The time base should be set to an amount of time that allows two to four events to be displayed. Sample time is millivolts per division (indicated as mV/div) and total time includes:

Ms/Division	Total Time
1	10 ms (0.010 sec)
10	100 ms (0.100 sec)
50	500 ms (0.500 sec)
100	1 sec (1.000 sec)
500	5 sec (5.0 sec)
1000	10 sec (10.0 sec)

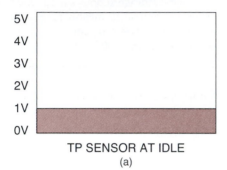

TP SENSOR AT IDLE

(a)

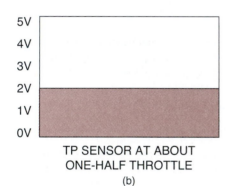

TP SENSOR AT ABOUT
ONE-HALF THROTTLE

(b)

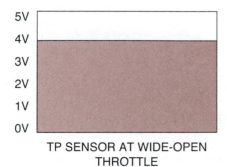

TP SENSOR AT WIDE-OPEN
THROTTLE

(c)

FIGURE 10-23 (a) On an analog scope, the voltage measured at the throttle-position signal wire is displayed on a horizontal line at about 0.5 volt. (b) As the throttle is opened, the horizontal line representing the voltage increases. (c) At wide-open throttle (WOT), the horizontal line indicates about 4.5 volts.

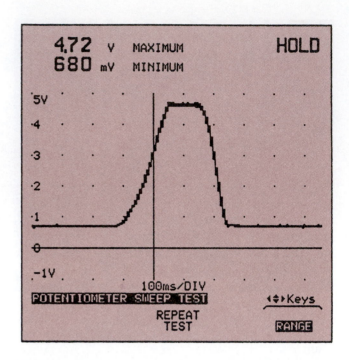

FIGURE 10-24 The display on a digital storage oscilloscope (DSO) displays the entire waveform from idle to WOT and then returns to idle. The display also indicates the maximum (4.72 volts) and minimum (680 mV or 0.68 volt) reading. The display does not show anything until the throttle is opened, because the scope has been set to start displaying a waveform after a certain voltage, or trigger, level has been reached. *(Courtesy of Fluke Corporation)*

FIGURE 10-25 A typical dual-trace bench scope. Notice the LCD frequency counter readout above the scope. This feature is useful for diagnosis of Ford MAP sensor or mass airflow (MAF) sensor outputs. (Some DMMs also include a frequency scale.)

NOTE: Increasing the time base reduces the number of samples per second.

The horizontal scale is divided into 10 divisions. If each division represented 1 sec of time, then the total time period displayed on the screen will be 10 sec. Time per division can vary greatly in automotive use, as follows:

Fuel injector—2 ms per division (20 ms total)
Throttle-position (TP) sensor—100 ms per division (1 sec total)
Oxygen sensor—1 sec per division (10 sec total)

The time per division is selected so that several events of the waveform are displayed. This allows comparisons to see if the waveform is consistent or is changing. Multiple waveforms shown on the display at the same time also allow for measurements to be seen more easily.

Commonly used time per division units for various component tests are as follows:

- Oxygen sensor—1 s/div
- TP sensor—100 ms/div
- MAP/MAF—2 ms/div
- Fuel injector—2 ms/div
- Stepper motor—10 ms/div
- Primary ignition—10 ms/div
- Dwell—20 ms/div
- Secondary ignition—10 ms/div
- Voltage measurements—5 ms/div
- Display diode test—50 ms/div

SETTING THE VOLTS PER DIVISION

The vertical scale has eight divisions. If each division is set to equal 1 volt, the display will show 0 to 8 volts. This is okay in a 0- to 5-volt variable sensor such as a TP sensor. The volts per division (V/div) should be set so that the entire anticipated waveform can be viewed. Examples include:

TP sensor	1 V/div (8 V total)
Battery, starting and charging	2 V/div (16 V total)
Oxygen sensor	200 mV/div (1.6 V total)

Notice from the examples that the total voltage to be displayed exceeds the voltage range of the component being tested. This ensures that all the waveform will be displayed. It also allows for some unanticipated voltage readings. For example, an oxygen sensor should read between 0 and 1 V (1000 mV). By setting the V/div to 200 mV, up to 1.6 V (1600 mV) will be displayed.

DC COUPLING

DC coupling allows the scope to display both AC and DC voltage signals and is the most used setting for automotive applications. An example of a DC voltage signal would be the starting and charging voltage measured at the battery.

A flat horizontal line across the display at a level of 12 volts indicates the DC voltage signal. When the starter motor is energized, a load is applied to the battery and the battery voltage drops to about 10.5 volts. This is displayed again as a horizontal line, but now at a level lower than previously seen. When the engine starts, the generator starts to charge the battery and the voltage increases to about 14.5 volts. Again, the display is a horizontal line, but with a higher level than before that shows the charging voltage. Any generator (alternator) ripple voltage caused by leaking diodes would be displayed as an AC signal on top of the DC waveform.

AC COUPLING

AC coupling allows the scope to read **alternating current (AC)** voltage signals and ignore any **direct current (DC)** voltage present in the circuit. For example, this setting allows the technician to view the ripple voltage of the charging circuit without seeing the 14 volts DC signal. For example, connect the scope probes to display 120 volts AC household voltage at an outlet.

CAUTION: 110 V AC can cause bodily injury. Always touch the rubber or plastic portions of the scope probes when making measurements of any circuit that exceed 30 volts (AC or DC). Some scopes cannot measure AC voltage higher than 30 volts. Always follow the scope manufacturer's operating instructions.

An AC voltage rises and falls above and below the zero level. To display several repeating continuously variable voltage signals, the proper time per division must be selected. Household electricity is 60 hertz (60 cycles per second) where 1 cycle requires just 18 ms (0.018 sec). One complete cycle displays as 0.2 ms/div (10 divisions × 2 ms/div = 20 ms). Because it is best to view two or three cycles, set the time base to 4 or 6 ms per division.

Setting the volts per division is a little tricky. A 120 V AC signal actually goes over 120 volts positive and down more than 120 volts negative. Therefore, to view the entire waveform, the total voltage range on the display must be greater than 240 volts. Because there are eight vertical grids, a setting of 50 volts per division would allow the scope to display a total of 400 volts (50 V × 8 = 400) with 200 volts positive and 200 volts negative.

PULSE TRAINS

A DC voltage that turns on and off in a series of pulses is called a **pulse train.** See Figure 10-26. Pulse train signals can vary in several ways.

Frequency

Frequency is the number of cycles per second, measured in hertz. Engine RPM signal is one example that can occur at various frequencies. At low engine speed, the ignition pulses occur fewer times per second (lower frequency) than when the engine is operated at higher engine speeds (RPMs).

Duty Cycle

Duty cycle refers to the percentage of on-time of the signal during one complete cycle. As on-time increases, the amount of time the signal is off decreases. Duty cycle is also called **pulse width modulation (PWM)** and can be measured in degrees. The General Motors computer-controlled carburetors are an example in which the carburetor mixture control solenoid is pulsed on and off with a variable duty cycle. The solenoid activation is constantly changing at 10 times per second (10 Hz), but the on-time varies. In this example, the duty cycle is measured in degrees. See Figure 10-27 on page 194.

Pulse Width

The **pulse width** is a measure of the actual on-time measured in milliseconds. Fuel injectors are usually controlled by varying the pulse width. See Figure 10-28 on page 194.

External Trigger

An **external trigger** is when the trace starts when a signal is received from another (external) source. A common example of an external trigger comes from the probe clamp around cylinder 1 spark plug wire to trigger the start of an ignition pattern.

Trigger Level

A scope will not start displaying a voltage signal until it is triggered or told to start. The **trigger level** must be set to start a stable display. In the example we want the pattern to start at 1 volt, then the trace will begin displaying on the left side of the screen *after* the trace has reached 1 volt.

Trigger Slope

The **trigger slope** is the voltage direction that a waveform requires to start display. Most often, the trigger to start a waveform display is taken from the signal itself. Besides trigger voltage level, most scopes can be adjusted to trigger only when the voltage rises past the trigger-level voltage, called a *positive slope*. When the trigger is activated by the voltage falling past the higher level, it is called a *negative slope*. The scope display indicates both a positive and a negative slope symbol. See Figure 10-29 on page 195.

For example, if a waveform such as a magnetic sensor used for crankshaft position or wheel speed starts moving upward, a positive slope should be selected. If a negative slope is selected, the waveform will not start showing until the voltage reaches the trigger level in a downward direction. A negative slope should be used when a fuel-injector circuit is being analyzed. In this circuit, the computer provides the ground and the voltage level drops when the computer commands the injector on. See the remaining chapters for examples of scope usage.

USING SCOPE LEADS

Most scopes, both analog and digital, normally use the same test leads. These leads usually attach to the scope through a **BNC connector,** a miniature standard coaxial cable connector named after its inventor, Baby Neil Councilman. BNC is an international standard that is used in the electronics industry. Each scope lead has an attached ground lead that should be connected to a good clean, metal engine ground. The probe of the scope lead attaches to the circuit or component being tested.

1. **Frequency** — Frequency is the number of cycles that take place per second. The more cycles that take place in one second, the higher the frequency reading. Frequencies are measured in hertz, which is the number of cycles per second. An eight hertz signal cycles eight times per second.

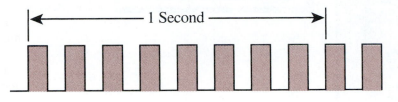

This is what an 8 hertz frequency signal would look like — 8 hertz means "8 cycles per second."

2. **Duty Cycle** — Duty cycle is a measurement comparing the signal on-time to the length of one complete cycle. As on-time increases, off-time decreases. Duty cycle is measured in percentage of on-time: A 60% duty cycle is a signal that's on 60% of the time, and off 40% of the time. Another way to measure duty cycle is dwell, which is measured in degrees instead of percent.

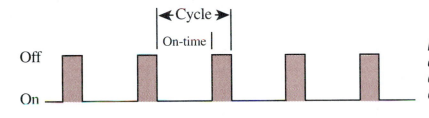

Duty cycle is the relationship between one complete cycle, and the signal's on-time. A signal can vary in duty cycle without affecting the frequency.

3. **Pulse Width** — Pulse width is the actual on-time of a signal, measured in milliseconds. With pulse width measurements, off-time doesn't really matter — the only real concern is how long the signal's on. This is a useful test for measuring conventional injector on-time, to see that the signal varies with load changes.

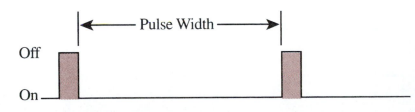

Pulse width is the actual time a signal's on, measured in milliseconds. The off-time doesn't affect signal pulse width at all — the only thing being measured is how long the signal's on.

FIGURE 10-26   A pulse train is any electrical signal that turns on and off, or goes high and low in a series of pulses. Igniter and fuel-injector pulses are examples of a pulse train signal. *(Courtesy of Fluke Corporation)*

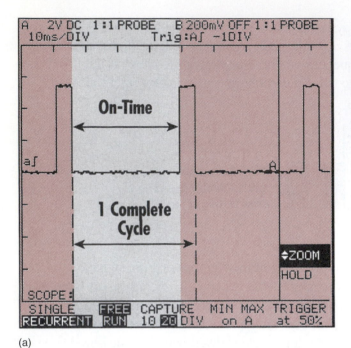

(a)

(b)

The "%" symbol in the upper right corner of the display tells you your meter's reading a duty cycle signal.

FIGURE 10-27   (a) A scope representation of a complete cycle showing both on-time and off-time. (b) A meter display indicating the on-time duty cycle in percent (%). Note the trigger and negative (−) symbol. This indicates that the meter started to record the percentage of on-time when the voltage dropped (start of on-time). *(Courtesy of Fluke Corporation)*

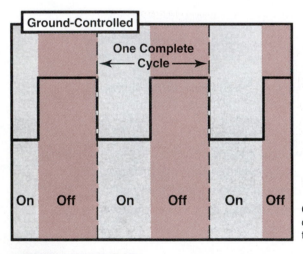

On a ground-controlled circuit, the on-time pulse is the lower horizontal pulse.

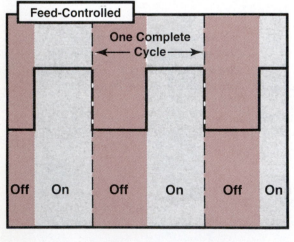

On a feed-controlled circuit, the on-time pulse is the upper horizontal pulse.

FIGURE   10-28   Most automotive computer systems control the device by opening and closing the ground to the component. *(Courtesy of Fluke Corporation)*

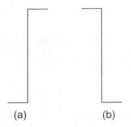

FIGURE 10-29 (a) A symbol for a positive trigger—a trigger that occurs at a rising (positive) edge of the signal (waveform). (b) A symbol for a negative trigger—trigger that occurs at a falling (negative) edge of the signal (waveform).

(a)   (b)

MEASURING BATTERY VOLTAGE WITH A SCOPE

One of the easiest things to measure and observe on a scope is battery voltage. A lower voltage can be observed on the scope display as the engine is started and a higher voltage should be displayed after the engine starts. See Figure 10-30.

An analog scope displays rapidly and cannot be set to show or freeze a display. Therefore, even though an analog scope shows all voltage signals, it is easy to miss a momentary glitch on an analog scope.

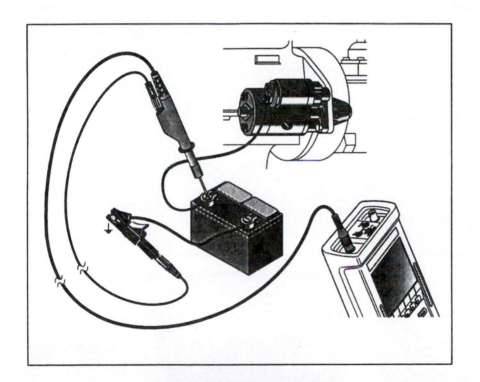

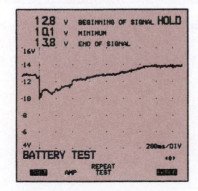

FIGURE 10-30 Battery voltage is represented by a flat horizontal line. In this example, the engine was started and the battery voltage dropped to about 10 volts as shown on the left side of the scope display. When the engine started, the generator (alternator) started to charge the battery and the voltage is shown as climbing. *(Courtesy of Fluke Corporation)*

◀ **SAFETY TIP** ▶

METER USAGE ON HYBRID VEHICLES

Many hybrid (gasoline and electric motor) powered vehicles are equipped with a generator that can exceed 400 volts DC. Be sure to follow all vehicle manufacturer's testing procedures and, if a voltage measurement is needed, be sure to use a meter and test leads that are designed to insulate against high voltages. The **International Electrotechnical Commission (IEC)** has several categories of voltage standards for meter and meter leads. These categories are ratings for overvoltage protection and are rated CAT I, CAT II, CAT III, and CAT IV. The higher the category, the greater the protection against voltage spikes. Under each category there are various voltage ratings.

CAT I   Typically a CAT I meter is used for low voltage measurements such as voltage measurements at wall outlets in the home. Meters with a CAT I rating are usually rated at 300 to 800 volts.

CAT II   A higher-rated meter that would be typically used for checking voltages at the fuse panel in the home. Meters with a CAT II rating are usually rated at 300 to 600 volts.

CAT III   The minimum rated meter that should be used for hybrid vehicles. This category is designed for voltage measurements at the service pole at the transformer. Meters with a CAT III rating are usually rated at 600 to 1000 volts.

CAT IV   CAT IV meters are for clamp-on meters only. If a clamp-on meter also has meter leads for voltage measurements, that part of the meter will be rated as CAT III.

NOTE: Always use the highest CAT rating meter, especially when working with hybrid vehicles. A CAT III 600-volt meter is safer than a CAT II 1000-volt meter because of the way the CAT rating is determined.

Therefore, for best personal protection, use only meters and meter leads that are CAT III or CAT IV rated when measuring voltage on a hybrid vehicle. See Figures 10-31 and 10-32.

FIGURE 10-31 Be sure to only use a meter that is CAT-III rated when taking electrical voltage measurements on a hybrid vehicle.

FIGURE 10-32 Always use meter leads that are CAT III-rated on a meter that is also CAT-III rated to maintain the protection needed when working on hybrid vehicles.

PHOTO SEQUENCE   Digital Meter Usage #1

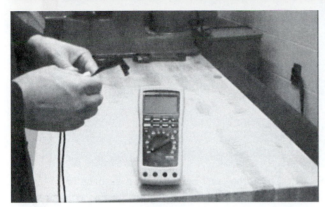

PS 6-1   Meter leads often become tangled. Start work with a digital meter by straightening the meter leads.

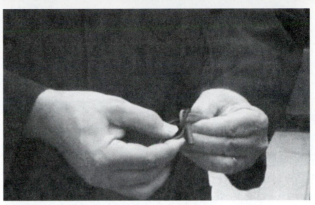

PS 6-2   To help prevent the leads from becoming tangled, tie a loose knot at the meter end of the leads.

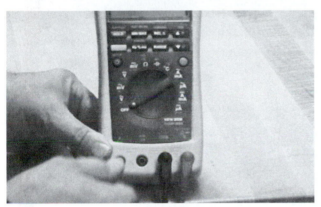

PS 6-3   For most electrical measurements, the black meter lead is inserted in the terminal labeled COM and the red meter lead is inserted into the terminal labeled V.

PS 6-4   To use a digital meter, turn the power switch on and select the unit of electricity to be measured. In this case, the rotary switch is turned to select DC volts, indicated by the letter V with a straight line and a straight dotted line over the V.

PS 6-5   If AC volts are selected (a V with a wavy line on top)—AC millivolts in this case—a reading usually appears on the display indicating an AC voltage is being induced in the meter leads from the fluorescent lights in the room.

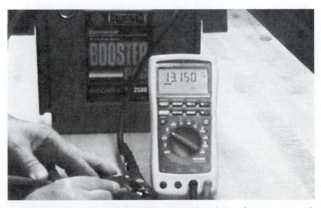

PS 6-6   Connect the red meter lead to the positive (+) terminal of a battery and the black meter lead to the negative (−) terminal of a battery. The meter reads the voltage difference between the leads.

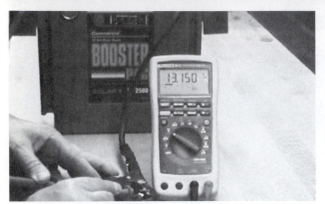

PS 6-7   For most automotive electrical use, select DC volts.

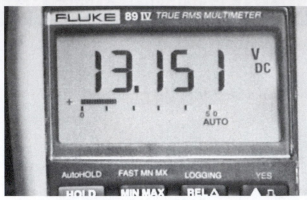

PS 6-8   This jump start battery unit measures 13.151 volts with the meter set on autoranging on the DC voltage scale. The accuracy of this meter (Fluke 89 IV) is greater than necessary for most automotive service work so the reading could be rounded to 13.2 V.

PS 6-9   Another meter (Fluke 87 III) displays four digits when measuring the voltage of the battery jump start unit.

PS 6-10   Both meters are displayed side-by-side to show the readings of both. The Fluke 89 IV (right) is capable of measuring down to 1/1000 of a volt.

PS 6-11   Meters can also be set to read different ranges. The "range" button was pressed once on the meter on the left. Notice that the meter is now set to read higher voltages. Note the added zero on the left of the display. The meter in this range setting cannot display any more accurately than 1/10 of a volt (13.1).

PS 6-12   Pressing the range button a second time on the meter results in the loss of 1/10 of a volt reading and the addition of another zero on the left of the display.

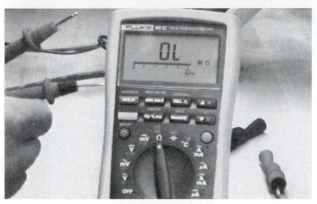

PS 6-13   To measure resistance, turn the rotary dial to the ohm (Ω) symbol. With the meter leads separated, the meter display reads OL (over limit), meaning that the resistance between the meter leads is higher than what is being read by the meter.

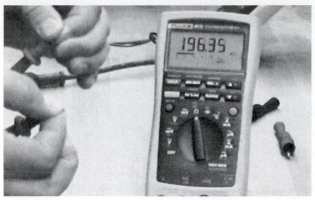

PS 6-14   The meter can read your own body resistance if you grasp the meter lead terminals with your fingers. The reading on the display indicates 196.35 kΩ or 196,350 ohms. Typical body resistance constantly changes and is usually between 100,000 and 300,000 ohms (100 kΩ to 300 kΩ).

PS 6-15   When measuring anything, be sure to read the meter face. In this case, the meter is reading 291.10 kΩ. The letter k represents 1000 ohms so the reading displayed is 291.10 thousand ohms or 291.100 ohms.

PS 6-16   A meter set on ohms can be used to check the resistance of a light bulb filament. In this case, the meter reads 3.15 ohms. If the bulb were bad (filament open), the meter would display OL.

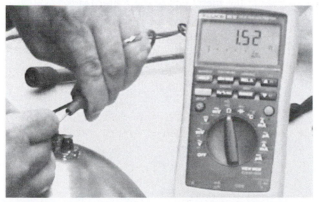

PS 6-17   A sealed beam headlight bulb is being measured. The filament being measured has 1.52 ohms. The only symbol in the window is the Ω symbol, which means that the display is showing the actual resistance in ohms (and not kΩ or MΩ).

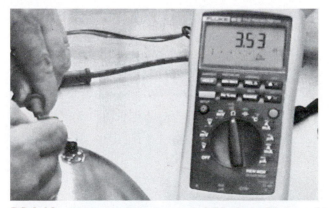

PS 6-18   The other filament reads 3.53 ohms. Obvious this filament is the low beam (high resistance means less current flow and a dimmer light).

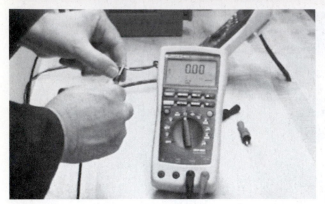

PS 6-19 A digital meter set to read ohms should measure 0.00 as shown when the meter leads are touched together. Some meters, such as this Fluke, have a relative button that can be pushed in order to zero the reading, if necessary, to compensate for the resistance of the meter leads.

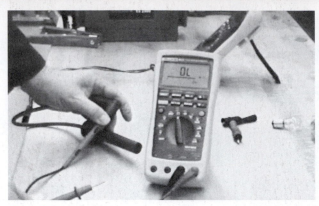

PS 6-20 To measure the resistance of a spark plug wire, attach one lead of the meter to one end and the other meter lead to the other end. The polarity (which meter lead is attached to which part of the component being measured) is not important when measuring resistance.

PS 6-21 The spark plug wire measures 5.900 kΩ (5900 ohms). This 1-foot-long spark plug wire is okay because it measures less than 10,000 ohms per foot of length (5900 ohms is less than 10,000 ohms).

PS 6-22 A digital multimeter can also be used to check the voltage of an electrical outlet. Set the meter to read AC volts. When measuring AC volts, either meter lead can be inserted in either outlet terminal. Just be careful not to touch either of the metal tips of the meter leads.

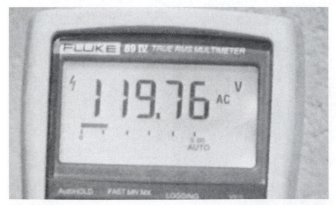

PS 6-23 The outlet voltage is 119.76 volts AC. Note the AC and V in the window display.

PS 7-1 An overall view of a typical digital multimeter. In the center is a rotary switch that can be turned to point to the various symbols around the switch. The symbols represent units of electricity that the meter can measure.

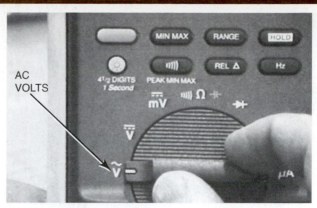

PS 7-2 The large letter V means volts and the wavy symbol over the V means that the meter measures alternating current (AC) voltage if this position is selected.

PS 7-3 Turning the meter on AC volts does show some voltage even if the leads are not connected to any vehicle or circuit. This small voltage is due to electromagnetic induction from the fluorescent lights and other electromagnetic sources.

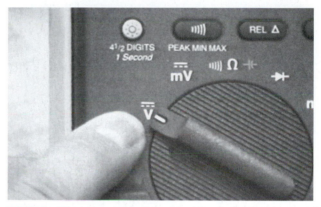

PS 7-4 The next symbol is a V with a dotted and a straight line overhead. This symbol stands for direct current (DC) volts. This position is most used for automotive service.

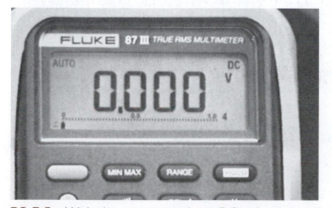

PS 7-5 With the rotary switch on DC volts, notice the display. The letters DC and V appear in the upper right of the display. Also note the word *auto* in the upper left. This indicates that the range (scale) of the meter will be automatically selected to best read the measured voltage.

PS 7-6 The symbol mV indicates millivolts or 1/1000 of a volt (0.001). The solid and dashed line above the mV means DC mV. This position is not normally used in most vehicle diagnostic or service work.

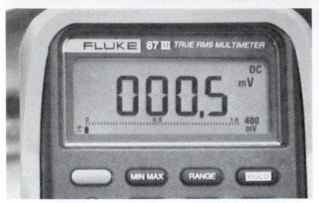

PS 7-7 This display is with DC mV selected. Notice the DC and mV in the display in the upper right. The display means that the meter is set to read up to 400 mV (0.400 V) DC.

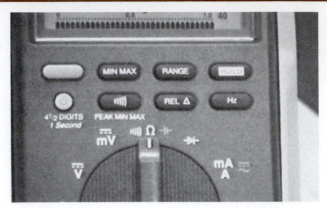

PS 7-8 The rotary switch is turned to Ω (ohms) unit of resistance measure. The symbol to the left of the Ω symbol is the beeper or continuity indicator. The meter will beep if there is continuity between the meter leads.

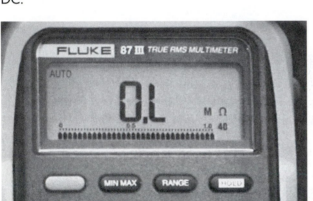

PS 7-9 Notice that auto is in the upper left and the MΩ is in the lower right. This MΩ means megohms or that the meter is set to read in millions of ohms.

PS 7-10 Another symbol to the right of the Ω symbol is the symbol for capacitance which is measured in microfarads. On this meter, the capacitor symbol is in blue, indicating that a blue button must be pushed for the meter to read capacitance.

PS 7-11 When the blue button is pushed and the rotary switch is still on ohms (Ω), the meter will read capacitance in microfarads.

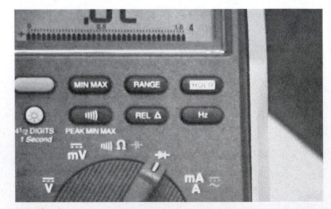

PS 7-12 The symbol shown is the symbol of a diode. In this position, the meter applies a voltage to a diode and the meter reads the voltage drop across the junction of a diode.

PS 7-13   Notice that in the diode check position, the display shows DCV in the upper right, indicating that the meter will be showing the voltage drop of a diode which is usually between 0.5 and 0.7 volt or 1.5 to 2.2 volts for a light-emitting diode (LED).

PS 7-14   The next position that the rotary knob is pointing to is the position used to measure amperes (A) and milliamperes (mA).

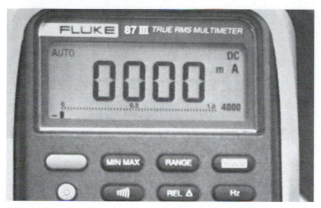

PS 7-15   Notice the display when mA and A are selected. The word *auto* in the upper left indicates that the meter is set to read whatever amperage is about to be measured.

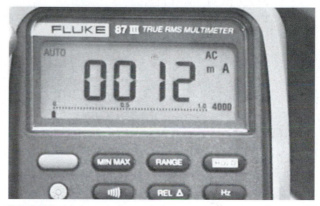

PS 7-16   By pushing the blue button, the meter is switched to read AC mA. Notice that although the meter is reading some current, even though the leads are not connected to a circuit, it is actually reading induced current in the leads from the fluorescent lights.

PS 7-17   The last position on the rotary switch is the symbol for microamperes (one millionth of an ampere or 0.000001 A). This position is not used for automotive service work.

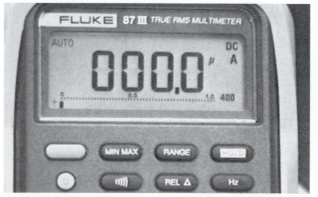

PS 7-18   Notice the symbol for microamperes (the Greek letter mu or μ) and DCA on the display.

PS 7-19   One of the most useful features of this meter is the MIN/MAX feature. By pushing the MIN/MAX button, the meter will be able to display the highest (MAX) and the lowest (MIN) reading of a voltage during a test. This is a great feature for finding intermittent problems.

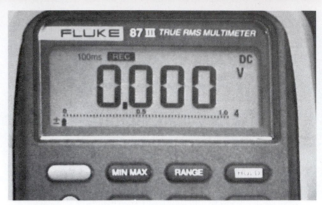

PS 7-20   Pushing the MIN/MAX button puts the meter into record mode. Note the 100 mS and "rec" on the display. In this position, the meter is capturing any voltage change that lasts 100 mS (0.1 sec) or longer.

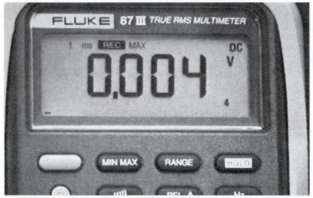

PS 7-21   Pushing the beeper button (below the MIN/MAX button) places the meter into a 1 mS (0.001 sec) capture mode.

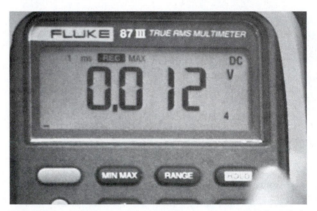

PS 7-22   The maximum reading is being displayed during the test. As long as the display shows "rec," it is recording any new high or low voltages that last longer than one-thousandth of a second (0.001 sec).

PS 7-23   To show the lowest voltage recorded, touch the MIN/MAX button. The lowest voltage will be displayed.

PS 7-24   Because some voltages or other signals change, it is often necessary to manually set the range of the meter. The range of this meter is displayed in the lower right. In this range (4 volts DC), the meter will read voltage up to 4 volts and will display OL if it detects any voltage above 4 volts.

PS 7-25   To increase the range of the meter, touch the range button. Now the meter is set to read voltage up to 40 volts DC. Notice that in this range the meter is able to display two decimal places (such as 12.36 volts).

PS 7-26   Pushing the range button one more time changes the meter scale to the 400-volt range. Notice that the decimal point has moved to the right, indicating that it can only read voltage to one-tenth of a volt (such as 12.4 volts).

PS 7-27   Pushing the range button again changes the meter to the 4000-volt range. Notice that the decimal point is missing and in this range the meter is not capable of displaying anything but full-volt units such as 12 volts. This range is not suitable to use in automotive applications.

PS 7-28   By pushing and holding the range button, the meter will reset to autorange. Autorange is the preferred setting for most automotive measurements except when using MIN/MAX record mode where the meter must be set to the range that will give the best results (usually the 40-volt range on a Fluke meter).

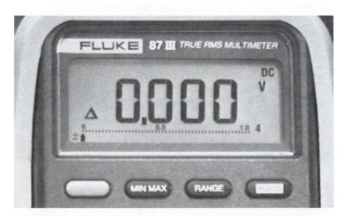

PS 7-29   The relative "rel" or (Δ) mode sets the meter display to zero and is useful for eliminating any resistance in the meter leads. The relative mode is also useful for voltage drop measurements. First measure the battery voltage and then push the "rel" button to put the meter back to zero and store the voltage as a reference. Then measure the voltage at the device. The meter will read the difference (voltage drop) between the battery and the device.

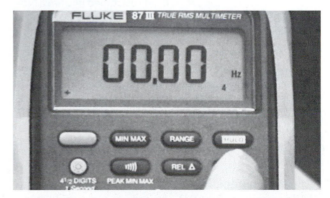

PS 7-30   Frequency of a changing voltage can also be measured by selecting hertz (Hz) while the rotary switch is on AC or sometimes DC volts. The Hz symbol will appear in the display.

PHOTO SEQUENCE   Digital Meter Usage #2—*Continued*

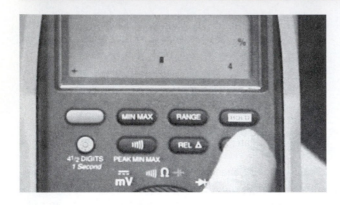

PS 7-31 Percent (%) of duty cycle (on-time of a signal) can be measured by pushing the Hz button. This feature allows the service technician to read the on-time of a mixture control solenoid or other device that is being turned on and off by the computer.

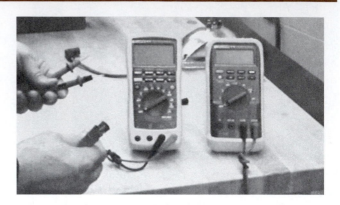

PS 7-32 Two meters are being set up to measure each other. A Fluke 89 is on the left and a Fluke 87 is on the right. By connecting the meter leads, one meter can measure the other meter.

PS 7-33 The meter on the left is set to read DC volts and the meter on the right is set to read resistance in ohms. Notice that the meter on the left is reading 0.6472 volts DC, indicating that the meter on the right is applying a voltage to measure resistance. Because the meter applies a voltage, the resistance of any computer circuit should never be attempted. The voltage applied by the meter, even though low, can damage electronic components.

PS 7-34 The meter on the right is reading 10.983 MΩ (10,983,000 ohms), indicating that the resistance of the meter itself is extremely high and will not affect the circuit being measured when the leads are attached. This is a high-impedance meter and the reading should be greater than 10 MΩ to be safely used on computer-controlled circuits. This high impedance is only effective on the voltage scales. This is why most vehicle manufacturers recommend checking voltages instead of current or resistance.

SUMMARY

1. Digital multimeter (DMM) and digital volt-ohm-milliammeter (DVOM) are terms commonly used for electronic high-impedance test meters.
2. Use of a high-impedance digital meter is required on any computer-related circuit or component.
3. Ammeters measure current and must be connected in series in the circuit.
4. Voltmeters measure voltage and are connected in parallel.
5. Ohmmeters measure resistance of a component and must be connected in parallel, with the circuit or component disconnected from power.
6. Logic probes can indicate the presence of both ground and power.

REVIEW QUESTIONS

1. Why are most digital meters called high-impedance meters?

2. How should an ammeter be connected to an electrical circuit?

3. Why must an ohmmeter be connected to a disconnected circuit or component?

4. How should a voltmeter be connected to an electrical circuit?

ASE CERTIFICATION-TYPE QUESTIONS

1. Inductive ammeters work because of what principle?
   a. Magic
   b. Electromagnetic induction
   c. A magnetic field surrounds any wire carrying a current
   d. Voltage drop as it flows through a conductor

2. A meter used to measure amperes is called _____.
   a. An amp meter
   b. An ampmeter
   c. An ammeter
   d. A coulomb meter

3. A voltmeter should be connected to the circuit being tested _____.
   a. In series
   b. In parallel
   c. Only when no power is flowing
   d. Both a and c

4. An ohmmeter should be connected to the circuit being tested _____.
   a. In series
   b. In parallel
   c. Only when no power is flowing
   d. Both b and c

5. A high-impedance meter _____.
   a. Measures a high amount of current flow
   b. Measures a high amount of resistance
   c. Can measure a high voltage
   d. Has a high internal resistance

6. A meter is set to read DC volts on the 4-volt scale. The meter leads are connected at a 12-volt battery. The display will read _____.
   a. 0.00
   b. OL
   c. 12 V
   d. 0.012 V

7. Technician A says an analog scope can store the waveform for viewing later. Technician B says that the trigger level has to be set on most scopes to view a changing waveform. Which technician is correct?
   a. Technician A only
   b. Technician B only
   c. Both Technicians A and B
   d. Neither Technician A nor B

8. The highest amount of resistance that can be read by the meter set to the 2-kΩ scale is _____.
   a. 2000 ohms
   b. 200 ohms
   c. 200 kΩ (200,000 ohms)
   d. 20,000,000 ohms

9. If a digital meter face shows 0.93 when set to read kilohms, the reading means _____.
   a. 93 ohms
   b. 930 ohms
   c. 9300 ohms
   d. 93,000 ohms

10. A reading of 432 shows on the face of the meter set to the millivolts scale. The reading means _____.
    a. 0.432 volt
    b. 4.32 volts
    c. 43.2 volts
    d. 4320 volts

◀ Chapter 11 ▶

COMPUTER FUNDAMENTALS

OBJECTIVES

After studying Chapter 11, the reader should be able to:

1. Prepare for ASE Electrical/Electronic Systems (A6) certification test content area "A" (General Electrical/Electronic Systems Diagnosis).
2. Explain the purpose and function of onboard computers.
3. List the various parts of an automotive computer.
4. List five input sensors.
5. List four devices controlled by the computer (output devices).

COMPUTER CONTROL

Modern automotive control systems consist of a network of electronic sensors, actuators, and computer modules designed to regulate the powertrain and vehicle support systems. The **powertrain control module (PCM)** is the heart of this system. It coordinates engine and transmission operation, processes data, maintains communications, and makes the control decisions needed to keep the vehicle operating.

Automotive computers use voltage to send and receive information. Voltage is electrical pressure and does not flow through circuits, but voltage can be used as a signal. A computer converts input information or data into voltage signal combinations that represent number combinations. The number combinations can represent a variety of information—temperature, speed, or even words and letters. A computer processes the input voltage signals it receives by computing what they represent, and then delivering the data in computed or processed form.

THE FOUR BASIC COMPUTER FUNCTIONS

The operation of every computer can be divided into four basic functions. See Figure 11-1.

- Input
- Processing
- Storage
- Output

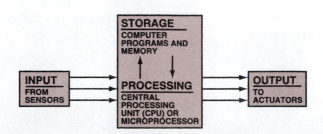

FIGURE 11-1 All computer systems perform four basic functions: input, processing, storage, and output.

These basic functions are not unique to computers; they can be found in many noncomputer systems. However, we need to know how the computer handles these functions.

Input

First, the computer receives a voltage signal (input) from an input device. The device can be as simple as a button or a switch on an instrument panel, or a sensor on an automotive engine. See Figure 11-2 for a typical type of automotive sensor.

Vehicles use various mechanical, electrical, and magnetic sensors to measure factors such as vehicle speed, engine RPM, air pressure, oxygen content of exhaust gas, air flow, and engine coolant temperature. Each sensor transmits its information in the form of voltage signals. The computer receives these voltage signals, but before it can use them, the signals must undergo a process called **input conditioning.** This process includes amplifying voltage signals that are too small for the computer circuitry to handle. Input conditioners generally are located inside the computer, but a few sensors have their own input-conditioning circuitry.

Processing

Input voltage signals received by a computer are processed through a series of electronic logic circuits maintained in its programmed instructions. These logic circuits change the input voltage signals, or data, into output voltage signals or commands.

Storage

The program instructions for a computer are stored in electronic memory. Some programs may require that certain input data be stored for later reference or future processing. In others, output commands may be delayed or stored before they are transmitted to devices elsewhere in the system.

Computers have two types of memory: permanent and temporary. Permanent memory is called **read-only memory (ROM)** because the computer can only read the contents; it cannot change the data stored in it. This data is retained even when power to the computer is shut off. Part of the ROM is built into the computer, and the rest is located in an IC chip called a **programmable read-only memory (PROM)** or calibration assembly. See Figure 11-3. Many chips are erasable, meaning that the program can be changed. These chips are called erasable programmable read-only memory or EPROM. Since the early 1990s most programmable memory has been electronically erasable, meaning that the program in the chip can be reprogrammed by using a scan tool and the proper software. This computer reprogramming is usually called *reflashing*. These chips are electrically erasable programmable read-only memory, abbreviated **EEPROM** or **E²PROM.** All vehicles equipped with onboard diagnosis second generation, called OBD II, are equipped with EEPROMs.

Temporary memory is called **random-access memory (RAM)** because the microprocessor can write or store new data into it as directed by the computer program, as well as read the data already in it. Automotive computers use two types of RAM memory: **volatile**

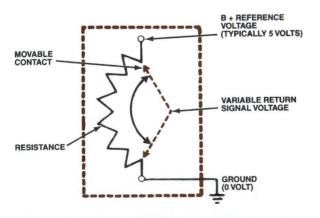

FIGURE 11-2 A potentiometer uses a movable contact to vary resistance and send an analog voltage right to the PCM.

FIGURE 11-3 A replaceable PROM used in an older General Motors computer. Notice that the sealed access panel has been removed to gain access.

and **nonvolatile.** Volatile RAM memory is lost whenever the ignition is turned off. However, a type of volatile RAM called **keep-alive memory (KAM)** can be wired directly to battery power. This prevents its data from being erased when the ignition is turned off. Both RAM and KAM have the disadvantage of losing their memory when disconnected from their power source. One example of RAM and KAM is the loss of station settings in a programmable radio when the battery is disconnected. Since all the settings are stored in RAM, they have to be reset when the battery is reconnected. System trouble codes are commonly stored in RAM and can be erased by disconnecting the battery.

Nonvolatile RAM memory can retain its information even when the battery is disconnected. One use for this type of RAM is the storage of odometer information in an electronic speedometer. The memory chip retains the mileage accumulated by the vehicle. When speedometer replacement is necessary, the odometer chip is removed and installed in the new speedometer unit. KAM is used primarily in conjunction with adaptive strategies.

Output

After the computer has processed the input signals, it sends voltage signals or commands to other devices in the system, such as system actuators. An **actuator** is an electrical or mechanical device that converts electrical energy into heat, light, or motion, such as adjusting engine idle speed, altering suspension height, or regulating fuel metering.

Computers also can communicate with, and control, each other through their output and input functions. This means that the output signal from one computer system can be the input signal for another computer system through a network.

Most all outputs work electrically in one of three ways:

- Switched
- Pulse width modulated
- Digital

A switched output is an output that is either on or off. In many circuits, the PCM uses a relay to switch a device on or off. This is because the relay is a low current device that can switch a higher current device. Most computer circuits cannot handle a lot of current. By using a relay circuit as shown in Figure 11-4, the PCM provides the output control to the relay, which in turn provides the output control to the device. The relay coil, which the PCM controls, typically draws less than 0.5 amps. The device that the relay controls may draw 30 amps or more.

These switches are actually transistors, often called **output drivers.**

Low-Side Drivers

Low-side drivers, often abbreviated **LSD,** are transistors that complete the ground path in the circuit. Ignition voltage is supplied to the relay as well as battery voltage. The computer output is connected to the ground side of the relay coil. The computer energizes the fuel pump relay by turning the transistor on and completing the ground path for the relay coil. A relatively low current flows through the relay coil and transistor that is inside the computer. This causes the relay to switch and provides the fuel pump with battery voltage. The majority of switched outputs have typically been low-side drivers. See Figure 11-5. Low-side drivers can often perform a diagnostic circuit check by monitoring the voltage from the relay to check that the control circuit for the relay is complete. A low-side driver, however, cannot detect a short-to-ground.

High-Side Drivers

High-side drivers, often abbreviated **HSD,** control the power side of the circuit. In these applications when the transistor is switched on, voltage is applied to the device. A ground has been provided to the device so when the high-side driver switches the device will be energized. In some applications, high-side drivers are used instead of low-side drivers to provide better circuit protection. General Motors vehicles have used a high-side driver to control the fuel pump relay instead of a low-side driver. In the event of an accident, should the circuit to the fuel pump relay become grounded, a high-side driver would cause a short circuit, which would cause the fuel pump relay to de-energize. High-

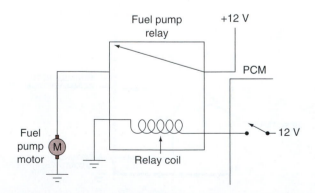

FIGURE 11-4 A typical output driver. In this case, the PCM applies voltage to the fuel pump relay coil to energize the fuel pump.

side drivers inside modules can detect electrical faults such as a lack of continuity when the circuit is not energized. See Figure 11-6.

Pulse Width Modulation

Pulse width modulation (**PWM**) is a method of controlling an output using a digital signal. Instead of just turning devices on or off, the computer can control output devices more precisely by using pulse width modulation. For example, a vacuum solenoid could be a pulse width modulated device. If the vacuum solenoid is controlled by a switched driver, switching ei-

ther on or off would mean that either full vacuum would flow through the solenoid or no vacuum would flow through the solenoid. However, to control the amount of vacuum that flows through the solenoid, pulse width modulation could be used. A PWM signal is a digital signal, usually 0 volts and 12 volts, that is cycling at a fixed frequency. Varying the length of time that the signal is on, provides a signal that can vary the on and off time of an output. The ratio of on-time relative to the period of the cycle is referred to as **duty cycle**. See Figure 11-7. Depending on the frequency of the signal, which is usually fixed, this signal would turn the device on and off a fixed number of times per second. When, for example, the voltage is high (12 volts) 90% of the time and low (0 volts) the other 10%

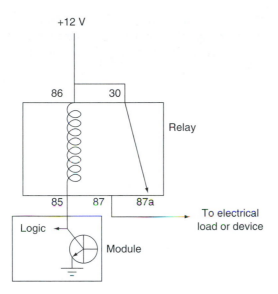

FIGURE 11-5   A typical low-side driver (LSD), which uses a control module to provide the ground path for the relay coil.

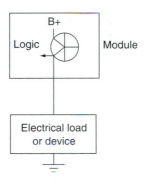

FIGURE 11-6   A typical module controlled high-side driver (HSD) where the module itself supplies the electrical power to the electrical device. The logic circuit inside the module can detect circuit faults including continuity of the circuit, and if there is a short-to-ground in the circuit being controlled.

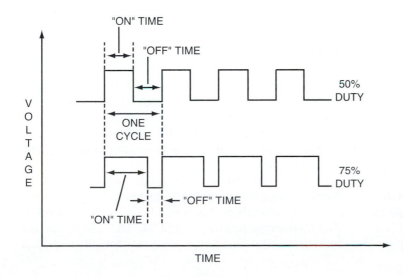

FIGURE 11-7   Both the top and bottom pattern have the same frequency. However, the amount of on-time varies. Duty cycle is the percentage of the time during a cycle that the signal is turned on.

of the time, the signal has a 90% duty cycle. In other words, if this signal were applied to the vacuum solenoid, the solenoid would be on 90% of the time. This would allow more vacuum to flow through the solenoid. The computer has the ability to vary this on and off time or pulse width modulation at any rate between 0 and 100%.

A good example of pulse width modulation is the cooling fan speed control. The speed of the cooling fan is controlled by varying the amount of on-time that the battery voltage is applied to the cooling fan motor.

100% duty cycle — the fan runs at full speed

75% duty cycle — the fan runs at ¾ speed

50% duty cycle — the fan runs at ½ speed

25% duty cycle — the fan runs at ¼ speed

The use of PMW, therefore, results in very precise control of an output device to achieve the amount of cooling needed and conserve electrical energy compared to simply timing the cooling fan on high when needed. PWM may be used to control vacuum through a solenoid, the amount of purge of the evaporative purge solenoid, the speed of a fuel pump motor, control of a linear motor, or even the intensity of a light bulb.

DIGITAL COMPUTERS

In a **digital** computer, the voltage signal or processing function is a simple high/low, yes/no, on/off signal. The digital signal voltage is limited to two voltage levels: high voltage and low voltage. Since there is no stepped range of voltage or current in-between, a digital binary signal is a "square wave."

The signal is called "digital" because the on and off signals are processed by the computer as the digits or numbers 0 and 1. The number system containing only these two digits is called the **binary** system. Any number or letter from any number system or language alphabet can be translated into a combination of binary 0s and 1s for the digital computer.

A digital computer changes the analog input signals (voltage) to digital bits (*bi*nary dig*its*) of information through an **analog-to-digital (AD) converter** circuit. The binary digital number is used by the computer in its calculations or logic networks. Output signals usually are digital signals that turn system actuators on and off.

The digital computer can process thousands of digital signals per second because its circuits are able to switch voltage signals on and off in billionths of a second. See Figure 11-8.

FIGURE 11-8 Many electronic components are used to construct a typical vehicle computer. Notice the quantity of chips, resistors, and capacitors used in this General Motors computer.

Parts of a Computer

The software consists of the programs and logic functions stored in the computer's circuitry. The hardware is the mechanical and electronic parts of a computer.

Central processing unit (CPU). The microprocessor is the **central processing unit (CPU)** of a computer. Since it performs the essential mathematical operations and logic decisions that make up its processing function, the CPU can be considered the heart of a computer. Some computers use more than one microprocessor, called a coprocessor.

Computer memory. Other IC devices store the computer operating program, system sensor input data, and system actuator output data, information that is necessary for CPU operation.

Computer Programs

By operating a vehicle on a dynamometer and manually adjusting the variable factors such as speed, load, and spark timing, it is possible to determine the optimum output settings for the best driveability, economy, and emission control. This is called **engine mapping.** See Figure 11-9.

Engine mapping creates a three-dimensional performance graph that applies to a given vehicle and powertrain combination. Each combination is mapped in this manner to produce a PROM. This allows an automaker to use one basic computer for all models; a

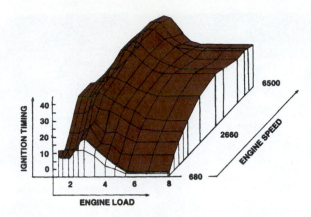

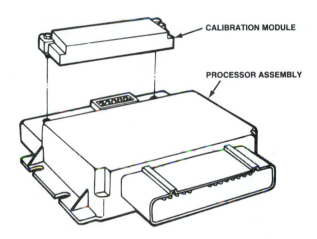

FIGURE 11-9 Typical ignition timing map developed from testing and used by the vehicle computer to provide the optimum ignition timing for all engine speeds and load combinations.

FIGURE 11-10 The calibration module on many Ford computers contains a system PROM.

unique PROM individualizes the computer for a particular model. Also, if a driveability problem can be resolved by a change in the program, the manufacturers can release a revised PROM to supersede the earlier part.

Many older vehicle computers used a single PROM that plugged into the computer. See Figure 11-10. Some Ford computers used a larger "calibration module" that contained the system PROM.

NOTE: If the onboard computer needs to be replaced, the PROM or calibration module must be removed from the defective unit and installed in the replacement computer. Since the mid-1990s, computers must be programmed or *flashed* before being put into service.

FIGURE 11-11 The clock generator produces a series of pulses that are used by the microprocessor and other components to stay in step with each other at a steady rate.

Clock Rates and Timing

The microprocessor receives sensor input voltage signals, processes them by using information from other memory units, and then sends voltage signals to the appropriate actuators. The microprocessor communicates by transmitting long strings of 0s and 1s in a language called binary code. But the microprocessor must have some way of knowing when one signal ends and another begins. That is the job of a crystal oscillator called a **clock generator.** See Figure 11-11. The computer's crystal oscillator generates a steady stream of one-bit-long voltage pulses. Both the microprocessor and the memories monitor the clock pulses while they are communicating. Because they know how long each voltage pulse should be, they can distinguish between a 01 and a 0011. To complete the process, the input and output circuits also watch the clock pulses.

Computer Speeds

Not all computers operate at the same speed; some are faster than others. The speed at which a computer operates is specified by the cycle time, or clock speed, required to perform certain measurements. Cycle time or clock speed is measured in megahertz (4.7 MHz, 8.0 MHz, 15 MHz, 18 MHz, etc.).

Baud Rate

The computer transmits bits of a serial datastream at precise intervals. The computer's processing speed is called the baud rate, or bits per second. Just as MPH helps in estimating the length of time required to travel a certain distance, the baud rate is useful in estimating how long a given computer will need to transmit a specified amount of data to another computer. Storage of a single character requires eight bits per byte, plus an additional two bits to indicate stop and start. This means that transmission of one character requires 10 bits. Dividing the baud rate by 10 tells us the maximum number of words per second that can be transmitted. For example, if the computer has a baud rate of 600, approximately 60 words can be received or sent per minute.

Automotive computers have evolved from a baud rate of 160 used in the early 1980s to a baud rate as high as 500,000 for some networks. The speed of data transmission is an important factor both in system operation and in system troubleshooting.

Control Module Locations

The onboard automotive computer has many names. It may be called an **electronic control unit (ECU), electronic control module (ECM), electronic control assembly (ECA),** or a **controller,** depending on the manufacturer and the computer application. The Society of Automotive Engineers (SAE) bulletin, J-1930, standardizes the name as a **powertrain control module (PCM).** The computer hardware is all mounted on one or more circuit boards and installed in a metal case to help shield it from electromagnetic interference (EMI). The wiring harnesses that link the computer to sensors and actuators connect to multipin connectors or edge connectors on the circuit boards.

Onboard computers range from single-function units that control a single operation to multifunction units that manage all of the separate (but linked) electronic systems in the vehicle. They vary in size from a small module to a notebook-sized box. Most other engine computers are installed in the passenger compartment either under the instrument panel or in a side kick panel where they can be shielded from physical damage caused by temperature extremes, dirt, and vibration, or interference by the high currents and voltages of various underhood systems. See Figures 11-12 and 11-13.

COMPUTER INPUT SENSORS

The vehicle computer uses the signals (voltage levels) from the following engine sensors.

- **Engine speed (RPM or revolutions per minute) sensor.** This signal comes from the primary signal in the ignition module.

FIGURE 11-12 This powertrain control module (PCM) is located under the hood on this Chevrolet pickup truck.

FIGURE 11-13 This PCM on a DaimlerChrysler vehicle can only be seen by hoisting the vehicle because it is located next to the radiator, and in the airflow to help keep it cool.

- **MAP (manifold absolute pressure) sensor.** This sensor detects engine load. The computer uses this information for fuel delivery and for onboard diagnosis of other sensors and systems such as the exhaust gas recirculation (EGR) system.
- **MAF (mass air flow) sensor.** This sensor measures the mass (weight and density) of the air entering the engine. The computer uses this information to determine the amount of fuel needed by the engine.

- **ECT (engine coolant temperature) sensor.** This sensor measures the temperature of the engine coolant needed by the computer to determine the amount of fuel and spark advance. This is a major sensor, especially when the engine is cold and when the engine is first started.
- **O2S (oxygen sensor).** This sensor measures the oxygen in the exhaust stream. These sensors are used for fuel control and to check other sensors and systems.
- **TP (throttle position) sensor.** This sensor measures the throttle opening and is used by the computer to control fuel delivery as well as spark advance and the shift points of the automotive transmission/transaxle.
- **VS (vehicle speed) sensor.** This sensor measures the vehicle speed using a sensor located at the output of the transmission/transaxle or by monitoring sensors at the wheel speed sensors.
- **Knock sensor.** The voltage signal from the knock sensor (**KS**) is sent to the PCM. The PCM retards the ignition timing until the knocking stops.

COMPUTER OUTPUTS

A vehicle computer can do just two things.

- Turn a device on.
- Turn a device off.

The computer can turn devices such as fuel injectors on and off very rapidly or keep them on for a certain amount of time. Typical output devices include the following.

- **Fuel injectors.** The computer can vary the amount of time the injectors are held open, thereby controlling the amount of fuel supplied to the engine.
- **Ignition timing.** The computer can trigger the signal to the ignition module to fire the spark plugs based on information from the sensors. The spark is advanced when the engine is cold and/or when the engine is operating under light load conditions.
- **Transmission shifting.** The computer provides a ground to the shift solenoids and torque converter clutch solenoid. The operation of the automatic transmission/transaxle is optimized based on vehicle sensor information.
- **Idle speed control.** The computer can pulse the idle speed control (ISC) or idle air control (IAC) device to maintain engine idle speed and to provide an

increased idle speed when needed, such as when the air-conditioning system is operating.
- **Evaporative emission control solenoids.** The computer can control the flow of gasoline fumes from the charcoal canister to the engine and seal off the system to perform a fuel system leak detection test as part of the OBD II onboard diagnosis.

MODULE COMMUNICATION

Since the 1990s, vehicles have used modules to control most of the electrical component operation. A typical vehicle will have 10 or more modules and they communicate with each other over data lines or hard wiring, depending on the application.

Serial Data

Serial data means that data is transmitted by a series of rapidly changing voltage signals pulsed from low to high or from high to low. Most modules are connected together in a network because of the following advantages.

- A decreased number of wires is needed, thereby saving weight and, cost, as well as helping with installation at the factory and decreased complexity, making servicing easier.
- Common sensor data can be shared with those modules that may need the information, such as vehicle, speed, outside air temperature, and engine coolant temperature.

Multiplexing

Multiplexing is the process of sending multiple signals of information at the same time over a signal wire and then separating the signals at the receiving end. This system of intercommunication of computers or processors is referred to as a **network.** By connecting the computers together on a communications network, they can easily share information back and forth. This multiplexing has a number of advantages, including:

- The elimination of redundant sensors and dedicated wiring for these multiple sensors.
- The reduction of the number of wires, connectors, and circuits.
- Addition of more features and option content to new vehicles.
- Weight reduction, increasing fuel mileage.
- Allows features to be changed with software upgrades instead of component replacement.

SAE COMMUNICATION CLASSIFICATIONS

The Society of Automotive Engineers (SAE) standards include three categories of in-vehicle network communications, including the following.

Class A

Low-speed networks (less than 10,000 bits per second [10 kbs]) are generally used for trip computers, entertainment, and other convenience features. Most low-speed Class A communication functions are performed using the following:

- UART standard (Universal Asynchronous Receive/Transmit) used by General Motors (8192 bps).
- CCD (Chrysler Collision Detection) used by DaimlerChrysler (7812.5 bps).

NOTE: The "collision" in CCD-type bus communication refers to the program that avoids conflicts of information exchange within the bus, and does not refer to airbags or other accident-related circuits of the vehicle.

- DaimlerChrysler SCI (Serial Communications Interface) is used to communicate between the engine controller and a scan tool (62.5 kbps).
- ACP (Audio Control Protocol) is used for remote control of entertainment equipment (twisted pairs) on Ford vehicles.

Class B

Medium-speed networks (10,000 to 125,000 bits per second [10 to 125 kbs]) are generally used for information transfer among modules, such as instrument clusters, temperature sensor data, and other general uses.

- General Motors GMLAN; both low- and medium-speed and Class 2, which uses 0- to 7-volt pulses with an available pulse width. Meets SAE 1850 variable pulse width (VPW).
- DaimlerChrysler Programmable Communication Interface (PCI). Meets SAE standard J-1850 pulse width modulated (PWM).
- Ford Standard Corporate Protocol (SCP). Meets SAE standard J-1850 pulse width modulated (PWM).

Class C

High-speed networks (125,000 to 1,000,000 bits per second [125,000 to 1,000,000 kbs]) are generally used for real time powertrain and vehicle dynamic control. Most high-speed bus communication is **controller area network** or **CAN.** See Figure 11-14.

◀ FREQUENTLY ASKED ▶ QUESTION

WHAT IS A BUS?

A bus is a term used to describe a communication network. Therefore, there are *connections to the bus* and *bus communications*, both of which refer to digital messages being transmitted among electronic modules or computers.

MODULE COMMUNICATION DIAGNOSIS

Most vehicle manufacturers specify that a scan tool be used to diagnose modules and module communications. Always follow the recommended testing procedures, which usually require the use of a factory scan tool.

Some tests of the communication bus (network) and some of the service procedures require the service technician to attach a DMM, set to DC volts, to monitor communications. A variable voltage usually indicates that messages are being sent and received.

Network Configurations

Multiplex networks can be configured differently. One method of configuring networks is the **loop configuration.** The loop configuration has two data lines attached to each controller. The controllers can communicate with other controllers in either direction. The advantage to this type of configuration is that an open in the data line will not affect the operation of the network. However, two opens in the data line will cause certain controllers to lose communication, depending on where the opens are. The disadvantage to this type of configuration is that if the entire network stops communicating due to a ground in the data line,

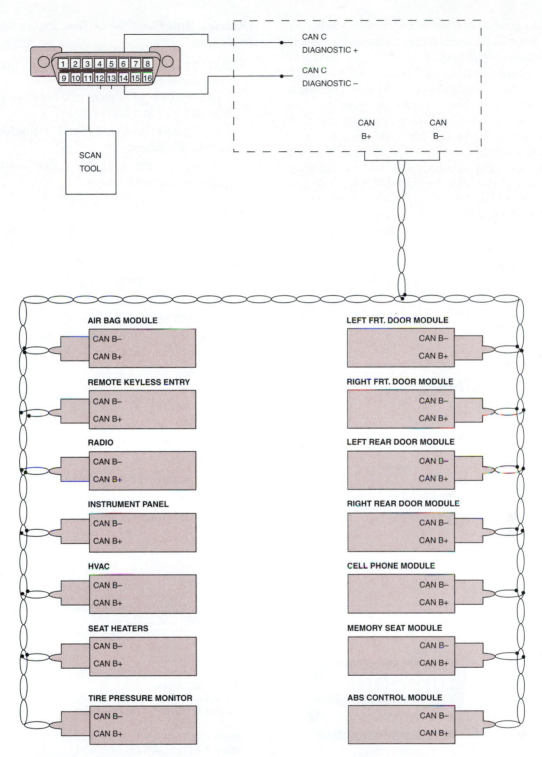

FIGURE 11-14 A typical bus system showing module CAN communications and twisted pairs of wire.

or a short-to-ground within a controller, each controller will have to be isolated individually by disconnecting to diagnose the fault.

Another more common method of configuring networks is the **star configuration.** In this configuration, each controller is connected to a single data line wire that is then routed back to a common junction. This junction may be in the form of a bus bar or a splice clip. If a splice clip is used, it is easier to diagnose a grounded data circuit due to the fact that each controller and circuit can be isolated from the network at a central point in the circuit. The disadvantage to this type of circuit is that any open in a data line will cause that controller to lose communication with the rest of the network.

In some applications, the manufacturer may use a combination of the two configurations. A portion of the network may be configured in the loop configuration and another portion of the network may be configured in the star configuration.

OBD II DATA LINK CONNECTOR

All OBD II Vehicles Use a 16-pin Connector that Includes: (See Figure 11-15.)

Pin 4 = chassis ground

Pin 5 = signal ground

Pin 16 = battery power (4A max)

Vehicles May Use One of Two Major Standards Including:

- **ISO 9141-2 Standard (ISO = International Standards Organization)**
  Pins 7 and 15 (or wire at pin 7 and no pin at 2 or a wire at 7 and at 2 and/or 10)
- **SAE J-1850 Standard (SAE = Society of Automotive Engineers)**
  Two types: **VPW** (variable pulse width) or **PWM** (pulse width modulated)
  Pins 2 and 10 (no wire at pin 7)

General Motors Vehicles Use:

- SAE J-1850 (VPW—Class 2—10.4 kb) standard, which uses pins 2, 4, 5, and 16 and not 10
- **GM Domestic OBD II**
  Pin 1 and 9—CCM (Comprehensive Component Monitor) slow baud rate—8192 UART
  Pins 2 and 10—OEM Enhanced—Fast Rate—40,500 baud rate
  Pins 7 and 15—Generic OBD II—ISO 9141—10,400 baud rate

DaimlerChrysler, European and Asian Vehicles Use:

- ISO 9141-2 standard, which uses pins 4, 5, 7, 15, and 16

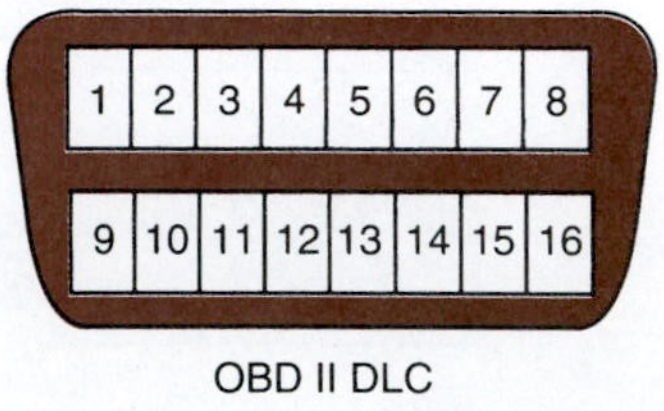

PIN NO.	ASSIGNMENTS
1.	MANUFACTURER'S DISCRETION
2.	BUS + LINE, SAE J1850
3.	MANUFACTURER'S DISCRETION
4.	CHASSIS GROUND
5.	SIGNAL GROUND
6.	MANUFACTURER'S DISCRETION
7.	K LINE, ISO 9141
8.	MANUFACTURER'S DISCRETION
9.	MANUFACTURER'S DISCRETION
10.	BUS–LINE, SAE J1850
11.	MANUFACTURER'S DISCRETION
12.	MANUFACTURER'S DISCRETION
13.	MANUFACTURER'S DISCRETION
14.	MANUFACTURER'S DISCRETION
15.	L LINE, ISO 9141
16.	VEHICLE BATTERY POSITIVE (4A MAX)

OBD II DLC

FIGURE 11-15 Sixteen-pin OBD II DLC with terminals identified. Scan tools use the power pin (16) and ground pin (4) for power so that a separate cigarette lighter plug is not necessary on OBD II vehicles.

- **Chrysler Group OBD II**
  Pins 2 and 10—CCM
  Pins 3 and 14—OEM Enhanced—60,500 baud rate
  Pins 7 and 15—Generic OBD II—ISO 9141—10,400 baud rate

Ford Vehicles Use:

- SAE J-1850 (PWM) (PWM—41.6 kb) standard, which uses pins 2, 4, 5, 10, and 16

- **Ford Domestic OBD II**
  Pins 2 and 10—CCM
  Pins 6 and 14—OEM Enhanced—Class C—40,500 baud rate
  Pins 7 and 15—Generic OBD II—ISO 9141—10,400 baud rate

SUMMARY

1. The Society of Automotive Engineers (SAE) standard J-1930 specifies that the term power train control module (PCM) be used for the computer that controls the engine and transmission in a vehicle.
2. The four basic computer functions include input, processing, storage, and output.
3. Read-only memory (ROM) can be programmable (PROM), erasable (EPROM), or electrically erasable (EEPROM).
4. Computer input sensors include engine speed (RPM), MAP, MAF, ECT, O2S, TP, and VS.
5. A computer can only turn a device on or turn a device off, but it can do the operation very rapidly.

REVIEW QUESTIONS

1. What part of the vehicle computer is considered to be the brain?
2. What is the difference between volatile and nonvolatile RAM?
3. List four input sensors.
4. List four output devices.

ASE CERTIFICATION-TYPE QUESTIONS

1. What unit of electricity is used as a signal for a computer?
   a. Volt
   b. Ohm
   c. Ampere
   d. Watt

2. The four basic computer functions include _____.
   a. Writing, processing, printing, and remembering
   b. Input, processing, storage, and output
   c. Data gathering, processing, output, and evaluation
   d. Sensing, calculating, actuating, and processing

3. All OBD II vehicles use what type of read-only memory?
   a. ROM
   b. PROM
   c. EPROM
   d. EEPROM

4. The "brain" of the computer is the _____.
   a. PROM
   b. RAM
   c. CPU
   d. AD converter

5. Computer processing speed is measured in _____.
   a. Baud rate
   b. Clock speed (Hz)
   c. Voltage
   d. Bytes

6. Which item is a computer input sensor?
   a. RPM
   b. Throttle position angle
   c. Engine coolant temperature
   d. All of the above

7. Which item is a computer output device?
   a. Fuel injector
   b. Transmission shift solenoid
   c. Evaporative emission control solenoid
   d. All of the above

8. The SAE term for the vehicle computer is _____.
   a. PCM
   b. ECM
   c. ECA
   d. Controller

9. What two things can a vehicle computer actually perform (output)?

   a. Store and process information

   b. Turn something on or turn something off

   c. Calculate and vary temperature

   d. Control fuel and timing only

10. Analog signals from sensors are changed to digital signals for processing by the computer through which type of circuit?

    a. Digital

    b. Analog

    c. AD converter

    d. PROM

◀ Chapter 12 ▶

TEMPERATURE SENSORS

OBJECTIVES

After studying Chapter 12, the reader should be able to:

1. Prepare for ASE Engine Performance (A8) certification test content area "E" (Computerized Engine Controls Diagnosis and Repair).
2. Explain the purpose and function of the ECT and IAT temperature sensors.
3. Describe how to test temperature sensors.
4. Discuss how automatic fluid temperature sensor valves can affect transmission operation.

ENGINE COOLANT TEMPERATURE SENSORS

Computer-equipped vehicles use an **engine coolant temperature (ECT)** sensor. When the engine is cold, the fuel mixture must be richer to prevent stalling and engine stumble. When the engine is warm, the fuel mixture can be leaner to provide maximum fuel economy with the lowest possible exhaust emissions. Because the computer controls spark timing and fuel mixture, it will need to know the engine temperature. An engine coolant temperature sensor (ECT) screwed into the engine coolant passage will provide the computer with this information. See Figure 12-1. This will be the most important (high authority) sensor while the engine is cold. The ignition timing can also be tai-

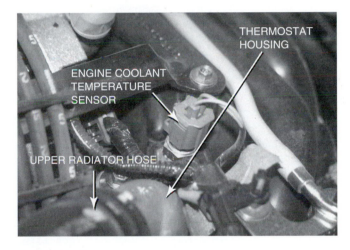

FIGURE 12-1 A typical engine coolant temperature (ECT) sensor. ECT sensors are located near the thermostat housing on most engines.

lored to engine (coolant) temperature. A hot engine cannot have the spark timing as far advanced as can a cold engine. The ECT sensor is also used as an important input for the following:

- Idle air control (IAC) position
- Oxygen sensor closed-loop status
- Canister purge on/off times
- Idle speed

Engine coolant temperature sensors are constructed of a semiconductor material that decreases in resistance as the temperature of the sensor increases. Coolant sensors have very high resistance when the coolant is cold and low resistance when the coolant is hot. This is referred to as having a **negative temperature coefficient (NTC),** which is opposite to the situation with most other electrical components. See Figure 12-2. Therefore, if the coolant sensor has a poor connection (high resistance) at the wiring connector, the computer will supply a richer-than-normal fuel mixture based on the resistance of the coolant sensor. Poor fuel economy and a possible-rich code can be caused by a defective

sensor or high resistance in the sensor wiring. If the sensor was shorted or defective and had too low a resistance, a leaner-than-normal fuel mixture would be supplied to the engine. A too-lean fuel mixture can cause driveability problems and a possible lean computer code.

STEPPED ECT CIRCUITS

Some vehicle manufacturers use a step-up resistor to effectively broaden the range of the ECT sensor. Daimler-Chrysler and General Motors vehicles use the same sensor as a non-stepped ECT circuit, but instead apply the sensor voltage through two different resistors.

- When the temperature is cold, usually below 120°F (50°C), the ECT sensor voltage is applied through a high-value resistor inside the PCM.
- When the temperature is warm, usually above 120°F (50°C), the ECT sensor voltage is applied through a much lower resistance value inside the PCM. See Figure 12-3.

The purpose of this extra circuit is to give the PCM a more accurate reading of the engine coolant temperature compared to the same sensor with only one circuit. See Figure 12-4.

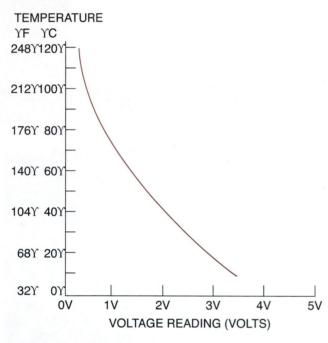

FIGURE 12-2 A typical ECT sensor temperature versus voltage curve.

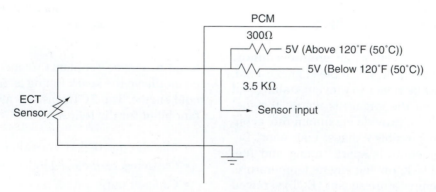

FIGURE 12-3 A typical two-step ECT circuit showing that when the coolant temperature is low, the PCM applies a 5-volt reference voltage to the ECT sensor through a higher resistance compared to when the temperature is higher.

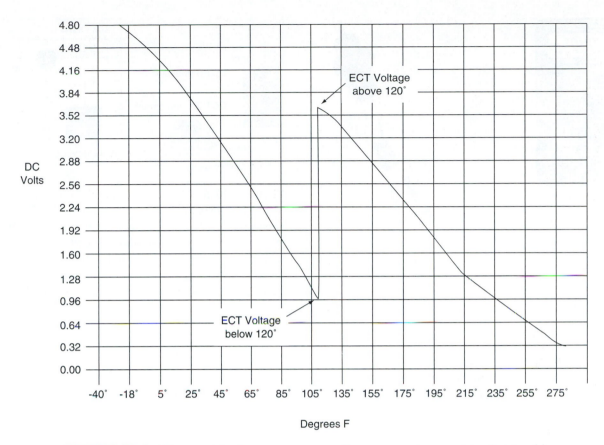

FIGURE 12-4   The transition between steps usually occur at a temperature that would not interfere with cold engine starts or the cooling fan operation. In this example, the transition occurs when the sensor voltage is about 1 volt and rises to about 3.6 volts.

TESTING THE ENGINE COOLANT TEMPERATURE SENSOR

Testing the Engine Coolant Temperature by Visual Inspection

The correct functioning of the engine coolant temperature (ECT) sensor depends on the following items that should be checked or inspected:

- **Properly filled cooling system.** Check that the radiator reservoir bottle is full and that the radiator itself is filled to the top.

CAUTION: Be sure that the radiator is cool before removing the radiator cap to avoid being scalded by hot coolant.

The ECT sensor must be submerged in coolant to be able to indicate the proper coolant temperature.

- **Proper pressure maintained by the radiator cap.** If the radiator cap is defective and cannot allow the cooling system to become pressurized, air pockets could develop. These air pockets could cause the engine to operate at a hotter-than-normal temperature and prevent proper temperature measurement, especially if the air pockets occur around the sensor.

- **Proper antifreeze-water mixture.** Most vehicle manufacturers recommend a 50/50 mixture of antifreeze and water as the best compromise between freezing protection and heat transfer ability.

- **Proper operation of the cooling fan.** If the cooling fan does not operate correctly, the engine may overheat.

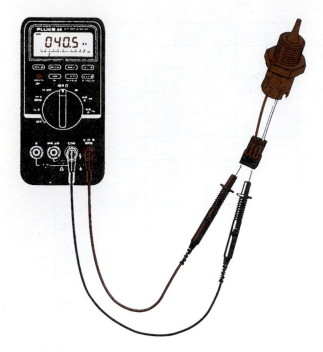

FIGURE 12-5 Measuring the resistance of the ECT sensor. The resistance measurement can then be compared with specifications. *(Courtesy of Fluke Corporation)*

Testing the ECT Using a Multimeter

Both the resistance (in ohms) and the voltage drop across the sensor can be measured and compared with specifications. See Figure 12-5. See the following charts showing examples of typical engine coolant temperature sensor specifications. Some vehicles use the PCM to attach another resistor in the ECT circuit to provide a more accurate measure of the engine temperature. See Figure 12-6.

General Motors ECT Sensor without Pull-up Resistor

°F	°C	Ohms	Voltage Drop Across Sensor
−40	−40	100,000 +	4.95
18	−8	14,628	4.68
32	0	9420	4.52
50	10	5670	4.25
68	20	3520	3.89
86	30	2238	3.46
104	40	1459	2.97
122	50	973	2.47
140	60	667	2.00

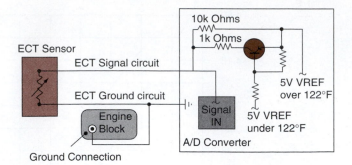

FIGURE 12-6 When the voltage drop reaches approximately 1.20 volts, the PCM turns on a transistor. The transistor connects a 1-kΩ resistor in parallel with the 10-kΩ resistor. Total circuit resistance now drops to around 909 ohms. This function allows the PCM to have full binary control at cold temperatures up to approximately 122°F, and a second full binary control at temperatures greater than 122°F.

158	70	467	1.59
176	80	332	1.25
194	90	241	0.97
212	100	177	0.75

General Motors ECT Sensor with Pull-up Resistor

°F	°C	Ohms	Voltage Drop Across Sensor
−40	−40	100,000	5
−22	−30	53,000	4.78
−4	−20	29,000	4.34
14	−10	16,000	3.89
32	0	9400	3.45
50	10	5700	3.01
68	20	3500	2.56
86	30	2200	1.80
104	40	1500	1.10

			Pull-Up Resistor Switched by PCM
122	50	970	3.25
140	60	670	2.88
158	70	470	2.56
176	80	330	2.24
194	90	240	1.70
212	100	177	1.42
230	110	132	1.15
248	120	100	.87

Ford ECT Sensor

°F	°C	Resistance (Ω)	Voltage (V)
50	10	58,750	3.52
68	20	37,300	3.06
86	30	24,270	2.26
104	40	16,150	2.16
122	50	10,970	1.72
140	60	7600	1.35
158	70	5370	1.04
176	80	3840	0.80
194	90	2800	0.61
212	100	2070	0.47
230	110	1550	0.36
248	120	1180	0.28

DaimlerChrysler ECT Sensor without Pull-up Resistor

°F	°C	Voltage (V)
130	54	3.77
140	60	3.60
150	66	3.40
160	71	3.20
170	77	3.02
180	82	2.80
190	88	2.60
200	93	2.40
210	99	2.20
220	104	2.00
230	110	1.80
240	116	1.62
250	121	1.45

DaimlerChrysler ECT Sensor with Pull-up Resistor

°F	°C	Volts
−20	−29	4.70
−10	−23	4.57
0	−18	4.45
10	−12	4.30
20	−7	4.10
30	−1	3.90
40	4	3.60
50	10	3.30

60	16	3.00
70	21	2.75
80	27	2.44
90	32	2.15
100	38	1.83

		Pull-Up Resistor Switched by PCM
110	43	4.20
120	49	4.10
130	54	4.00
140	60	3.60
150	66	3.40
160	71	3.20
170	77	3.02
180	82	2.80
190	88	2.60
200	93	2.40
210	99	2.20
220	104	2.00
230	110	1.80
240	116	1.62
250	121	1.45

Nissan ECT Sensor

°F	°C	Resistance (Ω)
14	−10	7000–11,400
68	20	2100–2900
122	50	680–1000
176	80	260–390
212	100	180–200

Mercedes ECT

°F	°C	Voltage (DCV)
60	20	3.5
86	30	3.1
104	40	2.7
122	50	2.3
140	60	1.9
158	70	1.5
176	80	1.2
194	90	1.0
212	100	0.8

European Bosch ECT Sensor

°F	°C	Resistance (Ω)
32	0	6500
50	10	4000
68	20	3000
86	30	2000
104	40	1500
122	50	900
140	60	650
158	70	500
176	80	375
194	90	295
212	100	230

Honda ECT Sensor (Resistance Chart)

°F	°C	Resistance (Ω)
0	−18	15,000
32	0	5,000
68	20	3,000
104	40	1,000
140	60	500
176	80	400
212	100	250

Honda ECT Sensor (Voltage Chart)

°F	°C	Voltage (V)
0	−18	4.70
10	−12	4.50
20	−7	4.29
30	−1	4.10
40	4	3.86
50	10	3.61
60	16	3.35
70	21	3.08
80	27	2.81
90	32	2.50
100	38	2.26
110	43	2.00
120	49	1.74
130	54	1.52
140	60	1.33
150	66	1.15
160	71	1.00
170	77	0.88
180	82	0.74
190	88	0.64
200	93	0.55
210	99	0.47

If resistance values match the approximate coolant temperature and there is still a coolant sensor trouble code, the problem is generally in the wiring between the sensor and the computer. Always consult the manufacturers' recommended procedures for checking this wiring. If the resistance values do not match, the sensor may need to be replaced.

Normal operating temperature varies with vehicle make and model. Some vehicles are equipped with a thermostat with an opening temperature of 180°F (82°C), whereas other vehicles use a thermostat that is 195°F (90°C) or higher. Before replacing the ECT sensor, be sure that the engine is operating at the temperature specified by the manufacturer. Most manufacturers recommend checking the ECT sensor after the cooling fan has cycled twice, indicating a fully warmed engine. See Figure 12-7.

NOTE: Many manufacturers install another resistor in parallel inside the computer to change the voltage drop across the ECT sensor. This is done to expand the scale of the ECT sensor and to make the sensor more sensitive. Therefore, if measuring *voltage* at the ECT sensor, check with the service manual for the proper voltage at each temperature.

Testing the ECT Sensor Using a Scan Tool

Follow the scan tool manufacturer's instructions and connect a scan tool to the data link connector (DLC) of the vehicle. Comparing the temperature of the engine coolant as displayed on a scan tool with the actual temperature of the engine is an excellent method to test an engine coolant temperature sensor.

1. Record the scan tool temperature of the coolant (ECT).
2. Measure the actual temperature of the coolant using an infrared pyrometer or contact-type temperature probe.

HINT: Often the coolant temperature gauge in the dash of the vehicle can be used to compare with the scan tool temperature. Although not necessarily accurate, it may help to diagnose a faulty sensor, especially if the temperature shown on the scan tool varies greatly from the temperature indicated on the dash gauge.

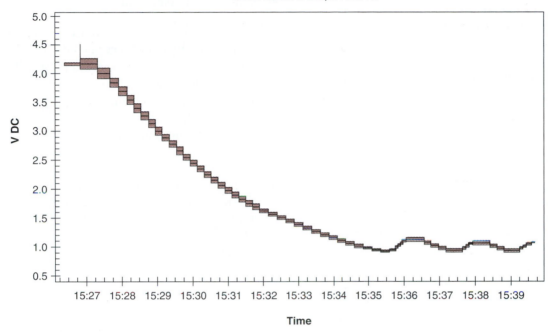

Generic Logging Form

Remarks: | ECT Voltage
2001 Jeep Wrangler Warm-up Cycle
AUTO 202 - Fuel and Emissions Systems

Form Saved Time: 2/18/04 4:11:55 PM
Upload Time: 2/18/04 4:09:05 PM
Meter ID: FLUKE 189 V2.02 0085510089

Show Data: All Graph View: All

FIGURE 12-7   A chart showing the voltage decrease of the ECT sensor as the temperature increases from a cold start. The bumps at the bottom of the waveform represent temperature decreases when the thermostat opens and is controlling coolant temperature.

The maximum difference between the two readings should be 10°F (5°C). If the actual temperature varies by more than 10°F from the temperature indicated on the scan tool, check the ECT sensor wiring and connector for damage or corrosion. If the connector and wiring are okay, check the sensor with a DVOM for resistance and compare to the actual engine temperature chart. If that checks out okay, check the computer.

NOTE: Some manufacturers use two coolant sensors, one for the dash gauge and another one for the computer.

◀ **TECH TIP** ▶

QUICK AND EASY ECT TEST

To check that the wiring and the computer are functioning, regarding the ECT sensor, connect a scan tool and look at the ECT temperature display.

Step 1.   Unplug the connector from the ECT sensor. The temperature displayed on the scan tool should read about −40.

NOTE: −40° Celsius is also −40° Fahrenheit. This is the point where both temperature scales meet.

Step 2.   With the connector still removed from the ECT sensor, use a fused jumper lead and connect the two terminals of the connector together. The scan tool should display about 285°F (140°C).

This same test procedure will work for the IAT and most other temperature sensors.

INTAKE AIR TEMPERATURE SENSOR

The intake air temperature (IAT) sensor is a negative temperature coefficient (NTC) thermistor that decreases in resistance as the temperature of the sensor increases. The IAT sensor can be located in one of the following locations:

- In the air cleaner housing
- In the air duct between the air filter and the throttle body, as shown in Figure 12-8
- Built into the mass air flow (MAF) or air flow sensor
- Screwed into the intake manifold where it senses the temperature of the air entering the cylinders

NOTE: An IAT installed in the intake manifold is the most likely to suffer damage due to an engine backfire, which can often destroy the sensor.

IAT SENSOR

FIGURE 12-8 The IAT sensor on this General Motors 3800 V-6 engine is in the air passage duct between the air cleaner housing and the throttle plate.

The purpose and function of the intake air temperature sensor is to provide the engine computer (PCM) the temperature of the air entering the engine. The IAT sensor information is used for fuel control (adding or subtracting fuel) and spark timing, depending on the temperature of incoming air.

- If the air temperature is cold, the PCM will modify the amount of fuel delivery and add fuel.
- If the air temperature is hot, the PCM will subtract the calculated amount of fuel.
- Spark timing is also changed, depending on the temperature of the air entering the engine. The timing is advanced if the temperature is cold and retarded from the base programmed timing if the temperature is hot.
- Cold air is more dense, contains more oxygen, and therefore requires a richer mixture to achieve the proper air-fuel mixture. Air at 32°F (0°C) is 14% denser than air at 100°F (38°C).
- Hot air is less dense, contains less oxygen, and therefore requires less fuel to achieve the proper air-fuel mixture.

The IAT sensor is a low-authority sensor and is used by the computer to modify the amount of fuel and ignition timing as determined by the engine coolant temperature sensor.

The IAT sensor is used by the PCM as a backup in the event that the ECT sensor is determined to be inoperative.

NOTE: Some engines use a **throttle-body temperature (TBT)** sensor to sense the temperature of the air entering the engine, instead of an intake air temperature sensor.

Engine temperature is most accurately determined by looking at the engine coolant temperature (ECT) sensor. In certain conditions, the IAT has an effect on performance and driveability. One such condition is a warm engine being stopped in very cold weather. In this case, when the engine is restarted, the ECT may be near normal operating temperature such as 200°F (93°C) yet the air temperature could be −20°F (−30°C). In this case, the engine requires a richer mixture due to the cold air than the ECT would seem to indicate.

POOR FUEL ECONOMY? BLACK EXHAUST SMOKE? LOOK AT THE IAT.

If the intake air temperature sensor is defective, it may be signaling the computer that the intake air temperature is extremely cold when in fact it is warm. In such a case the computer will supply a mixture that is much richer than normal.

If a sensor is physically damaged or electrically open, the computer will often set a diagnostic trouble code (DTC). This DTC is based on the fact that the sensor temperature did not change for a certain amount of time, usually about 8 minutes. If, however, the wiring or the sensor itself has excessive resistance, a DTC will not be set and the result will be lower-than-normal fuel economy, and in serious cases, black exhaust smoke from the tailpipe during acceleration.

Intake Air Temperature Sensor Temperature vs. Resistance and Voltage Drop (Approximate)

°C	°F	Ohms	Voltage Drop Across the Sensor
−40	−40	100,000	4.95
−8	+18	15,000	4.68
0	32	9400	4.52
10	50	5700	4.25
20	68	3500	3.89
30	86	2200	3.46
40	104	1500	2.97
50	122	1000	2.47
60	140	700	2.00
70	158	500	1.59
80	176	300	1.25
90	194	250	0.97
100	212	200	0.75

TESTING THE INTAKE AIR TEMPERATURE SENSOR

If the intake air temperature sensor circuit is damaged or faulty, a diagnostic trouble code (DTC) is set and the malfunction indicator lamp (MIL) may or may not turn on depending on the condition and the type and model of the vehicle. To diagnose the IAT sensor follow these steps:

Step 1 After the vehicle has been allowed to cool for several hours, use a scan tool, observe the IAT, and compare it to the engine coolant temperature (ECT). The two temperatures should be within 5°F of each other.

Step 2 Perform a thorough visual inspection of the sensor and the wiring. If the IAT is screwed into the intake manifold, remove the sensor and check for damage.

Step 3 Check the voltage and compare to the following chart.

WHAT EXACTLY IS AN NTC SENSOR?

A negative temperature coefficient (NTC) thermistor is a semiconductor whose resistance decreases as the temperature increases. In other words, the sensor becomes more electrically conductive as the temperature increases. Therefore, when a voltage is applied, typically 5 volts, the signal voltage is high when the sensor is cold because the sensor has a high resistance and little current flows through to ground. See Figure 12-9.

However, when the temperature increases, the sensor becomes more electrically conductive and takes more of the 5 volts to ground, resulting in a lower signal voltage as the sensor warms.

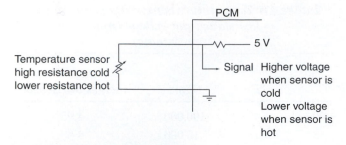

FIGURE 12-9 A typical temperature sensor circuit.

TRANSMISSION FLUID TEMPERATURE SENSOR

The transmission fluid temperature (TFT), also called transmission oil temperature (TOT), sensor is an important sensor for the proper operation of the automatic transmission. A TFT sensor is a negative temperature coefficient (NTC) thermistor that decreases in resistance as the temperature of the sensor increases.

General Motors

Transaxle Sensor—Temperature to Resistance to Voltage (approximate)

°C	°F	Resistance Ohms
0	32	7987–10,859
10	50	4934–6407
20	68	3106–3923
30	86	1991–2483
40	104	1307–1611
50	122	878–1067
60	140	605–728
70	158	425–507
80	176	304–359
90	194	221–259
100	212	163–190

DaimlerChrysler

Sensor Resistance (Ohms)— Transmission Temperature Sensor

°C	°F	Resistance Ohms
−40	−40	291,490–381,710
−20	−4	85,850–108,390
−10	14	49,250–61,430
0	32	29,330–35,990
10	50	17,990–21,810
20	68	11,370–13,610
25	77	9120–10,880
30	86	7370–8750
40	104	4900–5750
50	122	3330–3880
60	140	2310–2670
70	158	1630–1870
80	176	1170–1340
90	194	860–970
100	212	640–720
110	230	480–540
120	248	370–410

Ford

Transmission Fluid Temperature

°C	°F	Resistance Ohms
−40 to −20	−40 to −4	967K–284K
−19 to −1	−3 to 31	284K–100K
0 to 20	32 to 68	100K–37K
21 to 40	69 to 104	37K–16K
41 to 70	105 to 158	16K–5K
71 to 90	159 to 194	5K–2.7K
91 to 110	195 to 230	2.7K–1.5K
111 to 130	231 to 266	1.5K–0.8K
131 to 150	267 to 302	0.8K–0.54K

The transmission fluid temperature signal is used by the powertrain control module (PCM) to perform certain strategies based on the temperature of the automatic transmission fluid. For example:

- If the temperature of the automatic transmission fluid is low (typically below 32°F (0°C)), the shift points may be delayed and overdrive disabled. The torque converter clutch also may not be applied to assist in the heating of the fluid.
- If the temperature of the automatic transmission fluid is high (typically above 260°F (130°C)), the overdrive is disabled and the torque converter clutch is applied to help reduce the temperature of the fluid.

NOTE: Check service information for the exact shift strategy based on high and low transmission fluid temperatures for the vehicle being serviced.

Cylinder Head Temperature Sensor

Some vehicles are equipped with **cylinder head temperature (CHT)** sensors.

VW Golf	$14°F = 11,600 \, \Omega$
	$68°F = 2,900 \, \Omega$
	$176°F = 390 \, \Omega$

Engine Fuel Temperature (EFT) Sensor

Some vehicles, such as many Ford vehicles that are equipped with an electronic returnless type of fuel injection, use an engine fuel temperature (EFT) sensor to give the PCM information regarding the temperature and, therefore, the density of the fuel.

Exhaust Gas Recirculation (EGR) Temperature Sensor

Some engines, such as Toyota, are equipped with exhaust gas recirculation (EGR) temperature sensors. EGR is a well-established method for reduction of NOX emissions in internal combustion engines. The exhaust gas contains unburned hydrocarbons, which are recirculated in the combustion process. Recirculation is controlled by valves, which operate as a function of exhaust gas speed, load, and temperature. The gas reaches a temperature of about 850°F (450°C) for which a special heavy-duty glass-encapsulated NTC sensor is available.

The PCM monitors the temperature in the exhaust passage between the EGR valve and the intake manifold. If the temperature increases when the EGR is commanded on, the PCM can determine that the valve or related components are functioning.

Engine Oil Temperature Sensor

Engine oil temperature sensors are used on many General Motors' vehicles and are used as an input to the oil life monitoring system. The computer program inside the PCM calculates engine oil life based on run time, engine RPM, and oil temperature.

TEMPERATURE SENSOR DIAGNOSTIC TROUBLE CODES

The OBD II diagnostic trouble codes that relate to temperature sensors include both high- and low-voltage codes, as well as intermittent codes.

Diagnostic Trouble Code	Description	Possible Causes
P0112	IAT sensor low voltage	▪ IAT sensor internally shorted-to-ground ▪ IAT sensor wiring shorted-to-ground ▪ IAT sensor damaged by backfire (usually associated with IAT sensors that are mounted in the intake manifold) ▪ Possible defective PCM.
P0113	IAT sensor high voltage	▪ IAT sensor internally (electrically) open ▪ IAT sensor signal, circuit, or ground circuit open ▪ Possible defective PCM.
P0117	ECT sensor low voltage	▪ ECT sensor internally shorted-to-ground ▪ The ECT sensor circuit wiring shorted-to-ground ▪ Possible defective PCM.

Diagnostic Trouble Code	Description	Possible Causes
P0118	ECT sensor high voltage	• ECT sensor internally (electrically) open • ECT sensor signal, circuit, or ground circuit open

- Engine operating in an overheated condition.
- Possible defective PCM.

SUMMARY

1. The ECT sensor is a high-authority sensor at engine startup and is used for closed loop control, as well as idle speed.
2. All temperature sensors decrease in resistance as the temperature increases. This is called negative temperature coefficient (NTC).
3. The ECT and IAT sensors can be tested visually, as well as by using a digital multimeter or a scan tool.
4. Some vehicle manufacturers use a stepped ECT circuit inside the PCM to broaden the accuracy of the sensor.
5. Other temperature sensors include transmission fluid temperature (TFT), engine fuel temperature (EFT), exhaust gas recirculation temperature (EGR), and engine oil temperature.

REVIEW QUESTIONS

1. How does a typical NTC temperature sensor work?
2. What is the difference between a stepped and a non-stepped ECT circuit?
3. What temperature should be displayed on a scan tool if the ECT sensor is unplugged with the key on, engine off?
4. What are the three ways that temperature sensors can be tested?
5. If the transmission fluid temperature (TFT) sensor were to fail open (as if it were unplugged), what would the PCM do to the transmission shifting points?

ASE CERTIFICATION-TYPE QUESTIONS

1. The sensor that most determines fuel delivery when a fuel-injected engine is first started is the _____.
   a. O2S
   b. ECT sensor
   c. Engine MAP sensor
   d. IAT sensor

2. The SAE J-1930 standardized name for the sensor that measures the temperature of the air being drawn into the engine is called a(n) _____.
   a. Intake air temperature sensor (IAT)
   b. Air temperature sensor (ATS)
   c. Air charge temperature (ACT) sensor
   d. Manifold air temperature (MAT) sensor

3. Two technicians are discussing a stepped ECT circuit. Technician A says that the sensor used for a stepped circuit is different than one used in a non-stepped circuit. Technician B says that a stepped ECT circuit uses different internal resistance inside the PCM. Which technician is correct?
   a. Technician A only
   b. Technician B only
   c. Both Technicians A and B
   d. Neither Technician A nor B

4. When testing an ECT sensor on a vehicle, a digital multi-meter can be used and the signal wires back probed. What setting should the technician use to test the sensor?

   a. AC volts

   b. DC volts

   c. Ohms

   d. Hz (Hertz)

5. When testing the ECT sensor with the connector disconnected, the technician should select what position on the DMM?

   a. AC volts

   b. DC volts

   c. Ohms

   d. Hz (Hertz)

6. When checking the ECT sensor with a scan tool, about what temperature should be displayed if the connector is removed from the sensor with the key on, engine off?

   a. 284°F (140°C)

   b. 230°F (110°C)

   c. 120°F (50°C)

   d. −40°F (−40°C)

7. Two technicians are discussing the IAT sensor. Technician A says that the IAT sensor is more important to the operation of the engine (higher authority) than the ECT sensor. Technician B says that the PCM will add fuel if the IAT indicates that the incoming air temperature is cold. Which technician is correct?

   a. Technician A only

   b. Technician B only

   c. Both Technicians A and B

   d. Neither Technician A nor B

8. A typical IAT or ECT sensor reads about 3000 ohms when tested using a DMM. This resistance represents a temperature of about _____.

   a. −40°F (−40°C)

   b. 70°F (20°C)

   c. 120°F (50°C)

   d. 284°F (140°C)

9. If the transmission fluid temperature (TFT) sensor were to fail electrically open (infinity resistance), what would the PCM do to the shifts?

   a. Normal shifts and normal operation of the torque converter clutch

   b. Disable torque converter clutch; normal shift points

   c. Delayed shift points and torque converter clutch disabled

   d. Normal shifts but overdrive will be disabled

10. A P0118 DTC is being discussed. Technician A says that the ECT sensor could be shorted internally. Technician B says that the signal wire could be open. Which technician is correct?

   a. Technician A only

   b. Technician B only

   c. Both Technicians A and B

   d. Neither Technician A nor B

◄ Chapter 13 ►

THROTTLE POSITION (TP) SENSORS

OBJECTIVES

After studying Chapter 13, the reader should be able to:

1. Prepare for ASE Engine Performance (A8) certification test content area "E" (Computerized Engine Controls Diagnosis and Repair).
2. Discuss how throttle position sensors work.
3. List the methods that can be used to test TP sensors.
4. Describe the symptoms of a failed TP sensor.
5. List how the operation of the TP sensor affects vehicle operation.
6. Discuss TP sensor rationality tests.

FIGURE 13-1 A typical TP sensor mounted on the throttle plate of this port-injected engine.

THROTTLE POSITION SENSORS

Most computer-equipped engines use a **throttle position (TP)** sensor to signal to the computer the position of the throttle. See Figure 13-1. The TP sensor consists of a **potentiometer** a type of variable resistor.

Potentiometers

A potentiometer is a variable-resistance sensor with three terminals. One end of the resistor receives reference voltage, while the other end is grounded. The third terminal is attached to a movable contact that slides across the resistor to vary its resistance. Depending on whether the contact is near the supply end or the ground end of the resistor, return voltage is high or low. See Figure 13-2.

Throttle position (TP) sensors are among the most common potentiometer-type sensors. The computer uses their input to determine the amount of throttle opening and the rate of change.

A typical sensor has three wires:

- A 5-volt reference feed wire from the computer
- Signal return (A ground wire back to the computer)
- A voltage signal wire back to the computer; as the throttle is opened, the voltage to the computer changes

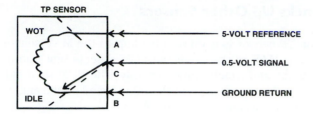

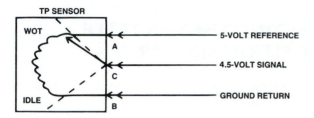

FIGURE 13-2 The signal voltage from a throttle position increases as the throttle is opened because the wiper arm is closer to the 5-volt reference. At idle, the resistance of the sensor winding effectively reduces the signal voltage output to the computer.

Normal throttle position voltage on most vehicles is about 0.5 volt at idle (closed throttle) and 4.5 volts at wide-open throttle (WOT).

HINT: The TP sensor voltage at idle is usually about 10% of the TP sensor voltage when the throttle is wide open, but can vary from as low as 0.3 volts to 1.2 volts, depending on the make and model of vehicle.

TP SENSOR COMPUTER INPUT FUNCTIONS

- The computer senses any change in throttle position and changes the fuel mixture and ignition timing. The actual change in fuel mixture and ignition timing is also partly determined by the other sensors, such as the manifold pressure (engine vacuum), engine RPM, the coolant temperature, and oxygen sensor(s). Some throttle position sensors are adjustable and should be set according to the exact engine manufacturer's specifications.
- The throttle position (TP) sensor used on fuel-injected vehicles acts as an "electronic accelerator pump." This means that the computer will pulse additional fuel from the injectors when the throttle is depressed. Because the air can quickly flow into the engine when the throttle is opened, additional fuel

must be supplied to prevent the air fuel mixture from going less, causing the engine to hesitate when the throttle is depressed. If the TP sensor is unplugged or defective, the engine may still operate satisfactorily, but hesitate upon acceleration.

- The PCM supplies the TP sensor with a regulated voltage that ranges from 4.8 to 5.1 volts. This reference voltage is usually referred to as a 5-volt reference or "Vref." The TP output signal is an input to the PCM, and the TP sensor ground also flows through the PCM.

See the Ford throttle position (TP) sensor chart for an example of how sensor voltage changes with throttle angle.

Ford Throttle Position (TP) Sensor Chart

Throttle Angle (Degrees)	Voltage (V)
0	0.50
10	0.97
20	1.44
30	1.90
40	2.37
50	2.84
60	3.31
70	3.78
80	4.24

NOTE: Generally, any reading higher than 80% represents wide-open throttle to the computer.

PCM USES FOR THE TP SENSOR

The TP sensor is used by the powertrain control module (PCM) for the following reasons.

Clear Flood Mode

If the throttle is depressed to the floor during engine cranking, the PCM will either greatly reduce or entirely eliminate any fuel-injector pulses to aid in cleaning a flooded engine. If the throttle is depressed to the floor and the engine is not flooded with excessive fuel, the engine may not start.

Torque Converter Clutch Engagement and Release

The torque converter clutch will be released if the PCM detects rapid acceleration to help the transmission deliver maximum torque to the drive wheels. The torque converter clutch is also disengaged when the accelerator pedal is released with the vehicle moving to help engine braking.

Rationality Testing for MAP and MAF Sensors

As part of the rationality tests for the MAP and/or MAF sensor, the TP sensor signal is compared to the reading from other sensors to determine if they match. For example, if the throttle position sensor is showing wide-open throttle (WOT), the MAP and/or MAF reading should also indicate that this engine is under a heavy load. If not, a diagnostic trouble code could be set for the TP, as well as the MAP and/or MAF sensors.

Automatic Transmission Shift Points

The shift points are delayed if the throttle is opened wide to allow the engine speed to increase, thereby producing more power and aiding in the acceleration of the vehicle. If the throttle is barely open, the shift point occurs at the minimum speed designed for the vehicle.

Target Idle Speed (Idle Control Strategy)

When the TP sensor voltage is at the idle, the PCM then controls idle speed using the idle air control (IAC) and/or spark timing variation to maintain the commanded idle speed. If the TP sensor indicates that the throttle has moved off idle, fuel delivery and spark timing are programmed for acceleration. Therefore, if the throttle linkage is stuck or binding, the idle speed may not be correct.

Air-Conditioning Compressor Operation

The TP sensor is also used as an input sensor for traction control and air-conditioning compressor operation. If the PCM detects that the throttle is at or close to wide open, the air-conditioning compressor is disengaged.

Backs Up Other Sensors

The TP sensor is used as a backup to the MAP sensor and/or MAF in the event the PCM detects that one or both are not functioning correctly. The PCM then calculates fuel needs and spark timing based on the engine speed (RPM) and throttle position.

TESTING THE THROTTLE POSITION SENSOR

A TP sensor can be tested using one or more of the following tools:

- A digital voltmeter with three test leads connected in series between the sensor and the wiring harness connector or back probing using T-pins.
- A scan tool or a specific tool recommended by the vehicle manufacturer.
- A breakout box that is connected in series between the computer and the wiring harness connector(s). A typical breakout box includes test points at which TP voltages can be measured with a digital voltmeter.
- An oscilloscope.

Use jumper wires, T-pins to back probe the wires, or a breakout box to gain electrical access to the wiring to the TP sensor. See Figure 13-3.

FIGURE 13-3 A meter lead connected to a T-pin that was gently pushed along the signal wire of the TP sensor until the point of the pin touched the metal terminal inside the plastic connector.

NOTE: The procedure that follows is the usual method used by many manufacturers. Always refer to service literature for the exact recommended procedure and specifications for the vehicle being tested.

The procedure for testing the sensor using a digital multimeter is as follows:

1. Turn the ignition switch on (engine off).
2. Measure the voltage between the signal wire and ground (reference low) wire. The voltage should be about 0.5 volt.

NOTE: Consult the service information for exact wire colors or locations.

3. With the engine still not running (but with the ignition still on), slowly increase the throttle opening. The voltage signal from the TP sensor should also increase. Look for any "dead spots" or open circuit readings as the throttle is increased to the wide-open position. See Figure 13-4 for an example of

how a good TP sensor would look when tested with a digital storage oscilloscope (DSO).

HINT: Use the accelerator pedal to depress the throttle because this applies the same forces on the TP sensor as the driver does during normal driving. Moving the throttle by hand under the hood may not accurately test the TP sensor.

4. With the voltmeter still connected, slowly return the throttle down to the idle position. The voltage from the TP sensor should also decrease evenly on the return to idle.

The TP sensor voltage at idle should be within the acceptable range as specified by the manufacturer. Some TP sensors can be adjusted by loosening their retaining screws and moving the sensor in relation to the throttle opening. This movement changes the output voltage of the sensor.

All TP sensors should also provide a smooth transition voltage reading from idle to WOT and back to idle. Replace the TP sensor if erratic voltage readings are obtained or if the correct setting at idle cannot be obtained.

```
A   1V DC  1:1 PROBE    B 200mV OFF 1:1 PROBE
200ms/DIV SINGLE  Trig:Aƒ -3DIV
```

FIGURE 13-4 A typical waveform of a TP sensor signal as recorded on a DSO when the accelerator pedal was depressed with the ignition switch on (engine off). Clean transitions and the lack of any glitches in this waveform indicate a good sensor. *(Courtesy of Fluke Corporation)*

TESTING A TP SENSOR USING THE MIN/MAX FUNCTION

Many digital multimeters are capable of recording voltage readings over time and then displaying the minimum, maximum, and average readings. To perform a min/max test of the TP sensor, manually set the meter to read higher than 4 volts.

Step 1   Connect the red meter lead to the signal wire and the black meter lead to a good ground on the ground return wire at the TP sensor.

Step 2   With the ignition on, engine off, slowly depress and release the accelerator pedal from inside the vehicle.

Step 3   Check the minimum and maximum voltage reading on the meter display. Any 0- or 5-volt reading would indicate a fault or short in the TP sensor.

◀ **TECH TIP** ▶

CHECK POWER AND GROUND BEFORE CONDEMNING A BAD SENSOR

Most engine sensors use a 5-volt reference and a ground. If the 5 volts to the sensor is too high (shorted to voltage) or too low (high resistance), then the sensor output will be **skewed** or out of range. Before replacing the sensor that did not read correctly, measure both the 5-volt reference and ground. To measure the ground, simply turn the ignition on (engine off) and touch one test lead of a DMM set to read DC volts to the sensor ground and the other to the negative terminal of the battery. Any reading higher than 0.2 volt (200 mV) represents a poor ground. See Figures 13-5 and 13-6.

FIGURE 13-6 Checking the voltage drop between the TP sensor ground and a good engine ground with the ignition on (engine off). A reading of greater than 0.6 volt (600 mV) represents a bad computer ground.

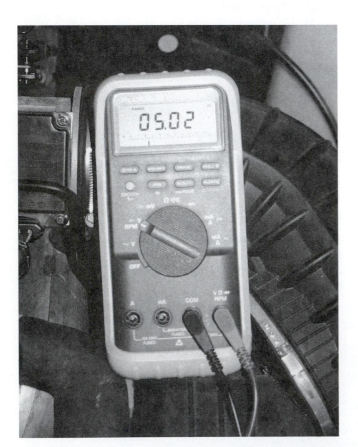

FIGURE 13-5 Checking the 5-volt reference from the computer being applied to the TP sensor with the ignition switch on (engine off).

TESTING THE TP SENSOR USING A SCAN TOOL

A scan tool can be used to check for proper operation of the throttle position sensor using the following steps.

Step 1 With the key on, engine off, the TP sensor voltage display should be about 0.5 volt, but can vary from as low as 0.3 volt to as high as 1.2 volts.

Step 2 Check the scan tool display for the percentage of throttle opening. The reading should be zero and gradually increase in percentage as the throttle is depressed.

Step 3 The idle air control (IAC) counts should increase as the throttle is opened and decrease as the throttle is closed. Start the engine and observe the IAC counts as the throttle is depressed.

Step 4 Start the engine and observe the TP sensor reading. Use a wedge or thin object to increase the throttle opening slightly. The throttle percentage reading should increase. Shut off and restart the engine. If the percentage of throttle opening returns to 0%, the PCM determines that the increased throttle opening is now the new minimum and resets the idle position of the TP sensor. Remove the wedge and cycle the ignition key. The throttle position sensor should again read zero percentage.

NOTE: Some engine computers are not capable of resetting the throttle position sensor.

TP SENSOR DIAGNOSTIC TROUBLE CODES

The diagnostic trouble codes (DTCs) associated with the throttle position sensor include the following.

Diagnostic Trouble Code	Description	Possible Causes
P0122	TP sensor low voltage	• TP sensor internally shorted-to-ground • TP sensor wiring shorted-to-ground • TP sensor or wiring open
P0123	TP sensor high voltage	• TP sensor internally shorted to 5-volt reference • TP sensor ground open • TP sensor wiring shorted-to-voltage
P0121	TP sensor signal does not agree with MAP	• Defective TP sensor • Incorrect vehicle-speed (VS) sensor signal • MAP sensor out-of-calibration or defective

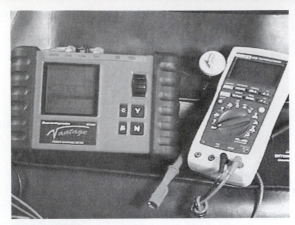

PS 8-1   Besides a scan tool, other equipment that can be used to check a throttle position (TP) sensor includes a scope or graphing multimeter, a digital multimeter equipped with MIN/MAX function, and T-pins to safely back-probe the sensor wires.

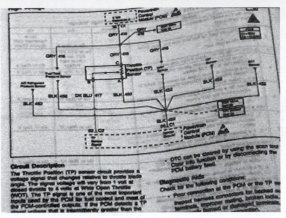

PS 8-2   Consult the factory service manual for the specifications and wire colors used for the TP sensor, as well as the recommended testing procedure.

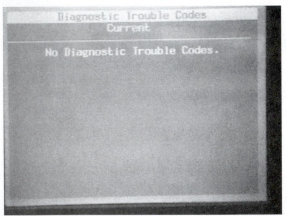

PS 8-3   A scan tool display showing no diagnostic trouble codes (DTCs). A fault could still exist even though a diagnostic trouble code is not set—it depends on the type of fault and when it occurs.

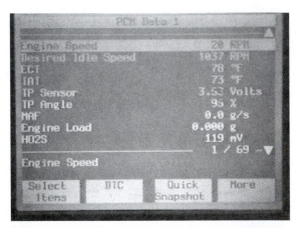

PS 8-4   A scan tool can be used to observe the output voltage and the calculated percentage (%) of throttle opening.

PS 8-5   Most throttle position sensors use a 5-volt reference voltage from the computer. To test that this signal is available at the sensor, carefully back-probe the 5-volt reference (gray on this General Motors vehicle) wire at the connector on the TP sensor. Simply push the T-pin alongside the wire until it touches the metal terminal inside the connector.

PS 8-6   Connect the red lead from the digital multimeter to the T-pin and attach the black meter lead to a good, clean engine ground.

PS 8-7   Select DC volts and turn the ignition key on (engine off). The meter reads slightly over 5 volts, confirming the computer is supplying the reference voltage to the TP sensor.

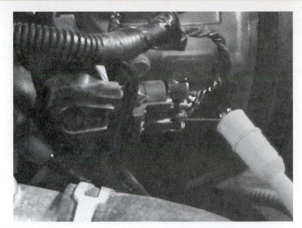

PS 8-8   Another important step when testing a TP sensor is to verify that the ground circuit is okay. To check the ground of the TP sensor, carefully back-probe the ground wire at the TP sensor connector (black on this General Motors vehicle) and connect the red meter lead to the T-pin.

PS 8-9   Attach the black meter lead to a good, clean engine ground.

PS 8-10   With the ignition on (engine off) and the digital meter still set to read DC volts, read the voltage drop of the TP sensor ground. General Motors specifies that this voltage drop should not exceed 35 mV (0.035V). This TP sensor ground shows 31.1 mV (0.031 IV).

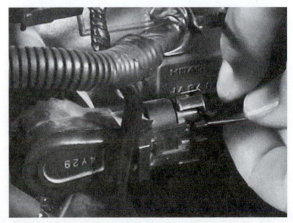

PS 8-11   To measure the signal voltage, back-probe the signal wire (dark blue on this General Motors vehicle).

PS 8-12   Select DC volts and manually range the meter. This Fluke meter changes from the 4-volt scale to the 40-volt scale as the sensor voltage goes slightly higher than 4 volts. For an instant, "OL" appears on the display as it switches ranges. This OL could also indicate a fault.

PS 8-13 Slowly move the throttle from idle speed to wide open and back to idle speed position. For best results, this test should be performed by depressing the accelerator pedal. This puts the same forces on the sensor as occurs during normal driving.

PS 8-14 The high reading for this sensor was 4.063 volts.

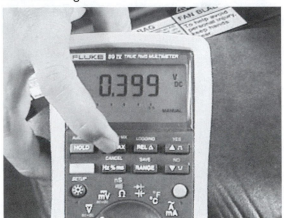

PS 8-15 Pushing the MIN/MAX button shows the minimum voltage the meter recorded during the test (0.399V).

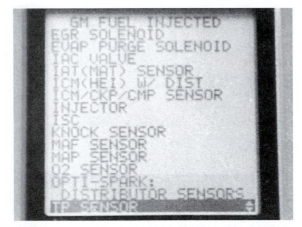

PS 8-16 A Snap-On Vantage graphing multimeter or digital storage oscilloscope can also be used to test a TP sensor. To test the sensor using the Snap-On Vantage, select TP sensor from the menu.

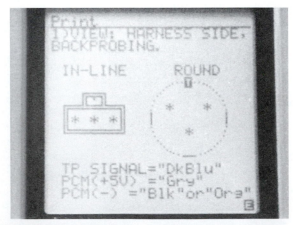

PS 8-17 The Vantage has a built-in database that can be accessed to show connector position and wire color information.

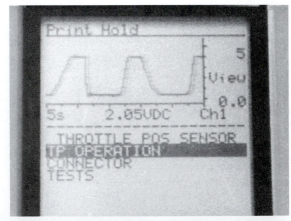

PS 8-18 After attaching the meter leads to the signal wire and ground (ignition key on, engine off), the graphing multimeter shows the waveform of the voltage signal as the throttle is depressed, released, and depressed again. These are normal for a TP sensor. A fault would show as a vertical line or dip in the waveform.

SUMMARY

1. A throttle position (TP) sensor is a three-wire variable resistor called a potentiometer.

2. The three wires on the TP sensor include a 5-volt reference voltage from the PCM, plus the signal wire to the PCM, and a ground, which also goes to the PCM.

3. The TP sensor is used by the PCM for clear flood mode, torque converter engagement and release, and automotive transmission shift points, as well as for rationality testing for the MAP and MAF sensor.

4. The TP sensor signal voltage should be about 0.5 volt at idle and increase to about 4.5 volts at wide-open throttle (WOT).

5. A TP sensor can be tested using a digital multimeter, a digital storage oscilloscope (DSO), or a scan tool.

REVIEW QUESTIONS

1. What is the purpose of each of the three wires on a typical TP sensor?

2. What all does the PCM do with the TP sensor signal voltage?

3. What is the procedure to follow when checking the 5-volt reference and TP sensor ground?

4. How can a TP sensor be diagnosed using a scan tool?

ASE CERTIFICATION-TYPE QUESTIONS

1. Which sensor is generally considered to be the electronic accelerator pump of a fuel-injected engine?
   a. O2S _____
   b. ECT sensor
   c. Engine MAP sensor
   d. TP sensor

2. Typical TP sensor voltage at idle is about _____.
   a. 2.50 to 2.80 volts
   b. 0.5 volt or 10% of WOT TP sensor voltage
   c. 1.5 to 2.8 volts
   d. 13.5 to 15.0 volts

3. A TP sensor is what type of sensor?
   a. Rheostat
   b. Voltage generating
   c. Potentiometer
   d. Piezoelectric

4. Which is *not* a function of a TP sensor?
   a. Torque converter clutch operation
   b. Clear flood mode operation
   c. Determining rich and lean air-fuel mixtures
   d. Air-conditioning compressor clutch operation

5. Which sensor does the TP sensor backup if the PCM determines that a failure has occurred?
   a. Oxygen sensor
   b. MAF sensor
   c. MAP sensor
   d. Either b or c

6. Which wire on a TP sensor should be back probed to check the voltage signal to the PCM?
   a. 5-volt reference (Vref)
   b. Signal
   c. Ground
   d. Meter should be connected between the 5-volt reference and the ground

7. After a TP sensor has been tested using the min/max function on a DMM, a reading of zero volts is displayed. What does this reading indicate?
   a. The TP sensor is open at one point during the test.
   b. The TP sensor is shorted.
   c. The TP sensor signal is shorted to 5-volt reference.
   d. Both b and c are possible.

8. After a TP sensor has been tested using the min/max function on a DMM, a reading of 5 volts is displayed. What does this reading indicate?
   a. The TP sensor is open at one point during the test.
   b. The TP sensor is shorted.
   c. The TP sensor signal is shorted to 5-volt reference.
   d. Both b and c are possible.

9. A technician attaches one lead of a digital voltmeter to the ground terminal of the TP sensor and the other meter lead to the negative terminal of the battery. The ignition is switched to on, engine off and the meter displays 37.3 mV. Technician A says that this is the signal voltage and is a little low. Technician B says that the TP sensor ground circuit has excessive resistance. Which technician is correct?

   a. Technician A only
   b. Technician B only
   c. Both Technicians A and B
   d. Neither Technician A nor B

10. A P0122 DTC is retrieved using a scan tool. This DTC means _____.

   a. The TP sensor voltage is low
   b. The TP sensor could be shorted-to-ground
   c. The TP sensor signal circuit could be shorted-to-ground
   d. All of the above are correct

◀ Chapter 14 ▶

MAP/BARO SENSORS

OBJECTIVES

After studying Chapter 14, the reader should be able to:

1. Prepare for ASE Engine Performance (A8) certification test content area "E" (Computerized Engine Controls Diagnosis and Repair).
2. Discuss how MAP sensors work.
3. List the methods that can be used to test MAP sensors.
4. Describe the symptoms of a failed MAP sensor.
5. List how the operation of the MAP sensor affects vehicle operation.
6. Discuss MAP sensor rationality tests.

AIR PRESSURE— HIGH AND LOW

You can think of an internal combustion engine as a big air pump. As the pistons move up and down in the cylinders, they pump in air and fuel for combustion and pump out exhaust gases. They do this by creating a difference in air pressure. The air outside an engine has weight and exerts pressure, as does the air inside an engine.

As a piston moves down on an intake stroke with the intake valve open, it creates a larger area inside the cylinder for the air to fill. This lowers the air pressure within the engine. Because the pressure inside the engine is lower than the pressure outside, air flows into the engine to fill the low-pressure area and equalize the pressure.

The low pressure within the engine is called **vacuum.** Vacuum causes the higher-pressure air on the outside to flow into the low-pressure area inside the cylinder. The difference in pressure between the two areas is called a **pressure differential.** See Figure 14-1.

PRINCIPLES OF PRESSURE SENSORS

Intake manifold pressure changes with changing throttle positions. At wide-open throttle, manifold pressure is almost the same as atmospheric pressure. On deceleration or at idle, manifold pressure is below atmospheric pressure, thus creating a vacuum. In cases where turbo or supercharging is used, under part or full load condition, intake manifold pressure rises above atmospheric. Also, oxygen content and barometric pressure change with differences in altitude and the computer must be able to compensate by making changes in the flow of fuel entering the engine. To provide the computer with changing air flow information, a fuel-injection system may use a:

- Manifold absolute pressure (MAP) sensor
- Manifold absolute pressure (MAP) sensor plus barometric absolute pressure (BARO) sensor
- Barometric and manifold absolute pressure sensors combined (BMAP).

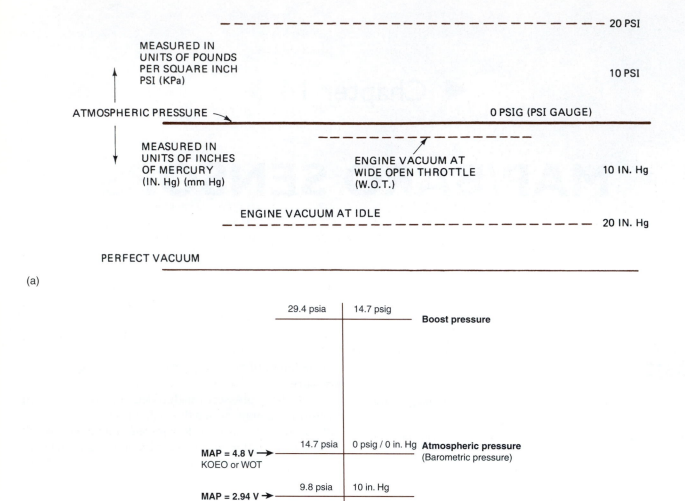

(a)

(b)

FIGURE 14-1 (a) As an engine is accelerated under a load, the engine vacuum drops. This drop in vacuum is actually an increase in absolute pressure in the intake manifold. A MAP sensor senses all pressures greater than that of a perfect vacuum. (b) The relationship between absolute pressure, vacuum and gauge pressure.

The **manifold absolute pressure (MAP)** sensor may be a ceramic capacitor diaphragm, an aneroid bellows, or a piezoresistive crystal. It has a sealed vacuum reference input on one side; the other side is connected (vented) to the intake manifold. This sensor housing also contains signal conditioning circuitry. See Figure 14-2. Pressure changes in the manifold cause the sensor to deflect, varying its analog or digital return signal to the computer. As

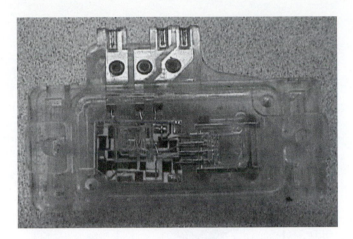

FIGURE 14-2 A plastic MAP sensor used for training purposes showing the electronic circuit board and electrical connections.

the air pressure increases, the MAP sensor generates a higher voltage or frequency return signal to the computer.

CONSTRUCTION OF MANIFOLD ABSOLUTE PRESSURE (MAP) SENSORS

The **manifold absolute pressure (MAP)** sensor is used by the engine computer to sense engine load. The typical MAP sensor consists of a ceramic or silicon wafer sealed on one side with a perfect vacuum and exposed to intake manifold vacuum on the other side. As the engine vacuum changes, the pressure difference on the wafer changes the output voltage or frequency of the MAP sensor.

A manifold absolute pressure (MAP) sensor is used on many engines for the PCM to determine the load on the engine. The relationship among barometer pressure, engine vacuum, and MAP sensor voltage includes:

- Absolute pressure is equal to barometric pressure minus intake manifold vacuum.
- A decrease in manifold vacuum means an increase in manifold pressure.
- The MAP sensor compares manifold vacuum to a perfect vacuum.
- Barometric pressure minus MAP sensor reading equals intake manifold vacuum. Normal engine vacuum is 17–21 in. Hg.

- Supercharged and turbocharged engines require a MAP sensor that is calibrated for pressures above atmospheric, as well as for vacuum.

Silicon-Diaphragm Strain Gauge MAP Sensor

This is the most commonly used design for a MAP sensor and the output is a DC analog (variable) voltage. One side of a silicon wafer is exposed to engine vacuum and the other side is exposed to a perfect vacuum.

There are four resistors attached to the silicon wafer which changes in resistance when strain is applied to the wafer. This change in resistance due to strain is called **piezoresistivity.** The resistors are electrically connected to a Wheatstone bridge circuit and then to a differential amplifier, which creates a voltage in proportion to the vacuum applied.

A typical General Motors MAP sensor voltage varies from 0.88 to 1.62 at engine idle.

- 17 in. Hg is equal to about 1.62 volts
- 21 in. Hg is equal to about 0.88 volts

Therefore, a good reading should be about 1.0 volt from the MAP sensor on a sound engine at idle speed.

Engine Load	Manifold Vacuum	Manifold Absolute Pressure	MAP Sensor Volt Signal
Heavy (WOT)	Low (almost 0 in. Hg)	High (almost atmospheric)	High (4.6–4.8 V)
Light (idle)	High (17–21 in. Hg)	Low (lower than atmospheric)	Low (0.8–1.6 V)

Capacitor—Capsule MAP Sensor

A capacitor-capsule is a type of MAP sensor used by Ford which uses two ceramic (alumina) plates with an insulating washer spacer in the center to create a capacitor. Changes in engine vacuum cause the plates to deflect, which changes the capacitance. The electronics in the sensor then generate a varying digital frequency output signal, which is proportional to the engine vacuum. See Figure 14-3. See Figure 14-4 for a scope waveform of a digital MAP sensor.

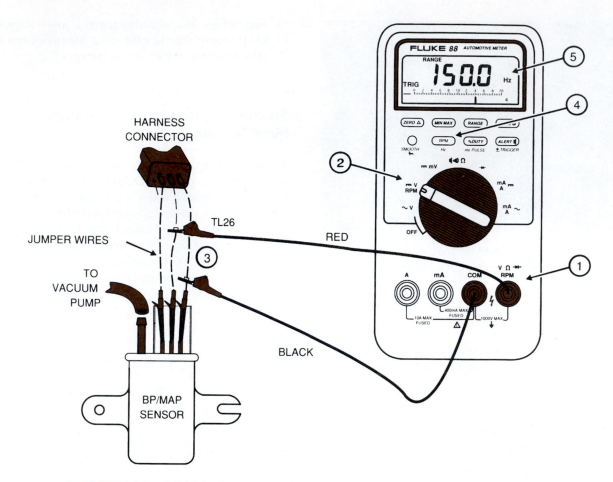

FIGURE 14-3 A DMM set to test a MAP sensor. (1) Connect the red meter lead to the V meter terminal and the black meter lead to the COM meter terminal. (2) Select DC volts. (3) Connect the test leads to the sensor signal wire and the ground wire. (4) Select hertz (Hz) if testing a MAP sensor whose output is a varying frequency; otherwise keep it on DC volts. (5) Read the change of frequency as the vacuum is applied to the sensor. Compare the vacuum reading and the frequency (or voltage) reading to the specifications. *(Courtesy of Fluke Corporation)*

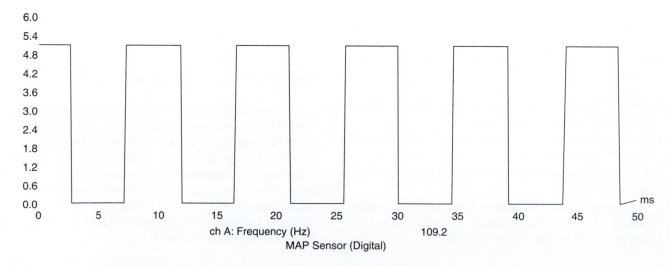

FIGURE 14-4 A waveform of a typical digital MAP sensor.

Ford MAP Sensor Chart

MAP Sensor Output (Hz)	Engine Operating Conditions	Intake Manifold Vacuum (in. Hg)
156–159 Hz	Key on, engine off	0 in. Hg
102–109 Hz	Engine at idle (sea level)	17–21 in. Hg
156–159 Hz	Engine at wide-open throttle (WOT)	About 0 in. Hg

◀ **TECH TIP** ▶

IF IT'S GREEN, IT'S A SIGNAL WIRE

Ford-built vehicles usually use a green wire as the signal wire back to the computer from the sensors. It may not be a solid green, but if there is green somewhere on the wire, then it is the signal wire. The other wires are the power and ground wires to the sensor.

Ceramic Disc Map Sensor

The ceramic disc MAP sensor is used by Daimler-Chrysler and it converts manifold pressure into a capacitance discharge. The discharge controls the amount of voltage delivered by the sensor to the PCM. The output is the same as the previously used strain gauge/Wheatstone bridge design and is interchangeable. See Figure 14-5.

DaimlerChrysler MAP Sensor Chart

Vacuum (in. Hg)	MAP Sensor Signal Voltage (V)
0.5	4.8
1.0	4.6
3.0	4.1
5.0	3.8
7.0	3.5
10.0	2.9
15.0	2.1
20.0	1.2
25.0	0.5

◀ **TECH TIP** ▶

USE THE MAP SENSOR AS A VACUUM GAUGE

A MAP sensor measures the pressure inside the intake manifold compared with absolute zero (perfect vacuum). For example, an idling engine that has 20 inches of mercury (in. Hg) of vacuum has a lower pressure inside the intake manifold than when the engine is under a load and the vacuum is at 10 in. Hg. A decrease in engine vacuum results in an increase in manifold pressure. A normal engine should produce between 17 and 21 in. Hg at idle. Comparing the vacuum reading with the voltage reading output of the MAP sensor indicates that the reading should be between 1.62 and 0.88 volt or 109 to 102 Hz or lower on Ford MAP sensors. Therefore, a digital multimeter (DMM), scan tool, or scope can be used to measure the MAP sensor voltage and be used instead of a vacuum gauge.

NOTE: This chart was developed by testing a MAP sensor at a location about 600 feet above sea level. For best results, a chart based on your altitude should be made by applying a known vacuum, and reading the voltage of a known-good MAP sensor. Vacuum usually drops about 1 inch per 1000 feet of altitude.

Vacuum (in. Hg)	GM (volts)	Ford (Hz)
0	4.80	156–159
1	4.52	
2	4.46	
3	4.26	
4	4.06	
5	3.88	141–143
6	3.66	
7	3.50	
8	3.30	
9	3.10	
10	2.94	127–130
11	2.76	
12	2.54	
13	2.36	
14	2.20	
15	2.00	114–117
16	1.80	
17	1.62	
18	1.42	108–109
19	1.20	
20	1.10	102–104
21	0.88	
22	0.66	

FIGURE 14-5 Shown is the electronic circuit inside a ceramic disc MAP sensor used on many DaimlerChrysler engines. The black areas are carbon resistors that are applied to the ceramic, and lasers are used to cut lines into these resistors during testing to achieve the proper operating calibration.

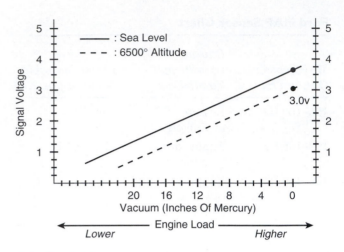

FIGURE 14-6 Altitude affects the MAP sensor voltage.

PCM USES OF THE MAP SENSOR

The PCM uses the MAP sensor to determine the following:

- **The load on the engine.** The MAP sensor is used on a speed density-type of fuel-injector system to determine the load on the engine, and therefore the amount of fuel needed. On engines equipped with a mass air flow (MAF) sensor, the MAP is used as a backup to the MAF, for diagnosis of other sensors, and systems such as the EGR system.
- **Altitude, fuel, and spark control calculations.** At key on, the MAP sensor determines the altitude (acts as a BARO sensor) and adjusts the fuel delivery and spark timing accordingly.
  - If the altitude is high, generally over 5000 feet (1500 meters), the PCM will reduce fuel delivery and advance the ignition timing.
  - The altitude is also reset when the engine is accelerated to wide-open throttle and the MAP sensor is used to reset the altitude reading. See Figure 14-6.
- **EGR system operation.** As part of the OBD II standards, the exhaust gas recirculation (EGR) system must be checked for proper operation. One method used by many vehicle manufacturers is to command the EGR valve on and then watch the MAP sensor signal. The opening of the EGR pistle should decrease engine vacuum. If the MAP sensor

does not react with the specified drop in manifold vacuum (increase in manifold pressure), an EGR flow rate problem diagnostic trouble code is set.

- **Detect deceleration (vacuum increases).** The engine vacuum rises when the accelerator is released, which changes the MAP sensor voltage. When deceleration is detected by the PCM, fuel is either stopped or greatly reduced to improve exhaust emissions.
- **Monitor engine condition.** As an engine wears, the intake manifold vacuum usually decreases. The PCM is programmed to detect the gradual change in vacuum and is able to keep the air-fuel mixture in the correct range. If the PCM were not capable of making adjustments for engine wear, the lower vacuum could be interpreted as increased load on the engine, resulting in too much fuel being injected, thereby reducing fuel economy and increasing exhaust emissions.
- **Load detection for returnless-type fuel injection.** On fuel delivery systems that do not use a return line back to the fuel tank, the engine load calculation for the fuel needed is determined by the signals from the MAP sensor.
- **Altitude and map sensor values.** On an engine equipped with a speed-density-type of fuel injection, the MAP sensor is the most important sensor needed to determine injection pulse width. Changes in altitude change the air density as well as weather conditions. Barometric pressure and altitude are inversely related:
  - As altitude increases—barometric pressure decreases
  - As altitude decreases—barometric pressure increases

As the ignition switch is rolled from off to the start position, the PCM reads the MAP sensor value to determine atmospheric and air pressure conditions. This barometric pressure reading is updated every time the engine is started and whenever wide-open throttle is detected. The barometric pressure reading at that time is updated. See the chart that compares altitude to MAP sensor voltage.

Altitude and MAP Sensor Voltage

Altitude	MAP Sensor Voltage (can vary due to atmospheric conditions)
Sea level	4.6 to 4.8 volts
2500 (760 m)	4.0 volts
5000 (1520 m)	3.7 volts
7500 (2300 m)	3.35 volts
10,000 (3050 m)	3.05 volts
12,500 (3800 m)	2.80 volts
15,000 (4600 m)	2.45 volts

BAROMETRIC PRESSURE SENSOR

A **barometric pressure (BARO) sensor** is similar in design, but senses more subtle changes in barometric absolute pressure (atmospheric air pressure). It is vented directly to the atmosphere. The **barometric manifold absolute pressure (BMAP)** sensor is actually a combination of a BARO and MAP sensor in the same housing. The BMAP sensor has individual circuits to measure barometric and manifold pressure. This input not only allows the computer to adjust for changes in atmospheric pressure due to weather, but also is the primary sensor used to determine altitude.

NOTE: A MAP sensor and a BARO sensor are usually the same sensor, but the MAP sensor is connected to the manifold and a BARO sensor is open to the atmosphere. The MAP sensor is capable of reading barometric pressure just as the ignition switch is turned to the on position before the engine starts. Therefore, altitude and weather changes are available to the computer. During mountainous driving, it may be an advantage to stop and then restart the engine so that the engine computer can take another barometric pressure reading and recalibrate fuel delivery based on the new altitude. See the Ford/BARO altitude chart for an example of how altitude affects intake manifold pressure. The computer on some vehicles will monitor the throttle position sensor and use the MAP sensor reading at wide-open throttle (WOT) to update the BARO sensor if it has changed during driving.

Ford MAP/BARO Altitude Chart

Altitude (feet)	Volts (V)
0	1.59
1000	1.56
2000	1.53
3000	1.50
4000	1.47
5000	1.44
6000	1.41
7000	1.39

NOTE: Some older Chrysler brand vehicles were equipped with a combination BARO and IAT sensor. The sensor was mounted on the bulkhead (firewall) and sensed the underhood air temperature.

◄ DIAGNOSTIC STORY ►

THE CAVALIER CONVERTIBLE STORY

The owner of a Cavalier convertible stated to a service technician that the "check engine" (MIL) was on. The technician found a diagnostic trouble code (DTC) for a MAP sensor. The technician removed the hose at the MAP sensor and discovered that gasoline had accumulated in the sensor and dripped out of the hose as it was being removed. The technician replaced the MAP sensor and test drove the vehicle to confirm the repair. Almost at once the check engine light came on with the same MAP sensor code. After several hours of troubleshooting without success in determining the cause, the technician decided to start over again. Almost at once, the technician discovered that no vacuum was getting to the MAP sensor where a vacuum gauge was connected with a T-fitting in the vacuum line to the MAP sensor. The vacuum port in the base of the throttle body was clogged with carbon. After a thorough cleaning, and clearing the DTC, the Cavalier again performed properly and the check engine light did not come on again. The technician had assumed that if gasoline was able to reach the sensor through the vacuum hose, surely vacuum could reach the sensor. The technician learned to stop assuming when diagnosing a vehicle and concentrate more on testing the simple things first.

TESTING THE MAP SENSOR

Most pressure sensors operate on 5 volts from the computer and return a signal (voltage or frequency) based on the pressure (vacuum) applied to the sensor. If a MAP sensor is being tested, make certain that the vacuum hose and hose fittings are sound and making a good, tight connection to a manifold vacuum source on the engine.

Four different types of test instruments can be used to test a pressure sensor:

1. A digital voltmeter with three test leads connected in series between the sensor and the wiring harness connector or back probe the terminals.
2. A scope connected to the sensor output, power, and ground.
3. A scan tool or a specific tool recommended by the vehicle manufacturer.
4. A breakout box connected in series between the computer and the wiring harness connection(s). A typical breakout box includes test points at which pressure sensor values can be measured with a digital voltmeter (or frequency counter, if a frequency-type MAP sensor is being tested).

NOTE: Always check service information for the exact testing procedures and specifications for the vehicle being tested.

Testing the MAP sensor using a DMM or scope

Use jumper wires, T-pins to back probe the connector, or a breakout box to gain electrical access to the wiring to the pressure sensor. Most pressure sensors use three wires:

1. A 5-volt wire from the computer
2. A variable-signal wire back to the computer
3. A ground or reference low wire

The procedure for testing the sensor is as follows:

1. Turn the ignition on (engine off)
2. Measure the voltage (or frequency) of the sensor output
3. Using a hand-operated vacuum pump (or other variable vacuum source), apply vacuum to the sensor

A good pressure sensor should change voltage (or frequency) in relation to the applied vacuum. If the signal does not change or the values are out of range according to the manufacturers' specifications, the sensor must be replaced.

◀ TECH TIP ▶

VISUAL CHECK OF THE MAP SENSOR

A defective vacuum hose to a MAP sensor can cause a variety of driveability problems including poor fuel economy, hesitation, stalling, and rough idle. A small air leak (vacuum leak) around the hose can cause these symptoms and often set a trouble code in the vehicle computer. When working on a vehicle that uses a MAP sensor, make certain that the vacuum hose travels consistently *downward* on its route from the sensor to the source of manifold vacuum. Inspect the hose, especially if another technician has previously replaced the factory-original hose. It should not be so long that it sags down at any point. Condensed fuel and/or moisture can become trapped in this low spot in the hose and cause all types of driveability problems and MAP sensor codes.

When checking the MAP sensor, if anything comes out of the sensor itself, it should be replaced. This includes water, gasoline, or any other substance.

TESTING THE MAP SENSOR USING A SCAN TOOL

A scan tool can be used to test a MAP sensor by monitoring the injector pulse width (in milliseconds) when vacuum is being applied to the MAP sensor using a hand-operated vacuum pump. See Figure 14-7.

Step 1 Apply about 20 in. Hg of vacuum to the MAP sensor and start the engine.

Step 2 Observe the injector pulse width. On a warm engine, the injector pulse width will normally be 1.5 to 3.5 ms.

Step 3 Slowly reduce the vacuum to the MAP sensor and observe the pulse width. A lower vacuum to the MAP sensor indicates a heavier load on the engine and the injector pulse width should increase.

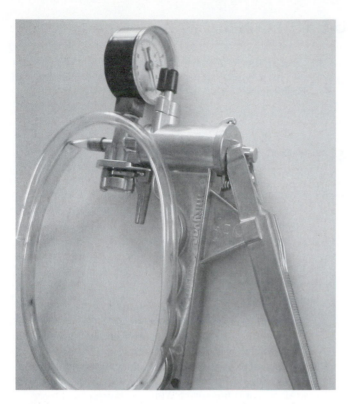

FIGURE 14-7 A typical hand-operated vacuum pump.

NOTE: If 23 in. Hg or more vacuum is applied to the MAP sensor with the engine running, this high vacuum will often stall the engine. The engine stalls because the high vacuum is interpreted by the PCM to indicate that the engine is being decelerated, which shuts off the fuel. During engine deceleration, the PCM shuts off the fuel injectors to reduce exhaust emissions and increase fuel economy.

FUEL-RAIL PRESSURE SENSOR

A fuel-rail pressure (FRP) sensor is used on some vehicles such as Fords that are equipped with electronic returnless fuel injection. This sensor provides fuel pressure information to the PCM for fuel injection pulse width calculations.

MAP/BARO DIAGNOSTIC TROUBLE CODES

The diagnostic trouble codes (DTCs) associated with the MAP and BARO sensors include:

Diagnostic Trouble Code	Description	Possible Causes
P0106	BARO sensor out-of-range at key on	• MAP sensor fault • MAP sensor O-ring damaged or missing
P0107	MAP sensor low voltage	• MAP sensor fault • MAP sensor signal circuit shorted-to-ground • MAP sensor 5-volt supply circuit open
P0108	Map sensor high voltage	• MAP sensor fault • MAP sensor O-ring damaged or missing • MAP sensor signal circuit shorted-to-voltage

SUMMARY

1. Pressure below atmospheric pressure is called vacuum and is measured in inches of mercury.
2. A manifold absolute pressure sensor uses a perfect vacuum (zero absolute pressure) in the sensor to determine the pressure.
3. Three types of MAP sensors include:
   - Silicon-diaphragm strain gauge
   - Capacitor-capsule design
   - Ceramic disc design
4. A heavy engine load results in low intake manifold vacuum and a high MAP sensor signal voltage.
5. A light engine load results in high intake manifold vacuum and a low MAP sensor signal voltage.
6. A MAP sensor is used to detect changes in altitude, as well as check other sensors and engine systems.
7. A MAP sensor can be tested by visual inspection, testing the output using a digital meter or scan tool.

REVIEW QUESTIONS

1. What is the relationship among atmospheric pressure, vacuum, and boost pressure in psi?

2. What are two types (construction) of MAP sensors?

3. What is the MAP sensor signal voltage or frequency at idle on a typical General Motors, DaimlerChrysler, and Ford engine?

4. What are three uses of a MAP sensor by the PCM?

ASE CERTIFICATION-TYPE QUESTIONS

1. As the load on an engine increases, the manifold vacuum decreases and the manifold absolute pressure _____.
   a. Increases
   b. Decreases
   c. Changes with barometric pressure only (altitude or weather)
   d. Remains constant (absolute)

2. A typical MAP compares the vacuum in the intake manifold to _____.
   a. Atmospheric pressure
   b. A perfect vacuum
   c. Barometric pressure
   d. The value of the IAT sensor

3. Which statement is *false?*
   a. Absolute pressure is equal to barometric pressure plus intake manifold vacuum.
   b. A decrease in manifold vacuum means an increase in manifold pressure.
   c. The MAP sensor compares manifold vacuum to a perfect vacuum.
   d. Barometric pressure minus the MAP sensor reading equals intake manifold vacuum.

4. Which design of MAP sensor produces a frequency (digital) output signal?
   a. Silicon-diaphragm strain gauge
   b. Piezo-resistivity design
   c. Capacitor-capsule
   d. Ceramic disc

5. The frequency output of a digital MAP sensor is reading 114 Hz. What is the approximate engine vacuum?
   a. Zero
   b. 5 in. Hg
   c. 10 in. Hg
   d. 15 in. Hg

6. Which is *not* a purpose or function of the MAP sensor?
   a. Measures the load on the engine
   b. Measures engine speed
   c. Calculates fuel delivery based on altitude
   d. Helps diagnose the EGR system

7. When measuring the output signal of a MAP sensor on a General Motors vehicle, the digital multimeter should be set to read _____.
   a. DC V
   b. AC V
   c. Hz
   d. DC A

8. Two technicians are discussing testing MAP sensors. Technician A says that the MAP sensor should be replaced if anything comes out of the sensor when the vacuum hose is removed from the sensor. Technician B says that the injector pulse width should increase when vacuum to the MAP sensor is increased. Which technician is correct?
   a. Technician A only
   b. Technician B only
   c. Both Technicians A and B
   d. Neither Technician A nor B

9. Technician A says that MAP sensors use a 5-volt reference voltage from the PCM. Technician B says that the MAP sensor voltage will be higher at idle at high altitudes compared to when the engine is operating at near sea level. Which technician is correct?
   a. Technician A only
   b. Technician B only
   c. Both Technicians A and B
   d. Neither Technician A nor B

10. A P0107 DTC is being discussed. Technician A says that a defective MAP sensor could be the cause. Technician B says that a MAP sensor signal wire shorted-to-ground could be the cause. Which technician is correct?
    a. Technician A only
    b. Technician B only
    c. Both Technicians A and B
    d. Neither Technician A nor B

◀ Chapter 15 ▶

MASS AIR FLOW SENSORS

OBJECTIVES

After studying Chapter 15, the reader should be able to:

1. Prepare for ASE Engine Performance (A8) certification test content area "E" (Computerized Engine Controls Diagnosis and Repair).
2. Discuss how MAF sensors work.
3. List the methods that can be used to test MAF sensors.
4. Describe the symptoms of a failed MAF sensor.
5. List how the operation of the MAF sensor affects vehicle operation.
6. Discuss MAF sensor rationality tests.

Engines that do not use an air flow meter or sensor rely on calculating the amount of air entering the engine by using the MAP sensor and engine speed as the major factors. The method of calculating the amount of fuel needed by the engine is called **speed density.**

AIR FLOW SENSORS

Port electronic fuel-injection systems that use air flow volume for fuel calculation usually have a movable vane in the intake stream. The vane is part of the **vane air flow (VAF)** sensor. The vane is deflected by intake air flow. See Figure 15-1.

The vane air flow sensor used in Bosch L-Jetronic, Ford, and most Japanese electronic port fuel-injection

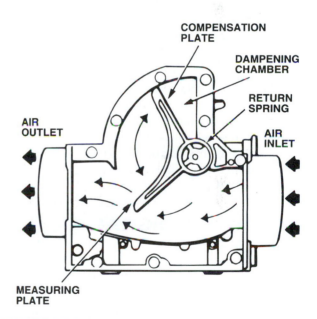

FIGURE 15-1 A vane air flow (VAF) sensor.

systems is a movable vane connected to a laser-calibrated potentiometer. The vane is mounted on a pivot pin and is deflected by intake air flow proportionate to air velocity. As the vane moves, it also moves the potentiometer. This causes a change in the signal voltage supplied to the computer. See Figure 15-2. For example, if the reference voltage is 5 volts, the potentiometer's signal to the computer will vary from a 0 voltage signal (no air flow) to almost a 5-volt signal (maximum air flow). In this way, the potentiometer provides the information the computer needs to vary the injector pulse width proportionate to air flow.

FIGURE 15-2 A typical air vane sensor with the cover removed. The movable arm contacts a carbon resistance path as the vane opens. Many air vane sensors also have contacts that close to supply voltage to the electric fuel pump as the air vane starts to open when the engine is being cranked and air is being drawn into the engine.

There is a special "dampening chamber" built into the VAF to smooth out vane pulsations which would be created by intake manifold air-pressure fluctuations caused by the valve opening and closing. Many vane air flow sensors include a switch to energize the electric fuel pump. This is a safety feature that prevents the operation of the fuel pump if the engine stalls.

ANALOG AND DIGITAL MAF SENSORS

Some MAF sensors produce a digital DC voltage signal whose frequency changes with the amount of air flow through the sensor. The frequency range also varies with the make of sensor and can range from 0- to 300-Hz for older General Motors MAF sensors to 1000- to 9000-Hz for most newer designs.

Some MAF sensors, such as those used by Ford and others, produce a changing DC voltage, rather than frequency, and range from 0- to 5-volts DC.

MASS AIR FLOW SENSOR TYPES

There are several types of mass air flow sensors.

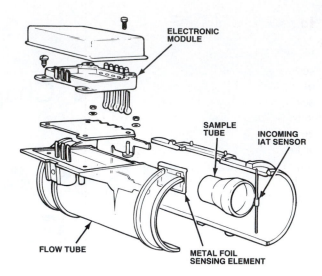

FIGURE 15-3 This five-wire mass air flow sensor consists of a metal foil sensing unit, an intake air temperature (IAT) sensor, and the electronic module.

Hot Film Sensor

The hot film sensor uses a temperature-sensing resistor (thermistor) to measure the temperature of the incoming air. Through the electronics within the sensor, a conductive film is kept at a temperature 70°C above the temperature of the incoming air. See Figure 15-3.

Because the amount and density of the air both tend to contribute to the cooling effect as the air passes through the sensor, this type of sensor can actually produce an output based on the *mass* of the air flow. *Mass equals volume times density.* For example, cold air is denser than warm air so a small amount of cold air may have the same mass as a larger amount of warm air. Therefore, a mass air flow sensor is designed to measure the mass, not the volume, of the air entering the engine.

The output of this type of sensor is usually a frequency based on the amount of air entering the sensor. The more air that enters the sensor, the more the hot film is cooled. The electronics inside the sensor, therefore, increase the current flow through the hot film to maintain the 70°C temperature differential between the air temperature and the temperature of the hot film. This change in current flow is converted to a frequency output that the computer can use as a measurement of air flow. Most of these types of sensors are referred to as **mass air flow (MAF) sensors** because, unlike the air vane sensor, the MAF sensor takes into account relative humidity, altitude, and temperature of the air. The denser the air, the greater the cooling effect on the hot film sensor and the greater the amount of fuel required for proper combustion.

Hot Wire Sensor

The hot wire sensor is similar to the hot film type, but uses a hot wire to sense the mass air flow instead of the hot film. Like the hot film sensor, the hot wire sensor uses a temperature-sensing resistor (thermistor) to measure the temperature of the air entering the sensor. See Figure 15-4. The electronic circuitry within the sensor keeps the temperature of the wire at 70°C above the temperature of the incoming air.

Both designs operate in essentially the same way. A resistor wire or screen installed in the path of intake air flow is heated to a constant temperature by electric current provided by the computer. Air flowing past the screen or wire cools it. The degree of cooling varies with air velocity, temperature, density, and humidity. These factors combine to indicate the mass of air entering the engine. As the screen or wire cools, more current is required to maintain the specified temperature. As the screen or wire heats up, less current is required. The operating principle can be summarized as follows:

- More intake air volume = cooler sensor, more current.
- Less intake air volume = warmer sensor, less current.

The computer constantly monitors the change in current and translates it into a voltage signal that is used to determine injector pulse width.

Burn-off circuit. Some MAF sensors use a burn-off circuit to keep the sensing wire clean of dust and dirt. A high current is passed through the sensing wire for a short time, but long enough to cause the wire to glow due to the heat. The burn-off circuit is turned on when the ignition switch is switched off after the engine has been operating long enough to achieve normal operating temperature.

KARMAN VORTEX SENSORS

In 1912, a Hungarian scientist named Theodore Van Karman observed that vortexes were created when air passed over a pointed surface. This type of sensor sends a sound wave through the turbulence created by incoming air passing through the sensor. Air mass is calculated based on the time required for the sound waves to cross the turbulent air passage.

There are two basic designs of Karman Vortex air flow sensors. The two types include:

- **Ultrasonic.** This type of sensor uses ultrasonic waves to detect the vortexes that are produced, and produce a digital (on and off) signal where frequency is proportional to the amount of air passing through the sensor. See Figure 15-5.
- **Pressure-type.** DaimlerChrysler uses a pressure-type Karman Vortex sensor that uses a pressure sensor to detect the vortexes. As the air flow through the sensor increases, so do the number of pressure variations. The electronics in the sensor convert these pressure variations to a square wave (digital DC voltage) signal, whose frequency is in proportion to the air flow through the sensor.

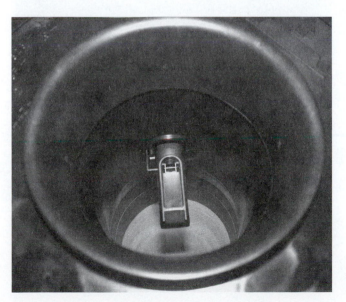

FIGURE 15-4 The sensing wire in a typical hot wire mass air flow sensor.

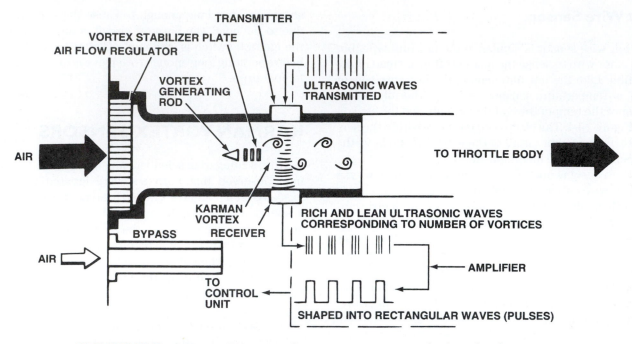

FIGURE 15-5 A Karman Vortex air flow sensor uses a triangle-shaped rod to create vortexes as the air flows through the sensor. The electronics in the sensor itself converts these vortexes to a digital square wave signal.

◀ DIAGNOSTIC STORY ▶

THE DIRTY MAF SENSOR STORY

The owner of a Buick Park Avenue equipped with a 3800 V-6 engine complained that the engine would hesitate during acceleration, showed lack of power, and seemed to surge or miss at times. A visual inspection found everything to be like new, including a new air filter. There were no stored diagnostic trouble codes (DTCs). A look at the scan data showed air flow to be within the recommended 3 to 7 grams per second. A check of the frequency output showed the problem.

Idle frequency = 2.177 kHz (2177 Hz)

Normal frequency at idle speed should be 2.37 to 2.52 kHz. Cleaning the hot wire of the MAF sensor restored proper operation. The sensor wire was covered with what looked like fine fibers, possibly from the replacement air filter.

NOTE: Older GM MAF sensors operated at a lower frequency of 32 to 150 Hz, with 32 Hz being the average reading at idle and 150 Hz for wide-open throttle.

PCM USES FOR AIR FLOW SENSORS

The PCM uses the information from the air flow sensor for the following purposes:

- Air flow sensors are used mostly to determine the amount of fuel needed and base pulse-width numbers. The greater the mass of the incoming air, the longer the injectors are pulsed on.

- Air flow sensors back up the TP sensor in the event of a loss of signal or an inaccurate throttle position sensor signal. If the MAF sensor fails, then the PCM will calculate the fuel delivery needs of the engine based on throttle position and engine speed (RPM).

◀ FREQUENTLY ASKED QUESTION ▶

WHAT IS MEANT BY A "HIGH-AUTHORITY SENSOR?"

A high-authority sensor is a sensor that has a major influence over the amount of fuel being delivered to the engine. For example, at engine start-up, the engine coolant temperature (ECT) sensor is a high-authority sensor and the oxygen sensor (O2S) is a low-authority sensor. However, as the engine reaches operating temperature, the oxygen sensor becomes a high-authority sensor and can greatly affect the amount of fuel being supplied to the engine. See the chart.

High-Authority Sensors	Low-Authority Sensors
ECT (especially when the engine starts and is warming up)	IAT (intake air temperature) sensors modify and backup the ECT
O2S (after the engine reaches closed-loop operation)	TFT (transmission fluid temperature)
MAP	PRNDL (shift position sensor)
MAF	KS (knock sensor)
TP (high authority during acceleration and deceleration)	EFT (engine fuel temperature)

TESTING MASS AIR FLOW SENSORS

Start the testing of a MAF sensor by performing a thorough visual inspection. Look at all the hoses that direct and send air, especially between the MAF sensor and the throttle body. Also check the electrical connector for:

- Corrosion
- Terminals that are bent or pushed out of the plastic connector
- Frayed wiring

◀ FREQUENTLY ASKED QUESTION ▶

WHAT IS FALSE AIR?

Air flow sensors and mass air flow (MAF) sensors are designed to measure *all* the air entering the engine. If an air inlet hose was loose or had a hole, extra air could enter the engine without being measured. This extra air is often called **false air.** See Figure 15-6. Because this extra air is unmeasured, the computer does not provide enough fuel delivery and the engine operates too lean, especially at idle. A small hole in the air inlet hose would represent a fairly large percentage of false air at idle, but would represent a very small percentage of extra air at highway speeds.

To diagnose for false air, look at long-term fuel trim numbers at idle and at 3000 RPM.

HINT: If the engine runs well in reverse, yet runs terrible in any forward gear, carefully look at the inlet hose for air leaks that would open when the engine torque moves the engine slightly on its mounts.

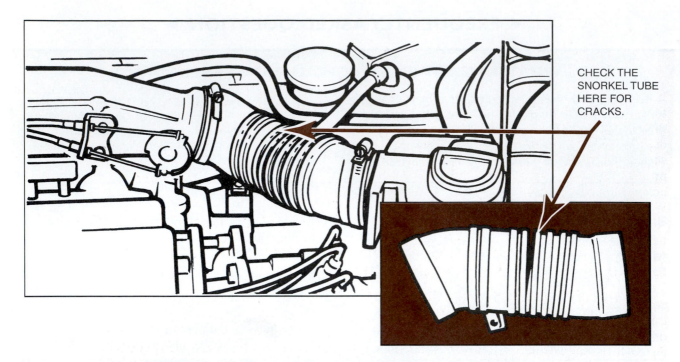

FIGURE 15-6 Carefully check the hose between the MAF sensor and the throttle plate for cracks or splits that could create extra (false) air into the engine that is not measured by the MAF sensor.

MAF Sensor Output Test

A digital multimeter can also be used to check the MAF sensor. See the chart that shows the voltage output compared with the grams per second of air flow through the sensor. Normal air flow is 3 to 7 grams per second.

Analog MAF Sensor Grams per Second/Voltage Chart

Grams per Second	Sensor Voltage
0	0.2
2	0.7
4	1.0
	(typical idle value)
8	1.5
15	2.0
30	2.5
50	3.0
80	3.5
110	4.0
150	4.5
175	4.8

Tap Test

With the engine running at idle speed, *gently* tap the MAF sensor with the fingers of an open hand. If the engine stumbles or stalls, the MAF sensor is defective. This test is commonly called the **tap test.**

Digital Meter Test of a MAF Sensor

A digital multimeter can be used to measure the frequency (Hz) output of the sensor and compare the reading with specifications.

The frequency output and engine speed in RPM can also be plotted on a graph to check to see if the frequency and RPM are proportional, resulting in a straight line on the graph.

◀ **TECH TIP** ▶

THE UNPLUG IT TEST

If a sensor is defective yet still produces a signal to the computer, the computer will often accept the reading and make the required changes in fuel delivery and spark advance. If, however, the sensor is not reading correctly, the computer will process this wrong information and perform an action assuming that information being supplied is accurate. For example, if a mass air flow (MAF) sensor is telling the computer that 12 grams of air per second is going into the engine, the computer will then pulse the injector for 6.4 ms or whatever figure it is programmed to provide. However, if the air going into the engine is actually 14 grams per second, the amount of fuel supplied by the injectors will not be enough to provide proper engine operation. If the MAF sensor is unplugged, the computer knows that the sensor is not capable of supplying air flow information, so it defaults to a fixed amount of fuel based on the values of other sensors such as the TP and MAP sensors. "If in doubt, take it out."

If the engine operates better with a sensor unplugged, then suspect that the sensor is defective. A sensor that is not supplying the correct information is said to be *skewed*. The computer will not see a diagnostic trouble code for this condition because the computer can often not detect that the sensor is supplying wrong information.

Contaminated Sensor

Dirt, oil, silicon, or even spider webs can coat the sensing wire. Because it tends to insulate the sensing wire at low air flow rates, a contaminated sensor often overestimates the amount of air entering the engine at idle, and therefore causes the fuel system to go rich. At higher engine speeds near wide-open throttle (WOT), the contamination can cause the sensor to underestimate the amount of air entering the engine. As a result, the fuel system will go lean, causing spark knock and lack of power concerns. To check for contamination, check the fuel trim numbers.

If the fuel trim is negative (removing fuel) at idle, yet is positive (adding fuel) at higher engine speeds, a contaminated MAF sensor is a likely cause. Other tests for a contaminated MAF sensor include:

- At WOT, the grams per second, as read on a scan tool, should exceed 100.
- At WOT, the voltage, as read on a digital voltmeter, should exceed 4 volts for an analog sensor.
- At WOT, the frequency, as read on a meter or scan tool, should exceed 7 kHz for a digital sensor.

If the readings do not exceed these values, then the MAF sensor is contaminated.

◀ **DIAGNOSTIC STORY** ▶

THE RICH RUNNING TOYOTA

A Toyota failed an enhanced emission test for excessive carbon monoxide, which is caused by a rich (too much fuel) air-fuel ratio problem. After checking all of the basics and not finding any fault in the fuel system, the technician checked the archives of the International Automotive Technicians Network (www.iatn.net) and discovered that a broken spring inside the air flow sensor was a possible cause. The sensor was checked and a broken vane return spring was discovered, as shown in Figure 15-7. Replacing the air flow sensor restored the engine to proper operating conditions and it passed the emission test.

MAF-Related Diagnostic Trouble Codes

The diagnostic trouble codes (DTCs) associated with the mass air flow and air vane sensors include:

Diagnostic Trouble Code	Description	Possible Cause
P0100	Mass or volume air flow circuit problems	- Open or short in mass air flow circuit - Defective MAF sensor
P0101	Mass air flow circuit range problems	- Defective MAF sensor (check for false air)

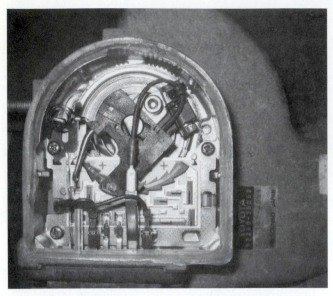

(a)

(b)

FIGURE 15-7 (a) Air flow sensor with the protective cover removed. (b) Broken air flow vane return spring.

P0102	Mass air flow circuit low output	• Defective MAF sensor • MAF sensor circuit open or shorted-to-ground • Open 12-volt supply voltage circuit
P0103	Mass air flow circuit high output	• Defective MAF sensor • MAF sensor circuit shorted-to-voltage

SUMMARY

1. A mass air flow sensor actually measures the density and amount of air flowing into the engine, which results in accurate engine control.

2. An air vane sensor measures the volume of the air, and the intake air temperature sensor is used by the PCM to calculate the mass of the air entering the engine.

3. A hot wire MAF sensor uses the electronics in the sensor itself to heat a wire 70°C above the temperature of the air entering the engine.

REVIEW QUESTIONS

1. How does a hot film MAF sensor work?

2. What type of voltage signal is produced by a MAF?

3. What change in the signal will occur if engine speed is increased?

4. How is a MAF sensor tested?

5. What is the purpose of a MAF sensor?

6. What are the types of air flow sensors?

ASE CERTIFICATION-TYPE QUESTIONS

1. A fuel-injection system that does not use a sensor to measure the amount (or mass) of air entering the engine is usually called a(n) _____ type of system.
   a. Air vane-controlled
   b. Speed density
   c. Mass air flow
   d. Hot wire

2. Which type of sensor uses a burn-off circuit?
   a. Hot wire MAF sensor
   b. Hot film MAF sensor
   c. Vane-type air flow sensor
   d. Both a and b

3. Which sensor has a switch that controls the electric fuel pump?
   a. VAF
   b. Hot wire MAF
   c. Hot filter MAF
   d. Karman Vortex sensor

4. Two technicians are discussing Karman Vortex sensors. Technician A says that they contain a burn-off circuit to keep them clean. Technician B says that they contain a movable vane. Which technician is correct?
   a. Technician A only
   b. Technician B only
   c. Both Technicians A and B
   d. Neither Technician A nor B

5. The typical MAF reading on a scan tool with the engine at idle speed and normal operating temperature is _____.
   a. 1 to 3 grams per second
   b. 3 to 7 grams per second
   c. 8 to 12 grams per second
   d. 14 to 24 grams per second

6. Two technicians are diagnosing a poorly running engine. There are no diagnostic trouble codes. When the MAF sensor is unplugged, the engine runs better. Technician A says that this means that the MAF is supplying incorrect air flow information to the PCM. Technician B says that this indicates that the PCM is defective. Which technician is correct?
   a. Technician A only
   b. Technician B only
   c. Both Technicians A and B
   d. Neither Technician A nor B

7. A MAF sensor on a General Motors 3800 V-6 is being tested for contamination. Technician A says that the sensor should show over 100 grams per second on a scan tool display when the accelerator is depressed to WOT on a running engine. Technician B says that the output frequency should exceed 7000 Hz when the accelerator pedal is depressed to WOT on a running engine. Which technician is correct?
   a. Technician A only
   b. Technician B only
   c. Both Technicians A and B
   d. Neither Technician A nor B

8. Which air flow sensor has a dampening chamber?
   a. A vane airflow
   b. A hot film MAF
   c. A hot wire MAF
   d. A Karman Vortex

9. Air that enters the engine without passing through the air flow sensor is called _____.
   a. Bypass air
   b. Dirty air
   c. False air
   d. Measured air

10. A P0102 DTC is being discussed. Technician A says that a sensor circuit shorted-to-ground can be the cause. Technician B says that an open sensor voltage supply circuit could be the cause. Which technician is correct?
    a. Technician A only
    b. Technician B only
    c. Both Technicians A and B
    d. Neither Technician A nor B

<h1>◄ Chapter 16 ►</h1>

<h1>OXYGEN SENSORS</h1>

OBJECTIVES

After studying Chapter 16, the reader should be able to:

1. Prepare for ASE Engine Performance (A8) certification test content area "E" (Computerized Engine Controls Diagnosis and Repair).
2. Discuss how O2S sensors work.
3. List the methods that can be used to test O2S sensors.
4. Describe the symptoms of a failed O2S sensor.
5. List how the operation of the O2S sensor affects vehicle operation.

OXYGEN SENSORS

Automotive computer systems use a sensor in the exhaust system to measure the oxygen content of the exhaust. These sensors are called **oxygen sensors (O2S)**. The oxygen sensor is installed in the exhaust manifold or located downstream from the manifold in the exhaust pipe. See Figure 16-1. The oxygen sensor is directly in the path of the exhaust gas stream where it monitors oxygen level in both the exhaust stream and the ambient air. In a zirconia oxygen sensor, the tip contains a thimble made of zirconium dioxide (ZrO_2), an electrically conductive material capable of generating a small voltage in the presence of oxygen.

Exhaust from the engine passes through the end of the sensor where the gases contact the outer side of the thimble. Atmospheric air enters through the other end of the sensor or through the wire of the sensor and contacts the inner side of the thimble. The inner and outer surfaces of the thimble are plated with platinum. The inner surface becomes a negative electrode; the outer surface is a positive electrode. The atmosphere contains a relatively constant 21% of oxygen. Rich exhaust gases contain little oxygen. Exhaust from a lean mixture contains more oxygen.

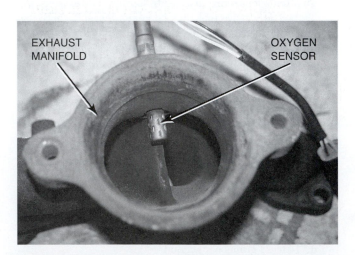

FIGURE 16-1 Many fuel-control oxygen sensors are located in the exhaust manifold near its outlet so that the sensor can detect the presence or absence of oxygen in the exhaust stream for all cylinders that feed into the manifold.

Negatively charged oxygen ions are drawn to the thimble where they collect on both the inner and outer surfaces. See Figure 16-2. Because the percentage of oxygen present in the atmosphere exceeds that in the exhaust gases, the atmosphere side of the thimble draws more negative oxygen ions than the exhaust side. The difference between the two sides creates an electrical potential, or voltage. When the concentration of oxygen on the exhaust side of the thimble is low (risk effort), a high voltage (0.60 to 1.0 volts) is generated between the electrodes. As the oxygen concentration on the exhaust side increases (lean exhaust), the voltage generated drops low (0.00 to 0.3 volts). See Figure 16-3.

This voltage signal is sent to the computer where it passes through the input conditioner for amplification. The computer interprets a high-voltage signal (low-oxygen content) as a rich air-fuel ratio, and a low-voltage signal (high oxygen content) as a lean air-fuel ratio. Based on the O2S signal (above or below 0.45 volts), the computer compensates by making the mixture either leaner or richer as required to continually vary close to a 14.7:1 air-fuel ratio to satisfy the needs of the three-way catalytic converter. The O2S is the key sensor of an electronically controlled fuel metering system for emission control.

An O2S does not send a voltage signal until its tip reaches a temperature of about 572°F (300°C). Also, O2 sensors provide their fastest response to mixture changes at about 1472°F (800°C). When the engine starts and the O2S is cold, the computer runs the engine in the open-loop mode, drawing on prerecorded data in the PROM for fuel control on a cold engine, or when O2S output is not within certain limits.

If the exhaust contains very little oxygen (O2S), the computer assumes that the intake charge is rich (too much fuel) and reduces fuel delivery. See Figure 16-4.

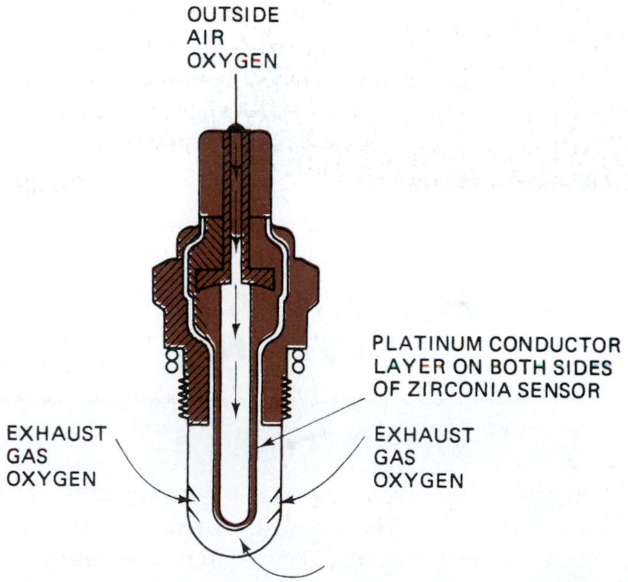

OXYGEN SENSOR ELEMENT

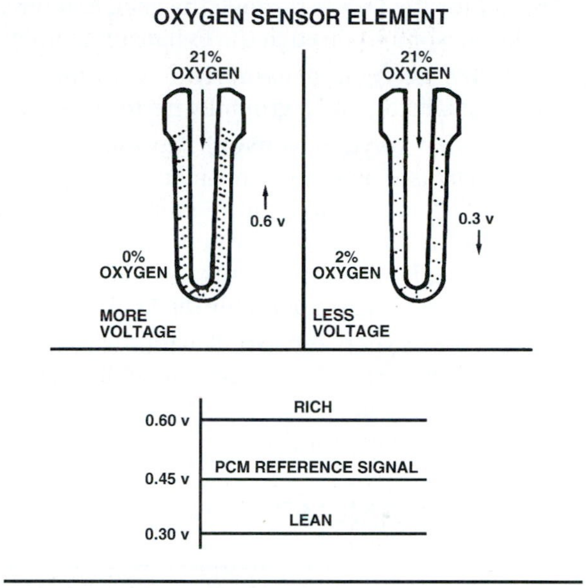

FIGURE 16-3 A difference in oxygen content between the atmosphere and the exhaust gases enables an O2S sensor to generate voltage.

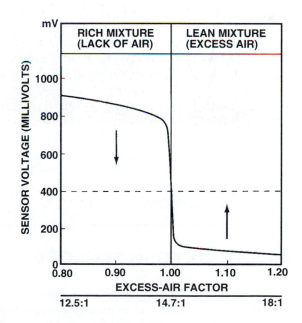

FIGURE 16-2 A cross-sectional view of a typical zirconia oxygen sensor.

FIGURE 16-4 The oxygen sensor provides a quick response at the stoichiometric air-fuel ratio of 14.7:1.

However, when the oxygen level is high, the computer assumes that the intake charge is lean (not enough fuel) and increases fuel delivery. There are several different designs of oxygen sensors, including:

- **One-wire oxygen sensor.** The one wire of the one-wire oxygen sensor is the O2S signal wire. The ground for the O2S is through the shell and threads of the sensor and through the exhaust manifold.
- **Two-wire oxygen sensor.** The two-wire sensor has a signal wire and a ground wire for the O2S.
- **Three-wire oxygen sensor.** The three-wire sensor design uses an electric resistance heater to help get the O2S up to temperature more quickly and to help keep the sensor at operating temperature even at idle speeds. The three wires include the O2S signal, the power, and ground for the heater.
- **Four-wire oxygen sensor.** The four-wire sensor is a heated O2S (HO2S) that uses an O2S signal wire and signal ground. The other two wires are the power and ground for the heater.

◀ DIAGNOSTIC STORY ▶

THE CHEVROLET PICKUP TRUCK STORY

The owner of a 1996 Chevrolet pickup truck complained that the engine ran terribly. It would hesitate and surge, yet there were no diagnostic trouble codes (DTCs). After hours of troubleshooting, the technician discovered while talking to the owner that the problem started after the transmission had been repaired, yet the transmission shop said that the problem was an engine problem and not related to the transmission.

A thorough visual inspection revealed that the front and rear oxygen sensor connectors had been switched. The computer was trying to compensate for an air-fuel mixture condition that did not exist. Reversing the O2S connectors restored proper operation of the truck.

ZIRCONIA OXYGEN SENSORS

The most common type of oxygen sensor is made from zirconia (zirconium dioxide). It is usually constructed using powder that is pressed into a thimble shape and coated with porous platinum material that acts as electrodes. All zirconia sensors use 18-mm-diameter threads with a washer. See Figure 16-5.

FIGURE 16-5 A typical zirconia oxygen sensor.

Zirconia oxygen sensors (O2S) are constructed so that oxygen ions flow through the sensor when there is a difference between the oxygen content inside and outside of the sensor. An ion is an electrically charged particle. The greater the differences between the oxygen content between the inside and outside of the sensor the higher the voltage created.

- **Rich mixture.** A rich mixture results in little oxygen in the exhaust stream. Compared to the outside air, this represents a large difference and the sensors create a relatively high voltage of about 1.0 volt (1000 mV).
- **Lean mixture.** A lean mixture leaves some oxygen in the exhaust stream that did not combine with the fuel. This leftover oxygen reduces the difference between the oxygen content of the exhaust compared to the oxygen content of the outside air. As a result, the sensor voltage is low or almost 0 volt.
- **O2S voltage above 450 mV** is produced by the sensor when the oxygen content in the exhaust is low. This is interpreted by the engine computer (PCM) as being a rich exhaust.
- **O2S voltage below 450 mV** is produced by the sensor when the oxygen content is high. This is interpreted by the engine computer (PCM) as being a lean exhaust.

◀ FREQUENTLY ASKED ▶ QUESTION

WHERE IS HO2S1?

Oxygen sensors are numbered according to their location in the engine. On a V-type engine, heated oxygen sensor number 1 (HO2S1) is located in the exhaust manifold on the side of the engine where the number one cylinder is located. See Figure 16-6.

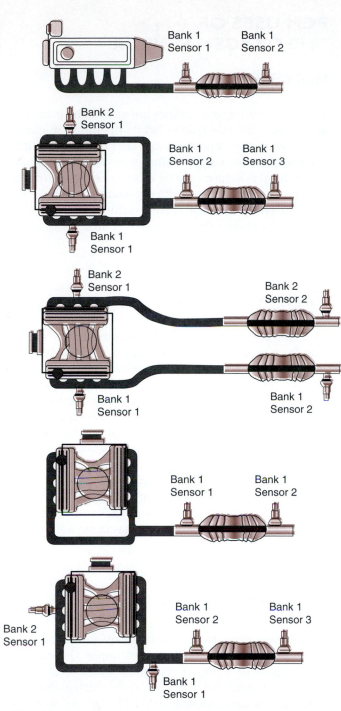

FIGURE 16-6 Number and label designations for oxygen sensors. Bank I is the bank where cylinder number I is located.

TITANIA OXYGEN SENSOR

The titania (titanium dioxide) oxygen sensor does not produce a voltage but rather changes in resistance with the presence of oxygen in the exhaust. All titania oxygen sensors use a four-terminal variable resistance unit with a heating element. A titania sensor samples exhaust air only and uses a reference voltage from the PCM. Titania oxide oxygen sensors use a 14-mm thread and are not interchangeable with zirconia oxygen sensors. One volt is applied to the sensor and the changing resistance of the titania oxygen sensor changes the voltage of the sensor circuit. As with a zirconia oxygen sensor, the voltage signal is above 450 mV when the exhaust is rich, and low (below 450 mV) when the exhaust is lean.

WIDE-BAND OXYGEN SENSORS

A **wide-band oxygen sensor,** also called a **lean air-fuel (LAF) ratio sensor** or a **linear air-fuel ratio sensor,** allows engines to operate as lean as 23:1 and still maintain closed-loop operation. This type of sensor usually uses five wires.

- One power wire
- One ground wire for the electric heater
- Three sensor wires

The three sensor wires are used to provide the PCM with a signal that more accurately reflects the oxygen content in the exhaust than a conventional oxygen sensor. A wide-band oxygen sensor can be best described as having two oxygen sensors mated together with a diffusion layer between the two components. Just as in a conventional zirconium dioxide oxygen sensor, current flows from one side to the other and produces a voltage. In a wide-band oxygen sensor, an oxygen pump uses a heated cathode and anode to pull oxygen from the exhaust into a diffusion gap. The diffusion layer and the oxygen sensor elements are electrically connected so that it takes a certain amount of current (in milliamperes) to maintain a balanced oxygen level in the diffusion layer. When the air-fuel mixture is perfectly balanced at 14.7:1, the sensor produces no output current. When the air-fuel mixture is rich, the sensor produces a negative current ranging from zero to about 2 milliamps, which represents an air-fuel ratio of about 12:1. When the air-fuel ratio is lean, the sensor produces a positive current that ranges from 0 to 1.5 milliamperes as the mixture gets leaner up to about 22:1.

Testing a wide-band oxygen sensor is usually achieved using a scan tool. Most PCMs display the rich and lean status of the exhaust, plus many show the operation of the oxygen sensor in millivolts from 0 to 1000 just as if the sensor were a conventional zirconia oxygen sensor.

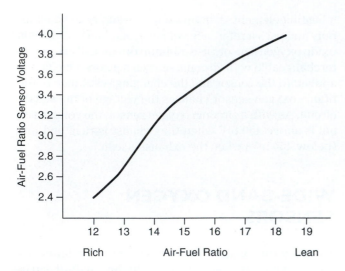

FIGURE 16-7   The output of a typical air-fuel mixture sensor showing that the voltage increases as the exhaust becomes leaner, which is opposite from normal oxygen sensors.

Wide-band oxygen sensors, just like conventional zirconia oxygen sensors, can be fooled by exhaust leaks upstream of the sensor, as well as from ignition misfires.

A linear air-fuel sensor is used on some Toyota brand vehicles and produces a voltage reading of 2.2 to 4.2 volts, depending on the oxygen content of the exhaust. This type of oxygen sensor is used to detect mixtures as rich as 12:1 and as lean as 18:1. See Figure 16-7.

CLOSED LOOP AND OPEN LOOP

The amount of fuel delivered to an engine is determined by the powertrain control module (PCM) based on inputs from the engine coolant temperature (ECT), throttle position (TP) sensor, and others until the oxygen sensor is capable of supplying a usable signal. When the PCM alone (without feedback) is determining the amount of fuel needed, it is called **open-loop operation.** As soon as the oxygen sensor (O2S) is capable of supplying rich and lean signals, adjustments by the computer can be made to fine-tune the correct air-fuel mixture. This checking and adjusting by the computer is called **closed-loop operation.**

PCM USES OF THE OXYGEN SENSOR

Fuel Control

The upstream oxygen sensors are among the main sensor(s) used for fuel control while operating in closed loop. Before the oxygen sensors are hot enough to give accurate exhaust oxygen information to the computer, fuel control is determined by other sensors and the anticipated injector pulse width determined by those sensors. After the control system achieves closed loop status, the oxygen sensor provides feedback with actual exhaust gas oxygen content.

Fuel Trim

Fuel trim is computer program that is used to compensate for a too rich or a too lean air-fuel exhaust as detected by the oxygen sensor(s). Fuel trim is necessary to keep the air-fuel mixture within limits to allow the catalytic converter to operate efficiently. If the exhaust is too lean or too rich for a long time, the catalytic converter can be damaged. The fuel trim numbers are determined from the signals from the oxygen sensor(s). If the engine has been operating too lean, short-term and long-term fuel time programming inside the PCM can cause an increase in the commanded injector pulse width to bring the air-fuel mixture back into the proper range. Fuel trim can be negative (subtracting fuel) or positive (adding fuel).

Diagnosis

The oxygen sensors are used for diagnosis of other systems and components. For example, the exhaust gas recirculation (EGR) system is tested by the PCM by commanding the valve to open during the test. Some PCMs determine whether enough exhaust gas flows into the engine by looking at the oxygen sensor response (fuel trim numbers). The upstream and downstream oxygen sensors are also used to determine the efficiency of the catalytic converter. See Figure 16-8.

◀ **FREQUENTLY ASKED** ▶
QUESTION

WHAT HAPPENS TO THE BIAS VOLTAGE?

Some vehicle manufacturers such as General Motors Corporation have the computer apply 450 mV (0.450 V) to the O2S signal wire. This voltage is called the **bias voltage** and represents the threshold voltage for the transition from rich to lean.

This bias voltage is displayed on a scan tool when the ignition switch is turned on with the engine off. When the engine is started, the O2S becomes warm enough to produce a usable voltage and bias voltage "disappears" as the O2S responds to a rich and lean mixture. What happened to the bias voltage that the computer applied to the O2S? The voltage from the O2S simply overcome the very weak voltage signal from the computer. This bias voltage is so weak that even a 20-megohm impedance DMM will affect the strength enough to cause the voltage to drop to 426 mV. Other meters with only 10 megohms of impedance will cause the bias voltage to read less than 400 mV.

Therefore, even though the O2S voltage is relatively low powered, it is more than strong enough to override the very weak bias voltage the computer sends to the O2S.

◀ **DIAGNOSTIC STORY** ▶

THE OXYGEN SENSOR IS LYING TO YOU

A technician was trying to solve a driveability problem with a V-6 passenger car. The car idled roughly, hesitated, and accelerated poorly. A thorough visual inspection did not indicate any possible problems and there were no diagnostic trouble codes stored.

A check was made on the oxygen sensor activity using a DMM. The voltage stayed above 600 mV most of the time. If a large vacuum hose was removed, the oxygen sensor voltage would temporarily drop to below 450 mV and then return to a reading of over 600 mV. Remember:

- High O2S readings = rich exhaust (low O_2 content in the exhaust)
- Low O2S readings = lean exhaust (high O_2 content in the exhaust)

As part of a thorough visual inspection, the technician removed and inspected the spark plugs. All the spark plugs were white, indicating a lean mixture, not the rich mixture that the oxygen sensor was indicating. The high O2S reading signaled the computer to reduce the amount of fuel, resulting in an excessively lean operation.

After replacing the oxygen sensor, the engine ran great. But what killed the oxygen sensor? The technician finally learned from the owner that the head gasket had been replaced over a year ago. The phosphate and silicate additives in the antifreeze coolant had coated the oxygen sensor. Because the oxygen sensor was coated, the oxygen content of the exhaust could not be detected—the result: a false rich signal from the oxygen sensor.

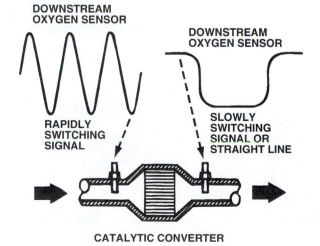

FIGURE 16-8 The OBD-II catalytic converter monitor compares the signals of the upstream and downstream oxygen sensor to determine converter efficiency.

◀ DIAGNOSTIC STORY ▶

THE MISSING FORD ESCORT

A Ford Escort was being analyzed for poor engine operation. The engine ran perfectly during the following conditions:

1. With the engine cold or operating in open loop
2. With the engine at idle
3. With the engine operating at or near wide-open throttle

After hours of troubleshooting, the cause was found to be a poor ground connection for the oxygen sensor. The engine ran okay during times when the computer ignored the oxygen sensor. Unfortunately, the service technician did not have a definite plan during the diagnostic process and as a result checked and replaced many unnecessary parts. An oxygen sensor test early in the diagnostic procedure would have indicated that the oxygen (O2S) signal was not correct. The poor ground caused the oxygen sensor voltage level to be too high, indicating to the computer that the mixture was too rich. The computer then subtracted fuel which caused the engine to miss and run rough as the result of the now too lean air-fuel mixture.

TESTING AN OXYGEN SENSOR USING A DIGITAL VOLTMETER

The oxygen sensor can be checked for proper operation using a digital high-impedance voltmeter.

1. With the engine off, connect the red lead of the meter to the oxygen sensor signal wire. See Figure 16-9.
2. Start the engine and allow it to reach closed-loop operation.
3. In closed-loop operation, the oxygen sensor voltage should be constantly changing as the fuel mixture is being controlled.

The results should be interpreted as follows:

- If the oxygen sensor fails to respond, and its voltage remains at about 450 millivolts, the sensor may be defective and require replacement. Before replacing the oxygen sensor, check the manufacturers' recommended procedures.
- If the oxygen sensor reads high all the time (above 550 millivolts), the fuel system could be supplying too rich a fuel mixture or the oxygen sensor may be contaminated.
- If the oxygen sensor voltage remains low (below 350 millivolts), the fuel system could be supplying

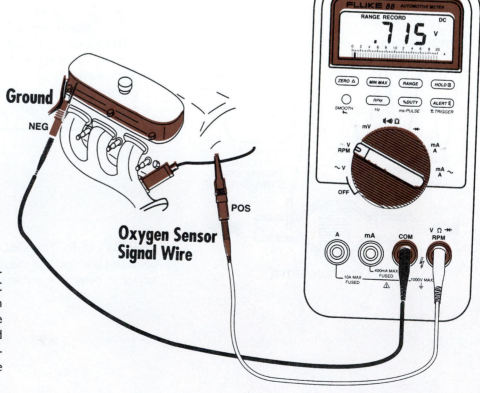

FIGURE 16-9 Testing an oxygen sensor using a DMM set on DC volts. With the engine operating in closed loop, the oxygen voltage should read over 800 mV and lower than 200 mV and be constantly fluctuating. *(Courtesy of Fluke Corporation)*

too lean a fuel mixture. Check for a vacuum leak or partially clogged fuel injector(s). Before replacing the oxygen sensor, check the manufacturer's recommended procedures.

TESTING THE OXYGEN SENSOR USING THE MIN/MAX METHOD

A digital meter set on DC volts can be used to record the minimum and maximum voltage with the engine running. A good oxygen sensor should be able to produce a value of less than 300 millivolts and a maximum voltage above 800 millivolts. Replace any oxygen sensor that fails to go above 700 millivolts or lower than 300 millivolts. See Figure 16-10.

◀ FREQUENTLY ASKED ▶ QUESTION

WHY DOES THE OXYGEN SENSOR VOLTAGE READ 5 VOLTS ON MANY CHRYSLER VEHICLES?

Many Chrysler (DaimlerChrysler) vehicles apply a 5-volt reference to the signal wire of the oxygen sensor. The purpose of this voltage is to allow the computer to detect if the oxygen sensor signal circuit is open or grounded.

- If the voltage on the signal wire is 4.5 volts or more, the computer assumes that the sensor is open.
- If the voltage on the signal wire is zero, the computer assumes that the sensor is shorted-to-ground.

If either condition exists, the computer can set a diagnostic trouble code (DTC).

TESTING AN OXYGEN SENSOR USING A SCAN TOOL

A good oxygen sensor should be able to sense the oxygen content and change voltage outputs rapidly. How fast an oxygen sensor switches from high (above 450 millivolts) to low (below 350 millivolts) is measured in oxygen sensor **cross counts.** Cross counts are the number of times an oxygen sensor changes voltage from high to low (from low to high voltage is not counted) in 1 second (or 1.25 second, depending on scan tool and computer speed).

MIN/MAX Oxygen Sensor Test Chart

Minimum Voltage	Maximum Voltage	Average Voltage	Test Results
Below 200 mV	Above 800 mV	400 to 500 mV	Oxygen sensor is okay.
Above 200 mV	Any reading	400 to 500 mV	Oxygen sensor is defective.
Any reading	Below 800 mV	400 to 500 mV	Oxygen sensor is defective.
Below 200 mV	Above 800 mV	Below 400 mV	System is operating lean[*].
Below 200 mV	Below 800 mV	Below 400 mV	System is operating lean. (Add propane to the intake air to see if the oxygen sensor reacts. If not , the sensor is defective.)
Below 200 mV	Above 800 mV	Above 500 mV	System is operating rich.
Above 200 mV	Above 800 mV	Above 500 mV	System is operating rich. (Remove a vacuum hose to see if the oxygen sensor reacts. If not, the sensor is defective.)

[*]Check for an exhaust leak upstream from the O2S or ignition misfire that can cause a false lean indication before further diagnosis.

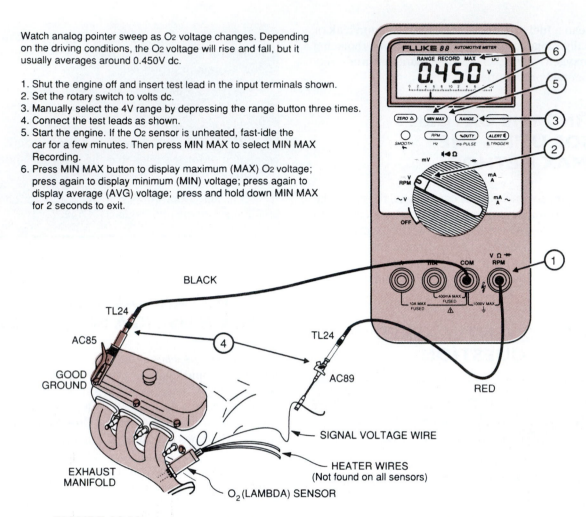

Watch analog pointer sweep as O₂ voltage changes. Depending on the driving conditions, the O₂ voltage will rise and fall, but it usually averages around 0.450V dc.

1. Shut the engine off and insert test lead in the input terminals shown.
2. Set the rotary switch to volts dc.
3. Manually select the 4V range by depressing the range button three times.
4. Connect the test leads as shown.
5. Start the engine. If the O₂ sensor is unheated, fast-idle the car for a few minutes. Then press MIN MAX to select MIN MAX Recording.
6. Press MIN MAX button to display maximum (MAX) O₂ voltage; press again to display minimum (MIN) voltage; press again to display average (AVG) voltage; press and hold down MIN MAX for 2 seconds to exit.

FIGURE 16-10 Using a digital multimeter to test an oxygen sensor using the min/max record function of the meter. *(Courtesy of Fluke Corporation)*

NOTE: On a fuel-injected engine at 2000 engine RPM, 8 to 10 cross counts is normal.

Oxygen sensor cross counts can only be determined using a scan tool or other suitable tester that reads computer data. See Figure 16-11.

If the cross counts are low (or zero), the oxygen sensor may be contaminated, or the fuel delivery system is delivering a constant rich or lean air-fuel mixture. To test an engine using a scan tool, follow these steps:

1. Connect the scan tool to the DLC and start the engine.
2. Operate the engine at a fast idle (2500 RPM) for 2 minutes to allow time for the oxygen sensor to warm to operating temperature.

FIGURE 16-11 A DaimlerChrysler DRB III scan tool is an excellent tool to use to test an oxygen sensor(s).

3. Observe the oxygen sensor activity on the scan tool to verify closed-loop operation. Select "snapshot" mode and hold the engine speed steady and start recording.

4. Play back snapshot and place a mark beside each range of oxygen sensor voltage for each frame of the snapshot.

A good oxygen sensor and computer system should result in most snapshot values at both ends (0 to 300 and 600 to 1000 mV). If most of the readings are in the middle, the oxygen sensor is not working correctly.

◀ TECH TIP ▶

THE KEY ON, ENGINE OFF OXYGEN SENSOR TEST

This test works on General Motors vehicles and may work on others if the PCM applies a bias voltage to the oxygen sensors. Zirconia oxygen sensors become more electrically conductive as they get hot. To perform this test, be sure that the vehicle has not run for several hours.

Step 1. Connect a scan tool and get the display ready to show oxygen sensor data.

Step 2. Key the engine on *without* starting the engine. The heater in the oxygen sensor will start heating the sensor.

Step 3. Observe the voltage of the oxygen sensor. The applied bias voltage of 450 mV should slowly decrease for all oxygen sensors as they become more electrically conductive and other bias voltage is flowing to ground.

Step 4. A good oxygen sensor should indicate a voltage of less than 100 mV after 3 minutes. Any sensor that displays a higher-than-usual voltage or seems to stay higher longer than the others could be defective or skewed high.

TESTING AN OXYGEN SENSOR USING A SCOPE

A scope can also be used to test an oxygen sensor. Connect the scope to the signal wire and ground for the sen-

sor (if it is so equipped). See Figure 16-12. With the engine operating in closed loop, the voltage signal of the sensor should be constantly changing. See Figure 16-13. Check for rapid switching from rich to lean and lean to rich and change between once every 2 seconds and five times per second (0.5 to 5.0 Hz). See Figures 16-14 and 16-15 on page 275, and Figure 16-16 on page 276.

NOTE: General Motors warns not to base the diagnosis of an oxygen sensor problem solely on its scope pattern. The varying voltage output of an oxygen sensor can easily be mistaken for a fault in the sensor itself, rather than a fault in the fuel delivery system.

◀ TECH TIP ▶

THE PROPANE OXYGEN SENSOR TEST

Adding propane to the air inlet of a running engine is an excellent way to check if the oxygen sensor is able to react to changes in air-fuel mixture. Follow these steps in performing the propane trick:

1. Connect a digital storage oscilloscope to the oxygen sensor signal wire.

2. Start and operate the engine until up to operating temperature and in closed-loop fuel control.

3. While watching the scope display, add some propane to the air inlet. The scope display should read full rich (over 800 mV), as shown in Figure 16-17 on page 276.

4. Shut off the propane. The waveform should drop to less than 200 mV (0.200 V), as shown in Figure 16-18 on page 276.

5. Quickly add some propane while the oxygen sensor is reading low and watch for a rapid transition to rich. The transition should occur in less than 100 milliseconds (ms).

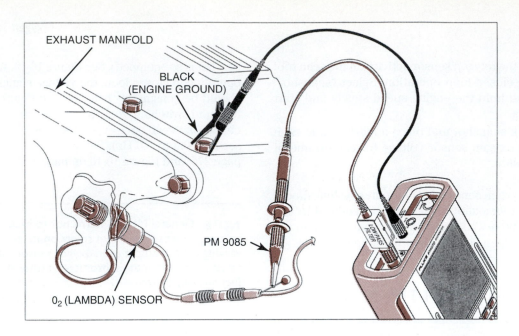

FIGURE 16-12 Connecting a handheld digital storage oscilloscope to an oxygen sensor signal wire. The use of the low-pass filter helps eliminate any low-frequency interference from affecting the scope display. *(Courtesy of Fluke Corporation)*

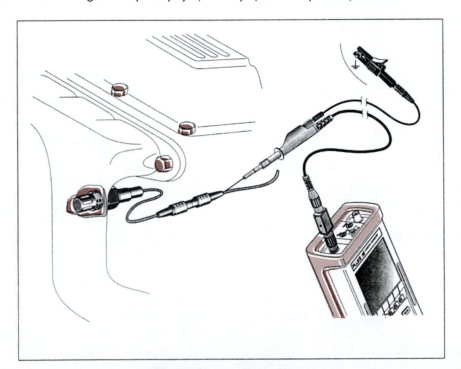

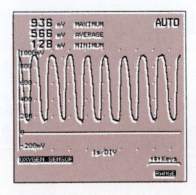

FIGURE 16-13 The waveform of a good oxygen sensor as displayed on a digital storage oscilloscope (DSO). Note that the maximum reading is above 800 mV and the minimum reading is less than 200 mV. *(Courtesy of Fluke Corporation)*

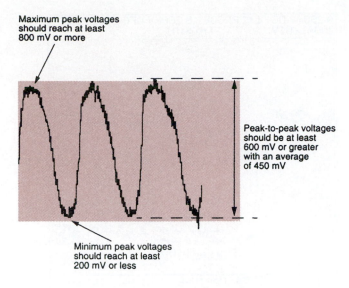

Maximum peak voltages
should reach at least
800 mV or more

Peak-to-peak voltages
should be at least
600 mV or greater
with an average
of 450 mV

Minimum peak voltages
should reach at least
200 mV or less

FIGURE 16-14 A typical good oxygen sensor waveform as displayed on a digital storage oscilloscope. Look for transitions that occur rapidly between 0.5 and 5.0 Hz. *(Courtesy of Fluke Corporation)*

FIGURE 16-15 Using the cursors on the oscilloscope, the high- and low-oxygen sensor values can be displayed on the screen. *(Courtesy of Fluke Corporation)*

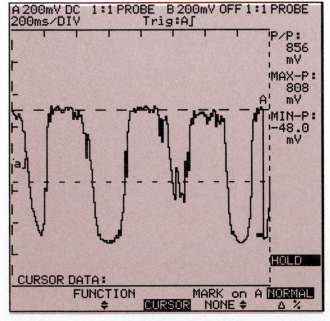

Once you've activated "Peak-to-Peak," "Max-Peak," and "Min-Peak," frame the waveform with the Cursors — look for the minimum and maximum voltages and the difference between them in the Right Display.

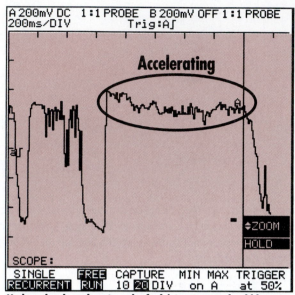

Under a hard acceleration, the fuel/air mixture should become rich — the voltages should stay fairly high.

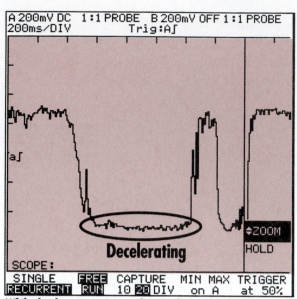

While decelerating, mixtures become lean. Look for low voltage levels.

FIGURE 16-16 When the air-fuel mixture rapidly changes such as during a rapid acceleration, look for a rapid response. The transition from low to high should be less than 100 ms. *(Courtesy of Fluke Corporation)*

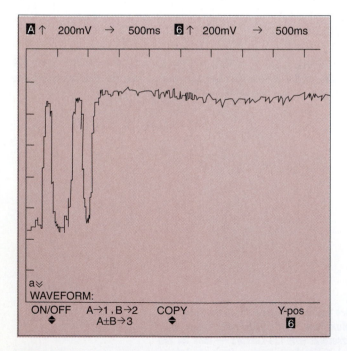

FIGURE 16-17 Adding propane to the air inlet of an engine operating in closed loop with a working oxygen sensor causes the oxygen sensor voltage to read high.

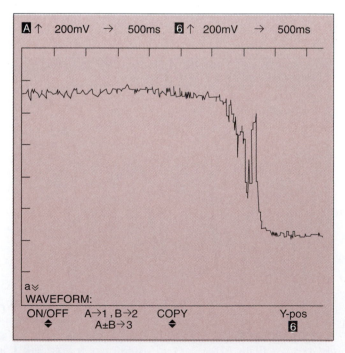

FIGURE 16-18 When the propane is shut off, the oxygen sensor should read below 200 mV.

◀ TECH TIP ▶

SENSOR OR WIRING?

When troubleshooting a diagnostic trouble code, it is sometimes difficult to determine if the sensor itself is defective or its wiring and ground connections are defective. For example, when diagnosing an O2S code, perform the following to check the wiring:

1. Connect a scan tool and observe the O2S voltage with the ignition on (engine off).
2. Disconnect the O2S pigtail to open the circuit between the computer and the O2S. The scan tool should read 450 mV if the wiring is okay and the scan tool is showing the bias voltage.

NOTE: Some vehicle manufacturers do not apply a bias voltage to the O2S and the reading on the scan tool may indicate zero and be okay.

3. Ground the O2S wire from the computer. The scan tool should read 0 volts if the wiring is okay.

OXYGEN SENSOR WAVEFORM ANALYSIS

As the O_2 sensor warms up, the sensor voltage begins to rise. When the sensor voltage rises above 450 mV, the PCM determines that the sensor is up to operating temperature, takes control of the fuel mixture, and begins to cycle rich and lean. At this point, the system is considered to be in closed loop. See Figure 16-19.

Frequency

The frequency of the O_2 sensor is important in determining the condition of the fuel control system. The higher the frequency the better, but the frequency must not exceed 6 Hz. For its OBD-II standards, the government has stated that a frequency greater than 6 Hz represents a misfire.

Throttle-Body Fuel-Injection Systems. Normal TBI system rich/lean switching frequencies are from about 0.5 Hz at idle to about 3 Hz at 2500 RPM. Additionally, due to the TBI design limitations, fuel distribution to individual cylinders may not always be equal (due to

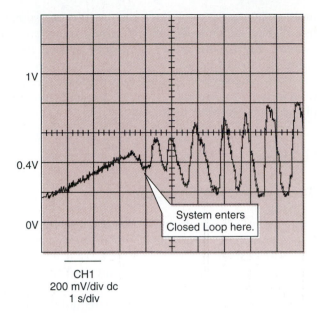

FIGURE 16-19 When the O2S voltage rises above 450 mV, the PCM starts to control the fuel mixture based on oxygen sensor activity.

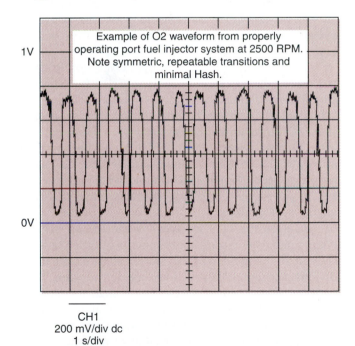

FIGURE 16-20 Normal oxygen sensor frequency is from about one to five times per second.

unequal intake runner length, etc.). This may be normal unless certain other conditions are present at the same time.

Port Fuel-Injection Systems. Specification for port fuel-injection systems is 0.5 Hz at idle to 5 Hz at 2500 RPM. See Figure 16-20. Port fuel-injection systems have more rich/lean O2S voltage transitions (cross counts) for a given amount of time than any other type of system, due to the greatly improved system design compared to TBI units.

Port fuel-injection systems take the least amount of time to react to the fuel adaptive command (for example, changing injector pulse width).

HASH

Background Information

Hash on the O2S waveform is defined as a series of high-frequency spikes, or the fuzz (or noise) viewed on some O2S waveforms, or more specifically, oscillation frequencies higher than those created by the PCM normal feedback operation (normal rich/lean oscillations).

Hash is the critical indicator of reduced combustion efficiency. Hash on the O2S waveform can warn of reduced performance in individual engine cylinders. Hash also impedes proper operation of the PCM feedback fuel control program. The feedback program is the active software program that interprets the O_2 sensor voltage and calculates a corrective mixture control command.

Generally, the program for the PCM is not designed to process O2S signal frequencies efficiently that result from events other than normal system operation and fuel control commands. The high-frequency oscillations of the hash can cause the PCM to lose control. This, in turn, has several effects. When the operating strategy of the PCM is adversely affected, the air-fuel ratio drifts out of the catalyst window, which affects converter operating efficiency, exhaust emissions, and engine performance.

Hash on the O2S waveform indicates an exhaust charge imbalance from one cylinder to another, or more specifically, a higher oxygen content sensed from an individual combustion event. Most oxygen sensors, when working properly, can react fast enough to generate voltage deflections corresponding to a single combustion event. The bigger the amplitude of the deflection (hash), the greater the differential in oxygen content sensed from a particular combustion event.

There are vehicles that will have hash on their O2S waveforms and are operating perfectly normal. Small amounts of hash may not be of concern and larger amounts of hash may be all important. A good rule concerning hash is, if engine performance is good, there are no vacuum leaks, and if exhaust HC (hydrocarbon) and oxygen levels are okay while hash is present on the O2S waveform, then the hash is nothing to worry about.

Causes of Hash

Hash on the O2S signal can be caused by the following:

1. Misfiring cylinders
   - Ignition misfire
   - Lean misfire
   - Rich misfire
   - Compression-related misfire
   - Vacuum leaks
   - Injector imbalance
2. System design, such as different intake runner length
3. System design amplified by engine and component degradation caused by aging and wear
4. System manufacturing variances, such as intake tract blockage and valve stem mismachining

The spikes and hash on the waveform during a misfire event are created by incomplete combustion, which results in only partial use of the available oxygen in the cylinder. The leftover oxygen goes out the exhaust port and travels past the oxygen sensor. When the oxygen sensor "sees" the oxygen-filled exhaust charge, it quickly generates a low voltage, or spike. A series of these high-frequency spikes make up what we are calling "hash."

CLASSIFICATIONS OF HASH

Class 1: Amplified and Significant Hash

Amplified hash is the somewhat unimportant hash that is often present between 300 and 600 millivolts on the O2S waveform. This type of hash is usually not important for diagnosis. That is because amplified hash is created largely as a result of the electrochemical properties of the O2S itself and many times not an engine or other unrelated problem. Hash between 300 and 600 mV is not particularly conclusive, so for all practical purposes it is insignificant. See Figure 16-21.

Significant hash is defined as the hash that occurs above 600 mV and below 300 mV on the O2S waveform. This is the area of the waveform that the PCM is watching to determine the fuel mixture. Significant hash is important for diagnosis because it is caused by a combustion event. If the waveform exhibits class 1 hash, the combustion event problem is probably occurring in only one of the cylinders. If the event happens in a greater number of the cylinders the waveform will become class 3 or be fixed lean or rich the majority of the time.

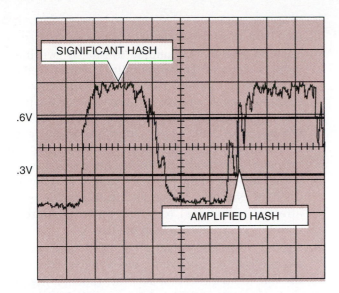

FIGURE 16-21 Significant hash can be caused by faults in one or more cylinders, whereas amplified hash is not as important for diagnosis.

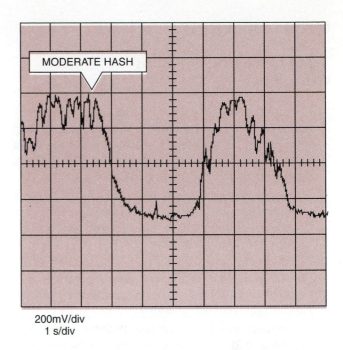

200mV/div
1 s/div

FIGURE 16-22 Moderate hash may or may not be significant for diagnosis.

Class 2: Moderate Hash

Moderate hash is defined as spikes shooting downward from the top arc of the waveform as the waveform carves its arc through the rich phase. Moderate hash spikes are not greater than 150 mV in amplitude. They may get as large as 200 mV in amplitude as the O2S waveform goes through 450 mV. Moderate hash may or may not be significant to a particular diagnosis. See Figure 16-22. For instance, most vehicles will exhibit more hash on the O2S waveform at idle. Additionally, the engine family or type of O2S could be important factors when considering the significance of moderate hash on the O2S waveform.

Class 3: Severe Hash

Severe hash is defined as hash whose amplitude is greater than 200 mV. Severe hash may even cover the entire voltage range of the sensor for an extended period of operation. Severe hash on the DSO display appears as spikes that shoot downward, over 200 mV from the top of the operating range of the sensor, or as far as to the bottom of the sensor's operating range. See Figure 16-23. If severe hash is present for several seconds during a steady state engine operating mode, say 2500 RPM, it is almost always significant to the diagno-

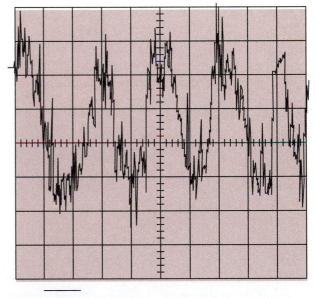

CH1
200 mV/div dc
500 ms/div

FIGURE 16-23 Severe hash is almost always caused by cylinder misfire conditions.

sis of any vehicle. Severe hash of this nature is almost never caused by a normal system design. It is caused by cylinder misfire or mixture imbalance.

HASH INTERPRETATION

Types of Misfires That Can Cause Hash

1. Ignition misfire caused by a bad spark plug, spark plug wire, distributor cap, rotor, ignition coil, or ignition primary problem. Usually an engine analyzer is used to eliminate these possibilities or confirm these problems. See Figure 16-24.

2. Rich misfire from an excessively rich fuel delivery to an individual cylinder (various potential root causes). Air-fuel ratio in a given cylinder ventured below approximately 13:1.

3. Lean misfire from an excessively lean fuel delivery to an individual cylinder (various potential root causes). Air-fuel ratio in a given cylinder ventured above approximately 17:1.

4. Compression-related misfire from a mechanical problem that reduces compression to the point that not enough heat is generated from compressing the air-fuel mixture prior to ignition, preventing combustion. This raises O2S content in the exhaust (for example, a burned valve, broken or worn ring, flat cam lobe, or sticking valve).

5. Vacuum leak misfire unique to one or two individual cylinders. This possibility is eliminated or confirmed by inducing propane around any potential vacuum leak area (intake runners, intake manifold gaskets, vacuum hoses, etc.) while watching the DSO to see when the signal goes rich and the hash changes from ingesting the propane. Vacuum leak misfires are caused when a vacuum leak unique to one cylinder or a few individual cylinders causes the air-fuel ratio in the affected cylinder(s) to venture above approximately 17:1, causing a lean misfire.

6. Injector imbalance misfire (on port fuel-injected engines only); one cylinder has a rich or lean misfire due to an individual injector(s) delivering the wrong quantity of fuel. Injector imbalance misfires are caused when an injector on one cylinder or a few individual cylinders causes the air-fuel ratio in its cylinder(s) to venture above approximately 17:1, causing a lean misfire, or below approximately 13.7:1, causing a rich misfire. See Figure 16-25.

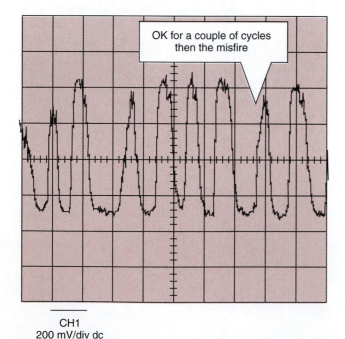

CH1
200 mV/div dc
500 ms/div

FIGURE 16-24 An ignition- or mixture-related misfire can cause hash on the oxygen sensor waveform.

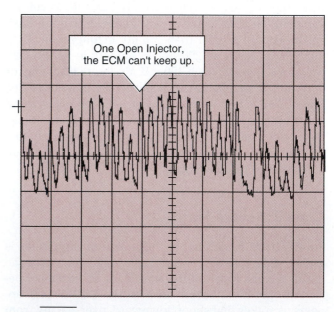

Memory 4
200 mV/div
200 ms/div

FIGURE 16-25 An injector imbalance can cause a lean or a rich misfire.

Other Rules Concerning Hash on the O2S Waveform

If there is significant hash on the O2S signal that is not normal for that type of system, it will usually be accompanied by a repeatable and generally detectable engine miss at idle (for example, a thump, thump, thump every time the cylinder fires). Generally, if the hash is significant, the engine miss will correlate in time with individual spikes seen on the waveform.

Hash that may be difficult to get rid of (and is normal in some cases) will not be accompanied by a significant engine miss that corresponds with the hash. When the individual spikes that make up the hash on the waveform do not correlate in time with an engine miss, less success can usually be found in getting rid of them by performing repairs.

A fair rule of thumb is if you are sure there are no intake vacuum leaks, and the exhaust gas HC (hydrocarbon) and oxygen levels are normal, and the engine does not run or idle rough, the hash is probably acceptable or normal.

NEGATIVE O2S VOLTAGE

When testing O2S waveforms, some O_2 sensors will exhibit some negative voltage. The acceptable amount of negative O2S voltage is $-.75$ mV, providing that the maximum voltage peak exceeds 850 mV. See Figure 16-26. Testing has shown that negative voltage signals from an O_2 sensor have usually been caused by the following:

1. Chemical poisoning of sensing element (silicon, oil, etc.)
2. Overheated engines
3. Mishandling of new O_2 sensors (dropped and banged around, resulting in a cracked insulator).
4. Poor O_2 sensor ground.

◀ GURU TIP ▶

In rare (very rare) instances, the metal shield on the exhaust side of the O_2 sensor (the shield over the zirconia thimble) may be damaged (or missing) and may create hash on the O2S waveform that could be mistaken for bad injectors or other misfires, vacuum leaks, or compression problems. After you have checked everything, and possibly replaced the injectors, pull the O2S to check for rare situations.

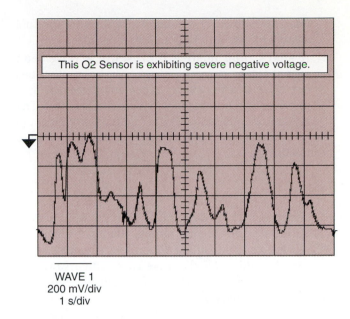

This O2 Sensor is exhibiting severe negative voltage.

WAVE 1
200 mV/div
1 s/div

FIGURE 16-26   Negative reading oxygen sensor voltage can be caused by several problems.

FALSE O2S READINGS

An oxygen sensor reading that is low could be due to other things besides a lean air-fuel mixture. Remember, an oxygen sensor senses oxygen, not unburned gas, even though a high reading generally indicates a rich exhaust (lack of oxygen) and a low reading indicates a lean mixture (excess oxygen).

False Lean

If an oxygen sensor reads low as a result of a factor besides a lean mixture, it is often called a **false lean indication.**

False lean indications (low O2S readings) can be attributed to the following:

1. **Ignition misfire.** An ignition misfire due to a defective spark plug wire, fouled spark plug, and so forth, causes no burned air and fuel to be exhausted past the O2S. The O2S "sees" the oxygen (not the unburned gasoline) and the O2S voltage is low.
2. **Exhaust leak in front of the O2S.** An exhaust leak between the engine and the oxygen sensor causes outside oxygen to be drawn into the exhaust and past the O2S. This oxygen is "read" by the O2S and produces a lower-than-normal voltage. The computer interrupts the lower-than-normal voltage signal from the O2S as meaning that the air-fuel

mixture is lean. The computer will cause the fuel system to deliver a richer air-fuel mixture.

3. **A spark plug misfire represents a false lean signal to the oxygen sensor.** The computer does not know that the extra oxygen going past the oxygen sensor is not due to a lean air-fuel mixture. The computer commands a richer mixture, which could cause the spark plugs to foul, increasing the rate of misfirings.

False Rich

An oxygen sensor reading that is high could be due to other things beside a rich air-fuel mixture. When the O2S reads high as a result of other factors besides a rich mixture, it is often called a **false rich indication.**

False rich indication (high O2S readings) can be attributed to the following:

1. Contaminated O2S due to additives in the engine coolant or due to silicon poisoning

2. A stuck-open EGR valve (especially at idle)

3. A spark plug wire too close to the oxygen sensor signal wire, which can induce a higher-than-normal voltage in the signal wire, thereby indicating to the computer a false rich condition

4. A loose oxygen sensor ground connection, which can cause a higher-than-normal voltage and a false rich signal

5. A break or contamination of the wiring and its connectors, which could prevent reference oxygen from reaching the oxygen sensor, resulting in a false rich indication (All oxygen sensors require an oxygen supply inside the sensor itself for reference to be able to sense exhaust gas oxygen.)

POST-CATALYTIC CONVERTER OXYGEN SENSOR TESTING

The oxygen sensor located behind the catalytic converter is used on OBD II vehicles to monitor converter efficiency. A changing air-fuel mixture is required for the most efficient operation of the converter. If the converter is working correctly, the oxygen content after the converter should be fairly constant. See Figure 16-27.

OXYGEN SENSOR INSPECTION

Whenever an oxygen sensor is replaced, the old sensor should be carefully inspected to help determine the cause of the failure. This is an important step because if the cause of the failure is not discovered, it could lead to another sensor failure.

Inspection may reveal the following:

1. **Black sooty deposits,** which usually indicate a rich air-fuel mixture.

2. **White chalky deposits,** which are characteristic of silica contamination. Usual causes for this type of sensor failure include silica deposits in the fuel or a technician having used the wrong type of silicone sealant during the servicing of the engine.

3. **White sandy or gritty deposits,** which are characteristic of antifreeze (ethylene glycol) contamination. A defective cylinder head or intake manifold gasket could be the cause, or a cracked cylinder head or engine block. Antifreeze may also cause the oxygen sensor to become green as a result of the dye used in antifreeze.

4. **Dark brown deposits,** which are an indication of excessive oil consumption. Possible causes include a defective positive crankcase ventilation (PCV) system or a mechanical engine problem such as defective valve stem seals or piston rings.

CAUTION: Do not spray any silicone spray near the engine where the engine vacuum could draw the fumes into the engine. This can also cause silica damage to the oxygen sensor. Also be sure that the silicone sealer used for gaskets is rated oxygen-sensor safe.

◀ FREQUENTLY ASKED ▶ QUESTION

WHAT IS LAMBDA?

An oxygen sensor is also called a lambda sensor because the voltage changes at the air-fuel ratio of 14.7:1, which is the stoichiometric rate for gasoline. If this mixture of gasoline and air is burned, all of the gasoline is burned and uses all of the oxygen in the mixture. This exact ratio represents a lambda of 1.0. If the mixture is richer (more fuel or less air), the number is less than 1.0, such as 0.850. If the mixture is leaner than 14.7:1 (less fuel or more air), the lambda number is higher than 1.0, such as 1.130. Often, the target lambda is displayed on a scan tool. See Figure 16-28 on page 284.

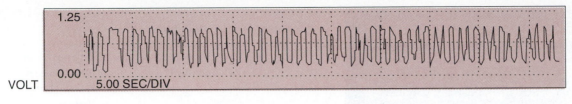

OXYGEN
SENSOR
BEFORE THE
CONVERTER

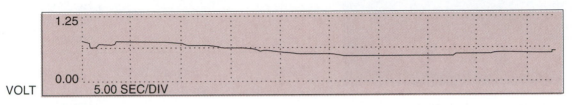

OXYGEN
SENSOR
AFTER THE
CONVERTER

GOOD (EFFICIENT) CONVERTER

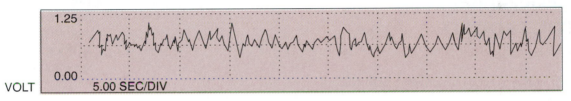

OXYGEN
SENSOR
AFTER THE
CONVERTER

BAD (INEFFICIENT) CONVERTER

FIGURE 16-27   The post-catalytic converter oxygen sensor should display very little activity if the catalytic converter is efficient.

◄ TECH TIP ►

GENERAL MOTORS FIELD SERVICE MODE

You are out in the middle of nowhere without any tools. Here's an easy test to see if the engine is operating rich or lean that can be performed on any General Motors fuel-injected vehicle manufactured between 1982 until 1995 (1992 on some models). All you need is a jumper wire or paper clip! Whether the engine is in closed loop or open loop, a rich or lean condition can easily be determined by connecting terminals A and B in the 12-pin DLC and starting the engine. (This test is not available on vehicles equipped with the 16-pin OBD II connector.) Check the operation of the "check engine" lamp (MIL). With the engine running and the diagnostic terminal B grounded (DLC terminal A con-

nected to B), the MIL lamp should be off when the exhaust is lean and on when it is rich. The procedure is called the **field service mode.**

1. **Open loop.** MIL lamp flashes at a rapid rate of two times per second.
2. **Closed loop.** MIL lamp flashes at a slower rate of one time per second.
3. **Lean exhaust.** MIL lamp is out all or most of the time.
4. **Rich exhaust.** MIL lamp is on all or most of the time.

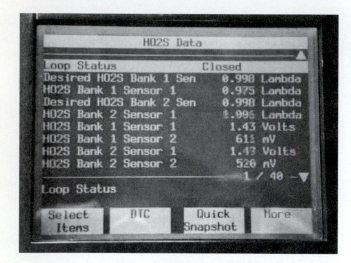

FIGURE 16-28 The target lambda on this vehicle is slightly lower than 1.0 indicating that the PCM is attempting to supply the engine with an air-fuel mixture that is slightly richer than stoichiometric. Multiply the lambda number by 14.7 to find the actual air-fuel ratio.

OXYGEN SENSOR-RELATED DIAGNOSTIC TROUBLE CODES

Diagnostic trouble codes (DTCs) associated with the oxygen sensor include:

Diagnostic Trouble Codes	Description	Possible Causes
P0131	Upstream HO2S grounded	▪ Exhaust leak upstream of HO2S (bank 1) ▪ Extremely lean air-fuel mixture ▪ HO2S defective or contaminated ▪ HO2S signal wire shorted-to-ground
P0132	Upstream HO2S shorted	▪ Upstream HO2S (bank 1) shorted ▪ Defective HO2S ▪ Fuel-contaminated HO2S
P0133	Upstream HO2S slow response	▪ Open or short in heater circuit ▪ Defective or fuel-contaminated HO2S ▪ EGR or fuel-system fault

PHOTO SEQUENCE   Oxygen Sensor Testing

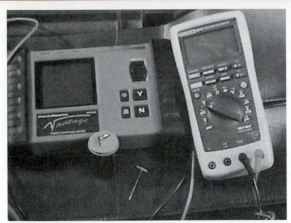

PS 9-1   Oxygen sensors can be tested using a digital multimeter or graphing multimeter using T-pins to back-probe the signal wire.

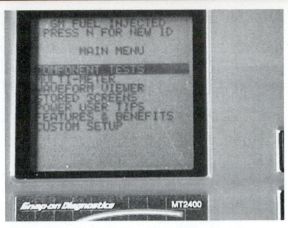

PS 9-2   Using a Snap-On Vantage, select "component tests" after selecting the vehicle manufacturer and year.

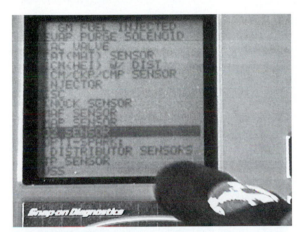

PS 9-3   Select "O2 sensor."

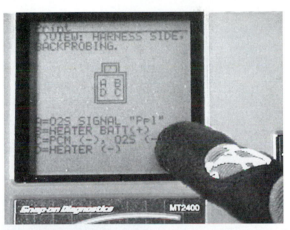

PS 9-4   Select four-wire sensor and then "connector" to view a sample oxygen sensor connector and the color of the signal wire (purple on this General Motors vehicle).

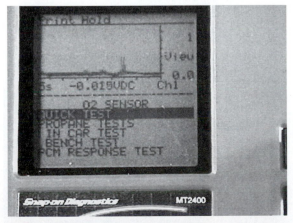

PS 9-5   To actually view the voltage signal from the oxygen sensor on the graphing multimeter, select "quick test."

PS 9-6   A T-pin was used to back-probe the purple signal wire at the connector near the oxygen sensor. The red test lead from the meter attaches to the T-pin.

PHOTO SEQUENCE   Oxygen Sensor Testing—*Continued*

PS 9-7   The black meter lead is attached to a good, clean engine ground.

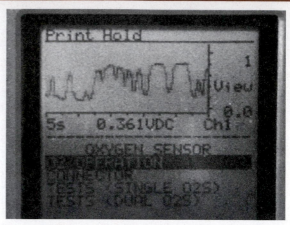

PS 9-8   The engine was started and allowed to operate until the oxygen sensor produced a changing voltage and closed-loop engine operation was achieved.

PS 9-9   A digital multimeter can also be used to check the operation of an oxygen sensor. Select "DC volts."

PS 9-10   Connect the red meter lead to the T-pin that is attached to the signal wire and attach the black meter lead to a good engine ground.

PS 9-11   Start the engine and select MIN/MAX.

PS 9-12   While the meter is recording, operate the engine for several minutes and then note the maximum reading (844.8 mV) which should be above 800 mV.

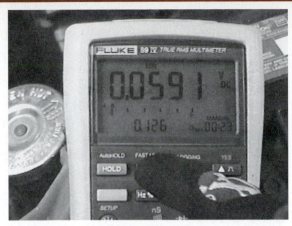

PS 9-13   Push the MIN/MAX button to view the minimum oxygen sensor voltage reading (59.1 mV). This minimum reading should be less than 200 mV.

PS 9-14   This reading (449.8 mV) is average and indicates that the engine is operating correctly. An average reading below 450 mV indicates that the engine is operating too lean whereas a reading higher than 450 mV indicates that the engine is operating too rich.

PS 9-15   After testing, carefully remove the meter, test leads, and T-pin used for testing.

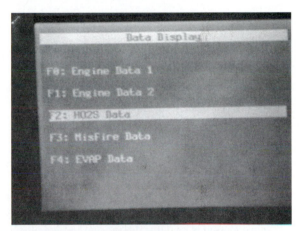

PS 9-16   A Tech 2 is being used on the OBD II vehicle and the screen showing oxygen sensor data should be selected before turning on the ignition (engine off).

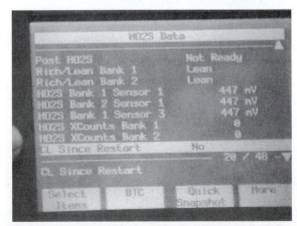

PS 9-17   Carefully watch the bias voltage sent to the oxygen sensors by the vehicle computer as the ignition is turned on (engine off). As the heater inside the oxygen sensors work, the sensors become more conductive to ground and the voltage should drop.

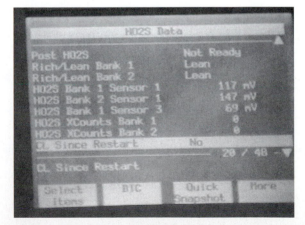

PS 9-18   After about three minutes, all sensors should show about the same low voltage. A sensor that remains high could be the cause of a hard-to-find driveability problem, yet not trigger a diagnostic trouble code (DTC).

SUMMARY

1. An oxygen sensor produces a voltage output signal based on the oxygen content of the exhaust stream.

2. If the exhaust has little oxygen, the voltage of the oxygen sensor will be close to 1 volt (1000 mV) and close to zero if there is high oxygen content in the exhaust.

3. Oxygen sensors can have one, two, three, four, or more wires, depending on the style and design.

4. A wide-band oxygen sensor, also called a lean air-fuel (LAF) or linear air-fuel ratio sensor, can detect air-fuel ratios from as rich as 12:1 to as lean as 18:1.

5. The oxygen sensor signal determines fuel trim, which is used to tailor the air-fuel mixture for the catalytic converter.

6. Conditions can occur that cause the oxygen sensor to be fooled and give a false lean or false rich signal to the PCM.

7. Oxygen sensors can be tested using a digital meter, a scope, or a scan tool.

REVIEW QUESTIONS

1. How does an oxygen sensor detect oxygen levels in the exhaust?

2. What are three basic designs of oxygen sensors and how many wires may be used for each?

3. What is the difference between open-loop and closed-loop engine operation?

4. What are three ways oxygen sensors can be tested?

5. How can the oxygen sensor be fooled and provide the wrong information to the PCM?

ASE CERTIFICATION-TYPE QUESTIONS

1. The sensor that must be warmed and functioning before the engine management computer will go to closed loop is the _____.
   a. O2S
   b. ECT sensor
   c. Engine MAP sensor
   d. BARO sensor

2. The voltage output of a zirconia oxygen sensor when the exhaust stream is lean (excess oxygen) is _____.
   a. Relatively high (close to 1 volt)
   b. About in the middle of the voltage range
   c. Relatively low (close to 0 volt)
   d. Either a or b, depending on atmospheric pressure

3. Which of the following describes acceptable oxygen sensor cross counts?
   a. 128 to 136
   b. A minimum of 8 at 2000 RPM
   c. 5 to 50 every 10 seconds
   d. Both b and c

4. A heated zirconia oxygen sensor will have how many wires?
   a. 2
   b. 3
   c. 4
   d. Either b or c

5. A high O2S voltage could be due to _____.
   a. A rich exhaust
   b. A lean exhaust
   c. A defective spark plug wire
   d. Both a and c

6. A low O2S voltage could be due to _____.
   a. A rich exhaust
   b. A lean exhaust
   c. A defective spark plug wire
   d. Both b and c

7. An oxygen sensor is being tested with digital multimeter (DMM), using the min/max function. The readings are: minimum = 78 mV; maximum = 932 mV; average = 442 mV. Technician A says that the engine is operating correctly. Technician B says that the oxygen sensor is skewed too rich. Which technician is correct?
   a. Technician A only
   b. Technician B only
   c. Both Technicians A and B
   d. Neither Technician A nor B

8. An oxygen sensor is being tested using a digital storage oscilloscope (DSO). A good oxygen sensor should display how many switches per second?
   a. 1 to 5
   b. 5 to 10
   c. 10 to 15
   d. 15 to 20

9. When testing an oxygen sensor using a digital storage oscilloscope (DSO), how quickly should the voltage change when either propane is added to the intake stream or when a vacuum leak is created?

    a. Less than 50 ms

    b. 1 to 3 seconds

    c. 100 to 200 ms

    d. 450 to 550 ms

10. A P0133 DTC is being discussed. Technician A says that a defective heater circuit could be the cause. Technician B says that a contaminated sensor could be the cause. Which technician is correct?

    a. Technician A only

    b. Technician B only

    c. Both Technicians A and B

    d. Neither Technician A nor B

CRANKSHAFT AND CAMSHAFT POSITION SENSORS

OBJECTIVES

After studying Chapter 17, the reader should be able to:

1. Prepare for ASE Engine Performance (A8) certification test content area "E" (Computerized Engine Controls Diagnosis and Repair).
2. Discuss how crankshaft position sensors work.
3. List the methods that can be used to test CKP sensors.
4. Describe the symptoms of a failed CMP sensor.
5. List how the operation of the CKP sensor affects vehicle operation.

The correct operation of computer-controlled engines depends on accurate and crankshaft- and camshaft-position sensors. Proper testing of these sensors is an important part of engine problem diagnosis and troubleshooting.

CRANKSHAFT AND CAMSHAFT POSITION SENSORS

Crankshaft position sensors are used to signal the position of the pistons in the cylinder. Most crankshafts use a series of notches or openings that are detected by the crankshaft position sensor, abbreviated **CKP.** See Figure 17-1. The position of the number one cylinder at top dead center (TDC) is used as a reference for the oth-ers in the firing order. The crankshaft position sensor is primarily responsible for the following.

- **Engine speed (RPM).** In older vehicles, before 1996, this function was usually achieved by signals from the pickup coil in the distributor.
- **Piston position for ignition timing control.** The primary use of the crankshaft position sensor is for ignition timing control because it accurately signals the position of the number one cylinder and every cylinder after that in the firing order.
- **Misfire detection.** Part of the requirements for all 1996 and newer vehicles equipped with on-board

FIGURE 17-1 A typical magnetic crankshaft position sensor used on a General Motors V-6 engine.

diagnosis, second generation (OBD II) is that the PCM be capable of detecting cylinder misfire. This is usually achieved by the PCM monitoring the crankshaft position sensor signal, and if there is a misfire, the interval between the firings of the cylinders will show as a time lag. This time lag indicates that the cylinder did not fire. The actual cylinder number is determined by comparing the crankshaft position sensor signal to the camshaft position sensor.

The camshaft position sensor, abbreviated **CMP**, is used with the CKP to detect which cylinder is firing for spark timing and as a reference to time the sequential fuel injection. See Figure 17-2. The camshaft position sensor is sometimes called the cylinder identification (CID) sensor. The PCM needs to see the signal from the CMP when the engine starts and, if absent, goes into a backup or limp-home mode. In this phase, the PCM "guesses" where the number one cylinder is located and

injects fuel based on the guess. If the engine runs correctly, then the PCM continues to inject fuel using only the crankshaft position sensor, and sets a CMP DTC. If the engine is not running correctly, the PCM will often guess again until the engine runs correctly.

Therefore, the symptom of a defective camshaft position (CMP) sensor is that the engine will crank without starting for an extended period up to 15 seconds until the PCM can identify the correct cylinder.

NOTE: Because the camshaft rotates at half engine speed, the number one cylinder notch appears once every crankshaft revolution, but only fires the spark plug once every other revolution. Two rotations of the crankshaft result in one revolution of the camshaft. Therefore, the camshaft notch for the number one cylinder is used to detect whether the number one cylinder is on the compression or the exhaust stroke.

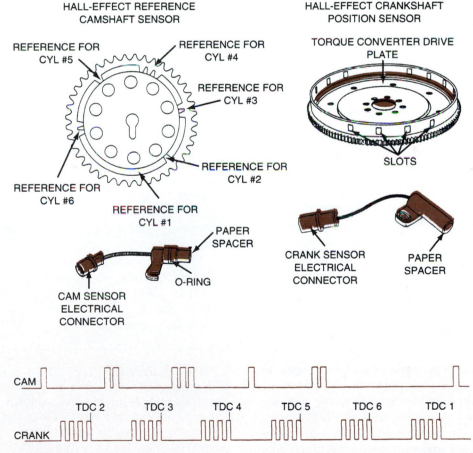

FIGURE 17-2 Some Hall-effect sensors look like magnetic sensors. This Hall-effect camshaft reference sensor and crankshaft position sensor have an electronic circuit built in that creates a 0- to 5-volt signal as shown at the bottom. These Hall-effect sensors have three wires: a power supply (8 volts) from the computer (controller); a signal (0 to 5 volts); and a signal ground.

MAGNETIC POSITION SENSOR

A magnetic sensor is constructed of a permanent magnet and a coil of wire. The sensor is mounted near a toothed-gear and an AC-voltage signal is generated in the coil as the gear teeth move past the sensor. The faster the gear rotates, the higher the signal frequency output of the sensor. When a tooth of a gear gets near the sensor, the magnetic field becomes stronger because metal is a better conductor of magnetic lines of force than air. Then, when the gear tooth moves away from the sensor, the magnetic field strength around the sensor decreases. It is this change in the magnetic field strength that creates the AC-voltage signal. A magnetic sensor is also called a **variable reluctance sensor** because the strength of the magnetic field (reluctance) is being changed as the gear tooth or notch passes near the sensor. Therefore, the notched or toothed wheel that rotates near a magnetic sensor is often called a **reluctor.** Some characteristics of a magnetic sensor include:

- **Two-wire sensors.** The two wires are often twisted to help prevent electrical interference from affecting the signal.
- **Sensors mounted near a gear or notched wheel.** A notch in a wheel or gear tooth will create the changing magnetic field strength needed for the sensor to create an AC-voltage signal. See Figure 17-3.
- **Sensors where the faster the toothed wheel moves past the sensor, the higher the frequency of the output signal.** Magnetic sensors are used for vehicle speed and input shaft speed, as well as for crankshaft and camshaft position.
- Magnetic position sensors generate a higher voltage signal with increased engine speed.

Testing Magnetic Position Sensors

A crankshaft position sensor will often set a diagnostic trouble code if the signal received by the PCM does not match the rationality parameters that would indicate that the engine speed or piston position is not correct. To diagnose a magnetic position sensor, a scope can be used to look for proper frequency and signal amplitude. If the scope pattern indicates a problem or a scope is not available, other tests include:

- **Check the sensor connection and wiring.** A fault, such as a loose or corroded connection, can cause excessive resistance in the circuit.
- **Check that the sensor itself is magnetic.** If the permanent magnet cracks, it becomes two weak magnets and the output of the sensor will be weaker than normal. See Figure 17-4.
- **Check the resistance of a magnetic sensor.** Magnetic sensors contain a coil of wire where the voltage is induced from the changing magnetic field. This coil winding should be checked for the specified resistance using an ohmmeter. Normal resistance can vary, but is generally in the range of 500 to 1500 ohms.
- **Scope testing a magnetic sensor.** A digital storage oscilloscope can be used to view the waveform of magnetic sensors. The waveform will be determined by the location and number of notches or teeth on the reluctor wheel. See Figures 17-5, 17-6, and 17-7.

◀ TECH TIP ▶

THE SOLDERING GUN TRICK

A magnetic sensor contains a coil of wire and a magnet. If the magnetic field changes in strength, a varying voltage will be induced in the coil windings of the sensor. A popular trick to test a magnetic sensor is to use a 110-volt electric soldering gun and hold it near the sensor. The soldering gun produces a varying magnetic field because the alternating current (AC) passes through a coil in the soldering gun to create heat.

To test a magnetic sensor, connect a DMM set to read AC volts or a scope. Turn on the soldering gun and hold it near the sensor. The meter or scope should display a signal that matches the 110-volt frequency of 60 Hz.

HINT: A soldering gun can also be used to check a magnetic vehicle speed sensor. If used on a General Motors vehicle, turn the ignition switch to on (key on-engine off) and turn the soldering gun on and place near the sensor. The speedometer should indicate 54 MPH, which corresponds to a frequency of 60 Hz.

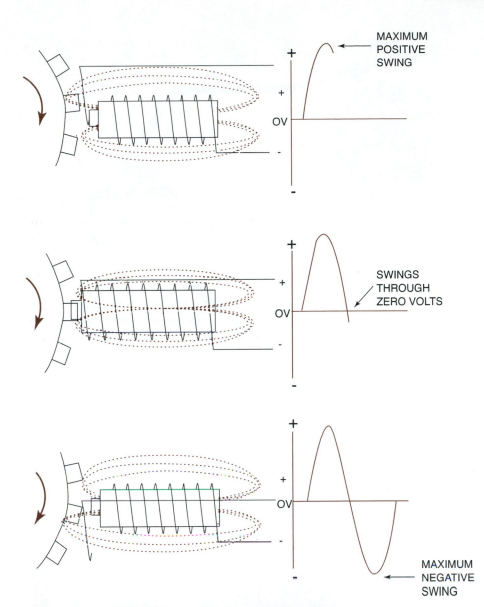

MAXIMUM
POSITIVE
SWING

SWINGS
THROUGH
ZERO VOLTS

MAXIMUM
NEGATIVE
SWING

FIGURE 17-3 A magnetic sensor uses a permanent magnet surrounded by a coil of wire. The notches of the crankshaft (or camshaft) create a variable magnetic field strength around the coil. When a metallic section is close to the sensor, the magnetic field is stronger because metal is a better conductor of magnetic lines of force than air.

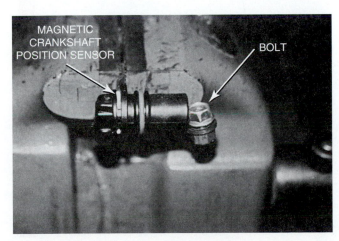

MAGNETIC
CRANKSHAFT
POSITION SENSOR

BOLT

FIGURE 17-4 A magnetic sensor being tested for magnetism. This sensor was able to hold a bolt and had about the same magnetic strength as a new sensor.

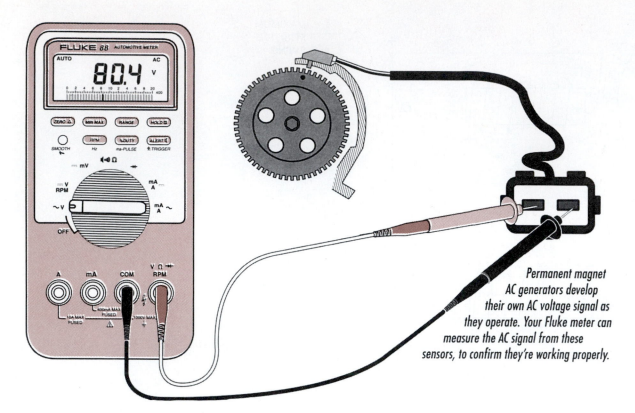

Permanent magnet
AC generators develop
their own AC voltage signal as
they operate. Your Fluke meter can
measure the AC signal from these
sensors, to confirm they're working properly.

FIGURE 17-5 An AC voltage is produced by a magnetic sensor. Most sensors should produce at least 0.1 volt AC while the engine is cranking if the pickup wheel has many teeth. If the pickup wheel has only a few teeth, you may need to switch the meter to read DC volts and watch the display for a jump in voltage as the teeth pass the magnetic sensor. *(Courtesy of Fluke Corporation)*

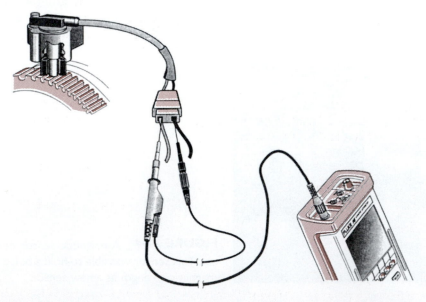

FIGURE 17-6 A magnetic sensor connected to a digital storage oscilloscope. *(Courtesy of Fluke Corporation)*

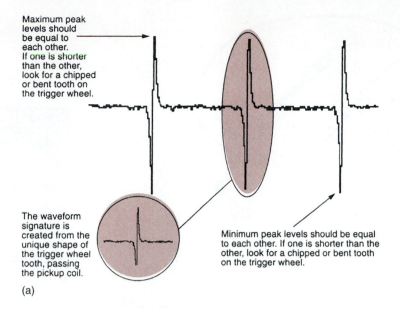

Maximum peak
levels should
be equal to
each other.
If one is shorter
than the other,
look for a chipped
or bent tooth on
the trigger wheel.

The waveform
signature is
created from the
unique shape of
the trigger wheel
tooth, passing
the pickup coil.

(a)

Minimum peak levels should be equal
to each other. If one is shorter than the
other, look for a chipped or bent tooth
on the trigger wheel.

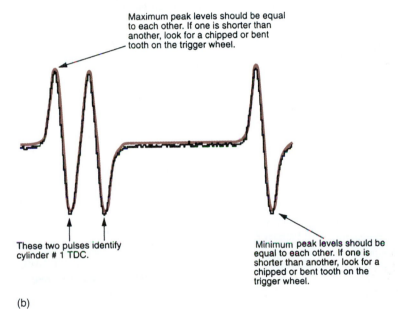

Maximum peak levels should be equal
to each other. If one is shorter than
another, look for a chipped or bent
tooth on the trigger wheel.

These two pulses identify
cylinder # 1 TDC.

Minimum peak levels should be
equal to each other. If one is
shorter than another, look for a
chipped or bent tooth on the
trigger wheel.

(b)

FIGURE 17-7   (a) Magnetic sensor waveform as shown on a digital storage oscilloscope. (b) A sync notch provides a signal to the computer that cylinder number one is at top dead center (TDC). *(Courtesy of Fluke Corporation)*

HALL-EFFECT DIGITAL SENSORS

The Hall effect was discovered in 1879 by Edwin H. Hall. He discovered that a voltage is produced if a magnetic field is exposed to a semiconductor. The voltage goes to zero if the magnetic field is removed or blocked. The typical Hall-effect sensor has three wires:

- Power (can be 8 to 12 volts)
- Ground
- Signal

The signal output is a digital (on/off) square wave. The signal is very accurate and will work at lower engine speeds than a magnetic sensor.

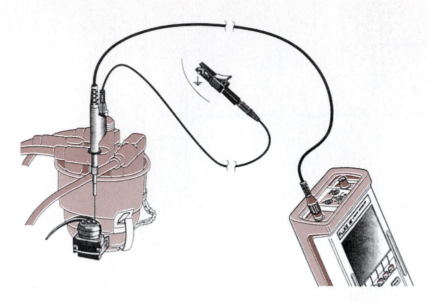

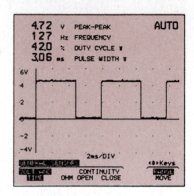

FIGURE 17-8 (a) The connection required to test a Hall-effect sensor. (b) A typical waveform from a Hall-effect sensor. *(Courtesy of Fluke Corporation)*

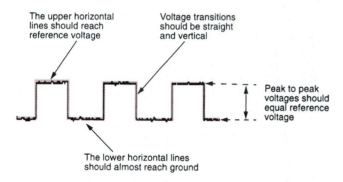

FIGURE 17-9 The waveform from a Hall-effect sensor (switch) should be checked for consistency and sharp transitions. *(Courtesy of Fluke Corporation)*

Testing Hall-Effect Sensors

A crankshaft position sensor will often set a diagnostic trouble code if the signal received by the PCM does not match the rationality parameters that would indicate that the engine speed or piston position is not correct. To diagnose a Hall-effect position sensor, a scope can be used to look for proper frequency and signal amplitude. See Figure 17-8. If the scope pattern indicates a problem or a scope is not available, other tests include:

- **Check the sensor connection and wiring.** A fault, such as a loose or corroded connection, can cause excessive resistance in the circuit.
- **Check the sensor damage.** If the sensor is damaged, the output of the sensor will be weaker than normal. See Figure 17-9.

MAGNETIC-RESISTIVE SENSORS

A magnetic-resistive sensor (abbreviated **MRE**) is similar to a magnetic sensor but, instead of producing an analog voltage signal, the electronics inside the sensor itself generate a digital on/off signal or an output. A magnetic-resistive sensor is more accurate than a magnetic sensor because it uses two magnets, both of which generate a waveform. A typical MRE sensor has three wires: a 12-volt supply, a ground, and a signal wire. The electronics inside the sensor convert these two separate signals into a digital signal. Some MRE sensors can detect the direction of rotation, as well as position and speed. Most MRE sensors use two wires.

Testing a Magnetic-Resistive Sensor

A MRE crankshaft position sensor will often set a diagnostic trouble code if the signal received by the PCM does not match the rationality parameters that would indicate that the engine speed or piston position is not correct. To diagnose a magnetic-resistive sensor, a scope can be used to look for proper frequency and signal amplitude. See Figure 17-10. If the scope pattern indicates a problem or a scope is not available, other tests include:

- **Check the sensor connection and wiring.** A fault, such as a loose or corroded connection, can cause excessive resistance in the circuit.

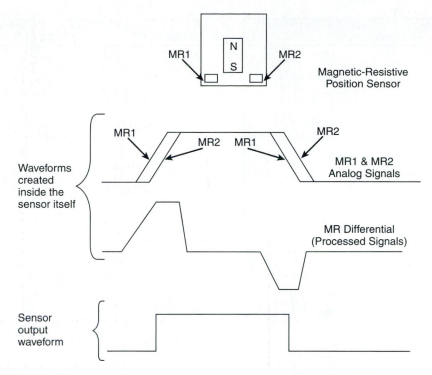

FIGURE 17-10 The input signals to a magnetic-resistive sensor and the electronic circuits inside the sensor convert them to a digital (on and off) signal.

- **Check that the sensor itself is magnetic.** If the permanent magnet cracks, it becomes two weak magnets and the output of the sensor will be weaker than normal.

OPTICAL SENSORS

Optical sensors typically use a photo diode and/or a photo transistor and a slotted disk to detect distributor position. The output is a digital on/off (square wave) signal that is very accurate. This type of sensor is so accurate that, in many applications, it can show each degree of crankshaft rotation (360 slits or holes for 360 degrees of crankshaft movement). Most optical sensor also include slots that are different sizes and are used by the computer to detect the various individual cylinders.

Testing Optical Sensors

A crankshaft position sensor will often set a diagnostic trouble code if the signal received by the PCM does not match the rationality parameters that would indicate that the engine speed or piston position is not correct. To diagnose an optical position sensor, a scope can be used to look for proper frequency and signal amplitude. See Figure 17-11. If the scope pattern indicates a problem or a scope is not available, other tests include:

- **Check the sensor connection and wiring.** A fault, such as a loose or corroded connection, can cause excessive resistance in the circuit.
- **Check the sensor or wiring for damage.** If the sensor or wiring are damaged, the output of the sensor will be weaker than normal or zero.

PCM USES OF THE CRANKSHAFT AND CAMSHAFT POSITION SENSOR

The crankshaft and camshaft position sensors are used by the powertrain control module for many functions including the following.

- The crankshaft position is normally used to determine engine speed (RPM). Engine speed is very important for the proper management of the fuel system, as well as the emission control systems.

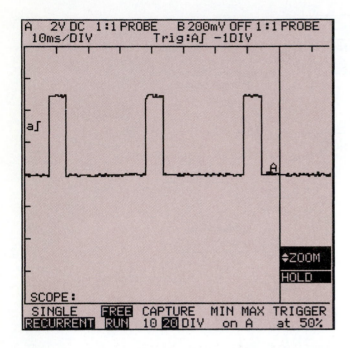

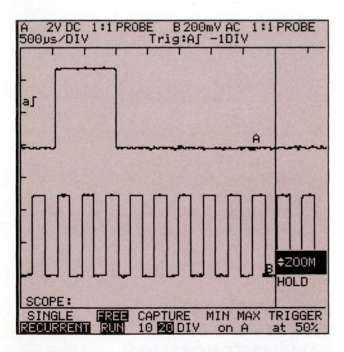

FIGURE 17-11 (a) The low-resolution signal has the same number of pulses as the engine has cylinders. (b) A dual trace pattern showing both the low-resolution signal and the high-resolution signals that usually represent 1 degree of rotation. *(Courtesy of Fluke Corporation)*

- Camshaft position sensor information is usually used to determine the cylinder position for fuel control (when to trigger the injectors). See Figure 17-12.

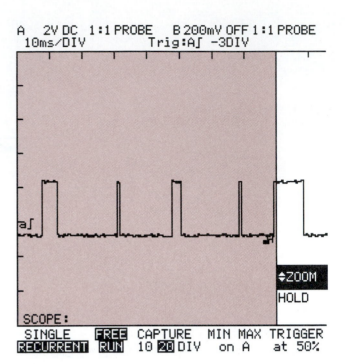

FIGURE 17-12 A General Motors camshaft sensor (CMP) pattern as shown on a digital storage oscilloscope. The camshaft sensor is used by the computer to help determine the engine crankshaft speed (OBD II) and camshaft position. Besides ignition timing and misfire input information, the camshaft sensor signal is also used for fuel-injection pulses. This signal uses different pulse widths to signal the computer the exact position of the distributor. *(Courtesy of Fluke Corporation)*

- Engine speed input is used to calculate IAC counts to maintain the target idle speed.
- Crankshaft position sensors are used primarily as the spark timing input sensor. In other words, the position of the piston in the cylinder is determined by the crankshaft position sensor.
- The crankshaft position sensor is used as an input for traction control. The engine speed (RPM) is one of the major inputs to the traction control system. If the engine speed is high, the PCM may retard ignition timing or shut off injectors to reduce engine torque to help restore traction of the drive wheels.

Re-Synchronizing the Crankshaft Position Sensor

Whenever the PCM or the crankshaft position sensor are replaced, the new part must be "learned" or synchronized before the engine will operate correctly. Most scan tools are capable of performing the re-learn process, which often calls for accelerating the engine for the new parameters to be learned. Always follow the vehicle manufacturer's recommended procedures.

Position Sensor-Related Diagnostic Trouble Codes (DTCs)

Diagnostic Trouble Codes	Description	Possible Causes
P0335	CKP sensor circuit problem	• CKP sensor circuit open or shorted • Reluctor wheel cracked, loose, or broken • Defective CKP sensor
P0336	CKP circuit out-of-range or performance fault	• Defective CKP • High resistance in the sensor wiring • Electromagnetic interference affecting sensor signal
P0337	CKP circuit low input	• Defective CKP • High resistance in the sensor wiring or connector • Broken or loose sensor reluctor wheel
P0338	CKP circuit high input	• Defective CKP sensor • Electromagnetic interference into sensor wiring
P0341	CMP sensor circuit fault	• Defective CMP sensor • Loose or corroded connections • Defective PCM
P0342	CMP sensor circuit low	• Defective CMP sensor • Loose or corroded connection • Defective PCM
P0343	CMP sensor circuit high	• Defective CMP sensor • Wiring shorted-to-voltage • Defective PCM

SUMMARY

1. The crankshaft position (CKP) sensor is used as an input sensor to the PCM for engine speed (RPM) and piston position for spark timing control.
2. A camshaft position sensor is also called a cylinder identification (CID) sensor and is primarily used to time the sequential fuel injection.
3. A magnetic position sensor generates an analog voltage signal.
4. A Hall-effect position sensor generates a digital (on and off) voltage signal.
5. A magnetic-resistive position sensor creates a digital output signal.
6. An optical position sensor creates a digital output signal.

REVIEW QUESTIONS

1. What is the primary purpose for a crankshaft position (CKP) sensor?
2. What is the primary purpose for a camshaft position (CMP) sensor?
3. How does a magnetic sensor work, and how is it tested?
4. How does a Hall-effect sensor work, and how is it tested?
5. How does a magnetic-resistive sensor work, and how is it tested?
6. How does an optical sensor work, and how is it tested?

ASE CERTIFICATION-TYPE QUESTIONS

1. A magnetic position sensor is being tested with an ohmmeter. The display reads 102 KΩ. Technician A says that the sensor resistance is within the normal range. Technician B says that the coil winding inside the sensor is shorted. Which technician is correct?
   a. Technician A only
   b. Technician B only
   c. Both Technicians A and B
   d. Neither Technician A nor B

2. Technician A says that the crankshaft position (CKP) sensor is used by the PCM to determine engine speed (RPM). Technician B says that the camshaft position (CMP) is used by the PCM to determine the timing of the fuel injectors. Which technician is correct?
   a. Technician A only
   b. Technician B only
   c. Both Technicians A and B
   d. Neither Technician A nor B

3. Which sensor produces an analog (varying voltage) output signal?
   a. Magnetic
   b. Hall-effect
   c. Optical
   d. Magnetic-resistive

4. Which type of sensor is most likely to be used to sense each degree of rotation of the crankshaft?
   a. Magnetic
   b. Hall-effect
   c. Optical
   d. Magnetic-resistive

5. A magnetic sensor usually has how many wires?
   a. 1
   b. 2
   c. 3
   d. 4

6. A Hall-effect sensor usually has how many wires?
   a. 1
   b. 2
   c. 3
   d. 4

7. In Figure 17-13, the top waveform is produced by what type of sensor?
   a. Magnetic
   b. Hall-effect
   c. Either a or b
   d. Neither a nor b

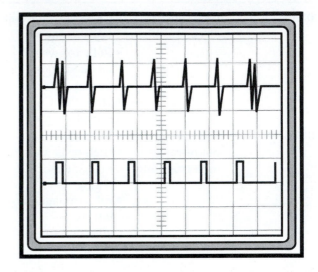

FIGURE 17-13 A typical crankshaft position waveform.

8. In Figure 17-13, the bottom waveform is produced by what type of sensor?
   a. Magnetic
   b. Hall-effect
   c. Either a or b
   d. Neither a nor b

9. Extending engine cranking before starting is a symptom of a defective _____ sensor.
   a. Crankshaft position (CKP)
   b. Camshaft position (CMP)
   c. Both CKP and CMP
   d. Neither CKP nor CMP

10. A P0337 DTC is being discussed. Technician A says that a broken CKP reluctor wheel could be the cause. Technician B says that a defective CKP could be the cause. Which technician is correct?
    a. Technician A only
    b. Technician B only
    c. Both Technicians A and B
    d. Neither Technician A nor B

◀ Chapter 18 ▶

FUEL PUMPS, LINES, AND FILTERS

OBJECTIVES

After studying Chapter 18, the reader should be able to:

1. Prepare for ASE Engine Performance (A8) certification test content area "C" (Fuel, Air Induction, and Exhaust Systems Diagnosis and Repair).
2. Describe how to check an electric fuel pump for proper pressure and volume delivery.
3. Explain how to check a fuel-pressure regulator.
4. Describe how to test fuel injectors.
5. Explain how to diagnose electronic fuel-injection problems.

FUEL DELIVERY SYSTEM

Creating and maintaining a correct air-fuel mixture requires a properly functioning fuel and air **delivery system.** Fuel delivery (and return) systems use many if not all of the following components to make certain that fuel is available under the right conditions to the fuel-injection system:

- Fuel storage tank, filler neck, and gas cap
- Fuel tank pressure sensor
- Fuel pump
- Fuel filter(s)
- Fuel delivery lines and fuel rail

- Fuel pressure regulator
- Evaporative emission controls (discussed in Chapter 19)
- Fuel return line

FUEL TANKS

A vehicle fuel tank is made of corrosion-resistant steel or polyethylene plastic. Some models, such as sport utility vehicles (SUVs) and light trucks, may have an auxiliary fuel tank.

Tank design and capacity are a compromise between available space, filler location, fuel expansion room, and fuel movement. Some later-model tanks deliberately limit tank capacity by extending the filler tube neck into the tank low enough to prevent complete filling, or by providing for expansion room. See Figure 18-1. A vertical **baffle** in this same tank limits fuel sloshing as the vehicle moves.

Regardless of size and shape, all fuel tanks incorporate most if not all of the following features:

- Inlet or filler tube through which fuel enters the tank
- Filler cap with pressure holding and relief features
- An outlet to the fuel line leading to the fuel pump or fuel injector
- Fuel pump mounted within the tank
- Tank vent system
- Fuel pickup tube and fuel level sending unit

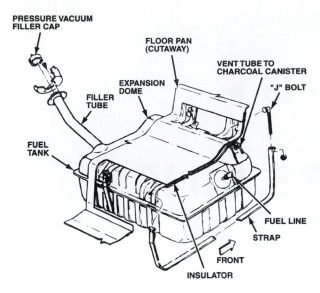

FIGURE 18-1   A typical fuel tank installation.

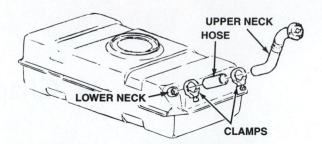

FIGURE 18-2   A three-piece filler tube assembly.

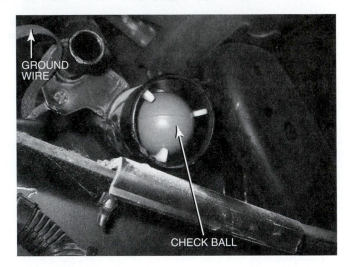

FIGURE 18-3   A view of a typical filler tube with the fuel tank removed. Notice the ground strap used to help prevent the buildup of static electricity as the fuel flows into the plastic tank. The check ball looks exactly like a ping-pong ball.

Tank Location and Mounting

Most vehicles use a horizontally suspended fuel tank, usually mounted below the rear of the floor pan, just ahead of or behind the rear axle. Fuel tanks are located there so that frame rails and body components protect the tank in the event of a crash. To prevent squeaks, some models have insulated strips cemented on the top or sides of the tank wherever it contacts the underbody.

Fuel inlet location depends on the tank design and filler tube placement. It is located behind a filler cap and is often a hinged door in the outer side of either rear fender panel.

Generally, a pair of metal retaining straps holds a fuel tank in place. Underbody brackets or support panels hold the strap ends using bolts. The free ends are drawn underneath the tank to hold it in place, then bolted to other support brackets or to a frame member on the opposite side of the tank.

Filler Tubes

Fuel enters the tank through a large tube extending from the tank to an opening on the outside of the vehicle. See Figure 18-2.

Effective in 1993, federal regulations require manufacturers to install a device to prevent fuel from being siphoned through the filler neck. Federal authorities recognized methanol as a poison, and methanol used in gasoline is a definite health hazard. Additionally, gasoline is a suspected carcinogen (cancer causing agent).

To prevent siphoning, manufacturers welded a filler-neck check-ball tube in fuel tanks. To drain check-ball-equipped fuel tanks, a technician must disconnect the check-ball tube at the tank and attach a siphon directly to the tank. See Figure 18-3.

Onboard refueling vapor recovery (ORVR) systems have been developed to reduce evaporative emissions during refueling. See Figure 18-4. These systems add components to the filler neck and the tank. One ORVR system utilizes a tapered filler neck with a smaller diameter tube and a check valve. When fuel flows down the neck, it opens the normally closed check valve. The vapor passage to the charcoal canister is opened. The decreased size neck and the opened air passage allow fuel and vapor to flow rapidly into the tank and the canister, respectively. When the fuel has reached a predetermined level, the check valve closes, and the fuel tank pressure increases. This forces the nozzle to shut off, thereby preventing the tank from being overfilled.

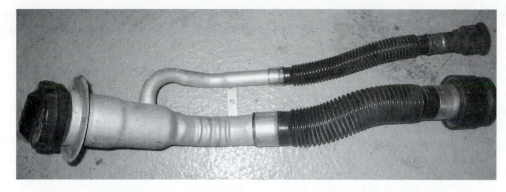

FIGURE 18-4   Vehicles equipped with onboard refueling vapor recovery usually have a reduced size fill tube.

Pressure-Vacuum Filler Cap

Fuel and vapors are sealed in the tank by the safety filler cap. The safety cap must release excess pressure or excess vacuum. Either condition could cause fuel tank damage, fuel spills, and vapor escape. Typically, the cap will release if the pressure is over 1.5 to 2.0 psi (10 to 14 kPa) or if the vacuum is 0.15 to 0.30 psi (1 to 2 kPa).

Fuel Pickup Tube

The fuel pickup tube is usually a part of the fuel sender assembly or the electric fuel pump assembly. Since dirt and sediment eventually gather on the bottom of a fuel tank, the fuel pickup tube is fitted with a filter sock or strainer to prevent contamination from entering the fuel lines. The woven plastic strainer also acts as a water separator by preventing water from being drawn up with the fuel. The filter sock usually is designed to filter out particles that are larger than 70 to 100 microns, or 30 microns if a geroter-type fuel pump is used. One micron is 0.000039 in. See Figure 18-5.

NOTE: The human eye cannot see anything smaller than about 40 microns.

The filter is made from woven Saran resin (copolymer of vinylidene chloride and vinyl chloride). The filter blocks any water that may be in the fuel tank, unless it is completely submerged in water. In that case, it will allow water through the filter. This filter should be replaced whenever the fuel pump is replaced.

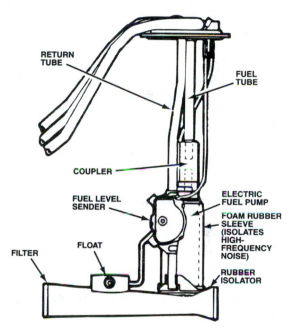

FIGURE 18-5   The fuel pickup tube is part of the fuel sender and pump assembly.

◀ **GURU TIP** ▶

The fuel pump strainer should be replaced with a new pump. In the case of a deflector shield, it should always be used to prevent fuel-return bubbles from blocking the fuel inlet to the pump.

Tank Venting Requirements

Fuel tanks must be vented to prevent a **vacuum lock** as fuel is drawn from the tank. As fuel is used and its level drops in the tank, the space above the fuel increases. As the air in the tank expands to fill this greater space, its pressure drops. Without a vent, the air pressure inside the tank would drop below atmospheric pressure, developing a vacuum which prevents the flow of fuel. Under extreme pressure variance, the tank could collapse. Venting the tank allows outside air to enter as the fuel level drops, preventing a vacuum from developing.

An EVAP system vents gasoline vapors from the fuel tank directly to a charcoal-filled vapor storage canister, and uses an unvented filler cap. Many filler caps contain valves that open to relieve pressure or vacuum above specified safety levels. Systems that use completely sealed caps have separate pressure and vacuum relief valves for venting.

Because fuel tanks are not vented directly to the atmosphere, the tank must allow for fuel expansion, contraction, and overflow that can result from changes in temperature or overfilling. One way is to use a dome in the top of the tank. Many General Motors (GM) vehicles use a design that includes a vertical slosh baffle which reserves up to 12% of the total tank capacity for fuel expansion.

Rollover Leakage Protection

All vehicles have one or more devices to prevent fuel leaks in case of vehicle rollover or a collision in which fuel may spill.

Variations of the basic one-way **check valve** may be installed in any number of places between the fuel tank and the engine. The valve may be installed in the fuel return line, vapor vent line, or fuel tank filler cap.

In addition to the rollover protection devices, some vehicles use devices to ensure that the fuel pump shuts off when an accident occurs. Some pumps depend upon an oil pressure or an engine speed signal to continue operating; these pumps turn off whenever the engine dies. On some air vane sensors, a microswitch is built into the sensor to switch on the fuel pump as soon as intake airflow causes the vane to lift from its rest position. See Figure 18-6.

Ford vehicles use an **inertia switch.** See Figure 18-7. The inertia switch is installed in the rear of the vehicle between the electric fuel pump and its power supply. With any sudden impact, such as a jolt from another vehicle in a parking lot, the inertia switch opens and shuts off power to the fuel pump. The switch must be reset manually by pushing a button to restore current to the pump.

FUEL LINES

Fuel and vapor lines made of steel, nylon tubing, or fuel-resistant rubber hoses connect the parts of the fuel system. Fuel lines supply fuel to the throttle body or fuel rail. They also return excess fuel and vapors to the tank. Depending on their function, fuel and vapor lines may be either rigid or flexible.

Fuel lines must remain as cool as possible. If any part of the line is located near too much heat, the gasoline passing through it vaporizes and **vapor lock** occurs. When this happens, the fuel pump supplies only vapor that passes into the injectors. Without liquid gasoline, the engine stalls and a hot restart problem develops.

The fuel delivery system supplies 10 to 15 psi (69 to 103 kPa) or up to 35 psi (241 kPa) to many throttle-body injection units and up to 50 psi (345 kPa) for multiport fuel-injection systems. Fuel-injection systems retain residual or rest pressure in the lines for a half hour or longer when the engine is turned off to prevent hot engine restart problems. Higher pressure systems such as these require special fuel lines.

Rigid Lines

All fuel lines fastened to the body, frame, or engine are made of seamless steel tubing. Steel springs may be wound around the tubing at certain points to protect against impact damage.

Only steel tubing, or that recommended by the manufacturer, should be used when replacing rigid fuel lines. *Never substitute copper or aluminum tubing for steel tubing.* These materials do not withstand normal vehicle vibration and could combine with the fuel to cause a chemical reaction.

Flexible Lines

Most fuel systems use synthetic rubber hose sections where flexibility is needed. Short hose sections often connect steel fuel lines to other system components. The fuel delivery hose inside diameter (ID) is generally larger (3/16- to 3/8-inches or 8 to 10 millimeters) than the fuel return hose ID (1/4-inches or 6 millimeters).

Fuel-injection systems require special-composition reinforced hoses specifically made for these higher-pressure systems. Similarly, vapor vent lines must be

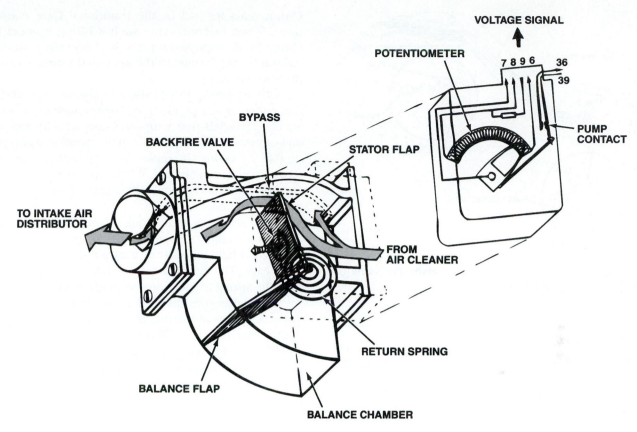

FIGURE 18-6 On some vehicles equipped with an airflow sensor, a switch is used to energize the fuel pump. In the event of a collision, the switch opens and the fuel flow stops.

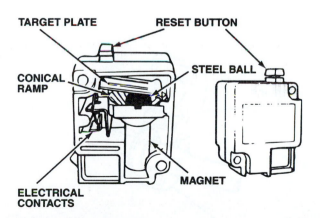

FIGURE 18-7 Ford uses an inertia switch to turn off the electric fuel pump in an accident.

made of materials that resist fuel vapors. Replacement vent hoses are usually marked with the designation "EVAP" to indicate their intended use.

Fuel Line Mounting

Fuel supply lines from the tank to a throttle body or fuel rail are routed to follow the frame along the underbody of the vehicle. Vapor and return lines may be routed with the fuel supply line. All rigid lines are fastened to the frame rail or underbody with screws and clamps, or clips. See Figure 18-8.

Fuel-Injection Lines and Clamps

Hoses used for fuel-injection systems are made of materials with high resistance to oxidation and deterioration. Replacement hoses for injection systems should always be equivalent to original equipment manufacturer (OEM) hoses.

Screw-type clamps are essential on injected engines and should have rolled edges to prevent hose damage.

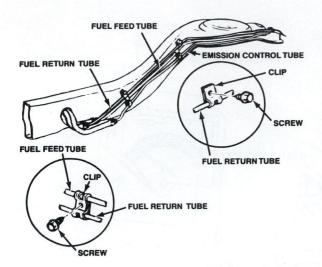

FIGURE 18-8   Fuel lines are routed along the frame or body and secured with clips.

CAUTION: *Do not use spring-type clamps on fuel-injected engines—they cannot withstand the fuel pressures involved.*

Fuel-Injection Fittings and Nylon Lines

Because of their operating pressures, fuel-injection systems often use special kinds of fittings to ensure leakproof connections. Some high-pressure fittings on GM vehicles with port fuel-injection systems use O-ring seals instead of the traditional flare connections. When disconnecting such a fitting, inspect the O-ring for damage and replace it, if necessary. *Always* tighten O-ring fittings to the specified torque value to prevent damage.

Other manufacturers also use O-ring seals on fuel line connections. In all cases, the O-rings are made of special materials that withstand contact with gasoline and oxygenated fuel blends. Some manufacturers specify that the O-rings be replaced every time the fuel system connection is opened. When replacing one of these O-rings, a new part specifically designed for fuel system service must be used.

Ford also uses spring-lock connectors to join male and female ends of steel tubing. See Figure 18-9. The coupling is held together by a garter spring inside a circular cage. The flared end of the female fitting slips behind the spring to lock the coupling together.

General Motors has used nylon fuel lines with quick-connect fittings at the fuel tank and fuel filter since the early 1990s. Like the GM threaded couplings used with steel lines, nylon line couplings use internal O-ring seals. Unlocking the metal connectors requires a special quick-connector separator tool; plastic connectors can be released without the tool. See Figures 18-10 and 18-11.

Fuel Line Layout

Fuel pressures have tended to become higher to prevent vapor lock, and a major portion of the fuel routed

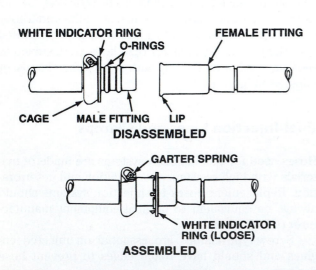

FIGURE 18-9   Some Ford metal line connections use spring-locks and O-rings.

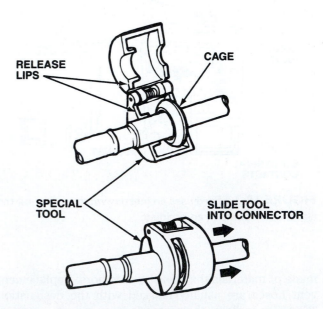

FIGURE 18-10   Ford spring-lock connectors require a special tool for disassembly.

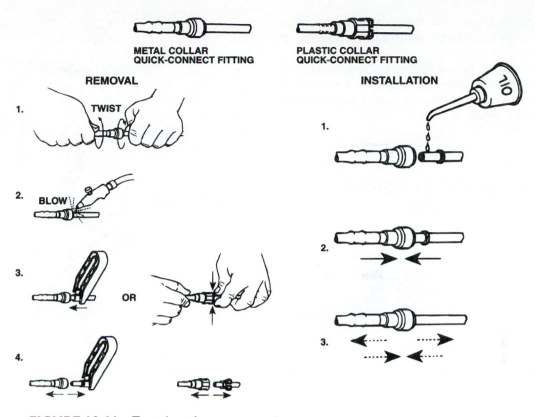

FIGURE 18-11 Typical quick-connect service steps.

to the fuel-injection system returns to the tank by way of a fuel return line or return-type systems. This allows better control, within limits, of heat absorbed by the gasoline as it is routed through the engine compartment. Throttle body and multiport injection systems have typically used a pressure regulator to control fuel pressure in the throttle body or fuel rail, and also allow excess fuel not used by the injectors to return to the tank. However, the warmer fuel in the tank may create problems, such as an excessive rise in fuel vapor pressures in the tank.

With late-model vehicles, there has been some concern about too much heat being sent back to the fuel tank, causing rising in-tank temperatures and increases in fuel vaporization and **volatile organic compound (VOC)** (hydrocarbon) emissions. To combat this problem, manufacturers have placed the pressure regulator back by the tank instead of under the hood on mechanical returnless systems. In this way, returned fuel is not subjected to the heat generated by the engine and the underhood environment. To prevent vapor lock in these systems, pressures have been

◀ FREQUENTLY ASKED QUESTION ▶

JUST HOW MUCH FUEL IS RECIRCULATED?

Approximately 80% of the available fuel pump volume is released to the fuel tank bypassing the fuel-pressure regulator at idle speed. As an example, a passenger vehicle cruising down the road at 60 mph gets 30 mpg. With a typical return style fuel system pumping about 30 gallons per hour from the tank, it would therefore burn 2 gallons per hour, and return about 28 gallons per hour to the tank!

raised in the fuel rail, and injectors tend to have smaller openings to maintain control of the fuel spray under pressure.

Not only must the fuel be filtered and supplied under adequate pressure, but there must also be a consistent *volume* of fuel to assure smooth engine performance even under the heaviest of loads.

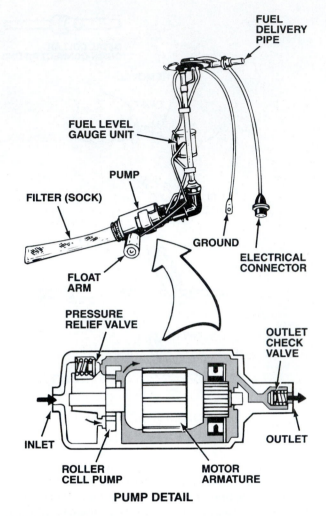

FIGURE 18-12 A roller cell-type electric fuel pump.

◄ FREQUENTLY ASKED ► QUESTION

HOW CAN AN ELECTRIC PUMP WORK INSIDE A GAS TANK AND NOT CAUSE A FIRE?

Even though fuel fills the entire pump, no burnable mixture exists inside the pump because there is no air and no danger of commutator brush arcing, igniting the fuel.

ELECTRIC FUEL PUMPS

The electric fuel pump is a pusher unit. When the pump is mounted in the tank, the entire fuel supply line to the engine can be pressurized. Because the fuel, when pressurized, has a higher boiling point, it is unlikely that vapor will form to interfere with fuel flow.

Most vehicles use the impeller or turbine pumps. See Figure 18-12. All electrical pumps are driven by a small electric motor, but the turbine pump turns at higher speeds and is quieter than the others.

Positive Displacement Pump

A positive displacement pump is a design that forces everything that enters the pump to leave the pump.

In the **roller cell** or vane pump, the **impeller** draws fuel into the pump, and then pushes it out through the fuel line to the injection system. All designs of pumps use a variable-sized chamber to draw in fuel. When the maximum volume has been reached, the supply port closes and the discharge opens. Fuel is then forced out the discharge as this volume decreases. The chambers are formed by rollers or gears in a rotor plate. Since this type of pump uses no valves to move the fuel, the fuel flows steadily through the pump housing. Since fuel flows steadily through the entire pump, including the electrical portion, the pump stays cool. Usually, only

when a vehicle runs out of fuel is there a risk of pump damage.

Most electric fuel pumps are equipped with a fuel outlet check valve that closes to maintain fuel pressure when the pump shuts off. **Residual** or **rest pressure** prevents vapor lock and hot-start problems on these systems.

Figure 18-13 shows the pumping action of a **rotary vane pump.** The pump consists of a central impeller disk, several rollers or vanes that ride in notches in the impeller, and a pump housing that is offset from the impeller centerline. The impeller is mounted on the end of the motor armature and spins whenever the motor is running. The rollers are free to slide in and out within the notches in the impeller to maintain sealing contact. Unpressurized fuel enters the pump, fills the spaces between the rollers, and is trapped between the impeller, the housing, and two rollers. An internal gear pump, called a **gerotor,** is another type of positive displace-

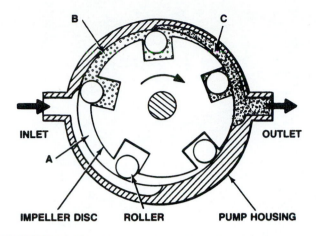

INLET

OUTLET

IMPELLER DISC   ROLLER   PUMP HOUSING

FIGURE 18-13 The pumping action of an impeller or rotary vane pump.

ment pump that is often used in engine oil pumps. It uses the meshing of internal and external gear teeth to pressurize the fuel. See Figure 18-14 for an example of a gerotor-type fuel pump that uses an impeller as the first stage and is used to move the fuel gerotor section where it is pressurized.

Hydrokinetic Flow Pump Design

The word *hydro* means liquid and the term *kinetic* refers to motion, so the term **hydrokinetic pump** means that this design of pump rapidly moves the fuel to create pressure. This design of pump is a nonpositive displacement pump design.

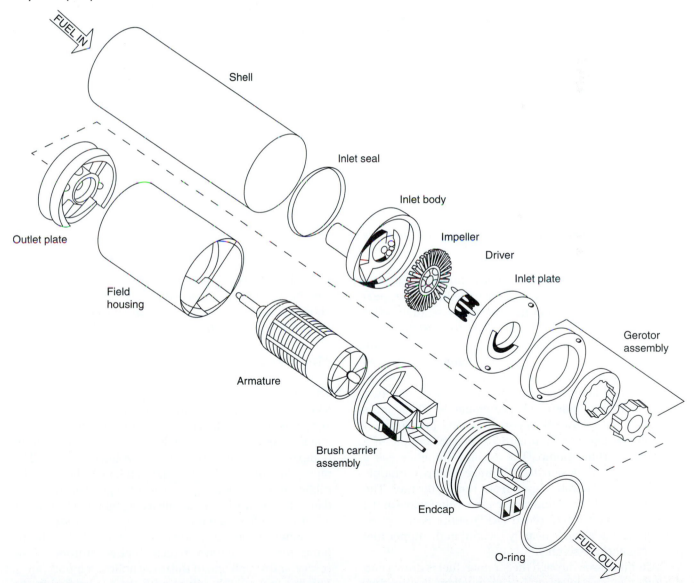

FIGURE 18-14 An exploded view of a gerotor electric fuel pump. The impeller draws fuel from the tank through the sock and into the gerotor pump area. The impeller is also used to expel any vapors that could be in the fuel.

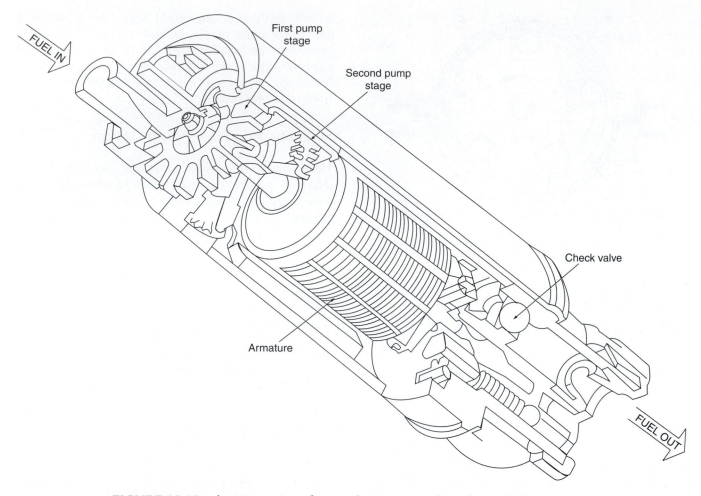

FIGURE 18-15 A cutaway view of a typical two-stage turbine electric fuel pump.

A **turbine pump** is the most common because it tends to be less noisy. Sometimes called **turbine, peripheral,** and **side-channel,** these units use an impeller that accelerates the fuel particles before actually discharging them into a tract where they generate pressure via pulse exchange. Actual pump volume is controlled by using a different number of impeller blades, and in some cases a higher number of impellers, or different shapes along the side discharge channels. These units are fitted more toward lower operating pressures of less than 60 psi. See Figure 18-15 for an example of a two-stage turbine pump. The turbine impeller has a staggered blade design to minimize pump harmonic noise and to separate vapor from the liquid fuel. The end cap assembly contains a pressure relief valve and a radio frequency interference (RFI) suppression module. The check valve is usually located in the upper fuel pipe connector assembly.

After it passes through the strainer, fuel is drawn into the lower housing inlet port by the impellers. It is pressurized and delivered to the convoluted fuel tube for transfer through a check valve into the fuel feed pipe. A typical electric fuel pump used on a fuel-injection system delivers about 40 to 50 gallons per hour or 0.6 to 0.8 gallons per minute at a pressure of 70 to 90 psi.

Modular Fuel Sender Assembly

The modular fuel sender consists of a replaceable fuel level sensor, a turbine pump, and a jet pump. The reservoir housing is attached to the cover containing fuel pipes and the electrical connector. Fuel is transferred from the pump to the fuel pipe through a convoluted (flexible) fuel pipe. The convoluted fuel pipe eliminates the need for rubber hoses, nylon pipes, and clamps. The reservoir dampens fuel slosh to maintain a constant fuel level available to the roller vane pump; it also reduces noise.

Some of the flow, however, is returned to the jet pump for recirculation. Excess fuel is returned to the reservoir through one of the three hollow support pipes. The hot fuel quickly mixes with the cooler fuel in the reservoir; this minimizes the possibility of vapor lock.

In these modules, the reservoir is filled by the jet pump. Some of the fuel from the pump is sent through the jet pump to lift fuel from the tank into the reservoir.

◀ FREQUENTLY ASKED ▶ QUESTION

WHY ARE MANY FUEL PUMP MODULES SPRING-LOADED?

Fuel modules that contain the fuel pickup sock, fuel pump, and fuel level sensor are often spring-loaded when fitted to a plastic fuel tank. The plastic material shrinks when cold and expands when hot, so having the fuel module spring-loaded ensures that the fuel pickup sock will always be the same distance from the bottom of the tank. See Figure 18-16.

Electric Pump Control Circuits

Fuel pump circuits are controlled by the fuel pump relay. Fuel pump relays are activated initially by turning the ignition key to on, which allows the pump to pressurize the fuel system. As a safety precaution, the relay de-energizes after a few seconds until the key is moved to the crank position. On some systems, once an ignition coil signal, or "tach" signal, is received by the engine control computer, indicating the engine is rotating, the relay remains energized even with the key released to the run position.

DaimlerChrysler

On DaimlerChrysler vehicles, the PCM must receive an engine speed (RPM) signal during cranking before it can energize a circuit driver inside the power module to activate an automatic shutdown (ASD) relay to power the fuel pump, ignition coil, and injectors. As a safety precaution, if the RPM signal to the logic module is interrupted, the logic module signals the power module to deactivate the ASD, turning off the pump, coil, and injectors. In some vehicles, the oil pressure switch circuit may be used as a safety circuit to activate the pump in the ignition switch run position.

General Motors

General Motors systems energize the pump with the ignition switch to initially pressurize the fuel lines, but then deactivate the pump if an RPM signal is not re-

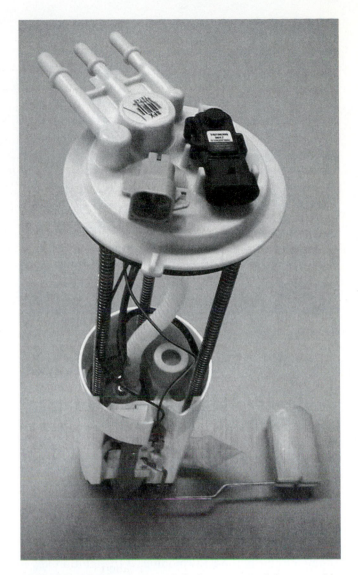

FIGURE 18-16 A typical fuel pump module assembly, which includes the pickup strainer and fuel pump, as well as the fuel-pressure sensor and fuel level sensing unit.

ceived within one or two seconds. The pump is reactivated as soon as engine cranking is detected. The oil pressure sending unit serves as a backup to the fuel pump relay on some vehicles. In case of pump relay failure, the oil pressure switch will operate the fuel pump once oil pressure reaches about 4 psi (28 kPa).

Fords

Most Fords with fuel injection have an inertia switch in the trunk between the fuel pump relay and fuel pump. When the ignition switch is turned to the ON position, the electronic engine control (EEC) power relay energizes, providing current to the fuel pump relay and a

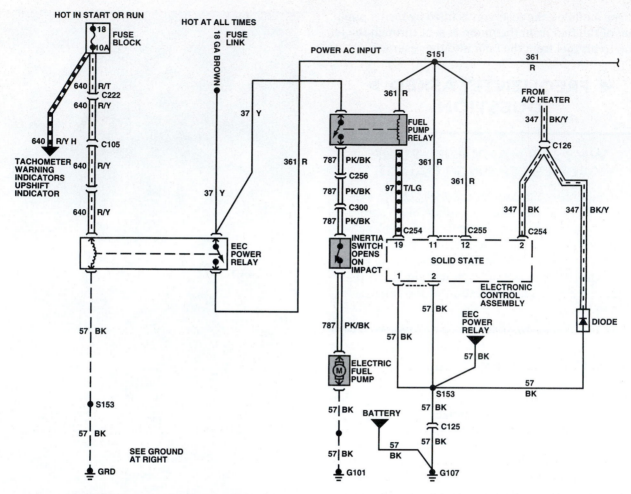

FIGURE 18-17 A schematic showing that an inertia switch is connected in series between the fuel pump relay and the fuel pump.

timing circuit in the EEC module. If the ignition key is not turned to the Start position within about one second, the timing circuit opens the ground circuit to de-energize the fuel pump relay and shut down the pump. This circuit is designed to pre-pressurize the system. Once the key is turned to the start position, power to the pump is sent through the relay and inertia switch.

The inertia switch opens under a specified impact, such as a collision. When the switch opens, current to the pump shuts off because the fuel pump relay will not energize. The switch must be reset manually by opening the trunk and depressing the reset button before current flow to the pump can be restored. See Figure 18-17 for a schematic of a typical fuel system that uses an injector switch in the power feed circuit to the electric fuel pump.

Pump Pulsation Dampening

Some manufacturers use an **accumulator** in the system to reduce pressure pulses and noise. Others use a pul-

sator located at the outlet of the fuel pump to absorb pressure pulsations that are created by the pump. These pulsators are usually used on roller vane pumps and are a source of many internal fuel leaks. See Figure 18-18.

NOTE: Some experts suggest that the pulsator be removed and replaced with a standard section of fuel line to prevent the loss of fuel pressure that results when the connections on the pulsator loosen and leak fuel back into the tank.

Variable Speed Pumps

Another way to help reduce noise, current draw, and pump wear is to reduce the speed of the pump when less than maximum output is required. Pump speed and pressure can be regulated by controlling the voltage supplied to the pump with a resistor switched into the circuit, or by letting the engine-control computer pulse-

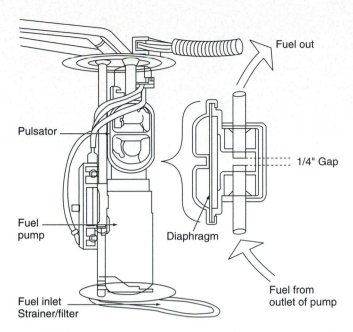

FIGURE 18-18 A typical fuel pulsator used mostly with roller vane-type pumps to help even out the pulsation in pressure that can cause noise.

FIGURE 18-19 Many fuel pump modules contain a non-replaceable fuel filter.

width modulate (PWM) the voltage supply to the pump, through a separate fuel pump driver electronic module. With slower pump speed and pressure, less noise is produced.

◄ **GURU TIP** ►

Fuel pumps need 1/4 tank or more of fuel for correct pump operating temperature. The fuel cools and lubricates the pump.

FUEL FILTERS

Despite the care generally taken in refining, storing, and delivering gasoline, some impurities get into the automotive fuel system. Fuel filters remove dirt, rust, water, and other contamination from the gasoline before it can reach the fuel injectors. Most fuel filters are de-

signed to filter particles that are 10 to 20 microns or larger in size. See Figure 18-19.

The useful life of all filters is limited, although Ford specifies that its filters, when used with some fuel-injection systems, should last the life of the vehicle. If fuel filters are not cleaned or replaced according to the manufacturer's recommendations, they can become clogged and restrict fuel flow.

In addition to using several different types of fuel filters, a single fuel system may contain two or more filters.

The inline filter is located in the line between the fuel pump and the throttle body or fuel rail. See Figure 18-20. This filter protects the system from contamination, but does not protect the fuel pump. The inline filter usually is a metal or plastic container with a pleated paper element sealed inside.

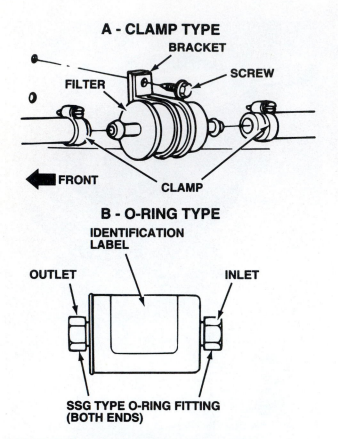

FIGURE 18-20 Inline fuel filters are usually attached to the fuel line with screw clamps or threaded connections. The fuel filter must be installed in the proper direction or a restricted fuel flow can result.

They may be mounted on a bracket on the fender panel, a shock tower, or another convenient place in the engine compartment. They may also be installed under the vehicle near the fuel tank. Fuel filters should be replaced according to the vehicle manufacturer's recommendations, which range from every 30,000 miles (48,000 km) to 100,000 miles (160,000 km) or larger. Fuel filters that are part of the fuel pump module assemblies usually do not have any specified service interval.

◄ GURU TIP ►

Fuel filter has flow direction; if it is installed backwards, the vehicle may act like a restricted exhaust (low power at higher engine speeds and loads).

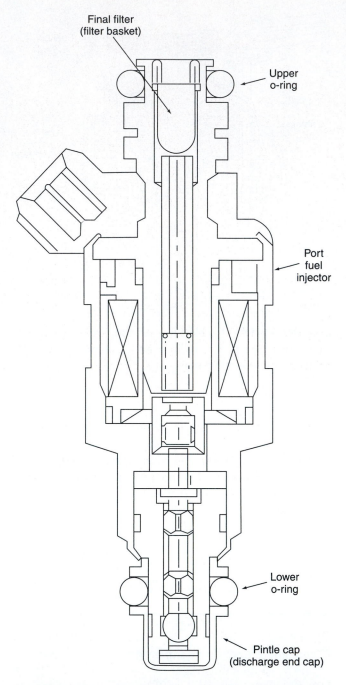

FIGURE 18-21 The final filter, also called a **filter basket,** is the last filter in the fuel system.

All injectors, throttle body or port, are fitted with one or more filter screens or strainers to remove any particles (generally 10 microns or 0.00039 in.) that might have passed through the other filters. These screens, which surround the fuel inlet, are on the side of throttle-body injectors and are inserted in the top of port injectors. See Figure 18-21

FUEL PUMP TESTING

Fuel pump testing includes many different tests and procedures. Even though a fuel pump can pass one test, it does not mean that there is not a fuel pump problem. For example, if the pump motor is rotating slower than normal, it may be able to produce the specified pressure, but not enough volume to meet the needs of the engine while operating under a heavy load.

◄ TECH TIP ►

THE EAR TEST

No, this is not a test of your hearing, but rather using your ear to check that the electric fuel pump is operating. The electric fuel pump inside the fuel tank is often difficult to hear running, especially in a noisy shop environment. A commonly used trick to better hear the pump is to use a funnel in the fuel filter neck. See Figure 18-22.

Testing Fuel-Pump Pressure

Fuel-pump-regulated pressure has become more important than ever with a more exact fuel control. Although an increase in fuel pressure does increase fuel volume to the engine, this is *not* the preferred method to add additional fuel as some units will not open correctly at the increased fuel pressure. On the other side of the discussion, many newer engines will not start when fuel pressure is just a few psi low. Correct fuel pressure is very important for proper engine operation. Most fuel-injection systems operate at either a low pressure of about 10 psi or a high pressure of between 35 and 45 psi.

Normal Operating Pressure	(psi)	Maximum Pump Pressure (psi)
Low-pressure TBI units	9–13	18–20
High-pressure TBI units	25–35	50–70
Port fuel-injection systems	35–45	70–90
Central port fuel injection (GM)	55–64	90–110

In both types of systems, maximum fuel-pump pressure is about double the normal operating pressure to ensure that a continuous flow of cool fuel is be-

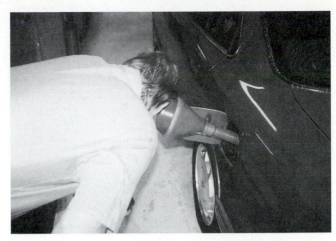

(a)

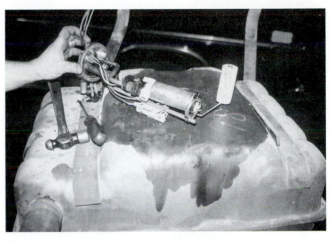

(b)

FIGURE 18-22 (a) A funnel helps in hearing if the electric fuel pump inside the gas tank is working. (b) If the pump is not running, check the wiring and current flow before going through the process of dropping the fuel tank to remove the pump.

ing supplied to the injector(s) to help prevent vapor from forming in the fuel system. Although vapor or foaming in a fuel system can greatly affect engine operation, the cooling and lubricating flow of the fuel must be maintained to ensure the durability of injector nozzles.

To measure fuel-pump pressure, locate the Schrader valve. See Figure 18-23. Attach a fuel-pressure gauge, as shown in Figure 18-24.

NOTE: Some vehicles, such as those with General Motors TBI fuel-injection systems, require a specific fuel-pressure gauge that connects to the fuel system. Always follow the manufacturers' recommendations and procedures.

◀ **TECH TIP** ▶

THE RUBBER MALLET TRICK

Often a no-start condition is due to an inoperative electric fuel pump. A common trick is to tap on the bottom of the fuel tank with a rubber mallet in an attempt to jar the pump motor enough to work. Instead of pushing a vehicle into the shop, simply tap on the fuel tank and attempt to start the engine. This is not a repair, but rather a confirmation that the fuel pump does indeed require replacement.

FIGURE 18-23   Typical fuel-pressure test Schrader valve.

FIGURE 18-24   A fuel-pressure gauge connected to the fuel-pressure tap (Schrader valve) on a port fuel-injected V-6 engine.

Rest Pressure Test

If the fuel pressure is acceptable, then check the system for leakdown. Observe the pressure gauge after five minutes. See Figure 18-25. The pressure should be the same as the initial reading. If not, then the pressure regulator, fuel-pump check valve, or the injectors are leaking down. To determine the reason for the drop in pressure, proceed as follows:

Step 1   Energize the fuel pump to pressurize the system. Use a fused jumper wire and connect the fuel pump test lead to the battery voltage on older General Motors vehicles. See Figure 18-26. To energize on other makes and models, remove the fuel pump relay and, using a fused jumper lead, jumper the power to load terminals (usually terminals 30 and 87).

Step 2   Restrict the return line. If the leakdown stops, then the regulator is defective.

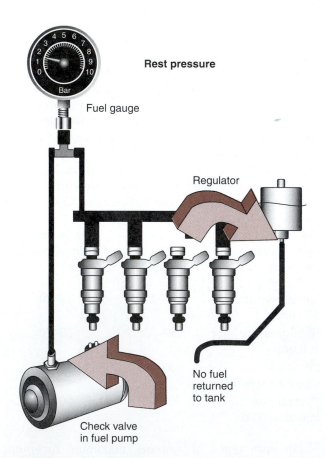

FIGURE 18-25   The fuel system should hold pressure if the system is leak free.

Step 3 If leakdown continues, then pressurize the system again and restrict the supply and return lines.

Step 4 If the leakdown stops now, then the fuel-pump check valve is defective.

Step 5 If leakdown continues, then the injectors are leaking. (Some pumps have an internal bleed orifice to prevent vapor lock and will not hold rest pressure. It is more important that the pump be able to supply instant pressure when the key is turned on. If the pump is capable of supplying the specified pressure immediately at start-up, the bleed-down is not important.

◄ GURU TIP ►

Do not test a fuel pump by clamping or shutting off the fuel return line (deadheading), as damage to the pump module can occur.

Dynamic Pressure Test

To test the pressure dynamically, start the engine. If the pressure is vacuum referenced, then the pressure should change when the throttle is cycled. If it does

not, then check the vacuum supply circuit. Remove the vacuum line from the regulator and inspect for any presence of fuel. See Figure 18-27. There should never be any fuel present on the vacuum side of the regulator diaphragm. When the engine speed is increased, the pressure reading should remain within the specifications.

Some engines do not use a vacuum-referenced regulator. The running pressure remains constant, which is typical for a mechanical returnless-type of fuel system. On these systems, the pressure is higher than on return-type systems to help reduce the formation of fuel vapors in the system.

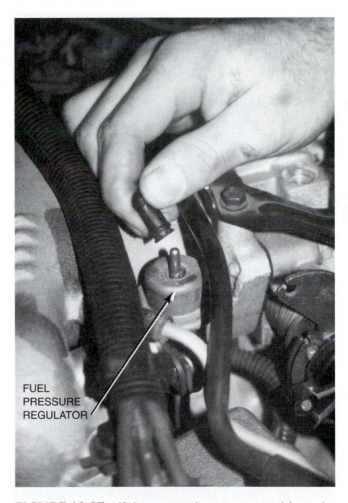

FIGURE 18-27 If the vacuum hose is removed from the fuel-pressure regulator when the engine is running, the fuel pressure should increase. If it does not increase, then the fuel pump is not capable of supplying adequate pressure or the fuel-pressure regulator is defective. If gasoline is visible in the vacuum hose, the regulator is leaking and should be replaced.

FIGURE 18-26 Many older General Motors fuel-injected vehicles are equipped with a fuel-pump test connector. The operation of the fuel pump can be checked by connecting a 12-volt test light to the positive (+) terminal of the battery and the point of the test light to the test connector. Turn the ignition to on (engine off). The light should either go out or come on for 2 seconds. This is a simple test to see if the computer can control the fuel-pump relay.

◄ TECH TIP ►

THE FUEL-PRESSURE STETHOSCOPE TEST

When the fuel pump is energized and the engine is not running, fuel should be heard flowing back to the fuel tank at the outlet of the fuel-pressure regulator. See Figure 18-28. If fuel is heard flowing through the return line, the fuel-pump pressure is higher than the regulator pressure. If no sound of fuel is heard, either the fuel pump or the fuel-pressure regulator is at fault.

FUEL PRESSURE REGULATOR

FUEL RETURN LINE TO TANK

FIGURE 18-28   Fuel should be heard returning to the fuel tank at the fuel return line if the fuel pump and fuel-pressure regulator are functioning correctly.

Testing Fuel-Pump Volume

Fuel pressure alone is not enough for proper engine operation. See Figure 18-29. Sufficient fuel capacity (flow) should be at least 2 pints (1 liter) every 30 seconds or 1 pint in 15 seconds. Fuel flow specifications are usually expressed in gallons per minute. A typical specification would be 0.5 gallons per minute or more. Volume testing shown in Figure 18-30 only confirms the volume through the regulator (a restriction) and is only part of

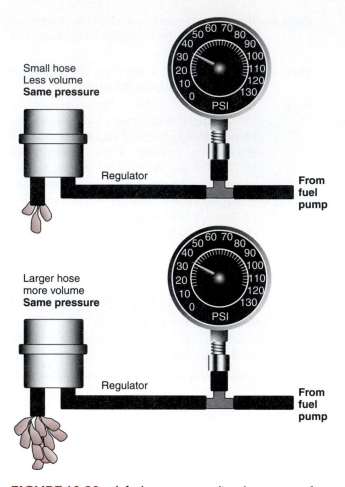

Small hose
Less volume
Same pressure

Regulator

From fuel pump

Larger hose
more volume
Same pressure

Regulator

From fuel pump

FIGURE 18-29   A fuel-pressure reading does not confirm that there is enough fuel volume for the engine to operate correctly.

the test. This test must also be measured in an open-loop (wide-open) test as well. The volume test shown in Figure 18-31 is a nonrestricted fuel pump actual delivery test. For example, specifications shown for one year truck is given at .85 to 1.00 U.S. gallons per hour (GPH) while another year truck specification is .92 to 1.08 GPH. This difference (however so slight) could cause a borderline problem with the vehicle if in fact the wrong pump has been installed. Case studies have shown this to happen quite a few times.

All fuel must be filtered to prevent dirt and impurities from damaging the fuel system components and/or engine. The first filter is inside the gas tank and is usually not replaceable separately but is attached to the fuel pump (if the pump is electric) and/or fuel gauge sending

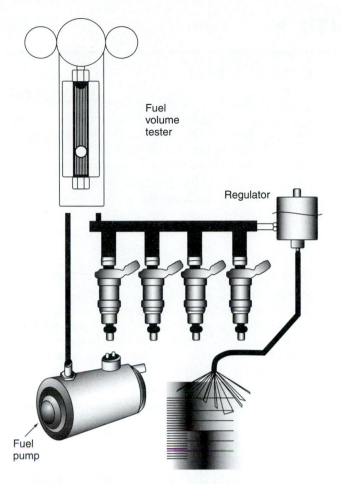

FIGURE 18-30 Measuring the volume of fuel flowing through the fuel-pressure regulator may not show the true volume capacity of the fuel pump.

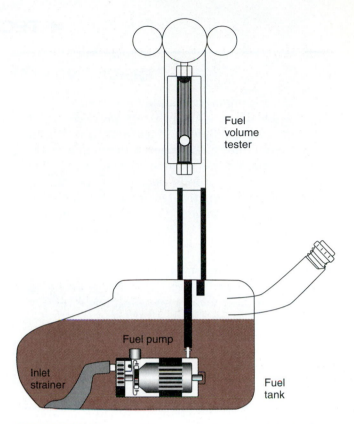

FIGURE 18-31 A nonrestricted (wide-open) fuel volume test using a fuel volume tester without the restriction of other components in the fuel system, such as the regulator.

unit. The replaceable fuel filter is usually located between the fuel tank and the fuel rail or inlet to the fuel-injection system. For long engine and fuel-system life and optimum performance, the fuel filter should be replaced every year or every 15,000 miles or 24,000 kilometers (km). (Consult vehicle manufacturers' recommendations for exact time and mileage intervals.)

If the fuel filter becomes partially clogged, the following are likely to occur:

1. There will be low power at higher engine speeds. The vehicle usually will not go faster than a certain speed (engine acts as if it has a built-in speed governor).
2. The engine will cut out or miss on acceleration, especially when climbing hills or during heavy-load acceleration.

A weak or defective fuel pump can also be the cause of the symptoms just listed. If an electric fuel pump for a fuel-injected engine becomes weak, additional problems include the following:

1. The engine may be hard to start.
2. There may be a rough idle and stalling.
3. There may be erratic shifting of the automatic transmission as a result of engine missing due to lack of fuel-pump pressure and/or volume.

CAUTION: Be certain to consult the vehicle manufacturers' recommended service and testing procedures before attempting to test or replace any component of a high-pressure electronic fuel-injection system.

◀ **TECH TIP** ▶

QUICK AND EASY FUEL VOLUME TEST

Testing for pump volume involves using a specialized tester or a fuel-pressure gauge equipped with a hose to allow the fuel to be drawn from the system into a container with volume markings to allow for a volume measurement. This test can be hazardous because of expanding gasoline. An alternative test involves connecting a fuel-pressure gauge to the system with the following steps:

Step 1   Start the engine and observe the fuel-pressure gauge. The reading should be within factory specifications (typically between 35 psi and 45 psi).

Step 2   Remove the hose from the fuel-pressure regulator. The pressure should increase if the system uses a demand-type regulator.

Step 3   Rapidly accelerate the engine while watching the fuel-pressure gauge. If the fuel volume is OK, the fuel pressure should not drop more than 2 psi. If the fuel pressure drops more than 2 psi, replace the fuel filter and retest.

Step 4   After replacing the fuel filter, accelerate the engine and observe the pressure gauge. If the pressure drops more than 2 psi, replace the fuel pump.

NOTE: The fuel pump could still be delivering less than the specified volume of fuel, but as long as the volume needed by the engine is met, the pressure will not drop. If, however, the vehicle is pulling a heavy load, the demand for fuel volume may exceed the capacity of the pump.

◀ **TECH TIP** ▶

REMOVE THE BED TO SAVE TIME?

The electric fuel pump is easier to replace on many General Motors pickup trucks if the bed is removed. Access to the top of the fuel tank, where the access hole is located, for the removal of the fuel tank sender unit and pump is restricted by the bottom of the pickup truck bed. Rather than drop the tank, it is often much easier to use an engine hoist or a couple of other technicians to lift the bed from the frame after removing only a few fasteners. See Figure 18-32.

CAUTION: Be sure to clean around the fuel pump opening so that dirt or debris does not enter the tank when the fuel pump is removed.

◀ **TECH TIP** ▶

THE ELECTRIC FUEL PUMP CLUE

The onboard computer controls the operation of the electric fuel pump, fuel-injection pulses, and ignition timing. With a distributorless ignition system, it is difficult at times to know what part in the system is not operating if there is no spark from any of the ignition coils. A fast-and-easy method for determining if the crankshaft sensor is operating is to observe the operation of the electric fuel pump. In most electronic fuel-injection systems, the computer will operate the electric fuel pump for only a short time (usually about 2 seconds) unless a crank pulse is received by the computer.

On most vehicles, if voltage is maintained to the pump during engine cranking for longer than 2 seconds, then the crankshaft sensor is working. If the pump only runs for 2 seconds and then turns off during cranking of the engine, the crankshaft sensor, wiring, or computer may be defective.

NOTE: Another way of testing is to use a scan tool or breakout box. If an RPM signal is processed and displayed by the computer, then the crank sensor is functioning.

Fuel pump

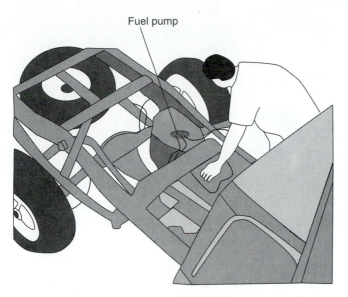

FIGURE 18-32   Removing the bed from a pickup truck makes gaining access to the fuel pump a lot easier.

FUEL-PUMP CURRENT DRAW TEST

Another test that can and should be performed on a fuel pump is to measure the current draw in amperes. This test is most often performed by connecting a digital multimeter set to read DC amperes and test the current draw. See Figure 18-33 for the hookup for General Motors vehicles with a fuel-pump test lead. See Figure 18-34 for the hookup for a typical Ford and Figure 18-35 for all vehicles equipped with a fuel-pump relay. Compare the reading to factory specifications. See the chart for an example of typical fuel-pump current draw readings.

◄ GURU TIP ►

Testing the current draw of an electric fuel pump may not indicate whether the pump is good. A pump that is not rotating may draw normal current.

Fuel-Pump Current Draw Table

Amperage Reading	*Expected Value*	*Amperage Too High*	*Amperage Too Low*
		▪ Check the fuel filter.	▪ Check for a high resistance connection.
Throttle-Body Fuel-Injection Engines	2 to 5 amps	▪ Check for restrictions in other fuel line areas.	▪ Check for a high resistance ground fault.
		▪ Replace the fuel pump.	▪ Replace the fuel pump.
Port Fuel-Injection Engines	4 to 8 amps	▪ Check the fuel filter. ▪ Check for restrictions in other fuel line areas. ▪ Replace the fuel pump.	▪ Check for a high resistance connection. ▪ Check for a high resistance ground fault. ▪ Replace the fuel pump.
Turbo Engines	6 to 10 amps	▪ Check the fuel filter. ▪ Check for restrictions in other fuel line areas. ▪ Replace the fuel pump.	▪ Check for a high resistance connection. ▪ Check for a high resistance ground fault. ▪ Replace the fuel pump.
GM CPI Truck Engines	8 to 12 amps	▪ Check the fuel filter. ▪ Check for restrictions in other fuel line areas. ▪ Replace the fuel pump.	▪ Check for a high resistance connection. ▪ Check for a high resistance ground fault. ▪ Replace the fuel pump.

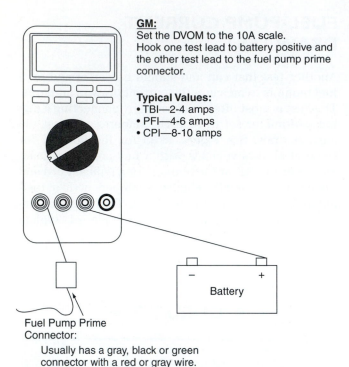

GM:
Set the DVOM to the 10A scale.
Hook one test lead to battery positive and
the other test lead to the fuel pump prime
connector.

Typical Values:
• TBI—2-4 amps
• PFI—4-6 amps
• CPI—8-10 amps

Battery

Fuel Pump Prime
Connector:

Usually has a gray, black or green
connector with a red or gray wire.

FIGURE 18-33 The hookup to test the current draw of
the fuel pump on a General Motors vehicle that is equipped
with a fuel-pump test lead (prime connector).

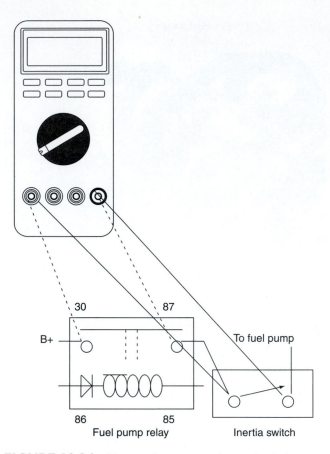

30   87

B+   To fuel pump

86   85
Fuel pump relay   Inertia switch

FIGURE 18-34 To test the current draw of a fuel pump
on a Ford vehicle, connect the meter leads at either the relay or the inertia switch.

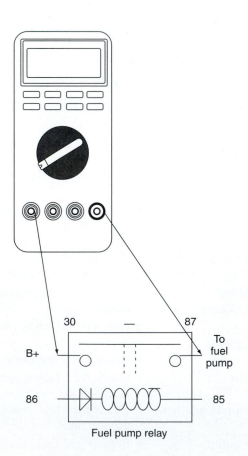

30   —   87
                To
B+   fuel
                pump

86   85
Fuel pump relay

FIGURE 18-35 Hookup for testing fuel pump current
draw on any vehicle equipped with a fuel pump relay.

FUEL-PUMP CURRENT RAMPING

Current ramping means to observe the current (amperes) waveform. By checking the current waveform of the fuel pump, possible problems can be detected. To perform a current ramping test, the following test equipment is required:

- Digital storage oscilloscope (See Figure 18-36.)
- Current probe

Current ramping is considered to be "nonintrusive," meaning that nothing has to be disconnected or disassembled in order to perform the test procedure. Most electric fuel pumps can be tested at one of three locations:

1. Fuel-pump test lead (most 1981–1995 General Motors fuel-injected vehicles)
2. Fuel-pump relay (use a fused jumper wire for the probe)
3. Fuel-pump fuse (use a fused jumper wire for the probe)

A current probe detects the current flow to the motor of the electric fuel pump. See Figure 18-37. The typical electric fuel pump motor has 8, 10, or 12 commutator segments and two brushes—a positive brush and a negative brush. See Figure 18-38. As the motor rotates, the

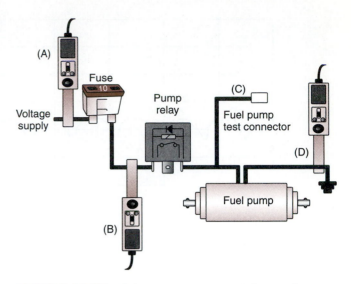

FIGURE 18-37 A low amp current probe can be connected anywhere in the fuel pump circuit that is the most convenient including: (a) at the fuse, (b) at the relay, (c) at the test connector or even the ground wire for the pump.

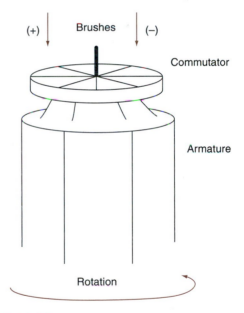

FIGURE 18-38 A typical electric fuel-pump motor that uses triangle-shaped commutator segments and horizontal brushes.

current through the brushes changes as the commutator segments rotate past the brushes. See Figure 18-39.

Scope Set-Up

The majority of scopes used for fuel-pump testing use a voltage setting of 100 mV per division and a time setting

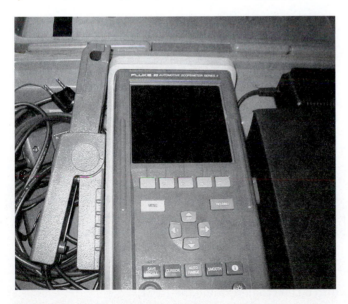

FIGURE 18-36 A digital storage oscilloscope, such as this Fluke 98-Series II and a low-current clamp, are necessary tools to perform current ramping.

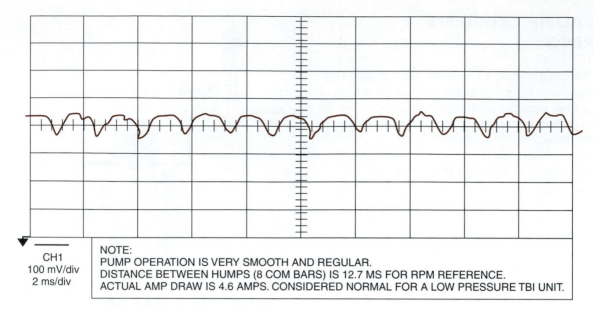

CH1
100 mV/div
2 ms/div

NOTE:
PUMP OPERATION IS VERY SMOOTH AND REGULAR.
DISTANCE BETWEEN HUMPS (8 COM BARS) IS 12.7 MS FOR RPM REFERENCE.
ACTUAL AMP DRAW IS 4.6 AMPS. CONSIDERED NORMAL FOR A LOW PRESSURE TBI UNIT.

FIGURE 18-39   As the fuel pump motor rotates, it produces a current waveform, as shown, as the brushes pass over the commutator segments.

of 2 ms. In some cases, the time base can be expanded to 5 ms for a better look at the waveform produced by the pump.

Current Draw

Current draw will increase with load and decrease with lack of load. Also, poor brush contact will lower current draw and brush spring tension is critical to the motor operation. The negative (ground) brush always seems to be the first to fail, and the spring behind the brushes will be the one to show heat and loss of spring tension.

Motor Commutator Bars and RPM

Most electric fuel pumps use a motor that has 8, 10, or 12 commutator segments. As the brushes pass over each commutator segment, a unique pattern is often visible. Counting the number of segments (usually eight) indicates one revolution of the pump motor. See Figure 18-40. Using that number and the time base of the scope, the actual operational RPM of the pump motor can be determined.

Pump Motor Speed

The speed of a good pump motor should be greater than 3000 RPM. Most pumps will operate from 3000 to

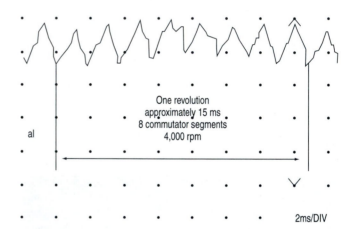

al

One revolution
approximately 15 ms
8 commutator segments
4,000 rpm

2ms/DIV

FIGURE 18-40   The speed of the fuel-pump motor can be determined by the time it takes the motor to make one revolution, as determined by looking for unique commutator segment patterns.

6000 RPM. A pump motor that is not rotating fast enough will not be able to supply the correct volume of fuel necessary for proper engine operation. To determine the speed of the pump motor, use the curves on the scope display and determine the time interval between the unique commutators and divide that number into 60,000 to determine the RPM.

$$\frac{60,000}{\text{time (ms)}} = \text{pump RPM}$$

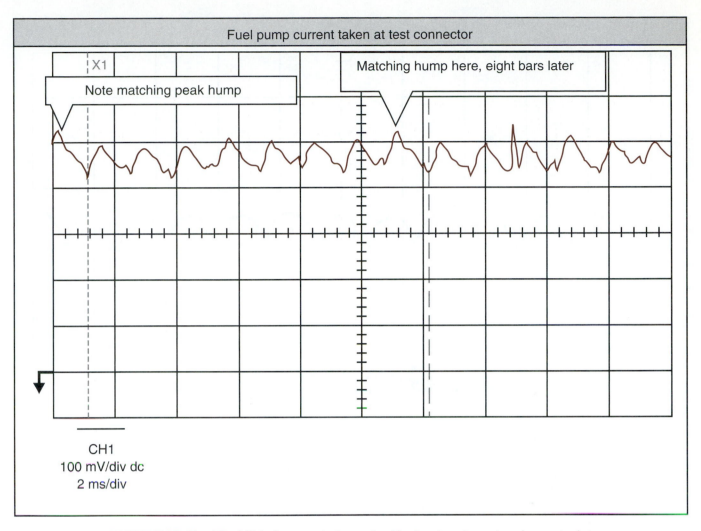

FIGURE 18-41 The RPM of a pump is determined by first locating unique humps in the voltage waveform. The time for one revolution is determined by counting the number of divisions between unique humps and then multiplying it by the time per division.

For example, if the pump motor rotates one revolution every 10 ms, then the motor is operating at 6000 RPM. See Figure 18-41. A pump that is operating at less than 3000 RPM will likely not be able to supply enough fuel, resulting in a driveability concern.

Case Study #1: Good Fuel Pump Waveform

See Figure 18-42. This is a known good pump with proper waveform. The waveform indicated that the amp draw is correct and within specifications for the vehicle being tested. Higher fuel pressure equals higher current draw or motor load. Also, the brush contact is very regular and consistent.

Case Study #2: Damaged Pump

See Figure 18-43 on page 327. The pump shows a damaged commutator section every eighth bar. This is a great example of a fuel pump that is showing some damage on one single section of the pump. Every eighth brush crossover to the next commutator bar shows some variation in current. This pump is not yet bad, but it would be wise to monitor it as time goes on and the vehicle returns for service.

Cash Study #3: Good Pressure, Low Volume

See Figure 18-44 on page 328. This pump motor is rotating at only 1300 RPM, indicating a very slow rotating pump.

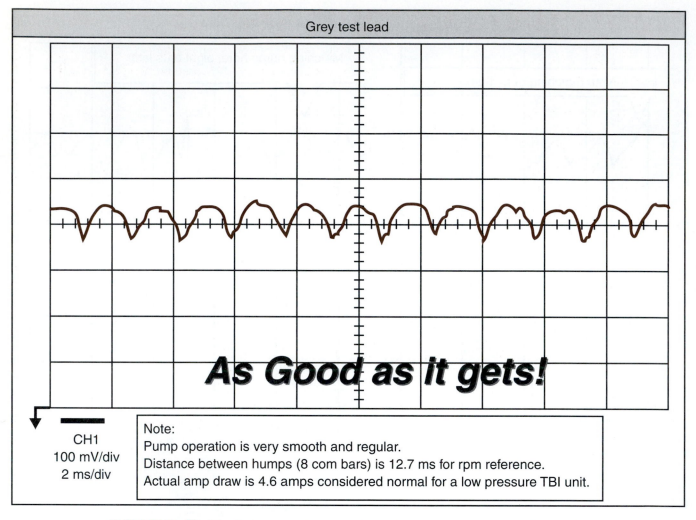

Grey test lead

CH1
100 mV/div
2 ms/div

Note:
Pump operation is very smooth and regular.
Distance between humps (8 com bars) is 12.7 ms for rpm reference.
Actual amp draw is 4.6 amps considered normal for a low pressure TBI unit.

As Good as it gets!

FIGURE 18-42 This fuel pump voltage waveform shows good pump speed (4724 RPM) and current draw.

◀ **GURU TIP** ▶

At idle, a typical V-8 engine requires 30 cc per minute of fuel, a V-6 engine about 25 cc per minute, a large 4-cylinder engine (2.5 liter) about 20 cc per minute, and a small 4-cylinder engine (1.8 liter) about 15 cc per minute.

FUEL-PUMP REPLACEMENT

The following recommendations should be followed whenever replacing an electric fuel pump.

- The fuel-pump strainer (sock) should be replaced with the new pump.

- If the original pump had a defector shield, it should always be used to prevent fuel return bubbles from blocking the inlet to the pump.
- Always check the interior of the fuel tank for evidence of contamination or dirt.
- Double-check that the replacement pump is correct for the application.

◀ **GURU TIP** ▶

Fuel-pump ground is more critical on high-output pumps.

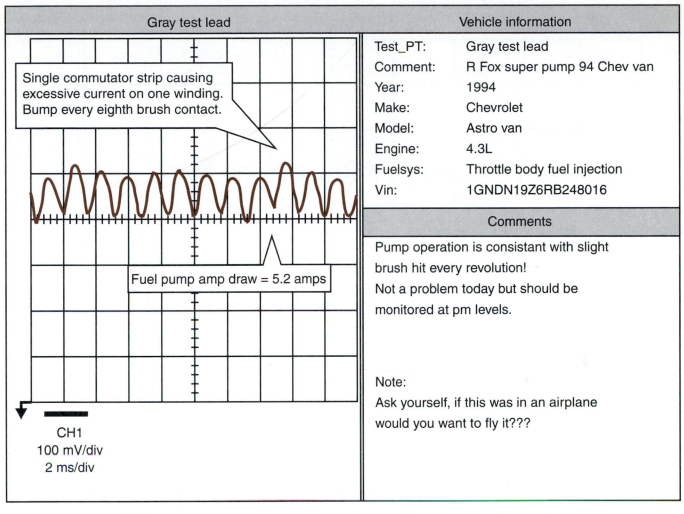

FIGURE 18-43   A pump motor that shows some damage, which could lead to failure in the future.

◄ GURU TIP ►

Fuel pump replacement is becoming more common as more vehicles acquire the mileage and lack of maintenance often leading to failure. Be careful to install the correct pump for each application. Misapplication is one of the leading causes of pump replacement!

FUEL SUPPLY-RELATED DIAGNOSTIC CHART

Problem	*Possible Causes*
Pressure too high after engine start-up.	1. Defective fuel-pressure regulator 2. Restricted fuel return line 3. Excessive system voltage 4. Restricted return line 5. Wrong fuel pump

(continued)

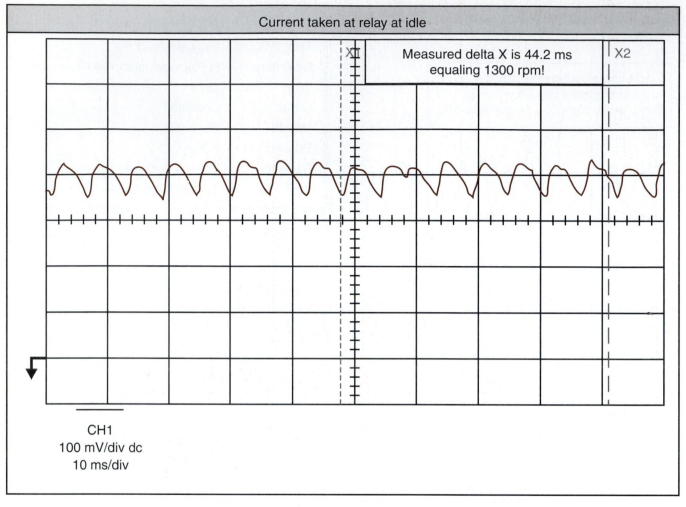

FIGURE 18-44 While the voltage waveform of this pump looks good, a calculation of the pump motor speed indicates that it is rotating far below the 3000 RPM minimum acceptable speed.

Problem	Possible Causes
Pressure too low after engine start-up.	1. Stuck-open pressure regulator
	2. Low voltage
	3. Poor ground
	4. Plugged fuel filter
	5. Faulty inline fuel pump
	6. Faulty in-tank fuel pump
	7. Partially clogged filter sock
	8. Faulty hose coupling
	9. Leaking fuel line
	10. Wrong fuel pump
	11. Leaking pulsator
	12. Restricted accumulator
	13. Faulty pump check valves
	14. Faulty pump installation

Problem	Possible Causes
Pressure drops off with key on/engine off. With key off, the pressure does not hold.	1. Leaky pulsator 2. Leaking fuel pump coupling hose 3. Faulty fuel pump (check valves) 4. Faulty pressure regulator 5. Leaking fuel injector 6. Leaking cold-start fuel injector 7. Faulty installation 8. Lines leaking

SUMMARY

1. The fuel delivery system includes the following items:
   - Fuel tank
   - Fuel pump
   - Fuel filter(s)
   - Fuel lines
2. A fuel tank is either constructed of steel with a tin plating for corrosion resistance or polyethylene plastic.
3. Fuel tank filler tubes contain an anti-siphoning device.
4. Accident and rollover protection devices include check valves and inertia switches.
5. Most fuel lines are made of nylon plastic.
6. Electric fuel pump types include: roller cell, gerotor, and turbine.
7. Fuel filters remove particles that are 10 to 20 microns or larger in size and should be replaced regularly.
8. Fuel pumps can be tested by checking:
   - Pressure
   - Volume
   - Pump motor speed (RPM) as determined by current ramping
   - Specified current draw

REVIEW QUESTIONS

1. What are the two materials used to construct fuel tanks?
2. What are the three most commonly used pump designs?
3. What is the proper way to disconnect and connect plastic fuel line connections?
4. Where are the fuel filters located in the fuel system?
5. What accident and rollover devices are installed in a fuel delivery system?
6. What four methods can be used to test a fuel pump?

ASE CERTIFICATION-TYPE QUESTIONS

1. The first fuel filter in the sock inside the fuel tank normally filters particles larger than _____.
   - **a.** 0.001 to 0.003 in.
   - **b.** 0.010 to 0.030 in.
   - **c.** 10 to 20 microns
   - **d.** 70 to 100 microns

2. Which type of safety device will keep the electric fuel pump from operating if it is tripped?
   - **a.** Roll-over valve
   - **b.** Inertia switch
   - **c.** Anti-siphoning valve
   - **d.** Check valve

3. Fuel lines are constructed from _____.
   a. Seamless steel tubing
   b. Nylon plastic
   c. Copper and/or aluminum tubing
   d. Both a and b are used

4. Which is not a commonly used type of fuel pump design?
   a. Gerotor
   b. Pulsating
   c. Rotor cell
   d. Turbine

5. A good fuel pump should be able to supply how much fuel per minute?
   a. ¼ pint
   b. ½ pint
   c. 1 pint
   d. 0.6 to 0.8 gallons

6. Technician A says that fuel pump modules are spring-loaded so that they can be compressed to fit into the opening. Technician B says that they are spring-loaded to allow for expansion and contraction of plastic fuel tanks. Which technician is correct?
   a. Technician A only
   b. Technician B only
   c. Both Technicians A and B
   d. Neither Technician A nor B

7. Most fuel filters are designed to remove particles larger than _____.
   a. 10 microns
   b. 20 microns
   c. 70 microns
   d. 100 microns

8. The amperage draw of an electric fuel pump is higher than specified. All of the following are possible causes *except:*
   a. Corroded electrical connections at the pump motor
   b. Clogged fuel filter
   c. Restriction in the fuel line
   d. Defective fuel pump

9. A fuel pump is being tested with an amp probe and a digital storage oscilloscope. Technician A says that most fuel pumps have four commutator segments. Technician B says that the speed of the pump motor should be higher than 3000 RPM. Which technician is correct?
   a. Technician A only
   b. Technician B only
   c. Both Technicians A and B
   d. Neither Technician A nor B

10. A fuel filter has been accidentally installed backwards. What is the most likely result?
    a. Nothing will be noticed
    b. Reduced fuel economy
    c. Lower power at higher engine speeds and loads
    d. Fuel system pulsation noises may be heard

EVAPORATIVE EMISSION CONTROL SYSTEMS

OBJECTIVES

After studying Chapter 19, the reader should be able to:

1. Prepare for the ASE Engine Performance (A8) certification test content area "D" (Emission Control Systems).
2. Describe the purpose and function of the evaporative emission control system.
3. Discuss how the evaporative emission control system is tested under OBD-II regulations.
4. Explain methods for diagnosing and testing faults in the evaporative emission control system.

NEED FOR EVAPORATIVE EMISSION CONTROL

The purpose of the **evaporative (EVAP)** emission control system is to trap and hold gasoline vapors. The charcoal canister is part of an entire system of hoses and valves called the **evaporative control system.** Before the early 1970s, most gasoline fumes were simply vented to the atmosphere.

The purpose of the EVAP system is to trap gasoline vapors—**volatile organic compounds,** or **VOCs**—that would otherwise escape into the atmosphere. These vapors are instead routed into a charcoal canister, from where they go to the intake airflow so they are burned in the engine.

◀ FREQUENTLY ASKED ▶ QUESTION

WHEN FILLING MY FUEL TANK, WHY SHOULD I STOP WHEN THE PUMP CLICKS OFF?

Every fuel tank has an upper volume chamber that allows for expansion of the fuel when hot. The volume of the chamber is between 10 and 20% of the volume of the tank. For example, if a fuel tank had a capacity of 20 gallons, the expansion chamber volume would be from 2 to 4 gallons. A hose is attached at the top of the chamber and vented to the charcoal canister. If extra fuel is forced into this expansion volume, liquid gasoline can be drawn into the charcoal canister. This liquid fuel can saturate the canister and create an overly rich air-fuel mixture when the canister purge valve is opened during normal vehicle operation. This extra-rich air-fuel mixture can cause the vehicle to fail an exhaust emissions test, reduce fuel economy, and possibly damage the catalytic converter. To avoid problems, simply add fuel to the next dime's worth after the nozzle clicks off. This will ensure that the tank is full, yet not overfilled.

Common Components

The fuel tank filler caps used on vehicles with modern EVAP systems are a special design. Most EVAP fuel tank filler caps have pressure-vacuum relief built into them. When pressure or vacuum exceeds a calibrated value, the valve opens. Once the pressure or vacuum has been relieved, the valve closes. If a sealed cap is used on an EVAP system that requires a pressure-vacuum relief design, a vacuum lock may develop in the fuel system, or the fuel tank may be damaged by fuel expansion or contraction. See Figure 19-1.

Various methods protect fuel tanks against fuel expansion and overflow caused by heat. When the fuel tank appears to be completely full—when it holds no more and the fuel gauge reads full—the expansion tank remains virtually empty. This provides enough space for fuel expansion and vapor collection if the vehicle is parked in the hot sun after filling the tank.

The dome design of the upper fuel tank section used in some late-model cars, or the overfill limiting valve contained within the vapor-liquid separator, eliminates the need for the overfill limiter tank used in earlier systems.

VAPOR CANISTER STORAGE

The canister is located under the hood or underneath the vehicle, and is filled with activated charcoal granules that can hold up to one-third of their own weight in fuel vapors. A vent line connects the canister to the fuel tank. See Figure 19-2. Some vehicles with large or dual fuel tanks may have dual canisters.

Activated charcoal is an effective vapor trap because of its great surface area. Each gram of activated charcoal has a surface area of 1100 square meters, or more than a quarter acre. Typical canisters hold either 300 or 625 grams of charcoal *with a surface area equivalent to 80 or 165 football fields.* **Adsorption** attaches the fuel vapor molecules to the carbon surface. This attaching force is not strong, so the system purges the vapor molecules quite simply by sending a fresh airflow through the charcoal. See Figure 19-3.

FIGURE 19-2 Charcoal canister as mounted under the hood (Jeep). Not all charcoal canisters are this accessible; in fact, most are hidden under the hood or in other locations on the vehicle.

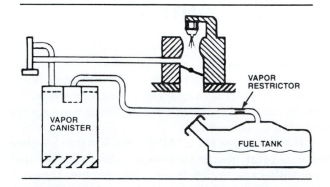

FIGURE 19-3 The evaporative emission control system includes all of the lines, hoses, and valves, plus the charcoal canister.

FIGURE 19-1 A typical bayonet-type gas cap.

VAPOR PURGING

During engine operation, stored vapors are drawn from the canister into the engine through a hose connected to the throttle body or the air cleaner. This "purging" process mixes HC vapors from the canister with the existing air-fuel charge.

Computer-Controlled Purge

Canister purging on engines with electronic fuel management systems is regulated by the powertrain control module (PCM). Control of this function is particularly important because the additional fuel vapors sent through the purge line can upset the air-fuel ratio provided by a fuel-injection system. Since air-fuel ratio adjustments are made many times per second, it is critical that vapor purging is controlled just as precisely. This is done by a microprocessor-controlled vacuum solenoid, and one or more purge valves. See Figure 19-4. Under normal conditions, most engine control systems permit purging only during closed-loop operation at cruising speeds. During other engine operation conditions, such as open-loop mode, idle, deceleration, or wide-open throttle, the PCM prevents canister purging.

EVAPORATIVE SYSTEM PRESSURE

Pressures can build inside the fuel system and are usually measured in units of inches of water, abbreviated in. H_2O. (28 inches of water equals one psi) Pressure buildup is a function of:

- Fuel evaporation rates (volatility)
- Gas tank size (fuel surface area and volume)
- Fuel level (liquid versus vapor)
- Fuel slosh (driving conditions)
- Temperature (ambient, in-tank, close to the tank)
- Returned fuel from the rail

Pressure Conversions

Psi	Inches Hg	Inches H_2O
14.7	29.93	407.19
1.0	2.036	27.7
0.9	1.8	24.93
0.8	1.63	22.16
0.7	1.43	19.39
0.6	1.22	16.62
0.5	1.018	13.85
0.4	0.814	11.08
0.3	0.611	8.31
0.2	0.407	5.54
0.1	0.204	2.77
0.09	0.183	2.49
0.08	0.163	2.22
0.07	0.143	1.94
0.06	0.122	1.66
0.05	0.102	1.385

1 psi = 28 inches of water
1/4 psi = 7 inches of water

NONENHANCED EVAPORATIVE CONTROL SYSTEMS

Prior to 1996, evaporative systems were referred to as evaporation (EVAP) control systems. This term refers to evaporative systems that had limited diagnostic capabilities. While they are often PCM controlled, their diagnostic capability is usually limited to their ability to detect if purge has occurred. Many systems have a diagnostic switch that could sense if purge is occurring and set a code if no purge is detected. See Figure 19-5. This system does not check for leaks. On some vehicles, the PCM also has the capability of monitoring the integrity of the purge solenoid and circuit. These systems' limitations are their ability to check the integrity of the evaporative system on the vehicle. They could not detect leaks or missing or loose gas caps that could lead to excessive evaporative emissions from the vehicle. Nonenhanced evaporative systems use either a canister purge solenoid or a vapor management valve to control purge vapor.

ENHANCED EVAPORATIVE CONTROL SYSTEM

Beginning in 1996 with OBD-II vehicles, manufacturers were required to install systems that are able to detect both purge flow and evaporative system leakage. The systems on models produced between 1996 and 2000 have to be able to detect a leak as small as .040 in. diameter. Beginning in the model year 2000, the enhanced systems started a phase-in of .020 in.-diameter leak detection.

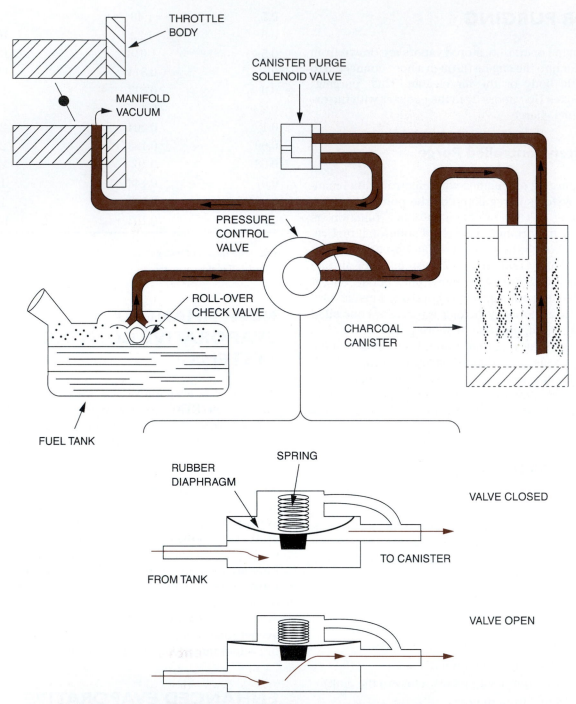

FIGURE 19-4 A typical evaporative emission control system. Note that when the computer turns on the canister purge solenoid valve, manifold vacuum draws any stored vapors from the canister into the engine. Manifold vacuum also is applied to the pressure control valve. When this valve opens, fumes from the fuel tank are drawn into the charcoal canister and eventually into the engine. When the solenoid valve is turned off (or the engine stops and there is no manifold vacuum), the pressure control valve is spring-loaded shut to keep vapors inside the fuel tank from escaping to the atmosphere.

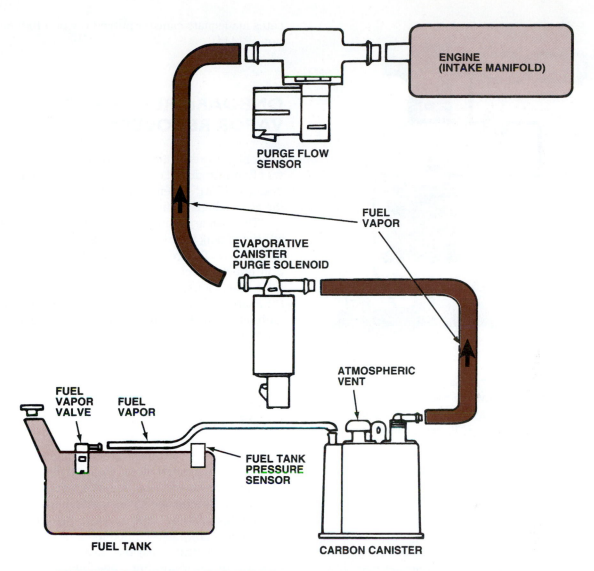

FIGURE 19-5 A typical OBD-II EVAP system which uses fuel tank pressure and purge flow sensors to detect leaks and measure purge flow. The purge flow sensor is similar to a mass air flow sensor and measures the amount of flow into the engine.

NOTE: DaimlerChrysler says that a 0.020 in.-diameter leak in an EVAP system can yield an average of about 1.35 grams of HC per mile driven.

All vehicles built after 1995 have enhanced evaporative systems that have the ability to detect purge flow and system leakage. If either of these two functions fails, the system is required to set a diagnostic trouble code and turn on the MIL light to warn the driver of the failure. See Figure 19-6.

Canister Vent Valve

The canister vent valve, also called the **vapor management valve (VMV)** output circuit is checked for opens and shorts internally in the PCM by monitoring the status of the duty-cycled output driver. When the output driver is fully energized, or de-energized, the feedback circuit voltage should respond high or low accordingly (P0443).

The vent valve functional check uses the idle airflow correction for the IAC solenoid to check for adequate purge flow. The vent valve is a source of engine airflow at idle; therefore, a change in VMV airflow will produce a corresponding change in IAC airflow.

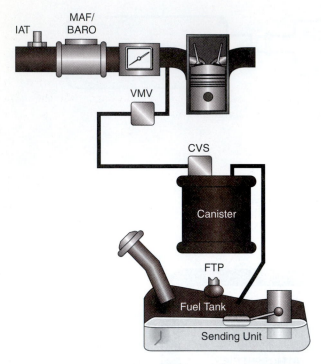

FIGURE 19-6 The vapor management valve (VMV) and the canister purge valve (CPV) are both PCM controlled and check for proper flow through the evaporative control system. The fuel tank pressure (FTP) sensor monitors vapor pressure inside the fuel tank.

The IAC airflow correction is checked while the VMV is normally open (greater than 75%), then checked again after the VMV is commanded closed (0%). If the difference in IAC airflow corrections is too small, it indicates inadequate VMV flow (P0441).

Canister Purge Solenoid (CPS)

The **canister purge (CANP)** solenoid output circuit is checked for opens and shorts internally in the PCM by monitoring the status of the duty-cycled output driver. When the output driver is fully energized, or de-energized, the feedback circuit voltage should respond high or low accordingly (P0443).

The canister purge solenoid functional check uses a **purge flow sensor (PFS)** to check for adequate purge flow. The PFS voltage is checked when the solenoid valve is normally open (less than 75%), then checked when the solenoid valve is commanded closed (0%). Too low a difference between the voltages indi-

cates inadequate canister purge flow or a PFS malfunction (P1443).

ONBOARD REFUELING VAPOR RECOVERY

The onboard refueling vapor recovery (ORVR) system was first introduced on some 1998 vehicles. Previously designed EVAP systems allowed fuel vapor to escape to the atmosphere during refueling.

The primary feature of most ORVR systems is the restricted tank filler tube, which is about 1 inch (25 mm) in diameter. This reduced filler tube creates an aspiration effect, which tends to draw outside air into the filler tube. During refueling, the fuel tank is vented to the charcoal canister, which captures the gas fumes and with air flowing into the filler tube, no vapors can escape to the atmosphere.

STATE INSPECTION EVAP TESTS

In some states, a periodic inspection and test of the fuel system are mandated along with a dynamometer test. The emissions inspection includes tests on the vehicle before and during the dynamometer test. Before the running test, the fuel tank and cap, fuel lines, canister, and other fuel system components must be inspected and tested to ensure that they are not leaking gasoline vapors into the atmosphere. See Figure 19-7.

First, the fuel tank cap is tested to ensure that it is sealing properly and holds pressure within specs. Next, the cap is installed on the vehicle, and using a special adapter, the EVAP system is pressurized to approximately 0.5 psi and monitored for two minutes. Pressure in the tank and lines should not drop below approximately 0.3 psi.

If the cap or system leaks, hydrocarbon emissions are likely being released, and the vehicle fails the test. If the system leaks, an ultrasonic leak detector may be used to find the leak.

Finally, with the engine warmed up and running at a moderate speed, the canister purge line is tested for adequate flow using a special flow meter inserted into the system. In one example, if the flow from the canister to the intake system when the system is activated is at least one liter per minute, then the vehicle passes the canister purge test.

FIGURE 19-7 A gas cap being testing by an inspector at an inspection station.

to a level below one pound per square inch or 1 psi (about 14 inches of water). The system is typically pressurized with nitrogen, a nonflammable gas that makes up 78% of our atmosphere. The pressure in the system is then shut off and the pressure monitored. If the pressure drops below a set standard, then the vehicle fails the test. This test determines if there is a leak in the system.

HINT: To help pass the evaporative section of an enhanced emissions test, arrive at the test site with less than a half-tank of fuel. This means that the rest of the volume of the fuel tank is filled with air. It takes longer for the pressure to drop from a small leak when the volume of the air is greater compared to when the tank is full and the volume of air remaining in the tank is small.

To test for proper airflow in the EVAP system, a **flow gauge** is required as shown in Figure 19-8. Most vehicle emission test sites require at least 1 liter of volume per purge during the 240-second (4-minute) test. Many vehicles today are capable of flowing up to 10 liters or more per minute.

Purge Command	Purge Flow (liters per minute)
10%	0 lpm
20%	14 lpm
40%	30 lpm
60%	40 lpm
80%	40 lpm
100%	Off the scale

DIAGNOSING THE EVAP SYSTEM

Before vehicle emissions testing began in many parts of the country, little service work was done on the evaporative emission system. Common engine-performance problems that can be caused by a fault in this system include:

- **Poor fuel economy.** A leak in a vacuum-valve diaphragm can result in engine vacuum drawing in a constant flow of gasoline vapors from the fuel tank. This usually results in a drop in fuel economy of 2 to 4 miles per gallon (MPG). Use a hand-operated vacuum pump to check that the vacuum diaphragm can hold vacuum.

- **Poor performance.** A vacuum leak in the manifold or ported vacuum section of vacuum hose in the system can cause the engine to run rough. Age, heat, and time all contribute to the deterioration of rubber hoses.

Enhanced exhaust emissions (I/M-240) testing tests the evaporative emission system. A leak in the system is tested by pressurizing the entire fuel system

LOCATING LEAKS IN THE SYSTEM

Leaks in the evaporative emission control system will cause the malfunction check gas cap indication light to come on in some vehicles. See Figure 19-9. A leak will also cause a gas smell, which would be most noticeable if the vehicle were parked in an enclosed garage. There are two methods that can be used to check for leaks in the evaporative system.

- **Smoke machine testing.** The most efficient method of leak detection is to introduce smoke under low pressure from a machine specifically designed for this purpose. See Figure 19-10.

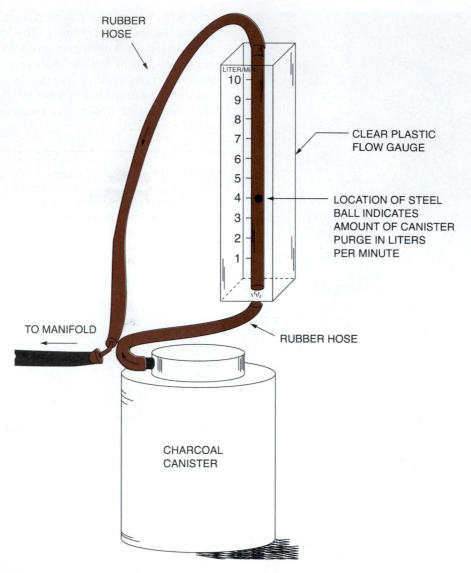

RUBBER
HOSE

LITER/MIN.
10
9
8
7
6
5
4
3
2
1

CLEAR PLASTIC
FLOW GAUGE

LOCATION OF STEEL
BALL INDICATES
AMOUNT OF CANISTER
PURGE IN LITERS
PER MINUTE

TO MANIFOLD

RUBBER HOSE

CHARCOAL
CANISTER

FIGURE 19-8 A typical purge flow tester connected in series between the intake manifold (or control solenoid) and the charcoal canister. Most working systems should be capable of flowing at least 1 L/min. Some vehicles must be test driven because their computers only purge after a certain road speed has been achieved.

FIGURE 19-9 Some vehicles will display a message if an evaporative control system leak is detected that could be the result of a loose gas cap.

- **Nitrogen gas pressurization.** This method uses nitrogen gas under a very low pressure (lower than 1 psi) in the fuel system. The service technician then listens for the escaping air, using amplified headphones. See Figure 19-11.

EVAPORATIVE SYSTEM MONITOR

OBD-II computer programs not only detect faults, but also *periodically test various systems* and alert the driver before emissions-related components are harmed

FIGURE 19-11 An emission tester that uses nitrogen to pressurize the fuel system.

systems are to be routinely tested *while underway* by the PCM management system.

All OBD-II vehicles—during normal driving cycles and under specific conditions—experience a canister purge system pressure test, as commanded by the PCM. While the vehicle is being driven, the vapor line between the canister and the purge valve is monitored for pressure changes. When the canister purge solenoid is open, the line should be under a vacuum since vapors must be drawn from the canister into the intake system. However, when the purge solenoid is closed, there should be no vacuum in the line. The pressure sensor detects if a vacuum is present or not, and the information is compared to the command given to the solenoid. If, during the canister purge cycle, no vacuum exists in the canister purge line, a code is set indicating a possible fault, which could be caused by an inoperative or clogged solenoid or a blocked or leaking canister purge fuel line. Likewise, if vacuum exists when no command for purge is given, a stuck solenoid is evident, and a code is set.

The EVAP system monitor tests for purge volume and leaks. Most applications purge the charcoal canister by venting the vapors into the intake manifold during cruise. To do this, the PCM typically opens a solenoid-operated purge valve installed in the purge line leading to the intake manifold.

A typical EVAP monitor first closes off the system to atmospheric pressure and opens the purge valve during cruise operation. A **fuel tank pressure (FTP)** sensor then monitors the rate with which vacuum increases in the system. The monitor uses this information to determine the purge volume flow rate. To test for leaks, the EVAP monitor closes the purge valve, creating a completely closed system. The fuel tank pressure sensor then monitors the leakdown rate. If the rate exceeds

(a)

(b)

FIGURE 19-10 (a) A typical EVAP diagnostic tester. (b) A smoke test shows a leaking gas cap.

by system faults. Serious faults cause a blinking malfunction indicator lamp (MIL) or even an engine shutdown; less serious faults may simply store a code but not illuminate the MIL.

The OBD-II requirements did not radically affect fuel system design. However, one new component, a fuel evaporative canister purge line pressure sensor, was added for monitoring purge line pressure during tests. The OBD-II requirements state that vehicle fuel

Evaporative System Components

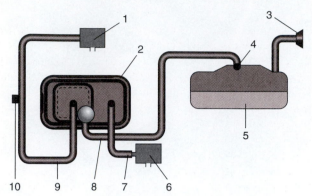

1. Canister purge valve (normally closed)
2. Canister
3. Fill neck and gas cap
4. Fuel Tank Pressure (FTP) and rollover valve
5. Fuel tank
6. Canister vent valve (normally open)
7. Vent line
8. Vapor line
9. Purge line
10. Service schrader

FIGURE 19-12 Typical evaporative system showing the valves and the normal position.

PCM-stored values, a leak greater than or equal to the OBD-II standard of 0.040 in. (1.0 mm) or 0.020 in. (0.5 mm) exists. After two consecutive failed trips testing either purge volume or the presence of a leak, the PCM lights the MIL and sets a DTC.

DaimlerChrysler vehicles use an electric pump, called a **leak defection pump (LDP),** to pressurize the fuel system to check for leaks by having the PCM monitor the fuel tank pressure sensor. The fuel tank pressure sensor is often the same part as the MAP sensor, and instead of monitoring intake manifold absolute pressure, it is used to monitor fuel tank pressure. See Figure 19-12.

Engine Off Natural Vacuum

System integrity (leakage) can also be checked after the engine is shut off. The premise is that a warm evaporative system will cool down after the engine is shut off and the vehicle is stable. A slight vacuum will be created in the gas tank during this cool-down period. If a specific level of vacuum is reached and maintained, the system is said to have integrity (no leakage).

FIGURE 19-13 An assortment of gas caps used during testing of the EVAP system.

◀ TECH TIP ▶

ALWAYS TIGHTEN "THREE CLICKS"

Many diagnostic trouble codes (DTCs) are set because the gas cap has not been properly installed. To be sure that a screw-type gas cap is properly sealed, tighten the cap until it clicks three times. The clicking is a ratchet device and the clicking does not harm the cap. Therefore, if a P0440 or similar DTC is set, check the cap. Test caps can also be used when diagnosing the system as shown in Figure 19-13.

GENERAL MOTORS ENHANCED EVAP

The PCM will run the EVAP monitor when the following enable criteria are met. Typical enable criteria include:

- Cold start
- BARO greater than 70 kPa (20.7 in. Hg or 10.2 psi)
- IAT between 39° and 86°F at engine start-up
- ECT between 39° and 86°F at engine start-up
- ECT and IAT within 39°F of each other at engine start-up
- Fuel level within 15 to 85%
- TP sensor between 9 and 35%

Running the EVAP Monitor

There are four tests which are performed during a typical GM EVAP monitor. A DTC is assigned to each test.

1. **Weak Vacuum Test (P0440—large leak).** This test identifies gross leaks. During the monitor, the vent solenoid is closed and the purge solenoid is duty cycled. The FTP should indicate a vacuum of approximately 6 to 10 in. H_2O.

2. **Small Leak Test (P0442—small leak).** After the large leak test passes, the PCM checks for a small leak by keeping the vent solenoid closed and closing the purge solenoid. The system is now sealed. The PCM measures the change in FTP voltage over time.

3. **Excess Vacuum Test (P0446).** This test checks for vent path restrictions. With the vent solenoid open and purge commanded, the PCM should not see excessive vacuum in the EVAP system. Typical EVAP system vacuum with the vent solenoid open is about 5 to 6 in. H_2O.

4. **Purge Solenoid Leak Test (P1442).** With the purge solenoid closed and vent solenoid closed, no vacuum should be present in the system. If there is vacuum present, the purge solenoid may be leaking.

FORD ENHANCED EVAP

The PCM will run the EVAP monitor when the following enable criteria are met.

- Cold start
- Inlet air temperature between 40° and 100°F
- 6-to-8 hour engine soak timer must expire

A PCM reset (without turning the ignition off) will bypass the 6-to-8 hour engine soak timer.

- Altitude less than 8000 feet
- Fuel level within 15 to 85% (40% min for 0.020 in. leak)
- 40 to 65 mph steady cruise
- 30-minute time limit for the monitor to run

The PCM will duty cycle the VMV to 75%. The FTP voltage should drop down in the 1.2 to 1.6 volt range. During the small leak check (0.040 inch), the FTP voltage should not increase more than 0.4 volts.

Typical Ford Strategy

Phase 0—Initial Vacuum Pulldown. First, the canister vent solenoid is closed to seal the entire EVAP system, then the VMV is opened to pull a 7 in. H_2O vacuum. If the initial vacuum could not be achieved, a large system leak is indicated (P0455). This could be caused by a fuel cap that was not installed properly, a large hole, an overfilled fuel tank, disconnected/kinked vapor lines, a canister vent solenoid that is stuck-open, or a VMV that is stuck closed. If the initial vacuum is excessive, a vacuum malfunction is indicated (P1450). This could be caused by kinked vapor lines or a stuck-open VMV. If a P0455 or P1450 code is generated, the EVAP test does not continue with subsequent phases of the small leak check, phases 1–4.

Phase 1—Vacuum Stabilization. If the target vacuum is achieved, the VMV is closed and vacuum is allowed to stabilize. This initial vacuum level is recorded.

Phase 2—Vacuum Hold and Decay. Next, the vacuum is held for a calibrated time and the vacuum level is again recorded at the end of this time period. The starting and ending vacuum levels are checked to determine if the change in vacuum exceeds the vacuum bleed-up criteria. Fuel level input is used to adjust the vacuum bleed-up criteria for the appropriate fuel tank vapor volume. Steady-state conditions must be maintained throughout this bleed-up portion of the test. The monitor will abort if there is an excessive change in load, fuel tank pressure, or fuel level input since these are all indicators of impending or actual fuel slosh. If the monitor aborts, it will attempt to run again (up to 8 or 10 times). If the vacuum bleed-up criteria is not exceeded, the small leak test is considered a pass. If the vacuum bleed-up criteria is exceeded on three successive monitoring events, a 0.040 in. diameter leak is likely and a final vapor generation check is done to verify the leak, phases 3–4. Excessive vapor generation can cause a false MIL.

Phase 3—Vacuum Release. The vapor generation check is done by releasing any vacuum, then closing the VMV, waiting for a period of time, and determining if tank pressure remains low or if it is rising due to excessive vapor generation.

Phase 4—Vapor Generation. If the pressure rise due to vapor generation is below the threshold limit for absolute pressure and change in pressure, a P0442 DTC is stored.

FIGURE 19-14 The fuel level must be above 15% and below 85% before the EVAP monitor will run on most vehicles.

DAIMLERCHRYSLER LEAK DETECTION PUMP SYSTEM

Many DaimlerChrysler vehicles use a **leak detection pump (LDP)** as part of the evaporative control system diagnosis equipment. See Figure 19-15. The system works as follows:

- The purge solenoid is normally closed. The conventional purge solenoid is ground-side controlled by the PCM. The proportional purge solenoid is feed-side controlled by the PCM. The PCM will energize the solenoid to purge fuel vapors from the canister and to lower tank pressure.
- The vent valve in the LDP is normally open. Filtered fresh air is drawn through the LDP to the canister.

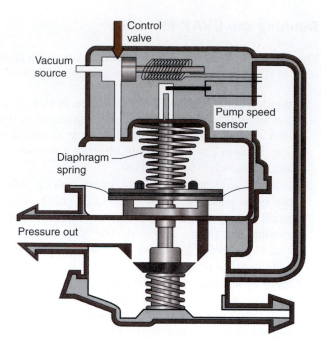

FIGURE 19-15 A leak detection pump (LDP) used on some DaimlerChrysler vehicles to pressurize (slightly) the fuel system to check for leaks.

- The solenoid on the LDP normally blocks manifold vacuum from the engine. When grounded by the PCM, manifold vacuum is allowed to pass through the solenoid and into the upper diaphragm chamber. Vacuum will pull the diaphragm back against spring pressure (rated at 7.5 in. H_2O). As the diaphragm is pulled up, fresh air is drawn into the pressure side of the LDP diaphragm through the inlet reed valve. This is the LDP intake stroke. When the diaphragm is pulled up against spring pressure, the normally closed contacts of the LDP reed switch open. The LDP reed switch is the only input regarding EVAP system pressure for the PCM. With the switch contacts open, the PCM knows the diaphragm has been drawn upwards. When the LDP solenoid is de-energized by the PCM, fresh air is allowed to enter the top side of the diaphragm chamber displacing the vacuum that was there. Spring pressure (7.5 in. H_2O) forces the air in the lower diaphragm chamber out through the outlet (exhaust) reed valve. This is the LDP exhaust stroke. The LDP switch contacts close once the diaphragm returns to its original at-rest position.
- The PCM checks for EVAP leaks by first de-energizing the purge solenoid (normally closed), and then rapidly cycling the LDP solenoid and watching the LDP switch. Once pressure (7.5 in. H_2O) is built up in the system, the diaphragm will be seated upwards against spring pressure. The PCM knows this since it is mon-

itoring the LDP switch. So, the PCM compares LDP switch position against LDP solenoid cycling time to determine if leakage is present.

- When manually checking for leaks (for example, smoke machine), the vent valve must be closed. Closing of the vent valve requires that the LDP solenoid be energized and that a vacuum source be applied to the LDP solenoid. This will enable the LDP diaphragm to stroke upwards, thereby allowing the vent valve spring to close the vent valve.

Pump Period

The time between LDP solenoid off and LDP switch close is called the pump period. This time period is inversely proportional to the size of the leak. The shorter the pump period, the larger the leak. The longer the pump period, the smaller the leak.

EVAP large leak (>0.080): less than 0.9 seconds
EVAP medium leak (0.040 to 0.080): 0.9 to 1.2 seconds
EVAP small leak (0.020 to 0.040): 1.2 to 6 seconds

EVAP SYSTEM-RELATED DIAGNOSTIC TROUBLE CODES (DTCs)

Diagnostic Trouble Code	Description	Possible Causes
P0440	Evaporative system fault	• Loose gas cap • Defective EVAP vent • Cracked charcoal canister • EVAP vent or purge vapor line problems
P0442	Small leak detected	• Loose gas cap • Defective EVAP vent or purge solenoid • EVAP vent or purge line problems
P0446	EVAP canister vent blocked	• EVAP vent or purge solenoid electrical problems • Restricted EVAP canister vent line

SUMMARY

1. The purpose of the evaporative emission (EVAP) control system is to reduce the release of volatile organic compounds (VOC) into the atmosphere.
2. A carbon (charcoal) canister is used to trap and hold gasoline vapors until they can be purged and run into the engine to be burned.
3. Pressures inside the EVAP system are low and are measured in inches of water (1 psi = 28 in. H_2O).
4. A typical EVAP system uses a canister purge valve, which is normally closed, and a canister vent valve, which is normally open.
5. OBD-II regulation requires that the evaporative emission control system be checked for leakage and proper purge flow rates.
6. External leaks can best be located by pressurizing the fuel system with low-pressure smoke.

REVIEW QUESTIONS

1. What components are used in a typical evaporative emission control system?
2. How does the computer control the purging of the vapor canister?
3. What is the difference between an enhanced and nonenhanced evaporative control system?
4. How is a flow gauge used to diagnose the evaporative emission control system?
5. What are the parameters (enable criteria) that must be met for the evaporative system monitor to run?

ASE CERTIFICATION-TYPE QUESTIONS

1. What is the substance used in a vapor canister to absorb volatile organic compounds?
   a. Desiccant
   b. Organic absorber
   c. Pleated paper
   d. Carbon

2. Which valve(s) is (are) normally closed?
   a. Canister purge valve
   b. Canister vent valve
   c. Both canister purge and canister vent valve
   d. Neither canister purge nor canister vent valve

3. All of the following can increase the pressure in the evaporative emission control system *except* _____.
   a. Fuel temperature
   b. Returned fuel from the fuel-injection system
   c. Inlet fuel to the fuel pump
   d. RVP of the fuel

4. Evaporative emission control systems operate on low pressure measured in inches of water (in. H_2O). One psi is equal to how many inches of water?
   a. 1
   b. 10
   c. 18
   d. 28

5. Inadequate purge flow rate will trigger which DTC?
   a. P0440
   b. P0441
   c. P0300
   d. P0301

6. Two technicians are discussing I/M 240 state emission testing. Technician A says that it is best to arrive at the test center with a low level of fuel instead of a high level of fuel to help pass the EVAP pressure test. Technician B says that a leaking gas cap can cause a failure of the EVAP test. Which technician is correct?
   a. Technician A only
   b. Technician B only
   c. Both Technicians A and B
   d. Neither Technician A nor B

7. A flow gauge is being used to check for proper canister pump flow rate. What is the specification used by most emission test sites?
   a. 10 liters per minute
   b. 5 liters per minute
   c. 1 liter in 4 minutes
   d. 0.5 liter per hour

8. Before an evaporative emission monitor will run, the fuel level must be where?
   a. At least 75% full
   b. Over 25%
   c. Between 15 and 85%
   d. The level of the fuel in the tank is not needed to run the monitor test

9. Technician A says that low pressure smoke installed in the fuel system can be used to check for leaks. Technician B says that nitrogen under low pressure can be installed in the fuel system to check for leaks. Which technician is correct?
   a. Technician A only
   b. Technician B only
   c. Both Technicians A and B
   d. Neither Technician A nor B

10. A small leak is detected by the evaporative emission control system monitor that could be caused by a loose gas cap. Which DTC will likely be set?
    a. P0440
    b. P0442
    c. P0446
    d. Either P0440 or P0442

◀ Chapter 20 ▶

FUEL-INJECTION COMPONENTS AND OPERATION

OBJECTIVES

After studying Chapter 20, the reader should be able to:

1. Prepare for ASE Engine Performance (A8) certification test content area "C" (Fuel, Air Induction, and Exhaust Systems Diagnosis and Repair).
2. Describe how a port fuel-injection system works.
3. Discuss the purpose and function of the fuel-pressure regulator.
4. List the types of fuel injection.

ELECTRONIC FUEL-INJECTION OPERATION

Electronic fuel-injection systems use the computer to control the operation of fuel injectors and other functions based on information sent to the computer from the various sensors. Most electronic fuel-injection systems share the following:

1. Electric fuel pump (usually located inside the fuel tank)
2. Fuel-pump relay (usually controlled by the computer)
3. Fuel-pressure regulator (mechanically operated spring-loaded rubber diaphragm maintains proper fuel pressure)
4. Fuel-injector nozzle or nozzles

See Figure 20-1. Most electronic fuel-injection systems use the computer to control these aspects of their operation:

1. **Pulsing the fuel injectors on and off.** The longer the injectors are held open, the greater the amount of fuel injected into the cylinder.
2. **Operating the fuel pump relay circuit.** The computer usually controls the operation of the electric fuel pump located inside (or near) the fuel tank. The computer uses signals from the ignition switch and RPM signals from the ignition module or system to energize the fuel-pump relay circuit.

NOTE: This is a safety feature, because if the engine stalls and the tachometer (engine speed) signal is lost, the computer will shut off (de-energize) the fuel pump relay and stop the fuel pump.

Computer-controlled fuel-injection systems are normally reliable systems if the proper service procedures are followed. Fuel-injection systems use the gasoline flowing through the injectors to lubricate and cool the injector electrical windings and pintle valves.

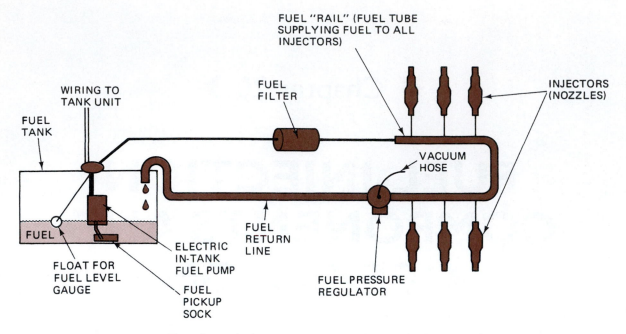

FIGURE 20-1 Typical port fuel-injection system, indicating the location of various components. Notice that the fuel-pressure regulator is located on the fuel *return* side of the system. The computer does not control fuel pressure, but does control the operation of the electric fuel pump (on most systems) and the pulsing on and off of the injectors.

◀ **TECH TIP** ▶

"TWO MUST DO'S"

For long service life of the fuel system always do the following:

1. Avoid operating the vehicle on a near-empty tank of fuel. The water or alcohol becomes more concentrated when the fuel level is low. Dirt that settles near the bottom of the fuel tank can be drawn through the fuel system and cause damage to the pump and injector nozzles.
2. Replace the fuel filter at regular service intervals.

NOTE: The fuel does not actually make contact with the electrical windings because the injectors have O-rings at the top and bottom of the winding spool to keep fuel out.

There are two types of electronic fuel-injection systems:

- **Throttle-body-injection (TBI)** type. A TBI system delivers fuel from a nozzle(s) into the air above the throttle plate. See Figure 20-2.
- **Port fuel-injection** type. A port fuel-injection design uses a nozzle for each cylinder and the fuel is squirted into the intake manifold about 2 to 3 inches (70 to 100 mm) from the intake valve. See Figure 20-3.

SPEED DENSITY FUEL-INJECTION SYSTEMS

Fuel-injection computer systems require a method for measuring the amount of air the engine is breathing in, in order to match the correct fuel delivery. There are two basic methods used:

1. Speed density
2. Mass airflow

The speed density method does not require an air quantity sensor, but rather calculates the amount of fuel required by the engine. The computer uses information from sensors such as the MAP and TP to calculate the needed amount of fuel.

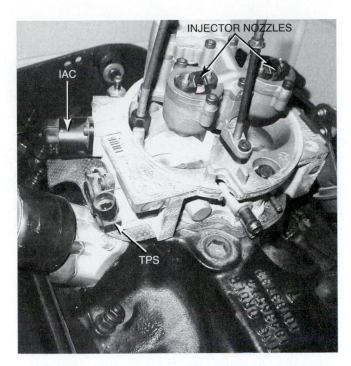

FIGURE 20-2 A dual-nozzle TBI unit on a Chevrolet 4.3-L V-6 engine.

- **MAP sensor.** The value of the intake (inlet) manifold pressure (vacuum) is a direct indication of engine load.
- **TP sensor.** The position of the throttle plate and its rate of change are used as part of the equation to calculate the proper amount of fuel to inject.

- **Temperature sensors.** Both engine coolant temperature (ECT) and intake air temperature (IAT) are used to calculate the density of the air and the need of the engine for fuel. A cold engine (low coolant temperature) requires a richer air-fuel mixture than a warm engine.

On speed-density systems, the computer calculates the amount of air in each cylinder by using manifold pressure and engine RPM. The amount of air in each cylinder is the major factor in determining the amount of fuel needed. Other sensors provide information to modify the fuel requirements. The formula used to determine the injector pulse width (PW) in milliseconds (ms) is:

$$\text{Injector pulse width} = \frac{\text{MAP}}{\text{BARO}} \times \frac{\text{RPM}}{\text{maximum RPM}}$$

The formula is modified by values from other sensors, including:

- Throttle position (TP)
- Engine coolant temperature (ECT)
- Intake air temperature (IAT)
- Oxygen sensor voltage (O2S)
- Adaptive memory

A fuel injector delivers atomized fuel into the airstream where it is instantly vaporized. All throttle-body (TB) fuel-injection systems and many multipoint (port) injection systems use the speed-density method of fuel calculation.

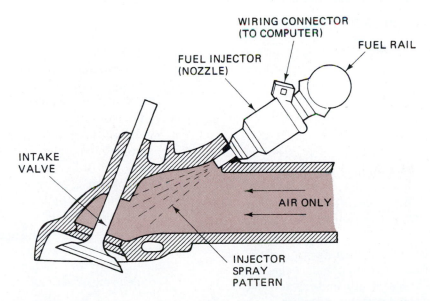

FIGURE 20-3 A typical port fuel-injection system squirts fuel into the low pressure (vacuum) of the intake manifold, about 3 in. (70 to 100 mm) from the intake valve.

MASS AIR FLOW FUEL-INJECTION SYSTEMS

The formula used by fuel-injection systems that use a mass air flow (MAF) sensor to calculate the injection base pulse width is:

Injector pulse width = airflow/RPM

The formula is modified by other sensor values such as:

- Throttle position
- Engine coolant temperature
- Barometric pressure
- Adaptive memory

NOTE: Many 4-cylinder engines do not use a MAF sensor because, due to the time interval between intake events, some reverse airflow can occur in the intake manifold. The MAF sensor would "read" this flow of air as being additional air entering the engine, giving the PCM incorrect airflow information. Therefore, most 4-cylinder engines use the speed density method of fuel control.

THROTTLE-BODY INJECTION

The computer controls injector pulses in one of two ways:

- Synchronized
- Nonsynchronized

If the system uses a synchronized mode, the injector pulses once for each distributor reference pulse. In some vehicles, when dual injectors are used in a synchronized system, the injectors pulse alternately. In a nonsynchronized system, the injectors are pulsed once during a given period (which varies according to calibration) completely independent of distributor reference pulses.

The injector always opens the same distance, and the fuel pressure is maintained at a controlled value by the pressure regulator. The regulators used on throttle-body injection systems are not connected to a vacuum like many port fuel-injection systems. The strength of the spring inside the regulator determines at what pressure the valve is unseated, sending the fuel back to the tank and lowering the pressure. See Figure 20-4. The amount of fuel delivered by the injector depends on the amount of time (on-time) that the nozzle is open. This is the injector pulse width—the on-time in milliseconds that the nozzle is open.

◄ FREQUENTLY ASKED QUESTION ►

HOW DO THE SENSORS AFFECT THE PULSE WIDTH?

The base pulse width of a fuel-injection system is primarily determined by the value of the MAF or MAP sensor and engine speed (RPM). However, the PCM relies on the input from many other sensors to modify the base pulse width as needed. For example,

- **TP Sensor**—This sensor causes the PCM to command up to 500% (5 times) the base pulse width if the accelerator pedal is depressed rapidly to the floor. It can also reduce the pulse width by about 70% if the throttle is rapidly closed.
- **ECT**—The value of this sensor determines the temperature of the engine coolant, helps determine the base pulse width, and can account for up to 60% of the determining factors.

- **BARO**—The BARO sensor compensates for altitude and adds up to about 10% under high-pressure conditions and subtracts as much as 50% from the base pulse width at high altitudes.
- **IAT**—The intake air temperature is used to modify the base pulse width based on the temperature of the air entering the engine. It is usually capable of adding as much as 20% if very cold air is entering the engine or reduce the pulse width by up to 20% if very hot air is entering the engine.
- **O2S**—This is one of the main modifiers to the base pulse width and can add or subtract up to about 20 to 25% or more, depending on the oxygen sensor activity.

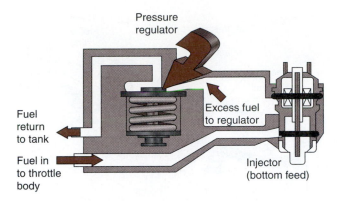

FIGURE 20-4   The tension of the spring in the fuel-pressure regulator determines the operating pressure on a throttle-body fuel-injection unit.

The PCM commands a variety of pulse widths to supply the amount of fuel that an engine needs at any specific moment.

- A long pulse width delivers more fuel.
- A short pulse width delivers less fuel.

◄ GURU TIP ►

GM dual TBI injectors should measure 2.2 ohms at 150°F.

◄ DIAGNOSTIC STORY ►

THE RICH-RUNNING CHRYSLER

A 4-cylinder Chrysler was running so rich that black smoke poured from the exhaust all the time. It was equipped with a TBI-type fuel-injector system, and the fuel pressure was fixed at about 38 psi—the same as the maximum fuel-pump pressure. A replacement fuel-pressure regulator did not correct the higher-than-normal fuel pressure. The fuel return line was also carefully inspected for a kink or other obstruction that may have caused excessive fuel pressure. The technician discovered the root cause of the problem to be a stuck shuttle valve, a part of many Chrysler brand TBI systems used to close off the fuel return to the tank. This keeps the pressure high to permit faster restarts when the engine is hot. See Figure 20-5. The shuttle valve simply slides downward on an incline to close off the fuel regulator return passage. The technician removed the shuttle valve and cleaned it. Vehicle operation then returned to normal and both the technician and the customer were satisfied that a low-cost and fast solution was found.

(a)

(b)

FIGURE 20-5   (a) Removing the fuel-pressure regulator from a Chrysler brand TBI unit. (b) A shuttle valve (if equipped) is located in this fuel return passage.

PORT FUEL INJECTION

The advantages of the port fuel-injection design also are related to characteristics of intake manifolds:

- Fuel distribution is equal to all cylinders because each cylinder has its own injector. See Figure 20-6.
- The fuel is injected almost directly into the combustion chamber, so there is no chance for it to condense on the walls of a cold intake manifold.
- Because the manifold does not have to carry fuel to properly position a TBI unit, it can be shaped and sized to tune the intake airflow to achieve specific engine performance characteristics.

An EFI injector is simply a specialized solenoid. See Figure 20-7. It has an armature winding to create a magnetic field, and a needle (pintle), a disc, or a ball valve. A spring holds the needle, disc, or ball closed against the valve seat, and when energized, the armature winding pulls open the valve when it receives a current pulse from the powertrain control module (PCM). When the solenoid is energized, it unseats the valve to inject fuel.

Electronic fuel-injection systems use a solenoid-operated injector to spray atomized fuel in timed pulses into the manifold or near the intake valve. See Figure 20-8. Injectors may be sequenced and fired in one of several ways, but their pulse width is determined and controlled by the engine computer.

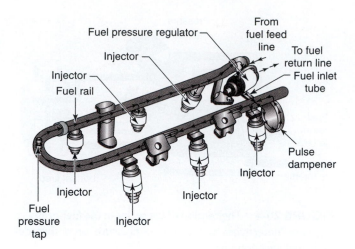

FIGURE 20-6 The injectors receive fuel and are supported by the fuel rail.

Port systems have an injector for each cylinder, but they do not all fire the injectors in the same way. Domestic systems use one of three ways to trigger the injectors:

- Grouped double-fire
- Simultaneous double-fire
- Sequential

Grouped Double-Fire

This system divides the injectors into two equalized groups. The groups fire alternately; each group fires once

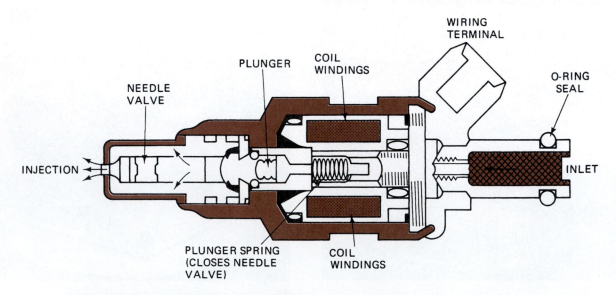

FIGURE 20-7 Cross-section of a typical port fuel-injection nozzle assembly. These injectors are serviced as an assembly only; no part replacement or service is possible except for replacement of external O-ring seals.

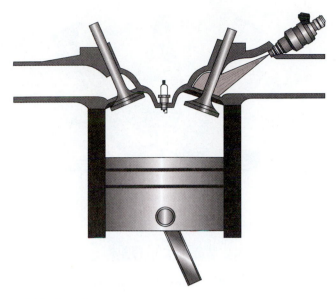

FIGURE 20-8 Port fuel injectors spray atomized fuel into the intake manifold about 3 inches (75 mm) from the intake valve.

each crankshaft revolution, or twice per 4-stroke cycle. The fuel injected remains near the intake valve and enters the engine when the valve opens. This method of pulsing injectors in groups is sometimes called **gang fired.**

Simultaneous Double-Fire

This design fires all of the injectors at the same time once every engine revolution: two pulses per 4-stroke cycle. Many port fuel-injection systems on 4-cylinder engines use this pattern of injector firing. It is easier for engineers to program this system and it can make relatively quick adjustments in the air-fuel ratio, but it still requires the intake charge to wait in the manifold for varying lengths of time.

Sequential

Sequential firing of the injectors according to engine firing order is the most accurate and desirable method of regulating port fuel injection. However, it is also the most complex and expensive to design and manufacture. In this system, the injectors are timed and pulsed individually, much like the spark plugs are sequentially operated in firing order of the engine. This system is often called **sequential fuel injection** or **SFI.** Each cylinder receives one charge every two crankshaft revolutions, just before the intake valve opens. This means that the mixture is never static in the intake manifold and mixture adjustments can be made almost instanta-

neously between the firing of one injector and the next. A camshaft position sensor (CmP) signal or a special distributor reference pulse informs the PCM when the No. 1 cylinder is on its compression stroke. If the sensor fails or the reference pulse is interrupted, some injection systems shut down, while others revert to pulsing the injectors simultaneously.

◄ GURU TIP ►

Shorted GM MULTECS injectors may cause a hesitation along with low O2S voltage.

◄ FREQUENTLY ASKED ► QUESTION

HOW CAN IT BE DETERMINED IF THE INJECTION SYSTEM IS SEQUENTIAL?

Look at the color of the wires at the injectors. If a sequentially fired injector is used, then one wire color (the pulse wire) will be a different color for each injector. The other wire is usually the same color because all injectors receive voltage from some source. If a group- or batch-fired injection system is being used, then the wire colors will be the same for the injectors that are group fired. For example, a V-6 group-fired engine will have three injectors with a pink and blue wire (power and pulse) and the other three will have pink and green wires.

The major advantage of using port injection instead of the simpler throttle-body injection is that the intake manifolds on port fuel-injected engines only contain air, not a mixture of air and fuel. This allows the engine design engineer the opportunity to design long, "tuned" intake-manifold runners that help the engine produce increased torque at low engine speeds. See Figure 20-9.

◄ GURU TIP ►

Do you detect a surge on a GM 3800 V-6 after the transmission shifts to high gear? Suspect the injectors are lean.

FIGURE 20-9 A port fuel-injected engine that is equipped with long-tuned intake manifold runners.

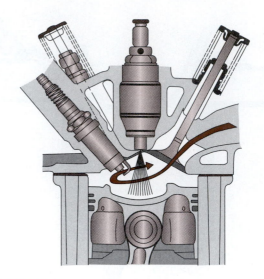

FIGURE 20-10 A gasoline direct-ignition system.

NOTE: Some port fuel-injection systems used on engines with four or more valves per cylinder may use two injectors per cylinder. One injector is used all the time, and the second injector is operated by the computer when high engine speed and high-load conditions are detected by the computer. Typically, the second injector injects fuel into the high-speed intake ports of the manifold. This system permits good low-speed power and throttle responses as well as superior high-speed power.

◀ TECH TIP ▶

NO SPARK, NO SQUIRT

Most electronic fuel-injection computer systems use the ignition primary (pickup coil or crank sensor) pulse as the trigger for when to inject (squirt) fuel from the injectors (nozzles). If this signal were not present, no fuel would be injected. Because this pulse is also necessary to trigger the module to create a spark from the coil, it can be said that "no spark" could also mean "no squirt." Therefore, if the cause of a no-start condition is observed to be a lack of fuel injection, do not start testing or replacing fuel-system components until the ignition system is checked for proper operation.

GASOLINE DIRECT INJECTION

Gasoline direct injection (GDI) systems inject fuel directly into the combustion chamber just before the spark. The fuel, under very high pressure, is injected in a fine mist into the closely packed air molecules. When ignition occurs, the fuel is moving under pressure throughout the cylinder. The flame front moves quickly through the compressed combustible-swirling mixture. Gasoline direct injection systems, like diesel systems, require very high fuel pressures to overcome the combustion chamber pressures during injection. See Figure 20-10.

FUEL-PRESSURE REGULATOR

The pressure regulator and fuel pump work together to maintain the required pressure drop at the injector tips. The fuel-pressure regulator typically consists of a spring-loaded, diaphragm-operated valve in a metal housing.

Fuel-pressure regulators on fuel-return-type fuel-injection systems are installed on the return (downstream) side of the injectors at the end of the fuel rail, or are built into or mounted upon the throttle-body housing. Downstream regulation minimizes fuel-pressure pulsations caused by pressure drop across the injectors as the nozzles open. It also ensures positive fuel pressure at the injectors at all times and holds residual pressure in the lines when the engine is off. On mechanical returnless systems, the regulator is located back at the tank with the fuel filter.

In order for excess fuel (about 80 to 90% of the fuel delivered) to return to the tank, fuel pressure must overcome spring pressure on the spring-loaded diaphragm to uncover the return line to the tank. This happens when system pressure exceeds operating requirements. With TBI, the regulator is close to the injector tip, so the regulator senses essentially the same air pressure as the injector.

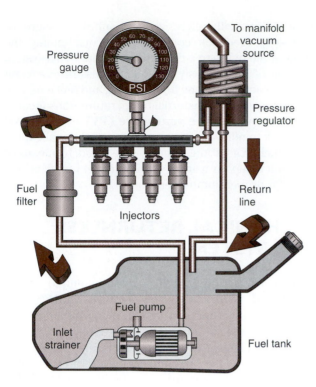

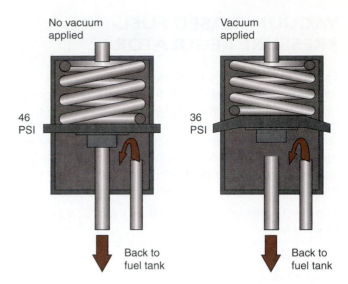

FIGURE 20-12 A typical fuel-pressure regulator that has a spring that exerts 46 pounds of force against the fuel. If 20 inches of vacuum are applied above the spring, the vacuum reduces the force exerted by the spring on the fuel, allowing the fuel to return to the tank at a lower pressure.

FIGURE 20-11 A typical port fuel-injected system showing a vacuum-controlled fuel-pressure regulator.

The pressure regulator used in a port fuel-injection system has an intake manifold vacuum line connection on the regulator vacuum chamber. This allows fuel pressure to be modulated by a combination of spring pressure and manifold vacuum acting on the diaphragm. See Figures 20-11 and 20-12.

In both TBI and port systems, the regulator shuts off the return line when the fuel pump is not running. This maintains pressure at the injectors for easy restarting after hot soak as well as reducing vapor lock.

NOTE: Some General Motors throttle-body units do not hold pressure and are called **nonchecking.**

Port fuel-injection systems generally operate with pressures at the injector of about 30 to 55 psi (207 to 379 kPa), while TBI systems work with injector pressures of about 10 to 20 psi (69 to 138 kPa). The difference in system pressures results from the difference in how the systems operate. Since injectors in a TBI system inject the fuel into the airflow at the manifold inlet (above the throttle), there is more time for atomization in the manifold before the air-fuel charge reaches the intake valve. This allows TBI injectors to work at lower pressures than injectors used in a port system.

◀ **TECH TIP** ▶

DON'T FORGET THE REGULATOR

Some fuel-pressure regulators contain a 10-micron filter. If this filter becomes clogged, a lack of fuel flow would result. See Figure 20-13.

FIGURE 20-13 A lack of fuel flow could be due to a restricted fuel-pressure regulator.

VACUUM-BIASED FUEL-PRESSURE REGULATOR

The primary reason why many port fuel-injected systems use a vacuum-controlled fuel-pressure regulator is to ensure that there is a constant pressure drop across the injectors. In a throttle-body fuel-injection system, the injector squirts into the atmospheric pressure regardless of the load on the engine. In a port fuel-injected engine, however, the pressure inside the intake manifold changes as the load on the engine increases.

Engine Operating Condition	Intake Manifold Vacuum	Fuel Pressure
Idle or cruise	High	Lower
Heavy load	Low	Higher

The computer can best calculate injector pulse width based on all sensors if the pressure drop across the injector is the same under all operating conditions. A vacuum-controlled fuel-pressure regulator allows the equal pressure drop by reducing the force exerted by the regulator spring at high vacuum (low load condition), yet allowing the full force of the regulator spring to be exerted when the vacuum is low (high engine load condition).

ELECTRONIC RETURNLESS FUEL SYSTEM

This system is unique because it does not use a mechanical valve to regulate rail pressure. Fuel pressure at the rail is sensed by a pressure transducer, which sends a low-level signal to a controller. The controller contains logic to calculate a signal to the pump power driver. The power driver contains a high-current transistor that controls the pump speed using pulse-width modulation (PWM). This system is called the **electronic returnless fuel system (ERFS)**. See Figure 20-14. This transducer can be differentially referenced to manifold pressure for closed-loop feedback correcting and maintaining the output of the pump to a desired rail setting. This system is capable of continuously varying rail pressure as a result of engine vacuum, engine fuel demand, and fuel temperature (as sensed by an external temperature transducer, if necessary). A **pressure vent valve (PVV)** is employed at the tank to relieve overpressure due to thermal expansion of fuel. In addition, a supply side bleed, by means of an in-tank reservoir using a supply side jet pump, is necessary for proper pump operation.

MECHANICAL RETURNLESS FUEL SYSTEM

The first production returnless systems employed the **mechanical returnless fuel system (MRFS)** approach. This system has a bypass regulator to control rail pressure that is located in close proximity to the fuel tank. Fuel is sent by the in-tank pump to a chassis-mounted inline filter with excess fuel returning to the tank through a short return line. See Figure 20-15. The inline filter may be mounted directly to the tank, thereby eliminating the shortened return line. Supply pressure is regulated on the downstream side of the inline filter to accommodate changing restrictions throughout the filter's service life. This system is limited to constant rail pressure (*CRP) system calibrations, whereas with ERFS, the pressure transducer can be referenced to atmospheric pressure for CRP systems or differentially referenced to intake manifold pressure for constant differential injector pressure (**CIP) systems.

NOTE: *CRP is referenced to atmospheric pressure, has lower operating pressure, and is desirable for calibrations using speed/air density sensing.
  **CIP is referenced to manifold pressure, varies rail pressure, and is desirable in engines that use mass airflow sensing.

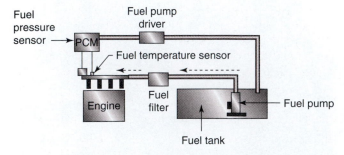

FIGURE 20-14 The fuel-pressure sensor and fuel-temperature sensor are often constructed together in one assembly to help give the PCM the needed data to control the fuel pump speed.

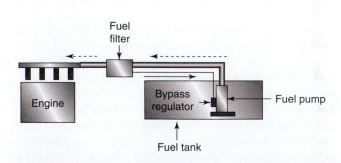

FIGURE 20-15 A mechanical returnless fuel system. The bypass regulator in the fuel tank controls fuel-line pressure.

DEMAND DELIVERY SYSTEM (DDS)

Given the experience with both ERFS and MRFS, a need was recognized to develop new returnless technologies that could combine the speed control and constant injector pressure attributes of ERFS together with the cost savings, simplicity, and reliability of MRFS. This new technology also needed to address pulsation damping/hammering and fuel transient response. Therefore, the **demand delivery system (DDS)** technology was developed. A different form of demand pressure regulator has been applied to the fuel rail. It mounts at the head or port entry and regulates the pressure downstream at the injectors by admitting the precise quantity of fuel into the rail as consumed by the engine. Having demand regulation at the rail improves pressure response to flow transients and provides rail pulsation damping. A fuel pump and a low-cost, high-performance bypass regulator are used within the appropriate fuel sender. See Figure 20-16. They supply a pressure somewhat higher than the required rail set pressure to accommodate dynamic line and filter pressure losses. Electronic pump speed control is accomplished using a smart regulator as an integral flow sensor. A **pressure control valve (PCV)** may also be used and can readily reconfigure an existing design fuel sender into a returnless sender.

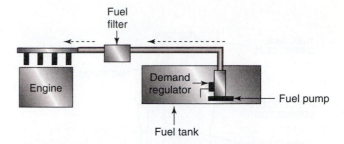

FIGURE 20-16 A demand delivery system uses an in-tank regulator.

FIGURE 20-17 A rectangular-shaped fuel rail is used to help dampen fuel system pulsations and noise caused by the injector opening and closing.

◀ FREQUENTLY ASKED ▶ QUESTION

WHY ARE SOME FUEL RAILS RECTANGULAR SHAPED?

A port fuel-injection system uses a pipe or tubes to deliver fuel from the fuel line to the intended fuel injectors. This pipe or tube is called the **fuel rail.** Some vehicle manufacturers construct the fuel rail in a rectangular cross-section. See Figure 20-17. The sides of the fuel rail are able to move in and out slightly, thereby acting as a fuel pulsator evening out the pressure pulses created by the opening and closing of the injectors to reduce underhood noise. A round cross-section fuel rail is not able to deform and, as a result, some manufacturers have had to use a separate dampener.

FUEL INJECTORS

EFI systems use solenoid-operated injectors. See Figure 20-18. This electromagnetic device contains an armature and a spring-loaded needle valve or ball valve assembly. When the computer energizes the solenoid, voltage is applied to the solenoid coil until the current reaches a specified level. This permits a quick pull-in of the armature during turn-on. The armature is pulled off of its seat against spring force, allowing fuel to flow through the inlet filter screen to the spray nozzle, where it is sprayed in a pattern that varies with application. See Figure 20-19. The injector opens the same amount each time it is energized, so the amount of fuel injected depends on the length of time the injector remains open.

By angling the director hole plates, the injector sprays fuel more directly at the intake valves, which further atomizes and vaporizes the fuel before it enters the combustion chamber.

PFI injectors typically are a top-feed design in which fuel enters the top of the injector and passes through its entire length to keep it cool before being injected.

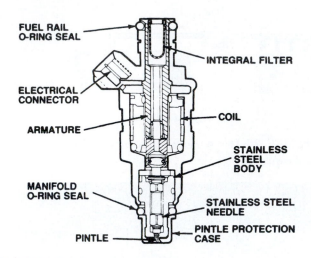

FIGURE 20-18 A multiport fuel injector. Notice that the fuel flows straight through and does not come in contact with the coil windings.

FIGURE 20-19 Each of the eight injectors shown are producing a correct spray pattern for the applications. While all throttle-body injectors spray a conical pattern, most port fuel injectors do not.

Ford introduced two basic designs of deposit-resistant injectors on some engines. The design, manufactured by Bosch, uses a four-hole director/metering plate similar to that used by the Rochester Multec injectors. The design manufactured by Nippondenso uses an internal upstream orifice in the adjusting tube. It also has a redesigned pintle/seat containing a wider tip opening that tolerates deposit buildup without affecting injector performance.

◀ GURU TIP ▶

All injectors have a final filter (approximately 10 microns) that will restrict over time!

◀ FREQUENTLY ASKED QUESTION ▶

HOW CAN THE PROPER INJECTION SIZE BE DETERMINED?

Most people want to increase the output of fuel to increase engine performance. Injector sizing can sometimes be a challenge, especially if the size of injector is not known. In most cases, manufacturers publish the rating of injectors, in pounds of fuel per hour (lb/hr). The rate is figured with the injector held open at 3 bars (43.5 psi). An important consideration is that larger flow injectors have a higher minimum flow rating. Here is a formula to calculate injector sizing when changing the mechanical characteristics of an engine.

Flow rate = HP × BSFC/# of cylinders × maximum duty cycle (% of or time of the injection)

- **HP** is the projected horsepower. Be realistic!
- **BSFC** is brake-specific fuel consumption in pounds per horsepower-hour. Calculated val-

ues are used for this, 0.4 to 0.8 lb. In most cases, start on the low side for naturally aspirated engines and the high side for engines with forced induction.

- **# of cylinders** is actually the number of injectors being used.
- **Maximum duty cycle** is considered at 0.8 (80%). Above this, the injector may overheat, lose consistency, or not work at all.

For example:

$$5.7 \text{ liter V-8} \frac{240 \text{ HP} \times 0.65}{8 \text{ cylinders} \times 0.8}$$

24.37 lb/hr injectors required

CENTRAL PORT INJECTION

A cross between port fuel injection and throttle-body injection, CPI was introduced in the early 1990s by General Motors. The CPI assembly consists of a single fuel injector, a pressure regulator, and six poppet nozzle assemblies with nozzle tubes. See Figure 20-20. The CSFI system has six injectors in place of the CPI's one.

When the injector is energized, its armature lifts off of the six fuel tube seats and pressurized fuel flows through the nozzle tubes to each poppet nozzle. The increased pressure causes each poppet nozzle ball to also lift from its seat, allowing fuel to flow from the nozzle. This hybrid injection system combines the single injector of a TBI system with the equalized fuel distribution of a PFI system. It eliminates the individual fuel rail while allowing more efficient manifold tuning than is otherwise possible with a TBI system. Newer versions use six individual solenoids to fire one for each cylinder. See Figure 20-21.

FUEL-INJECTION MODES OF OPERATION

All fuel-injection systems are designed to supply the correct amount of fuel under a wide range of engine operating conditions. These modes of operation include:

Starting (cranking)	Acceleration enrichment
Clear flood	Deceleration enleanment
Idle (run)	Fuel shutoff

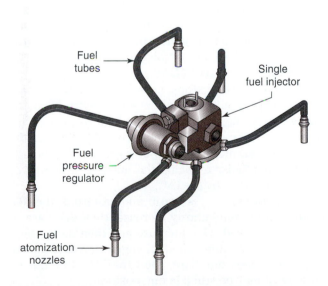

FIGURE 20-20   A central port fuel-injection system.

Fuel tubes
Single fuel injector
Fuel pressure regulator
Fuel atomization nozzles

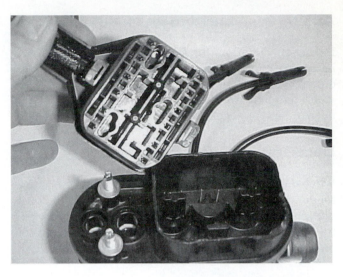

FIGURE 20-21   A view of a sequential central fuel-injection unit showing the electrical connections for the six individual solenoids.

Starting Mode

When the ignition is turned to the start (on) position, the engine cranks and the PCM energizes the fuel pump relay. The PCM also pulses the injectors on, basing the pulse width on engine speed and engine coolant temperature. The colder the engine is, the greater the pulse width. Cranking mode air-fuel ratio varies from about 1.5:1 at $-40°F$ ($-40°C$) to 14.7:1 at 200°F (93°C).

Clear Flood Mode

If the engine becomes flooded with too much fuel, the driver can depress the accelerator pedal to greater than 80% to enter the clear flood mode. When the PCM detects that the engine speed is low (usually below 600 RPM) and the throttle-position (TP) sensor voltage is high (WOT), the injector pulse width is greatly reduced or even shut off entirely, depending on the vehicle.

Open-Loop Mode

Open-loop operation occurs during warm-up before the oxygen sensor can supply accurate information to the PCM. The PCM determines injector pulse width based on values from the MAF, MAP, TP, ECT, and IAT sensors.

Closed-Loop Mode

Closed-loop operation is used to modify the base injector pulse width as determined by feedback from the oxygen sensor to achieve proper fuel control.

Acceleration Enrichment Mode

During acceleration, the throttle-position (TP) voltage increases, indicating that a richer air-fuel mixture is required. The PCM then supplies a longer injector pulse width and may even supply extra pulses to supply the needed fuel for acceleration.

Deceleration Enleanment Mode

When the engine decelerates, a leaner air-fuel mixture is required to help reduce emissions and to prevent deceleration backfire. If the deceleration is rapid, the injector may be shut off entirely for a short time and then pulsed on enough to keep the engine running.

Fuel Shut-Off Mode

Besides shutting off fuel entirely during periods of rapid deceleration, PCM also shuts off the injector when the ignition is turned off to prevent the engine from continuing to run.

◀ FREQUENTLY ASKED ▶ QUESTION

WHAT IS BATTERY VOLTAGE CORRECTION?

Battery voltage correction is a program built into the PCM that causes the injector pulse width to increase if there is a drop in electrical system voltage. Lower battery voltage would cause the fuel injectors to open slower than normal and the fuel pump to run slower. Both of these conditions can cause the engine to run leaner than normal if the battery voltage is low. Because a lean air-fuel mixture can cause the engine to overheat, the PCM compensates for the lower voltage by adding a percentage to the injector pulse width. This richer condition will help prevent serious engine damage. The idle speed is also increased to turn the generator (alternator) faster if low battery voltage is detected.

IDLE CONTROL

Port fuel-injection systems generally use an auxiliary air bypass. See Figure 20-22. This air bypass or regulator provides needed additional airflow, and thus

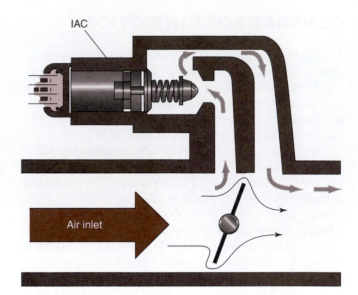

FIGURE 20-22 The small arrows indicate the air bypassing the throttle plate in the closed throttle position. This air is called minimum air. The air flowing through the IAC is the airflow that determines the idle speed.

more fuel. The engine needs more power when cold to maintain its normal idle speed to overcome the increased friction from cold lubricating oil. It does this by opening an intake air passage to let more air into the engine just as depressing the accelerator pedal would open the throttle valve, allowing more air into the engine. The system is calibrated to maintain engine idle speed at a specified value regardless of engine temperature.

Most PFI systems use an **idle air control (IAC)** motor to regulate idle bypass air. The IAC is computer-controlled, and is either a solenoid-operated valve or a stepper motor that regulates the airflow around the throttle. The idle air control valve is also called an **electronic air control (EAC)** valve.

When the engine stops, most IAC units will retract outward to get ready for the next engine start. When the engine starts, the engine speed is high to provide for proper operation when the engine is cold. Then, as the engine gets warmer, the computer reduces engine idle speed gradually by reducing the number of counts or steps commanded by the IAC.

When the engine is warm and restarted, the idle speed should momentarily increase, then decrease to normal idle speed. This increase and then decrease in engine speed is often called an engine **flare.** If the engine speed does not flare, then the IAC may not be working (it may be stuck in one position).

STEPPER MOTOR OPERATION

A digital output is used to control stepper motors. Stepper motors are direct current motors that move in fixed steps or increments from de-energized (no voltage) to fully energized (full voltage). A stepper motor often has as many as 120 steps of motion.

A common use for stepper motors is as an idle air control (IAC) valve, which controls engine idle speeds and prevents stalls due to changes in engine load. When used as an IAC, the stepper motor is usually a reversible DC motor that moves in increments, or steps. The motor moves a shaft back and forth to operate a conical valve. When the conical valve is moved back, more air bypasses the throttle plates and enters the engine, increasing idle speed. As the conical valve moves inward, the idle speed decreases.

When using a stepper motor that is controlled by the PCM, it is very easy for the PCM to keep track of the position of the stepper motor. By counting the number of steps that have been sent to the stepper motor, the PCM can determine the relative position of the stepper motor. While the PCM does not actually receive a feedback signal from the stepper motor, it does know how many steps forward or backward the motor should have moved.

A typical stepper motor uses a permanent magnet and two electromagnets. Each of the two electromagnetic windings is controlled by the computer. The computer pulses the windings and changes the polarity of the windings to cause the armature of the stepper motor to rotate 90 degrees at a time. Each 90-degree pulse is recorded by the computer as a "count" or "step;" therefore, the name given to this type of motor. See Figure 20-23.

Idle airflow in a TBI system travels through a passage around the throttle and is controlled by a stepper motor. In some applications, an externally mounted permanent magnet motor called the **idle speed control (ISC) motor** mechanically advances the throttle linkage to advance the throttle opening.

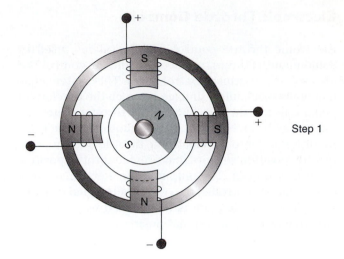

Step 1

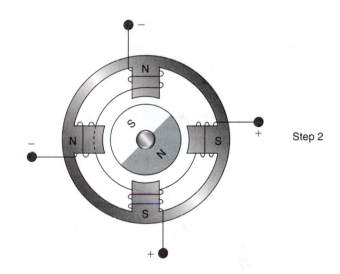

Step 2

FIGURE 20-23 Most stepper motors use four wires, which are pulsed by the computer to rotate the armature in steps.

◀ **FREQUENTLY ASKED QUESTION** ▶

WHY DOES THE IDLE AIR CONTROL VALVE USE MILLIAMPERES?

Some DaimlerChrysler vehicles, such as the Dodge Minivan, use linear solenoid idle air control valves (LSIAC). The PCM uses regulation current flow through the solenoid to control idle speed and the scan tool display is in milliamperes (mA).

Closed position = 180 to 200 mA
Idle = 300 to 450 mA
Light cruise = 500 to 700 mA
Fully open = 900 to 950 mA

Electronic Throttle Control

Electronic throttle control (ETC) systems, used by some manufacturers, replace the idle air control and also serve as a cruise control servo. This system eliminates the mechanical linkage between the accelerator pedal and the throttle plates. The throttle plates are controlled by an electric actuator motor and the PCM. Incorporated into the electronic throttle body are dual throttle position sensors that provide throttle position input to the PCM. The output is the electric actuator motor that is controlled by a duty-cycle signal from the PCM. The throttle plate is held closed by spring tension to a preset "limp home" position.

◄ GURU TIP ►

The injector O-rings do more than just seal the top and bottom of the injectors. They also act to isolate vibration and as heat shields. Always replace the injector O-ring whenever the injectors are removed and replaced, being certain to use the type and material as specified by the vehicle manufacturers.

Fuel Line Pressure

Abnormal scope patterns in fuel line or fuel rail pressures can reveal injector faults, pressure-regulator faults, and even imminent fuel pump failures from clogging, faulty brushes/commutator, and other faults. Again, a pressure transducer is used to input signals to the lab scope.

◄ TECH TIP ►

INJECTOR SPRAY PATTERNS

Not all injectors produce the same shape of spray pattern. See Figure 20-24 for an example of four different designs that produce four different spray patterns. Each engine design requires the specified injector spray pattern. Do not use a substitute injector unless specified by the vehicle manufacturer or injection supplier.

Conical seal pintle type hollow cone

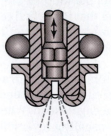

Conical seal dual pencil stream spray

Ball/seat seal single orifice pencil stream

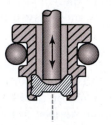

Ball/seat seal multi-orifice cone spray

FIGURE 20-24 Not all fuel injectors create a hollow cone discharge because the pattern depends on the design.

SUMMARY

1. A fuel-injection system includes the electric fuel pump and fuel pump relay, fuel-pressure regulator, and fuel injectors (nozzles).

2. The two types of fuel-injection systems are the throttle-body design and the port fuel-injection design.

3. The two methods of fuel-injection control are the speed density system, which uses the MAP to measure the load on the engine, and the mass air flow, which uses the MAF sensor to directly measure the amount of air entering the engine.

4. The amount of fuel supplied by fuel injectors is determined by how long they are kept open. This opening time is called the pulse width and is measured in milliseconds.

5. The fuel-pressure regulator is usually located on the fuel return on return-type fuel-injection systems.

6. TBI-type of fuel-injection systems do not use a vacuum-controlled fuel-pressure regulator, whereas many port fuel-injection systems use a vacuum-controlled regulator to monitor equal pressure drop across the injectors.

7. Other fuel designs include the electronic returnless, the mechanical returnless, and the demand delivery systems.

REVIEW QUESTIONS

1. What are the various types of fuel-injection systems?

2. What is the purpose of the vacuum-controlled (biased) fuel-pressure regulator?

3. How many sensors are used to determine the base pulse width on a speed density system?

4. How many sensors are used to determine the base pulse width on a mass air flow system?

5. Why should the fuel rail be inspected?

ASE CERTIFICATION-TYPE QUESTIONS

1. Technician A says that the fuel pump relay is usually controlled by the PCM. Technician B says that a TBI injector squirts fuel above the throttle into air at atmospheric pressure. Which technician is correct?
   a. Technician A only
   b. Technician B only
   c. Both Technicians A and B
   d. Neither Technician A nor B

2. Technician A says to avoid operating the vehicle with the fuel level low. Technician B says that the fuel filter or return-type fuel-injection system should be replaced regularly. Which technician is correct?
   a. Technician A only
   b. Technician B only
   c. Both Technicians A and B
   d. Neither Technician A nor B

3. Which fuel-injection system uses the MAP sensor as the primary sensor to determine the base pulse width?
   a. Speed density
   b. Mass air flow
   c. Demand delivery
   d. Mechanical returnless

4. Why is a vacuum line attached to a fuel-pressure regulator on many port fuel-injected engines?
   a. To draw fuel back into the intake manifold through the vacuum hose
   b. To create an equal pressure drop across the injectors
   c. To raise the fuel pressure at idle
   d. To lower the fuel pressure under heavy engine load conditions to help improve fuel economy

5. Which of the following has the greatest influence on injector pulse width besides the MAF sensor?
   a. IAT
   b. BARO
   c. ECT
   d. RPM

6. Technician A says that the wiring connectors are the same for all port fuel-injected engines and can be switched around without problems. Technician B says that sequential fuel injectors all use a different wire color on the injectors. Which technician is correct?
   a. Technician A only
   b. Technician B only
   c. Both Technicians A and B
   d. Neither Technician A nor B

7. Which type of port fuel-injection system uses a fuel temperature and/or fuel-pressure sensor?
   a. All port fuel-injected engines
   b. TBI units only
   c. Electronic returnless systems
   d. Demand delivery systems

8. Dampeners are used on some fuel rails to _____.
   a. Increase the fuel pressure in the rail
   b. Reduce (decrease) the fuel pressure in the rail
   c. Reduce noise
   d. Trap dirt and keep it away from the injectors

9. Where is the fuel-pressure regulator located on a vacuum-biased port fuel-injection system?
   a. In the tank
   b. At the inlet of the fuel rail
   c. At the outlet of the fuel rail
   d. Near or on the fuel filter

10. What type of device is used in a typical idle air control?
   a. DC motor
   b. Stepper motor
   c. Pulsator-type actuator
   d. Solenoid

◀ Chapter 21 ▶

FUEL-INJECTION SYSTEM DIAGNOSIS AND SERVICE

OBJECTIVES

After studying Chapter 21, the reader should be able to:

1. Prepare for ASE Engine Performance (A8) certification test content area "C" (Fuel, Air Induction, and Exhaust Systems Diagnosis and Repair).
2. Describe how to check an electric fuel pump for proper pressure and volume delivery.
3. Explain how to check a fuel-pressure regulator.
4. Describe how to test fuel injectors.
5. Explain how to diagnose electronic fuel-injection problems.

PORT FUEL-INJECTION PRESSURE REGULATOR DIAGNOSIS

Most port fuel-injected engines use a vacuum hose connected to the fuel-pressure regulator. At idle, the pressure inside the intake manifold is low (high vacuum). Manifold vacuum is applied above the diaphragm inside the fuel-pressure regulator. This reduces the pressure exerted on the diaphragm and results in a lower, about 10 psi (69 kPa), fuel pressure applied to the injectors. To test a vacuum-controlled fuel-pressure regulator, follow these steps:

1. Connect a fuel-pressure gauge to monitor the fuel pressure.
2. Locate the fuel-pressure regulator and disconnect the vacuum hose from the regulator.

NOTE: If gasoline drips out of the vacuum hose when removed from the fuel-pressure regulator, the regulator is defective and will require replacement.

---

3. With the engine running at idle speed, reconnect the vacuum hose to the fuel-pressure regulator while watching the fuel-pressure gauge. The fuel-pressure should drop (about 10 psi or 69 kPa) when the hose is reattached to the regulator.
4. Using a hand-operated vacuum pump, apply vacuum (20 in. Hg) to the regulator. The regulator should hold vacuum. If the vacuum drops, replace the fuel-pressure regulator. See Figure 21-1.

NOTE: Some vehicles do not use a vacuum-regulated fuel-pressure regulator. Many of these vehicles use a regulator located inside the fuel tank that supplies a constant fuel-pressure to the fuel injectors.

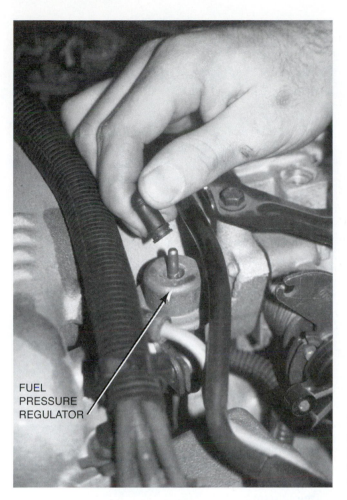

FUEL
PRESSURE
REGULATOR

PRESSURE TRANSDUCER FUEL PRESSURE TEST

Using a pressure transducer and a graphing multimeter (GMM) or digital storage oscilloscope (DSO) allows the service technician to view the fuel pressure over time. See Figure 21-2(a). Note that the fuel pressure dropped from 15 psi down to 6 psi on a TBI-equipped vehicle after just one minute. A normal pressure holding capability is shown in Figure 21-2(b) when the pressure dropped only about 10% after 10 minutes.

FIGURE 21-1 If the vacuum hose is removed from the fuel-pressure regulator when the engine is running, the fuel pressure should increase. If it does not increase, then the fuel pump is not capable of supplying adequate pressure or the fuel-pressure regulator is defective. If gasoline is visible in the vacuum hose, the regulator is leaking and should be replaced.

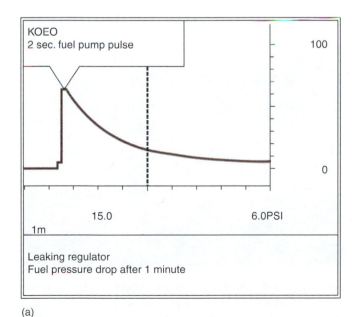

(a)

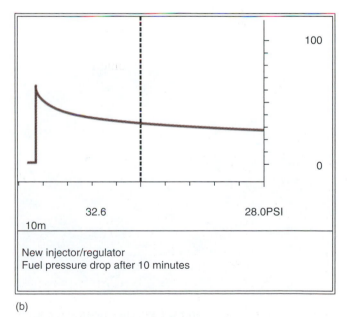

(b)

FIGURE 21-2 (a) A fuel-pressure graph after key on, engine off (KOEO). (b) Pressure drop after 10 minutes on a normal port fuel-injection system.

DIAGNOSING ELECTRONIC FUEL-INJECTION PROBLEMS USING VISUAL INSPECTION

All fuel-injection systems require the proper amount of clean fuel delivered to the system at the proper pressure and the correct amount of filtered air. The following items should be carefully inspected before proceeding to more detailed tests.

- Check the air filter and replace as needed.
- Check the air induction system for obstructions.
- Check the conditions of all vacuum hoses. Replace any hose that is split, soft (mushy), or brittle.
- Check the positive crankcase ventilation (PCV) valve for proper operation or replacement as needed. See Figure 21-3.

NOTE: The use of an incorrect PCV valve can cause a rough idle or stalling.

- Check all fuel-injection electrical connections for corrosion or damage.
- Check for gasoline at the vacuum port of the fuel-pressure regulator if the vehicle is so equipped. Gasoline in the vacuum hose at the fuel-pressure regulator indicates that the regulator is defective and requires replacement.

FIGURE 21-3 A clogged PCV system caused the engine oil fumes to be drawn into the air cleaner assembly. This is what the technician discovered during a visual inspection.

FIGURE 21-4 All fuel injectors should make the same sound with the engine running at idle speed. A lack of sound could indicate an electrically open injector, a break in the wiring, or a stuck closed injector. A defective computer could also be the cause of a lack of clicking (pulsing) of the injectors.

FUEL
PRESSURE
REGULATOR

FUEL
RETURN
LINE TO
TANK

FIGURE 21-5 Fuel should be heard returning to the fuel tank at the fuel return line if the fuel-pump and fuel-pressure regulator are functioning correctly.

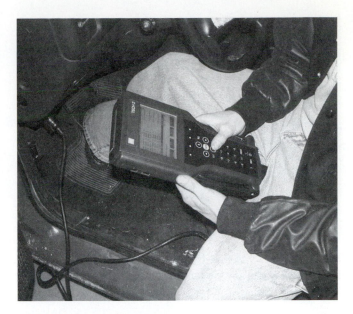

FIGURE 21-6 A scan tool can be used to help diagnose vacuum leaks by looking at the commanded IAC counts.

SCAN TOOL VACUUM LEAK DIAGNOSIS

If a vacuum (air) leak occurs on an engine equipped with a speed-density-type of fuel injection, the extra air would cause the following to occur:

- The idle speed increases due to the extra air just as if the throttle pedal was depressed.
- The MAP sensor reacts to the increased air from the vacuum leak as an additional load on the engine.
- The computer increases the injector pulse width slightly longer due to the signal from the MAP sensor.
- The air-fuel mixture remains unchanged.
- The idle air control (IAC) counts will decrease, thereby attempting to reduce the engine speed to the target idle speed stored in the computer memory. See Figure 21-6.

Therefore, one of the best indicators of a vacuum leak on a speed-density fuel-injection system is to look at the IAC counts or percentage. Normal IAC counts or percentage is usually 15 to 25. A reading of less than 5 indicates a vacuum leak.

If vacuum leak occurs on an engine equipped with a mass airflow-type fuel-injection system, the extra air causes the following to occur:

- The engine will operate leaner-than-normal because the extra air has not been measured by the MAF sensor.
- The idle speed will likely be lower due to the leaner-than-normal air-fuel mixture.
- The idle air control (IAC) counts or percentage will often increase in an attempt to return the engine speed to the target speed stored in the computer.

PORT FUEL-INJECTION SYSTEM DIAGNOSIS

To determine if a port fuel-injection system—including the fuel pump, injectors, and fuel-pressure regulator—are operating correctly, take the following steps.

1. Attach a fuel-pressure gauge to the Schrader valve on the fuel rail. See Figure 21-7.
2. Turn the ignition key on or start the engine to build up the fuel-pump pressure (to about 35 to 45 psi).
3. Wait 20 minutes and observe the fuel pressure retained in the fuel rail and note the psi reading. The fuel pressure should not drop more than 20 psi (140 kPa) in 20 minutes. If the drop is less than 20 psi in 20 minutes, everything is okay; if the drop is *greater*, then there is a possible problem with:
   - The check valve in the fuel pump
   - Leaking injectors, lines, or fittings
   - A defective (leaking) fuel-pressure regulator

FIGURE 21-7 A fuel-pressure gauge connected to the fuel-pressure tap (Schrader valve) on a port fuel-injected V-6 engine.

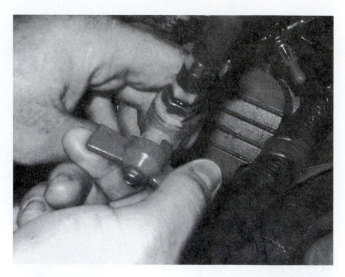

FIGURE 21-8 Shutoff valves must be used on vehicles equipped with plastic fuel lines to isolate the cause of a pressure drop in the fuel system.

To determine which unit is defective, perform the following:

- Reenergize the electric fuel pump.
- Clamp the fuel *supply* line, and wait 10 minutes (see caution box). If the pressure drop does not occur, replace the fuel pump. If the pressure drop still occurs, continue with the next step.
- Repeat the pressure buildup of the electric pump and clamp the fuel return line. If the pressure drop time is now okay, replace the fuel-pressure regulator.

- If the pressure drop still occurs, one or more of the injectors is leaking. Remove the injectors with the fuel rail and hold over paper. Replace those injectors that drip one or more drops after 10 minutes with pressurized fuel.

CAUTION: Do not clamp plastic fuel lines. Connect shutoff valves to the fuel system to shut off supply and return lines. See Figure 21-8.

DIAGNOSTIC STORY

THE QUAD 4 STORY

A service technician was diagnosing a rough-running condition on a General Motors Quad 4 engine. The paper test indicated a cylinder miss. To help determine which cylinder was possibly causing the problem, the technician used a scan tool and performed a power balance test. When the injector for cylinder 2 was canceled, the engine did not change in the way it was running. A compression test indicated that the cylinder had good compression. The technician removed the ignition cover and used conventional spark plug wires to connect the coils to the spark plugs. The technician then connected short lengths of rubber vacuum hose to each of the sparks. The technician then touched each rubber hose with a grounded test light to ground out each cylinder. Again, cylinder 2 was found to be completely dead.

Then the technician made the mistake of assuming that the fault had to be a defective fuel injector. A replacement fuel injector did not solve the problem. Further testing of the injectors revealed that injector 3 was shorted. Because both injectors 2 and 3 share the same driver inside the computer, the injector that was shorted electrically required more current than the normal good injector. Because the computer driver circuit controls and limits current flow, the defective (shorted) injector would fire (squirt), whereas the good injector did not have enough current to work.

GURU TIP

Defective or hardened injector O-rings can cause hard hot restart.

TESTING FOR AN INJECTOR PULSE

One of the first checks that should be performed when diagnosing a no-start condition is whether the fuel injectors are being pulsed by the computer. Checking for proper pulsing of the injector is also important in diagnosing a weak or dead cylinder.

A noid light is designed to electrically replace the injector in the circuit and to flash if the injector circuit is working correctly. See Figure 21-9. To use a noid light, disconnect the electrical connector at the fuel injector and plug the noid light into the injector harness connections. Crank or start the engine. The noid light should flash regularly.

NOTE: The term *noid* is simply an abbreviation of the word *solenoid*. Injectors use a movable iron core and are therefore solenoids. Therefore, a noid light is a replacement for the solenoid (injector).

Possible noid light problems and causes include the following:

1. **The light is off and does not flash.** The problem is an open in either the power side or ground side (or both) of the injector circuit.
2. **The noid light flashes dimly.** A dim noid light indicates excessive resistance or low voltage available to the injector. Both the power and ground side must be checked.
3. **The noid light is on and does not flash.** If the noid light is on, then both a power and a ground are present. Because the light does not flash (blink) when the engine is being cranked or started, then a short-to-ground fault exists either in the computer itself or in the wiring between the injector and the computer.

◀ GURU TIP ▶

A noid lamp must be used with caution. The computer may show a good noid light operation and have low supply voltage. See Figure 21-10.

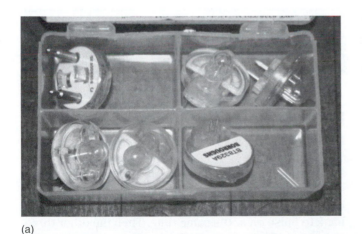
(a)

(b)

FIGURE 21-9 (a) Noid lights are usually purchased as an assortment so that one is available for any type or size of injector wiring connector. (b) The connector is unplugged from the injector and a noid light is plugged into the injector connector. The noid light should flash when the engine is being cranked if the power circuit and the pulsing to ground by the computer are functioning okay.

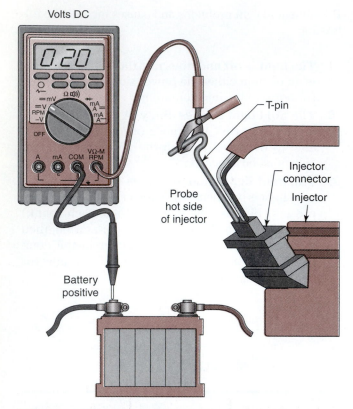

Volts DC

T-pin

Injector connector

Injector

Probe hot side of injector

Battery positive

FIGURE 21-10 Use a DMM set to read DC volts to check the voltage drop of the positive circuit to the fuel injector. A reading of 0.5 volt or less is generally considered to be acceptable.

CHECKING FUEL-INJECTOR RESISTANCE

Each port fuel injector must deliver an equal amount of fuel or the engine will idle roughly or perform poorly.

The electrical balance test involves measuring the injector coil-winding resistance. For best engine operation, all injectors should have the same electrical resistance. To measure the resistance, carefully release the locking feature of the connector and remove the connector from the injector.

NOTE: Some engines require specific procedures to gain access to the injectors. Always follow the manufacturers' recommended procedures.

GURU TIP

A good MULTEC will draw less than 1 amp of current; a bank of three must draw less than 3 amps.

With an ohmmeter, measure the resistance across the injector terminals. Be sure to use the low-ohms feature of the digital ohmmeter to read in tenths (0.1) of an ohm. See Figures 21-11 and 21-12. Check service information for the resistance specification of the injectors. Measure the resistance of all of the injectors. Replace any injector that does not fall within the resistance range of the specification. The resistance of the injectors should be measured twice—once when the engine (and injectors) are cold and once after the engine has reached normal operating temperature. If any injector measures close to specification, make certain that the terminals of the injector are electrically sound, and perform other tests to confirm an injector problem before replacement.

The resistance of the injectors should be measured twice—once when the engine (and injectors) are cold and once after the engine has reached normal operating temperature. If any injector measures close to specification, make certain that the terminals of the injector are electrically sound and perform other tests to confirm an injector problem before replacement.

◄ GURU TIP ►

A shorted injector may cause a problem on another cylinder due to injector pairings in a parallel circuit.

MEASURING RESISTANCE OF GROUPED INJECTORS

Many vehicles are equipped with a port fuel-injection system that "fires" two or more injectors at a time. For example, a V-6 may group all three injectors on one bank to pulse on at the same time. Then the other three injectors will be pulsed on. This sequence alternates. To measure the resistance of these injectors, it is often easiest to measure each group of three that is wired in parallel. The resistance of three injectors wired in parallel

Injector Resistance Table

Manufacturer	Injector Application	Resistance Values
General Motors		
	Quad 4	1.95–2.15 Ω
	CPI Vortec 4.3L	1.48–1.52 Ω
	MFI Bosch Style Injector (1985–1989) 2.8L	15.95–16.35 Ω
	MFI Black Multec Injector 2.8L, 3.1L, 3.3L, 3.4L	11.8–12.6 Ω
	MFI 3800	14.3–14.7 Ω
	MFI 3.8L, 5.0L, 5.7L	15.8–16.6 Ω
	MFI 5.7 LT5-ZR1	11.8–12.6 Ω
	TBI 220 Series 2.8L, 3.1L, 4.3L, 5.0L, 5.7L, 7.4L	1.16–1.36 Ω
	TBI 295 Series 4.3L, 6.0L, 7.0L	1.42–1.62 Ω
	TBI 700 Series 2.0L, 2.2L, 2.5L	1.42–1.62 Ω
Chrysler Brand		
	MFI Early Years through 1992 (majority of)	2.4 Ω
	MFI Later Years after 1992 (majority of)	14.5 Ω
	TBI Low-Pressure Systems (majority of)	1.3 Ω
	TBI High-Pressure Systems (majority of)	0.7 Ω
Ford		
	MFI 1.6L (1985)	2.0–2.7 Ω
	MFI 1.6L (1983–1985)	15.0–19.0 Ω
	MFI 2.3L T/C (1983–1988)	2.0–2.7 Ω
	MFI 2.3L (1989–1994)	15.0–18.0 Ω
	MFI 2.3L TK (1985–1994)	15.0–18.0 Ω
	MFI 3.0L (1986–1990)	15.0–18.0 Ω
	MFI 4.9L (1987–1988)	15.0–18.0 Ω
	MFI 5.0L (1985–1994)	15.0–18.0 Ω
	MFI 7.4L (1987–1994)	15.0–18.0 Ω
	TBI Low-Pressure 1.9L (1987–1990)	1.0–2.0 Ω
	TBI Low-Pressure 2.3L (1985–1987)	1.0–2.0 Ω
	TBI Low-Pressure 2.5L (1986–1990)	1.0–2.0 Ω
	TBI High-Pressure 3.8L (1984–1987)	1.5–2.5 Ω
	TBI High-Pressure 5.0L (1981–1985)	1.5–3.5 Ω

is one-third of the resistance of each individual injector. For example,

Injector resistance = 12 ohms (Ω)
Three injectors in parallel = 4 ohms (Ω)

A V-6 has two groups of three injectors. Therefore, both groups should measure the same resistance. If both groups measure 4 ohms, then it is likely that all six injectors are OK. However, if one group measures only 2.9 ohms and the other group measures 4 ohms, then it is likely that one or more fuel injectors are defective (shorted). This means that the technician now has reasonable cause to remove the intake manifold to get access to each injector for further testing. See Figure 21-13.

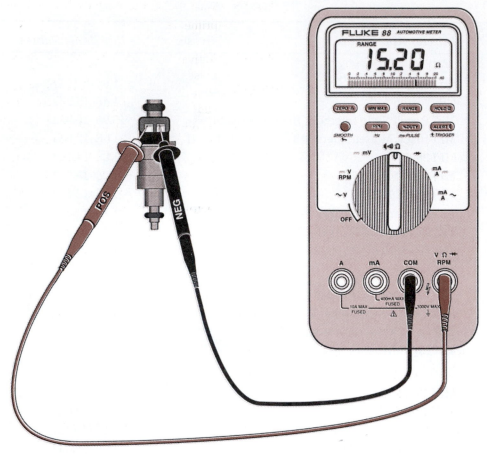

Your Fluke digital multimeter provides you with a low-ohms setting, which lets you measure low resistance components with much greater accuracy. Just hold the yellow key down as you power the meter up — that sets your meter to the low-ohms setting.

FIGURE 21-11   Connections and settings necessary to measure fuel-injector resistance. *(Courtesy of Fluke Corporation)*

FIGURE 21-12   To measure fuel-injector resistance, a technician constructed a short wiring harness with a double banana plug that fits into the V and COM terminals of the meter and an injector connector at the other end. This setup makes checking resistance of fuel injectors quick and easy.

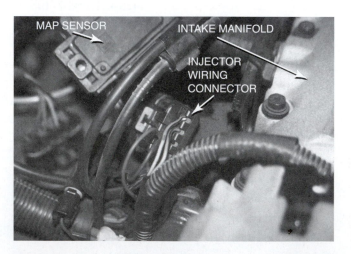

FIGURE 21-13   The fuel-injector wiring connector on an older General Motors 3.1-liter V-6 is hidden and attached to the rear of the intake manifold. Both groups of three injectors can be easily measured using an ohmmeter. Both groups of injectors should measure within 0.5 ohm of each other. Newer engines have a connector that is harder to reach. Check service information for details.

PRESSURE-DROP BALANCE TEST

The pressure balance test involves using an electrical timing device to pulse the fuel injectors on for a given amount of time, usually 500 ms or 0.5 second, and observing the drop in pressure that accompanies the pulse. If the *fuel flow* through each injector is equal, the drop in pressure in the system will be equal. Most manufacturers recommend that the pressures be within about 1.5 psi (10 kPa) of each other for satisfactory engine performance. This test method not only tests the electrical functioning of the injector (for definite time and current pulse), but also tests for mechanical defects that could affect fuel flow amounts.

The purpose of running this injector balance test is to determine which injector is restricted, inoperative, or delivering fuel differently than the other injectors. Replacing a complete set of injectors can be expensive. The basic tools needed are:

- Accurate pressure gauge with pressure relief
- Injector pulser with time control
- Necessary injector connection adapters
- Safe receptacle for catching and disposing of any fuel released

| Step 1 | Attach the pressure gauge to the fuel delivery rail on the supply side. Make sure the connections are safe and leakproof. |
| Step 2 | Attach the injector pulser to the first injector to be tested. |

FIGURE 21-14 Note the fuel pressure before and after pulsing the injector on for 500 ms to help determine if the injector is flowing the same amount of fuel as all of the other injectors.

Step 3	Turn the ignition key to the on position to prime the fuel-rail. Note the static fuel-pressure reading. See Figure 21-14.
Step 4	Activate the pulser for the timed firing pulses.
Step 5	Note and record the new static rail pressure after the injector has been pulsed.
Step 6	Re-energize the fuel pump and repeat this procedure for all of the engine injectors.
Step 7	Compare the two pressure readings and compute the pressure drop for each injector. Compare the pressure drops of the injectors to each other. Any variation in pressure drops will indicate an uneven fuel delivery rate between the injectors.

For example:

Injector	1	2	3	4	5	6
Initial Pressure	40	40	40	40	40	40
Second Pressure	30	30	35	30	20	30
Pressure Drop	10	10	5	10	20	10
Possible Problem	OK	OK	Restriction	OK	Leak	OK

INJECTOR VOLTAGE DROP TEST

Another test of injectors involves pulsing the injector and measuring the voltage drop across the windings as current is flowing. A typical voltage drop tester is shown in Figure 21-15. The tester, which is recommended for use by General Motors Corporation, pulses the injector while a digital multimeter is connected to the unit, which will display the voltage drop as the current flows through the winding.

CAUTION: Do not test an injector using a pulse-type tester more than one time without starting the engine to help avoid a hydrostatic lock caused by the flow of fuel into the cylinder during the pulse test.

Record the highest voltage drop observed on the meter display during the test. Repeat the voltage drop test for all of the injectors. The voltage drop across each injector should be within 0.1 volt of each other. If an injector has

FIGURE 21-15 This General Motors specified tester is used to measure not only the pressure drop caused by pulsing an injector on for 500 ms, but can also be used to measure the voltage drop across the windings.

a higher-than-normal voltage drop, the injector windings have higher-than-normal resistance.

EXHAUST GAS BALANCE TEST

The most accurate method is to perform a cylinder balance test with gases. This test is most accurate when taken in front of the catalytic converter. Due to this fact, it is the least used by technicians because they must tap into the vehicle's exhaust, which takes time, or they do not have a working gas analyzer.

Cylinder Balance with Gases

This is a great way to check an injector's contribution to each cylinder. The analyzer kills the spark for a period of time, usually 6 to 8 seconds, while watching the HC level at the tailpipe. The HC level is measured as a PPM number indicating the unburned fuel coming from the disabled cylinder.

Once an injector problem has been found, the service technician has to make the choice for proper service and repair. These choices may include:

- Replacement of the injector with a new OEM unit.
- Replacement of the injector with a new reconditioned unit.

- Service (clean) the injector on the vehicle.
- Have the injector serviced off the vehicle.

EXAMPLE 1 RPM—2200

Cylinder	1	2	3	4	5	6
HC	1711	1542	1500	1188	1147	1211

Notice that the injectors for cylinders 4, 5, and 6 are much lower than the other three. This can be caused by clogged injector basket filters or many other injector faults.

EXAMPLE 2

Cylinder	1	2	3	4	5	6
HC	1235	1323	1200	600	1312	1267

Injector 4 is restricted.

SCOPE TESTING FUEL INJECTORS

A scope (analog or digital storage) can be connected into each injector circuit. There are three types of injector-driven drive circuits and each type of circuit has its own characteristic pattern. See Figure 21-16 for an example of how to connect a scope to read a fuel-injector waveform.

Saturated Switch Type

In a saturated switch-type injector-driven circuit, voltage (usually a full 12 volts) is applied to the injector. The ground for the injector is provided by the vehicle computer. When the ground connection is completed, current flows through the injector windings. Due to the resistance and inductive reactance of the coil itself, it requires a fraction of a second (about 3 milliseconds or 0.003 seconds) for the coil to reach **saturation** or maximum current flow. Most saturated switch-type fuel injectors have 12 to 16 ohms of resistance. This resistance, as well as the computer switching circuit, control and limit the current flow through the injector. A voltage spike occurs when the computer shuts off (opens the injector ground-side circuit) the injectors. See Figures 21-17 and 21-18.

Peak-and-Hold Type

A peak-and-hold type is typically used for TBI and some port low-resistance injectors. Full battery voltage is applied to the injector and the ground side is controlled

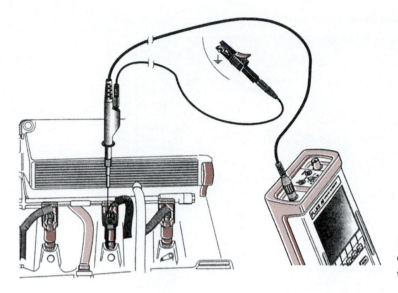

FIGURE 21-16 A digital storage oscilloscope can be easily connected to an injector by carefully back probing the electrical connector. *(Courtesy of Fluke Corporation)*

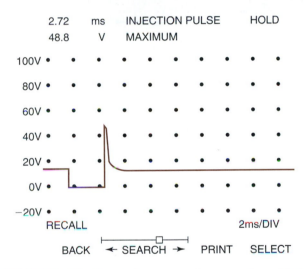

FIGURE 21-17 A typical injector voltage waveform. Notice that the battery voltage is reduced to zero when the injector is grounded by the computer. The injector on-time is then represented by the line near zero voltage. When the computer turns off the injector, a voltage spike is generated by the collapsing magnetic field created by the injector windings.

through the computer. The computer provides a high initial current flow (about 4 amperes) to flow through the injector windings to open the injector core. Then the computer reduces the current to a lower level (about 1 ampere). The hold current is enough to keep the injector open, yet conserves energy and reduces the heat buildup that would occur if the full current flow remains on as long as the injector is commanded on. Typical peak-and-hold type injector resistance ranges from 2 to 4 ohms.

The scope pattern of a typical peak-and-hold type injector shows the initial closing of the ground circuit, then a voltage spike as the current flow is reduced. Another

voltage spike occurs when the lower level current is turned off (opened) by the computer. See Figures 21-19, 21-20, and 21-21.

Pulse-Width Modulated Type

A pulse-width modulated type of injector drive circuit uses lower resistance coil injectors. Battery voltage is available at the positive terminal of the injector and the computer provides a variable-duration connection to ground on the negative side of the injector. The computer can vary the time intervals that the injector is grounded for very precise fuel control.

Each time the injector circuit is turned off (ground circuit opened), a small voltage spike occurs. It is normal to see multiple voltage spikes on a scope connected to a pulse-width modulated type of fuel injector. See Figure 21-22.

INJECTOR CURRENT RAMPING

Fuel injectors can be tested using a digital storage oscilloscope (DSO) connected to a current probe that is attached to one of the leads of the fuel injector. The term **current ranging** is used to describe the display of the current waveform on a DSO. The current flow through an injector rises gradually (or ranges upward) through the winding of the injector. This is due to **inductive reactance,** which means that as the current starts to flow through the coil windings, this current creates a current in the opposite direction. This causes a slight delay in reaching maximum current flow through the coil. The

Conventional (Saturated Switch Driver) Fuel Injector

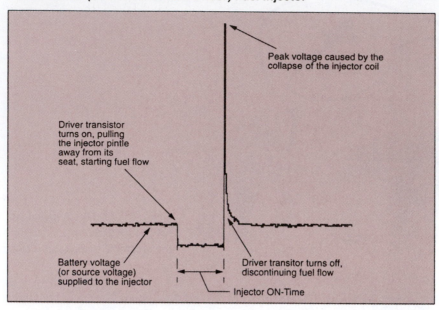

Peak voltage caused by the collapse of the injector coil

Driver transistor turns on, pulling the injector pintle away from its seat, starting fuel flow

Battery voltage (or source voltage) supplied to the injector

Driver transitor turns off, discontinuing fuel flow

Injector ON-Time

FIGURE 21-18 The injector on-time is called the *pulse width*. *(Courtesy of Fluke Corporation)*

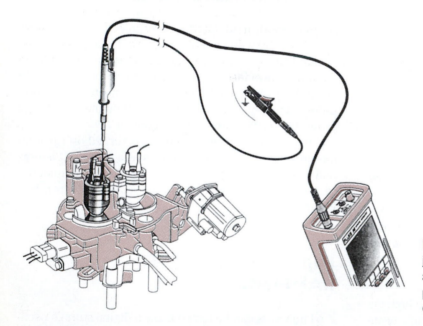

FIGURE 21-19 A peak-and-hold type of fuel injector such as this TBI can be easily connected to a digital storage oscilloscope by carefully back probing the electrical connector. *(Courtesy of Fluke Corporation)*

slope of the current pattern raises at about a 60-degree angle and then reaches the peak and levels off when it reaches **saturation** before dropping to zero when the injector is switched off. See Figure 21-23. The small hump in the pattern about two-thirds of the way up the range represents the point when the pintle of the injector actually opens. If the opening point of the injector pintle is

higher on the range than 70%, then there is a possible problem with one or more of the following:

- Drag caused by dirt in the pintle bore
- Excessive fuel pressure which can shut off an injector
- Spring tension on the pintle

Although the injector voltage pattern may not show a problem, the current ramp can detect these problems, and they often require that the injector be replaced. See Figure 21-24 for examples of injector current waveforms compared to the voltage waveforms.

Current-Controlled (Peak-and-Hold) Fuel Injector (Throttle Body and Port Fuel Injection Systems)

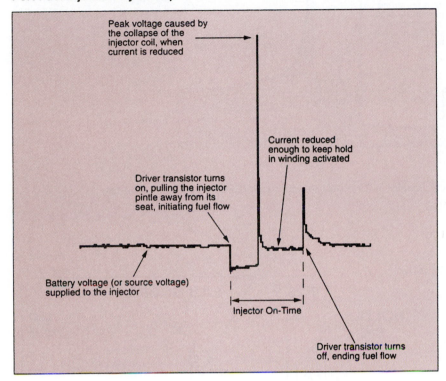

Peak voltage caused by the collapse of the injector coil, when current is reduced

Current reduced enough to keep hold in winding activated

Driver transistor turns on, pulling the injector pintle away from its seat, initiating fuel flow

Battery voltage (or source voltage) supplied to the injector

Injector On-Time

Driver transistor turns off, ending fuel flow

FIGURE 21-20 A typical peak-and-hold fuel-injector waveform. Most fuel injectors that measure less than 6 ohms will usually display a similar waveform. *(Courtesy of Fluke Corporation)*

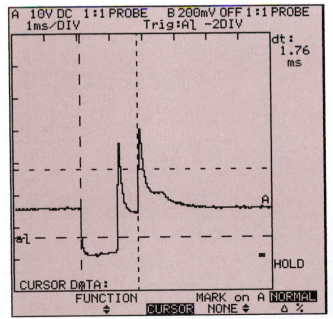

Peak-and-Hold injector waveforms have two voltage spikes — one when the high-current circuit de-energizes, and a second when the low-current, "Hold" circuit releases the injector. Measure the injector on-time from the falling edge of the on-time pulse to the second voltage spike.

FIGURE 21-21 A peak-and-hold injector waveform. *(Courtesy of Fluke Corporation)*

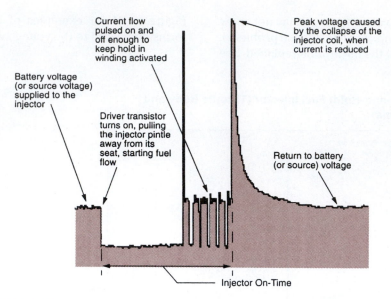

Current flow
pulsed on and
off enough to
keep hold in
winding activated

Peak voltage caused
by the collapse of the
injector coil, when
current is reduced

Battery voltage
(or source voltage)
supplied to the
injector

Driver transistor
turns on, pulling
the injector pintle
away from its
seat, starting fuel
flow

Return to battery
(or source) voltage

Injector On-Time

FIGURE 21-22 A typical waveform for a pulse-width modulated fuel injector. *(Courtesy of Fluke Corporation)*

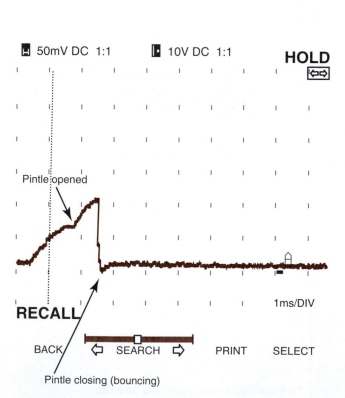

■ 50mV DC 1:1   ■ 10V DC 1:1

HOLD
⟨⇦⇨⟩

Pintle opened

RECALL

1ms/DIV

BACK   ⇦ SEARCH ⇨   PRINT   SELECT

Pintle closing (bouncing)

FIGURE 21-23 A typical waveform created by current ranging the operation of a fuel injector. The slight dip in the waveform, sometimes called the "gull wing", about two-thirds of the way up the "ramp" indicates when the pintle of the fuel injector actually opens. If it opens higher, a dirty pintle is indicated; if it opens lower, a worn injector pintle or a broken pintle return spring is indicated.

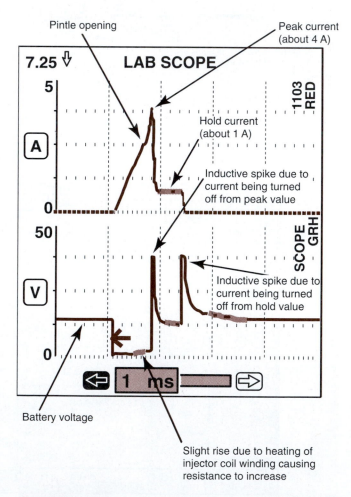

Pintle opening

Peak current
(about 4 A)

7.25 ⇩   **LAB SCOPE**

1103
RED

5

A

Hold current
(about 1 A)

Inductive spike due to
current being turned
off from peak value

0

50

SCOPE
GRH

V

Inductive spike due to
current being turned
off from hold value

0

⇦ **1 ms** ⇨

Battery voltage

Slight rise due to heating of
injector coil winding causing
resistance to increase

FIGURE 21-24 A comparison of a current waveform (top) and a voltage waveform (bottom) of a peak-and-hold TBI injector.

◄ FREQUENTLY ASKED ►
QUESTION

IF THREE OF SIX INJECTORS ARE DEFECTIVE, SHOULD I ALSO REPLACE THE OTHER THREE?

This is a good question. Many service technicians "recommend" that the three good injectors also be replaced along with the other three that tested as being defective. The reasons given by these technicians include:

- All six injectors have been operating under the same fuel, engine, and weather conditions.
- The labor required to replace all six is just about the same as replacing only the three defective injectors.
- Replacing all six at the same time helps ensure that all of the injectors are flowing the same amount of fuel so that the engine is operating most efficiently.

With these ideas in mind, the customer should be informed and offered the choice. Complete sets of injectors such as those in Figure 21-25 can be purchased at a reasonable cost.

◄ GURU TIP ►

Low IAC counts indicate a vacuum leak or misadjusted minimum air rate or low fuel pressure.

FIGURE 21-25   A set of six reconditioned injectors.

IDLE AIR SPEED CONTROL DIAGNOSIS

On an engine equipped with fuel injection (TBI or port injection), the idle speed is controlled by increasing or decreasing the amount of air bypassing the throttle plate. Again, an electronic stepper motor or pulse-width modulated solenoid is used to maintain the correct idle speed. This control is often called the **idle air control (IAC)**. See Figures 21-26 through 21-28.

When the engine stops, most IAC units will retract outward to get ready for the next engine start. When the engine starts, the engine speed is high to provide for proper operation when the engine is cold. Then, as the engine gets warmer, the computer reduces engine idle speed gradually by reducing the number of counts or steps commanded by the IAC.

When the engine is warm and restarted, the idle speed should momentarily increase, then decrease to normal idle speed. This increase and then decrease in engine speed is often called an engine **flare.** If the engine speed does not flare, then the IAC may not be working (it may be stuck in one position).

◄ GURU TIP ►

If there is high idle on dual TBI units, suspect a leaking base gasket.

◄ DIAGNOSTIC STORY ►

THERE IS NO SUBSTITUTE FOR A THOROUGH VISUAL INSPECTION

An intermittent "check engine" light and a random-misfire diagnostic trouble code (DTC) PO 300 was being diagnosed. A scan tool did not provide any help because all systems seemed to be functioning normally. Finally, the technician removed the engine cover and discovered a mouse nest. See Figure 21-29.

Cleaning the Throttle Plates of a Port Fuel-Injected Engine

The throttle plates of a port fuel-injected engine may require cleaning, especially if the following conditions exist:

- Rough idle
- Stalling

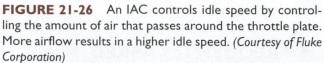

FIGURE 21-26 An IAC controls idle speed by controlling the amount of air that passes around the throttle plate. More airflow results in a higher idle speed. *(Courtesy of Fluke Corporation)*

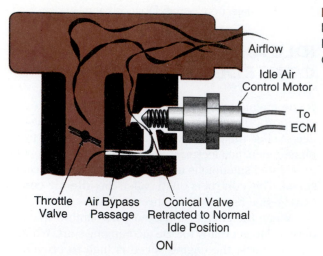

Airflow

Idle Air Control Motor

To ECM

Throttle Valve

Air Bypass Passage

Conical Valve Retracted to Normal Idle Position

ON

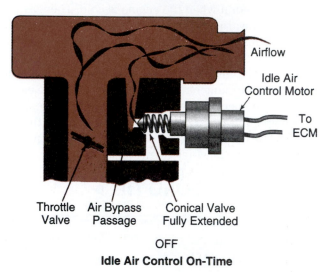

Airflow

Idle Air Control Motor

To ECM

Throttle Valve

Air Bypass Passage

Conical Valve Fully Extended

OFF

Idle Air Control On-Time

FIGURE 21-27 A typical IAC.

FIGURE 21-28 Some IAC units are purchased with the housing as shown. Carbon buildup in these passages can cause a rough or unstable idling or stalling.

(a)

(b)

FIGURE 21-29 (a) Nothing looks unusual when the hood is first opened. (b) When the cover is removed from the top of the engine, a mouse or some other animal nest is visible. The animal had already eaten through a couple of injector wires. At least the cause of the intermittent misfire was discovered.

(a)

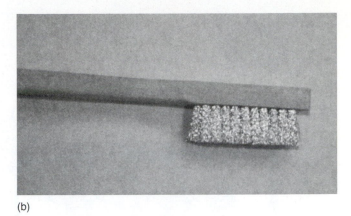

(b)

FIGURE 21-30   (a) Dirty throttle plate. This throttle plate was so dirty that the technician removed the entire throttle body to be sure it was thoroughly cleaned. (b) Most throttle plates can be cleaned on the vehicle using a brush and throttle body cleaner. Be sure the cleaner is safe for oxygen sensors.

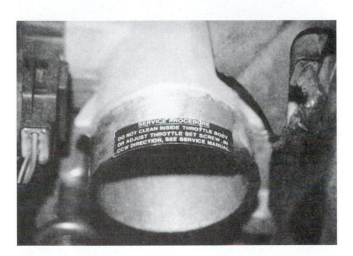

FIGURE 21-31   Some vehicles, such as this Ford, have labels on the throttle body to warn against cleaning of the throttle plates. A slippery coating is placed on the throttle plate and throttle bore that prevents deposits from sticking. Cleaning this type of housing can remove this protective coating.

- Surging at idle
- Hesitation during acceleration
- Higher-than-normal IAC counts as displayed on a scan tool

See Figures 21-30 and 21-31.

FUEL-INJECTION SERVICE

After many years of fuel-injection service, some service technicians still misunderstand the process of proper fuel system handling. Much has been said over the years with regard to when and how to perform injector cleaning. Some manufacturers have suggested methods of cleaning while others have issued bulletins to prohibit any cleaning at all.

All engines using fuel injection do require some type of fuel system maintenance. Normal wear and tear with today's underhood temperatures and changes in gasoline quality contribute to the buildup of olefin wax, dirt, water, and many other additives. Unique to each engine is an air-control design that also may contribute different levels of carbon deposits, such as oil control.

Fuel-injection system service should include the following operations:

1. **Check fuel pump operating pressure and volume.** The missing link here is volume. Most working technicians assume that if the pressure is correct, the volume is also OK. By hooking up a fuel-pressure tester to the fuel rail inlet to quickly test the fuel pressure with the engine running. At the same time, test the volume of the pump by sending fuel into the holding tank. (One ounce per second is the usual specification.) See Figure 21-32(a). A two-line system tester is the recommended procedure and use and is attached to the fuel inlet and the return on the fuel rail. The vehicle onboard system is looped and returns fuel to the tank.

2. **Test the fuel-pressure regulator for operation and leakage.** At this time, the fuel-pressure regulator would be tested for operational pressure and proper regulation, including leakage. (This works well as the operator has total control of rail pressure with a unit control valve.) Below are some points to ponder:

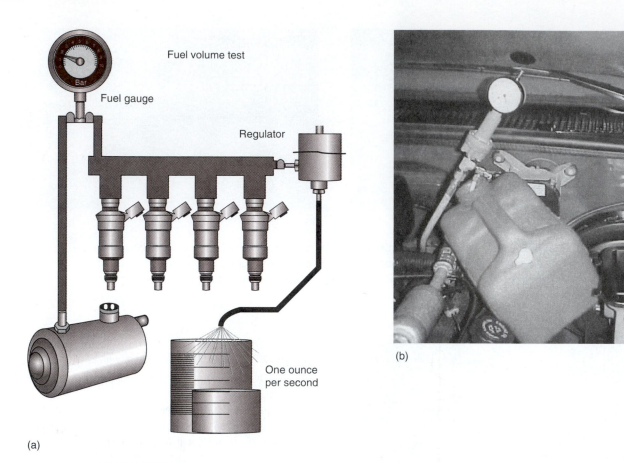

Fuel volume test

Fuel gauge

Regulator

One ounce per second

(a)

(b)

FIGURE 21-32 (a) Checking fuel pump value using a hose from the outlet of the fuel-pressure regulator into a calibrated container. (b) Testing fuel-pump volume using a fuel-pressure gauge with a bleed hose into a suitable container. The engine is running during this test.

- Good pressure does not mean proper volume. For example, a clogged filter may test OK on pressure but the restriction may not allow proper volume under load. See Figure 21-32(b).

- It is a good idea to use the vehicle's own gasoline to service the system versus a can of shop gasoline that has been sitting around for some time.

- Pressure regulators do fail and a lot more do not properly shut off fuel, causing higher-than-normal pump wear and shorter service life.

3. **Flush the entire fuel rail and upper fuel-injector screens including the fuel-pressure regulator.** Raise the input pressure to a point above regulator setting to allow a constant flow of fuel through the inlet pressure side of the system, through the fuel rail, and out the open fuel-pressure regulator. In most cases the applied pressure is 75 to 90 psi, but will be maintained by the presence of a regulator. At this point, cleaning chemical is added to the fuel at a 5:1 mixture and allowed to flow through the system

for 15 to 30 minutes. See Figure 21-33. Results are best on a hot engine with the fuel supply looped and the engine not running. Below are some points to ponder:

- This flush is the fix most vehicles need first. The difference is that the deposits are removed to a remote tank and filter versus attempting to soften the deposits and blow them through the upper screens.

- Most injectors use a 10-micron final filter screen. A 25% restriction in the upper screen would increase the injector on-time approximately 25%.

- Injectors have a working duty cycle like a welding machine. Extending the duty cycle (on-time) will shorten the life of the injector (coil or bobbin).

- Each engine has a pattern failure in the system. For example, Buick V-6 engines have problems with the injectors located on the end where the rail curves and the injector is next to the EGR

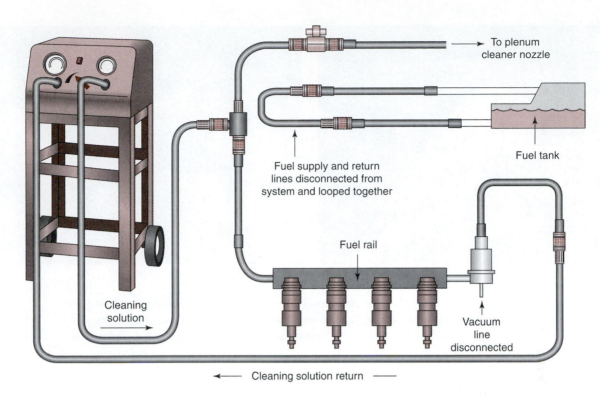

FIGURE 21-33 A typical two-line cleaning machine hookup, showing an extension hose that can be used to squirt a cleaning solution into the throttle body while the engine is running on the cleaning solution and gasoline mixture.

valve. Those three injectors will always show a restriction first.

4. **Clean the fuel injectors.** At this point in the service, start the engine and adjust the output pressure closer to regulator pressure or lower than in the previous steps. Lower pressure will cause the pulse width to open up somewhat longer and allow the injectors to be cleaned. Slow speed (idle) position will take a longer time frame and operating temperature will be reached. This is one place where time is required. Ever wonder how a can of injector cleaner could clean the entire injector in 9 minutes? It can't! Clean injectors are the objective, but the chemical should also decarbon the engine valves, pistons, and O2 sensor. Below are some points to ponder:

- Time is required to perform this service.
- Internal pintle cleaning is performed during this cycle.
- Fuel control is always in direct response to O2 response. For example, slow O2 − slow fuel control = poor performance.

5. **Decarbon the engine assembly.** On most vehicles, the injector spray will help the decarboning process. On others, you may need to enhance the operation with external addition of a mixture through the PCV hose, throttle plates, or idle air controls. Below are some points to ponder:

- Most technicians think carbon is an old outdated problem, but carbon is still a problem. Fuel volatility is lower and, in some cases, vehicles with high compression may experience a no-start situation.
- Proper compression = 14.7 × the compression ratio. Carbon buildup in the cylinder can raise the compression, and raise the required octane rating of the fuel to operate knock-free.

6. **Clean the throttle plate and idle air control passages.** Doing this service alone on most late model engines will show a manifold vacuum increase of up to 2. Stop the engine and clean the areas as needed then use a handheld fuel injector connected in parallel with the pressure hose, along with a pulser to allow cleaning of the throttle plates with the same chemical as injectors are running on. See Figure 21-34. This works well as air is drawn into IAC passages on a running engine and will clean the passages without IAC removal. Below are points to ponder:

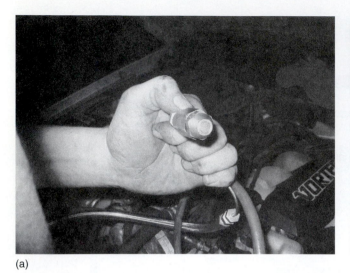

(a)

(b)

FIGURE 21-34 (a) A close up of an auxiliary nozzle from a fuel-injector cleaning machine used to clean the air intake. (b) The metal line is inserted into the throttle body and the engine is run with a combination of cleaner and gasoline flowing through the nozzle.

- A manifold vacuum increase tells the technician that the engine liked the service.
- Using the handheld injector will usually lower a GM IAC count from 40 to 15 without touching a thing.

◄ GURU TIP ►

Carbon on throttle plates causes extended crank time on a cold start.

7. **Check the minimum airflow rate and adjust if needed.** Most vehicles that have stalling problems are due to a misadjusted throttle plate or incorrect minimum air rate. Check service information for specifications. Below are points to ponder:

   - Delco makes a set of small tune-up booklets that do an excellent job of covering minimum air rate adjustment procedures.

8. **Relearn the onboard computer.** Some vehicles may have been running in such a poor state of operation that the onboard computer may need to be relearned. Consult the OEM-suggested relearn procedures for each particular vehicle.

This service usually takes approximately one hour for the vehicle to run out of fuel and the entire service to be performed. The good thing is that the technician may do other services while this is being performed. Some technicians may install a set of plugs or change the fuel filter while the engine is flushing. This service should restore the fuel system to original operations.

All of the previously listed steps may be performed using a *two-line* fuel-injector service unit such as: Carbon Clean, Auto Care, Injector Test, DeCarbon, or Motor-Vac.

◄ TECH TIP ►

BE SURE TO CLEAN THE FUEL RAIL

Whenever servicing the fuel injectors, or suspect that there may be a fuel-injector problem, remove the entire fuel rail assembly and check the passages for contamination. See Figure 21-35. Always thoroughly clean the rail when replacing fuel injectors.

◄ GURU TIP ►

A shorted injector may run OK under normal electrical loads and poorly under higher voltages. Lower voltage at the battery and listen at the tailpipe for a misfire.

(a)

(b)

FIGURE 21-35 (a) Always check the fuel rail for contamination. (b) Often an injector problem is a fuel rail problem instead.

◀ GURU TIP ▶

On an ignition scope, a plugged injector looks like a vacuum leak with a sloping upward spark line.

◀ GURU TIP ▶

Code 42 on an OBD-I GM vehicle can be caused by shorted injectors.

Fuel Symptoms/Action Chart

Symptom	Possible Causes
Hard cold starts	• Low fuel pressure
	• Leaking fuel injectors
	• Contaminated fuel
	• Low volatility fuel
	• Dirty Throttle Plate
Garage stalls	• Low fuel pressure
	• Insufficient fuel volume
	• Restricted fuel injector
	• Contaminated fuel
	• Low volatility fuel

◀ TECH TIP ▶

ALWAYS CHECK THE FUEL PRESSURE

General Motors vehicles equipped with TBI-type fuel injectors do not have a Schrader valve to check for the fuel pressure. As a result, the fuel pressure is not measured and it is "assumed" to be okay. See Figure 21–36 for an example of why the fuel pressure could be low and causing a lean condition.

Symptom	Possible Causes
Poor cold performance	• Low fuel pressure
	• Insufficient fuel volume
	• Contaminated fuel
	• Low volatility fuel
Tip-in hesitation (Hesitation just as the accelerator pedal is depressed)	• Low fuel pressure
	• Insufficient fuel volume
	• Intake valve deposits
	• Contaminated fuel
	• Low volatility fuel

FUEL-SYSTEM SCAN TOOL DIAGNOSTICS

Diagnosing a faulty fuel system can be a difficult task. However, it can be made easier by utilizing the information available via the serial datastream. By observing the long-term fuel trim and the short-term fuel trim, we can determine how the fuel system is performing. Short-term fuel trim and long-term fuel trim can help us to zero in on

FIGURE 21-36 This TBI pressure regulator spring came out in pieces when the regulator cover was removed.

specific areas of trouble. Readings should be taken at idle and at 3000 RPM. Use the following chart as a guide.

Condition	Long-Term Fuel Trim @ Idle	Long-Term Fuel Trim @ 3000 RPM
System normal	128 ± 8 or 0% ± 10%	128 ± 8 or 0% ± 10%
Vacuum leak	HIGH	OK
Fuel flow problem	OK	HIGH
Low fuel pressure	HIGH	HIGH
High fuel pressure	* OK or LOW	* OK or LOW

* High fuel pressure will affect trim at idle, at 3000, or both.

PS 10-1   The tools needed to diagnose a circuit containing a relay include a digital multimeter (DMM), a fused jumper wire, and an assortment of wiring terminals.

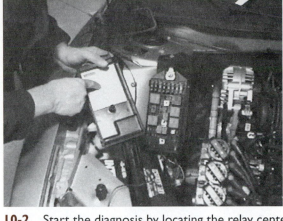

PS 10-2   Start the diagnosis by locating the relay center. It is under the hood on this General Motors vehicle, so access is easy. Not all vehicles are this easy.

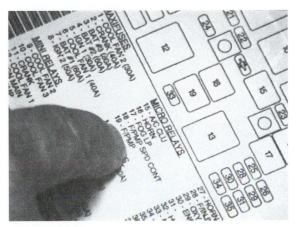

PS 10-3   The chart under the cover for the relay center indicates the location of the relay that controls the electric fuel pump.

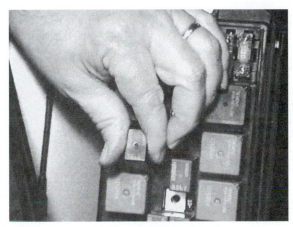

PS 10-4   Locate the fuel-pump relay and remove by using a puller if necessary. Try to avoid rocking or twisting the relay to prevent causing damage to the relay terminals or the relay itself.

PS 10-5   The schematic for the relay is printed on the side of the relay. Terminals 85 and 86 represent the coil inside the relay. Terminal 30 is the power terminal, 87a is the normally closed contact, and 87 is the normally open contact.

PS 10-6   The terminals are also labeled on most relays.

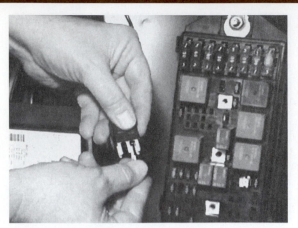

PS 10-7   To help make good electrical contact with the terminals without doing any harm, select the proper-size terminal from the terminal assortment.

PS 10-8   Insert the terminals into the relay socket in 30 and 87.

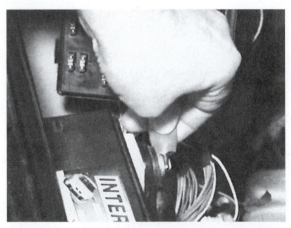

PS 10-9   To check for voltage at terminal 30, use a test light or a voltmeter. Start by connecting the alligator clip of the test light to the positive (+) terminal of the battery.

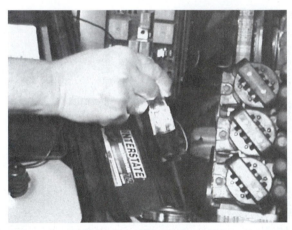

PS 10-10   Touch the test light to the negative (−) terminal of the battery or a good engine ground to check the test light.

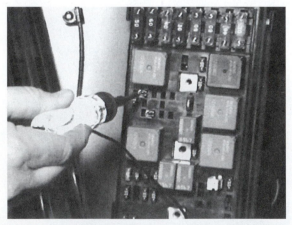

PS 10-11   Use the test light to check for voltage at terminal 30 of the relay. The ignition may have to be in the on (run) position.

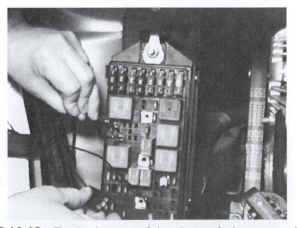

PS 10-12   To check to see if the electric fuel pump can be operated from the relay contacts, use a fused jumper wire and touch the relay contacts that correspond to terminals 30 and 87 of the relay. The fuel pump should be heard, and fuel pressure should rise to normal if the pump is operating correctly.

PS 10-13 Instead of a fused jumper wire, a digital multimeter could also be used to measure the current draw of the pump. Set the meter to read DC amperes and connect the leads of the meter to contacts 30 and 87 of the relay socket. The reading of 4.7 amperes is okay because the specification of this GM V-6 equipped with port fuel-injection is 4 to 8 amperes.

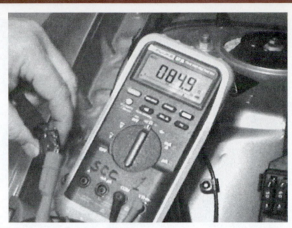

PS 10-14 The relay itself can also be tested using the digital multimeter. Set the meter to read ohms (Ω) and measure the resistance of the relay coil. The usual reading for most relays is between 60 and 100 ohms. This coil reads about 85 ohms and therefore has the proper resistance.

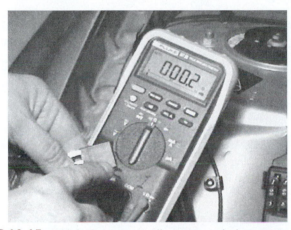

PS 10-15 With the meter still set to read ohms, measure between terminals 30 and 87a. Terminal 87a is the normally closed contact, and there should be little, if any, resistance between these two terminals, as shown.

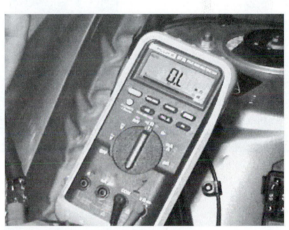

PS 10-16 To test the normally open contacts, connect one meter lead to terminal 30 and the other lead to terminal 87. The ohmmeter should show an open circuit by displaying OL.

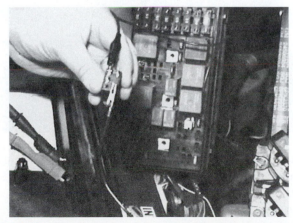

PS 10-17 To test to see if the relay clicks, connect a fused jumper wire to supply 12 volts to terminal 86 and a ground to terminal 85 of the relay. If the relay clicks, then the relay coil is able to move the armature (movable arm) of the relay.

PS 10-18 After testing, be sure to reinstall the relay and the relay cover.

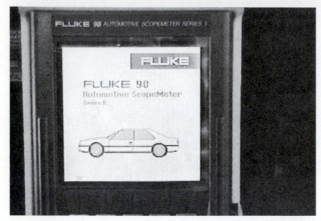

PS 11-1   This is the first screen you see when turning on a Fluke 98 scopemeter.

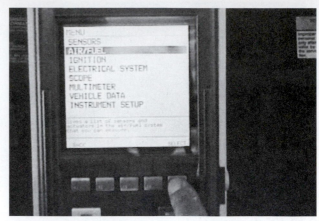

PS 11-2   Select "air/fuel" from the main menu.

PS 11-3   Select "fuel injector" from the air/fuel menu.

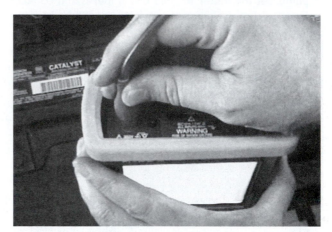

PS 11-4   The scopemeter will prompt you to connect the BNC test lead into the input A terminal.

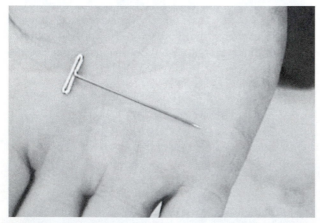

PS 11-5   Use a T-pin to back-probe the injector connector. These T-pins are usually available at discount stores and specialty shops in the craft area.

PS 11-6   Carefully insert the point of the T-pin into the back of the connector and lightly push on the T-pin until it contacts the metal terminal inside the connector.

PS 11-7   Attach the test probe from the scopemeter to the T-pin.

PS 11-8   Attach the ground test lead to a good, clean engine ground.

PS 11-9   Start the engine.

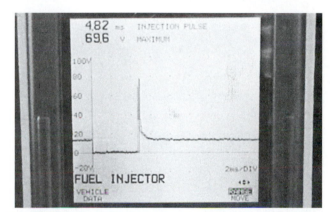

PS 11-10   Observe the waveform. If the waveform does not look similar to this, insert the T-pin into the other terminal of the connector. To achieve this pattern, the scopemeter should be connected to the terminal that is being pulsed on and off by the computer. The pulse width is longer than normal in this photo because the engine is cold and the computer is pulsing the injector on for a longer time to provide the engine with additional fuel.

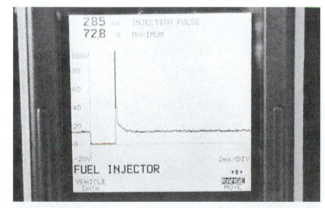

PS 11-11   Note the shortened pulse width compared to the previous photo. The engine is now at normal operating temperature and the injector pulse width should be 1.5 to 3.5 ms. Also look for consistent inductive voltage spikes for all injectors indicating that the injector coil is not shorted. Repeat the test on all of the injectors.

PS 11-12   Turn the engine off and disconnect the scopemeter.

PS 12-1 Start the fuel injector cleaning process by bringing the vehicle's engine up to operating temperature. Shut off the engine, remove the cap from the fuel rail test port, and install the appropriate adapter.

PS 12-2 The vehicle's fuel pump is disabled by removing its relay or fuse. In some cases, it may be necessary to disconnect the fuel pump at the tank if the relay or fuse powers more than just the pump.

PS 12-3 Turn the outlet valve of the canister to the OFF or CLOSED position.

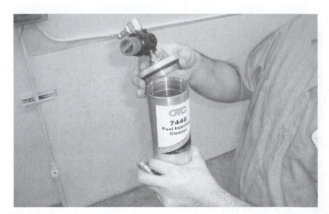

PS 12-4 Remove the fuel injector cleaning canister's top and regulator assembly. Note that there is an O-ring seal located here that must be in place for the canister's top to seal properly.

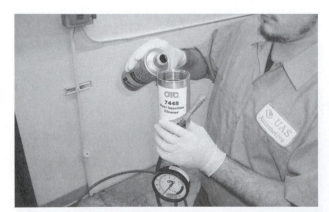

PS 12-5 Pour the injection system cleaning fluid into the open canister. Rubber gloves are highly recommended for this step as the fluid is toxic.

PS 12-6 Replace the canister's top (making sure it is tight) and connect its hose to the fuel rail adapter. Be sure that the hose is routed away from exhaust manifolds and other hazards.

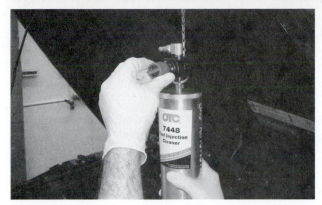

PS 12-7 Hang the canister from the vehicle's hood and adjust the air pressure regulator to full OPEN position (CCW).

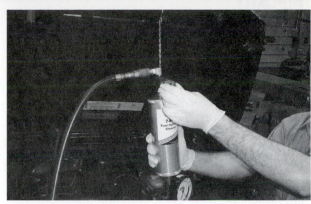

PS 12-8 Connect shop air to the canister and adjust the air pressure regulator to the desired setting. Canister pressure can be read directly from the gauge.

PS 12-9 Canister pressure should be adjusted to 5 psi below system fuel pressure. An alternative for return-type systems is to block the fuel return line to the tank.

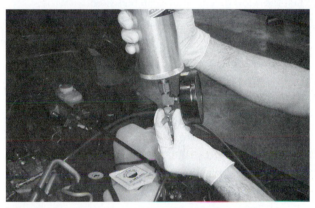

PS 12-10 Open the outlet valve on the canister.

PS 12-11 Start the vehicle's engine and let it run at 1000–1500 RPM. The engine is now running on fuel injector cleaning fluid provided by the canister.

PS 12-12 Continue the process until the canister is empty and the engine stalls. Remove the cleaning equipment, enable the vehicle's fuel pump, and run the engine to check for leaks.

SUMMARY

1. A typical throttle-body fuel injector uses a computer-controlled injector solenoid to spray fuel into the throttle-body unit above the throttle plates.

2. A typical port fuel-injection system uses an individual fuel injector for each cylinder and squirts fuel directly into the intake manifold about 3 inches (80 millimeters) from the intake valve.

3. Most electric fuel pumps can be tested for pressure, volume, and current flow.

4. A typical fuel-injection system fuel pressure should not drop more than 20 psi in 20 minutes.

5. A noid light can be used to check for the presence of an injector pulse.

6. Injectors can be tested for resistance and should be within 0.3 to 0.4 ohms of each other.

7. Different designs of injectors have a different scope waveform depending on how the computer pulses the injector on and off.

8. An idle air control unit controls idle speed and can be tested for proper operation using a scan tool or scope.

REVIEW QUESTIONS

1. List the ways fuel injectors can be tested.

2. List the steps necessary to test a fuel-pressure regulator.

3. Describe why it may be necessary to clean the throttle plate of a port fuel-injected engine.

ASE CERTIFICATION-TYPE QUESTIONS

1. Most port fuel-injected engines should be able to supply how much fuel pressure?
   a. 3 to 5 psi (21 to 35 kPa)
   b. 9 to 13 psi (62 to 90 kPa)
   c. 35 to 45 psi (240 to 310 kPa)
   d. 55 to 65 psi (380 to 450 kPa)

2. Fuel injectors can be tested using _____.
   a. An ohmmeter
   b. A stethoscope
   c. A scope
   d. All of the above

3. Throttle-body fuel-injection systems use what type of injector driver?
   a. Peak and hold
   b. Saturated switch
   c. Pulse-width modulated
   d. Pulsed

4. Port fuel-injection systems generally use what type of injector driver?
   a. Peak and hold
   b. Saturated switch
   c. Pulse-width modulated
   d. Pulsed

5. The vacuum hose from the fuel-pressure regulator was removed from the regulator and gasoline dripped out of the hose. Technician A says that is normal and that everything is okay. Technician B says that one or more of the injectors may be defective, causing the fuel to get into the hose. Which technician is correct?
   a. Technician A only
   b. Technician B only
   c. Both Technicians A and B
   d. Neither Technician A nor B

6. The fuel pressure drops rapidly when the engine is turned off. Technician A says that one or more injectors could be leaking. Technician B says that a defective check valve in the fuel pump could be the cause. Which technician is correct?
   a. Technician A only
   b. Technician B only
   c. Both Technicians A and B
   d. Neither Technician A nor B

7. In a typical port fuel-injection system, the fuel pressure is regulated _____.
   a. By a regulator located on the fuel return side of the fuel rail
   b. By a regulator located on the supply side of the fuel rail
   c. By the computer by pulsing the regulator on and off
   d. Either b or c

8. What component pulses the fuel injector on most vehicles?
   a. Electronic control unit (computer)
   b. Ignition module
   c. Crankshaft sensor
   d. Both b and c

9. Fuel injection service is being discussed. Technician A says the throttle plot(s) should be cleaned. Technician B says that the fuel rail should be cleaned. Which is correct?
   a. Technician A only
   b. Technician B only
   c. Both Technicians A and B
   d. Neither Technicians A nor B

10. If the throttle plate needs to be cleaned, what symptoms will be present regarding the operation of the engine?
    a. Stalls
    b. Rough idle
    c. Hesitation on acceleration
    d. All of the above

IGNITION SYSTEM COMPONENTS AND OPERATION

OBJECTIVES

After studying Chapter 22, the reader should be able to:

1. Prepare for ASE Engine Performance (A8) certification test content area "B" (Ignition System Diagnosis and Repair).
2. Explain how ignition coils create 40,000 volts.
3. Discuss crankshaft position sensor and pickup coil operation.
4. Describe the operation of waste-spark or coil-on-plug ignition systems.

The ignition system includes those parts and wiring required to generate and distribute a high voltage to the spark plugs. A fault anywhere in the primary (low-voltage) ignition circuit can cause a no-start condition. A fault anywhere in the secondary (high-voltage) ignition circuit can cause engine missing, hesitation, stalling, or excessive exhaust emissions.

IGNITION SYSTEM OPERATION

The ignition system includes components and wiring necessary to create and distribute a high voltage (up to 40,000 volts or more). All ignition systems apply battery voltage to the positive side of the ignition coil and pulse the negative side to ground except for capacitor-discharge systems used on some vehicles. When the coil negative lead is grounded, the primary (low-voltage) circuit of the coil is complete and a magnetic field is created by the coil windings. When the circuit is opened, the magnetic field collapses and induces a high-voltage in the secondary winding of the ignition coil which is used to generate a high-voltage are at the spark plug. Early ignition systems used a mechanically opened set of contact points to make and break the electrical connection to ground. Electronic ignition uses a sensor such as a pickup coil or trigger to signal an electronic module that makes and breaks the primary connection of the ignition coil.

NOTE: **Distributor ignition (DI)** is the term specified by the Society of Automotive Engineers (SAE) for an ignition system that uses a distributor. **Electronic ignition (EI)** is the term specified by the SAE for an ignition system that does not use a distributor.

IGNITION COILS

The heart of any ignition system is the **ignition coil.** The coil creates a high-voltage spark by electromagnetic induction. Many ignition coils for DI on some coil-on-plug systems contain two separate but electrically connected windings of copper wire. Other coils are true transformers in which the primary and secondary windings are not electrically connected. See Figure 22-1.

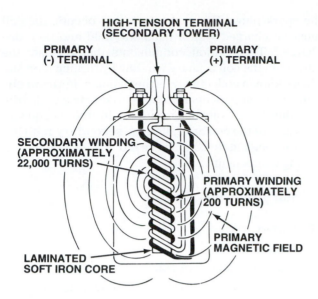

FIGURE 22-1 Internal construction of an oil-cooled ignition coil. Notice that the primary winding is electrically connected to the secondary winding. The polarity (positive or negative) of a coil is determined by the direction in which the coil is wound.

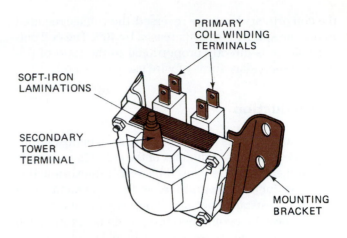

FIGURE 22-2 Typical air-cooled epoxy-filled E coil.

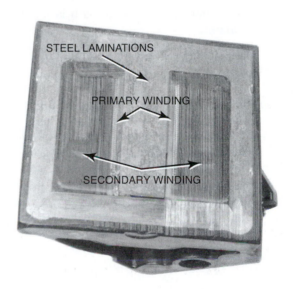

FIGURE 22-3 Cutaway of a General Motors Type II distributorless ignition coil. Note that the primary windings are inside of the secondary windings.

The center of an ignition coil contains a core of laminated soft iron (thin strips of soft iron). This core increases the magnetic strength of the coil. Surrounding the laminated core are approximately 20,000 turns of fine wire (approximately 42 gauge). These windings are called the **secondary** coil windings. Surrounding the secondary windings are approximately 150 turns of heavy wire (approximately 21 gauge). These windings are called the **primary** coil windings. The secondary winding has about 100 times the number of turns of the primary winding, referred to as the turn ratio (approximately 100:1). In many coils, these windings are surrounded with a thin metal shield and insulating paper, and are placed into a metal container. The metal container and shield help retain the magnetic field produced in the coil windings. The primary and secondary windings produce heat because of the electrical resistance in the turns of wire. Many coils contain oil to help cool the ignition coil. Other coil designs, such as those used on GM's **high energy ignition (HEI)** systems, use an air-cooled, epoxy-sealed **E coil.** The E coil is so named because the laminated, soft iron core is E shaped, with the coil wire turns wrapped around the center "finger" of the E and the primary winding wrapped inside the secondary winding. See Figures 22-2 and 22-3.

The primary windings of the coil extend through the case of the coil and the terminals and are labeled as positive and negative. The positive terminal of the coil attaches to the ignition switch, which supplies current from the positive battery terminal. The negative terminal is attached to an **electronic ignition module (or igniter),** which opens and closes the primary ignition circuit by opening or closing the ground return path of the circuit. When the ignition switch is on, voltage should be available at *both* the positive terminal and the negative terminal of the coil if the primary windings of the coil have continuity. The labeling of positive ($+$) and negative ($-$) of the coil indicates that the positive terminal is *more* positive (closer to the positive terminal of the battery) than the negative terminal of the coil. This condition is called the coil **polarity.** *The polarity of an ignition coil is determined by the direction of rotation of the coil windings.* The correct polarity is then indicated on the primary terminals of the coil. If the coil primary leads are reversed, the voltage required to fire the spark plugs is increased by 40%. The coil output voltage is directly proportional to the ratio of primary to secondary turns of wire used in the coil.

Self-Induction

When current starts to flow into a coil, an opposing current is created in the windings of the coil. This opposing current generation is caused by **self-induction** and is called **inductive reactance.** Inductive reactance is similar to resistance because it opposes any increase in current flow in a coil. Therefore, when an ignition coil is first energized, there is a slight delay of approximately 0.01 second before the ignition coil reaches its maximum magnetic field strength. The point at which a coil's maximum magnetic field strength is reached is called **saturation.**

Mutual Induction

In an ignition coil there are two windings, a primary and a secondary winding. When a *change* occurs in the magnetic field of one coil winding, a change also occurs in the other coil winding. Therefore, if the current is stopped from flowing (circuit is opened), the collapsing magnetic field cuts across the turns of the secondary winding and creates a high voltage in the secondary winding. Generating an electric current in both coil windings is called **mutual induction.** The collapsing magnetic field also creates a voltage of up to 250 volts in the primary winding.

How Ignition Coils Create 40,000 Volts

All ignition systems use electromagnetic induction to produce a high-voltage spark from the ignition coil. Electromagnetic induction means that a current can be created in a conductor (coil winding) by a moving magnetic field.

If the primary circuit is completed, current (approximately 2 to 6 A) can flow through the primary coil windings. This flow creates a strong magnetic field inside the coil. When the primary coil winding ground return path connection is opened, the magnetic field collapses and induces a voltage of from 250 to 400 volts in the primary winding of the coil and a high-voltage (20,000 to 40,000 volts) low-amperage (20 to 80 mA) current in the secondary coil windings. This high-voltage pulse flows through the coil wire (if the vehicle is so equipped), distributor cap, rotor, and spark plug wires to the spark plugs. For each spark that occurs, the coil must be charged with a magnetic field and then discharged. The ignition components that regulate the current in the coil primary winding by turning it on and off are known collectively as the **primary ignition circuit.** The components necessary to create and distribute the high voltage produced in the secondary windings of the coil are called the **secondary ignition circuit.** See Figure 22-4. These circuits include the following components.

Primary Ignition Circuit

1. Battery
2. Ignition switch
3. Primary windings of coil
4. Pickup coil (crank sensor) (module trigger)
5. Ignition module (igniter) (coil primary circuit switch)

Secondary Ignition Circuit

1. Secondary windings of coil
2. Distributor cap and rotor (if the vehicle is so equipped)
3. Spark plug wires
4. Spark plugs

◀ FREQUENTLY ASKED ▶ QUESTION

WHAT IS A "MARRIED" AND "DIVORCED" COIL DESIGN?

An ignition coil contains two windings: a primary winding and a secondary winding. These windings can be either connected together or kept separated.

- **Married.** These are also called a **tapped transformer** design. See Figure 22-5. The primary winding is electrically connected to the secondary winding. This method is commonly used in older distributor-type ignition system coils, as well as many coil-on-plug designs. The inductive kick, also called **flyback voltage,** created when the primary field collapses is used by the PCM to monitor secondary ignition performance.
- **Divorced.** These are also called a **true transformer** design and used by most waste-spark ignition coils to keep both the primary and secondary winding separated.

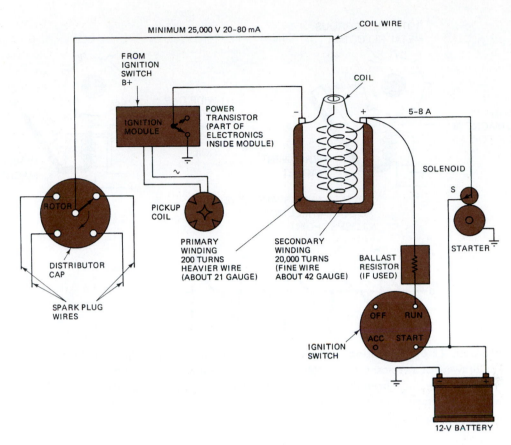

FIGURE 22-4 Typical primary and secondary electronic ignition using a ballast resistor and a distributor. To protect the ignition coil from overheating at lower engine speeds, many electronic ignitions do not use a ballast resistor, but use electronic circuits within the module.

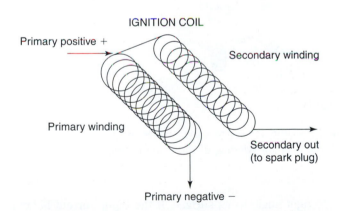

FIGURE 22-5 A tapped (married) type of ignition coil where the primary winding is tapped (connected) to the secondary winding.

PRIMARY CIRCUIT OPERATION

To get a spark out of an ignition coil, the primary coil circuit must be turned on and off. This primary circuit current is controlled by a **transistor** (electronic switch) inside the ignition module (or igniter) that in turn is controlled by one of several devices, including:

- **Pickup coil (pulse generator).** A simple and common ignition electronic switching device for DI systems is the magnetic pulse generator system. The rotation of the distributor shaft is used to time the voltage pulses. The **magnetic pulse** generator is installed in the distributor housing. The pulse generator consists of a trigger wheel (reluctor) and a pickup coil. The pickup coil consists of an iron core wrapped with fine wire, in a coil at one end and attached to a permanent magnet at the other end. The center of the coil is called the pole piece. The pickup coil signal triggers the transistor inside the module and is also

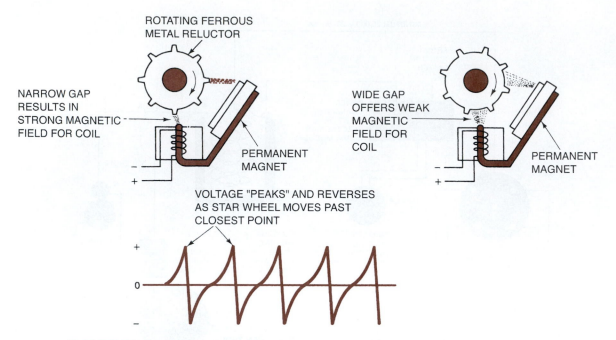

ROTATING FERROUS
METAL RELUCTOR

NARROW GAP
RESULTS IN
STRONG MAGNETIC
FIELD FOR COIL

WIDE GAP
OFFERS WEAK
MAGNETIC
FIELD FOR
COIL

PERMANENT
MAGNET

PERMANENT
MAGNET

VOLTAGE "PEAKS" AND REVERSES
AS STAR WHEEL MOVES PAST
CLOSEST POINT

FIGURE 22-6 Operation of a typical pulse generator (pickup coil). At the bottom is a line drawing of a typical scope pattern of the output voltage of a pickup coil. The module receives this voltage from the pickup coil and opens the ground circuit to the ignition coil when the voltage starts down from its peak (just as the reluctor teeth start moving away from the pickup coil).

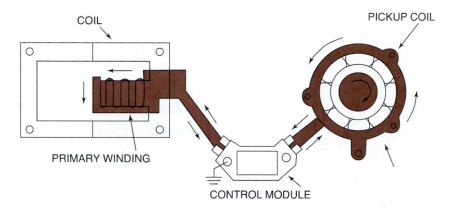

COIL

PICKUP COIL

PRIMARY WINDING

CONTROL MODULE

FIGURE 22-7 The varying voltage signal from the pickup coil triggers the ignition module. The ignition module grounds and ungrounds the primary winding of the ignition coil, creating a high-voltage spark.

used by the computer for piston position information and engine speed (RPM). See Figures 22-6 and 22-7.

- **Hall-effect switch.** This switch also uses a stationary sensor and rotating trigger wheel (shutter). See Figure 22-8. Unlike the magnetic pulse generator, the Hall-effect switch requires a small input voltage to generate an output or signal voltage. Hall effect is the ability to generate a voltage signal in semiconductor material (gallium arsenate crystal) by passing current through it in one direction and applying a magnetic field to it at a

right angle to its surface. If the input current is held steady and the magnetic field fluctuates, an output voltage is produced that changes in proportion to field strength. Most Hall-effect switches in distributors have a Hall element or device, a permanent magnet, and a rotating ring of metal blades (shutters) similar to a trigger wheel (another method uses a stationary sensor with a rotating magnet). Some blades, typically found in Bosch and DaimlerChrysler systems, are designed to hang down; others, typically found in GM and Ford

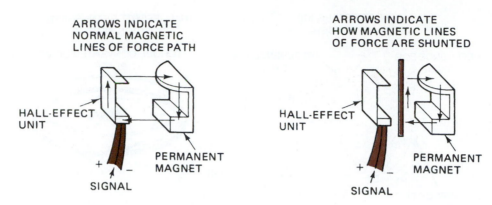

FIGURE 22-8   Hall-effect switches use metallic shutters to shunt magnetic lines of force away from a silicon chip and related circuits. All Hall-effect switches produce a square wave output for every accurate triggering.

FIGURE 22-9   Shutter blade of a rotor as it passes between the sensing silicon chip and the permanent magnet.

Hall-effect distributors, may be on a separate ring on the distributor shaft. When the shutter blade enters the gap between the magnet and the Hall element, it creates a magnetic shunt that changes the field strength through the Hall element, thereby creating an analog voltage signal. The Hall element contains a logic gate that converts the analog signal into a digital voltage signal, which triggers the switching transistor. The transistor transmits a digital square waveform at varying frequency to the ignition module or onboard computer. See Figures 22-9 and 22-10.

- **Magnetic crankshaft position sensors.** This sensor uses the changing strength of the magnetic field surrounding a coil of wire to signal the module and computer. This signal is used by the electronics in the module and computer as to piston position and engine speed (RPM). See Figure 22-11 on page 401.

- **Optical sensors.** These use light from a **LED** and a phototransistor to signal the computer. An interrupter disc between the LED and the phototransistor has slits that allow the light from the LED to trigger the phototransistor on the other side of the disc. Most optical sensors (usually located inside the distributor) use two rows of slits to provide individual cylinder recognition (low-resolution) and precise distributor angle recognition (high-resolution) signals. See Figure 22-12 on page 401.

◀ **TECH TIP** ▶

OPTICAL DISTRIBUTORS DO NOT LIKE LIGHT

Optical distributors use the light emitted from LEDs to trigger phototransistors. Most optical distributors use a shield between the distributor rotor and the optical interrupter ring. Sparks jump the gap from the rotor tip to the distributor cap inserts. This shield blocks the light from the electrical arc from interfering with the detection of the light from the LEDs.

If this shield is not replaced during service, the light signals are reduced and the engine may not operate correctly. See Figure 22-13 on page 401. This can be difficult to detect because nothing looks wrong during a visual inspection. Remember that all optical distributors must be shielded between the rotor and the interrupter ring.

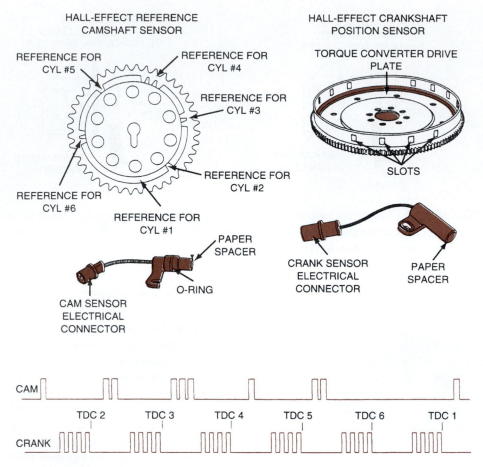

HALL-EFFECT REFERENCE
CAMSHAFT SENSOR

HALL-EFFECT CRANKSHAFT
POSITION SENSOR

REFERENCE FOR
CYL #5

REFERENCE FOR
CYL #4

REFERENCE FOR
CYL #3

REFERENCE FOR
CYL #6

REFERENCE FOR
CYL #2

REFERENCE FOR
CYL #1

TORQUE CONVERTER DRIVE
PLATE

SLOTS

PAPER
SPACER

O-RING

CAM SENSOR
ELECTRICAL
CONNECTOR

CRANK SENSOR
ELECTRICAL
CONNECTOR

PAPER
SPACER

CAM

TDC 2 · TDC 3 · TDC 4 · TDC 5 · TDC 6 · TDC 1

CRANK

FIGURE 22-10 Some Hall-effect sensors look like magnetic sensors. This Hall-effect camshaft reference sensor and crankshaft position sensor have an electronic circuit built in that creates a 0- to 5-volt signal as shown at the bottom. These Hall-effect sensors have three wires: a power supply (8 volts) from the computer (controller); a signal (0 to 5 volts); and a signal ground.

◀ TECH TIP ▶

THE TACHOMETER TRICK

When diagnosing a no-start or intermediate missing condition, check the operation of the tachometer. If the tachometer does not indicate engine speed (no-start condition) or drops toward zero (engine missing), then the problem is due to a defect in the *primary* ignition circuit. The tachometer gets its signal from the pulsing of the primary winding of the ignition coil. The following components in the primary circuit could cause the tachometer to not work when the engine is cranking.

- Pickup coil
- Crankshaft position sensor

- Ignition module (igniter)
- Coil primary wiring

If the vehicle is not equipped with a tachometer, connect a scan tool to monitor engine RPM. Remember the following:

No tachometer reading (RPM) means the problem is in the primary ignition circuit.

A tachometer reading OK means the problem is in the secondary ignition circuit or is a fuel-related problem.

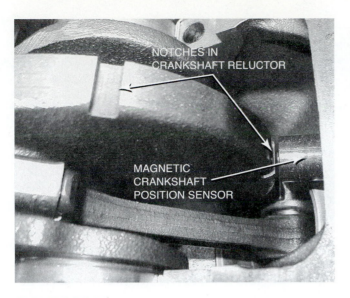

FIGURE 22-11 A typical magnetic crankshaft position sensor.

(a)

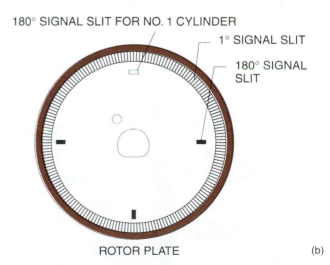

(b)

FIGURE 22-13 (a) An optical distributor on a Nissan 3.0 L V-6 shown with the light shield removed. (b) A light shield being installed before the rotor is attached.

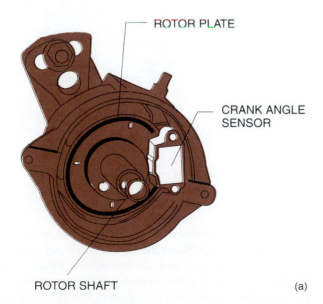

ROTOR PLATE

CRANK ANGLE SENSOR

ROTOR SHAFT

(a)

180° SIGNAL SLIT FOR NO. 1 CYLINDER

1° SIGNAL SLIT

180° SIGNAL SLIT

ROTOR PLATE

(b)

FIGURE 22-12 (a) Typical optical distributor. (b) A cylinder 1 slit signals the computer the piston position for cylinder 1. The 1-degree slits provide accurate engine speed information to the computer.

DISTRIBUTOR IGNITION

General Motors HEI Electronic Ignition

Some HEI models use an ignition coil inside the distributor cap and some use an externally mounted ignition coil. The operation of both styles is similar. The large-diameter distributor cap provides additional space between the spark plug connections to help prevent crossfire. See Figure 22-14. Most HEI distributors also use 8-mm-diameter spark plug wires that use female connections to the distributor cap towers. HEI coils must be replaced (if defective) with the exact replacement style. HEI coils differ and can be identified by the colors of the primary leads. The primary coil leads can be either white and red or yellow and red. The correct color of lead coil must be used for replacement. The colors of the leads in-dicate the direction in which the coil is wound, and therefore its polarity. See Figures 22-15 and 22-16.

Ford Electronic Ignition

Ford electronic ignition systems all function similarly, even though over the years the system has been called by various names.

The EEC IV system uses the thick-film-integration (TFI) ignition system. This system uses a smaller control module attached to the distributor, as well as an air-cooled epoxy E coil. See Figure 22-17. Thick-film integration means that all electronics are manufactured on small layers built up to form a thick film. Construction includes using pastes of different electrical resistances that

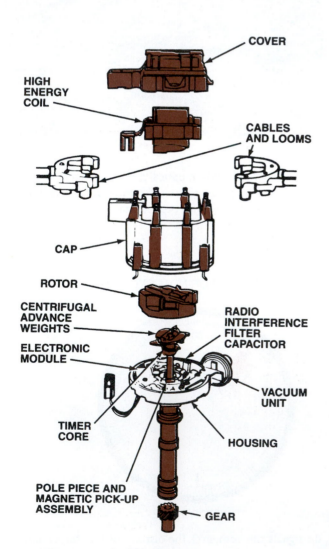

FIGURE 22-14 An HEI distributor.

FIGURE 22-15 A typical General Motors HEI coil installed in the distributor cap. When the coil or distributor cap is replaced, check that the ground clip is transferred from the old distributor cap to the new. Without proper grounding, coil damage is likely. There are two designs of HEI coils. One uses red and white wire as shown and the other design, which has reversed polarity, uses red and yellow wire for the coil primary.

are deposited on a thin, flat ceramic material by a process similar to silk-screen printing. These resistors are connected by tracks of palladium silver paste. Then the chips that form the capacitors, diodes, and integrated circuits are soldered directly to the palladium silver tracks. The thick-film manufacturing process is highly automated.

Operation of Ford Distributor Ignition

Ford DI systems function in basically the same way regardless of year and name. Under the distributor cap and rotor is a magnetic pickup assembly. This assembly produces a small alternating electrical pulse (approximately 1.5 volts) when the distributor armature rotates past the pickup assembly (stator). This low-voltage pulse is sent to the ignition module. The ignition module then switches (through transistors) off the primary ignition coil current.

FIGURE 22-16 This unit uses a remotely mounted ignition coil.

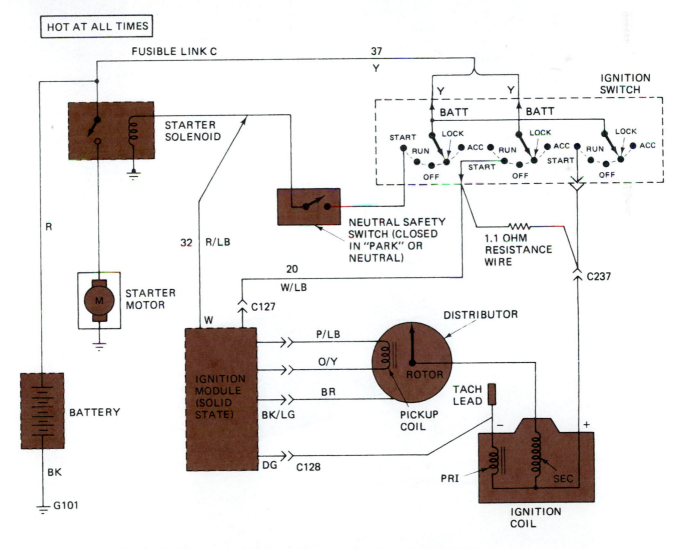

FIGURE 22-17 Wiring diagram of a typical Ford electronic ignition.

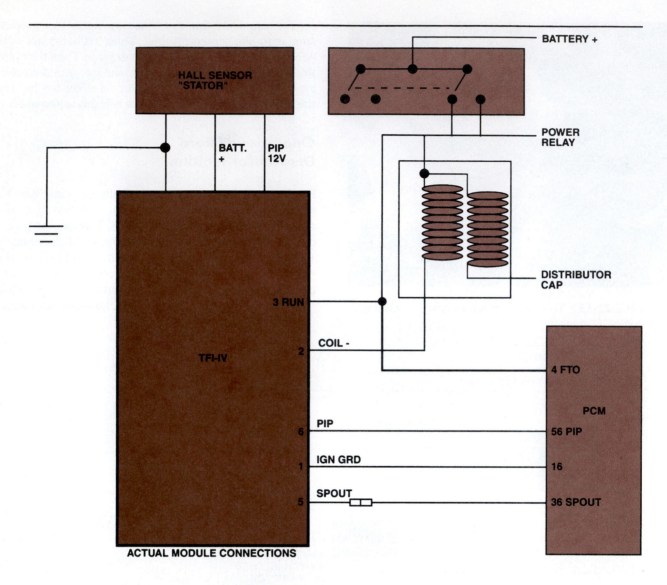

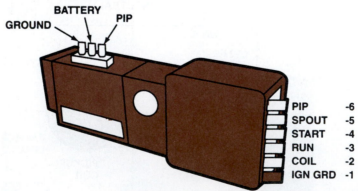

FIGURE 22-18 Schematic of a Ford TFI-IV ignition system. The SPOUT connector is unplugged when ignition timing is being set.

When the ignition coil primary current is stopped quickly, a high-voltage "spike" discharges from the coil secondary winding. Some Ford EI systems use a ballast resistor to help control the primary current through the ignition coil in the run mode (position); other Ford systems do not use a ballast resistor. The coil current is controlled in the module circuits by decreasing dwell (coil-charging time) depending on various factors determined by operating conditions. See Figure 22-18.

◀ TECH TIP ▶

IF IT'S SOFT, THROW IT AWAY

Ford uses a Hall-effect sensor in the distributor on most TFI module-equipped engines. The sensors were originally coated in a black plastic that would often become soft with age and break down electrically. The soft plastic sensor would also prevent proper connection to the TFI module, as shown in Figure 22-19. If a no-start or rough engine operation occurs, always check the Hall-effect sensor and the connections to the module. The original Hall-effect units were black plastic and more prone to failure. Ozone formed by the high-voltage arcing in the distributor cap is highly corrosive, and it chemically attaches to the plastic. The plastic then becomes soft and pliable, and similar to tar in feel and texture. If the sensor is soft-like tar, replace the Hall-effect switch assembly. Later production units use a more chemically stable white plastic material that is soft but not sticky.

DaimlerChrysler Distributor Ignition

DaimlerChrysler was the first domestic manufacturer to produce electronic ignition as standard equipment. The DaimlerChrysler system consists of a pulse generator unit in the distributor (pickup coil and reluctor). DaimlerChrysler's name for their electronic ignition is **electronic ignition system (EIS),** and the control unit (module) is called the **electronic control unit (ECU).**

The pickup coil in the distributor (pulse generator) generates the signal to open and close the primary coil circuit. See Figure 22-20.

FIGURE 22-19 Thick film-integrated type of Ford EI. Note how the module plugs into the Hall-effect switch inside the distributor. Heat-conductive silicone grease should be used between the module and the distributor mounting pad to help keep the electronic circuits inside the module cool.

FIGURE 22-20 A DaimlerChrysler electronic ignition distributor. This unit is equipped with a vacuum advance mechanism that advances the ignition timing under light engine load conditions.

WASTE-SPARK IGNITION SYSTEMS

Waste-spark ignition is another name for **distributorless ignition system (DIS)** or **electronic ignition (EI).** Waste-spark ignition was introduced in the mid-1980s and uses the onboard computer to fire the ignition coils. These systems were first used on some Saabs and General Motors engines. Some 4-cylinder engines use four coils, but usually a 4-cylinder engine uses two ignition coils and a 6-cylinder engine uses three ignition coils. Each coil is a true transformer in which the primary winding and secondary winding are not electrically connected. Each end of the secondary winding is connected to a cylinder exactly opposite the other in the firing order, which is called a **paired cylinder.** See Figure 22-21. This means that *both* spark plugs fire at the same time. When one cylinder (for example, 6) is on the compression stroke, the other cylinder (3) is on the exhaust stroke. The spark that occurs on the exhaust stroke is called the **waste spark,** because it does no useful work and is only used as a ground path for the secondary winding of the ignition coil. The voltage required to jump the spark plug gap on cylinder 3 (the exhaust stroke) is only 2 to 3 kV and provides the *ground circuit* for the secondary coil circuit. The remaining coil energy is used by the paired cylinder on its compression stroke. One spark plug of each pair fires straight polarity (from the top of the spark plug to the ground electrode) and the other cylinder fires reverse polarity (from the ground electrode to the center electrode). Spark plug life is not greatly affected by the reverse polarity. If there is only one defective spark plug wire or spark plug, two cylinders may be affected.

The coil polarity is determined by the direction the coil is wound (left-hand rule for conventional current flow) and cannot be changed. See Figure 22-22. Each spark plug for a particular cylinder will always be fired either with straight or reversed polarity, depending on

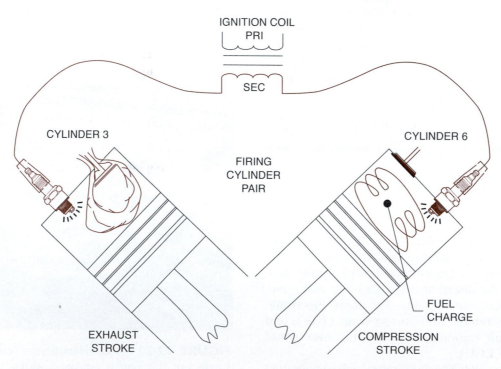

FIGURE 22-21 A waste-spark system fires one cylinder while its piston is on the compression stroke and into paired or companion cylinders while it is on the exhaust stroke. In a typical engine, it requires only about 2 to 3 kV to fire the cylinder on the exhaust strokes. The remaining coil energy is available to fire the spark plug under compression (typically about 8 to 12 kV).

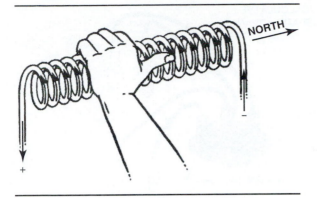

FIGURE 22-22 The left hand rule states that if a coil is grasped with the left hand, the fingers will point in the direction of current flow and the thumb will point toward the north pole.

its location in the engine and how the coils are wired. However, the compression and waste-spark condition flip-flops. When one cylinder is on compression, such as cylinder number 1, then the paired cylinder (number 4) is on the exhaust stroke. During the next rotation of the crankshaft, cylinder number 4 is on the compression stroke and cylinder number 1 is on the exhaust stroke.

Cylinder 1   Always fires straight polarity, one time, requiring 10 to 12 KV and one time, requiring 3 to 4 KV.

Cylinder 4   Always fires reverse polarity, one time, requiring 10 to 12 KV and one time, requiring 3 to 4 KV.

NOTE: With a distributor-type ignition system, the coil has two air gaps to fire: one between the rotor tip and the distributor insert (not under compression forces) and the other in the gap at the firing tip of the spark plug (under compression forces). A DIS also fires two gaps: one under compression (compression stroke plug) and one not under compression (exhaust stroke plug).

Waste-spark ignitions require a sensor (usually a crankshaft sensor) to trigger the coils at the correct time. See Figure 22-23. The crankshaft sensor cannot be moved to adjust ignition timing. Ignition timing is not adjustable. The slight adjustment of the crankshaft sensor is designed to position the sensor exactly in the middle of the rotating metal disc for maximum clearance. Some engines do not use a camshaft position sensor, but rather double Hall-effect crankshaft sensors. Again, ignition timing is not adjustable.

IGNITION CONTROL CIRCUITS

Ignition control (IC) is the OBD-II terminology for the output signal from the PCM to the ignition system that controls engine timing. Previously, each manufacturer used a different term to describe this signal. For instance, Ford referred to this signal as spark output (SPOUT) and General Motors referred to this signal as electronic spark timing (EST). This signal is now referred to as the ignition control (IC) signal. The ignition control signal is usually a digital output that is sent to the ignition system as a timing signal. If the ignition system is equipped with an

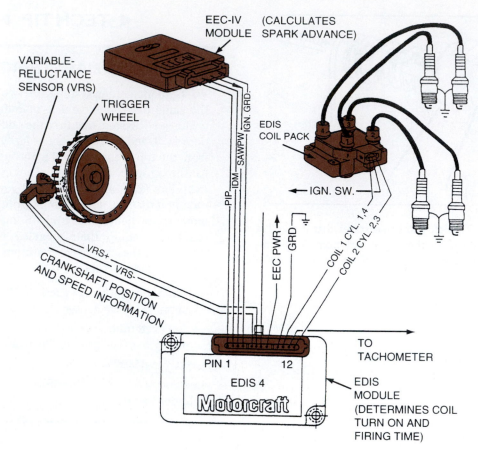

FIGURE 22-23 Typical Ford EDIS 4-cylinder ignition system. The crankshaft sensor, called a variable-reluctance sensor (VRS), sends crankshaft position and speed information to the EDIS module. A modified signal is sent to the computer as a profile ignition pickup (PIP) signal. The PIP is used by the computer to calculate ignition timing, and the computer sends a signal back to the EDIS module as to when to fire the spark plug. This return signal is called the spark angle word (SAW) signal.

ignition module, then this signal is used by the ignition module to vary the timing as engine speed and load changes. If the PCM directly controls the coils, such as most coil-on-plug ignition systems, then this IC signal directly controls the coil primary and there is a separate IC signal for each ignition coil. The IC signal controls the time that the coil fires; it either advances or retards the timing. On many systems, this signal controls the duration of the primary current flow in the coil, which is referred to as the **dwell**.

Bypass Ignition Control

A bypass-type of ignition control means that the engine starts using the ignition module for timing control and then switches to the PCM for timing control after

the engine starts. A bypass ignition is commonly used on General Motors engines equipped with distributor ignition (DI), as well as those equipped with waste-spark ignition. See Figure 22-24. The bypass circuit includes four wires:

- **Tach reference (purple/white).** This wire comes from the ignition control (IC) module and is used by the PCM as engine speed information.
- **Ground (black/white).** This ground wire is used to ensure that both the PCM and the ignition control module share the same ground.
- **Bypass (tan/black).** This wire is used to conduct a 5-volt DC signal from the PCM to the ignition control module to switch the timing control from the module to the PCM.

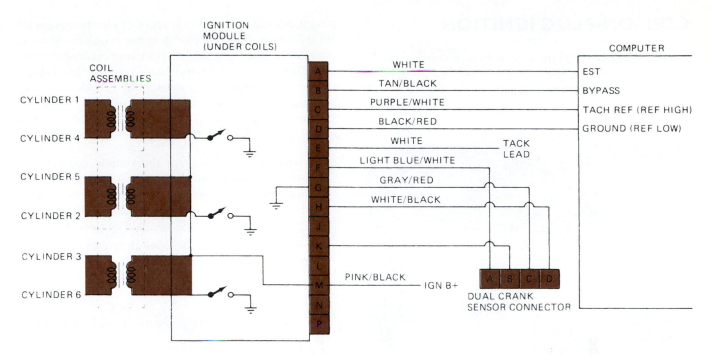

FIGURE 22-24 Typical wiring diagram of a V-6 distributorless (direct fire) ignition system. The computer applies 5 volts to the bypass wire when the engine starts. This signal changes the ignition timing function from the module to the computer (PCM).

NOTE: It is this bypass wire that is disconnected before the ignition timing can be set on many General Motors engines equipped with a distributor ignition.

- **EST (ignition control) (white wire).** This is the ignition timing control signal from the PCM to the ignition control module.

Diagnosing a Bypass Ignition System

One advantage of a bypass-type of ignition is that the engine will run without the computer because the module can do the coil switching and can, through electronic circuits inside the module, provide for some spark advance as the engine speed increases. This is a safety feature that helps protect the catalytic converter if the ignition control from the PCM is lost. Therefore, if there is a problem, use a digital meter and check for the presence of 5 volts on the tan bypass wire. If there is not 5 volts present with the engine running, then the PCM or the wiring is at fault.

Up-Integrated Ignition Control

Most coil-on-plug and many waste-spark-type ignition systems use the PCM for ignition timing control. This type of ignition control is called up-integrated because all tim-

ing functions are interpreted in the PCM, rather than being split between the ignition control module and the PCM. The ignition module, if even used, contains the power transistor for coil switching. The signal, as to when the coil fires, is determined and controlled from the PCM.

Unlike a bypass ignition control circuit, it is not possible to separate the PCM from the ignition coil control to help isolate a fault.

COMPRESSION SENSING IGNITION

Some waste-spark ignition systems, such as those used on Saturns, use the voltage required to fire the cylinders to determine cylinder position. It requires a higher voltage to fire a spark plug under compression than it does when the spark plug is being fired on the exhaust stroke. The electronics in the coil and the PCM can detect which of the two cylinders that are fired at the same time requires the higher voltage, which indicates the cylinder on the compression stroke. For example, a typical 4-cylinder engine equipped with a waste-spark ignition system will fire both cylinders 1 and 4. If cylinder number 4 requires a higher voltage to fire, as determined by the electronics connected to the coil, then the PCM assumes that cylinder number 4 is on the compression stroke. Engines equipped with compression sensing ignition systems, such as Saturns, do not require the use of a camshaft position sensor to determine cylinder number.

COIL-ON-PLUG IGNITION

Coil-on-plug (COP) ignition uses one ignition for each spark plug. This system is also called **coil-by-plug, coil-near-plug,** or **coil-over-plug** ignition. See Figures 22-25 and 22-26. The coil-on-plug system eliminates the spark

INDIVIDUAL COILS

ATTACHES TO TOP OF SPARK PLUG

COIL-ON-PLUG IGNITION COIL

FIGURE 22-25 A coil-on-plug ignition system.

plug wires which are often sources of **electromagnetic interference (EMI)** that can cause problems to some computer signals. The vehicle computer controls the timing of the spark. Ignition timing also can be changed (retarded or advanced) on a cylinder-by-cylinder basis for maximum performance and to respond to knock sensor signals. See Figure 22-27. There are two basic types of coil-on-plug ignition including:

- **2-wire.** This design uses the vehicle computer to control the firing of the ignition coil. The two wires include ignition voltage feed and the pulse ground wire, which is controlled by the computer. All ignition timing and dwell control are handled by the computer.

- **3-wire.** This design includes an ignition module at each coil. The three wires include:

  - Ignition voltage
  - Ground
  - Pulse from the computer to the built-in module

General Motors vehicles use a variety of coil-on-plug-type ignition systems. Many V-8 engines use a coil-near-plug system with individual coils and modules that are placed on the valve covers for each individual cylinder. Short secondary ignition spark plug wires are used to connect the output terminal of the ignition coil to the spark plug.

Most newer DaimlerChrysler engines use coil-over-plug-type ignition systems. Each coil is controlled by the PCM, which can vary the ignition timing separately for each cylinder based on signals the PCM receives from the knock sensor(s). For example, if the knock sensor detects that a spark knock has occurred after firing cylinder 3, then the PCM will continue to monitor cylinder 3 and retard timing on just this one cylinder if necessary to prevent engine-damaging detonation.

◀ SAFETY TIP ▶

NEVER DISCONNECT A SPARK PLUG WIRE WHEN THE ENGINE IS RUNNING!

Ignition systems produce a high-voltage pulse necessary to ignite a lean air-fuel mixture. If you disconnect a spark plug wire when the engine is running, this high-voltage spark could cause personal injury or damage to the ignition coil and/or ignition module.

COP IGNITION SCHEMATIC

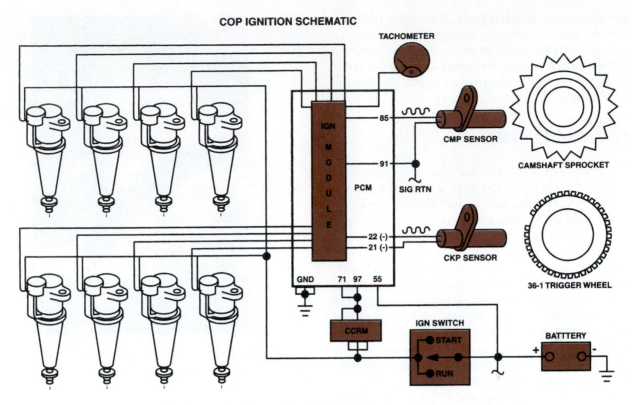

FIGURE 22-26 A typical coil-on-plug (COP) ignition system on a V-8 with a separate coil for each cylinder.

FIGURE 22-27 Individual coils with modules shown on the General Motors 4.2-L inline 6-cylinder light truck engine. Note the aluminum cooling fins (heat sink) on top of each assembly.

ION-SENSING IGNITION

In an ion-sensing ignition system, the spark plug itself becomes a sensor. The ignition control (IC) module applies a voltage of about 100 to 400 volts DC across the spark plug gap after the ignition to sense the plasma inside the cylinder. The coil discharge voltage (10 to 15 KV) is electrically isolated from the ion-sensing circuit. The combustion flame is ionized and will conduct some electricity, which can be accurately measured at the spark plug gap. The purposes of this circuit include:

- Misfire detection (required by OBD-II regulations)
- Knock detection (eliminates the need for a knock sensor)
- Ignition timing control (to achieve the best spark timing for maximum power with lowest exhaust emissions)
- Exhaust gas recirculation (EGR) control
- Air-fuel ratio control on an individual cylinder basis

Ion-sensing ignition systems still function the same as conventional coil-on-plug designs, but the engine does not need to be equipped with a camshaft position sensor or a knock sensor, because both of these faults are achieved using the electronics inside the ignition control circuits.

IGNITION TIMING

Ignition timing refers to when the spark plug fires in relation to piston position. The time when the spark occurs depends on engine speed, and therefore must be advanced (spark plugs fire some) as the engine rotates faster. The ignition in the cylinder takes a certain amount of time, usually 3 ms (0.003 or 3/1000 of a second). This burning time is relatively constant throughout the entire engine speed range. For maximum efficiency from the expanding gases inside the combustion chamber, the burning of the air-fuel mixture should end by about 10° after top dead center. If the burning of the mixture is still occurring after that point, the expanding gases do not exert much force on the piston because it is moving away from the gases.

Therefore, to achieve the goal of having the air-fuel mixture be completely burned by the time the piston reaches 10° after top dead center (ATDC), the spark must be advanced (occur sooner) as the engine speed increases. This timing advance is determined and controlled by the PCM on most vehicles. See Figure 22-28.

INITIAL TIMING

If the engine is equipped with a distributor, it may be possible to adjust the base or the initial timing. The initial timing is usually set to fire the spark plug between zero degrees (top dead center or TDC) or slightly before TDC (BTDC). Ignition timing does change as the timing chain or gear wears and readjustment is often necessary on high-mileage engines. See Figure 22-29. Waste-spark and coil-on-plug ignitions cannot be adjusted.

KNOCK SENSORS

Knock sensors are used to detect abnormal combustion, often called **ping, spark knock,** or **detonation.** Whenever abnormal combustion occurs, a rapid pressure increase occurs in the cylinder, creating a noise. It is this vibration that is detected by the knock sensor. The signal from the knock sensor is used by the PCM to retard

FIGURE 22-28 Ignition timing marks are found on the harmonic balancers that are equipped with distributor ignition.

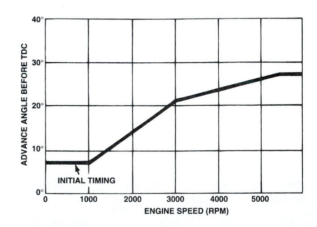

FIGURE 22-29 The initial timing is where the spark plug fires at idle speed. The computer then advances the timing based on engine speed and other factors.

the ignition timing until the knock is eliminated, thereby reducing the damaging effects of the abnormal combustion on pistons and other engine parts.

Inside the knock sensor is a piezoelectric element that generates a voltage when pressure or a vibration is applied to the unit. The knock sensor is tuned to the engine knock frequency, which is a range from 5 KHz to 10 KHz, depending on the engine design. The voltage signal from the knock sensor (**KS**) is sent to the PCM. The PCM retards the ignition timing until the knocking stops.

Diagnosing the Knock Sensor

If a knock sensor diagnostic trouble code (DTC) is present, follow the specified testing procedure in the service information. A scan tool can be used to check the operation of the knock sensor, using the following procedure.

Step 1 Start the engine and connect a scan tool to monitor ignition timing and/or knock sensor activity.

Step 2 Create a simulated engine knocking sound by tapping on the engine block or cylinder head with a soft-faced mallet.

Step 3 Observe the scan tool display. The vibration from the tapping should have been interpreted by the knock sensor as a knock, resulting in a knock sensor signal and a reduction in the spark advance.

A knock sensor can also be tested using a digital storage oscilloscope. See Figures 22-30 and 22-31.

NOTE: Some engine computers are programmed to ignore knock sensor signals when the engine is at idle speed to avoid having the noise from a loose accessory drive belt, or other accessory, be interpreted as engine knock. Always follow the vehicle manufacturer's recommended testing procedure.

Replacing a Knock Sensor

If replacing a knock sensor, be sure to purchase the exact replacement needed because they often look the same, but the frequency range can vary according to engine design, as well as where it is located on the engine. Always tighten the knock sensor using a torque wrench and tighten to the specified torque to avoid causing damage to the piezoelectric element inside the sensor.

SPARK PLUGS

Spark plugs are manufactured from ceramic insulators inside a steel shell. The threads of the shell are rolled and a seat is formed to create a gas-tight seal with the cylinder head. See Figure 22-32. The physical difference in spark plugs includes:

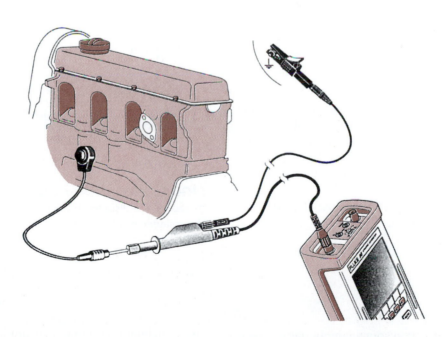

FIGURE 22-30 A knock sensor can be tested using a digital storage oscilloscope by first disconnecting the sensor lead from the vehicle computer and connecting the probe to the sensor. Also be sure the probe ground is attached to a good clean ground. *(Courtesy of Fluke Corporation)*

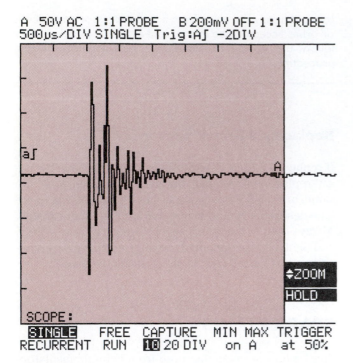

```
A 50V AC  1:1 PROBE   B 200mV OFF 1:1 PROBE
500µs/DIV SINGLE  Trig:A∫ -2DIV
```

```
                                          ⇕ZOOM
                                          HOLD
SCOPE:
SINGLE   FREE   CAPTURE   MIN MAX  TRIGGER
RECURRENT RUN   10 20 DIV  on A    at 50%
```

FIGURE 22-31 A typical waveform from a knock sensor during a spark knock event. This signal is sent to the computer which in turn retards the ignition timing. This timing retard is accomplished by an output command from the computer to either a spark advance control unit or directly to the ignition module. *(Courtesy of Fluke Corporation)*

- **Reach.** This is the length of the threaded part of the plug.
- **Heat range.** The heat range of the spark plug refers to how rapidly the heat created at the tip is transferred to the cylinder head. A plug with a long ceramic insulator path will run hotter at the tip than a spark plug that has a shorter path. See Figure 22-33.
- **Type of seat.** Some spark plugs use a gasket and others rely on a tapered seat to seal.

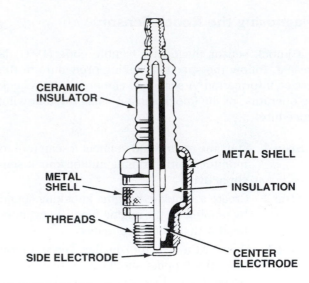

FIGURE 22-32 Parts of a typical spark plug.

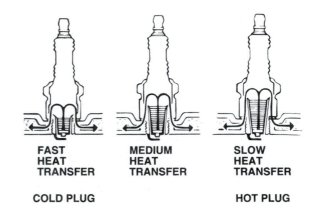

FIGURE 22-33 The heat range of a spark plug is determined by the distance the heat has to flow from the tip to the cylinder head.

SUMMARY

1. All inductive ignition systems supply battery voltage to the positive side of the ignition coil and pulse the negative side of the coil on and off to ground to create a high-voltage spark.

2. If an ignition system uses a distributor, it is a distributor ignition (DI) system.

3. If an ignition system does not use a distributor, it is called an electronic ignition (EI) system.

4. A waste-spark ignition system fires two spark plugs at the same time.

5. A coil-on-plug ignition system uses an ignition coil for each spark plug.

REVIEW QUESTIONS

1. How can 12 volts from a battery be changed to 40,000 volts for ignition?

2. How does a magnetic sensor work?

3. How does a Hall-effect sensor work?

4. How does a waste-spark ignition system work?

ASE CERTIFICATION-TYPE QUESTIONS

1. The primary (low-voltage) ignition system must be working correctly before any spark occurs from a coil. Which component is *not* in the primary ignition circuit?
   a. Spark plug wiring
   b. Ignition module (igniter)
   c. Pickup coil (pulse generator)
   d. Ignition switch

2. The ignition module has direct control over the firing of the coil(s) of an EI system. Which component(s) triggers (controls) the module?
   a. Pickup coil
   b. Computer
   c. Crankshaft sensor
   d. All of the above

3. Distributorless (waste-spark) ignition systems can be triggered by a _____.
   a. Hall-effect sensor
   b. Magnetic sensor
   c. Spark sensor
   d. Either a or b

4. HEI, Duraspark, and EIS are examples of _____.
   a. Waste-spark systems
   b. Coil-on-plug ignition systems
   c. Distributor ignition systems
   d. Pickup coil types

5. Coil polarity is determined by the _____.
   a. Direction of rotation of the coil windings
   b. Turn ratio
   c. Direction of laminations
   d. Saturation direction

6. Because of _____, an ignition coil cannot be fully charged (reach magnetic saturation) until after a delay of about 10 ms.
   a. Voltage drop across the ignition switch and related wiring
   b. Resistance in the coil windings
   c. Inductive reactance
   d. Saturation

7. The pulse generator _____.
   a. Fires the spark plug directly
   b. Signals the electronic control unit (module)
   c. Signals the computer that fires the spark plug directly
   d. Is used as a tachometer reference signal by the computer and has no other function

8. Two technicians are discussing distributor ignition. Technician A says that the pickup coil or optical sensor in the distributor is used to pulse the ignition module (igniter). Technician B says that some distributor ignition systems have the ignition coil inside the distributor cap. Which technician is correct?
   a. Technician A only
   b. Technician B only
   c. Both Technicians A and B
   d. Neither Technician A nor B

9. A waste-spark-type ignition system _____.
   a. Fires two spark plugs at the same time
   b. Fires one spark plug with reverse polarity
   c. Fires one spark plug with straight polarity
   d. All of the above

10. Technician A says that a defective crankshaft position sensor can cause a no-spark condition. Technician B says that a faulty ignition control module can cause a no-spark condition. Which technician is correct?
    a. Technician A only
    b. Technician B only
    c. Both Technicians A and B
    d. Neither Technician A nor B

IGNITION SYSTEM DIAGNOSIS AND SERVICE

OBJECTIVES

After studying Chapter 23, the reader should be able to:

1. Prepare for ASE Engine Performance (A8) certification test content area "B" (Ignition System Diagnosis and Repair).
2. Describe the procedure used to check for spark.
3. Discuss what to inspect and look for during a visual inspection of the ignition system.
4. List the steps necessary to check and/or adjust ignition timing on engines equipped with a distributor.
5. Describe how to test the ignition system using an oscilloscope.

CHECKING FOR SPARK

In the event of a no-start condition, the first step should be to check for secondary voltage out of the ignition coil or to the spark plugs. If the engine is equipped with a separate ignition coil, remove the coil wire from the center of the distributor cap, install a **spark tester,** and crank the engine. See the Tech Tip "Always Use a Spark Tester." A good coil and ignition system should produce a blue spark at the spark tester. See Figures 23-1 and 23-2.

If the ignition system being tested does not have a separate ignition coil, disconnect any spark plug wire from a spark plug and, while cranking the engine, test for spark available at the spark plug wire, again using a spark tester.

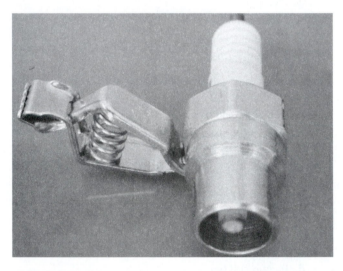

FIGURE 23-1 A spark tester looks like a regular spark plug with an alligator clip attached to the shell. This tester has a specified gap that requires at least 25,000 volts (25 kV) to fire.

NOTE: An intermittent spark should be considered a no-spark condition.

Typical causes of a no-spark (intermittent spark) condition include the following:

1. Weak ignition coil
2. Low or no voltage to the primary (positive) side of the coil

FIGURE 23-2 A close-up showing the recessed center electrode on a spark tester. It is recessed 3/8 in. into the shell and the spark must then jump another 3/8 in. to the shell for a total gap of 3/4 in.

3. High resistance or open coil wire, or spark plug wire
4. Negative side of the coil not being pulsed by the ignition module
5. Defective pickup coil
6. Defective module

IGNITION TROUBLESHOOTING PROCEDURE

When troubleshooting any electronic ignition system for no spark, follow these steps to help pinpoint the exact cause of the problem:

Step 1 Turn the ignition on (engine off) and, using either a voltmeter or a test light, test for battery voltage available at the positive terminal of the ignition coil. If the voltage is not available, check for an open circuit at the ignition switch or wiring. Also check the condition of the ignition fuse (if used).

NOTE: Many Chrysler brand products use an **automatic shutdown (ASD)** relay to power the ignition coil. The ASD relay will not supply voltage to the coil unless the engine is cranking and the computer senses a crankshaft sensor signal. This little fact has fooled many technicians.

Step 2 Connect the voltmeter or test light to the negative side of the coil and crank the engine. The voltmeter should fluctuate or the test light should blink, indicating that the primary coil current is being turned on and off. If there is no pulsing of the negative side of the coil, then the problem is a defective pickup, electronic control module, or wiring.

◀ TECH TIP ▶

ALWAYS USE A SPARK TESTER

A spark tester looks like a spark plug without a side electrode, with a gap between the center electrode and the grounded shell. The tester commonly has an alligator clip attached to the shell so that it can be clamped on a good ground connection on the engine. A good ignition system should be able to cause a spark to jump this wide gap at atmospheric pressure. Without a spark tester, a technician might assume that the ignition system is okay, because it can spark across a normal, grounded spark plug. The voltage required to fire a standard spark plug when it is out of the engine and not under pressure is about 3000 volts or less. An electronic ignition spark tester requires a minimum of 25,000 volts to jump the 3/4-in. gap. Therefore, never assume that the ignition system is okay because it fires a spark plug—always use a spark tester. *Remember that an intermittent spark across a spark tester should be interpreted as a no-spark condition.*

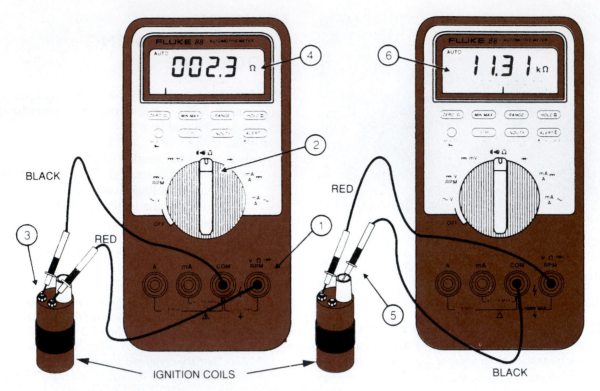

FIGURE 23-3   Checking an ignition coil using a multimeter set to read ohms. *(Courtesy of Fluke Corporation)*

IGNITION COIL TESTING USING AN OHMMETER

If an ignition coil is suspected of being defective, a simple ohmmeter check can be performed to test the resistance of the primary and secondary winding inside the coil. For accurate resistance measurements, the wiring to the coil should be removed before testing. To test the primary coil winding resistance, take the following steps (Figure 23-3):

Step 1   Set the meter to read low ohms.

Step 2   Measure the resistance between the positive terminal and the negative terminal of the ignition coil. Most coils will give a reading between 1 and 3 ohms; however, some coils should indicate less than 1 ohm. Check the manufacturer's specifications for the exact resistance values.

To test the secondary coil winding resistance, follow these steps:

Step 1   Set the meter to read kilohms (kΩ).

Step 2   Measure the resistance between either primary terminal and the secondary coil tower. The normal resistance of most coils ranges between 6000 and 30,000 ohms. Check the manufacturer's specifications for the exact resistance values.

NOTE: Many ignition coils use a screw that is inside the secondary tower of the ignition coil. If this screw is loose, an intermittent engine miss could occur. The secondary coil would also indicate high resistance if this screw was loose.

PICKUP COIL TESTING

The pickup coil, located under the distributor cap on many electronic ignition engines, can cause a no-spark condition if defective. The pickup coil must generate an AC voltage pulse to the ignition module so that the module can pulse the ignition coil.

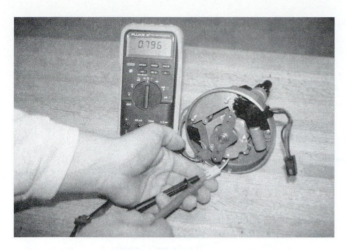

FIGURE 23-4 Measuring the resistance of an HEI pickup coil using a digital multimeter set to the ohms position. The reading on the face of the meter is 0.796 kΩ or 796 ohms in the middle of the 500- to 1500-ohm specifications.

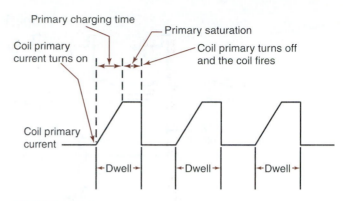

FIGURE 23-5 A waveform showing the primary current flow through the primary windings of an ignition coil.

A pickup coil contains a coil of wire, and the resistance of this coil should be within the range specified by the manufacturer. See Figure 23-4. Some common specifications include the following:

Manufacturer	Pickup Coil Resistance (Ohms)
General Motors	500–1500 (white and green leads)
Ford	400–1000 (orange and purple leads)
Chrysler brand	150–900 (orange and black leads)

If the pickup coil resistance is not within the specified range, replace the pickup coil assembly.

The pickup coil can also be tested for proper voltage output. During cranking, most pickup coils should produce a minimum of 0.25 volt AC. This can be tested with the distributor out of the vehicle by rotating the distributor drive gear by hand.

CURRENT RAMPING IGNITION COILS

Testing an ignition coil for resistance does not always find a coil problem that occurs under actual heat and loads. However, by using a digital storage oscilloscope and a low-current probe, the ignition system can be checked for module current limits and the charging rise time.

Ignition coil operation begins with the module completing the primary circuit through the ignition coil winding. This allows primary current to ramp upward (primary charging time) to a pre-set limit determined by the control module. Once ramped to the pre-set limit, the coil remains on for a set period of time (primary saturation), known as the dwell period. Coil current is then turned off (open circuit) allowing the magnetic field built up through the dwell cycle to collapse inward, cutting across many turns of secondary coil windings, inducing a higher output voltage to fire the coil. The ignition systems used today must provide voltages of 35,000 and maintain a spark duration of over 2 ms to assure good ignition over extended service intervals.

Using the digital storage oscilloscope and a current probe, a quick check can be made of the overall primary condition of the two most important parameters of the ignition circuit, the **module current limits** and the **charging rise time** of the circuit. Actual circuit operation of the primary current control is a very precise element in total ignition function and output. See Figure 23-5.

Every ignition system has a power feed circuit to the ignition coil. To perform current probe testing on the system, first locate the feed wire and make it current probe-accessible. See Figures 23-6 and 23-7. This will serve as a common point on all ignition systems to include both the DI and EI units.

Next, set up the scopes to read approximately 100 mV per division and 2 ms per division. This may be adjusted to suit the waveform, but will give a starting reference point.

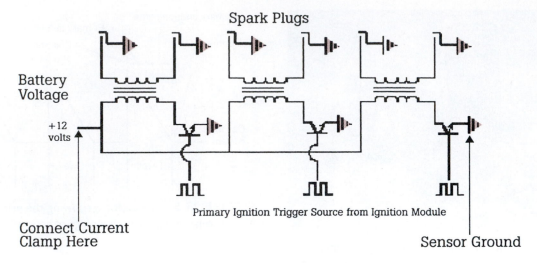

Spark Plugs

Battery Voltage

+12 volts

Connect Current Clamp Here

Primary Ignition Trigger Source from Ignition Module

Sensor Ground

FIGURE 23-6 Schematic of a typical distributorless ignition system showing the location for the power feed and grounds. *(Courtesy of Fluke Corporation)*

FIGURE 23-7 Connect the scopes current clamp around the feed wire for the primary side of the coil(s). Start the engine and view the current flow waveform. *(Courtesy of Fluke Corporation)*

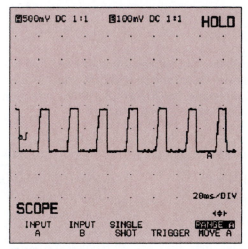

Good coil pattern

FIGURE 23-8 An example of a good coil current flow waveform pattern. Note the regular shape of the rise time and slope. Duration of the waveform may change as the module adjusts the dwell. The dwell is usually increased as the engine speed is increased. *(Courtesy of Fluke Corporation)*

Observed Current Ramp Times

GM electronic (DI) systems	3.6 ms
GM late 1996 and up (DI) systems	2.5 ms (OBD-II)
GM electronic (EI) systems	2.6 ms
Ford electronic (DI) systems	3.6 ms
Chrysler brand (DI) systems (ECM controlled)	3.8 ms

See Figures 23-8 and 23-9.

A pickup coil can also be checked on a scope. The waveform is created by the strengthening and weakening of the magnetic field as the points of time core rotates past the points of the pole pieces. See Figure 23-10.

The changing magnetic field is sent to the ignition control module where it turns off the current through the primary winding of the ignition coil. See Figure 23-11.

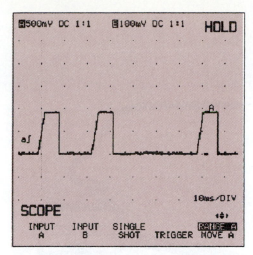

An open coil primary winding will be identified by a missing pulse in the current pattern.

(a)

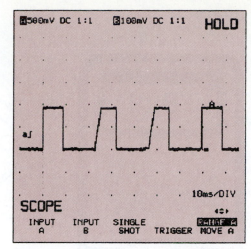

An shorted coil will have a square shaped current ramp (due to reduced primary coil resistance).

(b)

FIGURE 23-9 (a) A waveform pattern showing an open in the coil primary. (b) A shorted coil pattern waveform. *(Courtesy of Fluke Corporation)*

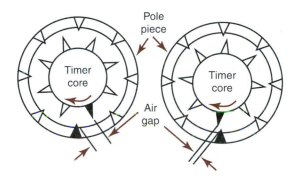

FIGURE 23-10 A typical pickup coil showing how the waveform is created as the timer core rotates inside the pole piece.

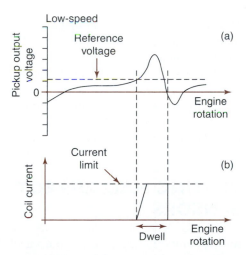

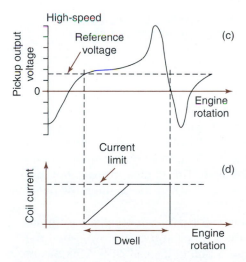

FIGURE 23-11 (a) A voltage waveform of a pickup coil at low engine speed. (b) A current waveform of the current through the primary windings of the ignition coil at low engine speed. (c) A voltage waveform of a pickup coil at high speed. (d) A current waveform through the primary winding of the ignition coil at high engine speed.

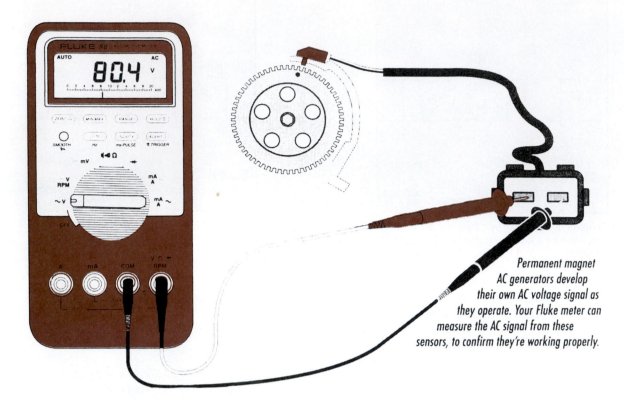

Permanent magnet AC generators develop their own AC voltage signal as they operate. Your Fluke meter can measure the AC signal from these sensors, to confirm they're working properly.

FIGURE 23-12 An AC voltage is produced by a magnetic sensor. Most sensors should produce at least 0.1 volt AC while the engine is cranking if the pickup wheel has many teeth. If the pickup wheel has only a few teeth, you may need to switch the meter to read DC volts and watch the display for a jump in voltage as the teeth pass the magnetic sensor. *(Courtesy of Fluke Corporation)*

◀ DIAGNOSTIC STORY ▶

THE WEIRD RUNNING CHEVROLET TRUCK

An older Chevrolet pickup truck equipped with a V-8 engine was towed into a shop because it would not start. A quick check of the ignition system showed that the pickup coil had a broken wire below the pickup coil and the ignition control module. The distributor was removed from the engine and cleaned, and a replacement pickup coil was installed. The engine started but ran rough and hesitated when the accelerator pedal was depressed.

After an hour of troubleshooting, a careful inspection of the new pickup coil showed that the time core had 6 points instead of 8. This meant that the new pickup coil that was installed was meant for a V-6 engine instead of a V-8. Replacing the pickup coil again solved the problem.

TESTING MAGNETIC SENSORS

Magnetic sensors must be magnetic. If the permanent magnet inside the sensor has cracked, the result is two weak magnets.

If the sensor is removed from the engine, hold a metal (steel) object against the end of the sensor. It should exert a strong magnetic pull on the steel object. If not, replace the sensor. Then, the sensor can be tested using a digital meter set to read AC volts. See Figure 23-12.

TESTING HALL-EFFECT SENSORS

As with any other sensor, the output of the Hall-effect sensor should be tested first. Using a digital voltmeter, check for the presence of a changing DC (digital hi-low) voltage when the engine is being cranked. The best test is to use an oscilloscope and observe the waveform. See Figure 23-13.

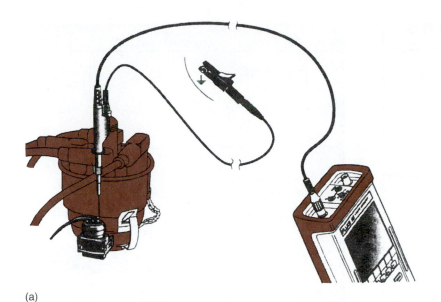

(a)

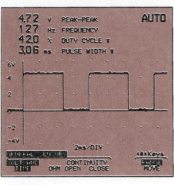

(b)

FIGURE 23-13   (a) The connection required to test a Hall-effect sensor. (b) A typical waveform from a Hall-effect sensor. *(Courtesy of Fluke Corporation)*

TESTING OPTICAL SENSORS

Optical sensors will not operate if dirty or covered in oil. Perform a thorough visual inspection to look for an oil leak that could cause dirty oil to get on the LED or phototransistor. Also be sure that the light shield is securely fastened and that the seal is lightproof. An opti-

cal sensor can also be checked using an oscilloscope. See Figure 23-14. Because of the speed of the engine and the number of slits in the optical sensor disk, a scope is about the only tool that could capture useful information. For example, a Nissan has 360 slits; if it is running at 2000 RPM, a signal is generated 720,000 times per minute or 12,000 times per second.

◄ TECH TIP ►

BAD WIRE? REPLACE THE COIL!

When performing engine testing (such as a compression test), always ground the coil wire. Never allow the coil to discharge without a path to ground for the spark. High-energy electronic ignition systems can produce 40,000 volts or more of electrical pressure. If the spark cannot spark to ground, the coil energy can (and usually does) arc inside the coil itself, creating a low-resistance path to the primary windings or the steel laminations of the coil. See Figure 23-15. This low-resistance path is called a **track** and could cause an engine miss under load even though all of the remaining component parts of the ignition system are functioning correctly. Often these tracks do not show up on any coil test, including most scopes. Because the track is a lower-resistance path to ground than normal, it requires that the ig-

nition system be put under a load for it to be detected, and even then, the problem (engine missing) may be intermittent.

Therefore, when disabling an ignition system, perform one of the following procedures to prevent possible ignition coil damage:

1. Remove the power source wire from the ignition system to prevent any ignition operation.

2. On distributor-equipped engines, remove the secondary coil wire from the center of the distributor cap and connect a jumper wire between the disconnected coil wire and a good engine ground. This ensures that the secondary coil energy will be safely grounded and prevents high-voltage coil damage.

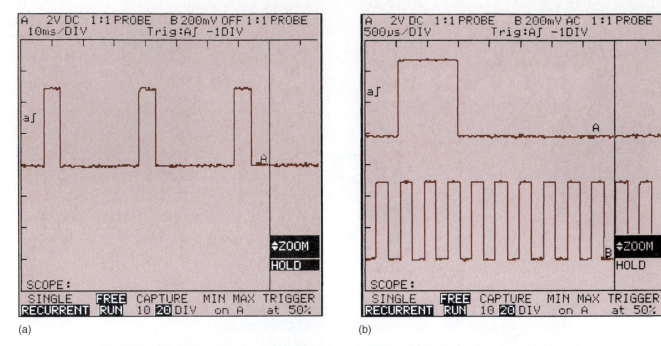

(a)

(b)

FIGURE 23-14 (a) The low-resolution signal has the same number of pulses as the engine has cylinders. (b) A dual-trace pattern showing both the low-resolution signal and the high-resolution signals that usually represent 1 degree of rotation. *(Courtesy of Fluke Corporation)*

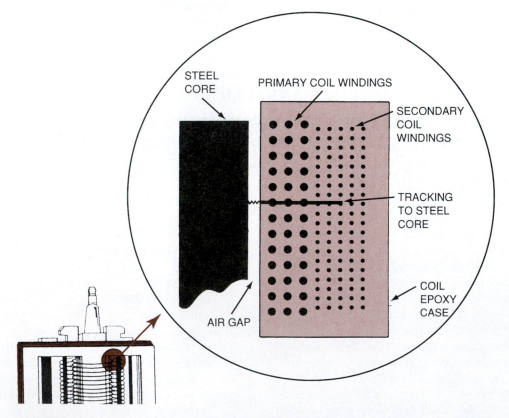

FIGURE 23-15 A track inside an ignition coil is not a short, but rather a low-resistance path or hole that has been burned through from the secondary wiring to the steel core.

DISTRIBUTOR INDEXING

A few engines still using a distributor also use a crank/cam shaft position sensor. Some of these engines use a positive distributor position notch or clamp that enables the distributor to be placed in only one position, while others use a method of indexing to verify the distributor position. See Figure 23-16.

A misindexed distributor may exhibit surging, light bucking, or intermittent engine misfiring. This will most likely occur when the vehicle is at operating temperature, and under a light load at approximately 2000 RPM. *This condition may be caused by a misindexed distributor.* The factory procedure must be used as outlined in the service information. Some of these may be indexed with a scan tool, while others require the use of a voltmeter to verify position. Jeep, late model Chrysler V-6 and V-8 engines, and some GM trucks require indexing. See Figures 23-17 and 23-18.

IGNITION SYSTEM DIAGNOSIS USING VISUAL INSPECTION

One of the first steps in the diagnosis process is to perform a thorough visual inspection of the ignition system, including the following items:

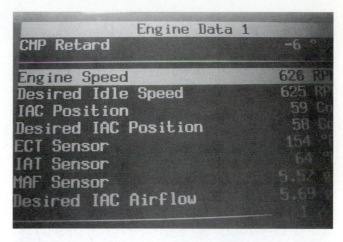

FIGURE 23-17 A scan tool displays the cam retard on a Chevrolet V-6. The cam retard value should be ± 2°.

FIGURE 23-18 A worn distributor drive gear can be the cause of an out-of-specification camshaft position (CMP) signal.

- Check all spark plug wires for proper routing. All plug wires should be in the factory wiring separator and be clear of any metallic object that could cause damage to the insulation and cause a short-to-ground fault.
- Check that all spark plug wires are securely attached to the spark plugs and to the distributor cap or ignition coil(s).
- Check that all spark plug wires are clean and free from excessive dirt or oil. Check that all protective covers normally covering the coil and/or distributor cap are in place and not damaged.
- Remove the distributor cap and carefully check the cap and distributor rotor for faults.
- Remove the spark plugs and check for excessive wear or other visible faults. Replace if needed.

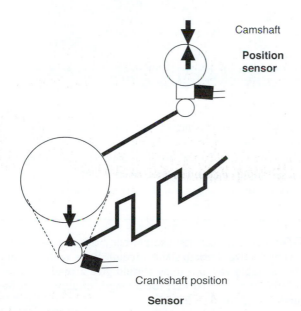

FIGURE 23-16 The relationship between the crankshaft position (CKP) sensor and the camshaft position (CMP) sensor is affected by wear in the timing gear and/or chain.

FIGURE 23-19 Keys used in a vehicle that had an ignition switch intermittent problem.

NOTE: According to research conducted by General Motors, about one-fifth (20%) of all faults are detected during a *thorough visual inspection!*

◄ TECH TIP ►

CHECK THE IGNITION KEYS

Some ignition-related faults are caused by a loose or worn lock cylinder and/or ignition switch assembly that can be caused by having an excessive amount of weight hanging from the key chain. See Figure 23-19.

TESTING FOR POOR PERFORMANCE

Many diagnostic equipment manufacturers offer methods for testing distributorless ignition systems on an oscilloscope. If using this type of equipment, follow the manufacturer's recommended procedures and interpretation of the specific test results.

A simple method of testing distributorless (waste-spark systems) ignition with the engine off involves removing the spark plug wires (or connectors) from the spark plugs (or coils or distributor cap) and installing short lengths (2 in.) of rubber vacuum hose in series.

FIGURE 23-20 A length of vacuum hose being used for a coil wire. The vacuum hose is conductive because of the carbon content of the rubber in the hose. This hose measures only 1000 ohms and was 1 ft long, which is lower resistance than most spark plug wires. Notice the spark from the hose's surface to the tip of a grounded screwdriver.

FIGURE 23-21 A distributorless ignition system (DIS) can be checked by unplugging *both* spark plug wires from one ignition coil and starting the engine. The spark should be able to jump the 1-in. (25-mm) distance between the terminals of the coil. No damage to the coil (or module) results because a spark occurs and does not find ground elsewhere.

NOTE: For best results, use rubber hose that is electrically conductive. Measure the vacuum hose with an ohmmeter. Suitable vacuum hose should give a reading of less than 10,000 ohms (10 kΩ) for a length of about 2 in. See Figures 23-20 through 23-22.

Step 1 Start the engine and ground out each cylinder one at a time by touching the tip of a grounded test light to the rubber vacuum hose. Even though the computer will in-

FIGURE 23-22 Using a vacuum hose and a grounded test light to ground one cylinder at a time on a DIS. This works on all types of ignition systems and provides a method for grounding out one cylinder at a time without fear of damaging any component.

crease idle speed and fuel delivery to compensate for the grounded spark plug wire, a technician should watch for a change in the operation of the engine. If no change is observed or heard, the cylinder being grounded is obviously weak or defective. Check the spark plug wire or connector with an ohmmeter to be certain of continuity.

Step 2 Check all cylinders by grounding them out one at a time. If one weak cylinder is found, check the other cylinder using the same ignition coil (except on engines that use an individual coil for each cylinder). If both cylinders are affected, the problem could be an open spark plug wire, defective spark plug, or defective ignition coil.

Step 3 To help eliminate other possible problems and determine exactly what is wrong, switch the suspected ignition coil to another position (if possible).

- If the problem now affects the other cylinders, the ignition coil is defective and must be replaced.
- If the problem does not "change positions," the control module affecting the suspected coil or either cylinder's spark plug or spark plug wire could be defective.

TESTING FOR A NO-START CONDITION

A no-start condition (with normal engine cranking speed) can be the result of either no spark or no fuel delivery.

Computerized engine control systems use the ignition primary pulses as a signal to inject fuel—a port or throttle-body injection (TBI) style of fuel-injection system. If there is no pulse, then there is no squirt of fuel. To determine exactly what is wrong, follow these steps:

Step 1 Test the output signal from the crankshaft sensor. Most computerized engines with distributorless ignitions use a crankshaft position sensor. These sensors are either the Hall-effect type or the magnetic type. The sensors must be able to produce a variable (either sine or digital) signal. A meter set on AC or DC volts should read a voltage across the sensor leads when the engine is being cranked. If there is no changing voltage output, replace the sensor.

Step 2 If the sensor tests okay in step 1, check for a changing AC voltage signal at the ignition module.

NOTE: Step 2 checks the wiring between the crankshaft position sensor and the ignition control module.

Step 3 If the ignition control module is receiving a changing signal from the crankshaft position sensor, it must be capable of switching the power to the ignition coils on and off. Remove a coil or coil package, and with the ignition switched to on (run), check for voltage at the positive terminal of the coil(s).

NOTE: Several manufacturers program the current to the coils to be turned off within several seconds of the ignition being switched to on if no pulse is received by the computer. This circuit design helps prevent ignition coil damage in the event of a failure in the control circuit or driver error, by keeping the ignition switch on (run) without operating the starter (start position). Some Chrysler brand engines do not supply power to the positive (+) side of the coil until a crank pulse is received by the computer.

If the module is not pulsing the negative side of the coil or not supplying battery voltage to the positive side of the coil, replace the ignition control module.

NOTE: Before replacing the ignition control module, be certain that it is properly grounded (where applicable) and that the module is receiving ignition power from the ignition circuit.

CAUTION: Most distributorless (waste-spark) ignition systems can produce 40,000 volts or more, with energy levels high enough to cause personal injury. Do not open the circuit of an electronic ignition secondary wire, because damage to the system (or to you) can occur.

IGNITION SYSTEM SERVICE

Most specifications are now commonly called *performance specifications*. Even though many electronic engine analyzers can help pinpoint suspected problem areas, close visual inspection of the distributor cap, rotor, spark plugs, and spark plug wires is still important.

FIRING ORDER

Firing order means the order that the spark is distributed to the correct spark plug at the right time. The firing order of an engine is determined by crankshaft and camshaft design. The firing order is determined by the location of the spark plug wires in the distributor cap of an engine equipped with a distributor. The firing order is often cast into the intake manifold for easy reference, as shown in Figure 23-23. Most service manuals also show the firing order and the direction of the distributor rotor rotation, as well as the location of the spark plug wires on the distributor cap.

CAUTION: Ford V-8s use two different firing orders depending on whether the engine is high output (HO) or standard. Using the incorrect firing order can cause the engine to backfire and could cause engine damage or personal injury. General Motors V-6s use different firing orders and different locations for cylinder 1 between the 60-degree V-6 and the 90-degree V-6. Using the incorrect firing order or cylinder number location chart could result in poor engine operation or a no start.

FIGURE 23-23 The firing order is cast or stamped on the intake manifold on most engines that have a distributor ignition.

Firing order is also important for waste-spark-type distributorless (direct-fire) ignition systems. The spark plug wire can often be installed on the wrong coil pack that can create a no-start condition or poor engine operation.

DISTRIBUTOR CAP AND ROTOR INSPECTION

Inspect a distributor cap for a worn or cracked center carbon insert, excessive side insert wear or corrosion, cracks, or carbon tracks, and check the towers for burning or corrosion by removing spark plug wires from the distributor cap one at a time. Remember, a defective distributor cap affects starting and engine performance, especially in high-moisture conditions. If a carbon track is detected, it is most likely the result of a high-resistance or open spark plug wire. Replacement of a distributor cap because of a carbon track without checking and replacing the defective spark plug wire(s) will often result in the new distributor cap failing in a short time. It is recommended that the distributor cap and rotor be inspected every year and replaced if defective. The rotor should be replaced every time the spark plugs are replaced, because all ignition current flows through the rotor. Generally, distributor caps should only need replacement after every 3 or 4 years of normal service. See Figures 23-24 through 23-27.

SPARK PLUG WIRE INSPECTION

Spark plug wires should be visually inspected for cuts or defective insulation and checked for resistance with an ohmmeter. Good spark plug wires should

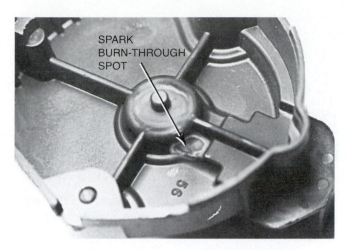

SPARK
BURN-THROUGH
SPOT

FIGURE 23-24 Note where the high-voltage spark jumped through the plastic rotor to arc into the distributor shaft. Always check for a defective spark plug(s) when a defective distributor cap or rotor is discovered. If a spark cannot jump to a spark plug, it tries to find a ground path wherever it can.

FIGURE 23-26 This rotor had arced through to the distributor shaft. The engine would not run above an idle speed and the spark from the coil could easily fire a spark tester.

FIGURE 23-25 This distributor cap should be replaced because of the worn inserts and excessive dusting inside the cap.

FIGURE 23-27 Carbon track in a distributor cap. These faults are sometimes difficult to spot and can cause intermittent engine missing. The usual cause of a tracked distributor cap (or coil, if it is a distributorless ignition) is a defective (open) spark plug wire.

◄ **TECH TIP** ►

LOOK BEFORE YOU PRY

Some distributor rotors are secured to the distributor shaft with a retaining screw, as shown in Figure 23-28. Serious damage can occur if excessive force is used to remove the rotor.

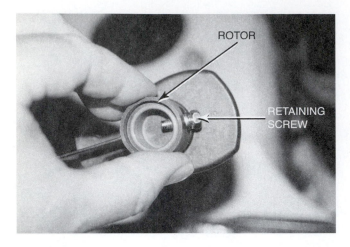

FIGURE 23-28 Some rotors are retained by a screw, so look before you pry.

FIGURE 23-29 With careful visual inspection, the technician discovered this defective spark plug wire.

measure less than 10,000 ohms per foot of length. See Figures 23-29 and 23-30. Faulty spark plug wire insulation can cause hard starting or no starting in damp weather conditions.

◄ TECH TIP ►

SPARK PLUG WIRE PLIERS ARE A GOOD INVESTMENT

Spark plug wires are often difficult to remove. Using good-quality spark plug wire pliers, such as shown in Figure 23-31, saves time and reduces the chance of harming the wire during removal.

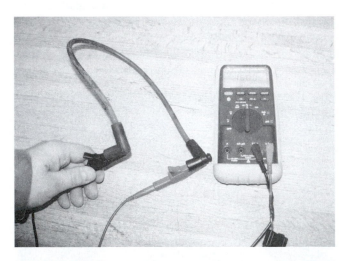

FIGURE 23-30 Measuring the resistance of a spark plug wire with a multimeter set to the ohms position. The reading of 16.03 kΩ (16,030 ohms) is okay because the wire is about 2-ft long. Maximum allowable resistance for a spark plug wire this long would be 20 kΩ (20,000 ohms).

◄ TECH TIP ►

ROUTE THE WIRES RIGHT!

High voltage is present through spark plug wires when the engine is running. Surrounding the spark plugs is a magnetic field that can affect other circuits or components of the vehicle. For example, if a spark plug wire is routed too closely to the signal wire from a mass air flow (MAF) sensor, the induced signal from the ignition wire could create a false MAF signal to the computer. The computer, not knowing the signal was false, would act on the MAF signal and command the appropriate amount of fuel based on the false MAF signal.

To prevent any problems associated with high-voltage spark plug wires, be sure to route them the same as the original plug wires, using all the factory holding brackets and wiring combs. See Figure 23-32. Most factory service manuals show the correct routing if the factory method is unknown.

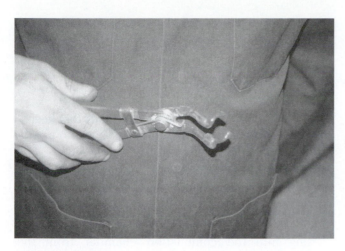

FIGURE 23-31   Spark plug wire boot pliers are a handy addition to any toolbox.

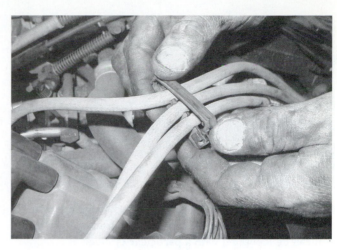

FIGURE 23-32   Always take the time to install spark plug wires back into the original holding brackets (wiring combs).

◄ TECH TIP ►

A CLEAN ENGINE IS A HAPPY ENGINE

Many technicians clean every engine before a tune-up or other engine service. Steam cleaners can be used, but steam tends to remove paint from the engine. A hot water wash, often found at coin-operated washes, does an excellent job of removing grease, oil, and dirt not only from the engine, but also from all underhood components, including the battery. Some technicians keep the engine running while cleaning it with hot water. If the engine stalls, yet restarts after drying of the spark plug wires and distributor cap, faulty spark plug wire insulation and/or a faulty distributor cap is indicated.

CAUTION: Avoid direct water spray to the air cleaner inlet and generator. Because water is thrown up on the engine components during normal driving on wet streets, no harm occurs from washing these parts as long as direct water sprays are avoided. Some diesel engine manufacturers do not recommend engine cleaning, due to the close tolerances of the parts commonly found in the injection pump.

A clean engine will run cooler and is much easier to service. Oil leaks can also be easier to locate on a clean engine. Most customers are impressed to find a clean engine compartment—it is one of the few tune-up items that is visible to the average owner.

SPARK PLUG SERVICE

Spark plugs should be inspected when an engine performance problem occurs and should be replaced regularly to ensure proper ignition system performance. Many spark plugs have a service life of over 20,000 miles (32,000 kilometers). Platinum-tipped original equipment spark plugs have a typical service life of 60,000 to 100,000 miles (100,000 to 160,000 kilometers). Used spark plugs should *not* be cleaned and reused unless absolutely necessary. The labor required to remove and replace (R & R) spark plugs is the same whether the spark plugs are replaced or cleaned. Although cleaning spark plugs often restores proper engine operation, the service life of cleaned spark plugs is definitely shorter than that of new spark plugs. *Platinum-tipped spark plugs should not be regapped!* Using a gapping tool can break the platinum after it has been used in an engine.

Be certain that the engine is cool before removing spark plugs, especially on engines with aluminum cylinder heads. To help prevent dirt from getting into the cylinder of an engine while removing a spark plug, use compressed air or a brush to remove dirt from around the spark plug before removal. See Figures 23-33 through 23-35.

Spark Plug Inspection

Spark plugs are the windows to the inside of the combustion chamber. A thorough visual inspection of the spark plugs can often lead to the root cause of an engine

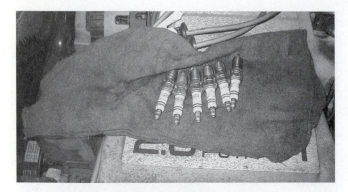

FIGURE 23-33 When removing spark plugs, it is wise to arrange them so that they can be compared and any problem can be identified with a particular cylinder.

FIGURE 23-34 A spark plug thread chaser is a low-cost tool that hopefully will not be used often, but is necessary to clean the threads before new spark plugs are installed.

FIGURE 23-35 Since 1991, General Motors engines have been equipped with slightly (1/8 in. or 3 mm) longer spark plugs. This requires that a longer spark plug socket should be used to prevent the possibility of cracking a spark plug during installation. The longer socket is shown next to a normal 5/8 in. spark plug socket.

performance problem. Two indications and their possible root causes include the following:

1. **Carbon fouling.** If the spark plug(s) has *dry black carbon* (soot), the usual causes include:
   - Excessive idling
   - Slow-speed driving under light loads that keeps the spark plug temperatures too low to burn off the deposits
   - Overrich air-fuel mixture
   - Weak ignition system output

2. **Oil fouling.** If the spark plug has *wet, oily* deposits with little electrode wear, oil may be getting into the combustion chamber from the following:
   - Worn or broken piston rings
   - Defective or missing valve stem seals

NOTE: If the deposits are heavier on the plug facing the intake valve, the cause is usually due to excessive valve stem clearance or defective intake valve stem seals.

When removing spark plugs, place them in order so that they can be inspected to check for engine problems that might affect one or more cylinders. All spark plugs should be in the same condition, and the color of the center insulator should be light tan or gray. If all the spark plugs are black or dark, the engine should be checked for conditions that could cause an overly rich air-fuel mixture or possible oil burning. If only one or a few spark plugs are black, check those cylinders for proper firing (possible defective spark plug wire) or an engine condition affecting only those particular cylinders. See Figures 23-36 through 23-39.

If all spark plugs are white, check for possible over-advanced ignition timing or a vacuum leak causing a lean air-fuel mixture. If only one or a few spark plugs are white, check for a vacuum leak affecting the fuel mixture only to those particular cylinders.

NOTE: The engine computer "senses" rich or lean air-fuel ratios by means of input from the oxygen sensor. If one cylinder is lean, the computer may make all other cylinders richer to compensate.

Inspect all spark plugs for wear by first checking the condition of the center electrode. As a spark plug wears, the center electrode becomes rounded. If the center electrode is rounded, higher ignition system voltage is required to fire the spark plug. When installing spark plugs, always use the correct tightening torque to ensure

FIGURE 23-36 An extended-reach spark plug that shows normal wear. The color and condition indicate that the cylinder is operating correctly.

FIGURE 23-38 Typical worn spark plug. Notice the rounded center electrode. The deposits indicate a possible oil usage problem.

FIGURE 23-37 Spark plug removed from an engine after a 500-mile race. Note the clipped side (ground) electrode. The electrode design and narrow (0.025 in.) gap are used to ensure that a spark occurs during extremely high engine speed operation. The color and condition of the spark plug indicate that near-perfect combustion has been occurring.

FIGURE 23-39 New spark plug that was fouled by a too-rich air-fuel mixture. The engine from which this spark plug came had a defective (stuck partially open) injector on this one cylinder only.

proper heat transfer from the spark plug shell to the cylinder head.

NOTE: General Motors does not recommend the use of antiseize compound on the threads of spark plugs being installed in an aluminum cylinder head, because the spark plug will be overtightened. This excessive tightening torque places the threaded portion of the spark plug too far into the combustion chamber where carbon can accumulate and result in the spark plugs being difficult to remove. If antiseize compound is used on spark plug threads, reduce the tightening torque by 40%. Always follow the vehicle manufacturer's recommendations.

◀ TECH TIP ▶

TWO-FINGER TRICK

To help prevent overtightening a spark plug when a torque wrench is not available, simply use two fingers on the ratchet handle. Even the strongest service technician cannot overtighten a spark plug by using two fingers.

QUICK AND EASY SECONDARY IGNITION TESTS

Most engine running problems are caused by defective or out-of-adjustment ignition components. Many ignition problems involve the high-voltage secondary ignition circuit. Following are some quick and easy secondary ignition tests.

Test 1 If there is a crack in a distributor cap, coil, or spark plug, or a defective spark plug wire, a spark may be visible at night. Because the highest voltage is required during partial throttle acceleration, the technician's assistant should accelerate the engine slightly with the gear selector in drive or second gear (if manual transmission) and the brake firmly applied. If any spark is visible, the location should be closely inspected and the defective parts replaced. A blue glow or "corona" around the shell of the spark plug is normal and not an indication of a defective spark plug.

◀ TECH TIP ▶

USE ORIGINAL EQUIPMENT MANUFACTURER'S SPARK PLUGS

A technician at an independent service center replaced the spark plugs in a Pontiac with new Champion brand spark plugs of the correct size, reach, and heat range. When the customer returned to pay the bill, he inquired as to the brand name of the replacement parts used for the tune-up. When told that Champion spark plugs were used, he stopped signing his name on the check he was writing. He said that he owned 1000 shares of General Motors stock, he owned two General Motors vehicles, and he expected to have General Motors parts used in his General Motors vehicles. The service manager had the technician replace the spark plugs with AC brand spark plugs because this brand was used in the engine when the vehicle was new. Even though most spark plug manufacturers produce spark plugs that are correct for use in almost any engine, many customers prefer that original equipment manufacturer (OEM) spark plugs be used in their engines.

Spark plug	Torque with torque wrench (lb-ft)		Torque without torque wrench (in turns)	
	Cast-iron Head	Aluminum Head	Cast-iron Head	Aluminum Head
Gasket				
14 mm	26–30	18–22	1/4	1/4
18 mm	32–38	28–34	1/4	1/4
Tapered seat				
14 mm	7–15	7–15	1/16 (snug)	1/16 (snug)
18 mm	15–20	15–20	1/16 (snug)	1/16 (snug)

Test 2   For intermittent problems, use a spray bottle to apply a water mist to the spark plugs, distributor cap, and spark plug wires. See Figure 23-40. With the engine running, the water may cause an arc through any weak insulating materials and cause the engine to miss or stall.

HINT: Adding a little salt or liquid soap to the water makes the water more conductive, and also makes it easier to find those hard-to-diagnose intermittent ignition faults.

Test 3   To determine if the rough engine operation is due to secondary ignition problems, connect a 6- to 12-volt test light to the negative side (sometimes labeled "tach") of the coil. Connect the other lead of the test light to the positive lead of the coil. With the engine running, the test light should be dim and steady in brightness. If there is high resistance in the secondary circuit (such as that caused by a defective spark plug wire), the test light will pulse brightly at times. If the test light varies noticeably, this indicates that the secondary voltage cannot find ground easily and is feeding back through the primary windings of the coil. This feedback causes the test light to become brighter.

IGNITION TIMING

Ignition timing should be checked and adjusted according to the manufacturer's specifications and procedures for best fuel economy and performance, and lowest exhaust emissions. Generally, for testing, engines must be at idle with computer engine controls put into **base timing,** the timing of the spark before the computer advances the timing. To be assured of the proper ignition timing, follow exactly the timing procedure indicated on the underhood emission decal. See Figure 23-41 for a typical ignition timing plate and timing mark.

FIGURE 23-40   A water spray bottle is an excellent diagnostic tool to help find an intermittent engine miss caused by a break in a secondary ignition circuit component.

0° (TDC) MARK

TIMING MARK ON HARMONIC BALANCER

FIGURE 23-41   Typical timing marks. The degree numbers are on the stationary plate and the notch is on the harmonic balancer.

NOTE: Most older engines equipped with a vacuum advance must have the vacuum hose removed and plugged before it is checked for timing.

If the ignition timing is too far *advanced*, for example, if it is set at 12 degrees before top dead center (BTDC) instead of 8 degrees BTDC, the following symptoms may occur:

1. Engine ping or spark knock may be heard, especially while driving up a hill or during acceleration.
2. Cranking (starting) may be slow and jerky, especially when the engine is warm.
3. The engine may overheat if the ignition timing is too far advanced.

If the ignition timing is too far *retarded*, for example, if it is set at 4 degrees BTDC instead of 8 degrees BTDC, the following symptoms may occur:

1. The engine may lack in power and performance.
2. The engine may require a long period of starter cranking before starting.
3. Poor fuel economy may result from retarded ignition timing.
4. The engine may overheat if the ignition timing is too far retarded.

Pretiming Checks

Before the ignition timing is checked or adjusted, the following items should be checked to ensure accurate timing results:

1. The engine should be at normal operating temperature (the upper radiator hose should be hot and pressurized).
2. The engine should be at the correct timing RPM (check the specifications).
3. Check the timing procedure specified by the manufacturer. This may include disconnecting a "set timing" connector wire, grounding a diagnostic terminal, disconnecting a four-wire connector, or similar procedure.

NOTE: General Motors specifies many different timing procedures depending on the engine and type of ignition system. Always consult the emission decal under the hood for the exact procedure to follow.

◄ TECH TIP ►

"TURN THE KEY" TEST

If the ignition timing is correct, a warm engine should start immediately when the ignition key is turned to the start position. If the engine cranks a long time before starting, the ignition timing may be retarded. If the engine cranks slowly, the ignition timing may be too far advanced. However, if the engine starts immediately, the ignition timing, although it may not be exactly set according to specification, is usually adjusted fairly close to specifications. When a starting problem is experienced, check the ignition timing first, before checking the fuel system or the cranking system for a possible problem. This procedure can be used to help diagnose a possible ignition timing problem quickly without tools or equipment.

Timing Light Connections

For checking or adjusting ignition timing, make the timing light connections as follows:

1. Connect the timing light battery leads to the vehicle battery: the red to the positive terminal and the black to the negative terminal.
2. Connect the timing light high-tension lead to spark plug cable 1.

Determining Cylinder 1

The following will help in determining cylinder 1.

1. Four- or six-cylinder engines. On all inline 4- and 6-cylinder engines, cylinder 1 is the *most forward* cylinder.
2. V-6 or V-8 engines. Most V-type engines use the left front (driver's side) cylinder as cylinder 1, except for Ford engines and some Cadillacs, which use the right front (passenger's side) cylinder.
3. Sideways (transverse) engines. Most front-wheel-drive vehicles with engines installed sideways use the cylinder to the far right (passenger's side) as cylinder 1 (plug wire closest to the drive belt[s]).

Follow this rule of thumb: If cylinder 1 is unknown for a given type of engine, it is the *most forward* cylinder as viewed from above (except in Pontiac V-8 engines). See Figure 23-42 for typical cylinder 1 locations.

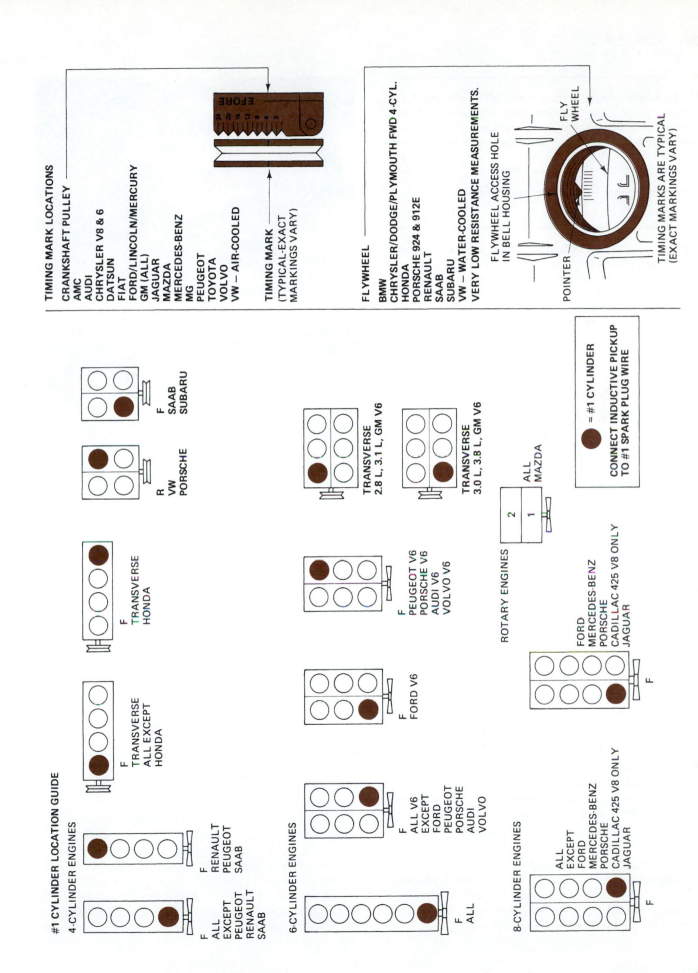

FIGURE 23-42 Cylinder l and timing mark location guide.

NOTE: Some engines are not timed off of cylinder 1. For example, Jaguar inline 6-cylinder engines before 1988 used cylinder 6, but the cylinders were numbered from the firewall (bulkhead) forward. Therefore, cylinder 6 was the most forward cylinder. Always check for the specifications and procedures for the vehicle being tested.

HINT: If cylinder 1 is difficult to reach, such as up against the bulkhead (firewall) or close to an exhaust manifold, simply use the opposite cylinder in the firing order (paired cylinder). The timing light will not know the difference and will indicate the correct position of the timing mark in relation to the pointer or degree mark.

Checking or Adjusting Ignition Timing

Use the following steps for checking or adjusting ignition timing:

1. Start the engine and adjust the speed to that specified for ignition timing.
2. With the timing light aimed at the stationary timing pointer, observe the position of the timing mark with the light flashing. Refer to the manufacturer's specifications on the underhood decal for the correct setting. See Figure 23-43.

NOTE: If the timing mark appears ahead of the pointer, in relation to the direction of crankshaft rotation, the timing is advanced. If the timing mark appears behind the pointer, in relation to the direction of crankshaft rotation, the timing is retarded.

3. To adjust timing, loosen the distributor locking bolt or nut and turn the distributor housing until the timing mark is in correct alignment. Turn the distributor housing in the direction of rotor rotation to retard the timing and against rotor rotation to advance the timing.
4. After adjusting the timing to specifications, carefully tighten the distributor locking bolt. It is sometimes necessary to readjust the timing after the initial setting because the distributor may rotate slightly when the hold-down bolt is tightened.

(a)

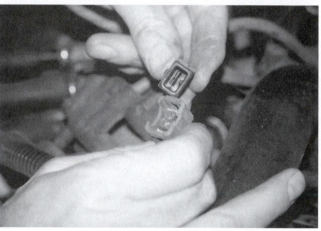

(b)

FIGURE 23-43 (a) Typical SPOUT connector as used on many Ford engines equipped with distributor ignition (DI). (b) The connector must be opened (disconnected) to check and/or adjust the ignition timing. On DIS/EDIS systems, the connector is called SPOUT/SAW (spark output/ spark angle word).

◀ TECH TIP ▶

TWO MARKS ARE THE KEY TO SUCCESS

When a distributor is removed from an engine, always mark the direction the rotor is pointing to ensure that the distributor is reinstalled in the correct position. Because of the helical cut on the distributor drive gear, the rotor rotates as the distributor is being removed from the engine. To help reinstall a distributor without any problems, simply make another mark where the rotor is pointing just as the distributor is lifted out of the engine. Then to reinstall, simply line up the rotor to the second mark and lower the distributor into the engine. The rotor should then line up with the original mark as a double-check. See Figure 23-44.

SCOPE-TESTING THE IGNITION SYSTEM

Any automotive scope will show an ignition system pattern. All ignition systems must charge and discharge an ignition coil. With the engine off, all scopes will display a horizontal line. With the engine running, this horizontal (zero) line is changed to a pattern that will have sections both above and below the zero line. Sections of this pattern that are above the zero line indicate that the ignition coil is discharging. Sections of the scope pattern below the zero line indicate charging of the ignition coil. The height of the scope pattern indicates voltage. The length (from left to right) of the scope pattern indicates time. See Figures 23-45 and 23-46 for typical scope hookups.

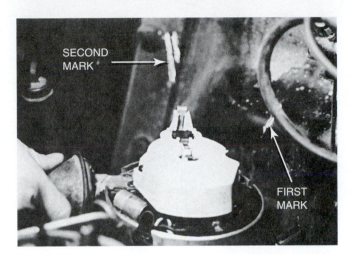

FIGURE 23-44 The first mark indicates the direction the rotor is pointing when the distributor is in the engine. The second mark indicates where the rotor is pointing just as it is pulled from the engine.

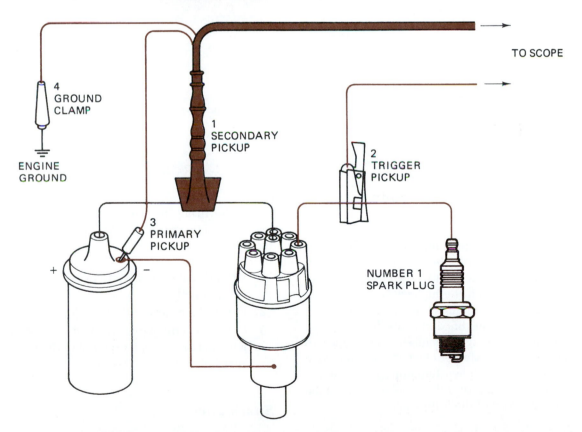

FIGURE 23-45 Typical engine analyzer hookup that includes a scope display. (1) Coil wire on top of the distributor cap if integral type of coil; (2) number 1 spark plug connection; (3) negative side of the ignition coil; (4) ground (negative) connection of the battery.

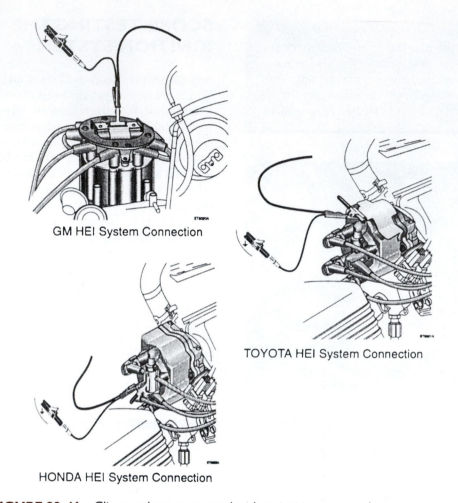

GM HEI System Connection

TOYOTA HEI System Connection

HONDA HEI System Connection

FIGURE 23-46 Clip-on adapters are used with an ignition system that uses an integral ignition coil. *(Courtesy of Fluke Corporation)*

Firing Line

The leftmost vertical (upward) line is called the **firing line.** The height of the firing line should be between 5000 and 15,000 volts (5 and 15 kV) with not more than a 3-kV difference between the highest and the lowest cylinder's firing line. See Figures 23-47 and 23-48.

The height of the firing line indicates the *voltage* required to fire the spark plug. It requires a high voltage to make the air inside the cylinder electrically conductive (to ionize the air). A higher-than-normal height (or height higher than that of other cylinders) can be caused by one or more of the following:

1. Spark plug gapped too wide
2. Lean fuel mixture
3. Defective spark plug wire

If the firing lines are higher than normal for *all* cylinders, then possible causes include one or more of the following:

1. Worn distributor cap and/or rotor (if the vehicle is so equipped)
2. Excessive wearing of all spark plugs
3. Defective coil wire (the high voltage could still jump across the open section of the wire to fire the spark plugs)

Spark Line

The **spark line** is a short horizontal line connected to the firing line. The height of the spark line represents the voltage required to maintain the spark across the spark

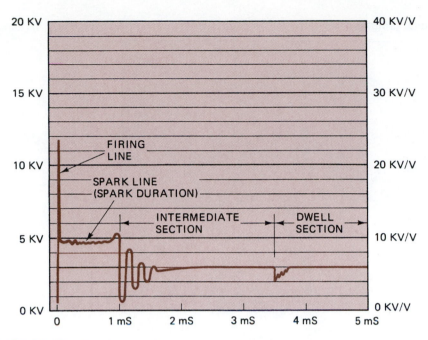

FIGURE 23-47 Typical secondary ignition oscilloscope pattern.

plug after the spark has started. The height of the spark line should be one-fourth of the height of the firing line (between 1.5 and 2.5 kV). The length (from left to right) of the line represents the length of time for which the spark lasts (duration). The spark duration should be between 0.8 and 2.2 milliseconds (usually between 1.0 and 2.0 ms). The spark stops at the end (right side) of the spark line as shown in Figure 23-49.

Intermediate Oscillations

After the spark has stopped, some energy remains in the coil. This remaining energy dissipates in the coil windings and the entire secondary circuit. The oscillations are also called the "ringing" of the coil as it is pulsed.

The secondary pattern amplifies any voltage variation occurring in the primary circuit because of the turns ratio between the primary and secondary windings of the ignition coil. A correctly operating ignition system should display five or more "bumps" (oscillations) (three or more for a GM HEI system).

Transistor-On Point

After the intermediate oscillations, the coil is empty (not charged), as indicated by the scope pattern being on the zero line for a short period. When the transistor turns on an electronic system, the coil is being charged. Note that the charging of the coil occurs slowly (coil-

charging oscillations) because of the inductive reactance of the coil.

Dwell Section

Dwell is the amount of time that the current is charging the coil from the transistor-on point to the transistor-off point. The end of the dwell section marks the beginning of the next firing line. This point is called "transistor off," and indicates that the primary current of the coil is stopped, resulting in a high-voltage spark out of the coil.

Pattern Selection

The entire pattern is not seen on a scope. Ignition oscilloscopes use three positions to view certain sections of the basic pattern more closely. These three positions are as follows:

1. **Superimposed.** This superimposed position is used to look at differences in patterns between cylinders in all areas except the firing line. There are no firing lines illustrated in superimposed positions. See Figure 23-50.
2. **Raster (stacked).** Cylinder 1 is at the bottom on most scopes. Use the raster (stacked) position to look at the spark line length and transistor-on point. The raster pattern shows all areas of the scope pattern except the firing lines. See Figure 23-51.

Secondary Conventional (Single)

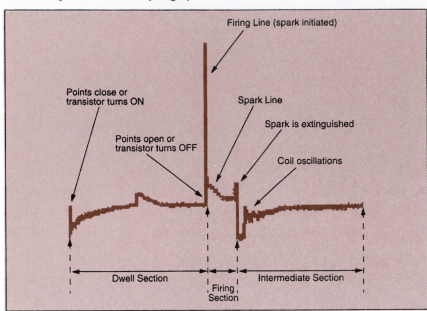

Secondary Conventional (Parade)

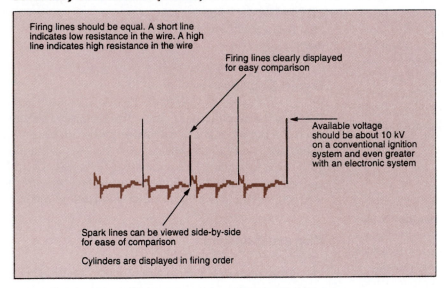

FIGURE 23-48 A single cylinder is shown at the top and a 4-cylinder engine at the bottom. *(Courtesy of Fluke Corporation)*

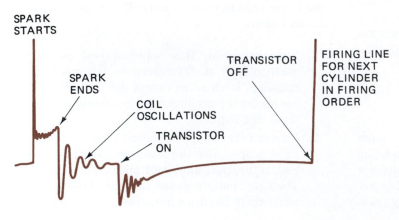

FIGURE 23-49 Drawing shows what is occurring electrically at each part of the scope pattern.

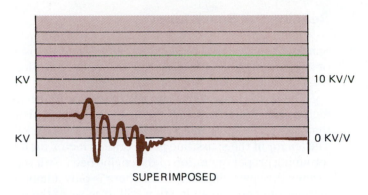

FIGURE 23-50 Typical secondary ignition pattern. Note the lack of firing lines on the superimposed pattern.

3. Display (parade). Display (parade) is the only position in which firing lines are visible. The firing line section for cylinder 1 is on the far right side of the screen, with the remaining portions of the pattern on the left side. This selection is used to compare the height of firing lines among all cylinders. See Figure 23-52.

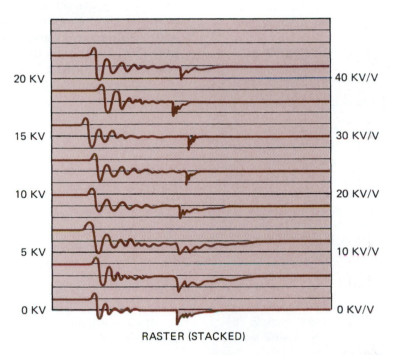

FIGURE 23-51 Raster is the best scope position to view the spark lines of all the cylinders to check for differences. Most scopes display cylinder 1 at the bottom. The other cylinders are positioned by firing order above cylinder 1.

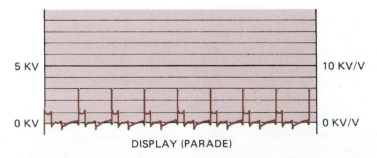

FIGURE 23-52 Display is the only position to view the firing lines of all cylinders. Cylinder 1 is displayed on the left (except for its firing line, which is shown on the right). The cylinders are displayed from left to right by firing order.

Reading the Scope on Display (Parade)

Start the engine and operate at approximately 1000 RPM to ensure a smooth and accurate scope pattern. Firing lines are visible only on the display (parade) position. The firing lines should all be 5 to 15 kV in height and be within 3 kV of each other. If one or more cylinders have high firing lines, this could indicate a defective (open) spark plug wire, a spark plug gapped too far, or a lean fuel mixture affecting only those cylinders.

A lean mixture (not enough fuel) requires a higher voltage to ignite because there are fewer droplets of fuel in the cylinder for the spark to use as "stepping stones" for the voltage to jump across. Therefore, a lean mixture is less conductive than a rich mixture.

◄ DIAGNOSTIC STORY ►

A TECHNICIAN'S TOUGHIE

A vehicle ran poorly, yet its scope patterns were "perfect." Remembering that the scope indicates only that a spark has occurred (not necessarily inside the engine), the technician grounded one spark plug wire at a time using a vacuum hose and a test light. Every time a plug wire was grounded, the engine ran worse, until the last cylinder was checked. When the last spark plug wire was grounded, the engine ran the same. The technician checked the spark plug wire with an ohmmeter; it tested within specifications (less than 10,000 ohms per foot of length). The technician also removed and inspected the spark plug. The spark plug looked normal. The spark plug was reinstalled and the engine tested again. The test had the same results as before—the engine seemed to be running on seven cylinders, yet the scope pattern was perfect.

The technician then replaced the spark plug for the affected cylinder. The engine ran correctly. Very close examination of the spark plug showed a thin crack between the wire terminal and the shell of the plug. Why didn't the cracked plug show on the scope? The scope simply indicated that a spark had occurred. The scope cannot distinguish between a spark inside and outside the engine. In this case, the voltage required to travel through the spark plug crack to ground was about the same voltage required to jump the spark plug electrodes inside the engine. The spark that occurred across the cracked spark plug, however, may have been visible at night with the engine running.

Reading the Spark Lines

Spark lines can easily be seen on either superimposed or raster (stacked) position. On the raster position, each individual spark line can be viewed.

The spark lines should be level and one-fourth as high as the firing lines (1.5 to 2.5 kV, but usually less than 2 kV). The spark line voltage is called the **burn kV.** The *length* of the spark line is the critical factor for determining proper operation of the engine because it represents the spark duration time. There is only a limited amount of energy in an ignition coil. If most of the energy is used to ionize the air gaps of the rotor and the spark plug, there may not be enough energy remaining to create a spark duration long enough to completely burn the air-fuel mixture. Many scopes are equipped with a **millisecond (ms) sweep.** This means that the scope will sweep only that portion of the pattern that can be shown during a 5- or 25-ms setting.

Following are guidelines for spark line length:

- 0.8 ms—too short
- 1.5 ms—average
- 2.2 ms—too long

If the spark line is too short, possible causes include the following:

1. Spark plug(s) gapped too widely
2. Rotor tip to distributor cap insert distance gapped too widely (worn cap or rotor)
3. High-resistance spark plug wire
4. Air-fuel mixture too lean (vacuum leak, broken valve spring, etc.)

If the spark line is too long, possible causes include the following:

1. Fouled spark plug(s)
2. Spark plug(s) gapped too closely
3. Shorted spark plug or spark plug wire

Many scopes do not have a millisecond scale. Some scopes are labeled in degrees and/or percentage (%) of dwell. The following chart can be used to determine acceptable spark line length.

Normal Spark Line Length (at 700 to 1200 RPM)

Number of Cylinders	Milliseconds	Percentage (%) of Dwell Scale	Degrees
4	1.0–2.0	3–6	3–5
6	1.0–2.0	4–9	2–5
8	1.0–2.0	6–13	3–6

Spark Line Slope

Downward-sloping spark lines indicate that the voltage required to maintain the spark duration is decreasing during the firing of the spark plug. This downward slope usually indicates that the spark energy is finding ground through spark plug deposits (the plug is fouled) or other ignition problems. See Figure 23-53.

An upward-sloping spark line usually indicates a mechanical engine problem. A defective piston ring or valve would tend to seal better in the increasing pressures of combustion. As the spark plug fires, the effective increase in pressures increases the voltage required to maintain the spark, and the height of the spark line rises during the duration of the spark. See Figure 23-54.

An upward-sloping spark line can also indicate a lean air-fuel mixture. Typical causes include:

1. Clogged injector(s)
2. Vacuum leak
3. Sticking intake valve

See Figure 23-55 for an example showing the relationship between the firing line and the spark line.

Reading the Intermediate Section

The intermediate section should have three or more oscillations (bumps) for a correctly operating ignition system. Because approximately 250 volts are in the primary ignition circuit when the spark stops flowing across the spark plugs, this voltage is reduced by about 75 volts per oscillation. Additional resistances in the primary circuit would decrease the number of oscillations. If there are fewer than three oscillations, possible problems include the following:

1. Shorted ignition coil
2. Leaky condenser (if point-type ignition)
3. Loose or high-resistance primary connections on the ignition coil or primary ignition wiring

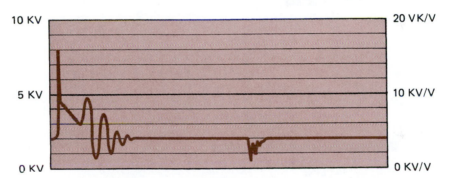

FIGURE 23-53 A downward-sloping spark line usually indicates high secondary ignition system resistance or an excessively rich air-fuel mixture.

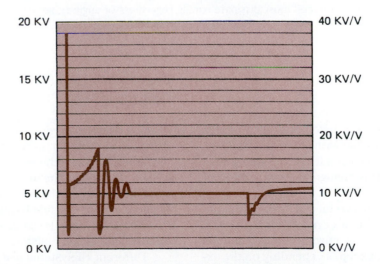

FIGURE 23-54 An upward-sloping spark line usually indicates a mechanical engine problem or a lean air-fuel mixture.

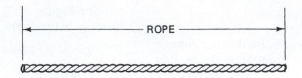

LENGTH OF ROPE REPRESENTS AMOUNT
OF ENERGY STORED IN IGNITION COIL

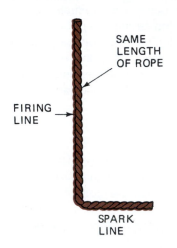

SAME LENGTH OF ROPE (ENERGY). IF HIGH VOLTAGE IS REQUIRED TO IONIZE SPARK PLUG CAP, LESS ENERGY IS AVAILABLE FOR SPARK DURATION. (A LEAN CYLINDER IS AN EXAMPLE OF WHERE HIGHER VOLTAGE IS REQUIRED TO FIRE WITH A SHORTER-THAN-NORMAL DURATION.)

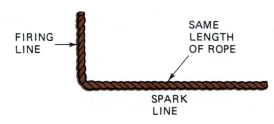

IF LOW VOLTAGE IS REQUIRED TO FIRE THE SPARK PLUG (LOW FIRING LINE), MORE OF THE COIL'S ENERGY IS AVAILABLE TO PROVIDE A LONG-DURATION SPARK LINE. (A FOULED SPARK PLUG IS AN EXAMPLE OF LOW VOLTAGE TO FIRE, WITH A LONGER-THAN-NORMAL DURATION.)

FIGURE 23-55 The relationship between the height of the firing line and length of the spark line can be illustrated using a rope. Because energy cannot be destroyed, the stored energy in an ignition coil must dissipate totally, regardless of engine operating conditions.

Electronic Ignition and the Dwell Section

Electronic ignitions also use a dwell period to charge the coil. Dwell is not adjustable with electronic ignition, but it does change with increasing RPM with many electronic ignition systems. This change in dwell with RPM should be considered normal.

Many EI systems also produce a "hump" in the dwell section, which reflects a current-limiting circuit in the control module. These current-limiting humps may have slightly different shapes depending on the exact module used. For example, the humps produced by various GM HEI modules differ slightly.

Dwell Variation (Distributor Ignition)

A worn distributor gear, worn camshaft gear, or other distributor problem may cause engine performance problems, because the signal created in the distributor will be affected by the inaccurate distributor operation. However, many electronic ignitions vary the dwell electronically in the module to maintain acceptable current flow levels through the ignition coil and module without the use of a ballast resistor.

Different EI systems use one of three different designs. The dwell change characteristic and the types of EI systems that use each design are as follows:

1. Dwell remains *constant* as the engine speed is increased. Types of ignition systems include:
   - Chrysler brand Hall-effect with EIS
   - Ford solid-state ignition
   - Ford Duraspark II
   - Ford EEC II

2. Dwell *decreases* as the engine speed is increased. Types of ignition systems include:
   - Chrysler brand electronic ignition system (EIS)
   - Chrysler brand electronic lean burn (ELB)
   - Chrysler brand electronic spark control (ESC)

3. Dwell *increases* as the engine speed is increased. Types of ignition systems include:
   - All GM HEI systems
   - Ford Duraspark I
   - Ford EEC III
   - Ford TFI
   - Chrysler brand Hall effect with ESC

NOTE: Distributorless ignition systems also vary dwell time electronically within the engine computer or ignition module.

Coil Polarity

With the scope connected and the engine running, observe the scope pattern in the superimposed mode. If the pattern is upside down, the primary wires on the coil may be reversed, causing the coil polarity to be reversed.

NOTE: Check the scope hookup and controls before deciding that the coil polarity is reversed.

Acceleration Check

With the scope selector set on the display (parade) position, rapidly accelerate the engine (gear selector in park or neutral with the parking brake on). The results should be interpreted as follows:

1. All firing lines should rise evenly (not to exceed 75% of maximum coil output) for properly operating spark plugs.
2. If the firing lines on one or more cylinders fail to rise, this indicates fouled spark plugs.

Rotor Gap Voltage

The rotor gap voltage test measures the voltage required to jump the gap (0.030 to 0.050 in. or 0.8 to 1.3 mm) between the rotor and the inserts (segments) of the distributor cap. Select the display (parade) scope pattern and remove a spark plug wire using a jumper wire to provide a good ground connection. Start the engine and observe the height of the firing line for the cylinder being tested. Because the spark plug wire is connected directly to ground, the firing line height on the scope will indicate the voltage required to jump the air gap between the rotor and the distributor cap insert. The normal rotor gap voltage is 3 to 7 kV, and the voltage should not exceed 8 kV. If the rotor gap voltage indicated is near or above 8 kV, inspect and replace the distributor cap and/or rotor as required.

SCOPE-TESTING A WASTE-SPARK IGNITION SYSTEM

A handheld digital storage oscilloscope can be used to check the pattern of each individual cylinder. Some larger scopes can be connected to all spark plug wires and therefore are able to display both power and waste-spark waveforms. See Figure 23-56. Because the waste spark does not require as high a voltage level as the cylinder on the power stroke, the waste-spark firing line will be normally lower.

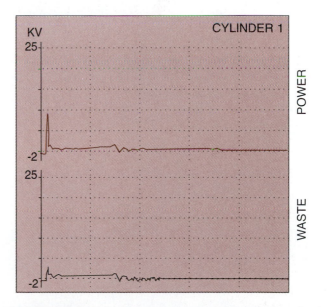

FIGURE 23-56 A dual-trace scope pattern showing both the power and the waste spark from the same coil (cylinders 1 and 6). Note that the firing line is higher on the cylinder that is under compression (power); otherwise, both patterns are almost identical.

IGNITION SYSTEM TROUBLESHOOTING GUIDE

The following list will assist technicians in troubleshooting ignition system problems.

Problem	Possible Causes and/or Solutions
No spark out of the coil	Possible open in the ignition switch circuit
	Possible defective ignition module (if electronic ignition coil)
	Possible defective pickup coil or Hall-effect switch (if electronic ignition)
	Possible shorted condenser
Weak spark out of the coil	Possible high-resistance coil wire or spark plug wire
	Possible poor ground between the distributor or module and the engine block
Engine missing	Possible defective (open) spark plug wire
	Possible worn or fouled spark plugs
	Possible defective pickup coil
	Possible defective module
	Possible poor electrical connections at the pickup coil and/or module

PS 13-1   The tools and supplies needed to test for a fault in the secondary ignition system include: spark plug boot removal pliers, spark tester, secondary ignition system voltage measuring tools, test light, short (2 inches long) pieces of 5/32 in. ID vacuum hose.

PS 13-2   The first step in the diagnosis of the ignition system is to check for adequate voltage from the coil(s). Using a spark plug wire boot removal tool, carefully remove the spark plug wire from the spark plug.

PS 13-3   Attach a spark tester to the end of the spark plug wire and then clip the spark tester to a good engine ground. Start the engine and observe the spark tester. A spark should consistently jump the gap indicating that the system is capable of supplying at least 25,000 volts (25 kV).

PS 13-4   Engine faults as well as ignition system faults can often be detected by using a tester capable of measuring spark plug firing voltage such as this unit from Snap-On tools. Connect the ground clip to a good engine ground and clip the probe around a spark plug wire.

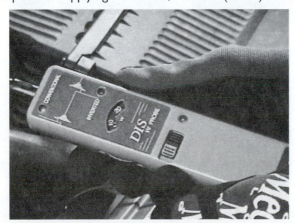

PS 13-5   Start the engine and rotate the thumb wheel until the red light emitting diode (LED) just flickers off and then read the firing voltage on the display. This cylinder shows about 12–13 kV with conventional firing. This reading is about normal (5 to 15 kV).

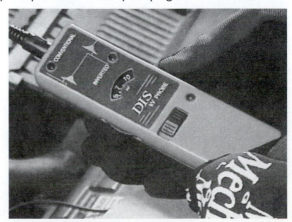

PS 13-6   This cylinder indicates a firing voltage of about 8 kV for the inverted spark on another cylinder. This cylinder is firing in the opposite polarity of the other cylinder (inverted). The firing voltage indicates a possible narrow gap or fouled spark plug.

PS 13-7   Another tester that can be used is one from OTC tools. To use this tester, connect the ground clip to a good engine ground and connect the test probe around a spark plug wire.

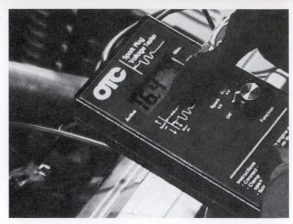

PS 13-8   Start the engine and select "spark kV." This is the voltage required to fire the spark plugs; this display indicates 16.4 kV. This is higher than normal and could be due to a high-resistance spark plug wire or a wide gap spark plug.

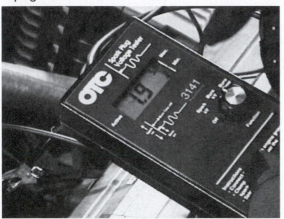

PS 13-9   Move the selector to read "burn kV." The reading indicates 1.9 kV. This is the voltage necessary to keep the spark firing after it has been started. It should be less than 2 kV for most vehicles.

PS 13-10   Move the selector to "burn time." The reading is 1.2 mS (milliseconds). This is the duration of the spark and it should be between 1 and 2 mS.

PS 13-11   Ground out a cylinder one at a time and observe if the engine speed or idle quality is affected. If one cylinder does not respond then this test can help pinpoint a fault in a particular cylinder. Insert 2-inch lengths of vacuum hose between the coil tower and the spark plug wires. This test can also be performed on vehicles equipped with a distributor.

PS 13-12   Use a grounded test light and touch the section of rubber hose with the tip. The high voltage will travel through the test light to ground and not fire the spark plug. This is an easy test to perform that does not require expensive test equipment to perform and can be done quickly to help isolate a cylinder that has a fault.

SUMMARY

1. A thorough visual inspection should be performed on all ignition components when diagnosing an engine performance problem.
2. Platinum spark plugs should not be regapped after use in an engine.
3. A secondary ignition scope pattern includes a firing line, spark line, intermediate oscillations, and transistor-on and transistor-off points.
4. The slope of the spark line can indicate incorrect air-fuel ratio or other engine problems.

REVIEW QUESTIONS

1. Why should a spark tester be used to check for spark rather than a standard spark plug?
2. How do you test a pickup coil for resistance and AC voltage output?
3. What harm can occur if the engine is cranked or run with an open (defective) spark plug wire?
4. What are the sections of a secondary ignition scope pattern?
5. What can the slope of the spark line indicate about the engine?

ASE CERTIFICATION-TYPE QUESTIONS

1. Technician A says that a pickup coil (pulse generator) can be tested with an ohmmeter. Technician B says that ignition coils can be tested with an ohmmeter. Which technician is correct?
   a. Technician A only
   b. Technician B only
   c. Both Technicians A and B
   d. Neither Technician A nor B

2. Technician A says that a defective spark plug wire can cause an engine miss. Technician B says that a defective pickup coil wire can cause an engine miss. Which technician is correct?
   a. Technician A only
   b. Technician B only
   c. Both Technicians A and B
   d. Neither Technician A nor B

3. The _____ sends a pulse signal to an electronic ignition module.
   a. Ballast resistor
   b. Pickup coil
   c. Ignition coil
   d. Condenser

4. Typical primary coil resistance specifications usually range from _____ ohms.
   a. 100 to 450
   b. 500 to 1500
   c. 1 to 3
   d. 6000 to 30,000

5. Typical secondary coil resistance specifications usually range from _____ ohms.
   a. 100 to 450
   b. 500 to 1500
   c. 1 to 3
   d. 6000 to 30,000

6. Technician A says that an engine will not start and run if the ignition coil is tracked. Technician B says that one wire of any pickup coil must be grounded. Which technician is correct?
   a. Technician A only
   b. Technician B only
   c. Both Technicians A and B
   d. Neither Technician A nor B

7. Technician A says that a GM HEI distributor rotor can burn through and cause an engine miss during acceleration. Technician B says that a defective distributor cap can cause an engine miss during acceleration. Which technician is correct?

   a. Technician A only

   b. Technician B only

   c. Both Technicians A and B

   d. Neither Technician A nor B

8. The secondary ignition circuit can be tested using _____.

   a. An ohmmeter

   b. A scope

   c. An ammeter

   d. Either a or b

9. Two technicians are discussing a no-start condition. During cranking, the tachometer on the dash moves and the engine backfires at times. Technician A says that a bad pickup coil or CKP sensor is the most likely cause. Technician B says that an open coil primary is the most likely cause. Which technician is correct?

   a. Technician A only

   b. Technician B only

   c. Both Technicians A and B

   d. Neither Technician A nor B

10. Which sensor produces a digital signal?

   a. Magnetic sensor

   b. Hall-effect sensor

   c. Pickup coil

   d. Both b and c

◄ Chapter 24 ►

OBD II

OBJECTIVES

After studying Chapter 24, the reader should be able to:

1. Prepare for the ASE Engine Performance (A8) certification test content area "E" (Computerized Engine Controls Diagnosis and Repair).
2. Explain the purpose and function of OBD II.
3. Describe how the PCM performs active and passive tests of the computerized engine controls system.
4. Describe the standardized OBD-II DTCs and terminology.
5. Discuss continuous and noncontinuous monitors.
6. Explain the difference between enhanced and generic OBD II.

ON-BOARD DIAGNOSTICS GENERATION-II (OBD-II) SYSTEMS

During the 1980s, most manufacturers began equipping their vehicles with full-function control systems capable of alerting the driver of a malfunction and of allowing the technician to retrieve codes that identify circuit faults. These early diagnostic systems were meant to reduce emissions and speed up vehicle repair.

The automotive industry calls these systems On-Board Diagnostics (OBDs). The California Air Resources Board (CARB) developed the first regulation requiring manufacturers selling vehicles in that state to install OBD. OBD Generation I (OBD I) applies to all vehicles sold in California beginning with the 1988 model year. It carries the following requirements:

1. An instrument panel warning lamp able to alert the driver of certain control system failures, now called a **malfunction indicator lamp (MIL).** See Figure 24-1.
2. The system's ability to record and transmit DTCs for emission-related failures.

FIGURE 24-1 A typical malfunction indicator lamp (MIL), often labeled "check engine."

3. Electronic system monitoring of the HO2S, EGR valve, and evaporative purge solenoid. Although not U.S. EPA required, during this time most manufacturers also equipped vehicles sold outside of California with OBD I.

By failing to monitor the catalytic converter, the evaporative system for leaks, and the presence of engine misfire, OBD I did not do enough to lower automotive emissions. This led the CARB and the EPA to develop OBD Generation II (OBD II).

OBD-II Objectives

Generally, the CARB defines an OBD-II-equipped vehicle by its ability to do the following:

1. Detect component degradation or a faulty emission-related system that prevents compliance with federal emission standards.
2. Alert the driver of needed emission-related repair or maintenance.
3. Use standardized DTCs and accept a generic scan tool.

These requirements apply to all 1996 and later model light duty vehicles. The Clean Air Act of 1990 directed the EPA to develop new regulations for OBD. The primary purpose of OBD II is emission related, whereas the primary purpose of OBD I (1988) was to detect faults in sensors or sensor circuits. OBD-II regulations require that not only sensors be tested but also all exhaust emission control devices, and that they be verified for proper operation.

All new vehicles must pass the **Federal Test Procedure (FTP)** for exhaust emissions while being tested for 505 seconds on rollers that simulate the urban drive cycle around downtown Los Angeles.

NOTE: IM 240 is simply a shorter 240-second version of the 505-second federal test procedure.

The regulations for OBD-II vehicles state that the vehicle computer must be capable of testing for, and determining, if the exhaust emissions are within 1.5 times the FTP limits. To achieve this goal, the computer must do the following:

1. Test all exhaust emission system components for correct operation.
2. Actively operate the system and measure the results.

3. Continuously monitor all aspects of the engine operation to be certain that the exhaust emissions do not exceed 1.5 times the FTP.
4. Check engine operation for misfire.
5. Turn on the MIL (check engine) if the computer senses a fault in a circuit or system.
6. Record a **freeze frame** which is a snapshot of all of the engine dots at the time the DTC was set.
7. Flash the MIL if an engine misfire occurs that could damage the catalytic converter.

DIAGNOSTIC EXECUTIVE AND TASK MANAGER

On OBD-II systems, the PCM incorporates a special segment of software. On Ford and GM systems, this software is called the **diagnostic executive.** On DaimlerChrysler systems, it is called the **task manager.** This software program is designed to manage the operation of all OBD-II monitors by controlling the sequence of steps necessary to execute the diagnostic tests and monitors.

MONITORS

A monitor is an organized method of testing a specific part of the system. Monitors are simply tests that the computer performs to evaluate components and systems. If a component or system failure is detected while a monitor is running, a DTC will be stored and the MIL illuminated by the second trip. The two types of monitors are continuous and noncontinuous.

Continuous Monitors

As required conditions are met, continuous monitors begin to run. These continuous monitors will run for the remainder of the vehicle drive cycle. The three continuous monitors are as follows:

- **Comprehensive component monitor (CCM).** This monitor watches the sensors and actuators in the OBD-II system. Sensor values are constantly compared with known-good values stored in the PCM's memory.

  The CCM is an internal program in the PCM designed to monitor a failure in any electronic component or circuit (including emission-related and non-emission-related circuits) that provide input or output signals to the PCM. The PCM considers that an input or output signal is inoperative when a failure exists due to an open circuit, out-of-range value, or if an onboard rationality check fails. If an emission-related fault is detected, the PCM will set a code and activate the MIL (requires two consecutive trips).

Many PCM sensors and output devices are tested at key-on or immediately after engine start-up. However, some devices, such as the IAC, are only tested by the CCM after the engine meets certain engine conditions. The number of times the CCM must detect a fault before it will activate the MIL depends upon the manufacturer, but most require two consecutive trips to activate the MIL. The components tested by the CCM include:

Four-wheel-drive low switch

Brake switch

Camshaft (CMP) and crankshaft (CKP) sensors

Clutch switch (manual transmissions/transaxles only)

Cruise servo switch

Engine coolant temperature (ECT) sensor

EVAP purge sensor or switch

Fuel composition sensor

Intake air temperature (IAT) sensor

Knock sensor (KS)

Manifold absolute pressure (MAP) sensor

Mass air flow (MAF) sensor

Throttle-position (TP) sensor

Transmission temperature sensor

Transmission turbine speed sensor

Vacuum sensor

Vehicle speed (VS) sensor

EVAP canister purge and EVAP purge vent solenoid

Idle air control (IAC) solenoid

Ignition control system

Transmission torque converter clutch solenoid

Transmission shift solenoids

- **Misfire monitor.** This monitor looks at engine misfire. The PCM uses the information received from the crankshaft position sensor (CPK) and is used to calculate the time between the edges of the reluctor, as well as the rotational speed and acceleration. By comparing the acceleration of each firing event, the PCM can determine if a cylinder is not firing correctly.

  Misfire type A. Upon detection of a misfire type A (200 revolutions), which would cause catalyst damage, the MIL will blink once per second during the actual misfire, and a DTC will be stored.

  Misfire type B. Upon detection of a misfire type B (1000 revolutions), which will exceed 1.5 times the EPA federal test procedure (FTP) standard or cause a vehicle to fail an inspection and maintenance tailpipe emissions test, the MIL will illuminate and a DTC will be stored.

  The DTC associated with multiple cylinder misfire for a type A or type B misfire is DTC P0300. The DTCs associated with an individual cylinder misfire for a type A or type B misfire are DTCs P0301, P0302, P0303, P0304, P0305, P0306, P0307, P0308, P0309, and P0310.

- **Fuel monitor.** The PCM continuously monitors short- and long-term fuel trim. Constantly updated adaptive fuel tables are stored in long-term memory (KAM), and used by the PCM for compensation due to wear and aging of the fuel system components. The MIL will illuminate when the PCM determines the fuel trim values have reached and stayed at their limits for too long a period of time.

Noncontinuous Monitors

Noncontinuous monitors run (at most) once per vehicle drive cycle. The noncontinuous monitors are as follows:

O2S monitor

O2S heater monitor

Catalyst monitor

EGR monitor

EVAP monitor

Secondary AIR monitor

Transmission monitor

PCV system monitor

Thermostat monitor

Once a noncontinuous monitor has run to completion, it will not be run again until the conditions are met during the next vehicle drive cycle. Also after a noncontinuous monitor has run to completion, the readiness status on your scan tool will show "complete" or "done" for that monitor. Monitors that have not run to completion will show up on your scanner as "incomplete."

DIAGNOSTIC TROUBLE CODE PRIORITY

CARB has also mandated that all diagnostic trouble codes (DTCs) be stored according to individual priority. DTCs with a higher priority overwrite those with a lower priority. The OBD-II System DTC Priority include:

- Priority 0—Non-emission related codes
- Priority 1—One-trip failure of two-trip fault for non-fuel, non-misfire codes
- Priority 2—One-trip failure of two-trip fault for fuel or misfire codes
- Priority 3—Two-trip failure or matured fault of non-fuel, non-misfire codes
- Priority 4—Two-trip failure or matured fault for fuel or misfire codes

OBD-II MONITOR INFORMATION SUMMARY

Comprehensive Components Monitor

- Monitor runs continuously
- Monitor includes sensors, switches, relays, solenoids, and PCM hardware
- All are checked for opens, shorts-to-ground, and shorts-to-voltage
- Inputs are checked for rationality
- Outputs are checked for functionality
- Most are 1-trip DTCs
- Freeze frame is priority 3
- Three consecutive good trips are used to extinguish the MIL
- Forty warm-up cycles are used to erase DTC and freeze frame
- Two minutes run time without reoccurrence of the fault constitutes a "good trip"

Continuous Running Monitors

- Monitors run continuously, only stop if fail
- Fuel system: rich/lean
- Misfire: catalyst damaging/FTP (emissions)
- Two-trip faults (except early generation catalyst damaging misfire)
- MIL, DTC, freeze frame after two consecutive faults
- Freeze frame is priority 2 on first trip
- Freeze frame is priority 4 on maturing trip
- Three consecutive good trips in a similar condition window are used to extinguish the MIL
- Forty warm-up cycles are used to erase DTC and freeze frame (80 to erase 1-trip failure if similar conditions cannot be met)

Once Per Trip Monitors

- Monitor runs once per trip, pass or fail
- O_2 response, O_2 heaters, EGR, purge flow EVAP leak, secondary air, catalyst are used
- Two-trip DTCs
- MIL, DTC, freeze frame after two consecutive faults
- Freeze frame is priority 1 on first trip
- Freeze frame is priority 3 on maturing trip
- Three consecutive good trips are used to extinguish the MIL
- Forty warm-up cycles are used to erase DTC and freeze frame

Exponentially Weighted Moving Average (EWMA) Monitors (mathematical method used to determine performance)

- Catalyst monitor
- EGR monitor
- PCM runs six consecutive failed tests; fails in 1-trip
- Three consecutive failed tests on next trip, then fails
- Freeze frame is priority 3
- Three consecutive good trips are used to extinguish the MIL
- Forty warm-up cycles are used to erase DTC and freeze frame

ENABLING CRITERIA

With so many different tests (monitors) to run, the PCM needs an internal director to keep track of when each monitor should run. As mentioned, different manufacturers have different names for this director, such as the **diagnostic executive** or the **task manager.** Each monitor has enabling criteria. These criteria are a set of conditions that must be met before the task manager will give the go-ahead for each monitor to run. Most enabling criteria follow simple logic; for example:

- The task manager will not authorize the start of the O2S monitor until the engine has reached operating temperature and the system has entered closed loop.
- The task manager will not authorize the start of the EGR monitor when the engine is at idle, because the EGR is always closed at this time.

Because each monitor is responsible for testing a different part of the system, the enabling criteria can differ greatly from one monitor to the next. The task manager must decide when each monitor should run, and in what order, to avoid confusion.

There may be a conflict if two monitors were to run at the same time. The results of one monitor might also be tainted if a second monitor were to run simultaneously. In such cases, the task manager decides which monitor has a higher priority. Some monitors also depend on the results of other monitors before they can run.

A monitor may be classified as pending if a failed sensor or other system fault is keeping it from running on schedule.

The task manager may suspend a monitor if the conditions are not correct to continue. For example, if the catalyst monitor is running during a road test and the PCM detects a misfire, the catalyst monitor will be suspended for the duration of the misfire.

◀ FREQUENTLY ASKED ▶ QUESTION

WHAT DOES "RATIONALITY CHECK" MEAN?

The PCM is programmed to detect faults that do not seem rational. For example, if the engine has been operating for 20 minutes and suddenly the engine coolant temperature changes from 195°F to −40°F, then the rationality test part of the computer program (CCM) determines that this is not possible (rational) and then defaults to a fail-safe operating temperature based largely on the IAT sensor. Before OBD-II regulations, if the ECT sensor became unplugged, the computer would increase the amount of fuel delivered to the engine because it was sure that the engine was in fact very cold. With rationality, the OBD-II computer can reason that there must be a fault and continue to deliver fuel for proper operation and not too much that could affect the exhaust emissions.

OBD-II DRIVE CYCLE

The vehicle must be driven under a variety of operating conditions for all active tests to be performed. OBD-II regulations also established a vehicle drive-cycle pattern that would allow the CCM and main monitors to run and complete their individual diagnostic tests. The OBD-II monitors that should run during the drive cycle include the CCM, EGR, EVAP, fuel system, misfire, O2S, and secondary AIR system. One manufacturer has a special code (Ford—DTC P1000) that sets if all the main monitors have not been run to completion.

A **trip** is defined as an engine-operating drive cycle that contains the necessary conditions for a particular test to be performed. These conditions are called the **enable criteria.** For example, for the EGR test to be performed, the engine must be at normal operating temperature and decelerating for a minimum amount of time. Some tests are performed when the engine is cold, whereas others require that the vehicle be cruising at a steady highway speed.

Warm-Up Cycle

Once a MIL is deactivated, the original code will remain in memory until 40 warm-up cycles are completed without the fault reappearing. A warm-up cycle is defined as a trip with an engine temperature increase of at least 40°F and where engine temperature reaches at least 160°F (71°C).

MIL Condition: Off

This condition indicates that the PCM has not detected any faults in an emissions-related component or system, or that the MIL circuit is not working.

MIL Condition: On Steady

This condition indicates a fault in an emissions-related component or system that could affect the vehicle emission levels.

MIL Condition: Flashing

This condition indicates a misfire or fuel control system fault that could damage the catalytic converter.

NOTE: In a misfire condition with the MIL on steady, if the driver reaches a vehicle speed and load condition with the engine misfiring at a level that could cause catalyst damage, the MIL would start flashing. It would continue to flash until engine speed and load conditions caused the level of misfire to subside. Then the MIL would go back to the on-steady condition. This situation might result in a customer complaint of a MIL with an intermittent flashing condition.

MIL: Off

The PCM will turn off the MIL if any of the following actions or conditions occur:

- The codes are cleared with a scan tool.
- Power to the PCM is removed at the battery or with the PCM power fuse for an extended period of time (may be up to several hours or longer).
- A vehicle is driven on three consecutive trips with a warm-up cycle and meets all code set conditions without the PCM detecting any faults.

The PCM will set a code if a fault is detected that could cause tailpipe emissions to exceed 1.5 times the FTP standard; however, the PCM will not deactivate the MIL until the vehicle has been driven on three consecutive trips with vehicle conditions similar to actual conditions present when the fault was detected. This is not merely three vehicle start-ups and trips. It means three trips during which certain engine operating conditions are met so that the OBD-II monitor that found the fault can run again and pass the diagnostic test.

OBD-II DTC NUMBERING DESIGNATION

A scan tool is required to retrieve DTCs from an OBD-II vehicle. Every OBD-II scan tool will be able to read all generic **Society of Automotive Engineers (SAE)**

DTCs from any vehicle. See Figures 24-2 and 24-3 for definitions and explanations of OBD alphanumeric DTCs.

The diagnostic trouble codes (DTCs) are grouped into major categories, depending on the location of the fault on the system involved.

Pxxx codes—powertrain DTCs (engine, transmission-related faults)

Bxxx codes—body DTCs (accessories, interior-related faults)

Cxxx codes—chassis DTCs (suspension and steering-related faults)

Uxxx codes—network DTCs (module communication-related faults)

DTC Numbering Explanation

The number in the hundredth position indicates the specific vehicle system or subgroup that failed. This position should be consistent for P0xxx and P1xxx type codes. The following numbers and systems were established by SAE:

- P0100—Air metering and fuel system fault
- P0200—Fuel system (fuel injector only) fault
- P0300—Ignition system or misfire fault
- P0400—Emission control system fault
- P0500—Idle speed control, vehicle speed (VS) sensor fault

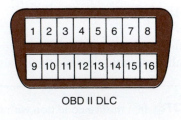

OBD II DLC

PIN NO.	ASSIGNMENTS
1.	MANUFACTURER'S DISCRETION
2.	BUS + LINE, SAE J1850
3.	MANUFACTURER'S DISCRETION
4.	CHASSIS GROUND
5.	SIGNAL GROUND
6.	MANUFACTURER'S DISCRETION
7.	K LINE, ISO 9141
8.	MANUFACTURER'S DISCRETION
9.	MANUFACTURER'S DISCRETION
10.	BUS–LINE, SAE J1850
11.	MANUFACTURER'S DISCRETION
12.	MANUFACTURER'S DISCRETION
13.	MANUFACTURER'S DISCRETION
14.	MANUFACTURER'S DISCRETION
15.	L LINE, ISO 9141
16.	VEHICLE BATTERY POSITIVE (4A MAX)

FIGURE 24-2 Sixteen-pin OBD-II DLC with terminals identified. Scan tools use the power pin (16) and ground pin (4) for power so that a separate cigarette lighter plug is not necessary on OBD-II vehicles.

EXAMPLE: P0302 = CYLINDER #2 MISFIRE DETECTED

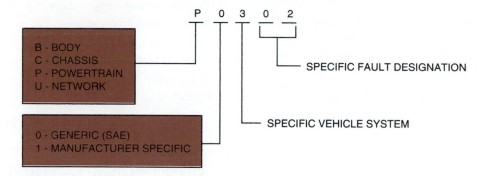

FIGURE 24-3 OBD-II DTC identification format.

- P0600—Computer output circuit (relay, solenoid, etc.) fault
- P0700—Transaxle, transmission faults

NOTE: The tens and ones numbers indicate the part of the system at fault.

Types of DTCs

Not all OBD-II DTCs are of the same importance for exhaust emissions. Each type of DTC has different requirements for it to set, and the computer will only turn on the MIL for emissions-related DTCs.

◄ FREQUENTLY ASKED QUESTION ►

IS THERE A GENERIC DRIVE CYCLE?

Readiness tests (sometimes called **flags**) are tests performed on all of the monitored systems as displayed on a scan tool. While there are published drive cycles for each vehicle manufacturer, this generic drive cycle usually allows all monitors to run. To run all tests, the engine coolant temperature should be less than 122°F (50°C) with the IAT within 11°F (6°C) of the ECT temperature and the fuel tank filled from 15% to 85% of capacity before starting the test. Proceed as follows:

1. *Start the engine and allow it to idle for 2.5 minutes.* This step tests the O2S heater, canister purge system, misfire, fuel trim, and time to closed-loop operation.
2. *Accelerate at one-half throttle to 55 mph (88 km/h).* This step tests for misfire, fuel trim diagnostics, and canister purge.
3. *Hold the speed steady for 3 minutes.* This step tests the O2S, EGR system, canister purge, misfire, and fuel trim diagnostics.
4. *Decelerate without using the brake or clutch (if equipped).* This step tests the EGR system, canister purge, and fuel trim diagnostics.
5. *Accelerate at three-fourths throttle to 55 to 60 mph (88 to 96 km/h).* This step tests for misfire, fuel trim diagnostics, and canister purge.
6. *Hold steady speed for 5 minutes.* This step tests the catalytic converter.
7. *Decelerate without using the brake or clutch, if equipped.* This step tests the EGR system, canister purge, and fuel trim diagnostics.

Type A Codes

A type A DTC is emission related and will cause the MIL to be turned on the *first trip* if the computer has detected a problem. Engine misfire or a very rich or lean air-fuel ratio, for example, would cause a type A DTC. These codes alert the driver to an emission problem that may cause damage to the catalytic converter.

Type B Codes

A type B code will be stored and the MIL will be turned on during the *second consecutive trip*, alerting the driver to the fact that a diagnostic test was performed and failed.

NOTE: Type A and B codes are emission-related codes that will cause the lighting of the malfunction indicator lamp (MIL), usually labeled "check engine" or "service engine soon."

Type C and D Codes

Type C and D codes are for use with non-emission-related diagnostic tests; they will cause the lighting of a "service" lamp (if the vehicle is so equipped). Type C codes are also called type C1 codes and D codes are also called type C0 codes.

OBD-II Freeze Frame

To assist the service technician, OBD II requires the computer to take a "snapshot" or freeze frame of all data at the instant an emission-related DTC is set. A scan tool is required to retrieve this data.

NOTE: Although OBD II requires that just one freeze frame of data be stored, the instant an emission-related DTC is set, vehicle manufacturers usually provide expanded data about the DTC beyond that required. However, retrieving this enhanced data usually requires the use of the vehicle-specific scan tool.

Freeze frame items include:

- Calculated load value
- Engine speed (RPM)
- Short-term and long-term fuel trim percent
- Fuel system pressure (on some vehicles)

- Vehicle speed (mph)
- Engine coolant temperature
- Intake manifold pressure
- Closed/open-loop status
- Fault code that triggered the freeze frame
- If a misfire code is set, identify which cylinder is misfiring

DON'T FORGET—THREE CLICKS

OBD II requires that the fuel system integrity be checked for possible leakage. If the fuel (gas) cap is not securely tightened, then a DTC such as P0442 may be set. To help prevent such false codes and to ensure that the gas cap is properly tightened, General Motors Corporation has printed on the cap itself a note that the cap should be tightened until three clicks are heard. This also applies to other screw-thread-type gas caps of all years and makes to be assured that the cap is tight.

NOTE: Gas caps are frequently tested as part of an exhaust emission test. Ask the person performing the test on your gas cap to tighten the cap three clicks to ensure a proper tightness. This will help prevent false defective test results.

FREEZE FRAME AND FAILURE RECORDS

A DTC should not be cleared from the vehicle computer memory unless the fault has been corrected and the technician is so directed by the diagnostic procedure. If the problem that caused the DTC to be set has been corrected, the computer will automatically clear the DTC after 40 consecutive warm-up cycles with no further faults detected (misfire and excessively rich or lean condition codes require 80 warm-up cycles). The codes can also be erased by using a scan tool.

NOTE: Disconnecting the battery may not erase OBD-II DTCs or freeze frame data. Most vehicle manufacturers recommend using a scan tool to erase DTCs rather than disconnecting the battery, because the memory for the radio, seats, and learned engine operating parameters are lost if the battery is disconnected.

◄ FREQUENTLY ASKED ► QUESTION

WHAT ARE PENDING CODES?

Pending codes are set when operating conditions are met and the component or circuit is not within the normal range, yet the conditions have not yet been met to set a DTC. For example, a sensor may require two consecutive faults before a DTC is set. If a scan tool displays a pending code or a failure, a driveability concern could also be present. The pending code can help the technician to determine the root cause before the customer complains of a check engine light indication.

THE NEED FOR FUEL TRIM

The purpose of fuel trim is to provide the catalytic converter with a rich *and* a lean air-fuel mixture. A rich mixture (lack of extra oxygen) is needed by the catalytic converter to reduce NO_X exhaust emissions. The catalytic converter, however, must also receive a lean mixture (excessive oxygen) to help oxidize **HC** and **CO** into harmless carbon dioxide (CO_2) and water (H_2O) vapor.

If the exhaust is always rich, the catalytic converter cannot reduce CO and HC emissions. If the exhaust is always lean, the catalytic converter cannot reduce NO_X emissions; therefore, the air-fuel mixture must alternate between rich and lean. The computer is therefore designed to provide this alternating mixture by using the oxygen sensor, short-term and long-term fuel trim program to accomplish this feat.

SHORT-TERM FUEL TRIM

Short-term fuel trim (**STFT**) is a percentage measurement of the amount the computer is adding or subtracting from a calculated value. Electronic fuel-injector systems use the oxygen sensor (O2S) to determine whether the exhaust is rich or lean. Without the O2S, the

MIL ON/OFF AND DRIVE CYCLES

Monitor Name	Monitor Type (How Often it Completes)	Number of Faults on Separate Drive Cycles to Set a DTC Pending	Number of Separate Consecutive Drive Cycles to Light MIL, Store a DTC	Number and Type of Drive Cycle with No Faults to Erase a Maturing DTC	Number and Type of Drive Cycle with No Fault to Turn the MIL Off	Number of Warm-Ups to Erase DTC After MIL is Turned Off
CCM	Continuous (when trip conditions allow it)	1	2	1—Trip	3—Trips	40
Catalyst	Once per drive cycle	1	3	1	3—OBD-II drive cycle	40
Misfire Type A	Continuous		1		3—Similar conditions	80
Misfire Type B	Continuous	1	2	1	3—Similar conditions	80
Fuel System	Continuous	1	2	1	3—Similar conditions	80
Oxygen Sensor	Once per trip	1	2	1—Trip	3—Trips	40
EGR	Once per trip	1	2	1—Trip	3—Trips	40
EVAP	Once per trip	1	1	1—Trip	3—Trips	40
AIR	Once per trip	1	2	1—Trip	3—Trips	40

control of the fuel delivery belongs to the computer alone using the programmed pulse width commands based on other sensor inputs such as engine coolant temperature (ECT), throttle position (TP), and engine load (MAP). When the engine is operating in closed loop, the O2S signal can modify or change the preprogrammed fuel delivery. Fuel trim is expressed as a percentage (%), either positive (+) or negative (−), and represents the amount of fuel different from the anticipated amount. For example, if a small vacuum leak were to occur, the O2S will produce a lower voltage signal which is interpreted by the computer as meaning the air-fuel mixture is too lean. As a result, the pulse width is increased slightly to compensate for this slight vacuum leak. The amount of this additional fuel added is seen on a scan tool as a positive short-term fuel trim.

NOTE: Before 1993, General Motors referred to short-term fuel trim as the **integrator** and expressed it in binary numbers that range from 0 to 255. A reading of 128 was the midpoint and a reading of ±10 from 128 (118–138) was usually considered to be a normal reading. See Figure 24-4 for a comparison between short-term trim in percentage versus binary numbers.

A short-term fuel trim of +20% indicates that 20% additional fuel had to be added to be able to achieve the proper air-fuel mixture. A −20% short-term fuel trim indicates that fuel had to be removed by shortening the injector pulse width to achieve the proper air-fuel mixture.

Short-term fuel trim represents actions by the computer over a relatively short time. The purpose of the STFT is to be able to provide a varying air-fuel mixture so that the catalytic converter can efficiently reduce HC, CO, and NO_X exhaust emissions. If, for example, a large vacuum leak were to occur, then the fuel delivery would have to be increased even more and for a longer time. Therefore, electronic fuel-injector system computers also incorporate a long-term fuel trim program.

LONG-TERM FUEL TRIM

Long-term fuel trim (**LTFT**) is designed to add or subtract fuel for a larger amount of time than short-term fuel trim. For this reason, LTFT should be looked at by the service technician as a guide to whether the computer has been adding or subtracting fuel in order to accomplish the proper air-fuel mixture. For example, if a vacuum hose split open, the engine will be leaner than normal. Short-term fuel trim will attempt to add fuel right away to adjust. If the resulting air (vacuum) leak remained for longer than a few seconds to a minute, the computer will revise the long-term fuel trim to compensate for the leak over a larger period of time.

When the LTFT makes an adjustment, the STFT can still make short and quick changes in the air-fuel mixture needed to provide the catalytic converter with an alternating rich, then lean, then rich, and so forth, exhaust.

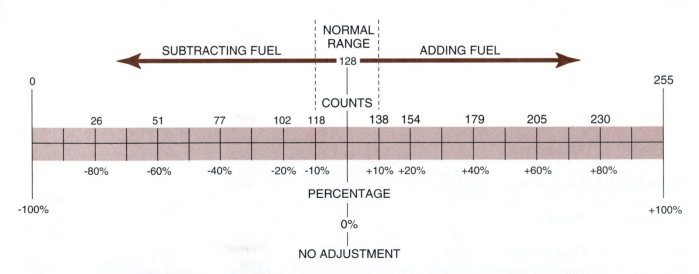

FIGURE 24-4 Both short-term fuel trim and long-term fuel trim use a percentage (%) of adding or subtracting fuel from normal values based on oxygen sensor activity. Many General Motors vehicles display counts instead of percentages. This chart plots both together so that a comparison can be made.

◄ **DIAGNOSTIC STORY** ►

THE RED S-10 PICKUP TRUCK STORY

A 4-cylinder 2.2-liter engine was replaced under the new vehicle warranty due to excessive oil consumption. The replacement engine never did run correctly, especially at idle and low speeds. The scan tool data showed a −100% long-term fuel trim, indicating that the oxygen sensor was measuring a very rich (low oxygen content) exhaust stream. Because the engine was operating so badly, the service technician believed the oxygen sensor was indicating a false rich condition. The service technician then checked the following:

- Poor O_2 sensor ground (this can cause a higher-than-normal O_2 sensor voltage)
- O_2 sensor wiring shorted to voltage or near a spark plug wire
- A contaminated (coated) O_2 sensor that will read higher than normal

None of the false rich conditions was found. Remembering that the engine runs terribly even when cold and the problem started after the engine was replaced, the technician started to look for faults that could have occurred when parts were switched from the original engine to the replacement engine. An incorrect EGR gasket was found. This caused exhaust gases to flow into the cylinders all the time. The exhaust gases also displaced the oxygen that normally would be in the cylinder, thereby reducing the amount of oxygen measured by the O_2 sensor. Replacing the EGR gasket restored proper engine operation.

USING FUEL TRIM AS A DIAGNOSTIC AID

Fuel trim values can only be observed with a scan tool. A scan tool will display both short-term and long-term fuel trim. For system diagnosis, refer to the long-term fuel trim because it represents a longer amount of time (history) and a greater amount of mixture correction.

NOTE: The object of STFT and LTFT is to be able to make corrections to the amount of fuel delivered to the engine to achieve the proper air-fuel mixture. For example, if a reading of +30% LTFT is indicated, it will require the computer to deliver 30% more than the calibrated amount of fuel to achieve the proper air-fuel mixture. This also means that the

engine is now operating with the correct air-fuel mixture. The LTFT number simply tells the technician what the computer had to do to achieve the proper mixture.

The following are three examples of readings and possible explanations:

Vehicle 1.   STFT = +5%, LTFT = 20%

Explanation: The computer is responding to a lean condition. The LTFT indicates that the programmed amount of fuel had to be increased by 20% to achieve the proper air-fuel mixture to the level where the STFT could "toggle" the mixture rich and lean for most catalytic converter efficiency. Look for a vacuum leak or low fuel pressure.

Vehicle 2.   STFT = +10%, LTFT = 0%

Explanation: Readings are perfect. It is normal for the STFT to add or subtract up to 20% to achieve the proper air-fuel mixture.

Vehicle 3.   STFT = −10%, LTFT = −30%

Explanation: The engine was rich because the LTFT had to remove 30% of the anticipated amount of fuel to achieve the proper air-fuel mixture. Look for a defective (stuck open) injector, defective fuel-pressure regulator, or a restriction in the intake air passage.

◄ **TECH TIP** ►

THINK OF A SMALL FAUCET AND A LARGE FAUCET

The purpose of fuel trim is to add or subtract fuel as needed to maintain the proper air-fuel mixture so the catalytic converter can operate properly. STFT is fast but can add or subtract a small amount of fuel. This can be visualized as being similar to a small water faucet adding water to a sink. For example, if a small vacuum hose were to become disconnected, the STFT will add a little extra fuel to compensate for the added amount of air being drawn into the engine. If a large hose were to be disconnected, the STFT cannot supply the needed fuel required so the LTFT is needed to supply additional fuel to overcome the large air leak. This can be visualized as being similar to a large water faucet adding a greater amount of water to a sink. Because the LTFT indicates a larger amount of fuel being added or subtracted, then STFT, many service technicians simply ignore the STFT readings and use the LTFT numbers to see if they are within 10%. If LTFT is greater than 10%, either positive (+) or negative (−), then a fault should be corrected.

FUEL TRIM CELLS

Both STFTs and LTFTs react to oxygen sensor voltage to modify fuel delivery. Most vehicles set aside different **cells** for each combination of engine speed (RPM) and load. The computer can then correct for slight differences in fuel mixture separately for each cell. For example, some General Motors vehicles use 16 cells plus 2 for deceleration and 2 for idle only.

12	13	14	15
8	9	10	11
4	5	6	7
0	1	2	3

RPM = 1400   1800   2200

Deceleration Cells:

greater than 1225 RPM = 17
less than 1225 RPM = 16

Idle Cells:

A/C on = 18
A/C off = 19

FUEL TRIM CELL DIAGNOSIS

To use fuel trim as a diagnostic aid, the data should be observed during the same condition as the problem. For example, notice that there are two cells for idle—one with air conditioning (A/C) on and one for the A/C off. If the problem or customer's concern only occurs when the A/C is on, then observe the fuel trim numbers on the scan tool with the engine operating at idle and with the A/C on.

The same thing is true of a problem that may be occurring at 55 mph (90 km/h). Looking at fuel trim in the service bay (stall) with the engine at idle will not help the technician at all. The vehicle must be driven under similar conditions to best duplicate the condition when the problem occurs. Only then will the correct fuel cell be displayed. Then the long-term fuel trim information should be valid. See the following fuel trim diagnostic chart.

Fuel Trim Diagnostic Chart

Fuel Trim @ Idle	Fuel Trim @ 3000 RPM	Possible Cause(s)
Adding fuel	No correction	Vacuum leak
No correction	Adding fuel	Low fuel volume, weak fuel pump, or restricted fuel filter
Adding fuel	Adding fuel	Dirty (clogged) fuel injectors, low fuel pump pressure
Subtracting fuel	No correction	Gasoline in the engine oil (drawn into the engine through the PCV valve)
Subtracting fuel	Subtracting fuel	High fuel pressure, defective fuel-pressure regulator, leaking or stuck open injector(s)

FUEL TRIM AND MISFIRE CODES

If a fuel control system (fuel trim) or misfire-related code sets, then the vehicle must be driven under conditions similar to when the fault was detected before the PCM will deactivate the MIL. Similar conditions are:

- The vehicle must be driven with engine speed within 375 RPM of the engine speed stored in the freeze frame data when the code set.
- The vehicle must be driven with engine load ±10% of the engine load value stored in the freeze frame data when the code set.
- The vehicle must be driven with engine temperature conditions similar to the temperature value stored in freeze frame data when the code set.

GENERIC OBD II

All OBD-II vehicles must be able to display data on a generic (also called **global**) scan tool under nine different modes of operation. These modes include:

Mode One	Current powertrain data (parameter identification display or **PID**)
Mode Two	Freeze frame data
Mode Three	Diagnostic trouble codes
Mode Four	Clear and reset diagnostic trouble codes (DTCs), freeze frame data, and readiness status monitors for noncontinuous monitors only
Mode Five	Oxygen sensor monitor test results
Mode Six	Onboard monitoring of test results for noncontinuous monitored systems
Mode Seven	Onboard monitoring of test results for continuously monitored systems

Mode Eight   Bidirectional control of onboard systems

Mode Nine   Module identification

The generic (global) data is used by most state emission programs. Generic OBD-II displays often use hexadecimal numbers, which use 16 numbers instead of 10. The numbers 0 to 9 (zero counts as a number) make up the first 10 and then capital letters A to F complete the 16 numbers. To help identify the number as being in a hexadecimal format, a dollar sign ($) is used in front of the number or letter. See the conversion chart below:

Decimal Number	Hexadecimal Code
0	$0
1	$1
2	$2
3	$3
4	$4
5	$5
6	$6
7	$7
8	$8
9	$9
10	$A
11	$B
12	$C
13	$D
14	$E
15	$F

Hexadecimal coding is also used to identify tests (**Test Identification [TID]** and **Component Identification [CID]**).

◀ FREQUENTLY ASKED ▶ QUESTION

HOW CAN YOU TELL GENERIC FROM FACTORY?

When using a scan tool on an OBD-II equipped vehicle, if the display asks for make, model, and year, then the factory or enhanced part of the PCM is being accessed. If the generic or global part of the PCM is being scanned, then there is no need to know the vehicle details.

DIAGNOSING PROBLEMS USING MODE SIX

Mode 6 information can be used to diagnose faults by following three steps.

Step 1   Check the monitor status before starting repairs. This step will show how the system failed.

Step 2   Look at the component or parameter that triggered the fault. This step will help pin down the root cause of the failure.

Step 3   Look to the monitor enable criteria, which will show what it takes to fail or pass the monitor.

SUMMARY

1. If the MIL is on, retrieve the DTC and follow the manufacturer's recommended procedure to find the root cause of the problem.
2. All monitors must have the enable criteria achieved before a test is performed.
3. OBD-II vehicles use a 16-pin DLC and common DTCs.
4. OBD II includes generic (SAE), as well as, vehicle manufacturer's specific DTCs and data display.

REVIEW QUESTIONS

1. What does the PCM do during a drive cycle to test emission-related components?
2. What is the difference between a type A and type B OBD-II DTC?
3. What is the difference between a trip and a warm-up cycle?
4. What could cause the MIL to flash?

ASE CERTIFICATION-TYPE QUESTIONS

1. A freeze frame is generated on an OBD-II vehicle _____.
   a. When a type C or D diagnostic trouble code is set
   b. When a type A or B diagnostic trouble code is set
   c. Every other trip
   d. When the PCM detects a problem with the O2S

2. An ignition misfire or fuel mixture problem is an example of what type of DTC?
   a. Type A
   b. Type B
   c. Type C
   d. Type D

3. How many terminals are in an OBD-II DLC?
   a. 5
   b. 9
   c. 12
   d. 16

4. OBD II has been on all passenger vehicles in the United States since _____.
   a. 1986
   b. 1991
   c. 1996
   d. 2000

5. A generic scan tool can access the same information at the same rate as an enhanced original equipment manufacturer's scan tool.
   a. True
   b. False

6. DTC P0302 is a _____.
   a. Generic DTC
   b. Vehicle manufacturer-specific DTC
   c. Idle speed-related DTC
   d. Transmission/transaxle-related DTC

7. The MIL is turned off if _____.
   a. The codes are cleared with a scan tool
   b. Power to the PCM is disconnected
   c. The vehicle is driven on three consecutive trips with a warm-up cycle and meets all code set conditions without the PCM detecting any faults
   d. All of the above occur

8. Which DTC could indicate that the gas cap is loose or defective?
   a. P0221
   b. P1301
   c. P0442
   d. P1603

9. The computer will automatically clear a DTC if there are no additional detected faults after _____.
   a. Forty consecutive warm-up cycles
   b. Eighty warm-up cycles
   c. Two consecutive trips
   d. Four key-on/key-off cycles

10. A pending code is set when a fault is detected on _____.
   a. A one-trip fault item
   b. The first fault of a two-trip failure
   c. The catalytic converter efficiency
   d. Thermostat problem (too long to closed-loop status)

◀ Chapter 25 ▶

EXHAUST EMISSION TESTING

OBJECTIVES

After studying Chapter 25, the reader should be able to:

1. Prepare for ASE A8 certification test content area "D" (Emissions Control Systems Diagnosis and Repair) and ASE L1 certification test content area "F" (I/M Failure Diagnosis)
2. Identify the reasons why excessive amounts of HC, CO, and NO_x exhaust emissions are created.
3. Describe how to baseline a vehicle after an exhaust emission failure.
4. List acceptable levels of HC, CO, CO_2, and O_2 with and without a catalytic converter.
5. List four possible causes for high readings for HC, CO, and NO_x.

EXHAUST ANALYSIS TESTING

The Clean Air Act Amendments require enhanced I/M programs in areas of the country that have the worst air quality and the Northeast Ozone Transport region. The states must submit to the EPA a **State Implementation Plan (SIP)** for their programs. Each enhanced I/M program is required to include as a minimum the following items:

- Computerized emission analyzers
- Visual inspection of emission control items

- Minimum waiver limit (to be increased based on the inflation index)
- Remote on-road testing of one-half of 1 percent of the vehicle population
- Registration denial for vehicles not passing an I/M test
- Denial of waiver for vehicles that are under warranty or that have been tampered with
- Annual inspections
- OBD-II systems check for 1996 and newer vehicles

Federal Test Procedure (FTP)

The **Federal Test Procedure (FTP)** is the test used to certify all new vehicles before they can be sold. Once a vehicle meets these standards, it is certified by the EPA for sale in the United States. The FTP test procedure is a loaded-mode test lasting for a total duration of 505 seconds and is designed to simulate an urban driving trip. A cold start-up representing a morning start and a hot start after a soak period is part of the test. In addition to this drive cycle, a vehicle must undergo evaporative testing. Evaporative emissions are determined using the **Sealed Housing for Evaporative Determination (SHED)** test, which measures the evaporative emissions from the vehicle after a heat-up period representing a vehicle sitting in the sun. In addition, the vehicle is driven and then tested during the hot soak period.

NOTE: A SHED is constructed entirely of stainless steel. The walls, floors, and ceiling, plus the door, are all constructed of stainless steel because it does not absorb hydrocarbons, which could offset test results.

The FTP is a much more stringent test of vehicle emissions than is any test type that uses equipment that measures percentages of exhaust gases. The federal emission standards for each model year vehicle are the same for that model regardless of what size engine the vehicle is equipped with. This is why larger V-8 engines often are equipped with more emission control devices than smaller 4- and 6-cylinder engines.

I/M Test Programs

- There are a variety of I/M testing programs that have been implemented by the various states. These programs may be centralized testing programs or decentralized testing programs. Each state is free to develop a testing program suitable to their needs as long as they can demonstrate to the EPA that their plan will achieve the attainment levels set by the EPA. This approach has led to a variety of different testing programs. See Figure 25-1.

Visual Tampering Checks

Visual tampering checks may be part of an I/M testing program and usually include checking for the following items:

- Catalytic converter
- Fuel tank inlet restrictor
- Exhaust gas recirculation (EGR)
- Evaporative emission system
- Air-injection reaction system (AIR)
- Positive crankcase ventilation (PCV)

If any of these systems are missing, not connected, or tampered with, the vehicle will fail the emissions test and will have to be repaired/replaced by the vehicle owner before the vehicle can pass the emission test. Any cost associated with repairing or replacing these components may not be used toward the waiver amount required for the vehicle to receive a waiver.

FIGURE 25-1 Photo of a sign taken at an emissions test facility.

One-Speed and Two-Speed Idle Test

The one-speed and two-speed idle test measures the exhaust emissions from the tailpipe of the vehicle at idle and/or at 2500 RPM. This uses stand-alone exhaust gas sampling equipment that measures the emissions in percentages. Each state chooses the standards which the vehicle has to meet in order to pass the test. The advantage to using this type of testing is that the equipment is relatively cheap and allows states to have decentralized testing programs because many facilities can afford the necessary equipment required to perform this test.

Loaded Mode Test

The loaded mode test uses a dynamometer that places a "single weight" load on the vehicle. The load applied to the vehicle varies with the speed of the vehicle. Typically, a 4-cylinder vehicle speed would be 24 mph, a 6-cylinder vehicle speed would be 30 mph, and an 8-cylinder vehicle speed would be 34 mph. Conventional stand-alone sampling equipment is used to mea-sure HC and CO emissions. This type of test is classified as a Basic I/M test by the EPA. See Figure 25-2.

FIGURE 25-2 A vehicle being tested during an enhanced emission test.

Acceleration Simulation Mode (ASM)

The ASM-type of test uses a dynamometer that applies a heavy load on the vehicle at a steady-state speed. The load applied to the vehicle is based on the acceleration rate on the second simulated hill of the FTP. This acceleration rate is 3.3 mph/sec./sec. (read as 3.3 mph per second per second, which is the unit of acceleration). There are different ASM tests used by different states.

The **ASM 50/15** test places a load of 50% on the vehicle at a steady 15 mph. This load represents 50% of the horsepower required to simulate the FTP acceleration rate of 3.3 mph/sec. This type of test produces relatively high levels of NO_X emissions; therefore, it is useful in detecting vehicles that are emitting excessive NO_X.

The **ASM 25/25** test places a 25% load on the vehicle while it is driven at a steady 25 mph. This represents 25% of the load required to simulate the FTP acceleration rate of 3.3 mph/sec. Because this applies a smaller load on the vehicle at a higher speed, it will produce a higher level of HC and CO emissions than the ASM 50/15. NO_X emissions will tend to be lower with this type of test.

I/M 240 Test

The I/M 240 test is the EPA's enhanced test. It is actually a portion of the 505-second FTP test used by the manufacturers to certify their new vehicles. The "240" stands for 240 seconds of drive time on a dynamometer. This is a loaded-mode transient test that uses constant volume sampling equipment to measure the exhaust emissions in mass just as is done during the FTP. The I/M 240 test simulates the first two hills of the FTP drive cycle. Figure 25-3 shows the I/M 240 drive trace.

OBD-II Testing

In 1999, the EPA requested that states adopt OBD-II systems testing for 1996 and newer vehicles. The OBD-II system is designed to illuminate the MIL light and store trouble codes any time a malfunction exists that would cause the vehicle emissions to exceed 1½ times the FTP limits. If the OBD-II system is working correctly, the system should be able to detect a vehicle failure that would cause emissions to increase to an unacceptable level. The EPA has determined that the OBD-II system should detect emission failures of a vehicle even before that vehicle would fail an emissions test of the type that most states are employing. Furthermore, the EPA has determined that, as the population of OBD-II equipped vehicles increases and the population of older non-OBD-II equipped vehicles decreases, tailpipe testing will no longer be necessary.

The OBD-II testing program consists of a computer that can scan the vehicle OBD-II system using the DLC connector. The technician first performs a visual check of the vehicle MIL light to determine if it is working correctly. Next, the computer is connected to the vehicle's DLC connector. The computer will scan the vehicle OBD-II system and determine if there are any codes stored that are commanding the MIL light on. In addition, it will scan the status of the readiness monitors and determine if they have all run and passed. If the readiness monitors have all run and passed, it indicates that the OBD-II system has tested all the components of the emission control system. An OBD-II vehicle would fail this OBD-II test if:

- The MIL light does not come on with the key on, engine off
- The MIL is commanded on
- A number (varies by state) of the readiness monitors have not been run

If none of these conditions are present, the vehicle will pass the emissions test.

Remote Sensing

The EPA requires that, in high-enhanced areas, states perform on-the-road testing of vehicle emissions. The state must sample 0.5% of the vehicle population base in high-enhanced areas. This may be accomplished by using

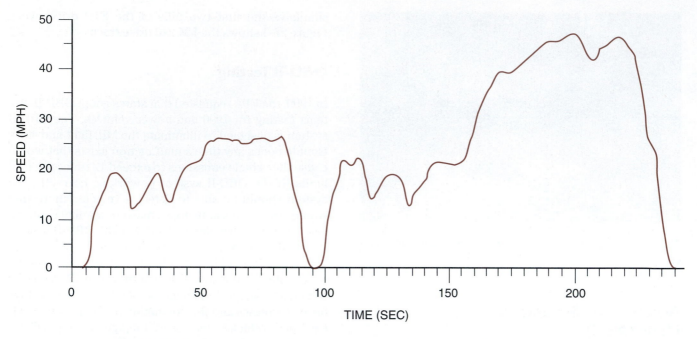

FIGURE 25-3 Trace showing the Inspection/Maintenance 240 test. The test duplicates an urban test loop around Los Angeles, California. The first "hump" in the curve represents the vehicle being accelerated to about 20 mph, then driving up a small hill to about 30 mph and coming to a stop. At about 94 seconds, the vehicle stops and again accelerates while climbing a hill and speeding up to about 50 mph during this second phase of the test.

a remote sensing device. This type of sensing may be done through equipment that projects an infrared light through the exhaust stream of a passing vehicle. The reflected beam can then be analyzed to determine the pollutant levels coming from the vehicle. If a vehicle fails this type of test, the vehicle owner will receive notification in the mail that he or she must take the vehicle to a test facility to have the emissions tested.

Random Roadside Testing

Some states may implement random roadside testing that would usually involve visual checks of the emission control devices to detect tampering. Obviously, this method is not very popular as it can lead to traffic tie-ups and delays on the part of commuters.

Exhaust analysis is an excellent tool to use for the diagnosis of engine performance concerns. In areas of the country that require exhaust testing to be able to get license plates, exhaust analysis must to be able to:

- Establish a baseline for failure diagnosis and service.
- Identify areas of engine performance that are and are not functioning correctly.
- Determine that the service and repair of the vehicle have been accomplished and are complete.

EXHAUST ANALYSIS AND COMBUSTION EFFICIENCY

A popular method of engine analysis, as well as emission testing, involves the use of five-gas exhaust analysis equipment. See Figure 25-4. The five gases analyzed and their significance are as follows.

Hydrocarbons

Hydrocarbons (HC) are unburned gasoline and are measured in parts per million (PPM). A correctly operating engine should burn (oxidize) almost all the gasoline; therefore, very little unburned gasoline should be present in the exhaust. Acceptable levels of HC are 50 PPM or less. High levels of HC could be due to excessive oil consumption caused by weak piston rings or worn valve guides. The most common cause of excessive HC emissions is a fault in the ignition system. Items that should be checked include:

- Spark plugs
- Spark plug wires
- Distributor cap and rotor (if the vehicle is so equipped)

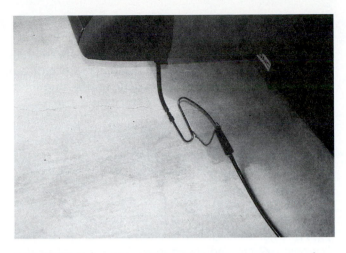

FIGURE 25-4 A typical partial stream sample type of exhaust probe used to measure exhaust gases in parts per million (PPM) or percentage (%).

- Ignition timing
- Ignition coil

◀ FREQUENTLY ASKED ▶
QUESTION

WHAT DOES NMHC MEAN?

NMHC means **non-methane hydrocarbon** and it is the standard by which exhaust emission testing for hydrocarbons is evaluated. Methane is natural gas and can come from animals, animal waste, and other natural sources. By not measuring methane gas, all background sources are eliminated, giving better results as to the true amount of unburned hydrocarbons that are present in the exhaust stream.

Carbon Monoxide

Carbon monoxide (CO) is unstable and will easily combine with any oxygen to form stable carbon dioxide (CO_2). The fact that CO combines with oxygen is the reason that CO is a poisonous gas (in the lungs, it combines with oxygen to form CO_2 and deprives the brain of oxygen). CO levels of a properly operating engine should be less than 0.5%. High levels of CO can be caused by clogged or restricted crankcase ventilation devices such as the PCV valve, hose(s), and tubes. Other items that might cause excessive CO include:

- Clogged air filter
- Incorrect idle speed

- Too-high fuel-pump pressure
- Any other items that can cause a rich condition

Carbon Dioxide (CO_2)

Carbon dioxide (CO_2) is the result of oxygen in the engine combining with the carbon of the gasoline. An acceptable level of CO_2 is between 12 and 15%. A high reading indicates an efficiently operating engine. If the CO_2 level is low, the mixture may be either too rich or too lean.

Oxygen

The next gas is oxygen (O_2). There is about 21% oxygen in the atmosphere, and most of this oxygen should be "used up" during the combustion process to oxidize all the hydrogen and carbon (hydrocarbons) in the gasoline. Levels of O_2 should be very low (about 0.5%). High levels of O_2, especially at idle, could be due to an exhaust system leak.

NOTE: Adding 10% alcohol to gasoline provides additional oxygen to the fuel and will result in lower levels of CO and higher levels of O_2 in the exhaust.

NO$_x$

An oxide of nitrogen (NO) is a colorless, tasteless, and odorless gas when it leaves the engine, but as soon as it reaches the atmosphere and mixes with more oxygen, nitrogen oxides (NO_2) are formed. NO_2 is reddish-brown and has an acid and pungent smell. NO and NO_2 are grouped together and referred to as NO_x, where x represents any number of oxygen atoms. NO_x, the symbol used to represent all oxides of nitrogen, is the fifth gas commonly tested using a five-gas analyzer. The exhaust gas recirculation (EGR) system is the major controlling device limiting the formation of NO_x.

Acceptable exhaust emissions include:

	Without Catalytic Converter	*With Catalytic Converter*
HC	300 PPM or less	30–50 PPM or less
CO	3% or less	0.3% to 0.5% or less
O$_2$	0% to 2%	0% to 2%
CO$_2$	12% to 15% or higher	12% to 15% or higher
NO$_x$	Less than 100 PPM at idle and less than 1000 PPM at WOT	Less than 100 PPM at idle and less than 1000 PPM at WOT

See Figure 25-5 on page 473.

◀ FREQUENTLY ASKED ▶ QUESTION

HOW CAN MY WORN OUT, OLD HIGH-MILEAGE VEHICLE PASS AN EXHAUST EMISSION TEST?

Age and mileage of a vehicle are generally not factors when it comes to passing an exhaust emission test. Regular maintenance is the most important factor for passing an enhanced Inspection and Maintenance (I/M) exhaust analysis test. Failure of the vehicle owner to replace broken accessory drive belts, leaking AIR pump tubes, defective spark plug wires, or a cracked exhaust manifold can lead to failure of other components such as the catalytic converter. Tests have shown that if the vehicle is properly cared for, even an engine that has 300,000 miles (483,000 km) can pass an exhaust emission test.

HC TOO HIGH

High hydrocarbon exhaust emissions are usually caused by an engine misfire. What burns the fuel in an engine? The ignition system ignites a spark at the spark plug to ignite the *proper* mixture inside the combustion chamber. If a spark plug does not ignite the mixture, the resulting unburned fuel is pushed out of the cylinder on the exhaust stroke by the piston through the exhaust valves and into the exhaust system. Therefore, if any of the following ignition components or adjustments are not correct, excessive HC emission is likely.

1. Defective or worn spark plugs
2. Defective or loose spark plug wires
3. Defective distributor cap and/or rotor
4. Incorrect ignition timing (either too far advanced or too far retarded)
5. A lean air-fuel mixture can also cause a misfire. This condition is referred to as a **lean misfire.**

HINT: To make discussion easier in future reference to these items, this list of ignition components and checks will be referred to simply as "spark stuff."

CO TOO HIGH

Excessive carbon monoxide is an indication of too rich an air-fuel mixture. High concentrations of CO indicate that not enough oxygen was available for the amount of fuel. Common causes of high CO include:

- Too-high fuel-pump pressure
- Defective fuel-pressure regulator
- Clogged air filter or PCV valve
- Defective injectors

HINT: One technician remembers "CO" as meaning "clogged oxygen" and always looks for restricted air flow into the engine whenever high CO levels are detected.

◀ TECH TIP ▶

CO EQUALS O_2

If the exhaust is rich, CO emissions will be higher than normal. If the exhaust is lean, O_2 emissions will be higher than normal. Therefore, if the CO reading is the same as the O_2 reading, then the engine is operating correctly. For example, if both CO and O_2 are 0.5% and the engine develops a vacuum leak, the O_2 will rise. If a fuel-pressure regulator were to malfunction, the resulting richer air-fuel mixture would increase CO emissions. Therefore, if both the rich indicator (CO) and the lean indicator (O_2) are equal, the engine is operating correctly.

MEASURING OXYGEN (O_2) AND CARBON DIOXIDE (CO_2)

Two gas exhaust analyzers (HC and CO) work well, but both HC and CO are consumed (converted) inside the catalytic converter. The amount of leftover oxygen coming out of the tailpipe is an indication of leanness. The higher the O_2 level, the leaner the exhaust. Oxygen therefore is the **lean indicator.** Acceptable levels of O_2 are 0 to 2%.

NOTE: A hole in the exhaust system can draw outside air (oxygen) into the exhaust system. Therefore, to be assured of an accurate reading, carefully check the exhaust system

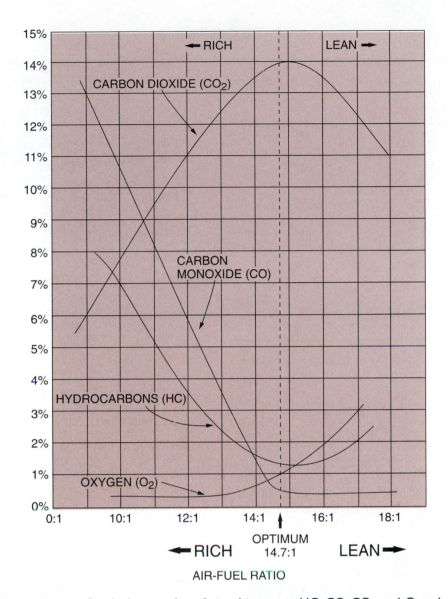

FIGURE 25-5 Graph showing the relationship among HC, CO, CO_2, and O_2 exhaust gases. Note that the higher the CO becomes, the richer the air-fuel mixture. This is why CO is called the *rich* indicator gas. Also note that the higher the O_2 levels, the leaner the air-fuel mixture. This is why O_2 is called the *lean* indicator gas.

for leaks. Using a smoke machine is an easy method to locate leaks in the exhaust system.

Carbon dioxide (CO_2) is a measure of efficiency. The higher the level of CO_2 in the exhaust stream, the more efficiently the engine is operating. Levels of 12 to 15% or higher are considered to be acceptable. Because CO_2 levels peak at an air-fuel mixture of 14.7:1, a lower level of CO_2 indicates either a too rich or a too lean condition. The CO_2 measurement by itself does not indicate which condition is present. For example:

CO_2 = 8% (This means efficiency is low and the air-fuel mixture is not correct.)
Look at O_2 and CO levels.
A high O_2 indicates lean and a high CO indicates rich.

◀ TECH TIP ▶

HOW TO FIND A LEAK IN THE EXHAUST SYSTEM

A hole in the exhaust system can dilute the exhaust gases with additional oxygen (O_2). See Figure 25-6.

This additional O_2 in the exhaust can lead the service technician to believe that the air-fuel mixture is too lean. To help identify an exhaust leak, perform an exhaust analysis at idle and at 2500 RPM (fast idle) and compare with the following:

- If the O_2 is high at idle and at 2500 RPM, the mixture is lean at both idle and at 2500 RPM.
- If the O_2 is low at idle and high at 2500 RPM, this usually means that the vehicle is equipped with a working AIR pump.
- If the O_2 is high at idle, but okay at 2500 RPM, a hole in the exhaust or a small vacuum leak that is "covered up" at higher speed is indicated.

◀ TECH TIP ▶

YOUR NOSE KNOWS

Using the nose, a technician can often hone in on a major problem without having to connect the vehicle to an exhaust analyzer. For example,

- The strong smell of exhaust is due to excessive unburned hydrocarbon (HC) emissions. Look for an ignition system fault that could prevent the proper burning of the fuel. A vacuum leak could also cause a lean misfire and cause excessive HC exhaust emissions.
- If your eyes start to burn or water, suspect excessive oxides of nitrogen (NO_x) emissions. The oxides of nitrogen combine with the moisture in the eyes to form a mild solution of nitric acid. The acid formation causes the eyes to burn and water. Excessive NO_x exhaust emissions can be caused by:

    A vacuum leak causing higher-than-normal combustion chamber temperature

    Overadvanced ignition timing causing higher-than-normal combustion chamber temperature

    Lack of proper amount of exhaust gas recirculation (EGR) (This is usually noticed above idle on most vehicles.)

- Dizzy feeling or headache. This is commonly caused by excessive carbon monoxide (CO) exhaust emissions. Get into fresh air as soon as possible. A probable cause of high levels of CO is an excessively rich air-fuel mixture.

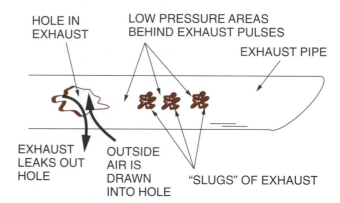

FIGURE 25-6 A hole in the exhaust system can cause outside air (containing oxygen) to be drawn into the exhaust system. This extra oxygen can be confusing to a service technician because the extra O_2 in the exhaust stream could be misinterpreted as a too lean air-fuel mixture.

PHOTOCHEMICAL SMOG FORMATION

Oxides of nitrogen are formed by high temperature—over 2500°F (1370°C)—and/or pressures inside the combustion chamber. Oxides of nitrogen contribute to the formation of photochemical **smog** when sunlight reacts chemically with NO_x and unburned hydrocarbons (HC). Smog is a term derived by combining the words *smoke* and *fog*. Ground-level ozone is a constituent of smog. **Ozone** is an enriched oxygen molecule with three atoms of oxygen (O_3) instead of the normal two atoms of oxygen (O_2).

Ozone in the upper atmosphere is beneficial because it blocks out harmful ultraviolet rays that contribute to skin cancer. However, at ground level, this ozone (smog) is an irritant to the respiratory system.

TESTING FOR OXIDES OF NITROGEN

Because the formation of NO_x occurs mostly under load, the most efficient method to test for NO_x is to use a portable exhaust analyzer that can be carried in the vehicle while the vehicle is being driven under a variety of conditions.

Specifications for NO_x

From experience, a maximum reading of 1000 parts per million (PPM) of NO_x under loaded driving conditions will generally mean that the vehicle will pass an enhanced I/M roller test. A reading of over 100 PPM at idle should be considered excessive.

NO_x is most likely to be created under the following conditions.

Under a Heavy Load

A heavy load creates high combustion pressure and temperatures which contribute to NO_x. Accelerating a vehicle on an entrance ramp to a highway is an excellent method to use to detect excessive NO_x emission.

NOTE: It requires about 15 seconds for any exhaust from the tailpipe to be drawn into the test equipment, analyzed, and the results displayed. For example, the reading for the acceleration on an entrance ramp may not occur until the vehicle is traveling at a constant speed under limited load after getting onto the highway.

Cruise Conditions

At a steady throttle under light loads, the ignition timing is advanced by the computer to optimize fuel economy. This advanced timing can cause high NO_x emission.

Carbon Deposits in the Combustion Chamber

Excessive carbon deposits inside the combustion chamber can cause hot spots, higher-than-normal compression, and spark knock. All these conditions can create excessive NO_x formation.

NOTE: High NO_x always accompanies engine ping (spark knock or detonation).

CORRECTING HIGH HC EMISSIONS

High HC emissions indicate an ignition misfire causing unburned gasoline (hydrocarbons or HC) to be pushed out the cylinder during the exhaust stroke. This can be caused by faults in the ignition system, such as:

- Fouled spark plug(s)
- Defective (open or grounded) spark plug wires
- Defective distributor cap or rotor
- Incorrect ignition timing (either too far advanced or too far retarded)
- Defective pickup coil or crankshaft position sensor
- Defective or intermittent ignition module (igniter)

Other causes of excessive HC exhaust emissions include an excessive lean air-fuel mixture. The mixture has to be so lean that the spark plug is not able to ignite it. Typical causes of an excessively lean air-fuel mixture on one or more cylinders include:

- Vacuum leak such as a split or broken vacuum hose
- Intake manifold leak
- Leaking throttle body or carburetor base gasket
- Weak or broken valve spring keeping an intake valve partially open at times

If the engine is operating at too low a temperature, the cooler cylinder walls can cause the vaporized fuel to condense. The flame started by the spark plug is quenched out when it reaches the sides or cooler surfaces of the combustion chamber. The area is called the **quench** area. Therefore, if a thermostat with too low a temperature rating is used (180°F instead of a 195°F, for example) increased HC emissions can be expected.

NOTE: HC emissions are unburned hydrocarbons (gasoline). Lowering HC exhaust emissions increases fuel economy. Otherwise, the engine is simply a large pump drawing in fuel from the fuel tank and exhausting it (unburned) out the tailpipe. Consumers are pleasantly surprised that the vehicle gets better fuel economy after an emission failure repair has been made.

CORRECTING HIGH CO EMISSIONS

Excessively high carbon monoxide (CO) emissions are usually due to an overly rich air-fuel mixture. Because CO is formed, a spark occurred because carbon is a by-product of combustion. If there was less fuel (a leaner mixture), there will be enough oxygen to change any CO into CO_2. Likely causes of excessive CO emissions include:

- Too high a fuel-pump pressure (pinched fuel return line)
- Defective (diaphragm leaking) fuel-pressure regulator
- Stuck carburetor choke (closed or partially closed)
- Defective charcoal canister purge system, allowing excessive fuel to be drawn into the intake manifold
- Defective mechanical fuel pump, allowing gasoline into the engine oil that is then drawn into the intake manifold through the PCV system
- Clogged air filter or air intake passage (See Tech Tip "Check for Dog Food?")

See Figure 25-7.

◀ TECH TIP ▶

CHECK FOR DOG FOOD?

A commonly experienced problem in many parts of the country involves squirrels and other animals placing dog food into the air intake ducts of vehicles. Dog food is often found packed tight in the ducts against the air filter. An air intake restriction occurs and drives the fuel mixture richer than normal and reduces engine power and vehicle performance as well as creating high CO exhaust emissions.

CORRECTING HIGH HC AND CO EMISSIONS

If both HC and CO emissions are excessive, the most likely cause is an excessively rich air-fuel mixture. See typical causes listed under high CO emissions. The high HC is often caused by the overly rich mixture causing the spark plugs to become fouled. A fouled spark plug does not ignite the mixture and, as a result, the unburned mixture is packed by the piston into the exhaust system on the exhaust stroke. The unburned air-fuel mixture is interpreted by the O2S as being too lean due to the amount of the oxygen level in the exhaust. This lean signal (low voltage) indicates to the vehicle computer that additional fuel should be supplied to the engine. This additional fuel causes an even greater amount of spark plug fouling and increases HC and CO emissions. Carefully inspect both the entire ignition and fuel systems for faults.

CORRECTING HIGH NO$_x$ EMISSIONS

Excessive oxides of nitrogen (NO_x) emissions are usually caused by two major problems:

1. Engine operating hotter than normal
2. Engine operating leaner than normal

If the engine operating temperature is higher than normal, the peak temperature inside the combustion chamber can exceed 2500°F and create excessive NO_x emissions. Exhaust gas recirculation (EGR) allows a small amount of exhaust gases into the combustion chamber to slow the burning rate of the air-fuel mixture. This effectively reduces the peak temperature inside the engine. See Figures 25-8 and 25-9.

A lean air-fuel mixture burns hotter than a normal mixture. A lean mixture contains less gasoline and, therefore, there is less volume of gasoline that requires vaporization. As gasoline vaporizes, it absorbs heat. Less gasoline means less heat is absorbed from the combustion chamber and the temperature is increased. The increased temperature creates excessive NO_x emissions. Items to check or service to reduce NO_x emissions include:

- EGR valve operation
- EGR passages for proper flow
- Decarbonization of the engine (one method is shown in Figure 25-10)
- Cooling system including flow through the radiator for proper operation
- Too lean air-fuel mixture

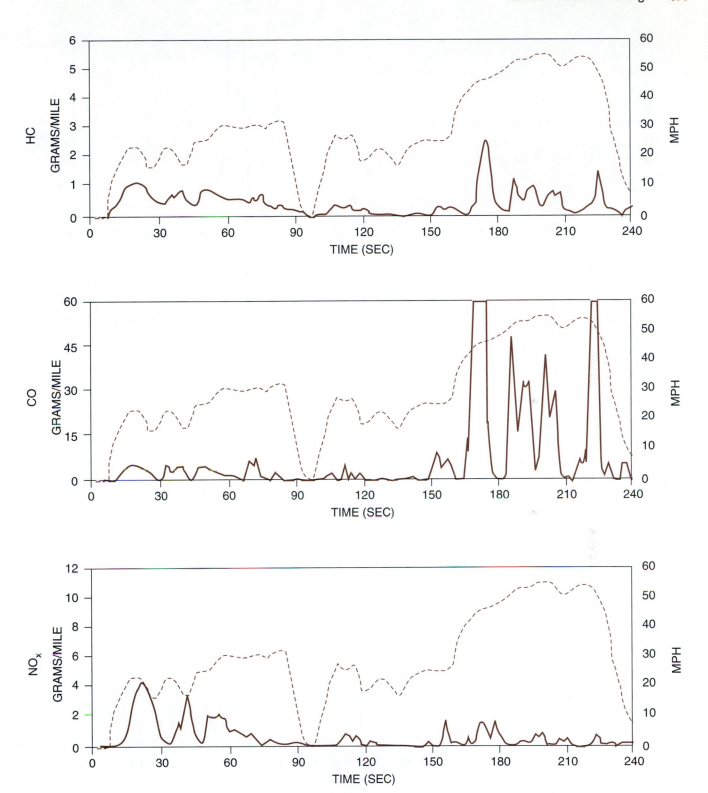

FIGURE 25-7 Excessive CO trace indicating that the major amount of CO emissions occurred during the second phase of the trace. During this phase, the vehicle was accelerated up a hill. Obviously, the engine was being supplied with a very rich air-fuel mixture during this phase of the test.

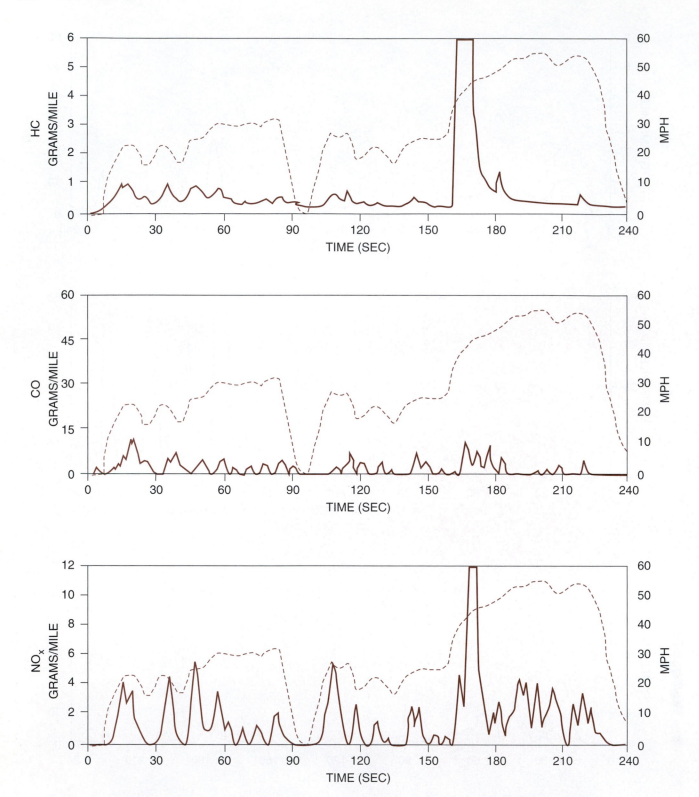

FIGURE 25-8 A typical enhanced exhaust emission test trace showing high HC and NO$_x$ emissions. Note that the CO is low. A lean misfire could be the cause of both gases being excessive.

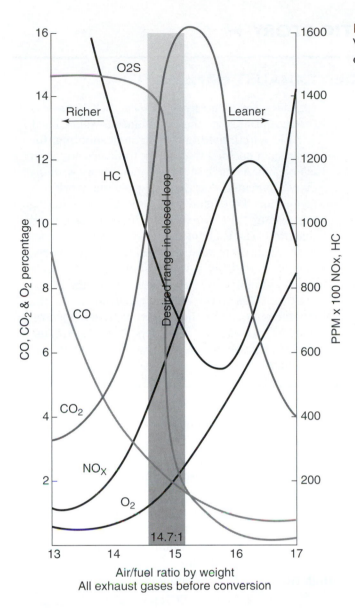

(a)

FIGURE 25-9 Exhaust emissions are very complex. When the air-fuel mixture becomes richer, some exhaust emissions are reduced while others increase.

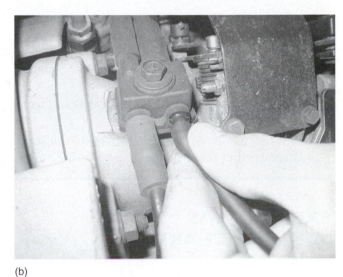

(b)

(c)

FIGURE 25-10 (a) A can of top engine cleaner is first poured into a container and the same volume of water is added to form an emulsion. (b) A 5/32-in. vacuum hose is connected to a manifold vacuum port. (c) The engine speed is raised to a fast idle until all of the mixture has been drawn into the engine. The engine is allowed to sit for about 30 minutes and then the vehicle is driven aggressively.

◀ DIAGNOSTIC STORY ▶

THE CASE OF THE RETARDED EXHAUST CAMSHAFT

A Toyota equipped with a double overhead camshaft (DOHC) inline 6-cylinder engine failed the state-mandated enhanced exhaust emission test for NO_x. The engine ran perfectly without spark knocking (ping), which is usually a major reason for excessive NO_x emissions. The technician checked the following:

- The ignition timing, which was found to be set to specifications (if too far advanced, it can cause excessive NO_x)
- The cylinders, which were decarbonized using top engine cleaner
- The EGR valve, which was inspected and the EGR passages cleaned

After all the items were completed, the vehicle was returned to the inspection station where the vehicle again failed for excessive NO_x emissions (better, but still over the maximum allowable limit).

After additional hours of troubleshooting, the technician decided to go back to basics and start over again. A check of the vehicle history with the owner indicated that the only previous work performed on the engine was a replacement timing belt over a year before. The technician discovered that the exhaust cam timing was retarded two teeth, resulting in late closing of the exhaust valve. The proper exhaust valve timing resulted in a slight amount of exhaust being retained in the cylinder. This extra exhaust was added to the amount supplied by the EGR valve and helped reduce NO_x emissions. After repositioning the timing belt, the vehicle passed the emissions test well within the limits.

EXHAUST GAS SUMMARY CHART

Gas	Cause and Correction
	Engine misfire or incomplete burning of fuel caused by:
High HC	1. Ignition system fault
	2. Lean misfire
	3. Too low an engine temperature (thermostat)
	Rich condition caused by:
High CO	1. Clogged air filter or PCV system
	2. Defective fuel-pressure regulator or injectors

Gas	Cause and Correction
	Excessively rich condition caused by:
High HC and CO	1. All items included under high CO
	2. Fouled spark plugs causing a misfire to occur
	3. Possible nonoperating catalytic converter
	Excessive combustion chamber temperature:
High NO_x	1. Nonoperating EGR valve
	2. Clogged EGR passages
	3. Engine operating temperature too high due to cooling system restriction, worn water pump impeller
	4. Lean air-fuel mixture or faults in the cooling system.

◀ DIAGNOSTIC STORY ▶

O2S SHOWS RICH, BUT PULSE WIDTH IS LOW

A service technician was attempting to solve a driveability problem. The computer did not indicate any diagnostic trouble codes (DTCs). A check of the oxygen sensor voltage indicated a higher-than-normal reading almost all the time. The pulse width to the port injectors was lower than normal. The lower-than-normal pulse width indicates that the computer is attempting to reduce fuel flow into the engine by decreasing the amount of on-time for all the injectors.

What could cause a rich mixture if the injectors were being commanded to deliver a lean mixture?

Finally the technician shut off the engine and took a careful look at the entire fuel-injection system. Although the vacuum hose was removed from the fuel-pressure regulator, fuel was found dripping from the vacuum hose. The problem was a defective fuel-pressure regulator that allowed an uncontrolled amount of fuel to be drawn by the intake manifold vacuum into the cylinders. While the computer tried to reduce fuel by reducing the pulse width signal to the injectors, the extra fuel being drawn directly from the fuel rail caused the engine to operate with too rich an air-fuel mixture.

◀ FREQUENTLY ASKED QUESTION ▶

WHAT DO ALL THESE EMISSION LABELS MEAN?

TLEV - Transitional Low-Emission Vehicle, car exhaust HC limited to 0.125 gram per mile

LEV - Low-Emission Vehicle, car exhaust HC 0.075 gpm

ULEV - Ultra Low-Emission Vehicle, car exhaust HC 0.040 gpm

SULEV - Super Ultra Low-Emission Vehicle, car exhaust HC 0.010 gpm

ZEV - Zero-Emission Vehicle

CEV - City Electric Vehicle, a miniature car, which could earn minor credit against ZEV quota

NEV - Neighborhood Electric Vehicle, similar to a golf cart, could earn minor credit against ZEV quota

PZEV - A near-zero emissions category, P is for partial; a PZEV would earn partial credit against manufacturers' ZEV quotas

AT-PZEV - A near-zero emissions category. AT is for advanced technology, meeting PZEV requirements using, for example, a low-emissions fuel cell running on methanol or an internal combustion engine running on natural gas.

PS 14-1 A typical portable exhaust gas analyzer that is capable of measuring unburned hydrocarbons (HCs), carbon monoxide (CO), oxides of nitrogen (NO$_x$), carbon dioxide (CO$_2$), and oxygen (O$_2$).

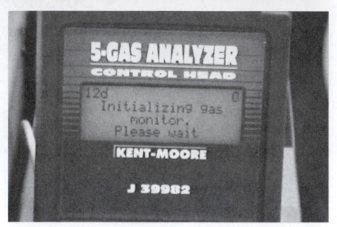

PS 14-2 After turning the unit one, most exhaust analyzers require a warm-up period.

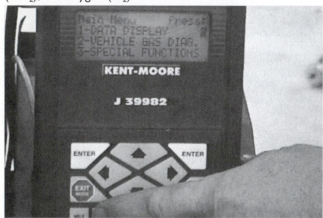

PS 14-3 To test the exhaust of a vehicle, select "data display" from the main menu.

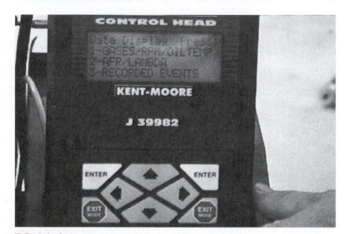

PS 14-4 Select "gases/RPM/oil temp" from the data display menu.

PS 14-5 Wait again! This is the reason why many service technicians turn on the exhaust gas analyzer at the beginning of each day and leave it on all day to avoid having to wait for the unit to become operational.

PS 14-6 The unit is now able to display exhaust gas readings. It has been about 15 minutes from the time the unit was first turned on!

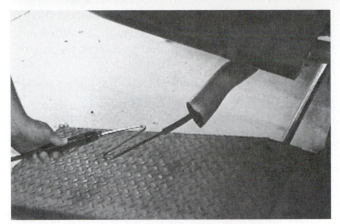

PS 14-7 Insert the test probe into the tailpipe.

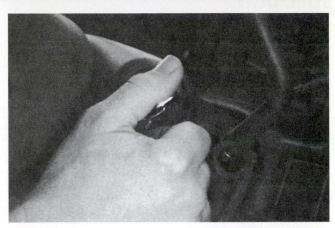

PS 14-8 Start the engine.

PS 14-9 Use the up and down arrow keys to scroll up and down the data list to observe the gases. This unit can only display four of the five gases at a time. Because we are not concerned with NO_x when the engine is not going to be driven, this technician selected this display showing CO, HC, CO_2, and O_2.

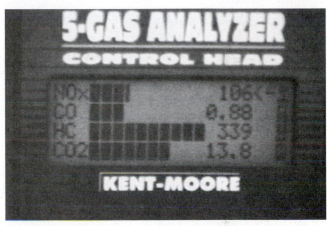

PS 14-10 This display shows a typical engine at idle after a cold start. Notice the higher-than-normal HC reading.

PS 14-11 To help get the engine, oxygen sensor, and catalytic converter up to operating temperature, operate the engine at 2000 RPM for several minutes.

PS 14-12 After the engine has reached operating temperature, the HC readings are now 13 PPM—well within the normal allowable limit of less than 50 PPM.

SUMMARY

1. Excessive hydrocarbon (HC) exhaust emissions are created by a lack of proper combustion such as a fault in the ignition system, too lean an air-fuel mixture, or too cold engine operation.

2. Excessive carbon monoxide (CO) exhaust emissions are usually created by a rich air-fuel mixture.

3. Excessive oxides of nitrogen (NO_x) exhaust emissions are usually created by excessive heat or pressure in the combustion chamber or a lack of the proper amount of exhaust gas recirculation (EGR).

4. Carbon dioxide (CO_2) levels indicate efficiency. The higher the CO_2, the more efficient the engine operation.

5. Oxygen (O_2) indicates leanness. The higher the O_2, the leaner the air-fuel mixture.

6. A vehicle should be driven about 20 miles, especially during cold weather, to allow the engine to be fully warm before an enhanced emission test.

REVIEW QUESTIONS

1. List the five exhaust gases and their maximum allowable readings for a fuel-injected vehicle equipped with a catalytic converter.

2. List two causes of a rich exhaust.

3. List two causes of a lean exhaust.

4. List those items that should be checked if a vehicle fails an exhaust test for excessive NO_x emissions.

ASE CERTIFICATION-TYPE QUESTIONS

1. Technician A says that high HC emission levels are often caused by a fault in the ignition system. Technician B says that high CO_2 emissions are usually caused by a richer-than-normal air-fuel mixture. Which technician is correct?

   a. Technician A only

   b. Technician B only

   c. Both Technicians A and B

   d. Neither Technician A nor B

2. HC and CO are high and CO_2 and O_2 are low. This could be caused by a _____.

   a. Rich mixture

   b. Lean mixture

   c. Defective ignition component

   d. Clogged EGR passage

3. Which gas is generally considered to be the rich indicator? (The higher the level of this gas, the richer the air-fuel mixture.)

   a. HC

   b. CO

   c. CO_2

   d. O_2

4. Which gas is generally considered to be the lean indicator? (The higher the level of this gas, the leaner the air-fuel mixture.)

   a. HC

   b. CO

   c. CO_2

   d. O_2

5. Which exhaust gas indicates efficiency? (The higher the level of this gas, the more efficient the engine operates.)

   a. HC

   b. CO

   c. CO_2

   d. O_2

6. All of the gases are measured in percentages except _____.

   a. HC

   b. CO

   c. CO_2

   d. O_2

7. After the following exhaust emissions were measured, how was the engine operating?

   HC = 766 PPM CO_2 = 8.2%   CO = 4.6%
   O_2 = 0.1%

   a. Too rich
   b. Too lean

8. Technician A says that carbon inside the engine can cause excessive NO_x to form. Technician B says that excessive NO_x could be caused by a cooling system fault causing the engine to operate too hot. Which technician is correct?

   a. Technician A only
   b. Technician B only
   c. Both Technicians A and B
   d. Neither Technician A nor B

9. A clogged EGR passage could cause excessive _____ exhaust emissions.

   a. HC
   b. CO
   c. NO_x
   d. CO_2

10. An ignition fault could cause excessive _____ exhaust emissions.

    a. HC
    b. CO
    c. NO_x
    d. CO_2

◀ Chapter 26 ▶

EXHAUST GAS RECIRCULATION (EGR) SYSTEMS

OBJECTIVES

After studying Chapter 26, the reader should be able to:

1. Prepare for the ASE Engine Performance (A8) certification test content area "D" (Emission Control Systems).
2. Describe the purpose and function of the exhaust gas recirculation system.
3. Discuss how the exhaust gas recirculation system is tested under OBD-II regulations.
4. Explain methods for diagnosing and testing for faults in the exhaust gas recirculation system.

Exhaust gas recirculation (EGR) is an emission control that lowers the amount of nitrogen oxides (NO_x) formed during combustion. In the presence of sunlight, NO_x reacts with hydrocarbons in the atmosphere to form ozone (O_3) or photochemical smog, an air pollutant.

NO$_x$ FORMATION

Nitrogen (N_2) and oxygen (O_2) molecules are separated into individual atoms of nitrogen and oxygen during the combustion process. These then bond to form NO_x (NO, NO_2). When combustion flame front temperatures exceed 2500°F (1370°C), NO_x formation increases dramatically.

CONTROLLING NO$_x$

The amounts of NO_x formed at temperatures below 2500°F (1370°C) can be controlled in the exhaust by a catalyst. To handle the amounts generated above 2500°F (1370°C), the following are some methods that have been used to lower NO_x formation:

- **Enrich the air-fuel mixture.** More fuel lowers the peak combustion temperature, but it raises hydrocarbon (HC) and carbon monoxide (CO) emissions. The reduction in fuel economy also makes this solution unattractive.

- **Lower the compression ratio.** This decreases NO_x levels somewhat but also reduces combustion efficiency. When the compression ratio becomes too low, HC and CO emissions rise.

- **Dilute the air-fuel mixture.** To lower emission levels further, engineers developed a system that introduces small amounts of exhaust gas into the engine intake. This lowers combustion temperatures by displacing some of the air and absorbs heat without contributing to the combustion process. Currently, this is one of the most efficient methods to meet NO_x emission level cut-points without significantly affecting engine performance, fuel economy, and other exhaust emissions. The EGR system routes small quantities, usually between 6% and 10%, of exhaust gas to the intake manifold.

FIGURE 26-1 Typical vacuum-operated EGR valve. The operation of the valve is controlled by the computer by pulsing the EGR control solenoid on and off.

EGR VALVE

EGR VALVE CONTROL SELENOID

Here, the exhaust gas mixes with and takes the place of some intake charge. This leaves less room for the intake charge to enter the combustion chamber. The recirculated exhaust gas is **inert** (chemically inactive) and does not enter into the combustion process. The result is a lower peak combustion temperature. As the combustion temperature is lowered, the production of oxides of nitrogen is also reduced.

The EGR system has some means of interconnecting the exhaust and intake manifolds. See Figure 26-1. The interconnecting passage is controlled by the EGR valve. On V-type engines, the intake manifold crossover is used as a source of exhaust gas for the EGR system. A cast passage connects the exhaust crossover to the EGR valve. The gas is sent from the EGR valve to openings in the manifold. On inline-type engines, an external tube is generally used to carry exhaust gas to the EGR valve. This tube is often designed to be long so that the exhaust gas is cooled before it enters the EGR valve.

NOTE: The amount of EGR is subtracted from the mass air flow calculations. While the EGR gases do occupy space, they do not affect the air-fuel mixture.

EGR SYSTEM OPERATION

Since small amounts of exhaust are all that is needed to lower peak combustion temperatures, the orifice that the exhaust passes through is small. See Figure 26-2.

Because combustion temperatures are low, EGR is usually not required during the following conditions.

- Idle speed
- When the engine is cold

The level of NO_x emission changes according to engine speed, temperature, and load. EGR is also not used at wide-open throttle (WOT) because it would reduce engine performance and the engine does not operate under these conditions for a long period of time.

In addition to lowering NO_x levels, the EGR system also helps control detonation. Detonation, or ping, occurs when high pressure and heat cause the air-fuel mixture to ignite. Detonation, or ping, occurs when high pressure and heat cause the air-fuel mixture to ignite at different times or locations in the combustion chamber by the spark plug. This uncontrolled combustion can severely damage the engine.

Using the EGR system allows for greater ignition timing advance and for the advance to occur sooner without detonation problems, which increases power and efficiency.

POSITIVE AND NEGATIVE BACK PRESSURE EGR VALVES

Many EGR valves are designed with a small valve inside that bleeds off any applied vacuum and prevents the valve from opening. Some EGR valves require a positive back pressure in the exhaust system. This is called a **positive back pressure** EGR valve. At low engine speeds and light engine loads, the EGR system is not needed, and the back pressure in it is also low. Without sufficient back pressure, the EGR valve does not open even though vacuum may be present at the EGR valve.

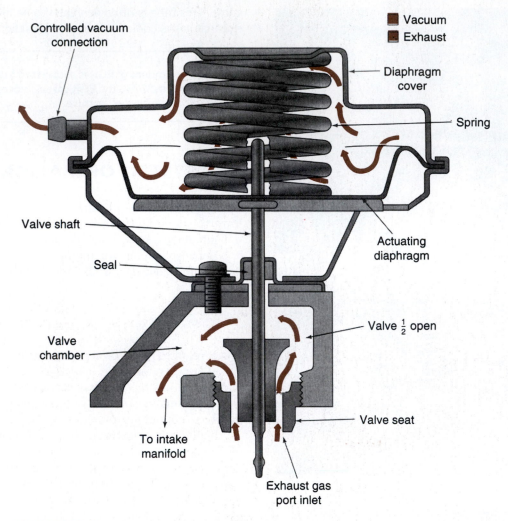

Vacuum
Exhaust

Controlled vacuum connection

Diaphragm cover

Spring

Valve shaft

Actuating diaphragm

Seal

Valve ½ open

Valve chamber

Valve seat

To intake manifold

Exhaust gas port inlet

FIGURE 26-2 When the EGR valve opens, exhaust flows through the valve and into passages in the intake manifold.

On each exhaust stroke, the engine emits an exhaust "pulse." Each pulse represents a positive pressure. Behind each pulse is a small area of low pressure. Some EGR valves react to this low pressure area by closing a small internal valve, which allows the EGR valve to be opened by vacuum. This type of EGR valve is called a **negative back pressure** EGR valve. See Figure 26-3. The following conditions must occur:

1. Vacuum must be applied to the EGR valve itself. This is usually ported vacuum on some TBI fuel-injected systems. The vacuum source is often manifold vacuum and is controlled by the computer through a solenoid valve.
2. Exhaust back pressure must be present to close an internal valve inside the EGR valve to allow the vacuum to move the diaphragm.

NOTE: The installation of a low-restriction exhaust system could prevent the proper operation of the back pressure controlled EGR valve.

COMPUTER-CONTROLLED EGR

Many computer-controlled EGR systems have one or more solenoids controlling the EGR vacuum. The computer controls a solenoid to shut off vacuum to the EGR valve at cold engine temperatures, idle speed, and wide-open throttle operation. If two solenoids are used, one acts as an off/on control of supply vacuum, while the

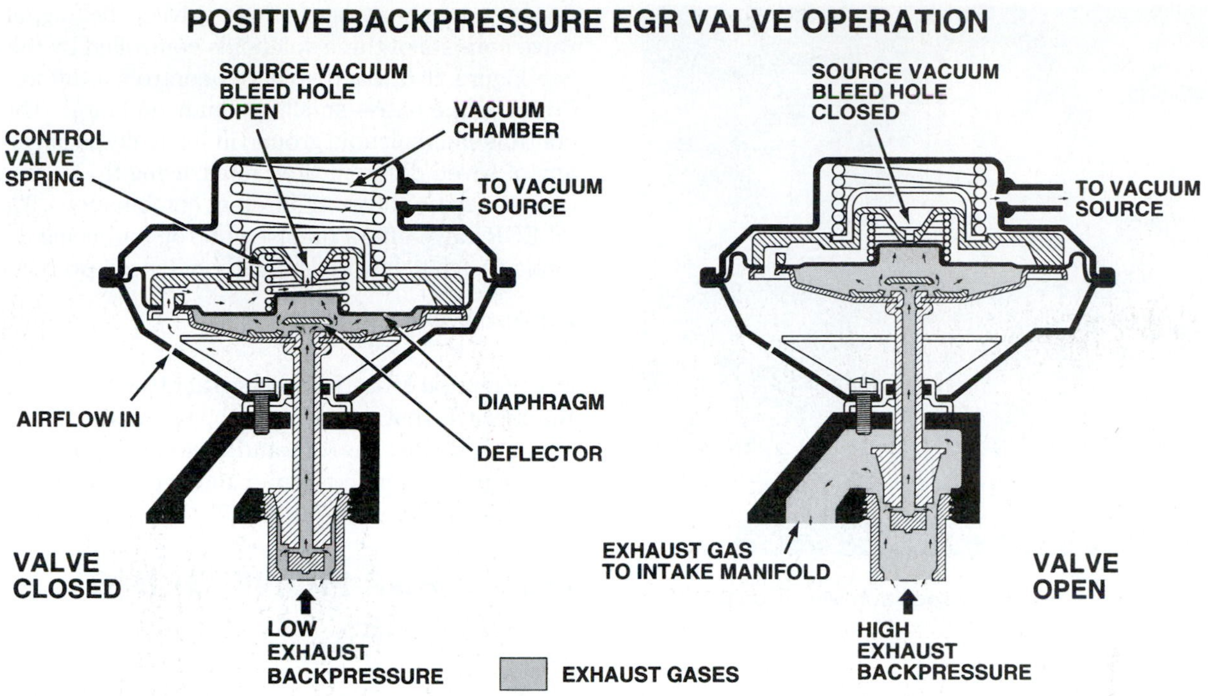

POSITIVE BACKPRESSURE EGR VALVE OPERATION

FIGURE 26-3 Back pressure in the exhaust system is used to close the control valve, thereby allowing engine vacuum to open the EGR valve.

second solenoid vents vacuum when EGR flow is not desired or needs to be reduced. The second solenoid is used to control a vacuum air bleed, allowing atmospheric pressure in to modulate EGR flow according to vehicle operating conditions.

EGR VALVE POSITION SENSORS

Late model computer-controlled EGR systems use a sensor to indicate EGR operation. On-Board Diagnostics Generation-II (OBD-II) EGR system monitors require an EGR to determine EGR gas flow. A linear potentiometer on the top of the EGR valve stem indicates valve position for the computer. This is called an **EGR valve position (EVP)** sensor. See Figure 26-4. Some later-model Ford EGR systems, however, use a feedback signal provided by an EGR exhaust back pressure sensor which converts the exhaust back pressure to a voltage signal. This sensor is called a **pressure feedback EGR (PFE)** sensor.

◀ **TECH TIP** ▶

FIND THE ROOT CAUSE

Excessive back pressure, such as could be caused by a partially clogged exhaust system, could cause the plastic sensors on the EGR valve to melt. Always check for a restricted exhaust whenever replacing a failed EGR valve sensor.

The GM-integrated electronic EGR valve uses a similar sensor. The top of the valve contains a vacuum regulator and EGR pintle-position sensor in one assembly sealed inside a non-removable plastic cover. The pintle-position sensor provides a voltage output to the PCM, which increases as the duty cycle increases, allowing the PCM to monitor valve operation. See Figure 26-5.

FIGURE 26-4 An EGR valve position sensor on top of an EGR valve.

Digital EGR Valves

GM introduced a completely electronic, digital EGR valve design on some 1990 engines. Unlike the previously men-tioned vacuum-operated EGR valves, the digital EGR valve consists of three solenoids controlled by the PCM. See Figure 26-6. Each solenoid controls a different size orifice in the base—small, medium, and large. The PCM controls each solenoid ground individually. It can produce any of seven different flow rates, using the solenoids to open the three valves in different combinations. The digital EGR valve offers precise control, and using a swivel pintle design helps prevent carbon deposit problems.

Linear EGR

Most General Motors and several others vehicles use a **linear** EGR that contains a stepper motor to precisely regulate exhaust gas flow and a feedback potentiometer that signals to the computer the actual position of the valve. See Figures 26-7 and 26-8.

OBD-II EGR MONITORING STRATEGIES

In 1996, the U.S. EPA began requiring OBD-II systems in all passenger cars and most light-duty trucks. These sys-tems include emissions system monitors that alert the driver and the technician if an emissions system is mal-functioning. To be certain the EGR system is operating,

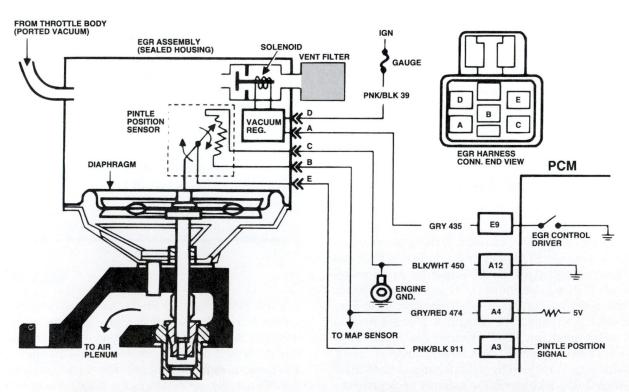

FIGURE 26-5 An integrated EGR valve system showing the pintle-position sensor and vacuum diaphragm.

FIGURE 26-6 This 3800 V-6 uses three solenoids for EGR. A scan tool can be used to turn on each solenoid to check if the valve is working and if the exhaust passages are capable of flowing enough exhaust to the intake manifold to affect engine operation when cycled.

the PCM runs a functional test of the system, when specific operating conditions exist. The OBD-II system tests by opening and closing the EGR valve. The PCM monitors an EGR function sensor for a change in signal voltage. If the EGR system fails, a diagnostic trouble code (DTC) is set. If the system fails two consecutive times, the malfunction indicator light (MIL) is lit.

Daimler Chrysler monitors the difference in the exhaust oxygen sensor's voltage activity as the EGR valve opens and closes. Oxygen in the exhaust decreases when the EGR is open and increases when the EGR valve is closed. The PCM sets a DTC if the sensor signal does not change.

Depending on the vehicle application, Ford uses at least one of two types of sensors to evaluate exhaust-gas flow. The first type uses a temperature sensor mounted in the intake side of the EGR passageway. The PCM monitors the change in temperature when the EGR valve is open. When the EGR is open and exhaust is flowing, the sensor signal is changed by the heat of the exhaust. The PCM compares the change in the sensor's signal with the values in its look-up table.

The second type of Ford EGR monitor test sensor is called a **Delta Pressure Feedback EGR (DPFE) sen-**

FIGURE 26-7 A General Motors linear EGR valve.

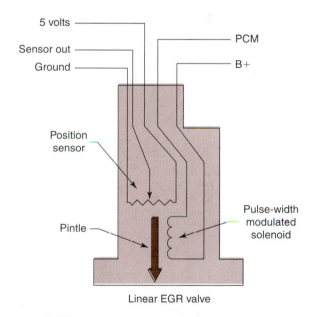

FIGURE 26-8 The EGR valve pintle is pulse-width modulated and a three-wire potentiometer provides pintle-position information back to the PCM.

sor. This sensor measures the pressure differential between two sides of a metered orifice positioned just below the EGR valve's exhaust side. Pressure between the orifice and the EGR valve decreases when the EGR opens because it becomes exposed to the lower pressure in the intake. The DPFE sensor recognizes this pressure drop, compares it to the relatively higher pressure on the exhaust side of the orifice, and signals the value of the pressure difference to the PCM. See Figure 26-9. When the EGR valve is closed, the exhaust-gas pressure on both sides of the orifice is equal.

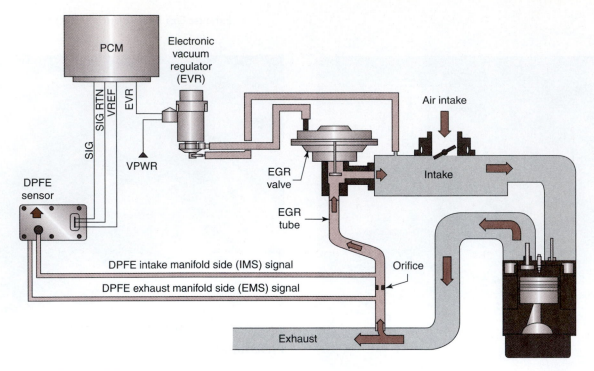

FIGURE 26-9 A DPFE sensor and related components.

DPFE EGR Sensor Chart

	Pressure		Voltage
Psi	*In. Hg*	*kPa*	*Volts*
4.34	8.83	29.81	4.56
3.25	6.62	22.36	3.54
2.17	4.41	14.90	2.51
1.08	2.21	7.46	1.48
0	0	0	0.45

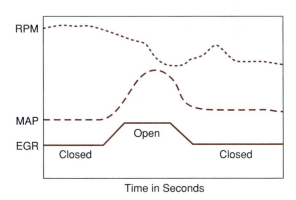

FIGURE 26-10 An OBD-II active test. The PCM opens the EGR valve and then monitors the MAP sensor and/or engine speed (RPM) to meet acceptable values.

The OBD-II EGR monitor for this second system runs when programmed operating conditions have been met. The monitor evaluates the pressure differential while the PCM commands the EGR valve to open. Like other systems, the monitor compares the measured value with the look-up table value. If the pressure differential falls outside the acceptable value, a DTC sets.

Several vehicle manufacturers use the manifold absolute pressure (MAP) sensor as the EGR monitor on some applications. After meeting the enable criteria (operating condition requirements), the EGR monitor is run. The PCM monitors the MAP sensor while it commands the EGR valve to open. The MAP sensor signal should change in response to the sudden change in manifold pressure or the fuel trim changes created by change in the oxygen sensor voltage. If the signal value falls outside the acceptable value in the look-up table, a DTC sets. See Figure 26-10. If the EGR fails on two consecutive trips the PCM lights the MIL.

DIAGNOSING A DEFECTIVE EGR SYSTEM

If the EGR valve is not opening or the flow of the exhaust gas is restricted, then the following symptoms are likely:

- Ping (spark knock or detonation) during acceleration or during cruise (steady-speed driving)
- Excessive oxides of nitrogen (NO_x) exhaust emissions

If the EGR valve is stuck open or partially open, then the following symptoms are likely:

- Rough idle or frequent stalling
- Poor performance/low power, especially at low engine speed
- To check for proper EGR flow, the engine vacuum should drop 6 to 8 in. Hg. when the EGR is commanded on by a scan tool when the engine is at idle speed.

◀ TECH TIP ▶

WATCH OUT FOR CARBON BALLS!

Exhaust gas recirculation (EGR) valves can get stuck partially open by a chunk of carbon. The EGR valve or solenoid will test as defective. When the valve (or solenoid) is removed, small chunks or balls of carbon often fall into the exhaust manifold passage. When the replacement valve is installed, the carbon balls can be drawn into the new valve again, causing the engine to idle roughly or stall.

To help prevent this problem, start the engine with the EGR valve or solenoid removed. Any balls or chunks of carbon will be blown out of the passage by the exhaust. Stop the engine and install the replacement EGR valve or solenoid.

◀ DIAGNOSTIC STORY ▶

THE BLAZER STORY

The owner of a Chevrolet Blazer equipped with a 4.3-L, V-6 engine complained that the engine would stumble and hesitate at times. Everything seemed to be functioning correctly, except that the service technician discovered a weak vacuum going to the EGR valve at idle. This vehicle was equipped with an EGR valve-control solenoid, called an **electronic vacuum regulator valve** or **EVRV** by General Motors Corporation. The computer pulses the solenoid to control the vacuum that regulates the operation of the EGR valve. The technician checked the service manual for details on how the system worked, and discovered that vacuum should be present at the EGR valve only when the gear selector indicates a drive gear (drive, low, reverse). Because the technician discovered the vacuum at the solenoid to be leaking, the solenoid was obviously defective and required replacement. After replacement of the solenoid (EVRV), the hesitation problem was solved.

NOTE: The technician also discovered in the service manual that blower-type exhaust hoses should not be connected to the tailpipe on any vehicle while performing an inspection of the EGR system. The vacuum created by the system could cause false EGR valve operation to occur.

The first step in almost any diagnosis is to perform a thorough visual inspection. To check for proper operation of a vacuum-operated EGR valve, follow these steps:

1. Check the vacuum diaphragm to see if it can hold vacuum.

NOTE: Because many EGR valves require exhaust back pressure to function correctly, the engine should be running at a fast idle.

2. Apply vacuum from a hand-operated vacuum pump and check for proper operation. The valve itself should move when vacuum is applied, and the engine operation should be affected. The EGR valve should be able to hold the vacuum that was applied. If the vacuum drops off, then the valve is likely to be defective. If the EGR valve is able to hold vacuum, but the engine is not affected when the valve is opened, then the exhaust passage(s) must be checked for restriction. See the Tech Tip "The Snake Trick." If the EGR valve will not hold vacuum, the valve itself is likely to be defective and may require replacement.

3. Connect a vacuum gauge to an intake manifold vacuum source and monitor the engine vacuum at idle (should be 17 to 21 in. Hg at sea level). Raise the speed of the engine to 2500 RPM and note the vacuum reading (should be 17 to 21 in. Hg or higher). Activate the EGR valve using a scan tool or vacuum pump, if vacuum controlled, and observe the vacuum gauge. The results are as follows:

   ▪ The vacuum should drop 6 to 8 in. Hg.
   ▪ If the vacuum drops less than 6 to 8 in. Hg, the valve or the EGR passages are clogged.

◀ DIAGNOSTIC STORY ▶

I WAS ONLY TRYING TO HELP!

On a Friday, an experienced service technician found that the driveability performance problem with a Buick V-6 was a worn EGR valve. When vacuum was applied to the valve, the valve did not move at all. Additional vacuum from the hand-operated vacuum pump resulted in the valve popping all the way open. A new valve of the correct part number was not available until Monday, yet the customer wanted the vehicle back for a trip during the weekend.

To achieve acceptable driveability, the technician used a small hammer and deformed the top of the valve to limit the travel of the EGR valve stem. The technician instructed the customer to return on Monday for the proper replacement valve.

The customer did return on Monday, but now accompanied by his lawyer. The engine had developed a hole in one of the pistons. The lawyer reminded the technician and the manager that an exhaust emission control had been "modified." The result was the repair shop paid for a new engine and the technician learned to always repair the vehicle correctly or not at all.

◀ TECH TIP ▶

THE SNAKE TRICK

The EGR passages on many intake manifolds become clogged with carbon, which reduces the flow of exhaust and the amount of exhaust gases in the cylinders. This reduction can cause spark knock (detonation) and increased emissions of oxides of nitrogen (NO_x) (especially important in areas with enhanced exhaust emissions testing).

To quickly and easily remove carbon from exhaust passages, cut an approximately 1-foot (30-cm) length from stranded wire, such as garage door guide wire or an old speedometer cable. Flare the end and place the end of the wire into the passage. Set your drill on reverse, turn it on, and the wire will pull its way through the passage, cleaning the carbon as it goes, just like a snake in a drain pipe. Some vehicles, such as Hondas, require that plugs be drilled out to gain access to the EGR passages, as shown in Figure 26-11.

FIGURE 26-11 Removing the EGR passage plugs from the intake manifold on a Honda.

EGR-RELATED OBD-II DIAGNOSTIC TROUBLE CODES

Diagnostic Trouble Code	Description	Possible Causes
P0400	Exhaust gas recirculation flow problems	• EGR valve • EGR valve hose or electrical connection • Defective PCM
P0401	Exhaust gas recirculation flow insufficient	• EGR valve • Clogged EGR parts or passages
P0402	Exhaust gas recirculation flow excessive	a. Stuck open EGR valve b. Vacuum hose(s) misrouted c. Electrical wiring shorted

SUMMARY

1. Oxides of nitrogen (NO_X) are formed inside the combustion chamber due to heat exceeding 2500°F.
2. Recirculating 6 to 10% inert exhaust gases back into the intake system reduces peak temperature inside the combustion chamber and reduces NO_x exhaust emissions.
3. EGR is usually not needed at idle, and not wanted, at wide-open throttle for maximum engine performance, or when the engine is cold.
4. Vacuum-operated EGR valves are usually exhaust back pressure controlled to help match EGR flow into the intake with the load on the engine.
5. Many EGR systems use a feedback potentiometer to signal the PCM about the position of the EGR valve pintle.
6. Some EGR valves are solenoids or pulse-width modulated pintles.
7. OBD II requires that the flow rate be tested and this can be achieved by opening the EGR valve and observing the reaction of the MAP sensor.

REVIEW QUESTIONS

1. What causes the formation of oxides of nitrogen?
2. How does the use of exhaust gas reduce NO_x exhaust emission?
3. How does the DPFE sensor work?
4. How does the PCM determine that the exhaust flow through the EGR system meets OBD-II regulations?

ASE CERTIFICATION-TYPE QUESTIONS

1. What causes the nitrogen and the oxygen in the air to combine and form NO_x?
   a. Sunlight
   b. Any spark will cause this to occur
   c. Heat above 2500°F (1370°C)
   d. Chemical reaction in the catalytic converter

2. Exhaust gas recirculation (EGR) is generally not needed under all the following conditions *except* _____.
   a. Idle speed
   b. Cold engine
   c. Cruise speed
   d. Wide-open throttle (WOT)

3. Technician A says that a low-restriction exhaust system could prevent a back pressure-type vacuum-controlled EGR valve from opening correctly. Technician B says restricted exhaust can cause the EGR valve position sensor to fail. Which technician is correct?
   a. Technician A only
   b. Technician B only
   c. Both Technicians A and B
   d. Neither Technician A nor B

4. EGR is used to control which exhaust emission?
   a. Unburned hydrocarbons (HC)
   b. Oxides of nitrogen (NO_x)
   c. Carbon monoxide (CO)
   d. Both NO_x and CO

5. A typical EGR pintle-position sensor is what type of sensor?
   a. Rheostat
   b. Piezoelectric
   c. Wheatstone bridge
   d. Potentiometer

6. OBD-II regulations require that the EGR system be tested. Technician A says that the PCM can monitor the commanded position of the EGR valve to determine if it is functioning correctly. Technician B says that the PCM can open the EGR valve and monitors for a change in the MAP sensor or oxygen sensor reading to detect if the system is functioning correctly. Which technician is correct?
   a. Technician A only
   b. Technician B only
   c. Both Technicians A and B
   d. Neither Technician A nor B

7. Two technicians are discussing clogged EGR passages. Technician A says clogged EGR passages can cause excessive NO_X exhaust emission. Technician B says that clogged EGR passages can cause the engine to ping (spark knock or detonation). Which technician is correct?
   a. Technician A only
   b. Technician B only
   c. Both Technicians A and B
   d. Neither Technician A nor B

8. An EGR valve that is partially stuck open would *most likely* cause what condition?

   a. Rough idle/stalling

   b. Excessive NO_x exhaust emissions

   c. Ping (spark knock or detonation)

   d. Missing at highway speed

9. When testing an EGR system for proper operation using a vacuum gauge, how much should the vacuum drop when the EGR is commanded on by a scan tool?

   a. 1 to 2 in. Hg

   b. 3 to 5 in. Hg

   c. 6 to 8 in. Hg

   d. 8 to 10 in. Hg

10. A P0401 DTC (exhaust gas recirculation flow insufficient) is being discussed. Technician A says that a defective EGR valve could be the cause. Technician B says that clogged EGR passages could be the cause. Which technician is correct?

    a. Technician A only

    b. Technician B only

    c. Both Technicians A and B

    d. Neither Technician A nor B

POSITIVE CRANKCASE VENTILATION (PCV) AND AIR-INJECTION REACTION (AIR) SYSTEMS

OBJECTIVES

After studying Chapter 27, the reader should be able to:

1. Prepare for the ASE Engine Performance (A8) certification test content area "D" (Emission Control Systems).
2. Describe the purpose and function of the positive crankcase ventilation and the air-injection reaction system.
3. Discuss how the PCV and AIR systems are tested under OBD-II regulations.
4. Explain methods for diagnosing and testing faults in the PCV and AIR systems.

The process of combustion produces power in an internal-combustion engine. Under perfect conditions, combustion would completely consume the air-fuel mixture, leaving only harmless by-products, such as water vapor (H_2O) and carbon dioxide (CO_2). Combustion of the air-fuel mixture is never perfect, however, and at best is incomplete. By-products other than H_2O and CO_2 remain after the combustion process and go out the tailpipe. These by-products of incomplete combustion include carbon monoxide (CO), hydrocarbons (HC), and oxides of nitrogen (NO_x). The PCV and AIR systems are designed to reduce CO and HC exhaust emissions.

CRANKCASE VENTILATION

The problem of crankcase ventilation has existed since the beginning of the automobile because no piston ring, new or old, can provide a perfect seal between the piston and the cylinder wall. When an engine is running, the pressure of combustion forces the piston downward. This same pressure also forces gases and unburned fuel from the combustion chamber, past the piston rings, and into the crankcase. This process of gases leaking past the rings is called **blow by,** and the gases form crankcase vapors.

These combustion by-products, particularly unburned hydrocarbons, caused by blow by must be ventilated from the crankcase. However, the crankcase cannot be vented directly to the atmosphere, because the hydrocarbon vapors add to air pollution. Positive crankcase ventilation (**PCV**) systems were developed to ventilate the crankcase and recirculate the vapors to the engine's induction system so they can be burned in the cylinders.

Closed PCV Systems

All systems use a PCV valve, calibrated orifice or separator, an air inlet filter, and connecting hoses. See Figure 27-1 An oil/vapor or oil/water separator is used

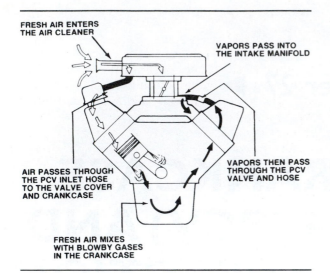

FRESH AIR ENTERS
THE AIR CLEANER

VAPORS PASS INTO
THE INTAKE MANIFOLD

AIR PASSES THROUGH
THE PCV INLET HOSE
TO THE VALVE COVER
AND CRANKCASE

VAPORS THEN PASS
THROUGH THE PCV
VALVE AND HOSE

FRESH AIR MIXES
WITH BLOWBY GASES
IN THE CRANKCASE

FIGURE 27-1 A PCV system includes a hose from the air cleaner assembly so that filtered air can be drawn into the crankcase. This filtered air is then drawn by engine vacuum through the PCV valve and into the intake manifold where the crankcase fumes are burned in the cylinder. The PCV valve controls and limits this flow of air and fumes into the engine and the valve closes in the event of a backfire to prevent flames from entering the crankcase area.

in some systems instead of a valve or orifice, particularly with turbocharged and fuel-injected engines. The oil/vapor separator lets oil condense and drain back into the crankcase. The oil/water separator accumulates moisture and prevents it from freezing during cold engine starts.

The air for the PCV system is drawn after or before, the air cleaner filter, which acts as a PCV filter.

NOTE: Some older designs drew from the dirty side of the air cleaner, where a separate crankcase ventilation filter was used. See Figure 27-2.

PCV VALVES

The PCV valve in most systems is a one-way valve containing a spring-operated plunger that controls valve flow rate. See Figure 27-3. Flow rate is established for each engine; a valve for a different engine should not be substituted. The flow rate is determined by the size of the plunger and the holes inside the valve. PCV valves usually are located in the valve cover or intake manifold.

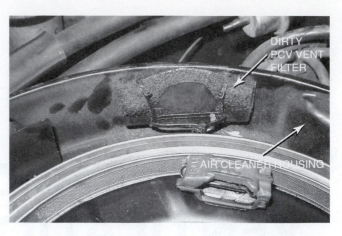

DIRTY
PCV VENT
FILTER

AIR CLEANER HOUSING

FIGURE 27-2 A dirty PCV vent filter inside the air cleaner housing. The air enters the crankcase through this filter and then is drawn into the engine through the PCV valve.

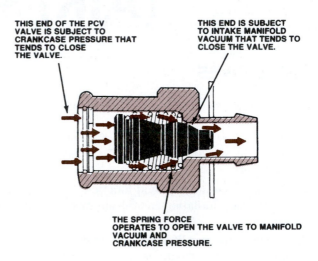

THIS END OF THE PCV
VALVE IS SUBJECT TO
CRANKCASE PRESSURE THAT
TENDS TO CLOSE
THE VALVE.

THIS END IS SUBJECT
TO INTAKE MANIFOLD
VACUUM THAT TENDS TO
CLOSE THE VALVE.

THE SPRING FORCE
OPERATES TO OPEN THE VALVE TO MANIFOLD
VACUUM AND
CRANKCASE PRESSURE.

FIGURE 27-3 Spring force, crankcase pressure, and intake manifold vacuum work together to regulate the flow rate through the PCV valve.

The PCV valve regulates air flow through the crankcase under all driving conditions and speeds. When manifold vacuum is high (at idle, cruising, and light-load operation), the PCV valve restricts the air flow to maintain a balanced air-fuel ratio. See Figure 27-4. It also prevents high intake manifold vacuum from pulling oil out of the crankcase and into the intake manifold. Under high speed or heavy loads, the valve opens and allows maximum air flow. See Figure 27-5. If the engine backfires, the valve will close instantly to prevent a crankcase explosion. See Figure 27-6.

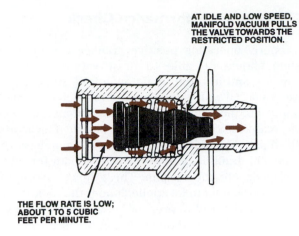

AT IDLE AND LOW SPEED, MANIFOLD VACUUM PULLS THE VALVE TOWARDS THE RESTRICTED POSITION.

THE FLOW RATE IS LOW; ABOUT 1 TO 5 CUBIC FEET PER MINUTE.

FIGURE 27-4 Air flows through the PCV valve during idle, cruising, and light-load conditions.

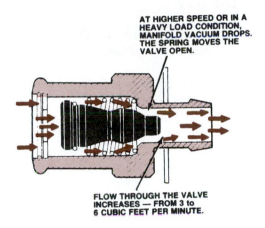

AT HIGHER SPEED OR IN A HEAVY LOAD CONDITION, MANIFOLD VACUUM DROPS. THE SPRING MOVES THE VALVE OPEN.

FLOW THROUGH THE VALVE INCREASES — FROM 3 to 6 CUBIC FEET PER MINUTE.

FIGURE 27-5 Air flows through the PCV valve during acceleration and when the engine is under a heavy load.

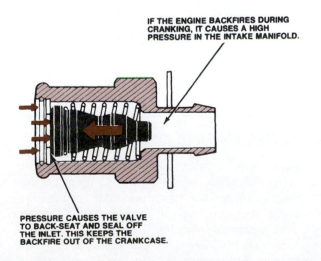

IF THE ENGINE BACKFIRES DURING CRANKING, IT CAUSES A HIGH PRESSURE IN THE INTAKE MANIFOLD.

PRESSURE CAUSES THE VALVE TO BACK-SEAT AND SEAL OFF THE INLET. THIS KEEPS THE BACKFIRE OUT OF THE CRANKCASE.

FIGURE 27-6 PCV valve operation in the event of a backfire.

ORIFICE-CONTROLLED SYSTEMS

The closed PCV system used on some 4-cylinder engines contains a calibrated orifice instead of a PCV valve. The orifice may be located in the valve cover or intake manifold, or in a hose connected between the valve cover, air cleaner, and intake manifold.

While most orifice flow control systems work the same as a PCV valve system, they may not use fresh air scavenging of the crankcase. Crankcase vapors are drawn into the intake manifold in calibrated amounts depending on manifold pressure and the orifice size. If vapor availability is low, as during idle, air is drawn in with the vapors. During off-idle operation, excess vapors are sent to the air cleaner as crankcase pressure increases oil, the gases backup.

At idle, PCV flow is controlled by a 0.050-inch (1.3-mm) orifice. As the engine moves off-idle, spark port vacuum pulls a spring-loaded valve off of its seat, allowing PCV flow to pass through a 0.090-inch (2.3-mm) orifice.

Separator Systems

Turbocharged and many fuel-injected engines use an oil/vapor or oil/water separator and a calibrated orifice instead of a PCV valve. In the most common applications, the air intake throttle body acts as the source for crankcase ventilation vacuum and a calibrated orifice acts as the metering device.

◀ DIAGNOSTIC STORY ▶

THE WHISTLING ENGINE

An older vehicle was being diagnosed for a whistling sound whenever the engine was running, especially at idle. It was finally discovered that the breather in the valve cover was plugged and caused high vacuum in the crankcase. The engine was sucking air from what was likely the rear main seal lip, making the 'whistle' noise. After replacing the breather and PCV, the noise stopped.

FIGURE 27-7 A visual inspection found this deteriorated PCV vacuum hose.

POSITIVE CRANKCASE VENTILATION (PCV) SYSTEM DIAGNOSIS

When intake air flows freely, the PCV system functions properly, as long as the PCV valve or orifice is not clogged. Modern engine design includes the air and vapor flow as a calibrated part of the air-fuel mixture. In fact, some engines receive as much as 30% of their idle air through the PCV system. For this reason, a flow problem in the PCV system results in driveability problems.

A blocked or plugged PCV system is a major cause of high oil consumption, and contributes to many oil leaks. Before expensive engine repairs are attempted, check the condition of the PCV system. See Figure 27-7.

PCV System Performance Check

A properly operating positive crankcase ventilation system should be able to draw vapors from the crankcase and into the intake manifold. If the pipes, hoses, and PCV valve itself are not restricted, vacuum is applied to the crankcase. A slight vacuum is created in the crankcase (usually less than 1 in. Hg if measured at the dipstick) and is also applied to other areas of the engine. Oil drain-back holes provide a path for oil to drain back into the oil pan. These holes also allow crankcase vacuum to be applied under the rocker covers and in the valley area of most V-type engines. There are several methods that can be used to test a PCV system.

The Rattle Test

The rattle test is performed by simply removing the PCV valve and shaking it in your hand. See Figure 27-8.

- If the PCV valve does *not* rattle, it is definitely defective and must be replaced.
- If the PCV valve *does* rattle, it does not necessarily mean that the PCV valve is good. All PCV valves contain springs that can become weaker with age and heating and cooling cycles. Replace any PCV valve with the *exact* replacement according to vehicle manufacturers' recommended intervals (usually every 3 years or 36,000 miles, or 60,000 km).

The 3 × 5 Card Test

Remove the oil-fill cap (where oil is added to the engine) and start the engine. See Figure 27-9.

◀ TECH TIP ▶

CHECK FOR OIL LEAKS WITH THE ENGINE OFF

The owner of an older vehicle equipped with a V-6 engine complained to his technician that he smelled burning oil, but only *after* shutting off the engine. The technician found that the rocker cover gaskets were leaking. But why did the owner only notice the smell of hot oil when the engine was shut off? Because of the positive crankcase ventilation (PCV) system, engine vac-uum tends to draw oil away from gasket surfaces. But when the engine stops, engine vacuum disappears and the oil remaining in the upper regions of the engine will tend to flow down and out through any opening. Therefore, a good technician should check an engine for oil leaks not only with the engine running but also shortly after shut-down.

FIGURE 27-8 A typical PCV valve. A defective or clogged PCV valve or hose can cause a rough idle or stalling problem. Because the air flow through the PCV valve accounts for about 20% of the air needed by the engine at idle, use of the incorrect valve for an application could have a severe effect on idle quality.

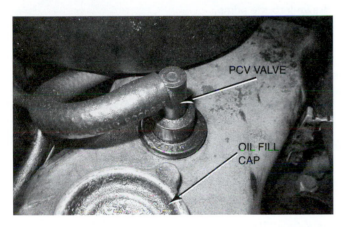

FIGURE 27-9 A typical PCV valve installed in a rubber grommet in the valve cover.

NOTE: Use care on some overhead camshaft engines. With the engine running, oil may be sprayed from the open oil-fill opening.

Hold a 3×5 card over the opening (a dollar bill or any other piece of paper can be used for this test).

- If the PCV system, including the valve and hoses, is functioning correctly, the card should be held down on the oil-fill opening by the slight vacuum inside the crankcase.
- If the card will not stay, carefully inspect the PCV valve, hose(s), and manifold vacuum port for carbon build-up (restriction). Clean or replace as necessary.

NOTE: On some 4-cylinder engines, the 3×5 card may vibrate on the oil-fill opening when the engine is running at idle speed. This is normal because of the time intervals between intake strokes on a 4-cylinder engine.

The Snap-Back Test

The proper operation of the PCV valve can be checked by placing a finger over the inlet hole in the valve when the engine is running and removing the finger rapidly. Repeat several times. The valve should "snap back." If the valve does not snap back, replace the valve.

Crankcase Vacuum Test

The PCV system can sometimes be checked by testing for a weak vacuum at the oil dipstick tube using an inches-of-water manometer or gauge as follows:

Step 1 Remove the oil filler cap and cover the opening.

Step 2 Remove the oil level indicator (dipstick).

Step 3 Connect a water manometer or gauge to the dipstick tube.

Step 4 Start the engine and observe the gauge at idle and at 2500 RPM. See Figure 27-10.

FIGURE 27-10 A water manometer being used to check for a slight vacuum when testing at the oil dipstick tube.

The gauge should show some vacuum, especially at 2500 RPM. If not, carefully inspect the PCV system for blockages or other faults.

◄ GURU TIP ►

The wrong PCV valve may cause low IAC counts and/or a rough unstable idle.

PCV MONITOR

All vehicles must be checked for proper operation of the PCV system starting with 2004 and newer vehicles. The PCV monitor will fail if the PCM detects an opening between the crankcase and the PCV valve or between the PCV valve and the intake manifold. Some vehicle manufacturers use a pressure sensor in the PCV system to monitor vacuum. Some manufacturers determine if the PCV system is functioning correctly by monitoring fuel trim.

PCV-RELATED DIAGNOSTIC TROUBLE CODE

Diagnostic Trouble Code	Description	Possible Causes
P1480	PCV solenoid circuit fault	• Defective PCV solenoid • Loose or corroded electrical connection • Loose, defective vacuum hoses/connections

AIR-PUMP SYSTEM

An air pump provides the air necessary for the oxidizing process inside the catalytic converter. See Figure 27-11.

NOTE: This system is commonly called AIR, meaning **air-injection reaction**. Therefore, an AIR pump does pump air.

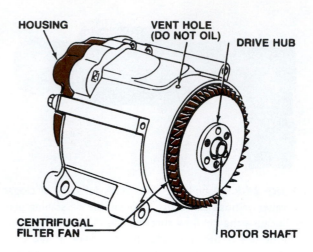

FIGURE 27-11 A typical belt-driven air pump. Air enters through the revolving fins. These fins act as a moving air filter because dirt is heavier than air and therefore the dirt in the air is deflected off the fins at the same time the air is drawn into the pump.

The AIR pump, sometimes referred to as a *smog pump* or *thermactor pump*, is mounted at the front of the engine and driven by a belt from the crankshaft pulley. It pulls fresh air in through an external filter and pumps the air under slight pressure to each exhaust port or the catalytic converter through connecting hoses or a manifold.

- A belt-driven pump with inlet air filter (older models), or
- An electronic air pump (newer models)
- One or more air distribution manifolds and nozzles
- One or more exhaust check valves
- Connecting hoses for air distribution
- Air management valves and solenoids on all newer applications

With the introduction of NO_x reduction converters (also called dual-bed, three-way converters, or TWC), the output of the AIR pump is sent to the center of the converter where the extra air can help oxidize HC and CO into H_2O and CO_2.

Air Switching Valves

The computer controls the air flow from the pump by switching on and off various solenoid valves. When the engine is cold, the air pump output is directed to the exhaust manifold to help provide enough oxygen to convert HC (unburned gasoline) and CO (carbon monoxide) to H_2O (water) and CO_2 (carbon dioxide). When the engine

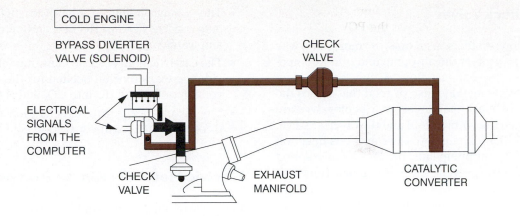

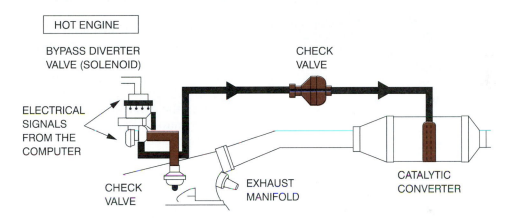

FIGURE 27-12   (a) When the engine is cold and before the oxygen sensor is hot enough to reach closed loop, the air flow is directed to the exhaust manifold(s) through one-way check valve(s). These valves keep exhaust gases from entering the switching solenoids and the air pump itself. (b) When the engine achieves closed loop, the air flows from the pump, is directed to the catalytic converter, and then moves through a check valve.

becomes warm and the engine is operating in closed loop, the computer operates the air valves so as to direct the air pump output to the catalytic converter. When the vacuum rapidly increases above the normal idle level, as during rapid deceleration, the computer diverts the air-pump output to the air cleaner assembly to silence the air. Diverting the air to the air cleaner prevents exhaust backfire during deceleration. See Figure 27-12.

AIR DISTRIBUTION MANIFOLDS AND NOZZLES

The air-injection system seals air from the pump to a nozzle installed near each exhaust port in the cylinder head. This provides equal air injection for the exhaust

from each cylinder and makes it available at a point in the system where exhaust gases are the hottest.

Air is delivered to the exhaust system in one of two ways:

- An external air manifold, or manifolds, distributes the air through injection tubes with stainless steel nozzles. The nozzles are threaded into the cylinder heads or exhaust manifolds close to each exhaust valve. This method is used primarily with smaller engines.
- An internal air manifold distributes the air to the exhaust ports near each exhaust valve through passages cast in the cylinder head or the exhaust manifold. This method is used mainly with larger engines.

Three basic types of air pumps are the belt-driven air pump, the pulse air-driven air pump, and the electric motor-driven air pump.

Exhaust Check Valves

All air-injection systems use one or more one-way check valves to protect the air pump and other components from reverse exhaust flow. A check valve contains a spring-type metallic disc or reed that closes the air line under exhaust back pressure. Check valves are located between the air manifold and the diverter valve. See Figure 27-13. If exhaust pressure exceeds injection pressure, or if the air pump fails, the check-valve spring closes the valve to prevent reverse exhaust flow. See Figure 27-14.

All air-pump systems use one-way check valves to allow air to flow into the exhaust manifold and to prevent the hot exhaust from flowing into the valves on the air pump itself.

NOTE: These check valves commonly fail, resulting in excessive exhaust emissions (CO especially). When the check valve fails, hot exhaust can travel up to and destroy the switching valve(s) and air pump itself.

Belt-Driven Air Pumps

The belt-driven air pump uses a centrifugal filter just behind the drive pulley. As the pump rotates, underhood air is drawn into the pump and is slightly compressed. See Figure 27-15. The air is then directed to

- The exhaust manifold when the engine is cold to help oxidize CO and HC into carbon dioxide (CO_2) and water vapor (H_2O).
- The catalytic converter on many models to help provide the extra oxygen needed for the efficient conversion of CO and HC into CO_2 and H_2O.
- The air cleaner during deceleration or wide-open throttle (WOT) engine operation. See Figure 27-16.

Electric Motor-Driven Air Pumps

This style of pump is generally used only during cold engine operation and is computer controlled.

Pulse Air-Driven Devices

The pulse air-driven air pump uses the exhaust system pulses to draw in the compressed air. See Figure 27-17. Pulse air or aspirator valves are similar in design to exhaust check valves. Each valve contains a spring-loaded diaphragm or reed valve and is connected by tubing to the exhaust port of each cylinder, or the exhaust manifold. Each time an exhaust valve closes, there is a period when exhaust manifold pressure

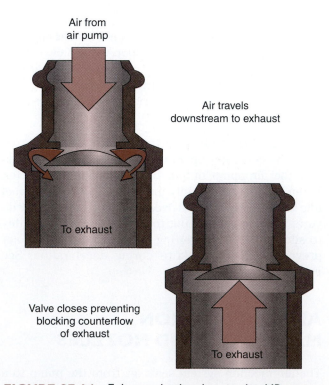

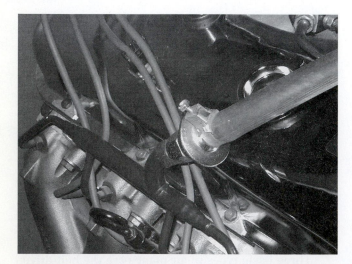

FIGURE 27-13 An AIR exhaust check valve between the rubber air hose and the metal discharge tubes.

FIGURE 27-14 Exhaust check valves in the AIR system allow air to flow in only one direction.

FIGURE 27-15 A typical belt-driven air pump used on an older model Chevrolet Corvette.

drops below atmospheric pressure. During these low-pressure (slight vacuum) pulses, the pulse valve opens to admit fresh air to the exhaust. When the exhaust valve opens and exhaust pressure rises above atmospheric pressure, the pulse air valve acts as a check valve and closes.

Pulse air injection works best at low engine speeds when extra air is needed most by the catalytic converter. At high engine speeds, the vacuum pulses occur too rapidly for the valve to follow, and the internal spring simply keeps the valve closed. Pulse air valves must be connected upstream in the exhaust system where negative pressure pulses are strongest. This means that pulse air cannot be switched downstream for use in the converter or between oxidation and reduction catalysts. The system is most effective on vehicles equipped with only an HC-CO oxidation catalyst.

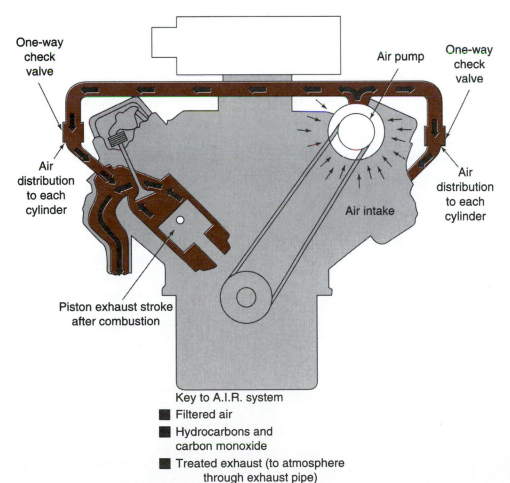

Key to A.I.R. system
- ■ Filtered air
- ■ Hydrocarbons and carbon monoxide
- ■ Treated exhaust (to atmosphere through exhaust pipe)

One-way check valve

Air distribution to each cylinder

Piston exhaust stroke after combustion

Air pump

One-way check valve

Air intake

Air distribution to each cylinder

FIGURE 27-16 The air pump supplies air to the exhaust port of each cylinder. Unburned HCs are oxidized into CO_2 and H_2O and CO is converted to CO_2.

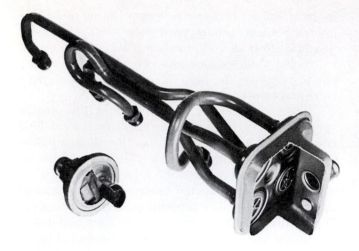

FIGURE 27-17 Cutaway of a pulse air-driven air device used on many older engines to deliver air to the exhaust port through the use of the exhaust pulses acting on a series of one-way check valves. Air from the air cleaner assembly moves through the system and into the exhaust port where the additional air helps reduce HC and CO exhaust emissions.

AIR-PUMP SYSTEM DIAGNOSIS

The air-pump system should be inspected if an exhaust emissions test failure occurs. In severe cases, the exhaust will enter the air cleaner assembly, resulting in a horribly running engine because the extra exhaust displaces the oxygen needed for proper combustion. With the engine running, check for normal operation:

Engine Operation	Normal Operation of a Typical Air-Injection Reaction (AIR) Pump System
Cold engine (open-loop operation)	Air is diverted to the exhaust manifold(s) or cylinder head
Warm engine (closed-loop operation)	Air is diverted to the catalytic converter
Deceleration	Air is diverted to the air cleaner assembly
Wide-open throttle	Air is diverted to the air cleaner assembly

Visual Inspection

Carefully inspect all air-injection reaction (AIR) system hoses and pipes. Any pipes that have holes and leak air or exhaust require replacement. The check valve(s) should be checked when a pump has become inoperative. Exhaust gases could have gotten past the check valve and damaged the pump. Check the drive belt on an engine-driven pump for wear and proper tension.

Four-Gas Exhaust Analysis

An AIR system can be easily tested using an exhaust gas analyzer. Follow these steps:

1. Start the engine and allow it to run until normal operating temperature is achieved.
2. Connect the analyzer probe to the tailpipe and observe the exhaust readings for hydrocarbons (HC) and carbon monoxide (CO).
3. Using the appropriate pinch-off pliers, shut off the air flow from the AIR system. Observe the HC and CO readings. If the AIR system is working correctly, the HC and CO should increase when the AIR system is shut off.
4. Record the O_2 reading with the AIR system still inoperative. Unclamp the pliers and watch the O_2 readings. If the system is functioning correctly, the O_2 level should increase by 1 to 4%.

AIR-RELATED DIAGNOSTIC TROUBLE CODE

Diagnostic Trouble Code	Description	Possible Causes
P1485	AIR solenoid circuit fault	• Defective AIR solenoid • Loose or corroded electrical connections • Loose, missing, or defective rubber hose(s)

SUMMARY

1. Positive crankcase ventilation (PCV) systems use a valve or a fixed orifice to control the fumes from the crankcase back into the intake system.

2. A PCV valve regulates the flow of fumes depending on engine vacuum and seals the crankcase vent in the event of a backfire.

3. As much as 30% of the air needed by the engine at idle speed flows through the PCV system.

4. PCV tests include the rattle test, card test, snap-back test, and crankcase vacuum test.

5. The AIR system forces air at low pressure into the exhaust to reduce CO and HC exhaust emissions.

6. Exhaust check valves are used between the AIR pump and the exhaust manifold to prevent exhaust gases from flowing into, and causing damage to, the AIR pump and valves.

REVIEW QUESTIONS

1. What exhaust emissions does the PCV valve and AIR system control?

2. How does a PCV valve work?

3. What does the abbreviation PCV mean?

4. What does the abbreviation AIR mean?

ASE CERTIFICATION-TYPE QUESTIONS

1. The PCV system controls which exhaust emission(s)?
   a. HC
   b. CO
   c. NO_x
   d. Both HC and CO

2. How much of the air needed by the engine flows through the PCV system when the engine is at idle speed?
   a. 1 to 3%
   b. 5 to 10%
   c. 10 to 20%
   d. Up to 30%

3. Technician A says that if the PCV system were defective or clogged, the engine could idle rough. Technician B says that the engine may stall. Which technician is correct?
   a. Technician A only
   b. Technician B only
   c. Both Technicians A and B
   d. Neither Technician A nor B

4. Technician A says that if a PCV valve rattles, then it is okay and does not need to be replaced. Technician B says that if a PCV valve does not rattle, it should be replaced. Which technician is correct?
   a. Technician A only
   b. Technician B only
   c. Both Technicians A and B
   d. Neither Technician A nor B

5. Technician A says that the PCV system should create a slight pressure in the crankcase at idle. Technician B says that the PCV system should create a slight vacuum in the crankcase at 2500 RPM. Which technician is correct?
   a. Technician A only
   b. Technician B only
   c. Both Technicians A and B
   d. Neither Technician A nor B

6. The AIR system is used to reduce which exhaust emission(s)?
   a. HC
   b. CO
   c. NO_x
   d. Both HC and CO

7. Two technicians are discussing exhaust check valves used in AIR systems. Technician A says that they are used to prevent the output from the AIR pump from entering the intake manifold. Technician B says the check valves are used to keep the exhaust from entering the AIR pump. Which technician is correct?
   a. Technician A only
   b. Technician B only
   c. Both Technicians A and B
   d. Neither Technician A nor B

8. Where is the output of the AIR pump directed when the engine is cold?

   a. Exhaust manifold

   b. Catalytic converter

   c. Air cleaner assembly

   d. To the atmosphere

9. The switching valves on the AIR pump have failed several times. Technician A says that a defective exhaust check valve could be the cause. Technician B says that a restricted exhaust system could be the cause. Which technician is correct?

   a. Technician A only

   b. Technician B only

   c. Both Technicians A and B

   d. Neither Technician A nor B

10. When checking for the proper operation of the AIR system using an exhaust gas analyzer, how much should the oxygen (O_2) levels increase when the pump is allowed to function?

    a. 1 to 4%

    b. 5 to 10%

    c. 10 to 20%

    d. Up to 30%

◀ Chapter 28 ▶

CATALYTIC CONVERTERS

OBJECTIVES

After studying Chapter 28, the reader should be able to:

1. Prepare for ASE Engine Performance (A8) certification test content area "D" (Emission Control Systems).
2. Describe the purpose and function of the catalytic converter.
3. Discuss how the catalytic converter is tested under OBD-II regulations.
4. Explain the method for diagnosing and testing the catalytic converter.

A **catalytic converter** is an aftertreatment device used to reduce exhaust emissions outside of the engine. This device is installed in the exhaust system between the exhaust manifold and the muffler, and usually is positioned beneath the passenger compartment. See Figure 28-1. The location of the converter is important, since as much of the exhaust heat as possible must be retained for effective operation. The nearer it is to the engine, the better.

CERAMIC MONOLITH CATALYTIC CONVERTER

Most catalytic converters are constructed of a ceramic material in a honeycomb shape with square openings for the exhaust gases. There are approximately 400 openings per square inch (62 per sq. cm) and the wall thickness is

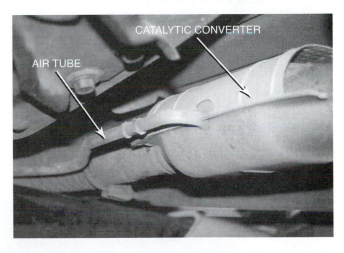

FIGURE 28-1 Typical catalytic converter. The small tube into the side of the converter comes from the air pump. The additional air from the air pump helps oxidize the exhaust into harmless H_2O and CO_2.

about 0.006 in. (1.5 mm). The substrate is then coated with a porous aluminum material called the **washcoat,** which makes the surface rough. The catalytic materials are then applied on top of the washcoat. The substrate is contained within a round or oval shell made by welding two stamped pieces of aluminum or stainless steel together. See Figure 28-2.

The ceramic substrate in monolithic converters is not restrictive, but breaks more easily when subject to shock or severe jolts, and is more expensive to manufacture. Monolithic converters can be serviced only as a unit.

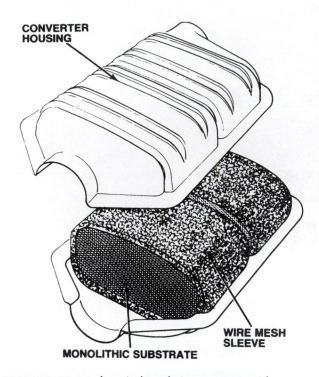

CONVERTER HOUSING

WIRE MESH SLEEVE

MONOLITHIC SUBSTRATE

FIGURE 28-2 A typical catalytic converter with a monolithic substrate.

An exhaust pipe is connected to the manifold or header to carry gases through a catalytic converter and then to the muffler or silencer. V-type engines usually route the exhaust into one catalytic converter.

Catalytic Converter Operation

The converter contains small amounts of **rhodium, palladium,** and **platinum.** These elements act as **catalysts.** A catalyst is an element that starts a chemical reaction without becoming a part of, or being consumed in, the process. In a three-way catalytic converter **(TWC),** three exhaust emissions (NO_x, HC, and CO) are converted to carbon dioxide (CO_2) and water (H_2O). See Figure 28-3. As the exhaust gas passes through the catalyst, oxides of nitrogen (NO_x) are chemically reduced (that is, nitrogen and oxygen are separated) in the first section of the catalytic converter. In the second section of the catalytic converter, most of the hydrocarbons and carbon monoxide remaining in the exhaust gas are oxidized to form harmless carbon dioxide (CO_2) and water vapor (H_2O). An air-injection system or pulse air system is used on some engines to supply additional air that may be needed in the oxidation process. See Figure 28-4.

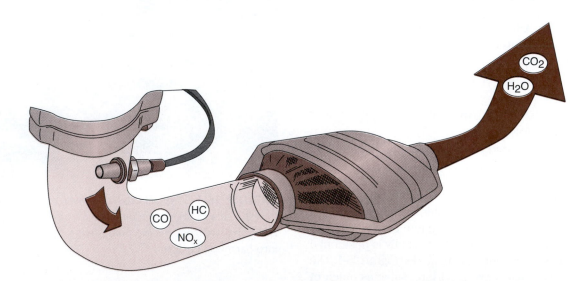

FIGURE 28-3 The three-way catalytic converter first separates the NO_x into nitrogen and oxygen and then converts the HC and CO into harmless water (H_2O) and carbon dioxide (CO_2).

FIGURE 28-4 A cutaway of a three-way catalytic converter showing the air tube in the center of the reducing and oxidizing section of the converter. Note the small holes in the tube to distribute air from the AIR pump to the oxidizing rear section of the converter.

NOTE: A two-way converter used in most vehicles from 1975 to 1980 only contained the oxidation portion.

Since the early 1990s, many converters also contain **cerium,** an element that can store oxygen. The purpose of the cerium is to provide oxygen to the oxidation bed of the converter when the exhaust is rich and lacks enough oxygen for proper oxidation. When the exhaust is lean, the cerium absorbs the extra oxygen. The converter must have a varying rich-to-lean exhaust for proper operation:

- A rich exhaust is required for reduction—stripping the oxygen (O_2) from the nitrogen in NO_x
- A lean exhaust is required to provide the oxygen necessary to oxidize HC and CO (combining oxygen with HC and CO to form H_2O and CO_2)

If the catalytic converter is not functioning correctly, check to see that the air-fuel mixture being supplied to the engine is correct and that the ignition system is free of defects.

Converter Light-Off

The catalytic converter does not work when cold and it must be heated to its **light-off** temperature of close to 500°F (260°C) before it starts working at 50% effectiveness. When fully effective, the converter reaches a temperature range of 900° to 1600°F (482° to 871°C). In spite of the intense heat, however, catalytic reactions do not generate the flame and radiant heat associated with a simple burning reaction. Because of the extreme heat (almost as hot as combustion chamber temperatures), a converter remains hot long after the engine is shut off. Most vehicles use a series of heat shields to protect the passenger compartment and other parts of the chassis from excessive heat. Vehicles have been known to start fires because of the hot converter causing tall grass or dry leaves beneath the just-parked vehicle to ignite.

Converter Usage

A catalytic converter must be located as close as possible to the exhaust manifold to work effectively. The farther back the converter is positioned in the exhaust system, the more gases cool before they reach the converter. Since positioning in the exhaust system affects the oxidation process, cars that use only an oxidation converter generally locate it underneath the front of the passenger compartment.

Some vehicles have used a small, quick heating oxidation converter called a **pre-converter, pup,** or **mini-converter** that connects directly to the exhaust manifold outlet. These have a small catalyst surface area close to the engine that heats up rapidly to start the oxidation process more quickly during cold engine warm-up. For this reason, they were often called **light-off converters,** or **LOC.** The oxidation reaction started in the LOC is completed by the larger main converter under the passenger compartment.

CATALYTIC CONVERTER WARM-UP TEST

The PCM determines if the catalytic converter is ready for testing based on the following conditions, which may vary by vehicle make, model, and year.

- Closed loop status achieved
- IAT sensor temperature higher than 32°F (0°C)
- ECT sensor temperature higher than 165°F (18°C)
- MAF sensor input from 15 to 32 grams per second
- Engine load less than 65% and steady
- Engine speed less than 4000 RPM
- All of the above conditions met for at least 4 minutes

These factors are the enable criteria that must be achieved before the OBD-II catalyst monitor will run.

OBD-II CATALYTIC CONVERTER PERFORMANCE

With OBD-II equipped vehicles, catalytic converter performance is monitored by a heated oxygen, (HO2S) sensor both before and after the converter. See Figure 28-5. The converters used on these vehicles have what is known as **OSC** or Oxygen Storage Capacity. OSC is due mostly to the cerium coating in the catalyst rather than the precious metals used. When the TWC is operating as it should, the post-converter HO2S is far less active than the pre-converter sensor. The converter stores, then releases, the oxygen during its normal reduction and oxidation of the exhaust gases, smoothing out the variations in O2 being released.

Where a cycling sensor voltage output is expected before the converter, because of the converter's action, the post-converter HO2S should read a steady signal without much fluctuation. See Figure 28-6. With the rapid light-off and more efficient converters used today, the air pump needs to supply only secondary air during the first few minutes of cold-engine operation.

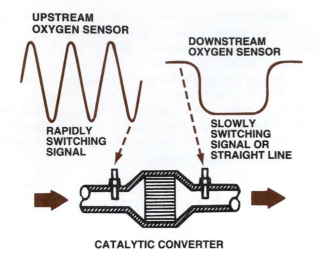

FIGURE 28-5 The OBD-II catalytic converter monitor compares the signals of the upstream and downstream HO2S to determine converter efficiency.

CONVERTER DAMAGING CONDITIONS

Since converters have no moving parts, they require no periodic service. Under federal law, catalyst effectiveness is warranted for 80,000 miles or eight years.

It is possible, however, to damage a converter. The three main causes of premature converter failure are:

- **Contamination.** Substances that can destroy the converter include exhaust that contains excess engine oil, antifreeze, sulfur (from poor fuel), and various other chemical substances.
- **Excessive temperatures.** Although a converter operates at a high temperature, it can be destroyed by excessive temperatures. This most often occurs either when too much unburned fuel enters the converter, or with excessively lean mixtures. Excessive temperatures may be caused by long idling periods on some vehicles, since more heat develops at those times than when driving at normal highway speeds. Severe high temperatures can cause the converter to melt down, leading to the internal parts breaking apart and either clogging the converter or moving downstream to plug the muffler. In either case, the restricted exhaust flow severely reduces engine power.
- **Improper air-fuel mixtures.** Rich mixtures or raw fuel in the exhaust can be caused by engine misfiring, or an excessively rich air-fuel mixture resulting from a defective coolant temp sensor or defective fuel injectors. Lean mixtures are commonly caused by intake manifold leaks. See Figure 28-7.

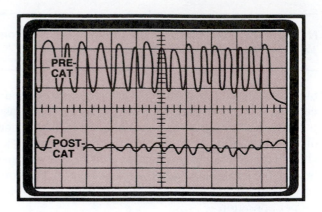

FIGURE 28-6 The waveform of an HO2S downstream from a properly functioning converter shows little, if any, activity.

When either of these circumstances occurs, the converter can become a catalytic furnace, causing the damage previously described.

To avoid excessive catalyst temperatures and the possibility of fuel vapors reaching the converter, follow these rules:

1. Do not try to start the engine on compression by pushing the vehicle. Use jumper cables instead.
2. Do not crank an engine for more than 40 seconds when it is flooded or firing intermittently.
3. Do not turn off the ignition switch when the car is in motion.
4. Do not disconnect a spark plug for more than 30 seconds to test the ignition.
5. Repair engine problems such as dieseling, misfiring, or stumbling from excess fuel that affect performance as soon as possible.

◀ FREQUENTLY ASKED ▶ QUESTION

CAN A CATALYTIC CONVERTER BE DEFECTIVE WITHOUT BEING CLOGGED?

Yes. Catalytic converters can fail by being chemically damaged or poisoned without being mechanically clogged. Therefore, the catalytic converter should not only be tested for physical damage (clogging) by performing a back pressure or vacuum test and a rattle test, but also for temperature rise, usually with a pyrometer or oxygen test, to check the efficiency of the converter.

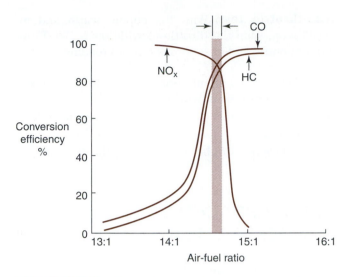

FIGURE 28-7 The highest catalytic converter efficiency occurs when the air-fuel mixture is about 14.7:1.

DIAGNOSING CATALYTIC CONVERTERS

The Tap Test

This simple test involves tapping (not pounding) on the catalytic converter using a rubber mallet. If the substrate inside the converter is broken, the converter will rattle when hit. If the converter rattles, a replacement converter is required. See Figure 28-8.

Testing Back Pressure with a Vacuum Gauge

A vacuum gauge can be used to measure manifold vacuum at a high idle (2000 to 2500 RPM). If the exhaust system is restricted, pressure increases in the exhaust system. This pressure is called **back pressure.** Manifold vacuum will drop gradually if the engine is kept at a constant speed if the exhaust is restricted.

The reason the vacuum will drop is that all the exhaust leaving the engine at the higher engine speed cannot get through the restriction. After a short time (within 1 minute), the exhaust tends to "pile up" above the restriction and eventually remains in the cylinder of the engine at the end of the exhaust stroke. Therefore, at the beginning of the intake stroke, when the piston traveling downward should be lowering the pressure (raising the vacuum) in the intake manifold, the extra exhaust in the cylinder *lowers* the normal vacuum. If the exhaust restriction is severe enough, the vehicle can become undriveable because cylinder filling cannot occur except at idle.

FIGURE 28-8 This catalytic converter blew up when gasoline from the excessively rich-running engine ignited. Obviously, raw gasoline was trapped inside and all it needed was a spark. No further diagnosis of this converter is necessary.

Testing Back Pressure with a Pressure Gauge

Exhaust system back pressure can be measured directly by installing a pressure gauge in an exhaust opening. This can be accomplished in one of the following ways:

1. To test an oxygen sensor, remove the inside of an old, discarded oxygen sensor and thread in an adapter to convert it to a vacuum or pressure gauge.

NOTE: An adapter can be easily made by inserting a metal tube or pipe. A short section of brake line works great. The pipe can be brazed to the oxygen sensor housing or it can be glued with epoxy. An 18-millimeter compression gauge adapter can also be adapted to fit into the oxygen sensor opening. See Figure 28-9.

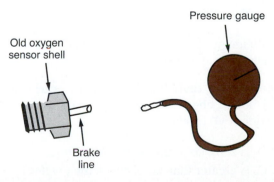

FIGURE 28-9 A back pressure tool can be easily made by attaching a short section of brake line to the shell of an old oxygen sensor. Braze or epoxy the tube to the shell.

2. To test an exhaust gas recirculation (EGR) valve, remove the EGR valve and fabricate a plate.

3. To test an air-injection reaction (AIR) check valve, remove the check valve from the exhaust tubes leading to the exhaust manifold. Use a rubber cone with a tube inside to seal against the exhaust tube. Connect the tube to a pressure gauge.

At idle the maximum back pressure should be less than 1.5 psi (10 kPa), and it should be less than 2.5 psi (15 kPa) at 2500 RPM.

Testing a Catalytic Converter for Temperature Rise

A properly working catalytic converter should be able to reduce NO_x exhaust emissions into nitrogen (N) and oxygen (O_2) and oxidize unburned hydrocarbon (HC) and carbon monoxide (CO) into harmless carbon dioxide (CO_2) and water vapor (H_2O). During these chemical processes, the catalytic converter should increase in temperature at least 10% if the converter is working properly. To test, operate the engine at 2500 RPM for at least 2 minutes to fully warm up the converter. Measure the inlet and the outlet temperatures using an infrared pyrometer as shown in Figure 28-10.

NOTE: If the engine is extremely efficient, the converter may not have any excessive unburned hydrocarbons or carbon monoxide to convert! In this case, a spark plug wire could be grounded out using a vacuum hose and a test light to create some unburned hydrocarbon in the exhaust. Do not ground out a cylinder for longer than 10 seconds or the excessive amount of unburned hydrocarbon could overheat and damage the converter.

Catalytic Converter Efficiency Tests

The efficiency of a catalytic converter can be determined using an exhaust gas analyzer.

Oxygen level test. With the engine warm and in closed loop, check the oxygen (O_2) and carbon monoxide (CO) levels.

- If O_2 is zero, go to the snap-throttle test.
- If O_2 is greater than zero, check the CO level.
- If CO is greater than zero, the converter is *not* functioning correctly.

Snap-throttle test. With the engine warm and in closed loop, snap the throttle to wide open (WOT) in park or neutral and observe the oxygen reading.

- The O_2 reading should not exceed 1.2%; if it does, the converter is not working.
- If the O_2 rises to 1.2%, the converter may have low efficiency.
- If the O_2% remains below 1.2%, then the converter is okay.

OBD-II CATALYTIC CONVERTER MONITOR

The catalytic converter monitor of OBD II uses an upstream and downstream HO2S to test catalytic efficiency. When the engine combusts a lean air-fuel mixture, higher amounts of oxygen flow through the exhaust into the converter. The catalyst materials absorb this oxygen for the oxidation process, thereby removing it from the exhaust stream. If a converter cannot absorb enough oxygen, oxidation does not occur. Engineers established a correlation between the amount of oxygen absorbed and converter efficiency.

The OBD-II system monitors how much oxygen the catalyst retains. A voltage waveform from the downstream HO2S of a good catalyst should have little or no activity. A voltage waveform from the downstream HO2S of a degraded catalyst shows a lot of activity. In other words, the closer the activity of the downstream HO2S matches that of the upstream HO2S, the greater the degree of converter degradation. In operation, the OBD-II monitor compares activity between the two exhaust oxygen sensors.

◄ TECH TIP ►

AFTERMARKET CATALYTIC CONVERTERS

Some replacement aftermarket (non-factory) catalytic converters do not contain the same amount of cerium as the original part. Cerium is the element that is used in catalytic converters to store oxygen. As a result of the lack of cerium, the correlation between the oxygen storage and the conversion efficiency may be affected enough to set a false diagnostic trouble code (P0422).

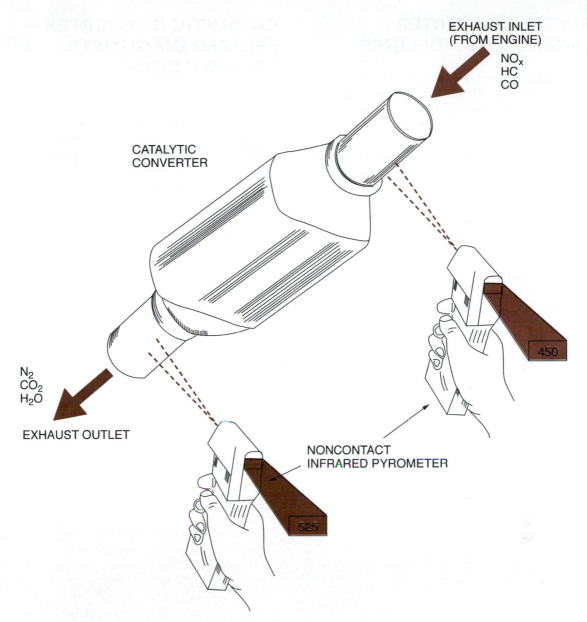

**EXHAUST INLET
(FROM ENGINE)**

NO$_x$
HC
CO

CATALYTIC
CONVERTER

N$_2$
CO$_2$
H$_2$O

EXHAUST OUTLET

NONCONTACT
INFRARED PYROMETER

450

525

FIGURE 28-10   The temperature of the outlet should be at least 10% hotter than the temperature of the inlet. This converter is very efficient. The inlet temperature is 450°F. Ten percent of 450° is 45° (45° + 450° = 495°). In other words, the outlet temperature should be at least 495°F for the converter to be considered okay. In this case, the outlet temperature of 525°F is more than the minimum 10% increase in temperature. If the converter is not working at all, the inlet temperature will be hotter than the outlet temperature.

CATALYTIC CONVERTER REPLACEMENT GUIDELINES

Because a catalytic converter is a major exhaust gas emission control device, the Environmental Protection Agency (EPA) has strict guidelines for its replacement, including:

- If a converter is replaced on a vehicle with less than 80,000/8 years, depending on the year of the vehicle, an original equipment catalytic converter *must* be used as a replacement.
- The replacement converter must be of the same design as the original. If the original had an air-pump fitting, so must the replacement.
- The old converter must be kept for possible inspection by the authorities for 60 days.
- A form must be completed and signed by both the vehicle owner and a representative from the service facility. This form must state the cause of the converter failure, and must remain on file for 2 years.

CATALYTIC CONVERTER RELATED DIAGNOSTIC TROUBLE CODE

Diagnostic Trouble Code	Description	Possible Causes
P0422	Catalytic converter efficiency failure	• Engine mechanical fault • Exhaust leaks • Fuel contaminants, such as engine oil, coolant, or sulfur

◀ TECH TIP ▶

CATALYTIC CONVERTERS ARE MURDERED

Catalytic converters start a chemical reaction but do not enter into the chemical reaction. Therefore, catalytic converters do not wear out and they do not die of old age. If a catalytic converter is found to be defective (nonfunctioning or clogged), look for the *root* cause. Remember this:

"Catalytic converters do not commit suicide—they're murdered."

Items that should be checked when a defective catalytic converter is discovered include all components of the ignition and fuel systems. Excessive unburned fuel can cause the catalytic converter to overheat and fail. The oxygen sensor must be working and fluctuating from 0.5 to 5 Hz (times per second) to provide the necessary air-fuel mixture variations for maximum catalytic converter efficiency.

SUMMARY

1. A catalytic converter is an aftertreatment device that reduces exhaust emissions outside of the engine.
2. The honeycomb shape of the catalytic converter is constructed of a ceramic material about 0.006-in. thick with small square openings.
3. A catalyst is an element that starts a chemical reaction but is not consumed in the process.
4. The catalyst materials used in a catalytic converter include rhodium, palladium, and platinum.
5. A catalytic converter has to be over 500°F (260°C) before it starts to become effective, and is therefore mounted as close as possible to the exhaust parts of the engine.
6. The OBD-II system monitor compares the relative activity of a rear oxygen sensor to the pre-catalytic oxygen sensor to determine catalytic converter efficiency.
7. Catalytic converters can be tested for restriction and for efficiency.

REVIEW QUESTIONS

1. What are the three most commonly used catalysts used in a catalytic converter?

2. How does a catalytic converter reduce NO_x to nitrogen and oxygen?

3. Why must a catalytic converter be mounted close to the exhaust ports of the engine?

4. How does the computer monitor catalytic converter performance?

5. What tests can be performed by a service technician to test the catalytic converter?

ASE CERTIFICATION-TYPE QUESTIONS

1. What is applied to the ceramic substrate to make the surface porous?
   a. Honeycomb filler
   b. Washcoat
   c. Aluminum
   d. Cerium

2. Two technicians are discussing catalytic converters. Technician A says that the exhaust mixture must fluctuate between rich and lean for the best efficiency. Technician B says that the air-fuel mixture must remain at exactly 14.7:1 for best performance from a three-way catalytic converter. Which technician is correct?
   a. Technician A only
   b. Technician B only
   c. Both Technicians A and B
   d. Neither Technician A nor B

3. A catalytic converter has to be at least how hot before it starts to work?
   a. 500°F (260°C)
   b. 1000°F (540°C)
   c. 1500°F (815°C)
   d. 2000°F (1100°C)

4. What two primary sensors does the PCM use to check the catalytic converter?
   a. Catalytic converter temperature sensor and rear oxygen sensor
   b. Pre-cat and post-cat oxygen sensor
   c. Pre-cat oxygen sensor and MAF
   d. MAP and TP

5. A catalytic converter can be harmed by _____.
   a. Excessive engine oil
   b. Antifreeze
   c. Sulfur from poor quality fuel
   d. Any of the above

6. Two technicians are discussing testing a catalytic converter. Technician A says that a vacuum gauge can be used and observed to see if the vacuum drops with the engine at idle for 30 seconds. Technician B says that a pressure gauge can be used to check for back pressure. Which technician is correct?
   a. Technician A only
   b. Technician B only
   c. Both Technicians A and B
   d. Neither Technician A nor B

7. A catalytic converter is being tested with an infrared pyrometer. Which is an acceptable (good converter) result?
   a. The inlet should be hotter than the outlet by 10%.
   b. The outlet should be hotter than the inlet by 10%.
   c. Both the inlet and the outlet should be the same temperature after the converter reaches operating temperature.
   d. The temperature of a catalytic converter is the best test to perform to locate a restricted (clogged) unit.

8. Which exhaust gas reading indicates a good catalytic converter?
   a. O_2 is zero
   b. CO is zero
   c. Both a and b
   d. Neither a nor b

9. A P0422 (catalytic converter efficiency failure) is set. What is a possible cause?
   a. Engine mechanical fault
   b. Exhaust leak
   c. Fuel contamination
   d. Any of the above

10. Technician A says that the catalytic converter is warranted for 8 years or 80,000 miles, whichever comes first. Technician B says that after replacing the catalytic converter, the old converter must be kept for possible inspection for 60 days. Which technician is correct?
    a. Technician A only
    b. Technician B only
    c. Both Technicians A and B
    d. Neither Technician A nor B

AUTOMOTIVE FUELS AND EMISSIONS

Answers to Even-Numbered ASE Certification-Type Questions

Chapter 1—2-d, 4-b, 6-b, 8-a, 10-d

Chapter 2—2-b, 4-a, 6-b, 8-b, 10-a

Chapter 3—2-b, 4-a, 6-b, 8-d, 10-d

Chapter 4—2-a, 4-c, 6-a, 8-b, 10-d

Chapter 5—2-c, 4-c, 6-a, 8-b, 10-a

Chapter 6—2-d, 4-b, 6-d, 8-c, 10-c

Chapter 7—2-b, 4-b, 6-b, 8-b, 10-c

Chapter 8—2-c, 4-d, 6-a, 8-a, 10-b

Chapter 9—2-a, 4-b, 6-a, 8-b, 10-a

Chapter 10—2-c, 4-d, 6-b, 8-a, 10-a

Chapter 11—2-b, 4-c, 6-d, 8-a, 10-c

Chapter 12—2-a, 4-b, 6-d, 8-b, 10-b

Chapter 13—2-b, 4-c, 6-b, 8-c, 10-d

Chapter 14—2-b, 4-c, 6-b, 8-c, 10-c

Chapter 15—2-a, 4-d, 6-a, 8-a, 10-c

Chapter 16—2-c, 4-d, 6-d, 8-a, 10-c

Chapter 17—2-a, 4-c, 6-c, 8-b, 10-c

Chapter 18—2-b, 4-b, 6-b, 8-a, 10-c

Chapter 19—2-a, 4-d, 6-c, 8-c, 10-b

Chapter 20—2-c, 4-b, 6-b, 8-c, 10-b

Chapter 21—2-d, 4-b, 6-c, 8-a, 10-d

Chapter 22—2-d, 4-c, 6-c, 8-c, 10-c

Chapter 23—2-a, 4-c, 6-d, 8-d, 10-b

Chapter 24—2-a, 4-c, 6-a, 8-c, 10-b

Chapter 25—2-a, 4-d, 6-a, 8-c, 10-a

Chapter 26—2-c, 4-b, 6-c, 8-a, 10-c

Chapter 27—2-c, 4-b, 6-d, 8-a, 10-a

Chapter 28—2-a, 4-b, 6-b, 8-c, 10-c

◀ Appendix I ▶

ENGINE PERFORMANCE (A8)

Sample ASE Certification Test

A8 ASE Test Specifications			
Content Area	*Questions in Test*	*Percentage of Test*	*Covered in Chapter #*
A. General Engine Diagnosis	10	17%	3, 4, 5, 6, 7, 8
B. Ignition System Diagnosis and Repair	10	17%	22, 23
C. Fuel, Air Induction, and Exhaust Systems Diagnosis and Repair	11	18%	6, 18, 20, 21
D. Emissions Control Systems Diagnosis and Repair **1.** Positive Crankcase Ventilation (1) **2.** Exhaust Gas Recirculation (3) **3.** Exhaust Gas Treatment (3) **4.** Evaporative Emission Controls (3)	9	15%	19, 25, 26, 27, 28
E. Computerized Engine Controls Diagnosis and Repair	16	26%	11, 12, 13, 14, 15, 16, 17
F. Engine Electrical Systems Diagnosis and Repair **1.** Battery (1) **2.** Starting System (1) **3.** Charging System (2)	4	7%	9, 10
TOTAL	**60**	**100%**	

(A) General Engine Diagnosis (10)

1. A smoothly operating engine depends on _____.
   a. High compression on most cylinders
   b. Equal compression among cylinders
   c. Cylinder compression levels above 100 psi (700 kPa) and within 70 psi (500 kPa) of each other
   d. Compression levels below 100 psi (700 kPa) on most cylinders

2. Technician A says that during a power balance test, the cylinder that causes the biggest RPM drop is the weak cylinder. Technician B says that if one spark plug wire is grounded out and the engine speed does not drop, a weak or dead cylinder is indicated. Which technician is correct?
   a. Technician A only
   b. Technician B only
   c. Both Technicians A and B
   d. Neither Technician A nor B

3. *Cranking* vacuum should be _____.
   a. 2.5 inches Hg or higher
   b. Over 25 inches Hg
   c. 17 to 21 inches Hg
   d. 6 to 16 inches Hg

4. Technician A says that white exhaust can be caused by a defective cylinder head gasket allowing coolant to enter the combustion chamber. Technician B says that white exhaust can be caused by the burning of automatic transmission fluid inside the engine. Which technician is correct?
   a. Technician A only
   b. Technician B only
   c. Both Technicians A and B
   d. Neither Technician A nor B

5. An engine is misfiring. A power balance test indicates that when the spark to cylinder #4 is grounded, there is no change in the engine speed. Technician A says that a burned valve is a possible cause. Technician B says that a defective cylinder #4 injector or spark plug wire could be the cause. Which technician is correct?
   a. Technician A only
   b. Technician B only
   c. Both Technicians A and B
   d. Neither Technician A nor B

6. An engine equipped with a turbocharger is burning oil (blue exhaust smoke all the time). Technician A says that a defective wastegate could be the cause. Technician B says that a plugged PCV system could be the cause. Which technician is correct?
   a. Technician A only
   b. Technician B only
   c. Both Technicians A and B
   d. Neither Technician A nor B

7. A compression test gave the following results:
   cylinder #1 = 155, cylinder #2 = 140, cylinder #3 = 110, cylinder #4 = 105

   Technician A says that a defective (burned) valve is the most likely cause. Technician B says that a leaking head gasket could be the cause. Which technician is correct?
   a. Technician A only
   b. Technician B only
   c. Both Technicians A and B
   d. Neither Technician A nor B

8. Two technicians are discussing a compression test. Technician A says that the engine should be turned over with the pressure gauge installed for "3 puffs." Technician B says that the maximum difference between the highest-reading cylinder and the lowest-reading cylinder should be 20%. Which technician is correct?
   a. Technician A only
   b. Technician B only
   c. Both Technicians A and B
   d. Neither Technician A nor B

9. During a cylinder leakage (leak-down) test, air is noticed coming out of the oil-fill opening. Technician A says that the oil filter may be clogged. Technician B says that the piston rings may be worn or defective. Which technician is correct?

   a. Technician A only
   b. Technician B only
   c. Both Technicians A and B
   d. Neither Technician A nor B

10. A cylinder leakage (leak-down) test indicates 30% leakage, and air is heard coming out of the air inlet. Technician A says that this is a normal reading for a slightly worn engine. Technician B says that one or more intake valves are defective. Which technician is correct?

    a. Technician A only
    b. Technician B only
    c. Both Technicians A and B
    d. Neither Technician A nor B

(B) Ignition System Diagnosis and Repair (10)

11. An engine will not start and a check of the ignition system output indicates no spark to any of the spark plugs. Technician A says that a defective crankshaft position sensor (CKP) could be the cause. Technician B says a defective ignition switch could be the cause. Which technician is correct?

    a. Technician A only
    b. Technician B only
    c. Both Technicians A and B
    d. Neither Technician A nor B

12. Technician A says that to check for spark, connect a spark tester to the end of a spark plug wire. Technician B says that a regular spark plug should be connected to the end of a spark plug wire to check for spark. Which technician is correct?

   a. Technician A only
   b. Technician B only
   c. Both Technicians A and B
   d. Neither Technician A nor B

13. An engine miss is being diagnosed. One spark plug wire measured "OL" on a digital ohmmeter set to the K ohm scale. Technician A says that the spark plug wire should be replaced. Technician B says that the spark plug wire is OK. Which technician is correct?

    a. Technician A only
    b. Technician B only
    c. Both Technicians A and B
    d. Neither Technician A nor B

14. Typical primary coil resistance specifications usually range from _____.

    a. 100 to 450 ohms
    b. 500 to 1500 ohms
    c. 1 to 3 ohms
    d. 6000 to 30,000 ohms

15. Which is the *least likely* to cause a weak spark at the spark plug?

    a. A shorted ignition coil
    b. A 12.2-volt battery voltage
    c. A high resistance spark plug wire(s)
    d. A voltage drop across the ignition switch

16. Which is *most likely* to cause an engine miss on one cylinder?

    a. An open spark plug wire
    b. A high resistance spark plug wire
    c. Excessive rotor gap
    d. A clogged fuel filter

17. A service technician should be sure to do all of the following when installing spark plugs *except* which one?

    a. The threads should be clean and dry.
    b. The spark plug should be tightened, and then loosened 1/16 turn.
    c. A torque wrench should be used to tighten the plugs.
    d. The gap should be checked before installing the plugs in the engine.

18. A no-start condition is being diagnosed on a vehicle equipped with a distributor ignition using a remotely mounted ignition coil. The coil wire is removed from the center of the distributor cap and a spark tester is used to check for spark. There is spark out of the coil but no spark is available to any of the spark plug wires. Technician A says the rotor is defective. Technician B says the spark plugs are fouled. Which technician is correct?

    a. Technician A only
    b. Technician B only
    c. Both Technicians A and B
    d. Neither Technician A nor B

19. All of the statements about spark plugs are correct *except* _____.
    a. Worn spark plugs decrease the voltage required to fire
    b. A cracked spark plug can cause an engine miss
    c. A platinum tip spark plug should not be regapped after being used in an engine
    d. Spark plugs should be torqued to factory specifications when installed

20. Which of these is *least likely* to be caused by incorrect ignition timing?
    a. Pinging (spark knock or detonation)
    b. Poor fuel economy
    c. Engine miss at idle or during acceleration
    d. Slow, jerky cranking when the engine is hot

(C) Fuel, Air Induction, and Exhaust Systems Diagnosis and Repair (11)

21. An engine equipped with a turbocharger is burning oil (blue exhaust smoke all the time). Technician A says that a defective wastegate could be the cause. Technician B says that a clogged PCV system could be the cause. Which technician is correct?
    a. Technician A only
    b. Technician B only
    c. Both Technicians A and B
    d. Neither Technician A nor B

22. An engine is idling too fast when the engine reaches operating temperature. Technician A says the engine could have a vacuum leak. Technician B says that the throttle linkage or cable could be stuck. Which technician is correct?
    a. Technician A only
    b. Technician B only
    c. Both Technicians A and B
    d. Neither Technician A nor B

23. A vehicle equipped with a mass air flow sensor as shown will stumble or stall when in "drive" but operate OK when driven in reverse. What is the *most likely* cause?
    a. A split or crack in the air intake hose
    b. A clogged fuel filter
    c. A restricted air filter
    d. A leaking fuel injector

24. Technician A says that the exhaust system can be checked for restriction by using a vacuum gauge attached to manifold vacuum and operating the engine at idle speed. Technician B says the exhaust is restricted if the vacuum increases at 2000 RPM. Which technician is correct?
    a. Technician A only
    b. Technician B only
    c. Both Technicians A and B
    d. Neither Technician A nor B

25. Excessive exhaust system back pressure has been measured. Technician A says that the catalytic converter may be clogged. Technician B says that the muffler may be clogged. Which technician is correct?
    a. Technician A only
    b. Technician B only
    c. Both Technicians A and B
    d. Neither Technician A nor B

26. Technician A says that catalytic converters should last the life of the vehicle unless damaged. Technician B says that catalytic converters wear out and should be replaced every 50,000 miles (80,000 kilometers). Which technician is correct?
    a. Technician A only
    b. Technician B only
    c. Both Technicians A and B
    d. Neither Technician A nor B

27. Which driver-controlled action is *not* harmful to electric fuel pumps?
    a. Operating the vehicle with a low fuel level
    b. Operating the vehicle in the city only; seldom driving at highway speeds
    c. Not replacing the fuel filter regularly
    d. Using alcohol-enhanced fuel

28. Two technicians are discussing plastic fuel lines. Technician A says that a special tool is often required to separate the connections at the fuel filter on vehicles using plastic fuel lines. Technician B says that some fuel filters use a ground strap that must be connected to a metal part of the vehicle. Which technician is correct?
    a. Technician A only
    b. Technician B only
    c. Both Technicians A and B
    d. Neither Technician A nor B

29. Two technicians are discussing the cracked exhaust manifold shown. Technician A says that the crack could cause noise. Technician B says that the crack could cause the O2S to read incorrectly, which could affect the engine operation. Which technician is correct?
    a. Technician A only
    b. Technician B only
    c. Both Technicians A and B
    d. Neither Technician A nor B

30. A lean air-fuel mixture is being diagnosed. Technician A says that a stuck IAC could be the cause. Technician B says that a hole in the air inlet between the MAF sensor and the throttle plate could be the cause. Which technician is correct?
    a. Technician A only
    b. Technician B only
    c. Both Technicians A and B
    d. Neither Technician A nor B

31. An engine is pinging (spark knock) during acceleration. What is the *most likely* cause?
    a. A vacuum leak
    b. A clogged air filter
    c. Using alcohol-enhanced fuel
    d. A partially clogged exhaust system

(D) Emissions Control System Diagnosis and Repair (9)

32. Technician A says that a defective one-way exhaust check valve could cause the air pump to fail. Technician B says that the air flow to the exhaust manifold when the engine is warm can cause a driveability problem. Which technician is correct?
    a. Technician A only
    b. Technician B only
    c. Both Technicians A and B
    d. Neither Technician A nor B

33. A vacuum-type EGR valve is being tested. Technician A says that the engine should be off to test the EGR valve. Technician B says a positive back pressure EGR valve will not hold vacuum if tested using a vacuum pump without the engine running. Which technician is correct?
    a. Technician A only
    b. Technician B only
    c. Both Technicians A and B
    d. Neither Technician A nor B

34. Technician A says the catalytic converter must be replaced if it rattles when tapped. Technician B says a catalytic converter can be defective and not be working yet not be clogged. Which technician is correct?
    a. Technician A only
    b. Technician B only
    c. Both Technicians A and B
    d. Neither Technician A nor B

35. A vehicle fails an emission test for excessive NO_x. Which exhaust control device has the greatest effect on the amount of NO_x produced by the engine?
    a. PCV
    b. Air pump
    c. Carbon (charcoal) canister
    d. EGR

36. A technician is testing the EGR valve. Technician A says that a vacuum EGR should be able to hold vacuum when tested with a hand-operated vacuum pump. Technician B says that the engine should stall if the EGR valve is opened all the way when the engine is idling if the passages are open and free of restrictions. Which technician is correct?
    a. Technician A only
    b. Technician B only
    c. Both Technicians A and B
    d. Neither Technician A nor B

37. The vacuum hose that attaches to the PCV has a split and allows air to enter the engine. Which is the *least likely* to occur?
    a. Rough, unstable idle
    b. Hesitation
    c. Spark knock (ping or detonation)
    d. Surging at highway speed

38. Two technicians are discussing the evaporative control system. Technician A says that the carbon (charcoal) canister should be replaced regularly as part of routine maintenance. Technician B says the carbon (charcoal) inside of the EVAP canister can dissolve in gasoline and leave a yellow deposit in the engine when burned. Which technician is correct?
    a. Technician A only
    b. Technician B only
    c. Both Technicians A and B
    d. Neither Technician A nor B

39. If a fuel line hose is used between the PCV valve and the intake manifold instead of using the proper vacuum hose, what is the *most likely* result?
    a. A collapsed hose and oil being forced out of the crankcase vent
    b. A vacuum leak when the hose collapses
    c. No harm will be done
    d. Exhaust back pressure will increase, which could clog the EGR valve

40. An EGR valve is stuck partially open. What is the *most likely* result?
    a. Pinging (spark knock)
    b. Rough idle—runs OK at highway speeds
    c. Fast idle
    d. Lack of power at highway speeds

(E) Computerized Engine Controls Diagnosis and Repair (16)

41. The connector to the throttle position (TP) sensor became disconnected. Technician A says that the engine will not idle correctly unless reconnected. Technician B says that the engine may hesitate on acceleration. Which technician is correct?
    a. Technician A only
    b. Technician B only
    c. Both Technicians A and B
    d. Neither Technician A nor B

42. An oxygen sensor (O2S) is being tested and the O2S voltage is fluctuating between 800 millivolts and 200 millivolts. Technician A says the engine is operating too lean. Technician B says the engine is operating too rich. Which technician is correct?
    a. Technician A only
    b. Technician B only
    c. Both Technicians A and B
    d. Neither Technician A nor B

43. The IAC counts are zero. Technician A says that the engine may have a vacuum leak or a stuck throttle cable. Technician B says the throttle plate(s) may be dirty or partially clogged. Which technician is correct?
    a. Technician A only
    b. Technician B only
    c. Both Technicians A and B
    d. Neither Technician A nor B

44. An engine is operating at idle speed with all accessories off and the gear selector in Park. Technician A says that a scan tool should display injector pulse width between 1.5 and 3.5 milliseconds. Technician B says that the oxygen sensor activity as displayed on a scan tool should indicate over 800 millivolts and less than 200 millivolts. Which technician is correct?
    a. Technician A only
    b. Technician B only
    c. Both Technicians A and B
    d. Neither Technician A nor B

45. Two technicians are discussing fuel trim. Technician A says that oxygen sensor activity determines short-term fuel trim numbers. Technician B says that a positive (+) long-term fuel trim means that the computer is adding fuel to compensate for a lean exhaust. Which technician is correct?
    a. Technician A only
    b. Technician B only
    c. Both Technicians A and B
    d. Neither Technician A nor B

46. A technician is looking to scan data and notices that the MAP sensor voltage reading is about 1.0 volt (18 in. Hg). Technician A says that the reading is normal. Technician B says that the reading indicates a possible MAP sensor fault. Which technician is correct?
    a. Technician A only
    b. Technician B only
    c. Both Technicians A and B
    d. Neither Technician A nor B

47. Typical TP sensor voltage at idle should measure _____.
    a. 2.50 to 2.80 volts
    b. 0.5 volt
    c. 1.5 to 2.8 volts
    d. 13.5 to 15.0 volts

48. Two technicians are discussing the diagnosis of a TP sensor voltage low fault stored diagnostic trouble code (DTC). Technician A says that if the opposite DTC (TP sensor high) can be set, the problem is the component itself. Technician B says if the opposite DTC cannot be set, the problem is with the wiring or the computer. Which technician is correct?
    a. Technician A only
    b. Technician B only
    c. Both Technicians A and B
    d. Neither Technician A nor B

49. This waveform of a fuel injector represents _____.
    a. A normal pattern
    b. A clogged injector
    c. A shorted injector
    d. An electrically open injector

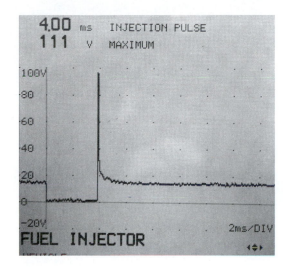

50. A vehicle fails an enhanced exhaust emission test for excessive oxides of nitrogen (NO_x) emission. Which is the *most likely* to be the cause?
    a. A defective cooling fan
    b. Excessively high fuel-pump pressure
    c. A defective AIR pump switching valve
    d. A clogged PCV valve

51. A vehicle fails an enhanced exhaust emission test for excessive carbon monoxide (CO) emission. Which is the *least likely* to be the cause?
    a. A defective fuel-pressure regulator (excessive pressure)
    b. A leaking fuel injector
    c. A stuck open purge valve
    d. A stuck closed EGR valve

52. A multiport fuel-injected V-8 engine has a rough and unstable idle and the customer states that it has stalled at times. There are no stored diagnostic trouble codes. Which is the *most likely* cause?
    a. A bad throttle position (TP) sensor
    b. An open fuel-injector winding
    c. An open oxygen sensor (O2S) lead
    d. A dirty throttle plate

53. The injector pulse width on a multiport fuel-injected engine is higher than normal. Technician A says that it could be caused by a vacuum leak. Technician B says that it can be caused by a clogged fuel injector. Which technician is correct?
    a. Technician A only
    b. Technician B only
    c. Both Technicians A and B
    d. Neither Technician A nor B

54. An engine equipped with multiport fuel injection runs rough when cold, but OK after it reaches normal operating temperature. Technician A says that the ECT may be at fault. Technician B says the cold start injector may be clogged. Which technician is correct?
    a. Technician A only
    b. Technician B only
    c. Both Technicians A and B
    d. Neither Technician A nor B

55. A customer complains of sluggish performance and poor fuel economy. A DTC for HO2S voltage low (lean exhaust) has been set. Technician A says that one or more fuel injectors could be clogged. Technician B says that the fuel return line from the regulator could be clogged. Which technician is correct?
    a. Technician A only
    b. Technician B only
    c. Both Technicians A and B
    d. Neither Technician A nor B

56. The idle speed on a port fuel-injected engine is too high. Which defective component is the *most likely* cause?
    a. MAP
    b. O2S
    c. IAT
    d. IAC

(F) Engine Electrical Systems Diagnosis and Repair (4)

57. A technician is checking the charging system for low output. A voltage drop of 1.67 volts is found between the generator (alternator) output terminal and the battery positive terminal. Technician A says that a corroded connector could be the cause. Technician B says that a defective rectifier diode could be the cause of the voltage drop. Which technician is correct?
    a. Technician A only
    b. Technician B only
    c. Both Technicians A and B
    d. Neither Technician A nor B

58. A driver turns the ignition switch to "start" and nothing happens (the dome light remains bright). Technician A says that dirty battery connections or a defective or discharged battery could be the cause. Technician B says that an *open* neutral safety switch could be the cause. Which technician is correct?
    a. Technician A only
    b. Technician B only
    c. Both Technicians A and B
    d. Neither Technician A nor B

59. The charging system voltage is found to be lower than specified by the vehicle manufacturer. Technician A says that a loose or defective drive belt could be the cause. Technician B says that a defective generator (alternator) could be the cause. Which technician is correct?

a. Technician A only

b. Technician B only

c. Both Technicians A and B

d. Neither Technician A nor B

60. If the starter turns slowly when engaged, which of the following is the *least likely* to be the cause?

a. A worn or defective starter drive

b. A defective solenoid

c. An open battery cable

d. An excessive voltage drop between the engine block and the battery negative cable

ANSWERS FOR ENGINE PERFORMANCE (A8)

Sample ASE Certification Test

1. b	21. b	41. b
2. b	22. c	42. d
3. a	23. a	43. a
4. c	24. d	44. c
5. c	25. c	45. c
6. b	26. a	46. a
7. b	27. b	47. b
8. b	28. c	48. c
9. b	29. c	49. a
10. b	30. b	50. a
11. c	31. a	51. d
12. a	32. c	52. d
13. a	33. b	53. c
14. c	34. c	54. a
15. b	35. d	55. a
16. a	36. c	56. d
17. b	37. d	57. a
18. a	38. d	58. b
19. a	39. a	59. c
20. c	40. b	60. c

◀ **Appendix 2** ▶

ENGINE PERFORMANCE (A8)

NATEF Correlation Chart

Engine Performance (A8)		
NATEF Task List		
NATEF Task List	*Textbook Page #*	*Worktext Page #*
A. General Engine Diagnosis		
1. Identify and interpret engine performance concerns; determine necessary action. P-1	124–149, 362–391 416–452	28
2. Research applicable vehicle and service information, such as engine management system operation, vehicle service history, service precautions, and technical service bulletins. P-1	1–4	5–7, 27, 29, 139–140, 164, 166
3. Locate and interpret vehicle and major component identification numbers (VIN, vehicle certification labels, and calibration decals). P-1	1–4	1–3, 12–18, 65
4. Inspect engine assembly for fuel, oil, coolant, and other leaks; determine necessary action. P-2	126–128	30–33
5. Diagnose abnormal engine noise or vibration concerns; determine necessary action. P-2	128–130	34–35
6. Diagnose abnormal exhaust color, odor, and sound; determine necessary action. P-2	125	36
7. Perform engine absolute (vacuum/boost) manifold pressure tests; determine necessary action. P-1	135–139	37
8. Perform cylinder power balance test; determine necessary action. P-1	135	40–42
9. Perform cylinder compression tests; determine necessary action. P-1	132–134	38–39, 42
10. Perform cylinder leakage test; determine necessary action. P-1	134–135	43
11. Diagnose engine mechanical, electrical, electronic, fuel, and ignition concerns with an oscilloscope and/or engine diagnostic equipment; determine necessary action. P-1	439–448	44– 46

NATEF Task List	Textbook Page #	Worktext Page #
12. Prepare four or five gas analyzer; inspect and prepare vehicle for test, and obtain exhaust readings; interpret readings, and determine necessary action. P-1	470–483	167–174
13. Verify engine operating temperature; determine necessary action. P-1	126, 141–142	47
14. Perform cooling system pressure tests; check coolant condition; inspect and test radiator, pressure cap, coolant recovery tank, and hoses; perform necessary action. P-1	126	48
15. Verify correct camshaft timing. P-2	298–299	53
B. Computerized Engine Controls Diagnosis and Repair		
1. Retrieve and record stored OBD-I diagnostic trouble codes; clear codes. P-2	454	66
2. Retrieve and record stored OBD-II diagnostic trouble codes; clean codes. P-1	453–465	67
3. Diagnose the causes of emissions or driveability concerns resulting from malfunctions in the computerized engine control system with stored diagnostic trouble codes. P-1	455–465	161–163, 168
4. Diagnose emissions or driveability concerns resulting from malfunctions in the computerized engine control system with no stored diagnostic trouble codes; determine necessary action. P-1	470–480	169
5. Check for module communication errors using a scan tool. P-2	458	64
6. Inspect and test computerized engine control system sensors, powertrain control module (PCM), actuators, and circuits using a graphing multimeter (GMM)/digital storage oscilloscope (DSO); perform necessary action. P-1	193–195, 227, 237, 252, 258, 273–282, 293–298 439–498	68–97, 99–102, 116–117, 121
7. Obtain and interpret scan tool data. P-1	221–284, 454–465	19, 98, 122–123, 165, 170
8. Access and use service information to perform step-by-step diagnosis. P-1	221–284	4
9. Diagnose driveability and emissions problems resulting from malfunctions of interrelated systems (cruise control, security alarms, suspension controls, traction controls, A/C automatic transmissions, non-OEM-installed accessories, or similar systems); determine necessary action. P-3	221–284	124, 171
C. Ignition System Diagnosis and Repair		
1. Diagnose ignition system related problems such as no starting, hard starting, engine misfire, poor driveability, spark knock, power loss, poor mileage, and emissions concerns on vehicles with electronic ignition (distributorless) systems; determine necessary action. P-1	416–449	141–146
2. Diagnose ignition system related problems such as no starting, hard starting, engine misfire, poor driveability, spark knock, power loss, poor mileage, and emissions concerns on vehicles with distributor ignition (DI) system; determine necessary action. P-1	416–449	147–148
3. Inspect and test ignition primary circuit wiring and solid-state components; perform necessary action. P-2	416–428	149
4. Inspect, test, and service distributor. P-3	428–430	150
5. Inspect and test ignition system secondary circuit wiring and components; perform necessary action. P-2	428–435	151–156

NATEF Task List	Textbook Page #	Worktext Page #
6. Inspect and test ignition coil(s); perform necessary action. P-1	418, 424, 439–446	157
7. Check and adjust ignition system timing and timing advance/retard (where applicable). P-3	435–439	158
8. Inspect and test ignition system pick-up sensor or triggering devices; perform necessary action. P-1	417–427	159
D. Fuel, Air Induction, and Exhaust Systems Diagnosis and Repair		
1. Diagnose hot or cold no starting, hard starting, poor driveability, incorrect idle speed, poor idle, flooding, hesitation, surging, engine misfire, power loss, stalling, poor mileage, dieseling, and emissions problems on vehicles with carburetor-type fuel systems; determine necessary action. P-3	470–472	138
2. Diagnose hot or cold no starting, hard starting, poor driveability, incorrect idle speed, poor idle, flooding, hesitation, surging, engine misfire, power loss, stalling, poor mileage, dieseling, and emissions problems on vehicles with injection-type fuel systems; determine necessary action. P-1	362–391	125–128
3. Check fuel for contaminants and quality; determine necessary action. P-3	86–87	14–17
4. Inspect and test mechanical and electrical fuel pumps and pump control systems for pressure, regulation, and volume; perform necessary action. P-1	315–328	103–107
5. Replace fuel filters. P-1	313–314	108
6. Inspect and test cold enrichment system and components; perform necessary action. P-3	367–372	118
7. Inspect throttle body, air induction system, intake manifold, and gaskets for vacuum leaks and/or unmetered air. P-2	259–261	119–120
8. Inspect and test fuel injectors. P-2	364–377	129–135
9. Check idle speed and fuel mixture. P-2	377–379	136–137, 172
10. Adjust idle speed and fuel mixture. P-3	377–379	173
11. Inspect the integrity of the exhaust manifold, exhaust pipes, muffler(s), catalytic converter(s), resonator(s), tailpipe(s), and heat shield(s); perform necessary action. P-2	474, 511–514	24–25
12. Perform exhaust system back pressure test; determine necessary action. P-1	513–514	190
13. Test the operation of turbocharger/supercharger systems; determine necessary action. P-3	116–120	26
E. Emissions Control Systems Diagnosis and Repair		
1. Positive Crankcase Ventilation		
1. Diagnose oil leaks, emissions, and driveability problems resulting from malfunctions in the positive crankcase ventilation (PCV) system; determine necessary action. P-2	498–501	183
2. Inspect, test, and service positive crankcase ventilation (PCV) filter/breather cap, valve, tubes, orifices, and hoses; perform necessary action. P-2	501–502	181–182

NATEF Task List	Textbook Page #	Worktext Page #
2. Exhaust Gas Recirculation		
1. Diagnose emissions and driveability problems caused by malfunctions in the exhaust gas recirculation (EGR) system; determine necessary action. P-1	492–495	175–177
2. Inspect, test, service, and replace components of the EGR system, including EGR tubing, exhaust passages, vacuum/pressure controls, filters, and hoses; perform necessary action. P-2	489–493	178
3. Inspect and test electrical/electronic sensors, controls, and wiring of exhaust gas recirculation (EGR) systems; perform necessary action. P-2	489–495	179–180
3. Exhaust Gas Treatment		
1. Diagnose emissions and driveability problems resulting from malfunctions in the secondary air injection and catalytic converter systems; determine necessary action. P-2	502–506	184, 187–188
2. Inspect and test mechanical components of secondary air-injection systems; perform necessary action. P-3	502–506	185
3. Inspect and test electrical/electronically operated components and circuits of air-injection systems; perform necessary action. P-3	504	186
4. Inspect and test catalytic converter performance. P-1	513–516	189
4. Intake Air Temperature Controls		
1. Diagnose emissions and driveability problems resulting from malfunctions in the intake air temperature control system; determine necessary action. P-3	99–101, 347	20
2. Inspect and test components of intake air temperature control system; perform necessary action. P-3	101	21
5. Early Fuel Evaporation (Intake Manifold Temperature) Controls		
1. Diagnose emissions and driveability problems resulting from malfunctions in the early fuel evaporation control system; determine necessary action. P-3	103–104	22
2. Inspect and test components of early fuel evaporation control system; perform necessary action. P-3	103–107	23
6. Evaporative Emissions Controls		
1. Diagnose emissions and driveability problems resulting from malfunctions in the evaporative emissions control system; determine necessary action. P-1	338–343	109–111
2. Inspect and test components and hoses of evaporative emissions control system; perform necessary action. P-2	331–338	112–113
3. Interpret evaporative emission-related diagnostic trouble codes (DTCs); determine necessary action. P-1	340–343	114
F. Engine Related Service		
1. Adjust valves on engines with mechanical or hydraulic lifters. P-1	128, 130	51
2. Remove and replace timing belt; verify correct camshaft timing. P-1	137, 298–299	52
3. Remove and replace thermostat. P-2	141–142, 221–227	54
4. Inspect and test mechanical/electrical fans, fan clutch, fan shroud/ducting, air dams, and fan control devices; perform necessary action. P-1	126	55

ENGINE PERFORMANCE (A8)

ASE Certification Test Correlation Chart

Automotive Engine Performance (A8)	
ASE Task List	*Textbook Page #*
A. General Engine Diagnosis	
1. Verify driver's complaint, perform visual inspection, and/or road test vehicle; determine needed action.	124–130
2. Research applicable vehicle and service information, such as engine management system operation, vehicle service history, service precautions, and technical service bulletins.	1–4
3. Diagnose noises and/or vibration problems related to engine performance; determine needed action.	128–130
4. Diagnose the cause of unusual exhaust color, odor, and sound; determine needed action.	125
5. Perform engine manifold vacuum or pressure tests; determine needed action.	135–139
6. Perform cylinder power balance test; determine needed action.	135
7. Perform cylinder cranking compression test; determine needed action.	132–134
8. Perform cylinder leakage/leak-down test; determine needed action.	134–135
9. Diagnose engine mechanical, electrical, electronic, fuel, and ignition problems with an oscilloscope and/or engine analyzer; determine needed action.	439–448
10. Prepare and inspect vehicle and analyzer for exhaust gas analysis; perform test and interpret exhaust gas readings.	470–483
11. Verify camshaft timing; determine needed action.	298–299
12. Verify engine operating temperature, check coolant level and condition, perform cooling system pressure test; determine needed repairs.	126, 141–142
13. Inspect and test mechanical/electrical fans, fan clutch, fan shroud/ducting, and fan control devices; determine needed repairs.	126

ASE Task List	Textbook Page #
B. Ignition System Diagnosis and Repair	
1. Diagnose ignition system related problems such as no starting, hard starting, engine misfire, poor driveability, spark knock, power loss, poor mileage, and emissions problems; determine root cause; determine needed repairs.	416–449
2. Interpret ignition system related diagnostic trouble codes (DTC); determine needed repairs.	298–299, 425
3. Inspect, test, repair, or replace ignition primary circuit wiring and components.	422–426
4. Inspect, test, and service distributor.	428–435
5. Inspect, test, service, repair, or replace ignition system secondary circuit wiring and components.	428–430
6. Inspect, test, and replace ignition coil(s).	418, 424, 434–446
7. Check and adjust, if necessary, ignition system timing and timing advance/retard.	435–439
8. Inspect, test, and replace ignition system pick-up sensor or triggering devices.	417–427
9. Inspect, test, and/or replace ignition control module (ICM)/powertrain control module (PCM).	419–421
C. Fuel, Air Induction, and Exhaust System Diagnosis and Repair	
1. Diagnose fuel system related problems, including hot or cold no starting, hard starting, poor driveability, incorrect idle speed, poor idle, flooding, hesitation, surging, engine misfire, power loss, stalling, poor mileage, dieseling and emissions problems; determine root cause; determine needed action.	362–391, 470–472
2. Interpret fuel or induction system related diagnostic trouble codes (DTCs); determine needed repairs.	453–464
3. Inspect fuel tank, filler neck, and gas cap; inspect and replace fuel lines, fittings and hoses; check fuel for contaminants and quality.	301–308
4. Inspect, test, and replace mechanical and electrical fuel pumps; inspect, service, and replace fuel filters.	315–328
5. Inspect and test fuel pump electrical control circuits and components; determine needed repairs.	321–328
6. Inspect, test, and repair or replace fuel-pressure regulation system components of fuel-injection systems.	317–318
7. Inspect, remove, service, or replace throttle body; make related adjustments.	259–261, 377–379
8. Inspect, test, clean, and replace fuel injectors.	364–377
9. Inspect, service, and repair or replace air filtration system components.	99–101
10. Inspect throttle body, air induction system, intake manifold, and gaskets for vacuum leaks and/or unmetered air.	259–261
11. Check and/or adjust idle speed where applicable.	377–379
12. Remove, clean, inspect, test, and repair or replace fuel system vacuum and electrical components and connections.	362–384
13. Inspect, service, and replace exhaust manifold, exhaust pipes, mufflers, resonators, catalytic converters, tailpipes, and heat shields.	107–111
14. Test for exhaust system restriction; determine needed action.	513–514
15. Inspect, test, clean and repair or replace turbocharger or supercharger and system components.	116–122

ASE Task List	Textbook Page #
D. Emissions Control Systems Diagnosis and Repair (including OBD II)	
1. Positive Crankcase Ventilation	
1. Test and diagnose emissions or driveability problems caused by positive crankcase ventilation (PCV) system.	498–501
2. Inspect, service, and replace positive crankcase ventilation (PCV) filter/breather cap, valve, tubes, orifices, and hoses.	501–502
2. Exhaust Gas Recirculation	
1. Test and diagnose emissions or driveability problems caused by the exhaust gas recirculation (EGR) system.	492–495
2. Interpret exhaust gas recirculation (EGR) related diagnostic trouble codes (DTCs); determine needed repairs.	489–493
3. Inspect, test, service, and replace components of the EGR system, including EGR tubing, exhaust passages, vacuum/pressure controls, filters, hoses, electrical/electronic-sensors, controls, solenoids, and wiring of exhaust gas recirculation (EGR) systems.	489–495
3. Secondary Air-Injection (AIR) and Catalytic Converter	
1. Test and diagnose emissions or driveability problems caused by the secondary air injection or catalytic converter systems.	502–506, 513–516
2. Interpret secondary air-injection system or catalytic converter-related diagnostic trouble codes; determine needed repairs.	506, 516
3. Inspect, test, service, and replace mechanical components and electrical/electronically operated components and circuits of secondary air-injection systems.	504
4. Inspect and test the catalytic converter(s).	513–516
4. Evaporative Emissions Controls	
1. Test and diagnose emissions or driveability problems caused by the evaporative emissions control system.	338–343
2. Interpret evaporative emission-related diagnostic trouble codes (DTCs); determine needed repairs.	340–343
3. Inspect, test, and replace mechanical and electrical components and hoses of evaporative emissions control systems.	331–338
E. Computerized Engine Controls Diagnosis and Repair (including OBD II)	
1. Retrieve and record diagnostic trouble codes (DTC) and freeze frame data if applicable.	458–461
2. Diagnose the causes of emissions or driveability problems resulting from failure of computerized engine controls with diagnostic trouble codes (DTC).	455–465
3. Diagnose the causes of emissions or driveability problems resulting from failure of computerized engine controls with no diagnostic trouble codes (DTC).	470–480
4. Use a scan tool, digital multimeter (DMM), or digital storage oscilloscope (DSO) to inspect or test computerized engine control systems sensors, actuators, circuits, and powertrain control module (PCM); determine needed repairs.	193–195, 227, 237, 252, 358, 293–298, 439–448
5. Measure and interpret voltage, voltage drop, amperage, and resistance using digital multimeter (DMM) readings.	177–189
6. Test, remove, inspect, clean, service, and repair or replace power and ground distribution circuits and connections.	157–173

ASE Task List	Textbook Page #
7. Practice recommended precautions when handling static sensitive devices and/or replacing the powertrain control module (PCM).	165
8. Diagnose driveability and emissions problems resulting from failures of interrelated systems (such as: cruise control, security alarms/theft deterrent, torque controls, suspension controls, traction controls, torque management, A/C, non-OEM installed accessories).	221–284
9. Diagnose the causes of emissions or driveability problems resulting from computerized spark timing controls; determine needed repairs.	416–449
10. Verify the repair, and clear diagnostic trouble codes (DTCs).	453–465
F. Engine Electrical Systems Diagnosis and Repair	
1. Battery	
1. Test and diagnose emissions or driveability problems caused by battery condition, connections, or excessive key-off battery drain; determine needed repairs.	189, 198
2. Starting System	
1. Perform starter current draw test; determine needed action.	179–181
2. Perform starter circuit voltage drop tests; determine needed action.	181–182
3. Inspect, test, and repair or replace components and wires in the starter control circuit.	171
3. Charging System	
1. Test and diagnose engine performance problems resulting from an undercharge, overcharge, or a no-charge condition; determine needed action.	211–212
2. Inspect, adjust, and replace alternator (generator) drive belts, pulleys, tensioners, and fans.	196
3. Inspect, test, and repair or replace charging circuit connectors and wires.	157–159

ENGLISH GLOSSARY

AIR   Air-injection reaction emission control system.

Air management system   The system of solenoids and valves that control the output of the air pump to the catalytic converter, air cleaner housing, or exhaust manifold.

Alnico   A permanent-magnet alloy of *al*uminum, *ni*ckel, and *co*balt.

Alternator   An electric generator that produces alternating current.

Ammeter   An electrical test instrument used to measure amperes (unit of the amount of current flow). An ammeter is connected in series with the circuit being tested.

Ampere   The unit of the amount of current flow. Named for André Ampère (1775–1836).

Ampere turns   The unit of measurement for electrical magnetic field strength.

Analog   A type of dash instrument that indicates values by use of the movement of a needle or similar device. An analog signal is continuous and variable.

Anode   The positive electrode; the electrode toward which electrons flow.

ANSI   American National Standards Institute.

Antimony   A metal added to nonmaintenance-free or hybrid battery grids to add strength.

Armature   The rotating unit inside a DC generator or starter, consisting of a series of coils of insulating wire wound around a laminated iron core.

ATC   After top center.

ATDC   After top dead center.

Atom   The smallest unit of matter that still retains its separate unique characteristics.

AWG   American Wire Gauge system.

Bakelite   A brand name of the Union Carbide Company for phenol formaldehyde resin plastic.

Ballast resistor   A variable resistor used to control the primary ignition current through the ignition coil. At lower engine speed, the temperature of the ballast resistor is high, as is its resistance. When engine RPM is high, the ballast resistance is low, permitting maximum current through the ignition coil.

BARO sensor   A sensor used to measure barometric pressure.

Base   The name for the section of a transistor that controls the current flow through the transistor.

Battery   A chemical device that produces a voltage created by two dissimilar metals submerged in an electrolyte.

Battery voltage correction factor   A computer problem that increases the fuel-injector pulse width if the battery voltage drops to compensate for the resulting slower opening of the injector(s).

Bias   In electrical terms, the voltage applied to a device or component to establish the reference point for operation.

Blower motor   An electric motor and squirrel cage type of fan moving air inside the car for heating, cooling, and defrosting.

BNC connector   A type of connector used on digital and analog scopes. Named for its inventor, Baby Neil Councilman.

Brushes   A copper or carbon conductor used to transfer electrical current from or to a revolving electrical part such as that used in an electric motor or generator.

BTDC   Before top dead center.

Burn in   A process of operating an electronic device for a period from several hours to several days.

CAFE   Corporate average fuel economy.

Calcium   A metallic chemical element added to the grids of a maintenance-free battery to add strength.

Capacitance   Electrical capacitance is a term used to measure or describe how much charge can be stored in a capacitor (condenser) for a given voltage potential difference. Capacitance is measured in farads or smaller increments of farads, such as microfarads.

Capacitor   A condenser; an electrical unit that can pass alternating current, yet block direct current. Used in electrical circuits to control fluctuations in voltage.

Carbon pile   An electrical test instrument used to provide an electrical load for testing batteries and the charging circuit.

Catalytic converter   An emission control device located in the exhaust system that changes HC and CO into harmless H_2O and CO_2. If a three-way catalyst, NO_x is also separated into harmless separate N and O.

Cathode   The negative electrode.

Cell   A group of negative and positive plates to form a cell capable of producing 2.1 volts. Each cell contains one more negative plate than positive plate.

CEMF   Counterelectromotive force.

Charging circuit   Electrical components and connections necessary to keep a battery fully charged. Components include the alternator, voltage regulator, battery, and interconnecting wires.

Chassis ground   In electrical terms, a ground is the desirable return circuit path. Ground can also be undesirable and provide a shortcut path for a defective electrical circuit.

Circuit   The path that electrons travel from a power source, through a resistance, and back to the power source.

Circuit breaker   A mechanical unit that opens an electrical circuit in the event of excessive flow.

CKP   Crankshaft position sensor.

CMOS   Complementary metal oxide.

CMP   Camshaft position sensor.

CO   Carbon monoxide.

Cold-cranking amperes (CCA)   The rating of a battery's ability to provide battery voltage during cold-weather operation. The number of amperes that a battery can supply at 0°F (-18°C) for 30 seconds and still maintain a voltage of 1.2 volts per cell (7.2 volts for a 12-volt battery).

Collector   The name of one section of a transistor.

Commutator   The name for the copper segments of the armature of a starter or DC generator. The revolving segments of the commutator collect the current from or distribute it to the brushes.

Compound wound   A type of electric motor where some field coils are wired in series and some field coils are wired in parallel with the armature.

Conductor   A material that conducts electricity and heat; a metal that contains fewer than four electrons in its atom's outer shell.

Conventional theory   The theory that electricity flows from positive ($+$) to negative ($-$).

Coulomb   A measurement of electrons. A coulomb is 6.28×10^1 (6.28 billion billion) electrons.

Courtesy light   General term used to describe all interior lights.

Cranking amperes   A battery specification abbreviated CA that refers to the number of amperes that a battery can supply at 32°F (0°C) for 30 seconds while still maintaining a voltage of 7.2 volts (1.2 volts per cell).

Cranking circuit   Electrical components and connections required to crank the engine to start. The circuit includes the starter motor, starter solenoid/relay, battery, neutral safety switch, ignition control switch, and connecting wires and cables.

CRT Cathode ray tube.

Cunife A magnetic alloy made from copper (Cu), nickel (Ni), and iron (Fe).

Current Electron flow through an electrical circuit; measured in amperes.

Current limiter One section of a voltage regulator for a DC generator charging system. The current limiter section opens the field current circuit when generator amperage output exceeds safe limits to protect the generator from overheating damage.

Deep cycling The full discharge and then the full recharge of a battery.

Delta wound A type of stator winding where all three coils are connected in a triangle shape. Named for the triangle-shaped Greek capital letter.

Digital A method of display that uses numbers instead of a needle or similar device.

Diode An electrical one-way check valve made from combining a P-type material and an N-type material.

Diode trio A group of three diodes grouped together with one output used to put out the charge indicator lamp and provide current for the field from the stator windings on many alternators.

Direct current Electric current that flows in one direction.

Distributor Electromechanical unit used to help create and distribute the high voltage necessary for spark ignition.

Doping The adding of impurities to pure silicon or germanium to form either P or N semiconductor materials.

DPDT switch Double-pole, double-throw switch.

Duty cycle Refers to the percentage of on-time of the signal during one complete cycle.

Dwell The number of degrees of distributor cam rotation that the points are closed.

Earth ground The most grounded ground. A ground is commonly used as a return current path for an electrical circuit.

EEPROM Electronically erasable programmable read-only memory.

EFI Electronic fuel injection.

EGR Exhaust gas recirculation. An emission control device to reduce NO_x (oxides of nitrogen).

Electricity The movement of free electrons from one atom to another.

Electrolyte Any substance which, in solution, is separated into ions and is made capable of conducting an electric current. The acid solution of a lead-acid battery.

Electromagnetic induction First discovered in 1831 by Michael Faraday, it is the generation of a current in a conductor that is moved through a magnetic field.

Electromagnetism A magnetic field created by current flow through a conductor.

Electromotive force The force (pressure) that can move electrons through a conductor.

Electron A negative-charged particle: 1/1800 the mass of a proton.

Electron theory The theory that electricity flows from negative $(-)$ to positive $(+)$.

Electronic circuit breaker See PTC.

Electronic ignition General term used to describe any of the various types of ignition systems that use electronic instead of mechanical components, such as contact points.

Element Any substance that cannot be separated into different substances.

EMF Electromotive force.

Emitter The name of one section of a transistor. The arrow used on a symbol for a transistor is on the emitter and the arrow points toward the negative section of the transistor.

EPROM Erasable programmable read-only memory.

ESC Electronic spark control. The computer system is equipped with a knock sensor that can retard spark advance if necessary to eliminate spark knock.

EST Electronic spark timing. The computer controls spark timing advance.

Farad A unit of capacitance named for Michael Faraday (1791–1867), an English physicist. A farad is the capacity to store 1 coulomb of electrons at 1 volt of potential difference.

Feedback The reverse flow of electrical current through a circuit or electrical unit that should not normally be operating. This feedback current (reverse-bias current flow) is most often caused by a poor ground connection for the same normally operating circuit.

FET Field effect transistor.

Fiber optics The transmission of light through special plastic that keeps the light rays parallel even if the plastic is tied in a knot.

Field coils Coils or wire wound around metal pole shoes to form the electromagnetic field inside an electric motor.

Forward bias   Current flow in normal direction.

Frequency   The number of cycles per second, measured in hertz.

Full fielding   The method of supplying full battery voltage to the magnetic field of a generator as part of the troubleshooting procedure for the charging system.

Fuse   An electrical safety unit constructed of a fine tin conductor that will melt and open the electrical circuit if excessive current flows through the fuse.

Fusible link   A type of fuse that will melt and open the protected circuit in the event of a short circuit, which could cause excessive current flow through the fusible link. Most fusible links are actually wires four gauge sizes smaller than the wire of the circuits being protected.

Gassing   The release of hydrogen and oxygen gas from the plates of a battery during charging or discharging.

Gauge   Wire sizes as assigned by the American Wire Gauge system; the smaller the gauge number, the larger the wire.

Gauss   A unit of magnetic induction or magnetic intensity named for Karl Friedrich Gauss (1777–1855), a German mathematician.

Generator   A device that converts mechanical energy into electrical energy.

Germanium   A semiconductor material.

Grid   The lead-alloy framework (support) for the active materials of an automotive battery.

Ground   The lowest possible voltage potential in a circuit. In electrical terms, a ground is the desirable return circuit path. Ground can also be undesirable and provide a shortcut path for a defective electrical circuit.

Hall-effect sensor   A type of electromagnetic sensor used in electronic ignition and other systems. Named for Edward H. Hall, who discovered the Hall effect in 1879.

Hash   An unclear or a messy section of a scope pattern.

Hazard flasher   Emergency warning flashers; lights at all four corners of the vehicle flash on and off.

HC   Hydrocarbon (unburned fuel); when combined with NO_x and sunlight, the properties form smog.

Heat sink   Usually, a metallic-finned unit used to keep electronic components cool.

HEI   High energy ignition. General Motors' name for their electronic ignition.

Hold-in winding   One of two electromagnetic windings inside a solenoid; used to hold the movable core into the solenoid.

Hole theory   A theory that states as an electron flows from negative (−) to positive (+), it leaves behind a hole. According to the hole theory, the hole would move from positive (+) to negative (−).

Horsepower   A unit of power; equals 33,000 ft-lb per minute; 1 hp equals 746 W.

Hydrometer   An instrument used to measure the specific gravity of a liquid. A battery hydrometer is calibrated to read the expected specific gravity of battery electrolyte.

IAC   Idle air control.

Ignition circuit   Electrical components and connections that produce and distribute high-voltage electricity to ignite the air-fuel mixture inside the engine.

Ignition coil   An electrical device that consists of two separate coils of wire: a primary and a secondary winding. The purpose of an ignition is to produce a high-voltage (20,000 to 40,000 volts), low-amperage (about 80 mA) current necessary for spark ignition.

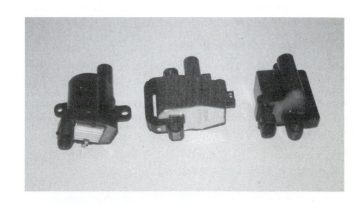

Ignition timing The exact point of ignition in relation to piston position.

Impurities Doping elements.

Inductive reactance An opposing current created in a conductor whenever there is a charging current flow in a conductor.

Insulator A material that does not readily conduct electricity and heat; a nonmetal material that contains more than four electrons in its atom's outer shell.

Ion An atom with an excess or deficiency of electrons forming either a negative- or a positive- charged particle.

Joule A unit of electrical energy. One joule equals 1 watt x 1 second ($1 V \times 1 A \times 1 s$).

Jumper cables Heavy-gauge (4 to 00) electrical cables with large clamps, used to connect a vehicle that has a discharged battery to a vehicle that has a good battery.

Junction The point where two types of materials join.

Kilo Means 1000; abbreviated k or K.

Knock sensor A sensor that can detect engine spark knock.

LCD Liquid crystal display.

Lead peroxide The positive plate of an automotive-style battery; the chemical symbol is $PbSO_4$.

Lead sulfate Both battery plates become lead sulfate when the battery is discharged. The chemical symbol for lead sulfate is $PBSO_4$.

Magnequench A magnetic alloy made from neodymium, iron, and boron.

Magnetic timing A method of measuring ignition that uses a magnetic pickup tool to sense the location of a magnet on the harmonic balancer.

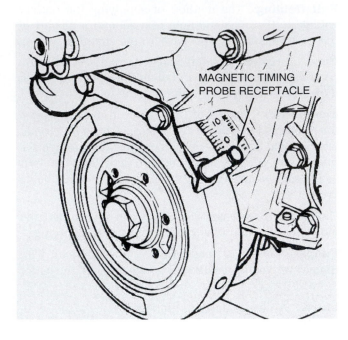

Manifold vacuum Low pressure (vacuum) measured at the intake manifold of a running engine (normally between 17 and 21 in. Hg at idle).

MAP Manifold absolute pressure.

Meniscus The puckering or curvature of a liquid in a tube. A battery is properly filled with water when the electrolyte first becomes puckered.

Module A group of electronic components functioning as a component of a larger system.

MOS Metal oxide semiconductor.

MOSFET Metal oxide semiconductor field-effect transistor.

Mutual induction The generation of an electric current due to a changing magnetic field of an adjacent coil.

Neutral safety switch A switch connected in series in the starter control circuit that allows operation of the starter motor to occur only when the gear selection is in neutral (N) or park (P).

Neutrons A neutral-charged particle; one of the basic particles of the nucleus of an atom.

NO_x Oxides of nitrogen; when combined with HC and sunlight, they form smog.

NTC Negative temperature coefficient. Usually used in reference to a temperature sensor (coolant or air temperature). As the temperature increases, the resistance of the sensor decreases.

N-type material Silicon or germanium doped with phosphorus, arsenic, or antimony.

Nucleus The central part of an atom which has a positive charge and contains almost all of the mass of the atom.

NVRAM Nonvolatile random-access memory.

Ohm The unit of electrical resistance. Named for Georg Simon Ohm (1787–1854).

Ohmmeter An electrical test instrument used to measure ohms (unit of electrical resistance). An ohmmeter uses an internal battery for power and must never be used when current is flowing through a circuit or component.

Ohm's law An electrical law that states, "It requires 1 volt to push 1 ampere through 1 *ohm* of resistance."

Omega The last letter of the Greek alphabet; a symbol for ohm, the unit for electrical resistance.

Open circuit An open circuit is any circuit that is not complete and in which no current flows.

Oscilloscope A visual display of electrical waves on a fluorescent screen or cathode ray tube.

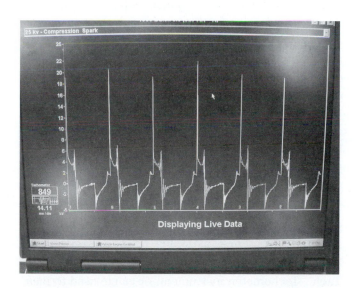

Displaying Live Data

Partitions Separations between the cells of a battery. Partitions are made of the same material as that of the outside case of the battery.

Pasting The process of applying active battery materials onto the grid framework of each plate.

PCV Positive crankcase ventilation.

Peak inverse voltage (PIV) The rating of resistance to reverse-bias voltage. Also called peak reverse voltage (PRV).

Permalloy A permanent-magnet alloy of nickel and iron.

Permeability The measure of a material's ability to conduct magnetic lines of force.

Photoelectric principle The production of electricity created by light striking certain sensitive materials, such as selenium or cesium.

Piezoelectric principle The principle by which certain crystals become electrically charged when pressure is applied.

Pinion gear A small gear on the end of the starter drive which rotates the engine flywheel ring gear for starting.

PM motor A permanent-magnet electric motor.

Polarity The condition of being positive or negative in relation to a magnetic pole.

Porous lead Lead with many small holes to make a surface porous for use in battery negative plates; the chemical symbol for lead is Pb.

Ported vacuum Low pressure (vacuum) measured above the throttle plates. As the throttle plates open, the vacuum increases and becomes of the same value as the manifold vacuum.

Power side The wires leading from the power source (battery) to the resistance (load) of a circuit.

PROM Programmable read-only memory.

Proton A positive-charged particle; one of the basic particles of the nucleus of an atom.

PRV See *peak inverse voltage.*

PTC Positive temperature coefficient. Normally used in reference to a conductor or electronic circuit breaker. As the temperature increases, the electrical resistance also increases.

P-type material Silicon or germanium doped with boron or indium.

Pull-in windings One of two electromagnetic windings inside a solenoid used to move a movable core.

Pulse generators An electromagnetic unit that generates a voltage signal used to trigger the ignition control module that controls (turns on and off) the primary ignition current of an electronic ignition system.

Pulse train DC voltage that turns on and off in a series of pulses.

Pulse width The amount of on-time of an electronic fuel injector.

Pulse width modulation (PWM) The control of a device by varying the amount of on-time current is flowing through the device.

Radial grid A lead-alloy framework for the active materials of a battery that has radial support spokes to add strength and to improve battery efficiency.

RAM Random-access memory.

Rectifier An electronic device that converts alternating current into direct current.

Rectifier bridge A group of six diodes, three positive (+) and three negative (−), commonly used in alternators.

Relay An electromagnetic switch that uses a movable arm.

Reluctance The resistance to the movement of magnetic lines of force.

Reserve capacity The number of minutes a battery can produce 25 A and still maintain a battery voltage of 1.75 volts per cell (10.5 volts for a 12-volt battery).

Residual magnetism Magnetism remaining after the magnetizing force is removed.

Resistance The opposition to current flow.

Reverse bias Current flow in the opposite direction from normal.

Rise time The time, measured in microseconds, for the output of a coil to rise from 10% to 90% of its maximum output.

ROM Read-only memory.

RPM Revolutions per minute.

RTV Room-temperature vulcanization.

Saturation The point of maximum magnetic field strength of a coil.

Sediment chamber A space below the cell plates of some batteries to permit the accumulation of sediment deposits flaking from the battery plates. Use of a sediment chamber keeps the sediment from shorting the battery plates.

Self-induction The generation of an electric current in the wires of a coil created when the current is first connected or disconnected.

Semiconductor A material that is neither a conductor nor an insulator; it has exactly four electrons in the atom's outer shell.

Separators In a battery, nonconducting porous, thin materials used to separate positive and negative plates.

Series wound In a starter motor, the field coils and the armature are wired in series. All current flows through the field coils, through the hot brushes, through the armature, then to the ground through the ground brushes.

Shelf life The length of time that something can remain on a storage shelf and not be reduced in performance level from that of a newly manufactured product.

Short circuit A circuit in which current flows, but bypasses some or all of the resistance in the circuit; a connection that results in a copper-to-copper connection.

Short to ground A short circuit in which the current bypasses some or all of the resistance of the circuit and flows to ground. Since ground is usually steel in automotive electricity, a short to ground (grounded) is a copper-to-steel connection.

Silicon A semiconductor material.

Smog The term used to describe a combination of *smoke* and *fog*. Formed by NO_x and HC with sunlight.

Solenoid An electromagnetic switch that uses a movable core.

Specific gravity The ratio of the weight of a given volume of a liquid divided by the weight of an equal volume of water.

Sponge lead Lead with many small holes used to make a surface porous or sponge-like for use in battery negative plates; the chemical symbol for lead is Pb.

Starter drive A term used to describe the starter motor drive pinion gear with overrunning clutch.

State of charge The degree or the amount that a battery is charged. A fully charged battery would be 100% charged.

Stator A name for three interconnected windings inside an alternator. A rotating rotor provides a moving magnetic field and induces a current in the windings of the stator.

Stepper motor A motor that moves a specified amount of rotation.

Stoichiometric An air-fuel ratio of exactly 14.7:1.

Stroboscopic A very bright pulsing light triggered from the firing of one spark plug. Used to check and adjust ignition timing.

Tach Tachometer, instrument, or gauge used to measure RPM.

TBI Throttle-body injection.

TDC Top dead center.

Tell-tale light Dash warning light.

TFI Thick-film integration. The name of a Ford electronic ignition system.

Transistor A semiconductor device that can operate as an amplifier or an electrical switch.

Vacuum Pressure below atmospheric pressure, measured in units of inches of Mercury (in. Hg).

Vacuum advance A spark advance unit that advances the ignition timing in relation to engine vacuum.

Vacuum kicker A computer-controlled throttle device used to increase idle RPM during certain operating conditions, such as when the air-conditioning system is operating.

Volt The unit of electrical pressure; named for Alessandro Volta (1745–1827).

Voltage drop A loss of voltage across a load or resistance when current is flowing through a circuit. Most of the voltage drop in a circuit should occur across the load.

Voltage regulator An electronic or mechanical unit that controls the output voltage of an electrical generator or alternator by controlling the field current of the generator.

Voltmeter An electrical test instrument used to measure volts (unit of electrical pressure); connected in parallel with the unit or circuit being tested.

Watt An electrical unit of power; 1 watt equals current (amperes) × voltage (1/746 hp). Named after James Watt (1736–1819), a Scottish inventor.

WOT Wide-open throttle.

Wye wound A type of stator winding in which all three coils are connected to a common center connection. Called a wye because the connections look like the letter Y.

Zener diode A specially constructed (heavily doped) diode designed to operate with a "reverse-bias" current after a certain voltage has been reached. Named for Clarence Melvin Zener (1905–1993).

Thermistor A resistor that changes resistance with temperature. A positive-coefficient thermistor has increased resistance with an increase in temperature. A negative-coefficient thermistor has increased resistance with a decrease in temperature.

Torque A twisting force which may or may not result in motion.

Transducer An electrical and mechanical speed-sensing and control unit used on cruise control systems.

SPANISH GLOSSARY

El controlador de la emisión de reacción de la inyección **de AIRE** Air.

El sistema de la gerencia de aire El sistema de solenoides y las válvulas que controlan la salida de la bomba de aire para el convertidor catalítico, airea al limpiador alojando, o el tubo múltiple eductor.

La aleación de imán permanente de la A **Alnico** de *al*uminio, *ní*quel, y el *co*balto.

El alternador Un generador eléctrico que produce corriente alterna.

El amperímetro Un instrumento experimental eléctrico es usado por medir amperios (la unidad de la cantidad de flujo actual). Un amperímetro está conectado en la serie con el circuito siendo probado.

El amperio La unidad de la cantidad de flujo actual. Nombrado para André Amp (1775–1836).

El amperio revuelve La unidad de medida para la fuerza magnética eléctrica del campo.

Analógico Un tipo de instrumento de arranque que indica aprecia por el uso del movimiento de una aguja o el dispositivo similar. Una señal analógica es continua y variable.

El ánodo El electrodo positivo; El electrodo hacia el cual los electrones fluyen.

El instituto de Estándares **ANSI** American National.

El metal de la A **de antimonio** acrecentó poco mantenimiento gratuitamente o cuadrículas híbridas de la batería para sumar fuerza.

El inducido La unidad rotativa dentro de un generador de CD o un arrancador, consistente en una serie de bobinas de herida aislante del alambre alrededor de un corazón laminado de hierro.

ATC Después de centro sobresaliente.

ATDC Después del punto muerto superior.

El átomo La unidad menor de materia que todavía retiene sus características únicas separadas.

El sistema del Calibrador para Alambres **AWG** American.

El nombre de marca de la A **de bakelita** de la Compañía Sindical de Carburo para plástico de resina del formaldehyde de fenol.

El reostato de variable de la A **del reostato del balasto** es usado por controlar la corriente primaria de ignición a través de la bobina de ignición. En la velocidad inferior del motor, la temperatura del reostato del balasto es alta, como es su resistencia. Cuando el motor RPM es alto, la resistencia del balasto es baja, permitiendo máxima corriente a través de la bobina de ignición.

El sensor de la A **del sensor BARO** es usado por medir presión barométrica.

Base El nombre para la sección de un transistor que controla el flujo actual a través del transistor.

El dispositivo del producto químico de la A **de la batería** que produce un voltaje creó por dos metales disímiles sumergidos en un electrólito.

El problema de la computadora de la A **de factor de corrección de voltaje de la batería** que aumenta la anchura de pulso del inyector de combustible si el voltaje de la batería desciende compensar la abertura más lenta resultante del inyector(es).

El prejuicio En los términos eléctricos, el voltaje se aplicó a un dispositivo o un componente para establecer el punto de referencia para la operación.

El motor del soplador Un motor eléctrico y una jaula de la ardilla determinan el tipo sanguíneo de abanico moviendo aire dentro del coche para calentándose, enfriándose, y descongelándose.

El tipo de la A **del conector BNC** de conector usado en los alcances digitales y analógicos. Denominado para su inventor, Baby Neil Councilman.

El cobre de la A **de cepillos** o el conductor de carbón solió transferir corriente eléctrica de o para una parte eléctrica giratoria tan como tan usado en un motor eléctrico o un generador.

BTDC Antes del punto muerto superior.

Arda en Un proceso de manejar un dispositivo electrónico para un período de varias horas para varios días.

La economía de combustible de promedio **del CAFÉ** Corporate.

La A **de calcio** que el elemento químico metálico le agregó a las cuadrículas de una batería libre de mantenimiento para sumar fuerza.

El Capacitance Electrical es un término usado para medir o describir cuánto el cargo puede ser almacenado en un condensador (el condensador) para una diferencia dada de potencial de voltaje. Capacitance es comedido en faradios o incrementos más pequeños de faradios, como microfarads.

El condensador de la A **del condensador;** una unidad eléctrica que puede pasarla corriente alterna, pero el bloque la CD. Usado en circuitos eléctricos para controlar fluctuaciones en el voltaje.

El montón de carbón que un instrumento experimental eléctrico usó para proveer una carga eléctrica para probar baterías y el circuito de carga.

El convertidor catalítico Un dispositivo de control de la emisión localizó en el sistema eductor que cambia a HC y CO en el inofensivo H_2O y CO_2. Si un catalizador de tres formas, NO_x está también separado en N separada inofensiva y O.

El cátodo El electrodo negativo.

El control de comando de computadora **CCC.** El nombre de controlador del motor de la computadora de la General Motors.

El grupo de la A **de la célula** de platos negativos y positivos para formar una celda capaz de voltios 2.1 productores. Cada celda contiene un plato negativo más que plato positivo.

CEMF Antagonice fuerza electromotriz.

Cobrando componentes **del circuito** Electrical y conexiones necesarias para mantener una batería completamente cobrada. Los componentes incluyen el alternador, el regulador de voltaje, la batería, y alambres que interconecta.

El chasis molido En los términos eléctricos, una tierra es el camino deseable del circuito de regreso. La tierra también puede ser indeseable y puede proveer un camino del atajo para un circuito eléctrico defectuoso.

Circunvale El camino del que los electrones viajan a través de una fuente de poder, a través de una resistencia, y de regreso a la fuente de poder.

La A **del cortacircuitos** la unidad mecánica que abre un circuito eléctrico en el caso del flujo excesivo.

El sensor de la posición **CKP** Crankshaft.

El óxido de metal **CMOS** Complementary.

El sensor de la posición **CMP** Camshaft.

El monóxido de carbono **de Colorado.**

Amperios (CCA) que hacen girar frío La valuación de habilidad de una batería para proveer voltaje de la batería durante la operación del clima frío. El número de amperios que una batería puede suministrar en 0°F (–18°C) para 30 segundos y el silencio mantienen un voltaje de 1.2 voltios por celda (7.2 voltios para una batería de 12 voltios).

El coleccionista El nombre de una sección de un transistor.

El conmutador El nombre para los segmentos de cobre del inducido de un arrancador o el generador de CD. Los segmentos giratorios del conmutador coleccionan la corriente de o se lo distribuyen para los cepillos.

Complique bobinado Un tipo de motor eléctrico donde algunas bobinas del campo están protegidas con alambre en la serie y algunas bobinas del campo son alambradas paralelamente con el inducido.

El material de la A **del conductor** que transmite electricidad y el calor; un metal que contiene menos que cuatro electrones en la concha exterior de su átomo.

La teoría convencional La teoría que la electricidad fluya de positivo (+) para negar (–).

La medida de la A **de culombio** de electrones. Un culombio es 6.28 letra x 101 (6.28 billones billones el billón) electrones.

El término **de luz de cortesía** General usó describir todas las luces interiores.

Hacer girar especificación de la batería de la A **de amperios** abrevió a CA que se refiere al número de amperios que una batería puede dar abasto en 32°F (0°C) para silencio de rato de 30 segundos manteniendo un voltaje de 7.2 voltios (1.2 voltios por celda).

Hacer girar componentes **del circuito** Electrical y las conexiones requirieron hacer girar el motor a iniciar. Incluye el arrancador, solenoide/relevador del arrancador del motor, batería, interruptor neutral de seguridad, interruptor de control de ignición, y a conectar alambres y cables.

CRT El tubo de rayos catódicos.

La A **Cunife** La aleación magnética hizo de cobre (Cu), níquel (Ni), y el hierro (Fe).

El flujo **actual** Electron a través de un circuito eléctrico; Medido en los amperios.

La sección **actual del limitador** de un regulador de voltaje para un generador de CD cobrando sistema. La sección actual del limitador abre el circuito de la corriente del campo cuándo la salida electrógena de amperaje excede límites seguros para proteger el generador de recalentar daño.

El ciclismo profundo La descarga completa y luego los llenos recargan de una batería.

El delta bobinó Un carácter de imprenta de estator serpenteando dónde todas las tres bobinas están conectado en una forma del triángulo. Denominado para la letra mayúscula del greco de la forma de triángulo.

El método **digital** de la A de despliegue que usa numera en lugar de una aguja o un dispositivo similar.

El diodo Un el cheque un eléctrico de forma que la válvula hizo de combinar un material de P-type y un material de N-type.

Los diodos del grupo de tres de la A **del trío del diodo** se agruparon con una salida usada para apagar la lámpara del señalizador de cargo y proveer corriente para el campo de los serpenteos del estator en muchos alternadores.

La corriente directa Electricidad que fluye en una dirección.

La unidad electromecánica **distribuidora** usó ayudar a crear y distribuir el alto voltaje necesario para el encendido de chispa.

Cayendo en cuenta de La adición de impurezas para el silicio puro o el germanio para forjar ya sea P o materiales del semiconductor N.

DPDT cambie polo doble, duplique interruptor de lanzamiento.

El ciclo arancelario Refers para el porcentaje de adelante cronometra de la señal durante un ciclo completo.

More El número de grados de rotación distribuidora de la leva que los puntos están cerrados.

Conecte a tierra tierra La tierra más puesta en tierra. Una tierra es comúnmente utilizada como un camino de la corriente de regreso para un circuito eléctrico.

EEPROM Memoria electrónica que se lee sólo programable borrable.

La inyección de combustible **EFI** Electronic.

EGR Agote recirculación del gas. Un dispositivo de control de la emisión para reducir a NO_x (los óxidos de nitrógeno).

La electricidad El movimiento de electrones gratis de un átomo para otro. **La sustancia**

de electrólito Cualequiera sustancia que, en la solución, está separada en iones y se hace capaz transmitiendo una corriente eléctrica. La solución ácida de una batería ácida en la pista.

La conscripción electromagnética Descubierto en 1831 por Michael Faraday, es la generación de una corriente en un conductor que se movió a través de un campo magnético.

La A de electromagnetismo que el campo magnético creó por el flujo actual a través de un conductor.

La fuerza electromotriz La fuerza (la presión) que puede mover electrones a través de un conductor.

La A del electrón la partícula de cargo negativo: El 1/1800 la masa de un protón.

La teoría del electrón La teoría que la electricidad fluya negativa (–) para positivo (+).

El cortacircuitos electrónico Vea PTC.

El término **electrónico de ignición** General usó describir cualquier de los tipos diversos de sistemas de ignición que usan electrónico en lugar de componentes mecánicos, como puntos de contacto.

La sustancia **del elemento** Cualquiera sustancia que se separó en sustancias diferentes.

EMF La fuerza electromotriz.

El emisor El nombre de una sección de un transistor. La flecha usada en un símbolo para un transistor está en el emisor y los puntos de la flecha hacia la sección negativa del transistor.

EPROM Memoria borrable que se lee sólo programable.

El control de la chispa **ESC** Electronic. El sistema de la computadora es equipado con un sensor de golpe que puede retardar avance de la chispa si es necesario para eliminar golpe de la chispa.

La chispa **EST** Electronic cronometrando. La computadora controla avance de oportunidad del momento de la chispa.

La unidad de la A **de faradio** de capacitance nombró para Michael Faraday (1791–1867), un físico inglés. Un faradio es la aptitud para almacenar 1 culombio de electrones en 1 voltio de diferencia potencial.

La información retroactiva El flujo inverso de corriente eléctrica a través de un circuito o una unidad eléctrica que normalmente no debería operar. Esta corriente de información retroactiva (el flujo actual diagonal en reverso) es más a menudo causada por una toma de tierra mala para lo mismo normalmente manejando circuito.

FET Fildee transistor de efecto.

La óptica de fibra La transmisión de luz por un plástico especial que mantiene el paralelo aun si el plástico está atado en un nudo.

Las bobinas **de bobinas del campo** o el alambre arrollado en polo de metal hierra a formar el campo electromagnético dentro de un motor eléctrico.

El flujo Actual **diagonal delantero** en la dirección normal.

La frecuencia El número de ciclos por segundo, midió en el hertz.

Dé amplitud a fildear El método de voltaje completo abastecedor de la batería para el campo magnético de un generador como parte del procedimiento del troubleshooting para el sistema embestidor.

Funda Una unidad de seguridad eléctrica construida de un conductor de hojalata fino que derretirá y abrirá el circuito eléctrico si flujos actuales excesivos a través del fusible.

El tipo **fusible** de la A **del enlace** de fusible que derretirá y abrirá el circuito protegido en el acontecimiento de un corto circuito, que podría causar flujo actual excesivo a través del enlace fusible. La mayoría de enlaces fusibles son de hecho alambres cuatro tamaños de calibre más pequeños que el alambre de los circuitos siendo protegen.

Asfixiando con gas La liberación del gas de hidrógeno y de oxígeno de los platos de una batería durante ir a la carga o la desvinculación.

El calibre Wire dimensiona tan asignado por el sistema americano del calibrador para alambres; mientras más pequeño el número de calibre, mayor el alambre.

La unidad de la A **de gauss** de conscripción magnética o intensidad magnética nombró para Karl Friedrich Gauss (1777–1855), un matemático alemán.

El dispositivo **electrógeno** de la A que convierte energía mecánica en la energía eléctrica.

El material del semiconductor de la A **del germanio**.

La cuadrícula El armazón de la aleación de pista (el soporte) para los materiales activos de una batería automotora.

Ponga en tierra El potencial posible mínimo de voltaje en un circuito. En los términos eléctricos, una tierra es el camino deseable del circuito de regreso. La tierra también puede ser indeseable y puede proveer un camino del atajo para un circuito eléctrico defectuoso.

El tipo de la A **del sensor de efecto del vestíbulo** de sensor electromagnético usado en ignición electrónica

y otros sistemas. Nombrado para Edward H. Hall, quién hallado el efecto Hall en 1879.

Pique en trocitos Una poco claro o una sección confusa de un patrón de alcance.

Destellador de peligro advirtiendo destelladores; Ilumina alguno cuatro esquinas del destello del vehículo de vez en cuando.

HC Hydrocarbon (el combustible que no está quemado); estando combinadas con NO_x y luz del sol, las propiedades forman humo y niebla.

Caliente fregadero una unidad de aleta metálica usó conservar calma electrónica de componentes.

La ignición de energía **HEI** El nombre de la General Motors para su ignición electrónica.

Refrene ventilando Uno de dos serpenteos electromagnéticos dentro de un solenoide; Usado para sujetar el corazón móvil en el solenoide.

La teoría de la A **de teoría del hueco** que indica como un electrón fluye negativa (–) para positivo (+), deja atrás un hueco. Según la teoría del hueco, el hueco se movería de positivo (+) para la negativa (–).

La unidad de la A **de caballo de fuerza** de poder; Corresponde a 33,000 ft-lb por minuto; Iguales 1 hp 746 W.

El hidrómetro Un instrumento usó medir la densidad específica de un líquido. Un hidrómetro de la batería es calibrado para leer la esperada densidad específica de electrólito de la batería.

El control de aire **IAC** idle.

Los componentes **del circuito de ignición** Electrical y las conexiones que produce y distribuye electricidad de alto voltaje enciende la mezcla de combustible de aire dentro del motor.

La bobina de ignición Un dispositivo eléctrico consta de dos bobinas separadas de alambre: Un primario y un serpenteo secundario. El propósito de una ignición es producir una corriente de alto voltaje (20,000 para 40,000 voltios), **low-amperage** (acerca de 80 mA del amperaje bajo necesaria para el encendido de chispa.

La ignición cronometrando El punto exacto de ignición en relación a posición del pistón.

El control de carga **ILC** idle.

Las impurezas Dopando elementos.

La reactancia inductiva que Una corriente contraria creó en un conductor cada vez que hay un flujo actual embestidor en un conductor.

El material de la A **del aislador** que fácilmente no transmite electricidad y el calor. Un material del elemento no metálico que contiene más que cuatro electrones en la concha exterior de su átomo.

El ion   Un átomo con un exceso o la deficiencia de electrones formando ya sea una negativa o una partícula de cargo positivo.

El control de velocidad ISC Idle.

La unidad de la A **de julio** de energía eléctrica. Iguales de un julio 1 letra x de vatio 1 secundan (1 letra x V 1 UNA letra x 1 s).

El calibre **de cables puente de batería** Heavy (4 para 00) los cables eléctricos con tenazas grandes, usadas para conectar un vehículo que tiene una batería muerta para un vehículo que tiene una buena batería.

El empalme   El punto donde dos tipos de materiales se asocien.

La Manera **de Kilo** 1000; la k o K abreviada.

El sensor de la A **del sensor de golpe** que puede detectar motor dar inicio al golpe.

El despliegue **electroluminiscente** del cristal líquido.

Cubra con plomo peróxido   El plato positivo de una batería de estilo automotor, el símbolo químico es $PbSO_4$.

Cubra con plomo   platos de la batería **de sulfato** Both sulfato en el quese convirtió de la pista cuando la batería es muerta. El símbolo químico para sulfato de la pista es $PbSO_4$.

La A **Magnequench** la aleación magnética hizo de neodymium, hierro, y boro.

El método **magnético** de la A **de oportunidad del momento** de ignición medidora que usa una herramienta magnética de arresto para sentir la posición de un imán en el balanceador armónico.

La presión baja **de vacío** (normalmente entre 17 y 21 adentro (el vacío) **múltiple** medida en la toma múltiple de un motor encendido. Hg en desocupado).

El MAPA   Manifold presión absoluta.

El menisco   El fruncimiento o la curvatura de un líquido en un tubo. Una batería se llena correctamente de agua cuando la primera parte de electrólito se vuelve arrugada.

El grupo de la A **de módulo** de componentes electrónicos funcionando como un componente de un mayor sistema.

El semiconductor de óxido **MOS** Metal.

El transistor de efecto de campo del semiconductor de óxido **MOSFET** Metal.

La conscripción mutual   La generación de una corriente eléctrica debido a un campo magnético cambiante de una bobina adyacente.

El interruptor de la A **del interruptor de seguridad neutral** conectado en la serie en el circuito de control del arrancador que consiente operación del arrancador motora para ocurrir sólo cuando la selección del engranaje está de moda neutral (N) o el parque (P).

La A de neutrones la partícula de cargo neutral; Una de las partículas básicas del núcleo de un átomo.

El NO_x   Oxides de nitrógeno; Estando combinado con HC y luz del sol, forme humo y niebla.

NTC   Niegue coeficiente de temperatura. Usualmente usado con atención a un sensor de temperatura. (La temperatura de líquido de refrigeración o de aire). Como la temperatura aumenta, la resistencia del sensor disminuye.

El material de N-Type   Silicon o germanio dopó con fósforo, arsénico, o antimonio.

El núcleo   La parte central de un átomo que tiene un cargo del positivo y contienen casi toda la masa del átomo.

La memoria de acceso al azar **NVRAM** nonvolatile.

El ohm   La unidad de resistencia eléctrica. Nombrado para Georg Simon Ohm (1787–1854).

Ohmmeter   Un instrumento experimental eléctrico usó medir ohmes (la unidad de resistencia eléctrica). Un ohmmeter destina una batería interna para poder y nunca debe ser usado cuando la corriente fluye a través de un circuito o componente.

La ley de Ohm   Una ley eléctrica que indica, "requiere 1 voltio para empujar 1 amperio a través de 1 *ohm* de resistencia."

La omega   La última carta del alfabeto griego; un símbolo para el ohm, la unidad para resistencia eléctrica.

Abra circuito   Un circuito abierto es cualquier circuito que no es completo y en el cual ninguna corriente fluye.

La A **Oscilloscope** el despliegue visual de ondas eléctricas en una pantalla fluorescente o un tubo de rayos catódicos.

Divide en partes a   Separations entre las celdas de una batería. Las particiones están hechas del mismo material como eso del caso exterior de la batería.

Empastando   El proceso de aplicar materiales activos de la batería encima del armazón cuadriculado de cada plato.

La ventilación del cárter **PCV** Positive.

Maximice voltaje inverso (PIV)   La valuación de resistencia para el voltaje diagonal en reverso. También el voltaje inverso culminante designado (PRV).

La aleación de imán permanente de la A **Permalloy** de níquel y hierro.

La permeabilidad   La medida de habilidad de un material para transmitir líneas magnéticas de fuerza.

El principio fotoeléctrico   La producción de electricidad creó por luz golpeando ciertos materiales sensitivos, como selenio o cesio.

El principio piezoeléctrico   El principio por el cual ciertos cristales se ponen eléctricamente cobrados cuando presión es aplicada.

El engranaje de la parte pequeña de la A **del engranaje del piñón** en el fin del paseo en coche del arrancador que rota el engranaje del anillo del volante del motor para empezar.

De la noche motor   Un imán permanente motor eléctrico.

La polaridad   La condición de ser positivo o negativo en relación a un polo magnético.

La pista porosa   Pista con muchos hoyos pequeños para hacer una superficie porosa para el uso en platos de negativa de la batería; el símbolo químico para pista es Pb.

La presión baja **de vacío** (el vacío) **exportada** medida por encima de los platos del obturador. Como el claro de platos del obturador, los incrementos de vacío y es del mismo valor como el vacío múltiple.

Parte de poder   Los alambres llevando la delantera de la fuente de poder (la batería) para la resistencia (la carga) de un circuito.

El Baile de graduación   Programmable memoria que se lee sólo.

La A **del protón** la partícula de cargo positivo; Una de las partículas básicas del núcleo de un átomo.

PRV   Vea *voltaje inverso culminante*.

El coeficiente de temperatura **PTC** positive. Normalmente usado con atención a un conductor o el cortacircuitos electrónico. Como la temperatura aumenta, la resistencia eléctrica también aumenta.

El material de P-type   Silicon o germanio dopado con boro o indium.

Serpenteos de apartaderos   Uno de dos serpenteos electromagnéticos dentro de un solenoide solió mover un corazón móvil.

Los generadores de pulso   Una unidad electromagnética que genera una señal de voltaje usó provocar el módulo de control de ignición que controla (las vueltas de vez en cuando) la corriente primaria de ignición de un sistema electrónico de ignición.

El voltaje de CD **del tren de pulso** que cambia de dirección de vez en cuando en una serie de pulsos.

La anchura de pulso   La cantidad de adelante cronometra de un inyector electrónico de combustible.

La modulación de anchura de pulso (PWM)   El control de un dispositivo variando la cantidad de corriente adelante cronometre es fluir a través del dispositivo.

Radial cuadriculado   Un armazón de la aleación de pista para los materiales activos de una batería que hace nervio radial soportar enraya para sumar fuerza y mejorar eficiencia de la batería.

La memoria de acceso al azar **de RAM.**

El rectificador   Un dispositivo electrónico que convierte corriente alterna en CD.

El grupo de la A **del puente del rectificador** de seis diodos, tres positivo (+) y tres niegan (–) comúnmente usado en alternadores.

Transmita   Un interruptor electromagnético que usa un brazo móvil.

La renuencia   La resistencia para el movimiento de líneas magnéticas de fuerza.

Reserve aptitud   El número de minutos que una batería puede producir 25 UNO y todavía puede mantener un voltaje de la batería de 1.75 voltios por celda (10.5 voltios para una batería de 12 voltios).

Magnetismo residual   Magnetism quedando después de la fuerza magnetizante está removido.

La resistencia   La oposición para el flujo actual.

Ponga al revés   flujo Actual **diagonal** en dirección opuesta de normalidad.

El reostato   Un reostato variable de 2 alambres regulable.

El tiempo de subida   El tiempo, medido en los microsegundos, para la para salida de una para bobina levantarse de 10% para 90% de su máxima salida.

ROM   memoria que se lee sólo.

Las revoluciones por minuto **RPM.**

La vulcanización de temperatura **RTV** Room.

La saturación   El punto de máxima fuerza magnética del campo de una bobina.

El espacio de la A **de la cámara del sedimento** debajo de los platos de la célula de algunas baterías para aceptar la acumulación de sedimento deposita descascarillado de los platos de la batería. El uso de una cámara del sedimento libra el sedimento de poner en cortocircuito los platos de la batería.

La autoinducción   que la generación de una corriente eléctrica en los alambres de una bobina creó cuando la corriente está primero conectado o desconectado.

El material **semiconductor** de la A que no es ni un conductor ni un aislador; tiene exactamente cuatro electrones en la concha exterior del átomo.

Los separadores En una batería, poco transmitiendo materiales porosos, delgados usados para poner aparte platos positivos y negativos.

La serie bobinada En un motor del arrancador, el campo se enrolla y el inducido está protegido con alambre en la serie. Toda corriente fluye a través de las bobinas del campo, directo los cepillos calientes, a través del inducido, luego al suelo a través de los cepillos de la tierra.

La durabilidad La longitud de tiempo que algo pueda quedar en un estante de almacenamiento y no se acorte en nivel de actuación de eso de un producto recién confeccionado.

El circuito **pequeño** de la A **del circuito** en el cual los flujos actuales, excepto carreteras de circunvalación un poco o toda la resistencia en el circuito; una conexión que resulta en un cobre cubrir de cobre conexión.

Ponga en cortocircuito para poner en tierra Un corto circuito en el cual la corriente pasa por encima de una cierta cantidad o toda la resistencia del circuito y los flujos para poner en tierra. Desde que la tierra es usualmente acerada en electricidad automotora, un cortocircuito a poner en tierra (encallado) es un cobre para acerar conexión.

El material del semiconductor de la A **de silicio.**

El humo y niebla El término usó describir una combinación de humo y niebla. Formado por NO_x y HC con la luz del sol.

El solenoide Un interruptor electromagnético que usa un corazón móvil.

La densidad específica que la proporción del peso de un volumen dado de un líquido dividió por el peso de un volumen igual de agua.

El plomo esponjoso Pista con muchos hoyos pequeños usó hacer una superficie porosa o una esponja análoga para el uso en platos de negativa de la batería; El símbolo químico para pista es Pb.

El término de la A **de paseo en coche del arrancador** usó describir el engranaje del piñón de accionamiento por motor del arrancador con invadir embrague.

Indique de cargo El grado o la cantidad que una batería es cobrada. Una batería con creces cobrada sería 100% cobrado.

El nombre de la A **del estator** para tres serpenteos interconectados dentro de un alternador. Un rotor rota-

tivo provee un campo magnético emocionante e induce una corriente en los serpenteos del estator.

Stepper transporte por vehículo UN motor que mueve una cantidad especificada de rotación.

Stoichiometric Una proporción de combustible de aire de exactamente 14.7:1.

La A **estroboscópica** muy brillante pulsar con poco equipaje provocó del tiroteo de una bujía del motor. Usado para comprobar y ajustar oportunidad del momento de ignición.

Tach Tachometer, instrumente, o el calibre usó medir RPM.

TBI Estrangule inyección del cuerpo.

TDC Corone punto muerto.

Dice luz de cuento Dash dando aviso con poco equipaje.

La integración de la película **TFI** Thick. El nombre de un sistema electrónico Ford de ignición.

El reostato de la A **Thermistor** que cambia resistencia con temperatura. Un thermistor de coeficiente positivo ha aumentado resistencia con un incremento en la temperatura. Un thermistor de coeficiente negativo ha aumentado resistencia con una disminución en la temperatura.

La fuerza de contorsión de la A **de fuerza de torsión** que puede o no puede resultar en marcha.

El transductor Una velocidad eléctrica y mecánica sintiendo y la unidad de control usada en controladores de crucero.

El dispositivo del semiconductor de la A **del transistor** que puede operar como un amplificador o un interruptor eléctrico.

Limpie con aspiradora presión atmosférica de abajo y Pressure, medida en unidades de pulgadas de mercurio (pulgadas de Hg).

La unidad de avance de la chispa de la A **de avance de vacío** que adelanta la oportunidad del momento de ignición en relación a vacío del motor.

La A **del pateador de vacío** que el dispositivo del obturador controlado por computadora usó para aumentar a RPM desocupado durante ciertas condiciones operativas, como cuando el sistema del aire acondicionado funciona.

El voltio La unidad de presión eléctrica; nombrado para Alessandro Volta (1745–1827).

La pérdida de la A **de caída de voltaje** de voltaje a través de una carga o la resistencia cuando la corriente fluya a través de un circuito. La mayor parte de la caída de voltaje en un circuito debería ocurrir a través de la carga.

El regulador de voltaje Una unidad electrónica o mecánica que controla el voltaje de salida de un alternador o generador eléctrico controlando el campo actual del generador.

El voltímetro Un instrumento experimental eléctrico usó medir voltios (la unidad de presión eléctrica); conectado de adentro iguala con la unidad o circuito siendo experimentado.

El vatio Una unidad eléctrica de poder; voltaje de la letra x de la corriente de iguales (1/746 hp) (los amperios) de 1 vatios. Nombrado después de James Watt (1736–1819), un inventor escocés.

El obturador del claro **WOT** Wide.

Wye bobinó Un carácter de imprenta de estator enrollando cuál todas las tres bobinas está conectado para una conexión central común. Designado un wye porque las conexiones se parezcan a la letra: "Y".

La A **del diodo Zener** en especial construyó (pesadamente dopado) diodo diseñado para funcionar con una corriente diagonal en reverso después de que un cierto voltaje ha sido alcanzado. Nombrado para Clarence Melvin Zener (1905–1993).

INDEX